ITALICA PRESS STUDIES IN ART AND HISTORY

THIS SERIES presents selected volumes in the art and cultural history of the Middle Ages and Renaissance, edited and written by some of the most distinguished scholars now working in these fields. Subjects include medieval and Renaissance painting, sculpture, architecture and urbanism; iconography and emblematica; cultural studies; history and historiography, philosophy and religion; manuscript studies and the history of the book.

The series aims to present the most rigorous scholarship to both an academic and a general audience with well edited and produced volumes at reasonable prices. These volumes are now available in hardcover, paperback and in a variety of digital formats, including Kindle, JSTOR and ProQuest versions. For more information see http://www.italicapress.com/index009.html.

Volumes include:

Florilegium Columbianum: Essays in Honor of Paul Oskar Kristeller
Edited by Karl-Ludwig Selig & Robert Somerville. 1987.

The Verbal & the Visual: Essays in Honor of William Sebastian Heckscher
Edited by Karl-Ludwig Selig & Elizabeth Sears. 1990.

Aldus and His Dream Book
By Helen Barolini. 1992.

Renaissance Society & Culture: Essays in Honor of Eugene F. Rice, Jr.
Edited by John Monfasani & Ronald G. Musto. 2004.

Kristeller Reconsidered: Essays on His Life and Scholarship
Edited by John Monfasani. 2006.

Rome Italy Renaissance: Essays Honoring Irving Lavin
Edited by Marilyn Aronberg Lavin. 2008.

Medieval Renaissance Baroque: A Cat's Cradle in Honor of Marilyn Aronberg Lavin
Edited by David A. Levine & Jack Freiberg. 2009.

A Scarlet Renaissance: Essays in Honor of Sarah Blake McHam
Edited by Arnold Victor Coonin. 2013.

Petrarch's Two Gardens: Landscape and the Image of Movement
By William Tronzo. 2013.

Patronage, Gender & the Arts in Early Modern Italy:
Essays in Honor of Carolyn Valone
Edited by Katherine A. McIver & Cynthia Stollhans. 2015.

The Art of Commemoration in the Renaissance
By Irving Lavin. Edited by Marilyn Aronberg Lavin. 2021.

Writing Southern Italy Before the Renaissance:
Trecento Historians of the Mezzogiorno.
By Ronald G. Musto. 2022.

The Mellon Lectures: More than Meets the Eye
By Irving Lavin. Edited by Marilyn Aronberg Lavin.
Forthcoming 2022.

WRITING SOUTHERN ITALY BEFORE THE RENAISSANCE

Frontispiece: Royal procession. *Meliadus de Leonnois*, c.1352. London, British Library, MS Add 12228, fol. 212v. Public Domain Mark. www.bl.uk/manuscripts/Viewer.aspx?ref=add_ms_12228_f212v

WRITING SOUTHERN ITALY BEFORE THE RENAISSANCE
TRECENTO HISTORIANS OF THE MEZZOGIORNO

RONALD G. MUSTO

Second Revised Edition

ITALICA PRESS
NEW YORK & BRISTOL
2022

Copyright © 2019 by Taylor & Francis
First published 2019 by Routledge.
Italica Press Second Revised Edition 2022
© Ronald G. Musto 2022

All rights reserved. No part of this book may be reprinted or reproduced or utilised in any form or by any electronic, mechanical, or other means, now known or hereafter invented, including photocopying and recording, or in any information storage or retrieval system, without prior permission in writing from Italica Press.

Library of Congress Cataloging-in-Publication Data
Names: Musto, Ronald G., author.
Title: Writing Southern Italy before the Renaissance : trecento historians of the Mezzogiorno / by Ronald G. Musto. Includes bibliographical references and index. |

ISBN 9781599104614 (hbk.) | ISBN 9781599104638 (ebk.)
ISBN 9781599104126 (pbk.) | ISBN 9781599104621(Kindle)
Subjects: LCSH: Italy, Southern—Historiography. | Italy, Southern—History—1268-1735.
Classification: LCC DG829 (ebook) | LCC DG829 .M87 2019 (print) | DDC 945/.705072—dc23
LC record available at https://lccn.loc.gov/2018040745

Cover image: Angevin Pictorial Genealogy. *Anjou Bible,* c.1340. Leuven, Maurits Sabbe 1, fol. 4r. Public domain, via Wikimedia Commons.

This book is dedicated to the memory of Ronald G. Witt.

CONTENTS

List of Figures and Tables	XII
List of Abbreviations	XIV
Preface	XXVI
Acknowledgments	XXXII
1. Introduction	1
Acknowledgments	9
Notes	9
Works Cited	11
2. The Historians: Their Lives and Works	14
Introduction	14
Southern Italy: Who Wrote?	14
Other Southern Historians	22
Northen Italy: Who Wrote?	22
Northern Europe: Who Wrote?	32
Notes	35
Works Cited	38
3. Sources	43
Introduction	43
The Classical Tradition: Texts	44
The Classical Tradition: Ancient Remains	49
Early Medieval Historiography	50
Arabic, Jewish, Greek Sources	51
Literary Sources	52
Religious Sources	52
Archival Sources	53
Cosmology, Science, Medicine	55
Folklore, Popular Memory and Orality	57
Conclusions	68
Notes	68
Works Cited	77
4. Narrative Communities and Strategies	80
Introduction: Narrative Communities	80
Language Choice	81
Latin Histories	82
Vernacular Histories	87
Narrative Structures	92

Narrative Forms or Modes	103
Conclusions	110
Notes	111
Works Cited	118

5. The Impact of Romance — 122

Introduction	122
Accused Queens	125
The Reign of Giovanna I of Naples	125
Giovanna I: The Falsely Accused Queen	128
Romance Models	129
Conclusions	142
Notes	142
Works Cited	146

6. Visual Evidence — 152

Introduction	152
Trecento Visual Language and Its Themes	153
Angevin Manuscripts and the Visualization of Power	178
Conclusions	188
Notes	189
Works Cited	194

7. Case Studies — 199

Introduction	199
Ceremony and Ritual	199
Rituals of Punishment	200
Prison Dialogues	216
Conclusions	221
Notes	222
Works Cited	226

8. Constructing Grand Narratives: The Black Legend of the Angevins — 229

Introduction	229
Infamy: Women Murderers	232
Hungarian Royal Propaganda	233
Petrarch	235
Villani	247
Domenico da Gravina	248
Boccaccio	250
Conclusions	252
Notes	253
Works Cited	256

9. Medieval to Renaissance: The Historiographical Question — 258

Renaissance Historiography	258
Historical Introduction	260
Humanist Historians of the Quattrocento: Flavio Biondo	262

CONTENTS

Humanists at the Neapolitan Court	266
Civic Historians of the Quattrocento	273
Conclusions	278
Notes	279
Works Cited	283
10. Conclusions	289
Notes	292
Chronology	293
Bibliography	297
Manuscript & Archival Materials	297
Primary Sources	297
Secondary Works	303
Index	334

FIGURES

Frontispiece: Royal procession. *Meliadus de Leonnois*, c.1352. London, British Library, MS Add 12228, fol. 212v. Public Domain Mark. www.bl.uk/manuscripts/Viewer.aspx?ref=add_ms_12228_f212v.   VI

6.1. Francesco da Barberino, "Iustitia." From *Documenti d'amore*. Vatican. Biblioteca Apostolica Vaticana. MS Vat. Barb. 4076, fol.87v. Autograph, c.1310. By permission of Biblioteca Apostolica Vaticana, with all rights reserved.   154

6.2. Ambrogio Lorenzetti. "Iusticia." From the *Allegory of Good Government*. Siena, Palazzo Pubblico, 1338–39. Public domain, via Wikimedia Commons.   156

6.3. Giotto. *Allegory of Iustitia*. Padua, Arena Chapel, c.1305. Public domain, via Wikimedia Commons.   158

6.4. *Nine Heroes Tapestry* (detail), 1400–1410. The Cloisters Museum, New York. Munsey Fund, 1932; Gift of John D. Rockefeller Jr., 1947. Accession No. 32.130.3a; 47.101.4. Public Domain Mark.   160

6.5. Cola di Rienzo and the Capitoline Painting by Lodovico Pogliaghi. *L'Illustrazione Italiana* 22.17 (April 28, 1895). Author's Collection.   166

6.6. Giotto, *Navicella* mosaic, Old St. Peter's, c. 1420. Copy by Parri Spinelli (1387–1453). New York, Metropolitan Museum of Art. Accession No. 19.76.2. Hewitt Fund, 1917. The file of this image was donated to Wikimedia Commons as part of a project by the Metropolitan Museum of Art.   167

6.7. Rome as an aged widow. From the *Carmina regia* or *Panegyric to Robert of Anjou from the Citizens of Prato*, c.1335. London, British Library, MS Royal 6.E.IX, fol. 11v. Public Domain Mark. www.bl.uk/catalogues/illuminatedmanuscripts/ILLUMIN.ASP?Size=mid&IllID=50479.   168

6.8. Apocalyptic Christ, *Maiestas*. Anagni Cathedral Crypt, Chapel of St. Magnus, c.1250. Photograph by author.   172

6.9. Pietro Cavallini, *Last Judgement*. Naples, Sta. Maria Donna Regina, 1317–23. Photograph by author.   173

6.10. Madonna of the Apocalypse. Cavallini workshop. Sta. Maria Donna Regina, Naples. 1317–23. Image courtesy of the Complesso Monumentale Donna Regina.   173

6.11. Passion cycle, Sta. Maria Donna Regina, Naples. Cavallini workshop. 1317–23. Photograph by author. 174

6.12. Pietro Cavallini, *Apocalypse*. Naples, Sta. Maria Donna Regina, Loffredo Chapel, 1317–23. Photograph by author. 175

6.13. Maso di Banco, *St. Silvester and the Dragon*. Bardi di Vernio Chapel, Sta. Croce, Florence. c. 1340. Photograph by author. 176

6.14. *The Stuttgart Apocalypse*. Neapolitan Master (now attributed to Giotto and studio), Apocalypse of John (a) Chapters 1–13, c.1332/34. (b) Chapters 14–22, c.1330/40. Staatsgalerie Stuttgart, Inv. Nr. 3100. Tempera, 34.9 × 86.3 cm. Photo: © Staatsgalerie Stuttgart. Used by permission of Staatsgalerie Stuttgart. 177

6.15. Robert of Anjou and Giovanna I. *Anjou Bible*, c.1340. Leuven, Maurits Sabbe 1, fol. 309r. Public domain, via Wikimedia Commons 181

6.16. Double portrait of Giovanna I and Louis of Taranto. *Statutes of the Order of the Holy Spirit*. c.1352. Paris, Bibliothèque nationale de France, MS fr. 4274, fol. 2v. ark:/12148/btv1b8551130g. Public Domain. Source: gallica.bnf.fr/BnF. 183

6.17. Royal procession. *Meliadus de Leonnois*, c.1352. London, British Library, MS Add 12228, fol. 212v–213r. Detail. Public Domain Mark. www.bl.uk/manuscripts/Viewer.aspx?ref=add_ms_12228_f212v 185

6.18. Louis of Taranto. *Meliadus de Leonnois*, c.1352. London, British Library, MS Add 12228, fol. 4r. Public Domain Mark. www.bl.uk/manuscripts/Viewer.aspx?ref=add_ms_12228_f004r. 186

6.19. Meliadus bearing Angevin royal arms. *Meliadus de Leonnois*, c.1352. London, British Library, MS Add 12228, fol. 68v. Public Domain Mark. www.bl.uk/manuscripts/Viewer.aspx?ref=add_ms_12228_f068v. 188

TABLE

4.1. Epideictic Form in Boccaccio's *Vita* of Giovanna I. 105

ABBREVIATIONS

Ainsworth (1990)	Ainsworth, Peter F. 1990. *Jean Froissart and the Fabric of History: Truth, Myth, and Fiction in the Chroniques.* Oxford: Clarendon Press.
Ainsworth (2013)	Ainsworth, Peter F. 2013. "Jean Froissart: Chronicler, Poet and Writer." In Froissart (2013).
Ainsworth (2003.1)	Ainsworth, Peter. 2003.1. "Contemporary and 'Eyewitness' History." In Deliyannis (2003), 249–76.
Anjou Bible	*The Anjou Bible: A Royal Manuscript Revealed, Naples 1340.* 2010. Lieve Watteeuw and Jan Ven der Stock, ed. Leuven: Peeters.
A&N	*Avignon & Naples: Italy in France, France in Italy in the Fourteenth Century.* 1997. Marianne Pade et al., ed. Rome: "L'Erma" di Bretschneider.
AR	*Anonimo romano: Cronica.* 1979. Giuseppe Porta, ed. Milan: Adelphi.
Arens	Arens, William. 1979. *The Man-Eating Myth: Anthropology and Anthropophagy.* Oxford: Oxford University Press.
Armstrong (2015)	Armstrong, Guyda. 2015. With Rhiannon Daniels and Stephen J. Milner, ed. *The Cambridge Companion to Boccaccio.* Cambridge: Cambridge University Press.
Ascoli–Falkeid	Ascoli, Albert Russell. 2015. With Unn Falkeid. *The Cambridge Companion to Petrarch.* Cambridge: Cambridge University Press.
ASPN	*Archivio storico per le province napoletane.*
BA	Alfano, Giancarlo, et al., ed. 2012. *Boccaccio angioino: Materiali per la storia culturale di Napoli nel Trecento.* Brussels: Peter Lang.
Bacco	Bacco, Enrico. 1991. With C. d'Engenio Caracciolo. *Naples: An Early Guide.* Eileen Gardiner, ed. and trans. Introductions by Caroline Bruzelius and Ronald G. Musto. New York: Italica Press.
Barbato (2017)	Barbato, Marcello. 2017. "Testo e codice: Le cronache volgari fino a Villani." In Francesconi–Miglio, 89–115.
Bentley	Bentley, Jerry H. 1987. *Politics and Culture in Renaissance Naples.* Princeton: Princeton University Press.

ABBREVIATIONS

Bertelli (2001)	Bertelli, Sergio. 2001. *The King's Body: Sacred Rituals of Power in Medieval and Early Modern Europe*. R. Burr Litchfield, trans. State College: Pennsylvania State University Press.
Black (2003)	Black, Nancy B. 2003. *Medieval Narratives of Accused Queens*. Gainesville: University Press of Florida.
Boccaccio (1983.1)	Boccaccio, Giovanni. 1983. *De casibus virorum illustrium*. Pier Giorgio Ricci and Vittorio Zaccaria, ed. Milan: Mondadori.
Boccaccio (1987)	Boccaccio, Giovanni. 1987. *Eclogues*. Janet Levarie Smarr, trans. New York: Garland.
Boccaccio (1992)	Boccaccio, Giovanni. 1992. *Rime, Carmina, Epistole e lettere, Vite, De Canaria*. In *Tutte le opere* 5.1. Vittore Branca et al., ed. Milan: Mondadori.
Boccaccio (2003)	Boccaccio, Giovanni. 2003. *Famous Women*. Virginia Brown, ed. and trans. Cambridge, MA: Harvard University Press.
Boccaccio (2011)	Boccaccio, Giovanni. 2011. *On Famous Women*. Guido A. Guarino, ed. and trans. New York: Italica Press.
Boccaccio (2018)	Boccaccio, Giovanni. 2018. *The Downfall of the Famous*. Louis Brewer Hall, ed. and trans.; rev. ed. New York: Italica Press.
Bologna	Bologna, Ferdinando. 1969. *I pittori alla corte angioina di Napoli, 1266–1414, e un riesame dell'arte nell'età fridericiana*. Rome: Ugo Bozzi.
Brandt	Brandt, William J. 1966. *The Shape of Medieval History: Studies in Modes of Perception*. New Haven: Yale University Press.
Breisach	Breisach, Ernst. 1985. *Classical Rhetoric & Medieval Historiography*. Kalamazoo, MI: Medieval Institute Publications.
Bruzelius (2004)	Bruzelius, Caroline. 2004. *The Stones of Naples: Church Building in Angevin Italy, 1266–1343*. New Haven: Yale University Press.
Buc	Buc, Philippe. 2001. *The Dangers of Ritual: Between Early Medieval Texts and Social Scientific Theory*. Princeton, NJ: Princeton University Press.
Buccio (1907)	Buccio di Ranallo. 1907. *Cronaca aquilana rimata di Buccio di Ranallo di Popplito di Aquila*. Vincenzo De Bartholomaeis, ed. Rome: Forzani.
Buccio (2008)	Buccio di Ranallo. 2008. *Cronica*. Carlo De Matteis, ed. Florence: SISMEL-Edizioni del Galluzzo.

Cammarosano	Cammarosano, Paolo, ed. 1994. *Le forme della propaganda politica nel Due e nel Trecento.* Rome: École Française de Rome.
Candido (2018)	Candido, Igor. 2018. *Petrarch and Boccaccio: The Unity of Knowledge in the Pre-Modern World.* Berlin: De Gruyter.
Capasso	Capasso, Bartolomeo. 1902. *Le fonti della storia delle provincie napolitane dal 568 al 1500.* Naples: Riccardo Marghieri.
Carratelli (1992)	Carratelli, Giovanni Pugliese. 1992. *Storia e civiltà della Campania.* 2 *Il medioevo.* Naples: Electa.
Casteen (2015)	Casteen, Elizabeth. 2015. *From She-Wolf to Martyr: The Reign and Disputed Reputation of Johanna I of Naples.* Ithaca, NY: Cornell University Press.
Casteen (2018)	Casteen, Elizabeth. 2018. "On She-Wolves and Famous Women: Boccaccio, Politics and the Neapolitan Court." In Holmes–Stewart, 219–45.
Cavallo (1992–93)	Cavallo, Guglielmo, et al., ed. 1992–93. *Lo spazio letterario del medioevo: Il medioevo latino* 1. *La produzione del testo.* Rome: Salerno.
Celenza (2017)	Celenza, Christopher. 2017. *Petrarch: Everywhere a Wanderer.* London: Reaktion Books.
Chronicon Estense	*Chronicon Estense.* 1908. RIS 15.3, fasc. 1–2.
Chronicon Mutinense	Giovanni da Bazzano. 1917. *Chronicon Mutinense AA. 1188–1363.* Tommaso Casini, ed. RIS 15:551–634.
Cronicon siculum	De Blasiis, Giuseppe, ed. 1887. *Cronicon siculum incerti authoris ab anno 340 ad annum 1396 in forma diary [sic]: Ex inedito Codice ottoboniano vaticano.* Naples: Giannini.
Chronicon Suessanum	In Pellicia, 1:51–78.
Clareno (1999)	Clareno, Angelo. 1999. *Historia septem tribulationum Ordinis minorum.* Orietta Rossini, with Hanno Helbling, ed. Rome: ISIME.
Clareno (2005)	Clareno, Angelo. 2005. *A Chronicle or History of the Seven Tribulations of the Order of Brothers Minor.* David Burr and E. R. Daniel, ed. and trans. St. Bonaventure, NY: Franciscan Institute.
Clarke (2007)	Clarke, Paula. 2007. "The Villani Chronicles." In Dale (2007), 113–43.
Cochrane	Cochrane, Eric. 1980. *Historians and Historiography in the Italian Renaissance.* Chicago: University of Chicago Press.

ABBREVIATIONS

Coluccia (2017)	Coluccia, Rosario. 2017. "Testi storici e fatti linguistici." In Francesconi–Miglio, 117–36.
Crassullo	Crassullo, Angelo. *Annales de rebus tarentinis*. In Pelliccia, 5:111–25.
Cronaca Senese	Dei, Andrea, and Agnolo di Tura del Grasso. *Cronaca Senese*. RIS 15.6:253–94.
Dale (2007)	Dale, Sharon, et al., ed. 2007. *Chronicling History: Chroniclers and Historians in Medieval and Renaissance Italy*. University Park: Pennsylvania State University Press.
DBI	*Dizionario Biografico dei Italiani*. 1961–. Rome: Istituto della Enciclopedia Italiana.
De Blasi (2012)	De Blasi, Nicola. 2012. *Storia linguistica di Napoli*. Rome: Carocci.
De Caprio (2012)	De Caprio, Chiara. 2012. *Scrivere la storia a Napoli tra Medioevo e prima età moderna: Tre studi*. Rome: Salerno.
De Caprio (2014)	De Caprio, Chiara. 2014. "Spazi comunicativi, tra dizioni narrative e storiografia in volgare: Il Regno negli anni delle guerre d'Italia." *Filologia e Critica* 39:39–72.
De Caprio (2015)	De Caprio, Chiara. 2015. "La storiografia angioina in volgare: Lessico metaletterario, modalità compositive e configurazioni stilistiche nella *Cronaca di Partenope*." In BA, 427–48.
De Caprio (2017)	De Caprio, Chiara. 2017. "La scrittura cronachistica nel Regno: Scriventi, tesi e stili narrativi." In Francesconi–Miglio, 227–68.
Delle Donne (2001)	Delle Donne, Fulvio. 2001. *Politica e letteratura nel Mezzogiorno medievale: La cronachistica dei secoli XII–XV*. Salerno: Carlone.
Delle Donne (2001a)	Delle Donne, Fulvio. 2001. "Austerità espositiva e reelaborazione creatrice nel *Chronicon* di Domenico da Gravina." In Delle Donne (2001), 1 28–46.
Delle Donne (2015.1)	Delle Donne, Fulvio. 2015. "*Virgiliana Neapolis Urbs*: Receptions of Classical Naples in the Swabian and Early Angevin Ages." In Hughes-Buongiovanni, 152–69.
Dell Donne (2015.2)	Delle Donne, Fulvio. 2015. *Alfonso il Magnanimo e l'invenzione dell'Umanesimo monarchico*. Rome: ISIME.
Delle Donne (2021)	Delle Donne, Fulvio. 2021. With Guido M. Cappelli. *Nel regno delle lettere: Umanesimo e politica nel Mezzo giorno aragonese*. Rome: Carocci.
Del Re	Del Re, Giuseppe. 1868. *Cronisti e scrittori sincroni napoletani*. Naples: Iride.

Del Treppo (2006)	Del Treppo, Mario. 2006. *Storiografia nel Mezzogiorno*. Naples: Guida.
Deliyannis (2003)	Deliyannis, Deborah Mauskopf, ed. 2003. *Historiography in the Middle Ages*. Leiden: Brill.
Diurnali	Monteleone, Duca di. 1895. *Diurnali detti del Duca di Monteleone*. Nunzio Federico Faraglia, ed. Naples: Società Napoletana di Storia Patria.
Dunbabin (2011)	Dunbabin, Jean. 2011. *The French in the Kingdom of Sicily, 1266–1305*. Cambridge: Cambridge University Press.
EA	*L'état Angevin: pouvoir, culture et société entre XIIIe et XIVe siècle: Actes du colloque international organisé par l'American Academy in Rome (Rome–Naples, 7–11 novembre 1995)*. Rome: École française de Rome & ISIME, 1998.
Elliott–Warr	Elliott, Janis, ed. 2004. With Cordelia Warr. *The Church of Santa Maria Donna Regina: Art, Iconography, and Patronage in Fourteenth-Century Naples*. Burlington, VT: Ashgate.
EMC	*Encyclopedia of the Medieval Chronicle*. 2015. Graeme Dunphy et al., ed. Brill Online.
Enders (1999)	Enders, Jody. 1999. *The Medieval Theater of Cruelty: Rhetoric, Memory, Violence*. Ithaca, NY: Cornell University Press.
Falconieri (2017)	Falconieri, Tommaso di Carpegna. 2017. "Note sulla cronachistica in volgare a Roma." In Francesconi–Miglio, 215–26.
Feniello (2015)	Feniello, Amedeo. 2015. *Napoli 1343: Le origini medievali di un sistema criminale*. Milan: Mondadori.
Ferguson (1948)	Ferguson, Wallace K. 1948. *The Renaissance in Historical Thought: Five Centuries of Interpretation*. Boston: Houghton Mifflin.
Fleck (2010.1)	Fleck, Cathleen A. 2010. *The Clement Bible at the Medieval Courts of Naples and Avignon: A Story of Papal Power, Royal Prestige, and Patronage*. Farnham: Ashgate.
Fleck (2010.2)	Fleck, Cathleen A. 2010. "Patronage, Art, and the Anjou Bible in Angevin Naples (1266–1352)." In *Anjou Bible*, 37–51.
Fleck (2010.3)	Fleck, Cathleen A. 2010. "The Rise of the Court Artist: Cavallini and Giotto in Fourteenth-Century Naples." In Warr–Elliott, 38–61.
Formentin (2012.a)	Formentin, Victor. 2012. "Approssimazioni al testo e alla lingua della *Cronica* d'Anonimo romano." In idem, *Leggere gli apparati: Testi e testimoni dei classici italiani*. Milan: Unicopli, 27–71.

Francesconi–Miglio	Francesconi, Giampaolo. 2017. With Massimo Miglio, ed. *Le cronache volgari in Italia: Atti della VI Settimana di studi medievali (Roma, 13–15 maggio 2015)*. Rome: ISIME.
Froissart (2013)	Froissart, Jean, 2013. *The Online Froissart*. Peter Ainsworth and Godfried Croenen, ed. At https://www.dhi.ac.uk/onlinefroissart.
Gaglione (2009)	Gaglione, Mario. 2009. *Converà ti que aptengas la flor: Profili di sovrani angioini, da Carlo I a Renato (1266–1442)*. Milan: Lampi di stampa.
Gehl (1993)	Gehl, Paul F. 1993. *A Moral Art: Grammar, Society, and Culture in Trecento Florence*. Ithaca, NY: Cornell University Press.
Gardiner (1993)	Gardiner, Eileen. 1993. *Medieval Visions of Heaven and Hell: A Sourcebook*. New York: Garland.
Gardiner–Musto (2015)	Gardiner, Eileen. 2015. With Ronald G. Musto. *The Digital Humanities: A Primer for Students and Scholars*. New York: Cambridge University Press.
Gravina (1903)	Gravina, Domenico da. 1903. *Dominici de Gravina notarii Chronicon de rebus in Apulia gestis (aa. 1333–1350)*. RIS 12.3.
Gravina (2022)	Gravina, Domenico da. 2022. *Chronicon de rebus in Apulia gestis*. Fulvio Delle Donne et al., ed. Florence: SISMEL-Edizioni del Galluzzo.
Green (1972)	Green, Louis. 1972. *Chronicle into History: An Essay on the Interpretation of History in Florentine Fourteenth-Century Chronicles*. Cambridge: Cambridge University Press.
Grendler (1989)	Grendler, Paul F. 1989. *Schooling in Renaissance Italy: Literacy and Learning, 1300–1600*. Baltimore: Johns Hopkins University Press.
Grendler (2002)	Grendler, Paul F. 2002. *The Universities of the Italian Renaissance*. Baltimore: Johns Hopkins University Press.
Gualdo (2017)	Gualdo, Riccardo. 2017. "Le cronache dell'Italia mediana." In Francesconi–Miglio, 187–213.
Hall–Willette	Hall, Marcia B. 2017. With Thomas Willette, ed. *Artistic Centers of the Italian Renaissance: Naples*. New York: Cambridge University Press.
Hanning	Hanning, Robert W. 1966. *The Vision of History in Early Britain: From Gildas to Geoffrey of Monmouth*. New York: Columbia University Press.
Hay (1977)	Hay, Denys. 1977. *Annalists and Historians: Western Historiography from the Eighth to the Eighteenth Centuries*. London: Methuen.

Holmes–Stewart	Holmes, Olivia, and Dana E. Stewart, ed. 2018. *Reconsidering Boccaccio: Medieval Contexts and Global Intertexts.* Toronto: University of Toronto Press.
Holstein (2006)	Holstein, Alizah. 2006. "Rome During Avignon: Myth, Memory, and Civic Identity in Fourteenth-Century Roman Politics." Ph.D. diss., Cornell University.
Hughes–Buongiovanni	Hughes, Jessica. 2015. With Claudio Buongiovanni, ed. *Remembering Parthenope: The Reception of Classical Naples from Antiquity to the Present.* Oxford: Oxford University Press.
Internullo (2016)	Internullo, Dario. 2016. *Ai margini dei giganti: La vita intellettuale dei romani nel Trecento (1305–1367 ca.).* Rome: Viella.
ISIME	Istituto Storico Italiano per il Medio Evo.
Kelly (2003)	Kelly, Samantha. 2003. *The New Solomon: Robert of Naples (1309–1343) and Fourteenth-Century Kingship.* Leiden: Brill.
Kelly (2011)	Kelly, Samantha, ed. 2011. *Cronaca di Partenope: An Introduction to and Critical Edition of the First Vernacular History of Naples (c.1350).* Leiden: Brill.
Kempshall	Kempshall, Matthew. 2011. *Rhetoric and the Writing of History, 400–1500.* Manchester: Manchester University Press.
Kirkham (2009)	Kirkham, Victoria. 2009. With Armando Maggi, ed. *Petrarch: A Critical Guide to the Complete Works.* Chicago: University of Chicago Press.
Kirkham (2013)	Kirkham, Victoria, et al., ed. 2013. *Boccaccio: A Critical Guide to the Complete Works.* Chicago: University of Chicago Press.
Laureys (1997)	Laureys, Marc. 1997. "Between *Mirabilia* and *Roma Instaurata:* Giovanni Cavallini's *Polistoria.*" In A&N, 100–115.
Léonard	Léonard, Emile G. 1932–37. *Histoire de Jeanne I, reine de Naples, comtesse de Provence (1343–1382): Mémoires et documents historiques.* 3 vols. Paris–Monaco: Imprimerie de Monaco. 1. *La jeunesse de la reine Jeanne.*
Leone De Castris (2006)	Leone De Castris, Pierluigi. 2006. *Giotto a Napoli.* Naples: Electa.
Lummus (2013)	Lummus, David. 2013. "The Changing Landscape of the Self *(Bucolicum carmen).*" In Kirkham (2013), 155–69.
Merback	Merback, Mitchell B. 1999. *The Thief, the Cross, and the Wheel: Pain and the Spectacle of Punishment in Medieval and Renaissance Europe.* Chicago: University of Chicago Press.

Moe	Moe, Nelson. 2002. *The View from Vesuvius: Italian Culture and the Southern Question.* Berkeley: University of California Press.
Montuori (2012.1)	Montuori, Francesco. 2012. "Immagini di Napoli fra trecento e quattrocento." In *Il viaggio a Napoli tra letteratura e arti*. Pasquale Sabbatino, ed. Naples: Edizioni Scientifiche Italiane, 13–37.
Montuori (2017)	Montuori, Francesco. 2017. "Come 'si costruisce' una cronaca." In Francesconi–Miglio, 31–87.
Morosini	Morosini, Roberta. 2012. "La 'bona sonoritas' di Calliopo: Boccaccio a Napoli, la polifonia di Partenope e i silenzi dell'Acciaiuoli." In BA, 69–87.
Musca (1985)	Musca, Giosuè. 1985. "Cronisti meridionali nell'età angioina." In *Civiltà del Mezzogiorno: La cultura angioina*. Milan: Silvana, 31–74.
Murphy (1974)	Murphy, James Jerome. 1974. *Rhetoric in the Middle Ages: A History of Rhetorical Theory from Saint Augustine to the Renaissance.* Berkeley: University of California Press.
Musto (1983)	Musto, Ronald G. 1983. "Angelo Clareno, O.F.M.: Fourteenth-Century Translator of the Greek Fathers. A Checklist of Manuscripts and Printings of His 'Scala paradisi'." *Archivum Franciscanum Historicum* 76:589–645.
Musto (1985)	Musto, Ronald G. 1985. "Queen Sancia of Naples (1286–1345) and the Spiritual Franciscans." In *Women of the Medieval World: Essays in Honor of John H. Mundy*. Julius Kirshner and Suzanne F. Wemple, ed. New York: Blackwell, 179–214.
Musto (1997)	Musto, Ronald G. 1997. "Franciscan Joachimism at the Court of Naples, 1305–1345: A New Appraisal." *Archivum Franciscanum Historicum* 90.3–4:1–86.
Musto (2003)	Musto, Ronald G. 2003. *Apocalypse in Rome: Cola di Rienzo and the Politics of the New Age.* Berkeley: University of California Press.
Musto (2013)	Musto, Ronald G. 2013. *Medieval Naples: A Documentary History, 400–1400.* New York: Italica Press.
Musto (2016)	Musto, Ronald G. 2016. "The Visualization of Power in the Reign of Giovanna I of Naples." *Visual History* 2:105–24.
Musto (2017)	Musto, Ronald G. 2017. "Naples in Myth and History." In Hall–Willette, 1–33.
Otter (2005)	Otter, Monica. 2005. "Functions of Fiction in Historical Writing." In Partner (2005), 109–30.

Palmer (2021)	Palmer, James A., ed. and trans. 2021. *The Chronicle of an Anonymous Roman: Rome, Italy, and Latin Christendom, c.1325–1360*. New York: Italica Press.
Palmieri (1934)	Palmieri, Matteo. 1934. *Vita Nicolai Acciaioli*. Gino Scaramella, ed. RIS 13.2.
Palmieri (2001)	Palmieri, Matteo. 2001. *La vita di Niccolò Acciaioli*. Alessandra Mita Ferraro, ed. Bologna: Il Mulino.
Partner (1985)	Partner, Nancy F. 1985. "The New Cornificius: Medieval History and the Artifice of Words." In Breisach, 5–59.
Partner (2005)	Partner, Nancy F., ed. 2005. *Writing Medieval History*. London: Hodder Arnold.
Pelliccia	Pelliccia, Alessio A. 1780–81. *Raccolta di varie croniche, diarj, ed altri opuscoli cosi italiani, come latini appartenenti alla storia del regno di Napoli*. 5 vols. Naples: Perger.
Perriccioli Saggese (2010)	Perriccioli Saggese, Alessandra. 2010. "Cristophoro Orimina: An Illustrator at the Angevin Court of Naples." In *Anjou Bible*, 113–25.
Petrarch (1974)	Petrarch, Francesco. 1974. *Petrarch's Bucolicum Carmen*. Thomas Goddard Bergin, trans. New Haven: Yale University Press.
Petrarch (1996)	Petrarch, Francesco. 1996. *The Revolution of Cola di Rienzo*. Mario Emilio Cosenza, ed. 3rd rev. ed. Ronald G. Musto, ed. New York: Italica Press.
Petrarch (2002)	Petrarch, Francesco. 2002. *Guide to the Holy Land: Itinerary to the Sepulcher of Our Lord Jesus Christ*. Theodore J. Cachey, Jr., ed. and trans. Notre Dame, IN: University of Notre Dame Press.
Petrarch (2004.1)	Petrarch, Francesco. 2004. *Le familiari: Familiarium rerum libri*. Latin ed., Vittorio Rossi and Umberto Bosco. Italian trans., Ugo Dotti and Felicita Audisio. 5 vols. Turin: N. Aragno.
Petrarch (2004.2)	Petrarch, Francesco. 2004. *Le senili: Rerum senilium libri*. Latin ed., Elvira Nota. Italian trans., Ugo Dotti. 3 vols. Turin: N. Aragno.
Petrarch (2005.1)	Petrarch, Francesco. 2005. *Letters of Old Age: Rerum senilium libri*. 2 vols. Aldo S. Bernardo et al., trans. New York: Italica Press.
Petrarch (2005.2)	Petrarch, Francesco. 2005. *Letters on Familiar Matters: Rerum familiarium libri*. 3 vols. Aldo S. Bernardo, trans. New York: Italica Press.
Pryds	Pryds, Darleen. 2000. *The King Embodies the Word: Robert d'Anjou and the Politics of Preaching*. Leiden: Brill.

ABBREVIATIONS

Ragone (1998)	Ragone, Franca. 1998. *Giovanni Villani e i suoi continuatori: La scrittura delle cronache a Firenze nel Trecento*. Rome: ISIME.
RIS	Muratori, Ludovico Antonio, ed. 1723–51. *Rerum Italicarum Scriptores*. 25 vols. Milan: RIS, 5th ed. Giosuè Carducci and Vittorio Fiorini, ed. Bologna: N. Zanichelli, 1931–33.
Rizzi (2017)	Rizzi, Andrea. 2017. *Vernacular Translators in Quattrocento Italy: Scribal Culture, Authority, and Agency*. Turnhout: Brepols.
Romano (2017)	Romano, Serena. 2017. "Patrons and Paintings from the Angevins to the Spanish Hapsburgs." In Hall–Willette, 171–232.
Rudolph (2006)	Rudolph, Conrad. 2006. *A Companion to Medieval Art: Romanesque and Gothic in Northern Europe*. Malden, MA: Blackwell.
Sabatini (1975)	Sabatini, Francesco. 1975. *Napoli angioina: Cultura e società*. Naples: Edizioni scientifiche italiane.
Seibt	Seibt, Gustav. 2000. *Anonimo romano: Scrivere la storia alle soglie del Rinascimento*. Rome: Viella.
Senatore (2014)	Senatore, Francesco. 2014. "Fonti documentarie e costruzione della notizia nelle cronache cittadine dell'Italia meridionale (secoli XV–XVI)." *Bullettino ISIME* 116:279–333.
Senatore (2017)	Senatore, Francesco. 2017. "Cronaca e cancellerie." In Francesconi–Miglio, 285–99.
SN	*Storia di Napoli*. 1967–74. Ernesto Pontieri, ed. 6 vols. Naples: Società Editrice Storia di Napoli.
Spiegel (1997)	Spiegel, Gabrielle M. 1997. *The Past as Text: The Theory and Practice of Medieval Historiography*. Baltimore: Johns Hopkins University Press.
Stock (1990)	Stock, Brian. 1990. *Listening for the Text: On the Uses of the Past*. Philadelphia: University of Pennsylvania Press.
Strohm (1992)	Strohm, Paul. 1992. *Hochon's Arrow: The Social Imagination of Fourteenth-Century Texts*. Princeton, NJ: Princeton University Press.
TMC	*The Medieval Chronicle*. 1999–2020. Erik Cooper, ed. 13 vols. to date. Amsterdam: Rodopi.
Trovato–Gonelli	Trovato, Paolo, and Lida Maria Gonelli, ed. 1993. *Lingue e culture dell'Italia meridionale, 1200–1600*. Rome: Bonacci.
Varvaro	Varvaro, Alberto. 1997. "L'Italia meridionale nelle cronache di Jean Froissard." In A&N, 131–39.

Villani (1906)	Villani, Giovanni. 1906. *Selections from the First Nine Books of the* Croniche Fiorentine. Rose E. Selfe, trans. Philip H. Wicksteed, ed. London: Archibald Constable.
Villani (1991)	Villani, Giovanni. 1990–91. *Cronica Nuova.* Giuseppe Porta, ed. 3 vols. Parma: Guanda.
Villani (1995)	Villani, Matteo and Filippo Villani. 1995. *Cronica.* Giuseppe Porta, ed. 2 vols. Parma: Guanda.
Walsingham (1864)	Walsingham, Thomas. 1864. *Thomae Walsingham, quondam monachi S. Albani, historia anglicana.* Henry Thomas Riley, ed. London: Longman, Green.
Walsingham (2003–11)	Walsingham, Thomas. 2003–11. *The St Albans Chronicle: The* Chronica Maiora *of Thomas Walsingham.* John Taylor et al., ed. and trans. 2 vols. Oxford: Clarendon Press.
Warr–Elliott	Warr, Cordelia. 2010. With Janis Elliott. *Art and Architecture in Naples, 1266–1713.* Malden, MA: Wiley-Blackwell.
White (1987)	White, Hayden. 1987. *The Content of the Form: Narrative Discourse and Historical Representation.* Baltimore: Johns Hopkins University Press.
White (2010)	White, Hayden. 2010. *The Fiction of Narrative: Essays on History, Literature, and Theory, 1957–2007.* Robert Doran, ed. Baltimore: Johns Hopkins University Press.
Wickham (2015)	Wickham, Chris. 2015. *Sleepwalking into a New World: The Emergence of the Italian City Communes in the Twelfth Century.* Princeton, NJ: Princeton University Press.
Winterthur	Winterthur, Johanns von. 1982. *Die Chronik Johanns von Winterthur.* Friedrich Baethgen and C. Brun, ed. MGH n.s. 3. Berlin: Weidmann.
Witt (2009)	Witt, Ronald G. 2009. "The Rebirth of the Romans as Models of Character *(De viris illustribus).*" In Kirkham (2009), 103–11.
Witt (2012)	Witt, Ronald G. 2012. *The Two Latin Cultures and the Foundation of Renaissance Humanism in Medieval Italy.* Cambridge: Cambridge University Press.
Wright	*The Life of Cola di Rienzo.* 1975. John Wright, ed. and trans. Toronto: Pontifical Institute of Mediaeval Studies.
Zabbia (1997)	Zabbia, Marino. 1997. *Notai-cronisti nel Mezzogiorno svevo-angioino: Il "Chronicon" di Domenico da Gravina.* Salerno: Laveglia, 1997.
Zabbia (1999)	Zabbia, Marino. 1999. *I notai e la cronachistica cittadina italiana nel Trecento.* Rome: ISIME.

Zabbia (2001)	Zabbia, Marino. 2001. "Giovanni da Bazzano." DBI 55. At www.treccani.it/ enciclopedia/giovannida bazzano_(Dizionario_Biografico).
Zabbia (2017)	Zabbia, Marino. 2017. "Cronaca e mondo notarile." In Francesconi–Miglio, 271–84.
Zorzi (1994)	Zorzi, Andrea. 1994. "Rituali di violenza, ceremoniali penali, rappresentazioni della Giustizia nelle città italiane centro-settentrionali (secoli xiii–xv)." In Cammarosano, 395–425.

PREFACE

This book examines the writers and forms of history writing of the trecento that helped shape our modern perceptions of southern Italy (the Mezzogiorno). These perceptions include popular ideas about the South encountered in daily reportage and scholarly discourse around culture and its representations. The following pages synthesize both synchronic issues — comparisons between the historiography produced within the Regno and that of the north of Italy and the rest of Europe during the trecento — and the diachronic issues around the transition from trecento historiography to the humanist works of the quattrocento.

These chapters draw on over four decades of my research on medieval Rome, on medieval and early modern Naples, and on the cultural and religious history of the trecento. Beginning with work on Angelo Clareno OFM, Petrarch, Cola di Rienzo and the medieval concept of Rome and its revival, I had the opportunity to examine both narrative and archival sources for Rome and to compare them with narrative accounts from both northern and southern Italy. I followed a similar path in studying the history of Naples, first tracing the influence of the Spiritual Franciscans on the thought and patronage of Queen Sancia of Majorca, then on the court of Sancia and King Robert the Wise and their heirs. This work led me to issues in the late medieval, and then early modern historiography of Naples and the South. My *Medieval Naples: A Documentary History 400–1400* surveyed both the variety of source materials available for study — archival, narrative, archeological and visual — and the range of historical interpretation around them. Many of these themes were then synthesized in my Introduction to *Artistic Centers of the Italian Renaissance: Naples,* edited by Marcia B. Hall and Thomas Willette.[1]

While researching these topics, I was struck by certain similarities among primary sources that dealt with widely different places, people and events in the trecento. These similarities reflect broad social, political and structural patterns across Italy on the verge of the the early modern period: the realities of urban life and governance; dynastic conflict; warfare, disease and natural calamities; the role of women; ritual, crime and punishment; the place of humanity in the universe. But they also reveal common modes of thinking and writing about these realities. These modes appeared as much in narrative styles and language as in reoccurrences of unusual and startling episodes, and in echoes — uncanny resonances — of familiar motifs, fables and literary and visual works of the late Middle Ages.

Study of historiography in the northern communes[2] has demonstrated that the writers who composed these histories were citizens of the same Italian urban and political culture as their contemporary romance writers and poets, painters, architects, theologians and lawyers, and that they rarely worked in isolation. Though most were neither academics nor clerics, as educated laypeople during a time of rapid cultural change, they were aware of both timeless legends and tales and of the latest works of art and literature, of the most current speculations by religious, philosophical and scientific writers, and of the newest inquiries into the recent and classical past. They were educated from the earliest age in the rules of grammar and rhetoric, and if *latinantes* (literate in Latin), they would have studied all the major classical authors then available in their grammar textbooks, their rhetoric handbooks, or as the core of their mature reading. If fluent in vernacular literacy, they would have used many translations of the classics and been familiar with courtly romance and *chansons de gestes* and their formal structure and linguistic and narrative strategies.[3]

These historians lived in tightly knit urban communities, in cities of rarely over 25,000 in population, in the same neighborhoods *(rioni, contrade* or *seggi),* amid long-lasting, thick social fabrics, in which most people knew hundreds of their neighbors.[4] Their social communication was performed through meeting and conversation on the street, in shops, at feasts, processions, baptisms, weddings and funerals, ceremonies in church or in public spaces and buildings. Their textual communities were reinforced by oral tradition, active networks of neighborhood and urban news, gossip and rumor, by the notary's documentation of daily life, property holdings, family records, contracts and civic events, by large and small commercial transactions, by official proclamations and written decrees.

While the *piazze, larghi* and *campi* of Florence, Siena, Rome or Venice still exist and continue to provide physical spaces for social encounter and performance, their touristic and transitory functions have long diminished such daily urban interaction as permanent community gives way to international residence and tourism. One must reside in some of Italy's smaller cities, especially in the less touristed South, to understand these patterns of formal news and ceremony, regular meeting and chance encounter, greeting, conversation, information-sharing that continue to create and reinforce these thick social networks. More broadly, this medieval urban society saw the literate elite's children, brothers and sisters, cousins, aunts and uncles, their patrons and clients filling many of the public offices and chief roles in government, church, cultural and intellectual life. Few could really claim ignorance of what their relatives, friends and neighbors were doing, saying or thinking. Their accounts were also heavily colored by their commonly inherited ways of conceiving of, and their tools for remembering and recording, the events of the distant and more recent past.

But this raises the question of whether the medieval Mezzogiorno — and its historians — share these characteristics of urban society with the more intensely studied and visited cities of the North. The research presented in the following chapters makes the strong argument that they did so in several areas key to history writing in the South and to this study. First, the South possessed similar classes of literate writers *(latinantes)*. These were drawn largely from the notarial and other professional and administrative groups. Second, these writers reflected the values of the local urban cultures of the South. They placed heavy emphasis on civic virtues and vices and framed their narratives most frequently in classical terms both pagan and early Christian. Third, their audiences were largely urban, lay and professional for whom these narratives resonated in ways that paralleled that of the North: civic pride, the origins and development of their political and cultural institutions, collective memory and the virtues or vices of leading individuals. Finally, trecento history writing in the South had already adopted many of the key principles we associate with Renaissance historiography: classical language, style and citation, the use of historical exempla, skillful deployment of classical rhetorical modes and structures, broad thematic organization, and a focus on individual actions and lives. In the works of writers like the Anonimo romano and Domenico da Gravina, they reached levels of sophistication and narrative power that match or exceed many of their contemporary urban chroniclers of the North. In many ways, the works we will examine below constructed the Mezzogiorno that we imagine today.

Over the past generation the linguistic turn has invited us to recognize that all historiography is a construct: not in inventing past facts and events — those facts are solid historical objects and not the inventions of poets, novelists or propagandists — but in the methods a historian uses to narrate these events, how they are emploted, presented as coherent, ordered in time, delineated as cause and effect.[5] Narratives, in the Middle Ages, as in antiquity and today, are a form of rhetoric,[6] with the same tool kit of words, sentences, syntax and construction, images, symbols, metaphors and allegories that poets and fiction writers use in their writing. In the following book we hope to bring to bear the tools, theoretical frames and insights developed over the last generation to analyze these forms of narrative and invention.

Since the nineteenth century, intense study of southern Italian history and historiography, institutions and culture has produced a substantial and important body of work that matches that of the North in rigor and intensity.[7] Several such works have informed this book throughout. In 1902, Bartolomeo Capasso's *Le fonti della storia dell provincie napolitane dal 568 al 1500* established the basic typologies, specific research and broad methods that have informed all later historiographical research into the Mezzogiorno. In addition, the sources of southern history — from the Normans through the Angevin, Aragonese and Spanish periods — have also received a modern revitalization[8] with new editions of texts and the digital dissemination of vast archival resources for the kingdom of Naples, many now available freely online.[9]

These findings have been enriched by contemporary Italian scholars who have brought the methods and insights of numerous disciplines to bear on these texts and on the historical issues that they raise. These scholars include Vittorio Formentin, Chiara De Caprio, Francesco Senatore, Francesco Montuori, Fulvio Delle Donne, and Dario Internullo, among others. Much of this research was incorporated in 2017 into *Le cronache volgari in Italia*, edited by Giampaolo Francesconi and Massimo Miglio.[10] Its influence is apparent throughout the following pages.

I examined the tradition of Anglophone scholarship on medieval Italy and its historiography elsewhere,[11] but its legacy of ignoring or undervaluing the historians of the South remains strong. The most influential study of Italian historiography for this period remains Eric Cochrane's 1980 *Historians and Historiography in the Italian Renaissance*,[12] which judged these trecento southern historians barely worth the mention. Cochrane remains important because few other works have examined southern Italian historiography. In 2007, *Chronicling History: Chroniclers and Historians in Medieval and Renaissance Italy*[13] presented eleven essays covering many aspects of the peninsula from Venice, Genoa and Milan to Florence. But the Mezzogiorno is covered in only one essay[14] and that for the Norman period (c.1100–c.1200). This reflects a long-standing historiographical focus on the achievements of these "northerners" in southern Italian history "as founders and organizers of states and contributors to European culture."[15] According to this volume, "the Norman histories of Italy more resembled their English counterparts than the communal annals of Lombardy."[16] The Angevin period, from the mid-thirteenth to the end of the fifteenth century, is overlooked.[17] Likewise Matthew Kempshall's exhaustive analysis of the impact of rhetoric on medieval historiography[18] makes scant mention of Italian work and discusses Neapolitan historiography only in the context of quattrocento humanism.[19]

Ronald G. Witt's *The Two Latin Cultures and the Foundation of Renaissance Humanism in Medieval Italy*[20] of 2012 summed up this line of interpretation:

> Communal historiography thrived in northern Italy.... These histories had been preceded by a rich tradition of city chroniclers in northern and central Italy beginning in the mid-twelfth century.[21]

Witt also explicitly sets his horizons north of the Tiber. He posits two main reasons: first, because humanism developed out of a lay Italian culture that did not penetrate the South,[22] and, second, because this "Italy" was restricted to the Carolingian *regnum*, that is, Italy north of the Tiber, excluding the papal states and the southern Regno. Witt reiterates

> that cultural developments in the lower half of the peninsula were so unlike those in the north that they were in effect those of other societies.... Unless otherwise indicated 'Italy' and 'Italian' refer to the regnum [of the north].[23]

As recently as 2015, Chris Wickham's *Sleepwalking into a New World: The Emergence of the Italian City Communes in the Twelfth Century* excludes everything south of Rome, even in his broad analysis of "Italy."[24] These broader European dichotomies have been reformulated and served up again as recently as 2016 in Quinones' *North/South*.[25]

The Anglophone scholarship that these works reflect maintains a concentration on the North and a continuation of the venerable dichotomy between its republican, communal and lay culture — a new "Italy" derived from and continuing a new political, cultural and linguistic freedom[26] — and the "other" Italy, the supposedly tradition-bound, clerical, royal and autocratic culture of the South. This southern culture is posited as having inhibited secular history writing, literary life, true classical study, urban liberty and society until the arrival of "Renaissance humanism" under the Aragonese.[27] Even within Italy, historiographical research has sometimes tended to reinforce this northern "hegemony."[28]

It therefore seems appropriate that one now turns to the chroniclers and historians of the South during the trecento in order to examine the series of questions posed by these dichotomies. Did the material, political and cultural structures of the South during the trecento create a historiography substantially different from that of the North? How different were their authors, their methods and scope, their sources, their rhetorical and other narrative tools and skills? How different were their audiences and the purposes to which these works were applied? How self-conscious were these trecento authors of their art and of their intent? Congruently, how air-tight are our current divisions between Northern and Southern writers discussed here?

On another level, we will examine the verbal and visual tools and theoretical insights that we deploy today to reveal the culture and history of the South of Italy and its reception in later centuries, including our own. Throughout this book, I will emphasize that the Mezzogiorno is a historical construct. Thus "writing" addresses both what trecento historians constructed and how modern scholars and critics have interpreteted these writings and their contexts. We have therefore taken care to cite modern scholars and their debates throughout our discussions in order to trace how the works of the trecento have been received and interpreted and how the nature and scope of this construct have been born and have evolved.

Such analyses provide us with new and meaningful understanding of the period and culture, of its relationship to later historiography and of cultural forms of the Italian South into the modern period. Just as importantly, we hope to demonstrate how our present understanding of the South has affected readers' understanding of its past and of historians' own attitudes toward this region, its history and its sources.

These are among the themes and questions that underlay the following book. We will address most of these questions explicitly, while others will remain implicit in our conclusions. We hope that this process will provide Anglophone readers with both ground- and frame-work for an initial synthesis and new interpretation of this large body of material.

※

This second, revised edition is published by Italica Press by special arrangement with Routledge. It presents revised text; revised and updated notes; a chronology of person and events; and a complete, updated, and comprehensive bibliography. For consistency of reference, all numbering of chapters, subsections, annotation, and pagination remain the same as in the original hardcover edition. This edition also takes into account suggestions and criticisms of certain editorial and interpretive issues in the first hardcover edition published by Routledge. It adds selected new materials published since that first edition, most especially the new, complete translation of the *Cronica* of the Anonimo romano by James A. Palmer published by Italica Press in 2021, which now supercedes Wright's partial translation of 1975. References to Wright's edition are retained and supplemented by Palmer's new edition. It also incorporates the new edition of Domenico da Gravina's *Chronicon* by Fulvio Delle Donne et al. published in 2022. In Chapter 6 it takes into consideratioin new research on Francesco da Barberino and his relationship to Giotto, Dante, and Villani. Other recent research is incorporated throughout.

※

ACKNOWLEDGMENTS

This book builds upon and synthesizes the research, writing and methodologies of experts in a wide variety of fields from history and historiography, through philology and codicology, literary and visual studies, to political science, anthropology and gender studies. I hope that I have incorporated these into this book fairly and comprehensively and that I have correctly interpreted the current state of research in areas that are not my specialty. All translations from the Latin and Italian, unless otherwise specified, are my own.

Several chapters of this book have built on my previously published work. These include my *Medieval Naples*[29] and my Introduction to *Artistic Centers of the Italian Renaissance Naples*.[30]

Parts of Chapter 5 are an expansion of a conference presentation and a seminar delivered at the Università degli Studi di Napoli Federico II in December 2014 at the conference entitled Scrivere la storia tra Medioevo ed età moderna: Autorialità e progettualità del testo storico. My thanks to conference organizers Giancarlo Abbamonte, Chiara De Caprio, Andrea Mazzucchi, Francesco Montuori and Francesco Senatore for the invitation to present my initial research findings and for their generous remarks and hospitality. Much of this work was subsequently published in *Visual History*.[31]

I presented parts of Chapter 6, on visual evidence, at the Early Modern Rome 3 conference at the University of California, Rome Center in October 2017. I would like to thank Sharon Dale, Alizah Holstein, Tommaso di Carpegna Falconieri and session attendees for their comments. My thanks also to conference organizers Julia Hairston and Paolo Alei for their invitation to speak. At the American Academy in Rome, my thanks to Director John Ochsendorf and Deputy Director Cristina Puglisi for their hospitality to a returning Fellow during and after this meeting and the many opportunities to continue to discuss my work there with other scholars of the trecento. Prof. Julia Holloway and Prof. Janis Elliott have also read and commented on sections of this chapter. Prof. Elliott has also called my attention to several of the images that were used for Chapter 6.

Large parts of Chapter 8, on the Black Legend of the Angevins, build on work appearing between 2013 and 2018.[32] All materials quoted from Petrarch's *Familiares* are from Francesco Petrarch, *Letters on Familiar Matters (Rerum Familiarium Libri)*, edited & translated by Aldo S. Bernardo (New York: Italica Press, 2005). Copyright 2005 by Aldo S. Bernardo. Used by permission of Italica Press.

❧ PREFACE & ACKNOWLEDGMENTS

My thanks to Prof. Gabrielle M. Spiegel of Johns Hopkins University for invaluable advice at the early stages of this project. At the University of Bristol, my appreciation is to Prof. George Ferzoco, Prof. Carolyn Muessig, the director of the Centre for Medieval Studies, and to Prof. Yasmin Haskell, the director of the Institute of Greece, Rome and the Classical Tradition for inviting me to speak on various aspects of my research for this book and for their warm welcome to Bristol and encouragement at important junctures of my research and writing. My thanks again to Prof. Chiara De Caprio for her careful reading and critique of preliminary chapters in this book. My thanks also to Prof. Fulvio Delle Donne for access to his new edition the *Chronicon* of Domenico da Gravina and for his heplful editorial suggestions. Dr. Eileen Gardiner read and advised each draft of this manuscript in the midst of her own research and other professional responsibilities. To her, as always, I offer my deepest appreciation and gratitude.

NOTES

1. Musto (2017).
2. See Green (1972), Dale (2007), Cochrane, Witt (2012), Francesconi–Miglio.
3. Kempshall, 450–56; Mortensen (2015).
4. One of the best treatments of this thick social context remains Brentano (1974). For more recent treatments, see Rehberg–Modigliani (2004). See also Musto (2003), 23–33, 208–11 et passim; Palmer (2019) and Palmer (2021). Boccaccio's works, including the *Corbaccio, Decameron* and *Fiammetta*, provide a similar sense for Naples.
5. This study is indebted to several fundamental works of medieval and Renaissance historiography, including Ferguson (1948), Brandt (1966), Guenée (1973), Hay (1977), Cochrane, Fleischman (1983), Partner (1986), Partner (2005), White (1987), White (2010), Stock (1990), Strohm (1992), Spiegel (1997), Spiegel (2005).
6. Knape (2002).
7. Musca (1985); Zabbia (1997); Zabbia (1999); Delle Donne (2001); Delle Donne (2011); De Caprio (2012); Montuori (2012); Francesconi-Miglio; Gonelli (1993) surveys nineteenth-century editions.
8. Del Treppo (2006); Senatore (2014); Francesconi-Miglio.
9. For example, the ALIM project: Archivio della Latinità Italiana del Medioevo, at http://alim.dfll.univr.it.
10. Francesconi–Miglio.
11. Musto (2017); Musto (2018).
12. Cochrane. See Chapter 9, pp. 259–60.
13. Dale (2007). For earlier work, Green (1967), 161–78; Green (1972).
14. Loud (2007).
15. This classic statement is from Haskins (1915), vii. Searle (1988) offered a revisionist view. See Musto (2003), xviii–xx, xli–xlvi on this Norman/Northern perspective.
16. Dale (2007), xi.
17. In Deliyannis (2003) twelve essays cover many aspects of European medieval

history and chronicle writing, both secular and religious. Italian historiography, even of the cities, however, is restricted to northern Italy, with the exception of the "Roman *Cronica*" (Anonimo romano) in Vasina (2003), 388–41.
18. Kempshall (2011).
19. Kempshall (2011), 496–506 et passim.
20. Witt (2012).
21. Witt (2009a), 103–4; and "The Return to Antiquity," Witt (2012), 438–71.
22. Witt (2012), 1–2.
23 Witt (2012), 13. For a corrective to the teleological view of the modern Italian nation as normative of late medieval ideas and realities, see Airò (2013).
24. Wickham (2015), 161–205.
25. Quinones (2016).
26. See also Faini (2008); Mortensen (2015), 25–26.
27. Witt (2012), 1–3. The same is also true for some European historiography. Most recently, Baker-Maxson (2015) makes no mention of Naples or the South.
28. Francesconi (2017), 165. See also Vasina (2003), who explains (341 n. 61) his decision to dismiss "the historiographical traditions of southern and insular Italy after 1000 (indeed, urban chronicle-writing had a very limited fortune, since the cities belonged to the royal demesne)."
29. Musto (2013).
30. Musto (2017).
31. Musto (2016).
32. Musto (2013), lvi–lxi; Musto (2017), 11–25; Musto (2018).

WORKS CITED

Baker, Nicholas Scott, 2015. With Brian Jeffrey Maxson. *After Civic Humanism: Learning and Politics in Renaissance Italy.* Toronto: Centre for Reformation and Renaissance Studies.

Brentano, Robert. 1974. *Rome before Avignon: A Social History of Thirteenth-Century Rome.* New York: Basic Books.

Faini, Enrico. 2008. "Alle origini della memoria comunale: Prime ricerche." *Quellen und Forschungen aus italienischen Archiven und Bibliotheken* 88:61–81.

Fleischman, Suzanne. 1983. "On the Representation of History and Fiction in the Middle Ages." *History and Theory* 22:278–310.

Guenée, Bernard. 1973. "Histoire, Annales, Chroniques: Essai sur les genres historiques au moyen âge." *Annales: Economies, Sociétés, Civilisations* 4:997–1016.

Knape, Joachim. 2002. "Historiography as Rhetoric." *TMC* 2:117–29.

Loud, Graham. 2007. "History Writing in the Twelfth-Century Kingdom of Sicily." In Dale (2007), 29–54.

Mortensen, Lars Boje. 2015. "Comparing and Connecting: The Rise of Fast Historiography in Latin and Vernacular (12th–13th cent.)." *Medieval Worlds* 1:25–39.

Musto, Ronald G. 2016. "The Visualization of Power in the Reign of Giovanna I of Naples." *Visual History* 2:105–24.

Palmer, James A. 2019. *The Virtues of Economy: Governance, Power and Piety in Late Medieval Rome.* Ithaca, NY: Cornell University Press.

Partner, Nancy F. 1986. "Making Up Lost Time: Writing on the Writing of History." *Speculum* 61:90–117.

Quinones, Ricardo J. 2016. *North/South: The Great European Divide.* Toronto: University of Toronto Press.

Rehberg, Andreas. 2004. With Anna Modigliani. *Cola di Rienzo e il Comune di Roma.* 2 vols. Rome: Inedita.

Spiegel, Gabrielle M. 1997. *The Past as Text: The Theory and Practice of Medieval Historiography.* Baltimore: Johns Hopkins University Press.

—. 2005. *Practicing History: New Directions in Historical Writing after the Linguistic Turn.* New York: Routledge.

White, Hayden. 1987a. "The Value of Narrativity in the Representation of Reality." In White (1987), 1–25.

1. INTRODUCTION

The following book offers an introduction and detailed analysis of historiography in the South of Italy (the Mezzogiorno) during the fourteenth century (trecento). It focuses on a group of historians who wrote on events and individuals key to the history of the Angevin dynasty of the kingdom of Naples (the Regno). It will focus less on the events described in their works, which cover the entire range of Angevin rule from 1266 to 1442, and more on historiography and it methods of representation. The following chapters will attempt to delineate the nature of this southern historiography by deploying a variety of methods and theoretical frames to its sources; elements, style and structure; literary, artistic and historical influences; case studies of this work; and theoretical frames for understanding it. These frames will include recent literary work on textualities, authorship and reception; feminist theory of queenship and misogynistic literary traditions; research on alterity, orientalism and eco-criticism; anthropological studies of ritual and punishment; scholarship on visuality and orality; new codicological theory and work; and interpretations of humanism and other cultures of the book.

This analysis also follows Mario Del Treppo's distinction among trecento historians both "from/in" *(nel)* and "about" *(sul)* the South.[1] The difference is an important one, since this book will synthesize not only history writing emerging *from* the South and its traditions but also the writings of late medieval historians and chroniclers *about* the South. It will also trace their impact on the emerging concept of the Mezzogiorno and the "Question of the South," first in Italian and then in European and North American historiographies. Their roots, I argue, can be traced directly to both these groups of historians.

The following chapters also distinguish between the mainland Mezzogiorno and Sicily, focusing on the first and only indirectly on Sicily[2] as it affects the history of the Regno during the trecento. The reasons for this distinction are several. Geographically, the "South" poses a question first taken up during the Risorgimento. For our purposes, the "South" begins with the historical District of Rome and includes the entire historical mainland of the Regno. It largely excludes Sicily, both because the island remained independent from the mainland throughout the trecento and because its historiography very often diverges from that of the mainland Mezzogiorno. The southern kingdom had it roots in the original Norman conquest of Apulia, Calabria and then Sicily. While the Normans had conquered all of the South, including Naples, by 1139, their kingdom maintained its identity as that "of Sicily." It retained this name under the successors of the Normans: the German Hohenstaufen emperors (1194–1266) and their French Angevin conquerors, who took the kingdom from the heirs of Emperor Frederick II in 1265/66. But with the revolt of Sicily from King Charles II in 1282, an event known as the Sicilian Vespers, the history of Sicily began to diverge from that of the mainland in significant ways[3] that only served to deepen and expand the already obvious cultural differences of what would later be designated as the "Two Sicilies."[4] The Angevin monarchs of Naples continued to refer to their kingdom as that of "Sicily" in order to maintain their claims to what even King Robert the Wise (1309–43) called its "mutilated" lost limb.[5]

For trecento writers, Sicily's separation from the southern mainland was very real. Both political and economic realities clearly marked these two as separate in the minds of contemporaries. Literature also reflected this difference. In many of the tales in his *Decameron*, for example, Giovanni Boccaccio (1313–75)[6] reflects the permanence of the Aragonese regime of Sicily, and beyond that its Norman and Hohenstaufen past. It was also common among northern writers to refer to the mainland kingdom of Naples as that of "Apulia," reinforcing its origins first in Byzantine domination, then in the Norman conquests of Apulia and Calabria and their distinction from Sicily.

Linguistic studies also distinguish between the medieval Regno[7] and Sicily, as have recent cultural studies.[8] New administrative definitions under both the Italian National Institute of Statistics (ISTAT)[9] and the European Union's NUTS designations for the European Parliament clearly separate them.[10]

The geographical and cultural boundaries of this mainland Mezzogiorno were, and remain, a question of lively discussion, debate and continuing controversy in Italy over regional and national history,[11] often posed as the problem of "where does the South begin?" For the Piedmontese of the early and mid-nineteenth century, the South was thought to begin at the Po Valley.[12] For many modern Florentines, it still begins south of the Arno. In this book we will take it to mean the medieval District of Rome[13] and the Regno of Naples,[14] thus the region extending from the Tiber Valley to the southernmost points of Calabria and Apulia. Geographically, this remains the region generally considered the mainland Mezzogiorno today, the region that historically was accorded a different identity from the communal cities and regions of Tuscany and the North. As recently as 2012, Ronald G. Witt

CHAPTER 1 ❧ INTRODUCTION

reinforced this distinction, referring to the "Italy" of his research as the medieval "regnum," north of the Tiber.[15]

During the trecento, the District of Rome also maintained close family ties, political connections and cultural affinities with the Regno of Naples.[16] There is also some reason to treat these two regions as separate culturally and linguistically from the North, as both Romanesco[17] and the various southern dialects, including Neapolitan,[18] have long been taken as distinguishing cultural markers with ancient antecedents and medieval influences different from the Tuscan of Dante, Petrarch and Boccaccio.[19] Indeed, the Latin culture of the South also had quite a different history from that of Florence or Milan, for example, influenced directly as it was by Basilian and Benedictine monasticism; late ancient, Lombard and Byzantine scribal cultures;[20] and then by successive Norman, Hohenstaufen and Angevin domination.

In previous work, we examined the problem inherent in the historiography of the Italian South,[21] especially in Anglophone writing of the past fifty years, and its ramifications on the still prevalent view of the Mezzogiorno. We noted that these issues include the general neglect of the trecento Mezzogiorno in Anglophone historiography and the emphasis on the origins and development of northern Italian "Renaissance humanism" as a teleological projection of Anglo-American urban, commercial and democratic culture, of a "civic humanism."[22] More mundane reasons also contribute to this neglect of Neapolitan history, including the changing tourist image of Italy first formed by Anglophones with the end of the Grand Tour into the late nineteenth century and the development of twentieth-century tourism.[23]

As Nelson Moe[24] and others have discussed in great detail, these factors have been compounded and embedded into the historiography of the "Southern Question" and its cultural manifestation, *meridionalismo*.[25] This politico-economic discourse is also reflected in scholarly opinion on the autonomy of Naples as cultural "capital."[26] Another aspect of this historiographical tendency to stress the alterity of Naples is the theory of the Angevin dynasty's attempts to legitimize its tenuous conquest of the South via a variation of Renaissance "self-fashioning"[27] and the search for legitimacy.[28] Variants of this interpretation emphasize the imported foreignness of Neapolitan and southern artistic styles beginning with the Angevin conquest, seeking to redo the South according to the French Gothic model and so again bolster the conquerors' legitimacy on their tenuous thrones.[29]

A more purely methodological issue compounds these theoretical frames: the relative but very real paucity of Neapolitan archival sources for the study of the later Middle Ages. More than other Italian and European centers, Naples and its Regno have suffered repeated ravages to its historical records for the medieval[30] and early modern periods.[31]

Building on recent trends in historiographical, textual, literary, orientalist and gender studies, this book argues that these Anglophone attitudes are directly related to the Italian "Southern Question" that emerged from the Risorgimento and the absorption of the kingdom of Naples into the new Italian nation. However, it departs from the historical consensus in seeking the roots of the negative attitudes of northern Italian writers not in nineteenth-century nationalist, racialist theory of the "other" but in far older and deeper intellectual and cultural modes that have their origins in the late Middle Ages, especially in the trecento.

※

This book examines the two major historiographical questions embodied in its title "Writing Southern Italy before the Renaissance." The first is to emphasize that southern Italy is a cultural artifact, an idea resulting from the writing of historians, poets and political thinkers who consciously constructed an identity for this area of Italy over and above its geographical location. In addition, this construct is the result of the very process of historical writing, and thus both the action of writing and the object of that writing bring together notions of the active agency of the author (and *scriptor* and reader)[32] in creating a narrative of the Mezzogiorno. The second part of the title, "before the Renaissance," carries two meanings. The first is chronological: the century leading up to the Aragonese conquest (1442) of the kingdom of Naples and then its annexation by the Spanish Empire (1504). The other meaning of "before" is spatial and performative, that is, "in the face of" the now debated term "Renaissance" as both a chronological period and yet another historical construct. Though many would prefer to call the period "early modern," I retain the term "Renaissance" in the title and in certain discussions of historiography to extend our study of such constructs.

"Writing Southern Italy" is thus an act that must take into account how we characterize both a region and a century that turns from late medieval into early modern and how that affects our understandings, interpretations and our very choice of places, events, personalities and works of verbal and visual art to construct our narratives.[33] Beyond all these considerations, this book seeks to introduce readers to these writers and their narratives of events, issues and historical figures. Throughout, this book addresses the traditional division among medieval annalists, chroniclers and historians.[34]

Medieval historiography has been studied so intensively over the past two generations, however, that one can no longer confidently use this three-fold division.[35] This is particularly true of the fourteenth century throughout Europe when the chronicle emerged as a form that included aspects of both the annal and the history, and its writers made it clear that many genre distinctions were artificial and permeable.[36]

※

CHAPTER 1 ❧ INTRODUCTION

A synopsis of later chapters follows. Chapter 2 provides a basic survey of the historians, their lives, work and impact. Historians and works in southern Italy[37] include Angelo Clareno OFM, the *Chronicon Suessanum*, the *Cronica di Partenope*, Domenico da Gravina, the Anonimo romano, Buccio di Ranallo, the *Chronicon siculum incerti authoris*, Angelo Crassullo, the *Diurnale* of the Duca di Monteleone, as well as mention of a few minor southern historians. While Saba Malaspina's chronicle formed an important source for Niccolò di Iamsilla[38] and helped form later views of the Angevins, neither can be considered among trecento historians.

By contrast, the historians of northern Italy are often far better known both to medievalists and to nonspecialists, a result of both the historiographical issues we discussed above and because of the wider scope of their work. Among these are Giovanni da Bazzano, the *Chronicon Estense*, the Villani, the *Cronica Sanese*, Petrarch and Boccaccio. The last two had first-hand familiarity with Naples, its court and culture; and their work often crosses the modern border between the literary and the historical. Matteo Palmieri's *Vita Nicolai Acciaioli* contains a good deal of Acciaiuoli's own letters. He is also illustrative of the humanist historiography that we analyze to compare with trecento works in Chapter 9. This book excludes other major writers like Brunetto Latini, Dante and Birgitta of Sweden because their work lacks this first-hand knowledge, because they could not be considered historiography or because they fall outside our chronological limits. Likewise, while historians like Bartolomeo of Neocastro or the various versions of *Rebellamentu di Sichilia* offer compelling and important accounts that touch on such major events as the Vespers and the Angevin-Aragonese wars, these were works of the duecento and their analysis more properly belongs to a study of Sicilian historiography.

Finally, this chapter introduces historians from northern Europe who included Italian and southern Italian events and personalities in their works with more than glancing interest. These include Johanns von Winterthur, Jean Froissart and Thomas Walsingham. While the three were remote from events in the Regno, as representative examples of northern historiography they can offer comparison and further contextualization for the Italians into more broadly studied fields of medieval history writing. In addition, their northern perspectives and historiographical traditions helped influence views of the Regno and provide useful points of comparison to the Italians included here, especially in their reliance on second-hand (often falsified) report, rumor and literary invention. Since these writers are generally better known to medievalists, they also offer objective correlatives to the conclusions drawn for the Italian writers discussed in the pages below. Those familiar with all these historians and their works may want to move on quickly to Chapter 3; but I suspect that many professional medievalists may be unfamiliar with the writers discussed in Chapter 2 or the contexts into which I place them.

Chapter 3 looks at sources. These include the classical tradition in both texts and archeological remains, earlier medieval historiography, and other Mediterranean sources. As Chapter 5 examines at length, literary sources were often integrated seamlessly into accounts to lend authenticity to particular episodes and to establish larger truth claims. Religious sources could include Scripture, sermons and saints' lives as well as canon law and some theological work. In addition, many of these historians discussed here, whether lay or religious, urban or court writers, had access to large amounts of archival material, ranging from private and public correspondence to commercial, notarial, legal, diplomatic and administrative records. These historians also reveal a sophisticated knowledge of contemporary law, science, medicine and cosmology, and these influences were brought to bear on both larger narrative schemes and on particular details of plot and character. Finally, much of the narration in these southern histories includes the strong presence of first-hand testimony. This chapter consequently traces the roles of orality, folk and popular memory and eyewitness accounts both to analyze narratives and to help define the textual communities active in the South. Here again, the consensus account that northern historiography reflected urban and lay outlooks and that southern reflected religious and monarchical outlooks falls short. In this regard, Chapter 3 also reviews the role of notaries, administrators and other professionals in establishing verifiable documentary history, as well as in bridging the gap between oral traditions, urban narrative and learned histories.

Chapter 4 focuses on the formal characteristics of these works and will range from philological considerations to broader narrative strategies. It covers narrative communities; language choice; Latin histories written either by ecclesiastics or lay writers, and their style and quality. It also analyzes vernacular histories, whether in French, Tuscan, Romanesco or Neapolitan. It then reviews narrative structures. Following rhetorical practice well known to these writers, this chapter divides these structures into paratactic, thematic and symbolic/figurative. Finally, Chapter 4 also attempts to classify these works into various narrative forms, again following rhetorical divisions into the epideictic, judicial or forensic/deliberative modes.

Relying on recent work in textualities and rhetorical traditions, this chapter examines how such forms both derive from, and set the context for, a certain professional habitus of discourse and varying narrative structures. These can range from the religious, including the confessional, homiletic, sermon and scholastic; to the aristocratic *chansons de geste* and romance; to the commercial, urban, legal, notarial and other scribal cultures; to court, archival, ambassadorial and diplomatic forms; to early humanist lettres, biographies and classically inspired treatises and histories. Each can be distinguished on philological and technical grounds, and each can be recognized as influencing the forms and impact of these histories.

CHAPTER 1 ❧ INTRODUCTION

Chapter 5 examines the impact of romance literature on narrative structures, motifs and character construction. It draws its chief examples from the life and reign of Queen Giovanna I of Naples (1343–82). After reviewing the literature on falsely accused queens, it discusses the trecento historiography around Giovanna I as heavily influenced by such narratives. It also places this historiography within the context of literary romance models. These include The *Empress of Rome, Constance, La Manekine, The Countess of Anjou, Melusine, Meliadus* and Boccaccio's life of Giovanna I in *De mulieribus claris*. Here it probes the permeable boundaries between fictive and factual narratives. This porosity allowed writers such as the Villani and Gravina in their chronicles, Petrarch in his *Familiares* and Boccaccio in his *De mulieribus claris* to employ a vocabulary and grammar of literary plot elements, characters, motifs and devices to provide the details of interior thought and motivation, to provide uncanny resonances, to "fill in the gaps," to supply missing details of events, and to extend characterization beyond the available conventions of hagiography and royal biography. In so doing, these writers were able to construct dramas of female inheritance, male privilege, dynastic conflict, female perversion, integrity and nobility that were readily recognizable to their audiences.

Chapter 6 analyzes visual evidence as sources for trecento historiography and for its language of civic virtue and vice. The first part of this chapter examines both extant and lost frescoes as autonomous visual texts and their possible impact on trecento writers' narrative structures, characterizations and framing techniques. It offers close readings of these paintings and attempts to apply the latest visual theory. Visual sources include Ambrogio Lorenzetti's *Good and Bad Government* frescoes in Siena, the Anonimo romano's account and ekphrasis of Rienzo's political frescoes in Rome and Giotto's *De viris illustribus* cycle in Naples. The second half of the chapter looks at Angevin manuscripts and their visualization of power. It probes the visual uses of the *Anjou Bible* (Maurits Sabbe 1), the *Statutes of the Order of the Holy Spirit* or *Knot* (BNF 4274), and *Meliadus de Leonnois* (BL Add 12228) to demonstrate the ease with which Angevin rulers crossed the boundary between fiction and fact by inserting themselves into the fabric of chivalric romance and sacred history to bolster dynastic claims at home and abroad.

Chapter 7 provides comparative case studies. After summarizing interpretations of medieval ceremony and ritual — including those of criminal executions and accounts of ritual dismemberment and cannibalism — it offers examples of the literary forms and tropes that appear in these historical works, including what I have termed "rituals of punishment." Among these case studies are the fall of the Duke of Athens in Florence, the punishment of Giovanna I's courtiers in Naples, the execution of Judge Martuccio in Apulia and the murder of Cola di Rienzo in Rome.

The chapter then proceeds to what I have termed "prison dialogues." Our historians offer these as supposedly private and candid exchanges among men and women locked away in prison and awaiting punishment. These dialogues include accounts of the Roman barons arrested by Cola di Rienzo, of Fra Morreale and his companions awaiting execution in Rome and of Giovanna I's courtiers awaiting their execution in Naples. Since such dialogues break the rules for reliable witness and stretch credibility, this chapter uses these accounts as tests of literary borrowing, verisimilitude and truth claims in trecento historiography.

Chapter 8 traces the construction of a single grand narrative: what I have termed "the black legend of the Angevins." After an introduction laying out the narrative of this black legend, this chapter moves on to the infamy of Queen Giovanna I and how it was devised by her political enemies and turned into a consistent narrative by trecento historians. Analysis includes research on *infamia* and the theme of women murderers. It traces the development of this black legend in Hungarian royal propaganda against Giovanna, in Petrarch's letters and other works and in the historiographical development of the theme in Villani, Domenico da Gravina and Boccaccio. This chapter argues that these writers constructed a narrative and a permanent legacy not only for Queen Giovanna I but also for the Regno that has influenced both historiography and popular thought on the Mezzogiorno to our own day.

Chapter 9 returns the conversation to territory more familiar to most Italianists and students of history: humanist historiography. It concentrates on the Aragonese court at Naples and compares its humanist writing to the contemporary "civic chronicles" of Naples. This chapter summarizes previous scholarship on both sides of the Atlantic and draws appropriate comparisons with our own findings. One of its key interpretative issues is the concept of "civic humanism" and how it relates to the Regno.

This chapter also brings to bear recent work on authorship and the book, comparing the consensus view of humanist historiography as privileging a comprehensive, unified and single-authored work with that of new research into the civic historians of Naples, reflecting a multipolarity of authorship, sources and voices that in some ways mirrors our modern distinction between print and digital cultures.

After a brief introduction to the consensus view of Renaissance historiography and a historical introduction to the Regno under the Aragonese, Chapter 9 examines humanist historians of the quattrocento. Beginning with Flavio Biondo's construct of the South in his *Italia Illustrata*, it moves on to the humanist historians at the Neapolitan court: Panormita, Bartolomeo Facio, Lorenzo Valla, Giannozzo Manetti and Giovanni Pontano. Neapolitan civic historians include Loise de Rosa, the Notar Giacomo and Ferraiolo.

Areas of comparison include style, language and sources; truth claims; technique and structure; character and motivation; the individual and the citizen, *virtù* and *fortuna*; and the grand sweep of historical periodization. It also addresses recent research on the genres of such historiography, including important Italian work on form, codicology, language and sources. Based on these findings, Chapter 9 approaches the underlying question of whether one can, in fact, draw sharp contrasts between the historiography of the Angevin and Aragonese periods, that is, between late medieval and "Renaissance" historiography in southern Italy, or between the supposedly urban, mercantile historiography of the North and the purportedly royal, ecclesiastical writing of the South. The chapter concludes with some remarks on what these findings might mean for our understanding of historiography on both sides of this long-held divide. A brief Chapter 10, Conclusions, recaps these themes and also draws some comparisons between trecento historiography and that of the twenty-first century, reflecting several influences, including gender studies and the digital and material turns.

ACKNOWLEDGMENTS

Parts of this chapter are based on my "Introduction" in *Artistic Centers of the Italian Renaissance: Naples,* Marcia B. Hall and Thomas Willette, ed. (New York: Cambridge University Press, 2017). Copyright © 2017 Cambridge University Press, reprinted with permission.

NOTES

1. Del Treppo (2006), 7.
2. Musca (1985), 47–68 for Sicilian historians.
3. Epstein (1992); Peri (1981); and Abulafia (1997), esp. 66–81, 156–71.
4. The official name, "Kingdom of the Two Sicilies," came only with the mainland kingdom of Naples' reunification with the kingdom of Sicily in 1816 after the Napoleonic wars and the restoration of the Bourbon monarchy. Santore (2001), xxxiii–xli, 97–136. On the practical distinctions for historiography, see Moe, 41–45.
5. In his own final will and testament of 1343, par. 14. Musto (2013), 247.
6. Days 2.6; 4.1, 4.4, 4.5, 5.2, 5.6, 5.7, 8.10, 10.7. See also Santini (1940); Abulafia (1979); Mazzamuto (1983); Kirkham (2013).
7. For example, Capasso; Capano–Varvaro (1981); De Caprio (2017) with ample supporting bibliography on 227–28 n. 2 et passim.
8. Moe, 41–46.
9. www.istat.it/en.
10. This distinguishes the South from the islands of Sicily and Sardinia. See http://ec.europa.eu/eurostat/web/nuts/national-structures-eu.
11. Del Treppo (2006), esp. 8–14, 34–39, 149–65, 177–82.
12. Moe, 38–40. The quip, "Africa starts south of Rome," still reflects the racialist formulation essential to the Southern Question and some Italians' continuing anxiety over their new global context.
13. Cola di Rienzo, using well-known legal and historical precedent going back to at least Emperor Otto IV in 1201, defined it in article 7 of the *Ordinances of the Buono Stato* as "from the Ponte di Ceperano all the way to the Ponte della Paglia." Musto (2003), 145.

14. Defined in Robert of Anjou's will of 1343 as the territory from the borders of the papal state "all the way to the Faro," or Reggio Calabria. See Musto (2013), 241 and n. 113.
15. Witt (2012), 1–3.
16. Zabbia (1997), 58–59, sees important connections; as does Internullo (2016), 53–54, 369–76. Gualdo (2017), 192–93, views Roman historiography as distinct from that of either the North or the Regno.
17. Felici (1972); D'Achille (2012).
18. Sabatini (1975); De Blasi (2012).
19. L. Petrucci (1993); Sabatini (1993); Coluccia (1994); De Blasi (2012); Alfano (2012). Boccaccio documented this linguistic difference in his well-known Neapolitan letter. See below Chapter 2, p. 31.
20. Cilento (1969); Ambrasi (1969); Rosa (1987); Carratelli (1992); Musto (2013), lxxiii–lxxvi.
21. Musto (2017).
22. See Chapter 9, pp. 260, 266, 272.
23. Black (2003); Hendrix (2015).
24. Moe, 5–6, 178–79 et passim; Santore (2001), 187–211.
25. Moe, 83–183, distinguishes between the Southern Question itself and *meridionalismo* in his chapter 7, esp. at 224. See Moe for earlier discussions of the issue of the Mezzogiorno and its cultural otherness and orientalism. For later work see Nitti (2004); Vitolo (2004); Musella (2005); Marco (2008). Ongoing research also reflects a new revisionism away from *meridionalismo* and toward a study of the South less as the North's "other" and more on its own terms. See Lumley (1997); and the positive reassessment in Senatore (2012), 45–49. Biddick (1994), 24, notes how orientalism has also produced "a fantastic scholarly geography of the origins of Europe. Within European national histories, orientalism produced knowledge of certain epochs, places, and social groups as an orientalism within." On efforts to stress the *Italianità* of the South during the Risorgimento, Marzano (2015).
26. The nature of Naples as artistic capital is key to the essays in Hall–Willette.
27. One can trace this to the newly self-conscious "Renaissance man" in Burckhardt (1958) and Greenblatt (1980).
28. Dunbabin (1998), 9–20, esp. 18; Kelly (2003), 119–32; Dunbabin (2011), 189–98.
29. A theme first formulated in the Anglophone scholarship by Gardner (1976) and restated most recently in Gardner (2004), 196–97; Bruzelius (2004); Kelly (2004). This view has been modified in Bruzelius–Tronzo (2011), 55–112. Hersey (1969), vi, 1 et passim, emphasized it as a key element of Aragonese cultural and political policy.
30. The bibliography on this topic is large. See Kiesewetter (1998); and Musto (2013), xvii–xviii.
31. Bentley, *Politics*, 49 n. 2, estimated that 90% of the Aragonese archives were lost. See also Senatore (2014).
32. For distinctions between the traditional *auctor* as creator of texts and the *scriptor* as transmitter, reassembler of existing texts, see Cavallo (1992–93); Holtz (1992–93); Petrucci (1992–93); Troncarelli (1992–93).
33. On early modern historiography of the South, see Marino (2013).
34. The distinctions made by Dale (2007), ix–xii et passim, where it is the

contribution of the northern Normans, once again, to write "history," and not the "annals" of the southern monks or communes. One does not have to agree with Hayden White's emphasis on moral imperative to acknowledge the value of seeing the annal, chronicle and history as differing, yet valid, forms of historical representation. White (1987a) et passim in that collection. For a summation of current consensus on these forms, Foote (2005); Arnaldi (1992–93); Mortensen (2015). On the chronicle form, Hay (1977), 38–86; Dumville (2002). On the annal, Burgess (2013).

35. Kempshall emphasizes the fluidity among these three forms in medieval historiography and argues for the inclusion of the visual as well. See 34–35, 88–91, 428–29, 441–56.
36. Kempshall, 449–53, 479–84.
37. The most useful guide remains Capasso, esp. 118–68.
38. Delle Donne (2015) examines the re-use and modification of Saba's work as part of Iamsilla's pro-Hohenstaufen history.

WORKS CITED

Abulafia, David. 1979. "The Reputation of a Norman King in Angevin Naples." *Journal of Medieval History* 5.2:135–47.

—. 1997. *The Western Mediterranean Kingdoms 1200–1500: The Struggle for Dominion*. Harlow: Longman.

Alfano, Giancarlo, et al., ed. 2012. *Boccaccio angioino: Materiali per la storia culturale di Napoli nel Trecento*. Brussels: Peter Lang.

Ambrasi, Domenico. 1969. "La vita religiosa." SN 3:437–574.

Arnaldi, Girolamo. 1992–93. "Annali, Cronache, Storie." In Cavallo (1992–93), 2:463–513.

Biddick, Kathleen. 1994. "Bede's Blush: Postcards from Bali, Bombay, and Palo Alto." In *The Past and Future of Medieval Studies*. John Van Engen, ed. Notre Dame: University of Notre Dame Press, 16–44.

Black, Jeremy. 2003. *Italy and the Grand Tour*. New Haven: Yale University Press.

Blunt, Anthony. 1974. *Naples as Seen by French Travellers 1630–1780*. Oxford: Clarendon Press.

—. 1975. *Neapolitan Baroque and Rococo Architecture*. London: Zwemmer.

Bruzelius, Caroline. 1991. "Art, Architecture and Urbanism in Naples." In Bacco, lxv–lxxix.

—. 2011. With William Tronzo. *Medieval Naples: An Architectural & Urban History, 400–1400*. New York: Italica Press.

Burckhardt, Jacob. 1958. *The Civilization of the Renaissance in Italy*. S.G.C. Middlemore, trans. New York: Harper & Row.

Burgess, Richard W. 2013. With Michael Kulikowski. "Medieval Historiographical Terminology: The Meaning of the Word *Annales*." TMC 8:165–92.

Capano, A.M. Compagna Perrone. 1981. With Alberto Varvaro. "Capitoli per la storia linguistica dell'Italia meridionale e della Sicilia." *Medioevo romanzo* 8:91–132.

Cilento, Nicola. 1969. "La cultura e gli inizi dello studio." SN 2.2:521–640.

Coluccia, Rosario. 1994. "Il volgare nel Mezzogiorno." In *Storia della lingua italiana*. L. Serianni and P. Trifone, ed. 3. *Le altre lingue*. Turin: Einaudi, 373–405.
D'Achille, Paolo, et al., ed. 2012. *Lasciatece parlà: Il romanesco nell'Italia di oggi*. Rome: Carocci.
Dumville, David. 2002. "What Is a Chronicle?" TMC 2:1–27
Dunbabin, Jean. 1998. *Charles I of Anjou: Power, Kingship and State-Making in Thirteenth-Century Europe*. London: Longman.
—. 2011. *The French in the Kingdom of Sicily, 1266–1305*. Cambridge: Cambridge University Press.
Epstein, Stephan R. 1992. *An Island for Itself: Economic Development and Social Change in Late Medieval Sicily*. Cambridge: Cambridge University Press.
Felici, Lucio. 1972. "Le vicende del dialetto romanesco." *Capitolium* 47.4:26–33.
Foote, Sarah. 2005. "Finding the Meaning of Form: Narrative in Annals and Chronicles." In Partner (2005), 88–108.
Francesconi, Giampaolo. 2017. "Una toscana senza autori: Siena e dintorni." In Francesconi–Miglio, 165–86.
Gardner, Julian. 1976. "Saint Louis of Toulouse, Robert of Anjou, and Simone Martini." *Zeitschrift für Kunstgeschichte* 39:12–33.
—. 2004. "Santa Maria Donna Regina in Its European Context." In Elliott–Warr, 195–201.
Greenblatt, Stephen. 1980. *Renaissance Self-Fashioning: From More to Shakespeare*. Chicago: University of Chicago Press.
Hendrix, Harald. 2015. "City Branding and the Antique: Naples in Early Modern City Guides." In Hughes-Buongiovanni, 217–41.
Hersey, George L. 1969. *Alfonso II and the Artistic Renewal of Naples, 1485–1495*. New Haven: Yale University Press.
—. 1973. *The Aragonese Arch at Naples, 1443–1475*. New Haven: Yale University Press.
Holtz, Louis. 1992–93. "Autore, Copista, Anonimo." In Cavallo (1992–93), 1:325–52.
Kelly, Samantha. 2004. "Religious Patronage and Royal Propaganda in Angevin Naples: Santa Maria Donna Regina in Contexts." In Elliott–Warr, 27–43.
Kiesewetter, Andreas. 1998. "La cancelleria angioina." In EA, 360–415.
Lumley, Robert. 1997. With Jonathan Morris, ed. *The New History of the Italian South: The Mezzogiorno Revisited*. Exeter: University of Exeter Press.
Marco, Costantino. 2008. *Meridione e meridionalismo: Dal mito storiografico alla politica della formazione civile*. Lungro di Cosenza: Ibis.
Marino, John A. 2013. "Constructing the Past of Early Modern Naples: Sources and Historiography." In *A Companion to Early Modern Naples*. Tommaso Astarita, ed. Leiden: Brill, 11–34.
Marzano, Annalisa. 2015. "Reshaping the Past, Shaping the Present: Andrea de Jorio and Naples' Classical Heritage." In Hughes–Buongiovanni, 266–83.

Mazzamuto, Pietro. 1983. "Il cronotopo dell'isola nel *Decameron* e la vicenda siciliana di Lisabetta." In *Boccaccio e dintorni: Miscellanea di studi in onore di Vittore Branca*. Florence: Olschki, 161–68.
Mortensen, Lars Boje. 2015. "Comparing and Connecting: The Rise of Fast Historiography in Latin and Vernacular (12th–13th cent.)." *Medieval Worlds* 1:25–39.
Musella, Luigi. 2005. *Meridionalismo: Percorsi e realtà di un'idea, 1885–1944*. Naples: Guida.
Musto, Ronald G. 1991. "An Introduction to Neapolitan History." In Bacco, xix–lxii.
Nitti, Francesco Saverio. 2004. With Domenico De Masi. *Napoli e la questione meridionale, 1903–2005*. Naples: Guida.
Peri, Illuminato. 1981. *La Sicilia dopo il Vespro: Uomini, città e campagne, 1282–1376*. Bari: Laterza.
Petrucci, Armando. 1992–93. "Dalla minuta al manoscritto d'autore." In Cavallo (1992–93), 1:353–72.
Petrucci, Livio. 1993. "Il volgare a Napoli in età angioina." In Trovato–Gonelli (1993), 27–72.
Rosa, Alberto Asor, ed. 1987. *Storia e geografia 1. L'età medievale*. Turin: Einaudi.
Sabatini, Francesco. 1993. "Volgare 'civile' e volgare cancelleresco nella Napoli angioina." In Trovato–Gonelli (1993), 109–32.
Santini, Emilio. 1940. "La Sicilia nel *Decameron*." *Archivio storico per la Sicilia* 6:239–52.
Santore, John. 2001. *Modern Naples: A Documentary History, 1799–1999*. New York: Italica Press.
Senatore, Francesco. 2012. "The Kingdom of Naples." In *The Italian Renaissance State*. Andrea Gamberini and Isabella Lazzarini, ed. New York: Cambridge University Press, 30–49.
Troncarelli, Fabio. 1992–93. "L'attribuzione, il plagio, il falso." In Cavallo (1992–93), 1:373–90.
Vitolo, Giovanni. 2004. With Aurelio Musi. *Il Mezzogiorno prima della questione meridionale*. Florence: Le Monnier.

2. THE HISTORIANS: THEIR LIVES AND WORKS

INTRODUCTION

This chapter provides basic information on the most important writers of the late medieval Mezzogiorno, on their works and on their survival in manuscript and print. We will focus on textual sources, whether chronicles, histories, literary inventions or some hybrids of these. Though we will include our authors' use of archival materials here and in subsequent chapters and briefly discuss the literary nature of certain archival sources, we maintain our focus on historiography where authorial intent — and the medieval understanding of *auctoritas* — largely determined the forms and scope of these works. We will examine the nature of compilations and the nature of the "codex-archive" in Chapter 9.

This chapter discusses three broad cultural maps: southern Italy, northern Italy and then northern Europe. As we noted in Chapter 1, we have defined the South to include the medieval District of Rome and the Regno of Naples after the Sicilian Vespers "mutilated" Sicily from the mainland. Within each group we have arranged these works chronologically — roughly by the end date of the history in question. We will address influences, common thematic and technical elements in later chapters.

Except for comparison to humanist historiography in Chapter 9, we have restricted the authors under discussion to those writing in the trecento. In addition, all the authors considered here were male. While this gendering is nothing unusual for the trecento sources, issues of female literacy, and this lack of female narrative agency, will color everything in these histories from rhetorical strategies and forms; to views of religion and worldview, politics and rulership; to notions of embodiment, agency and character.

SOUTHERN ITALY: WHO WROTE?

With the exception of the works of Angelo Clareno and possibly the author of the *Chronicon Suessanum*, trecento historiography in the South was lay and urban. Some writers, including Domenico da Gravina, Giovanni da Bazzano and Angelo Filippo

CHAPTER 2 ⚜ THE HISTORIANS

Crassullo, were notaries — skilled in the arts of legal documentation, rhetoric and civic Latin — often with high-profile positions in the urban administrations of their *universitates*.[1] The anonymous author of the *Diurnale (Diario) di Duca di Monteleone* and Bartolomeo Caracciolo-Carafa were nobles attached to the royal court. We know that the Anonimo romano was university educated, and other notaries may well have been. While often influenced by literary genres and conventions of romance and other chivalric forms, most maintained their civic identities and focus, even while sometimes clearly partisan of various royal and baronial elites.

All were active members of the late medieval communities of which they wrote, often as important agents in the political and cultural events that they describe. All had a professional knowledge of the building blocks of history: eyewitness accounts, oral tradition, verifiable firsthand testimony, archival documents, letters, reports and narrative sources, including both classical and medieval histories. They all used these materials to explain historical structures, events and individual motivations and character. While we will discuss their differences with humanist historians in Chapter 9, we should note that they were consciously aware of the narrative forms that they used and of their limitations.

ANGELO DA CLARENO, OFM

Despite his lifelong desire for obscurity, Angelo da Clareno OFM (c.1255–1337, abbreviated "Clareno" hereafter)[2] is among the most studied trecento writers. Born Pietro da Fossombrone in the March of Ancona c.1255, he entered the Franciscan Order c.1270. By 1274 he had joined the emerging Spiritual Franciscan movement. After spending the years 1279–90 in a Franciscan prison for their position, Clareno and his companions were sent on missionary work to Cilician Armenia. They returned to Italy in 1294 with great expectations for the pontificate of Celestine V, forming their own Order of Poor Hermits of Pope Celestine under the protection of the prominent Roman cardinal Napoleone Orsini. But Celestine's sudden abdication in Naples in 1295 and the election of Boniface VIII again thrust the emerging Spirituals into exile, this time to Greece. In 1309 Clareno traveled to Avignon to lobby for his new order before Pope Clement V and found himself allied with the Colonna, Boniface VIII's former enemies and supporters of the reformers and later the patrons of Petrarch in Avignon. The election of John XXII and the death of Cardinal Giacomo Colonna, however, forced Clareno to escape to Italy in 1318. There he gained the protection of the abbot of Subiaco, remaining at that Benedictine monastery until 1334 when he was again forced to flee, this time to Basilicata, where he died at Sta. Maria dell'Aspro on June 15, 1337.

While in Avignon, Clareno was well positioned to meet and to observe many of the most important ecclesiastical and secular leaders of the time. He also spent much of his later life on the borders of Lazio and the kingdom of Naples and recorded both religious and secular events there during the Angevin period. He corresponded actively with, or had substantial influence upon, many members of the Neapolitan court, including Queen Sancia[3] and, indirectly through his later followers in the Abruzzi, on Cola di Rienzo.[4] Abbot Bartolomeo of Subiaco probably urged him to commit his important knowledge and first-hand experience to writing, and Clareno composed his *Historia* during his years there, probably in the mid-1320s.

His *Historia septem tribulationum ordinis minorum*[5] traces a history of the Spiritual wing of the Franciscan Order from Francis of Assisi to about 1320. It is of major importance for trecento historiography for several reasons. First, it presents a grand historical narrative of trecento church history seen from the margins. Clareno's seven tribulations take their cue indirectly from Joachim of Fiore's seven periods within the second grand age of universal history. They are thematically linked around a central thesis: the unfolding history of church decline and renewal as outlined by Joachim. Clareno's work is therefore less a medieval chronicle than a unified history. Secondly, Clareno's well-informed narrative of events within the Franciscan Order, and more broadly within the Church, sheds important light on larger cultural contexts within trecento Italy, southern France and the Regno. He was friends with many of the most important religious dissenters of the period, and his work is thus a vivid account of the spiritual turmoil of the time that is vividly expressed in more literary form by Dante and Petrarch. Third, Clareno's work was heavily influenced by the written sources for the Franciscan tradition, by his own translations of the Greek Fathers — among the very first of the trecento — and by oral sources. His history thus amply demonstrates the interaction among written, translated and oral memory in creating a textual community. His incorporation of lengthy speeches, purporting to be accurate accounts, recall the ancient classical tradition of historiography and may have been influenced by his readings in classical Latin and Greek texts while in Greece and in the kingdom of Naples.

CHRONICON SUESSANUM

Written in and around the cathedral of Sessa Aurunca, on the Via Appia close to the northern border of Campania, this chronicle was begun in 1103 but contains useful detail only for the Angevin dynasty. It continues until 27 August 1348, when it ends abruptly with the departure of Queen Giovanna I and Louis of Taranto from Naples and Lewis of Hungary's invasion.[6] The anonymous chronicler provides both useful and intense details of the reign of Giovanna I, the murder of Andrew of Hungary and Lewis of Hungary's military

CHAPTER 2 ※ THE HISTORIANS

intervention, with particular interest in events around Sessa Aurunca, Fondi, Gaeta and northern Campania.

Cronaca di Partenope

One of the more useful narrative sources for the history of the later Angevins is the *Cronaca di Partenope,* titled after the ancient Greek name for Naples. Composed in Neapolitan, it is one of the earliest written documentations of that language, albeit in a later redacted form. Bartolommeo Capasso[7] and Francesco Sabatini[8] speculated that the text we now possess was the work of several authors and was composed between 1326 and 1380. It contains four main sections: (1) on ancient Naples, replete with references to the medieval Virgilian tradition,[9] (2) the *Breve informazione* from the Normans to the accession of Giovanna I in 1343, (3) the "Southern Villani," a set of long excerpts from the *Nuova Cronica* and (4) a continuation to 1382.[10] In her recent edition, Samantha Kelly[11] contended that parts one and two were written by a single author, Bartolomeo Caracciolo-Carafa (d. 1362), who completed the text between the summer of 1348 and that of 1350. This hypothesis has been challenged by Francesco Montuori,[12] Francesco Senatore[13] and Chiara De Caprio,[14] who offer an enhanced version of Capasso's and Sabatini's reconstructions. Whatever the solution to the question of authorship, scholars of the text agree that it is heavily indebted to Giovanni Villani's *Nuova Cronica* for much of its material in the 1330s and 1340s[15] and that Caracciolo-Carafa remains associated with the second part.

Available evidence indicates that Caracciolo-Carafa was a member of the lay urban patriciate. He was an educated man who knew Latin, was able to translate many of his sources from classical compendia into Neapolitan and took great pride in Naples' urban culture and heritage. He and his father were both royal officials. He may have represented the *seggio* of Nido in King Robert's parliament of 1332 and again in 1350. He probably served as a royal justiciar in Basilicata in 1333 and was chamberlain at the royal court for Prince Andrew of Hungary from at least 1334. From 1343 until his death in 1362 he served as *magister rationalis* or royal treasurer; and during the Hungarian invasion of the Regno in 1348, he was a member of Naples' civic council.[16] Caracciolo-Carafa was a well-informed narrator of the events unfolding during his own lifetime, knew many of their chief protagonists first-hand, used local oral traditions and Neapolitan topography well and had easy access to many forms of royal documents. He was decidedly pro-Angevin and dedicated at least his portions of the *Cronaca* to Louis of Taranto, consort to Queen Giovanna I and claimant to her throne.[17]

Scholars of the *Cronaca* agree that while it contains much pro-Angevin material, due to the complexity of its compilation, it also stands as one of the best representatives of a lay, urban historiography of the trecento.

The *Cronaca* thus offers a valuable corrective to the sharp distinction made between northern lay, civic and southern clerical and monarchical traditions.[18] This tension between civic and dynastic history[19] makes the *Cronaca* one of the most accessed and repurposed works of late medieval and early modern historiography in the South and makes its complexity the subject of ongoing research and scholarly debate.

Domenico da Gravina

Domenico da Gravina (c.1300–c.1351, abbreviated "Gravina" hereafter) was a notary who wrote the *Chronicon de rebus in Apulia gestis*, covering the years 1333–1350, which survives in a single manuscript.[20] He was born in Gravina in the rich agricultural border region between Lucania (Basilicata) and Apulia. He provided an unofficial history, away from the centers of power in Naples, from the perspective of the provincial elite. Gravina was not a first-hand witness to most of the events that he describes in Naples that form the first part of his chronicle but relied instead on contemporary sources. These included official documents perhaps provided by Gravina's overlord, Gianni Pipino of Altamura, the notarial records of the trials of Queen Giovanna I's couriers and pro-Hungarian[21] sources that were hostile to Giovanna and often inaccurate.[22] Gravina was an adherent of the house of Durazzo, and then of Hungary, and he painted a picture of corruption and misrule under Giovanna I, which he contrasts to Robert the Wise's reign of peace and justice.[23] This part of the *Chronicon* covers in detail the years following the wedding of Andrew of Hungary and Giovanna I in 1333 to Andrew's assassination in September 1345 through the two invasions by Lewis of Hungary.

The second part relates the struggle in Apulia between Maria of Anjou, Queen Giovanna's sister and widow of Charles of Durazzo — who held the city of Gravina as a fief from Giovanna — and the Hungarians under King Lewis' voivoda Stephan Laczkfy. Gravina's references to his own life and that of his neighbors clearly reflect the confused impact of invasion and civil war among constantly changing circumstances and factions. Because of his role as a public notary, he was entrusted with a variety of administrative positions and had a relatively high profile in Gravina. He was an adherent of Andrew of Hungary; but in late 1345, he was accused of belonging to the conspiracy to murder the prince consort. Shortly after the arrival of Lewis of Hungary's troops in Apulia, he declared for the invaders, but the citizens of Gravina sided with Duchess Maria of Durazzo and ultimately with the Neapolitan Angevins. His home and property were therefore expropriated, and he escaped from Gravina. He and his family settled in Bitonto, where he wrote the first part of the *Chronicon* in June and July 1349, focusing on the marriage of Andrew and Giovanna I and its aftermath. He composed the second part in 1350/51, concentrating on Apulia and the impact of civil war and invasion. His descriptions are personal, vivid and bitter.

CHAPTER 2 — THE HISTORIANS

According to recent analyses of his work, Gravina used few written sources for this part and relied on his own memory of events and the testimony of other eyewitnesses.[24] But his narrative seems to have been heavily influenced by both the *chansons de geste* for his battle and other action scenes and by the romances for his more complex plot devices and character portrayals. The Neapolitan court was certainly permeated with this chivalric culture and took pride in its French roots, and the Angevin court actively patronized courtly romance writers throughout Robert's reign.[25] Although Gravina was never a member of the court, his work would have received a sympathetic and knowing reading there.

THE ANONIMO ROMANO

Sometime between 1358 and July 1359, a *Vita* of Cola di Rienzo was completed within a larger *Cronaca* that set out to record the events of Europe. The *Cronaca*[26] covers such events as the Duke of Athens' rule and fall in Florence, Emperor Lewis of Bavaria's descent on Rome, the peace pilgrimage of Fra Venturino, the crusade to Izmir and politics and people in Lombardy, Spain and France. It also focuses on Naples from the death of Robert the Wise to the invasion of Lewis of Hungary, and on Rome and its district between 1325 and 1357/58. Rienzo's *Vita* was only one — but the major — part (chapters 18 and 26–27) of this larger history of which the consensus long held that only 19 of its 28 chapters survived.[27] As such these have often been edited separately as the *Vita* and divided into four books. Giuseppe Billanovich attributed the overall work to Bartolomeo di Iacovo da Valmontone (c.1310–c.1360), an acquaintance in Avignon of both Petrarch and Rienzo, though no firm identity has been definitively accepted.[28] This Anonimo romano was probably born in Rome to a lower noble or upper-middle-class family[29] between 1318 and 1320, in the *rione* Regola, and was thus a close neighbor of Rienzo's. He was living in Rome in 1334 and began his medical studies at the University of Bologna in 1338/39. Internal evidence tells us that he returned to Rome in the 1340s and practiced medicine.[30] He was therefore a trained professional with a good foundation in the available corpus of Latin classics and Latin and Greek sciences. Sometime in the 1350s, he moved to Tivoli, where he died around October 1360.

Whoever he was, and as sharp as his observations were, he was no political insider.[31] Although he faithfully reported events in Rome with keen judgment and a reporter's sense of personality and drama, he relied on others' accounts for events away from Lazio — for French affairs, for Rienzo's stays in Avignon or Prague and for events in Naples, for example — and for many of the central events that took place in Rome itself. While he used some of the best sources of the time, including the *Chronicle* of Martin of Troppau, the Mirabilian descriptions of Rome, medieval reinterpretations of ancient historians found in the *Liber ystoriorum* and at least some of Rienzo's own letters, his viewpoint was that of the public witness, not the personal intimate or the confidant of the key figures he discusses. Like the civic historians of Naples treated in Chapter 9,[32] he could also have had access to Rome's public records.[33]

The anonymous Roman historian also relied on both the psychological interpretations and the historical conventions available to him in the mid-fourteenth century. Most of these were derived from his classical sources: Livy, Sallust, Lucan, Valerius Maximus, Cicero and the minor Roman historians. Gustav Seibt has also argued for the contemporary influences of Rolandino da Padova and against any direct traces of the Villani chronicles. Whatever his sources,[34] the Anonimo romano was a brilliant storyteller and a great historian offering starkly dramatic scenarios of major events and deeply human portraits of individuals, infusing his narrative with a winning combination of deep skepticism and high ideals.

Buccio di Ranallo

Except for internal references in his work, little is known about Boezio di Rainaldo di Poppleto (c.1294–1363), known as Buccio di Ranallo.[35] He was born into a family of the lower nobility in the S. Pietro quarter of Aquila in the Abruzzi, probably at the time of the coronation of Pope Celestine V. Buccio was also the author of a verse *Leggenda di Santa Caterina d'Alessandria,* commissioned by a local confraternity c.1330. The poem shows some knowledge of Dante, most especially the *Inferno*. Beginning in 1338, he composed a series of twenty-one political sonnets. In these Buccio advised frugality during the famine of 1340. He later exhorted his fellow citizens to avoid the factional conflict of the barons, a goal only achieved with the assassination of the city's new lord, Pietro (Lallo) Camponeschi, in 1354 and the establishment of a communal council in 1355, of which Buccio was a member.

This interest in the *"bono stato"* and its communal virtues continued as he began composing the first part of his *Cronaca aquilana rimata* in Alexandrine verse c.1355. It covers the history of Aquila and the Abruzzi from the foundation of the city in 1254 to 1362. It becomes increasingly more accurate after 1310, covering events in the Abruzzi and further afield in the Regno, including the rule of the Angevins and their bureaucratic abuses, the Black Death of 1348, the Italian earthquake of 1349 and the Rome Jubilee of 1350, which he may have attended. Buccio supported Louis of Taranto's claims to the Neapolitan crown and lauded his role in overturning the Camponeschi and restoring order to Aquila. According to his son Antonio and other evidence, Buccio died in Aquila in 1363 with the return of the plague. Antonio continued the chronicle to 1387. A prose continuation was composed by Nicolò di Borbona who again began in 1363 and ended in 1424, broadening the scope of the work to cover much of the Regno. The work circulated widely in manuscript into the fifteenth and sixteenth centuries and has remained a fundamental source for the history of Aquila and the Abruzzi.

CHAPTER 2 ⚜ THE HISTORIANS

CRONICON SICULUM INCERTI AUTHORIS

This Latin work covers the years 340–1396, with a continuation of interpolations called the *Aliud Diarium*, probably by the same author, presented in somewhat random chronological order but focused mainly on the 1370s and 1380s.[36] The unknown author of both parts devoted only two pages in the printed edition to the earlier centuries from 340 — mainly a chorographical survey of the South — before launching into the history of the Normans. The *Chronicon*'s title uses "Sicily" in the medieval sense of the Angevin kingdom and southern mainland. It focuses particularly on Neapolitan events under the Angevins, especially from the reign of Giovanna I to the end of the trecento. The author sometimes covers events on an almost daily basis in Naples itself, in the Regno during the Hungarian invasion and during the campaign of Giovanna and Louis of Taranto to win it back. Similar detail appears in sections covering the 1370s and 1380s.

The author appears to have been Neapolitan from a noble family of the Capua and Nido *seggi* who was clear about his class allegiances. Kelly speculates that the author may have been a member of the noble Brancaccio family[37] and has demonstrated the clear reliance of the *Chronicon* on the *Cronaca di Partenope* and its sources, while also noting the author's original research and personal memory of events. Though it has survived in a unique manuscript, this text was widely known, read and annotated by later Neapolitan writers.[38]

ANGELO CRASSULLO

Angelo Filippo Crassullo[39] was born into a professional family of notaries, attorneys and judges in Taranto, was a notary himself in Taranto and is recorded there in 1365 authenticating a document. Crassullo's *Annales de rebus tarentinis*[40] survived in several early modern manuscripts whose exemplars are now lost.[41] The *Annales* were written in notarial Latin and cover the years between 1352, when Philip and Robert of Taranto returned from their forced exile in Hungary, and the execution on October 1, 1415 of Pandolfello Alopo, grand chamberlain and favorite of Queen Giovanna II. Composed as a series of almost random notices, it covers almost exclusively the region of Taranto and Apulia and offers important information on the Angevins' last years there.

DIURNALI (DIARIO) OF THE DUCA DI MONTELEONE

First mentioned by the sixteenth-century historian Angelo di Costanzo as the *Cronaca* or *Storia d'incerto autore*, this annal covers the period 1265–1420 with extensions to 1458.[42] It falls into three distinct sections. The first covers the period from the reign of Charles I to 1371. The second, from 1371 to the accession of Alfonso I in 1443, is the most accurate and useful. It reflects a single, if uneven, voice, perhaps someone attached to the royal court in Naples at Castel Capuano, either a literate soldier or a notary. A third section, from 1443, was compiled in Bari by an adherent of the house of Taranto and contains a collection of notices of varying value. The different parts also reflect changing political allegiances: moving from a pronounced pro-Angevin stance in the first part to a strong apologetic tone toward the Aragonese in the last. The compilation relied on a wide variety of sources for Naples and the South, including Guglielmo Marramaldo's *Breve chronicon de rebus neapolitanis,* Tommaso Loffredo's *Annales* and the *Diarium regum Neapolis et Siciliae.*

It reached a level of popularity in manuscript and was so named not because of any known authorship but because it was owned by Duke Ettore III Pignatelli, the second duke of Monteleone (Vibo Valentia) in Calabria. Its authenticity had been contested into the late nineteenth century until Capasso argued in its favor from the extant manuscripts and when the text received its first modern critical edition.

OTHER SOUTHERN HISTORIANS

While several other sources add information, confirmatory or contradictory reports and narratives, we do not analyze them here due to their limited value as history writing. Guglielmo Marramaldo's *Breve chronicon de rebus neapolitanis* was written by a friend of Petrarch at the Neapolitan court. The Marramaldo were a noble family from the *seggi* of Porto and Nido of special prominence throughout the trecento.[43] Guglielmo himself was a court attendant to Giovanna I.[44] Landolfo[45] (c.1350–1415), perhaps his son, was a cardinal who played a significant role during the Great Schism and the Council of Constance. Guglielmo's chronicle dealt with the reigns of Robert of Anjou and Giovanna I and would therefore have been highly informative. There are, however, no extant manuscripts. Tommaso Loffredo's *Annales* covered the period from 1300 to 1450, but once again there are no surviving manuscripts, and it is known to us only from citations in other sources, especially the *Diurnale (Diario) di Duca di Monteleone.*[46]

NORTHERN ITALY: WHO WROTE?

Events in the kingdom of Naples had a tremendous impact on the rest of the peninsula, and the historians of several northern centers, including Florence, Siena, Modena and Ferrara, wrote lengthy sections on Neapolitan affairs and personalities both for these reasons and for the more immediate impact on their own cities. Robert of Anjou's and Giovanna I's extensive economic and political clout were important factors in Florentine and Sienese affairs, and Lewis of Hungary's invasion of the Regno and the subsequent anarchy in the South, inflamed by the great mercenary

CHAPTER 2 ⚔ THE HISTORIANS

companies, were of grave concern to governments and citizens in the Romagna and Tuscany. Most of these writers shared the misogyny of their age and found the rule of Giovanna I over the largest, most powerful and richest area of Italy to be both scandalous and deeply troubling.[47] These writers had first-hand knowledge of the people and events about which they wrote, relying sometimes on their own and sometimes on others' eyewitness accounts, secondary reports from friends and associates, primary-source documents, such as royal and church archives, letters and memoranda, and on the work of other contemporary historians.

For this reason, we have also included Petrarch and Boccaccio. While known to us primarily for their literary achievements, they also composed history in their biographical and poetic works, which were modeled on ancient forms. We have excluded Dante, even though he was a master of grand narrative and helped shape the dark cultural memory regarding the early Angevins.[48] He had neither Petrarch's or Boccaccio's first-hand experience of Naples and its court, and much of what he recounted in the *Commedia* found a place in the Villani's chronicles. His role as a historian has been discussed fully elsewhere.[49] For similar reasons we have excluded Birgitta of Sweden. While her *Revelationes* document her knowledge of Naples and its court and are quite important sources for the reign of Giovanna I, they are not historiography per se but more like moral critique. We have also excluded such sources as the *Chronicon Neritinium*[50] as being both historically unreliable and derivative of other sources. While Paolino da Venezia (c.1270–1344)[51] wrote most of his works while bishop of Pozzuoli and an advisor to King Robert of Anjou, these were largely cartography and universal history that offer little useful information on the Regno.

GIOVANNI DA BAZZANO, CHRONICON MUTINENSE

This compilation focuses on events in Modena and further afield when they affected that city. Based on the *Annales veteres* and the *Chronica circularis*, it covers the years from 1109 but offers more detailed and accurate annals of the city's rectors and podestàs beginning in 1188 and concluding in 1347. It becomes more detailed up to about 1272, with sparse information until 1303, and then again with increasing detail to 1347. Giovanni da Bazzano wrote a continuation for the years 1348–63.[52]

He was born Giovanni di Guido Barbieri in Bazzano c.1285 and moved to Modena, where his father is documented from at least 1300. Giovanni was educated in the urban literacy of his time, learned Latin and served as a notary from at least 1318. Giovanni apparently worked professionally with fellow notary Bonifacio da Morano, the author of the *Chronica circularis*. In 1349 Giovanni handled Bonifacio's will upon his death (perhaps from the Black Death). It appears probable that Giovanni decided to continue his friend's chronicle, and he borrowed wholesale from the *Chronica circularis* for the period 1285–1347, adding his own materials for 1348–63. He died that year or in 1364, perhaps from a recurrence of the Black Death.

Since Modena was involved in the march of Lewis of Hungary through Italy to claim the throne of Naples, the *Chronicon* concerns itself with the murder of Andrew of Hungary and its aftermath. Giovanni da Bazzano probably obtained his account of Prince Andrew's murder from the Hungarian propagandists passing through Modena. He was able to follow events through Lewis' conquest, his return to Hungary, the removal of his royal Angevin prisoners there in 1348 and their release in 1352. He is also well informed about the rise of Cola di Rienzo and the *buono stato* in Rome in 1347, perhaps also from Hungarian sources during Lewis' alliance with Rienzo or from available diplomatic correspondence.

The *Chronicon Mutinense* survived into its modern edition via a single manuscript, and thus cannot be said to have had a wide influence on historiography. However, it does reflect the viewpoint of contemporaries in northern Italy, especially around the events of the Hungarian invasion of the Regno.

CHRONICON ESTENSE

Very little is known about the author of this universal chronicle, which covers the years 328–1354, with continuations to 1478.[53] It is assumed that the author was connected to the court of the Este in Ferrara, and the history of that city and region comes into full detail from around 1207. The *Chronicon* was very well informed about events in Rome and in the Regno from the 1340s on, covering the period from the death of Robert of Anjou through the restoration of Giovanna I. The author's command of Roman events is remarkable, covering Cola di Rienzo's abdication and flight from Rome in December 1347 on a day-to-day basis, in a form that most closely resembles diplomatic dispatch.[54] Coverage of events in Naples has almost the same immediacy for Prince Andrew's murder, Giovanna's reaction, subsequent events in Naples and Lewis of Hungary's invasion, which the chronicle covers again with an almost daily report. This lends support to the possibility that the author was involved in the diplomatic relations between the court of Ferrara, the invading Hungarian army and many of the Este's rivals in the northern Romagna. Benjamin Kohl speculated that the author was a notary working in the Este chancellery who therefore had ready access to all sorts of official and secret correspondence.

CHAPTER 2 ❧ THE HISTORIANS

THE VILLANI

The most important narrative source for trecento Italy is the *Nuova Cronica*[55] composed by the Villani: Giovanni, his brother Matteo and Matteo's son Filippo. The Villani were a prosperous Florentine merchant family with widespread business and political contacts. Giovanni (c.1280–1348)[56] became a shareholder of the Peruzzi bank in 1300, traveling for them as an agent throughout Italy and as far north as Flanders. He returned to Florence in 1307 and entered public service and diplomacy. He was one of the city's priors in 1316/17 and again in 1321, oversaw the mint in 1316 and the reconstruction of the city walls in 1324 and in 1330/31 supervised construction projects on the Baptistry and the Badia. From 1329 to 1330 Giovanni coordinated relief efforts for the thousands of impoverished Florentines facing famine. By the 1320s, the Villani had shifted their banking investments to the Buonaccorsi firm, but the wave of bankruptcies that swept through Florence's banking sector in the 1340s — due to over-expansion and unpaid loans from England and Naples — eventually led to Giovanni's imprisonment in 1346. He witnessed and described most of the major developments of trecento Florentine history, including the Black Death of 1348, to which he succumbed.

In both his career and chronicle, Villani took an anti-*popolani* viewpoint. He worked with the government of Charles, prince of Calabria and heir to Naples, who was elected *signore* of Florence in 1326 but who died in 1328. In 1342 Walter VI of Brienne, the Duke of Athens and a close ally of the Angevins of Naples, was named governor of Florence, and Giovanni Villani was implicated in Brienne's mismanagement and misrule that ended in the duke's violent overthrow in July 1343.

Giovanni Villani claimed that he was inspired to write his *Nuova Cronica* after visiting Rome for the Jubilee of 1300 and taking in the city's ancient remains and its fallen splendor. Scholars, however, conclude that the work was begun no earlier than the 1320s.[57] His *Cronica* was composed in Tuscan and derives from a long tradition of medieval writing, recording an ongoing narrative from antiquity to the author's own time on a year-by-year basis, becoming more detailed and less derivative of other sources and full of local memory and legend as events approached Villani's own period. He covered not only the history of Florence but that of England, France and the Low Countries during the early phases of the Hundred Years War, the continued struggle of the empire and papacy, the Avignon papacy and the history of Rome and the kingdom of Naples. His descriptions of Roman events in the era of Cola di Rienzo and of Naples under Robert the Wise and Giovanna I are among our most important sources.

Villani supplemented his annals with many rich details of politics, religion and natural phenomena. His work is characterized by a strong Guelph affinity, an early interest in the classics and the works of contemporary humanists, including Dante and Brunetto Latini, and a moralistic sense of equilibrium that balanced Christian virtues and vices. Every success and new height in human events would be followed swiftly in Villani's accounts by decline and ruin as God would punish sin as surely as he rewarded virtue and intelligence. Villani was heavily influenced by the classical notion of *fortuna* as well, and his Christian moralism often is indistinguishable from a sense of the turning Wheel of Fate. Giovanni also reveals a keen interest in natural events and causalities, including a fascination with prodigies and monstrosities common to late medieval chroniclers, as well as a strong belief in the efficacy of astrology and the impact of planetary events on human actions. Giovanni was acutely aware of his form and the art of history writing as a literary as well as a civic activity.

Giovanni covered Neapolitan events throughout book XIII. While a great deal of scholarship has been published tracing the influence of Villani on later Neapolitan histories, such as the *Cronaca di Partenope*,[58] little has been done to trace Villani's Neapolitan sources.[59] He was, however, particularly well informed about events in the South. This was probably due to his wide network of banking and merchant contacts and through connections to the court, perhaps through the circle of the Florentine Niccolò Acciaiuoli.[60] We do not know whether he had access to any other written or oral[61] narrative sources for the South.

Giovanni's work was continued by his brother Matteo (d. 1363) and Matteo's son Filippo. We know little about Matteo Villani, except that he was widowed and remarried. He began his portion with a vivid description of the Black Death of 1348 and brought the work up to 1363, when he died in the recurrence of the plague. His portions of the chronicle are far more pessimistic of human nature and of any divine plan for humanity and — in keeping with the shifting mood in Florence itself — far more critical of the Church and less accepting of the Guelph allegiance. They emphasized instead the growing conflict between republican government and the rise of tyranny abroad and oligarchy at home. Matteo therefore tended to downplay both the moral categories and astrological determinism of his brother and to focus more on the dynamic between *fortuna* and *virtù* in individual behavior. Like Giovanni, Matteo included lengthy sections on Neapolitan events, especially around the career there of the Florentine Niccolò Acciaiuoli.

Matteo's son Filippo took up his uncle's and father's work, but his interests lay more in the new humanism being created by Petrarch, Boccaccio and their circle. His work often concentrates on this emerging group with discursive biographies of Giotto, Francesco Landini and others. It also shared the emerging humanist preference for Latin over the vernacular as the best form of expression. He continued the *Cronica* only up until 1364.

CHAPTER 2 ❧ THE HISTORIANS

CRONACA SENESE

One of the earliest surviving examples of the Sienese Tuscan vernacular,[62] the *Cronaca Senese* covers the years 1186–1381. Its authorship has long been contested on paleographical, codicological and philological grounds,[63] and scholars now see it as an assemblage of three or more historians in two main manuscript redactions. A writer who identified himself as "Andrea Dei," presumably from the lower nobility, began the chronicle and covered the years 1186–1325, offering lists of Sienese consuls and podestàs from 1186 with increased historical detail and narrative from 1251. But this is less a comprehensive narrative than a collection of news items, public documents, private records and borrowings from Giovanni Villani. Agnolo di Tura del Grasso, a shoemaker and tax collector for the commune, then brought the collection to 1351, including a first-hand narrative of the Black Death of 1348 in Siena. Aside from that entry, whether he was simply a copyist or an active author of the continuation is debated.[64] A continuation, generally known as the *Diario*, dealt with the years 1352–81 and is attributed to Donato di Neri and his son Neri di Donato di Neri. As its title indicates, the *Cronaca* focuses on events in Siena and its territory from the late duecento into the late trecento. It also covers several important episodes in the mid-trecento, including the murder of Andrew of Hungary — offering grisly details not found elsewhere — the Black Death and the role of the mercenary companies.

PETRARCH

Because of his key role in developing what we term the "black legend of the Angevins"[65] and his impact on all later historiography of the Mezzogiorno, we will discuss Petrarch and his successor Giovanni Boccaccio at some length. Petrarch was born in Arezzo in 1304.[66] His father, Pietro di Parenzo (Ser Petracco), was a notary. Like his acquaintance, Dante Alighieri, he was a political exile from Florence. In 1312 Petracco moved to Avignon and settled his family in nearby Carpentras. Francesco was expected to follow in his father's footsteps, so he studied law both at the University of Montpellier (1316–20) and then at the University of Bologna (1320–26). There he became friends with fellow students Giacomo and Agapito Colonna of the powerful Roman family. In 1326, on his father's death, Francesco returned to Avignon, already determined to forge a career as a lyric poet and scholar. He had inherited his father's love of classical learning, especially of Cicero; but in April 1327, he began something new: his famous series of Italian sonnets in honor of Laura, who was married to another man. These courtly poems of unrequited love, written in the language of Dante but set in a new "Petrarchan" form, brought him instant fame throughout Italy and Europe. Rejecting careers in law and medicine, he entered the lower clergy to support his literary interests.

From 1330 his deep friendship and loyalty to the Colonna family were solidified when Cardinal Giovanni Colonna invited him into his household service or *familia* in Avignon. In 1333 Petrarch took the first of his literary journeys to northern Europe, stopping into monastic libraries in search of manuscripts of the ancient pagan and Christian classics, thus establishing a pattern for humanist scholars ever since. By that time, he had also begun his editions of Virgil and Livy, which earned him a solid reputation for scholarship and a new understanding of the past. In late 1336 and early 1337, he made his first visit to Rome as a guest of the Colonna. Late in 1337 he began work on his *De viris illustribus*, and in 1338/39 he began his incomplete Latin epic *Africa*, on the life of Scipio Africanus, which placed him at the center of the classical revival. From late 1339 or early 1340, Francesco, now calling himself by the more Latin "Petrarca," began campaigning for the poet laureate's crown. In the fall of 1340, he arrived in Naples. There he and King Robert held lengthy discussions on antiquity and the various legends associated with Virgil's presence in and around the city.[67] Robert decided to bestow the laurel crown on Petrarch on the Capitoline in Rome on Easter Sunday, April 8, 1341. On that day Petrarch delivered his *Collatio laureationis* on the revival of ancient learning.[68]

The 1340s saw Petrarch moving on both physically and intellectually. He began visiting Parma at the invitation of its Coreggio princes and began an unsuccessful study of ancient Greek. In the spring of 1343, he first met Cola di Rienzo during the latter's embassy to Avignon on behalf of the new Roman commune and forged a long-lasting friendship over their mutual ideals of Roman revival.[69] Later that year he visited Naples on behalf of Pope Clement VI and Giovanni Colonna and came away with his mission unsuccessful and with the first of his pessimistic views of the city under Queen Giovanna I. Petrarch warmly embraced Rienzo's revolution of May 1347 and the establishment of the *buono stato*, breaking with the Colonna. He then began making more frequent visits to Parma and Verona and beginning his association with the Carrara lords of Padua.

By the 1350s Petrarch's status as the leading figure of the revived learning attracted a new generation of followers, including Giovanni Boccaccio. It also saw him dissociating himself from Cola di Rienzo, rekindling hopes for an imperial return to Rome and moving on to new and controversial associations with Emperor Charles IV and with Italy's emerging tyrants. In 1351 he turned down a post as papal secretary in Avignon and a professorship at the University of Florence, finally leaving Avignon for good and accepting a diplomatic post with the Visconti in Milan that he held until 1361. In the 1360s Petrarch's fame brought him as far afield as Paris and a five-year stay in Venice (1362–67), then in Padua (to 1370) and finally to Arquà near Padua, where he died on July 18/19, 1374.

CHAPTER 2 ✤ THE HISTORIANS

Petrarch traveled extensively to Rome and in and around Naples and its bay, reporting first-hand their topography, monuments, legends, personalities and natural and political disasters.[70] His correspondence with and about Cola di Rienzo and the establishment of the short-lived *buono stato* in Rome remain some of our best historical sources. He wrote several works bearing on Naples and its contemporary and later image. These include his Letters, especially his *Familiares*[71] and *Seniles*,[72] his *Itinerary*[73] and his *Eclogues*.[74]

As a household member (*familiaris*) of both the papal and Colonna courts at Avignon, Petrarch was privy to many of their deliberations on the South. He also served in diplomatic capacities for both pope and cardinals and enjoyed a wide circle of colleagues, informants and admirers in Rome and Naples. These included Cola di Rienzo and members of his circle, King Robert himself and members of his and Giovanna I's court, including Philippe de Cabassoles, Giovanni Barrili and Barbato da Sulmona. He knew the workings of the Angevin royal circle, its system of justice and its mechanisms of public discourse and diplomacy.[75]

Except perhaps for his narration of events during Rienzo's career and his city descriptions in the *Itinerary*, his writing were not historical in a modern sense. Yet his use of classical sources and tropes, his thorough knowledge of the topography, personalities, cultural heritage, trends and politics of Rome and the Regno, his influence on contemporaries and his enduring legacy make his writing an essential if overlooked source for the historiography of the Mezzogiorno.[76] If, as Albert Ascoli argues,[77] the entire corpus of the *Familiares* is a "macrotext," a structured narrative of both personal and political development, then Petrarch's writing becomes a consciously framed political history for the South and the Angevins.[78]

BOCCACCIO

The author of the *Decameron*, Giovanni Boccaccio was widely seen as Petrarch's successor in the work of literary and cultural revival. Born at Certaldo,[79] Boccaccio grew up in Florence and in 1327 moved with his family to Naples, where his father opened a branch of the Bardi bank. He studied canon law at the University of Naples and was introduced by his father to the court of Robert the Wise. There he befriended Niccolò Acciaiuoli, Barbato da Sulmona, Giovanni Barrili, Cino da Pistoia, Graziolo de' Bambaglioli, the astronomer Andalo da Negro, the Greek Calabrian monk and tutor Barlaam, King Robert's librarian Paolo da Perugia and other members of the intellectual circle of King Robert the Wise and then of his granddaughter and heir Queen Giovanna I. At the Angevin royal library, he first encountered the French chivalric romances that would help form his fictional style. He was also present in the city during Giotto's work there, most likely on the now-lost frescos in the Capella Palatina of Castel Nuovo.[80] He considered Naples his spiritual and creative home and sought to make it his permanent residence,[81] spending the years 1327–41, 1355, 1362–63 and 1370–71 there in private and diplomatic capacities, moving freely through the city's merchant and noble circles and closely observing the Angevin court, its daily life and its public rituals.

Boccaccio quickly came under the spell of Petrarch and his revival of ancient literature and learning, beginning his biography of Petrarch, the *De vita moribus Francisci Petracchi de Florentia,* as early as 1341 when he first moved back to Florence and while Petrarch was in residence at Avignon.[82] Boccaccio remained in Florence, writing and corresponding until 1347, when he set a precedent for humanists by becoming the chancellor for Francesco Ordelaffi in Forlì. Boccaccio was back in Florence during the Black Death of 1348, which he describes so vividly (using ancient models) in the opening of his *Decameron* (first composed 1349–51 and revised until 1372). In October 1350, when he and other young humanists met Petrarch there, he and Petrarch began a lifelong friendship and intellectual collaboration, corresponding, exchanging texts and searching for manuscripts of the classics.

In the 1350s Boccaccio served as a high-ranking ambassador for Florence, including missions to Pope Innocent VI at Avignon, in diplomacy with Queen Giovanna I of Naples, with Ludwig of Brandenburg and with the Visconti in Lombardy.[83] He gradually moved away from his elegant Italian poetry and social satire to concentrate more and more on religious themes and on classically inspired works in the Latin style espoused by Petrarch. But Boccaccio forged his own classicism, independent of Petrarch, and went well beyond him in his study of Greek, which he had first begun during his early years in Naples. During the 1360s Boccaccio's literary activities only intensified as he worked on redactions of Dante's *Commedia,* began his own *De mulieribus claris,* perhaps in imitation of Petrarch's *De viris illustribus,* and continued work on his most classically inspired and executed work, his *Genealogia deorum gentilium.*[84] At the same time, his civic duties for Florence continued, both in administration and diplomacy. By the 1370s Boccaccio had achieved the highest prominence in Florence, celebrated and honored as he instituted his series of lectures on Dante and furthered the humanist agenda. In 1371 Queen Giovanna I and her court honored him with an invitation to take up residence in Naples once again, but he demurred. He died on December 21, 1375 at Certaldo.

Boccaccio did not escape elements of the misogyny of his times.[85] Yet the image of Naples that we derive from the *Decameron,* his *Fiammetta, Amorosa Visione,* the *Caccia di Diana* and the *Filocolo* is one distinctly different from Petrarch's view of corruption and decline after Robert of Anjou's death. Here again is a city full of bustling commerce and urban life, of a *"lieta brigata"* of young noblemen and women, of song and dance and a playful lightness of being.[86] He based several of the characters in these works on his first-hand acquaintance with well-known women at the Neapolitan court — royal servants, courtiers and women of the royal family.

Boccaccio was also thoroughly familiar with the city of Naples and its language. His *Decameron* II.5 recounts the story of Andreuccio da Perugia, in which precise details of Naples' urban topography, recent history and art are essential to the story.[87] His Neapolitan letter to Francesco de' Bardi of 1339 displays both a thorough command of the Neapolitan language and of Naples' particular form of comedic irony.[88] His *Ninfe fiorentine* includes passages on Naples' mythological foundations that parallel those of the *Cronaca di Partenope*.[89] His account of the punishment of Queen Giovanna I's household officials Filippa, Sancia and Roberto de'Cabanni in his *De casibus virorum illustrium*[90] and his "Life of Queen Giovanna I," the final chapter of his *De mulieribus claris*,[91] are also solidly grounded in Neapolitan culture and recent history.

Though chancellor to Francesco Ordelaffi of Forlì, Boccaccio did not accompany that lord when he joined Lewis of Hungary's invasion of the Regno in 1347/48, but his Neapolitan *Eclogues* (3–6)[92] do trace the history of the court and city from Robert of Anjou's death through Andrew of Hungary's murder, the invasion of Lewis of Hungary and the flight and return of Queen Giovanna I and Louis of Taranto. Much like Petrarch's letters and his eclogue "Argus," which Boccaccio knew only later, they trace a picture of decline in Angevin Naples after Robert of Anjou's death. *Eclogue* 8, "Midas," is a bitter indictment of Niccolò Acciaiuoli's role in Neapolitan affairs. Though not narrative history in the modern sense, Boccaccio's blend of urban memory, reportage from friends in the Regno, romance literature, fable, classically inspired poetry and biography collectively form an essential element of all contemporary and later views of trecento Naples.

MATTEO PALMIERI

Niccolò Acciaiuoli was one of the most important figures of the Neapolitan trecento. His own archives are an important primary source for this period. His *Vita*[93] was written in Latin by fellow Florentine Matteo Palmieri (1406–75)[94] and covered the years 1310–66. Palmieri was among the second generation of Florentine humanists. He was raised in an upper-middle class Florentine family and was an apothecary by profession and a member of the city's governing elite. In the 1420s he attended the *studium* (university) of Florence where he studied grammar, rhetoric and poetry. He soon joined a brilliant generation of Florentines who devoted themselves to the study of both the Latin and Greek classics. He served as *gonfalonier di compagnia*, prior, *gonfalonier di giustizia* and several times as an ambassador, including to the court of Alfonso I in Naples. In 1444 he succeeded Leonardo Bruni as chancellor of Florence, thus reaching the apogee of humanist status. Drawing heavily on the classical tradition, Palmieri composed several works in both Latin and Italian, the most famous of which was the *Della vita civile (On Civic Life)* of 1429, which circulated in manuscript among his humanist circle. Vespasiano da Bisticci included him among his *Vite di uomini illustri*.

Palmieri's *Vita* extolled the role of Acciaiuoli in Naples from his arrival through his rise in royal service to his fall. Palmieri took up a favorite theme among humanists: focusing on Acciaiuoli's *virtù* in his pursuit of eminence. The *Vita* presents a complex portrait of Acciaiuoli, mixing his great talents with his ambition and moral shortcomings, but it is decidedly on the side of Louis of Taranto in the dispute over the Regno's rule, relegating Giovanna I's role to that of a plotting murderer and extolling Niccolò's role in preserving the Regno both before and after Lewis of Hungary's invasion. Palmieri's work is also important to trecento historiography since it includes a good number of Acciaiuoli's original letters. A Tuscan translation of the *Vita* was later completed by Donato Acciaiuoli.

NORTHERN EUROPE: WHO WROTE?

Brief mentions — and sometimes detailed narratives — of Italian affairs and personalities were not unusual for northern chroniclers throughout the late Middle Ages, but here we concentrate on three non-Italian historians of the trecento who helped shape our views of Naples and the South. These treated aspects of Angevin history ranging from the conquest of the Regno almost to the end of the dynasty. They claim attention both for their subject matter and their methodology. They all wrote traditional chronicles rather than the histories and classically inspired biographies and memoirs written by the Italians. All depended on first-hand testimony, whether from the principles involved, from other eyewitnesses or from important documentary evidence for matters close to home. But their sources and reliability started to fall off when dealing with Italian matters and may have included outright falsifications passed on to them by enemies of the Angevins. As important, since they were external observers of the South, their viewpoints helped shape northern perceptions of Naples from the trecento onward. Consequently they offer us useful contrasts to Italian works and provide an index of the effects of distance on the accuracy and verisimilitude of medieval historical narrative. As we have already noted, since these writers are generally better known to medievalists, they also offer objective correlatives to our conclusions drawn for the Italian writers discussed in the subsequent chapters.

CHAPTER 2 ⚜ THE HISTORIANS

JOHANNS VON WINTERTHUR

Johanns (Iohannes Vitodurandi) was born c.1300 in Winterthur in Switzerland and educated there beginning c.1309. By 1328 he was at the Franciscan convent in Basel, at Schaffhouse by 1335 and at Lindau from 1340 until his death, probably in 1348, perhaps from the Black Death. He wrote his *Chronicon a Friderico II Imperatore ad annum 1348*[95] between 1340 and its last entry for June 4, 1348. A universal history, its two parts cover Creation to the reign of Innocent III (1198–1216) and the foundation of the Franciscan Order, and from then to 1348. While focusing primarily on the region around Lake Constance and tracing the early development of the Swiss Confederation, Johanns also wrote of people and events much further afield, including Italy, especially relating to the Franciscan Order. He drew from a variety of sources, including contemporary histories and documents. Johanns is important for his knowledge of Neapolitan matters, and he included in his discussion of Franciscan affairs direct borrowings from the letters of Queen Sancia of Majorca[96] and a description of her death and burial. His *Chronicon* offers important collaborative evidence of Sancia's crucial role in Franciscan affairs. Johanns' sympathy for Naples' queens also seems to have extended to Giovanna, who, he notes, escaped her husband Andrew's assassins only through flight.[97]

JEAN FROISSART

Jean Froissart[98] (1337–c.1404) was born in Valenciennes in Hainault, but little more is known of his early life. In 1362, he dedicated a verse chronicle to Philippa of Hainault, queen of King Edward III of England, and was attached to her court until her death in 1369. He then entered the service of Joanna, duchess of Brabant. Froissart traveled extensively through Britain, France, the Low Countries and Spain, searching for documents and first-hand oral testimony. He probably knew Geoffrey Chaucer and may have met Petrarch in Milan in 1368. He returned to England briefly in 1395, and he probably died in 1404 at Chimay in Hainault.

Froissart's *Chroniques* were among the most popular and lavishly illustrated works of the later Middle Ages, with over 100 surviving manuscripts. They are known both for their scrupulous attention to the details of court life, diplomacy and military affairs, especially around the Hundred Years' War, and for their overlap between factual historical account and chivalric romance. It is largely through Froissart's *Chroniques* that most modern readers have gained their sense of the "chivalrous" nature of late medieval aristocratic life, governance and warfare. He included references to well-known romances such as *Mélusine* within his narrative,[99] and he attempted to revive a more pure form for his literary ambitions with his own chivalric romance,

Meliador.[100] Yet Froissart was acutely aware of the waning literary conventions that he was applying to his historiography.

While Froissart focused on England and France and their conflicts, he did cover events in Italy, including Giovanna I's role in the Great Schism and her alliance with the Avignon antipope Clement VII, her marriage to Otto of Brunswick and Louis of Anjou's campaign in the Regno up until Charles III of Durazzo's conquest of Naples. Froissart's characterization of Naples as a magical and mysterious land is also important for what it reveals about the impact of second-hand (and falsified) reports and the influence of literary romance on historical narrative. Because of Froissart's great popularity with modern audiences, largely through Barbara Tuchman's reliance on his narrative in her *A Distant Mirror: The Calamitous Fourteenth Century*,[101] his views of events and historical figures in the Mezzogiorno are also critical to any historiographical study.

THOMAS WALSINGHAM

Walsingham was born c.1340, educated at Oxford and spent his life as a priest at the monastery of St. Albans. He directed the monastery's scriptorium from 1380 to 1396 and from 1394 to 1396 he served as prior of Wymondham Abbey in Norfolk. He devoted his other energies to historical and literary works, several of which were steeped in the Latin classical tradition. He died c.1422.

Given the importance of St. Albans as a pilgrimage site close to London and its ties to the monarchy and court, Walsingham was well informed of major political events in England from the testimony of first-hand acquaintances and from other written sources. His knowledge of Italian affairs also seems to have derived from official documents, including papal bulls, curial letters, public dispatches and the reports of English clergy resident in Rome with connections to St. Albans.

The *Chronica* was written in Latin and covers the years 1376–1420 and is one of our major sources for Richard II's reign. Book II[102] discusses many topics on the Continent, including the progress of the Great Schism. Walsingham therefore devotes some attention to the end of Giovanna I's reign, including her alliance with Avignon antipope Clement VII, her naming Louis of Anjou as her heir, Louis' expedition to Naples, Charles III of Durazzo's conquest of the Regno, Giovanna's death, Charles III's death and the rule of King Ladislaus. Walsingham's work provides us with important synchronic evidence of the effects of distance on medieval historiography. In an age when news, official reports and written texts needed to traverse physical and temporal boundaries, an author's reliability was bound to his skills in assembling narrative from such fragmentary and second-hand sources.

CHAPTER 2 ⚜ THE HISTORIANS

NOTES

1. Zabbia (1997) and Zabbia (2017) emphasize their similarities to the notarial class of northern Italy's communes.
2. The literature on Clareno, his works and his contexts is large. The best introduction remains Potestà (1990). For the most recent work, see Sancricca (2015).
3. Musto (1985); Musto (1997).
4. Musto (2003), 269–307.
5. There have been several editions of the *History*: Clareno (1959); Clareno (1998); Clareno (1999). For English translations, see Clareno (1983); Clareno (2005).
6. Capasso, 121. Edited in Pelliccia, 1:51–78.
7. Capasso, 131–37.
8. Sabatini (1975), 133–40, 160–61; Sabatini (1992), 543.
9. Hughes–Buongiovanni; Delle Donne (2015.1); Abbamonte (2015).
10. Montuori (2017), 5–15, 30–38.
11. Kelly (2011), 11–26.
12. Montuori (2012.2), 180–81; Montuori (2017), 15–18, 25.
13. Senatore (2014), 331–32 n. 107.
14. De Caprio (2012), 1–27, esp. 21–24 nn. 14–16; De Caprio (2014), 431–34; De Caprio (2017), 15–21.
15. Kelly (2013); Montuori (2017), 30–38.
16. Kelly (2011), 19–26.
17. Montuori (2017), 15–18.
18. De Caprio (2014), 427–30.
19. Montuori (2017), 23–26, 44–45.
20. Edited in Gravina (1781); Gravina (1903); Gravina (2022). An Italian edition with facing Latin was published in Gravina (1890). For recent analyses, Caravale (1991); Delle Donne (2001), 127–46; Zabbia (1997), 12–49; Gravina (2022), "Introduzione." For the text with Italian translation, textual and contextual notes, Gravina (2022), "Nota al testo" et passim. For background, Moretti (1989).
21. Zabbia (1997), 24–25, 31–32.
22. Zabbia (1997), 25–26.
23. Zabbia (1997), 23–26. Strohm (1992), 34, makes the point concerning Thomas Walsingham's treatment of the Peasant's Revolt in England that much of the intent of such narratives is to justify broader political opposition and hostility toward their objectified subjects.
24. Zabbia (1997), 30–46.
25. Chapter 5, pp. 122–51.
26. Edited by Porta (1979), henceforth AR. We have preferred this to Mazzali (1999). See now Palmer (2021) for a complete English translation.
27. Formentin (2012.1), 38–46, questions the existence of a larger original text.
28. The fundamental study of the Anonimo romano is Seibt (2000). See Formentin (2008); Formentin (2012.1); Campanelli (2014); Internullo (2016), 184–90, 310–15 et passim. Falconieri (2017) places him in the context of other Roman chroniclers.
29. Falconieri (2017), 219–20 and n. 20, states that the Anonimo was "certainly from an aristocratic family" based on the Anonimo's reference to his own "*ientilezza*."
30. Internullo (2016), 189, suggests that he may have worked for the commune.

31. See Chapter 6, 163–78.
32. Pp. 273–78.
33. Internullo (2016), 313.
34. Holstein (2006), 138–51 traces the common use of these sources among Roman trecento historians; as does Internullo (2016), passim. Formentin (2012.1), 36–37, calls for a new edition of the Anonimo to examine these sources more fully.
35. Edited in Buccio (1907); Buccio (2008). See Capasso, 122–24; Mutini (1972); Zabbia (1997), 49–58; De Caprio (2017), 9–15. Formentin (2010) provides detailed criticism of Buccio (2008).
36. Edited in De Blasiis (1887).
37. De Blasiis (1887), 90.
38. De Blasiis (1887), 72, 88–95.
39. De Nichilo (1984).
40. Edited by Pelliccia, 5:111–25.
41. Edizione nazionale dei testi della Storiografia umanistica (2008).
42. Edited in RIS 21, repr. Duca di Monteleone (1960); Duca di Monteleone (1895); Duca di Monteleone (1958). See Capasso, 137–42; De Caprio (2017), 22–24.
43. Spinelli (1874), 39; Capasso, 143.
44. De Blasiis (1887), 24 n. 1.
45. Girgensohn (2007).
46 Capasso, 143–44.
47. Amply documented and argued in Casteen (2015).
48. As for example in *Purgatorio* 20.79. See "Angevin Dynasty" in Lansing (2000), 45–46. We have also excluded a major source for Dante, Brunetto Latini. Though an important source for the Sicilian Vespers and other Angevin events, he died in 1294.
49. For recent evaluations, see Anselmi (2017); Cracco (2017).
50. Capasso, 125–26.
51. Fontana (2014).
52. Giovanni da Bazzano (1917); Arnaldi (1970); Andreolli (1991), 211–21; Zabbia (2001).
53. Bertino (1937). There is little critical analysis on the *Chronicon*. See Kohl (2015).
54. Musto (2013), 245–46.
55. Edited by Giuseppe Porta, Villani (1991) for Giovanni, and Villani (1995) for Matteo and Filippo. For a new English translation of book XII, 1341–48, see Villani (2016).
56. For introductions to the Villani's work and contexts, Green (1972), 9–85; Ragone (1998); Clarke (2007); Barbato (2017).
57. Green (1972), Appendix 2, 164–69.
58. Kelly (2011), 11–21.
59. But see Porta (1989); Porta (1999).
60. Tocco (2001).
61. On Villani's oral sources, Menache (2009).
62. See Francesconi (2017), 174–79.
63. *Cronaca Senese*. For authorship and versions, Bertolini (1988).
64. One of the more recent trends in medieval manuscript studies and historiography is the distinction between author and copyist and the relative roles played by each in the creation of our extant sources. See, for example, Emerson (2001).
65. See Chapter 8.

66. Kirkham (2009), xv–xxii; Wilkins (1961).
67. The story is recounted in his *Guide to the Holy Land*. Petrarch (2002), 9.8–10.1.
68. Recounted in the *Familiares* IV.8 to Barbato da Sulmona, Petrarch (2004.1), 1:528–31; Petrarch (2005.2), 1:196. See Godi (1970); Looney (2009); Celenza (2017), 69–76.
69. Petrarch (1996); Musto (2003). Celenza (2017), 76–83 et passim sees Rienzo through the eyes of an earlier historiography as "a truly unbalanced figure, a rabble-rousing demagogue" (76).
70. For recent research on Petrarch's relations with the city and Regno, Kiesewetter (2005); Cataudella (2006); Mercuri (1997).
71. Petrarch (2004.1); Petrarch (2005.2).
72. Petrarch (2004.2). English translation in Petrarch (2005.1).
73. Translated in Petrarch (2002).
74. Petrarch (1974).
75. On the forms of such public discourse, Feo (1994); Barbero (1994); Mercuri (1997); Kelly (2004).
76. Summit (2000).
77. Ascoli (2011), 120 and n. 3.
78. Hooper (2016), 1219, stresses Petrarch's insistence on authorship as an *officium* (civic office).
79. Smarr (1987); Smarr (2013); Kirkham (2013a); "Chronology," in Armstrong (2015), xxix–xxxv; the essays in Candido (2018).
80. Chapter 6, pp. 157–63.
81. The "Premessa" to BA, 11–14.
82. Petrarch's influence has been questioned. See Zak (2015). Celenza (2017), 140–71, summarizes the philological approach to their relationship. Mazzotta (2018) focuses on important intellectual differences over language, scientific knowledge of the world, the relationship between nature, fortune and history, the self, the authoritative voice and the writer's relationship to political power. Bragantini (2018) examines divergent attitudes towards the vernacular and implications for *historia* and *fabula*.
83. On Boccaccio's public service and politics, see Armstrong, Daniels and Milner (2015), 6–10; Zak (2015), 146–49.
84. For Boccaccio's classicism, see Gittes (2008); Solomon (2013); Gittes (2015); Petoletti (2018).
85. We discuss this at greater length in Chapter 5, pp. 125, 138–42.
86. Morosini (2012), 73–75, 80–85.
87. See Aceto (2012).
88. His letter 2, edited in Boccaccio (1949); Boccaccio (1983.2); Boccaccio (1992), 864. It has been partially translated into English by Eileen Gardiner in Musto (2013), 224–27. See Gaglione (2009), 262–63; Boli (2013), 295–96, 458.
89. Montuori (2012.1), 14–21.
90. IX.26, Boccaccio (1983.1), 856–65; Boccaccio (2018), 222–28.
91. Chapter 5, pp. 138–42 below.
92. Boccaccio (1987), 201–4. See Smarr, "Introduction," in Kirkham (2013), 10–11. Casteen (2018) summarizes scholarship tracing Boccaccio's changing attitudes towards Giovanna, concentrating on the early years of her reign from the negative impressions of the *Eclogues* through his praise in *De mulieribus claris*. She attributes this change (p. 231) to a desire for royal patronage and as a result of

Giovanna's changing "public persona" and reassumption of real power.
93. Edited in Palmieri (1934); Palmieri (2001).
94. Carpetto (1984); Taylor (1986); Ferraro (2005).
95. German translation in Winterthur (1866); edited in Winterthur (1982).
96. Heullant-Donat (2005).
97. Winterthur (1982), 260.
98. Editions and translations of Froissart's *Chroniques* include Froissart (2013). For detailed studies, Palmer (1981); Ainsworth (1990); Varvaro (1997); Maddox (1998); Wood (1998); Skorge (2006); Ainsworth (2013). For comprehensive bibliography, Froissart (2013).
99. Harf-Lancner (1999); and Chapter 5, pp. 135–38.
100. Dembowski (1983).
101. Tuchman (1978), reprinted as recently as 2017 by Penguin Books.
102. See Walsingham (1864); Walsingham (2005); Walsingham (2003–11).

WORKS CITED

Abbamonte, Giancarlo. 2015. "Naples, A Poet's City: Attitudes towards Statius and Virgil in the Fifteenth Century." In Hughes-Buongiovanni, 170–88.

Aceto, Francesco. 2012. "Boccaccio e l'arte: La novella di Andreuccio da Perugia (*Decameron* II, 5) e il sepulcro di Filippo Minutolo." In BA, 289–302.

Ainsworth, Peter F. 2013. "Jean Froissart: Chronicler, Poet and Writer." In Froissart (2013).

Andreolli, Bruno. 1991. *Repertorio della cronachistica emiliano-romagnola: Secc. IX–XV.* Rome: ISIME.

Anonimo Romano. Cronica: Vita di Cola di Rienzo. 1999. Ettore Mazzali, ed. Milan: Rizzoli.

Anselmi, Gian Mario. 2017. "Cronaca e narrazione: Dante e l'interpretazione della storia fra impero romano, Europa cristiana e Mediterraneo islamico." In Francesconi–Miglio, 11–27.

Armstrong, Guyda, et al. 2015. "Boccaccio as Cultural Mediator." In Armstrong (2015), 3–19.

Arnaldi, Girolamo. 1970. "Bonifacio da Morano." In DBI 12 (1970): 188–90.

Ascoli, Albert. 2011. "Petrarch's Private Politics: *Rerum Familiarium Libri* 19." In idem, *'A Local Habitation and a Name': Imagining History in the Italian Renaissance.* New York: Fordham University Press, 118–60.

Barbero, Alessandro. 1994. "La propaganda di Roberto d'Angiò, re di Napoli." In Cammarosano, 111–31.

Bertino, G. 1937. *Chronicon Estense cum additamentis usque ad annum 1478.* RIS 15.3, fasc. 1–2.

Bertolini, Paolo. 1988. "Dei, Andrea." DBI 36. At www.treccani.it/enciclopedia/andrea-dei_(Dizionario_Biografico).

Boccaccio, Giovanni, 1949. Letter 2. "Neapolitan." In *Testi Napoletani dei secoli XIII e XIV.* Antonio Altamura, ed. Naples: Libreria Perrella, 143–47.

—. 1983.2. Letter 2. "Neapolitan." "Prospettive sul parlato nella storia linguistica italiana, con una lettura dell' Epistola napoletana del Boccaccio." In *Italia Linguistica: Idee, Storia, Strutture.* Francesco Sabatini, ed. Bologna: Il Mulino, 167–201.

—. 1987. *Eclogues.* Janet Levarie Smarr, trans. New York: Garland.

—. 1992. *Lettere*. Ginetta Auzzas, ed. and Italian trans. *Tutte le opere* 5.1. Milan: Mondadori, 857–78.

—. 2018. *The Downfall of the Famous*. Louis Brewer Hall, ed. and trans. Rev. ed. New York: Italica Press.

Boli, Todd. 2013. "Personality and Conflict *(Epistole, Lettere)*." In Kirkham (2013), 295–306.

Bragantini, Renzo. 2018. "Petrarch, Boccaccio, and the Space of Vernacular Literature." In Candido (2018), 313–39.

Buccio di Ranallo. 1907. *Cronaca aquilana rimata di Buccio di Ranallo di Popplito di Aquila*. Vincenzo De Bartholomaeis, ed. Rome: Forzani.

—. 1969. *Poemetti sacri dei secoli XIV e XV.* Erasmo Pèrcopo, ed. Bologna: Commissione per i testi di lingua.

Campanelli, Maurizio. 2014. "The Anonimo Romano at His Desk: Recounting the Battle of Crécy in Fourteenth-Century Italy." TMC 9:33–78.

Candido, Igor, ed. 2018. *Petrarch and Boccaccio: The Unity of Knowledge in the Pre-Modern World*. Berlin: De Gruyter.

Caravale, Mario. 1991. "Domenico da Gravina." DBI 40. At www.treccani. it/enciclopedia/domenico-da-gravina_(Dizionario_Biografico).

Carpetto, George M. 1984. *The Humanism of Matteo Palmieri*. Rome: Bulzoni.

Cataudella, Michele. 2006. *Petrarca e Napoli: Atti del convegno, Napoli, 8–11 dicembre 2004*. Pisa: Istituti editoriali e poligrafici internazionali.

Clareno, Angelo. 1959. *Chronicon seu Historia septem tribulationum ordinis minorum*. Alberto Ghinato, ed. Rome: Pontificia Ateneo Antoniano.

—. 1983. *The Chronicle or History of the Seven Tribulations of the Order of Friars Minor*. Mary Bartholomew McDonald, OSF and George Marcil, OFM, trans. St. Bonaventure, NY: Franciscan Institute.

—. 1998. *Liber chronicorum sive tribulationum ordinis minorum*. Giovanni Boccali, OFM and Felice Accrocca, ed. Marino Bigaroni, OFM, Italian trans. Assisi: Edizioni Porziuncula.

Clark, James G. 2004. *A Monastic Renaissance at St. Albans: Thomas Walsingham and His Circle, c.1350–1440*. Oxford: Clarendon Press.

Cracco, Giorgio. 2017. "Dante e le cronache dell'Italia settentrionale." In Francesconi–Miglio, 139–63.

Crassullo, Angelo. *Annales de rebus tarentinis*. In Pelliccia, 5:111–25.

Dembowski, Peter F. 1983. *Jean Froissart and His Meliador: Context, Craft, and Sense*. Lexington: French Forum.

De Caprio, Chiara. 2014. "Spazi comunicativi, tradizioni narrative e storiografia in volgare: Il Regno negli anni delle guerre d'Italia." *Filologia e Critica* 39:39–72.

De Nichilo, Mauro. 1984. "Angelo Filippo Crassullo." DBI 30. At www.treccani. it/enciclopedia/angelo-filippo-crassullo_(Dizionario_Biografico).

Edizione nazionale dei testi della Storiografia umanistica. 2008. At www. ilritornodeiclassici.it/ensu/index.php?type=opera&op=fetch&id=478&lang=it.

Emerson, Catherine, ed. 2001. With Edward A. O'Brien and Laurent Semichon. *Auctoritas: Authorship and Authority*. Glasgow: University of Glasgow French and German Publications.

Falconieri, Tommaso di Carpegna. 2017. "Note sulla cronachistica in volgare a Roma." In Francesconi–Miglio, 215–26.
Feo, Michele. 1994. "L'epistola come mezzo di propaganda politica in Francesco Petrarca." In Cammarosano, 203–26.
Ferraro, Alessandra Mita. 2005. *Matteo Palmieri: Una biografia intellettuale*. Genoa: Name.
Fontana, Emanuele. 2014. "Paolino da Venezia, vescovo di Pozzuoli." DBI 81. At www.treccani.it/enciclopedia/paolino-da-venezia-vescovo-di-pozzuoli_(Dizionario-Biografico).
Formentin, Vittorio. 2008. "Schede lessicali e grammaticali per la *Cronica* d'Anonimo romano." *La Lingua Italiana* 4:25–43.
—. 2010. "Sfortuna di Buccio di Ranallo." *Lingua e Stile* 45.2:185–221.
Froissart, Jean. 1901–3. *The Chronicle of Froissart*. John Bourchier Berners and W.P. Ker, ed. 1901; The Chronicle of Froissart. 6 vols. London: David Nutt. Repr. New York: AMS, 1967.
—. 1991. *Chroniques*. George T. Diller, ed. Geneva: Droz.
—. 2003–15. *Chroniques de Jean Froissart*. Nathalie Desgrugillers-Billard, ed. Clermont-Ferrand: Éditions Paléo.
—. 2013–. *The Online Froissart*. Peter Ainsworth and Godfried Croenen, ed. v. 1.5 (Sheffield: HRIOnline, 2013), www.hrionline.ac.uk/onlinefroissart/apparatus.jsp?type=intros&intro=f.intros.PFA-Froissart.
Giovanni da Bazzano. 1917. *Chronicon Mutinense* AA. 1188–1363. Tommaso Casini, ed. RIS 15.
Girgensohn, Dieter. 2007. "Maramaldo (Maramauro), Landolfo." DBI 69. At www.treccani.it/enciclopedia landolfo-maramaldo_(Dizionario-Biografico).
Gittes, Tobias F. 2008. *Boccaccio's Naked Muse: Eros, Culture, and the Mythopoetic Imagination*. Toronto: University of Toronto Press.
—. 2015. "Boccaccio and Humanism." In Armstrong (2015), 155–70.
Godi, Carlo. 1970. "La *Collatio laureationis* del Petrarca." *Italia medioevale e umanistica* 13:1–27.
Gravina, Domenico da. 1781. "Chronicon de rebus in Apulia gestis." In Pelliccia, 3:193–486.
—. 1890. *Chronicon e rebus in Apulia gestis*. Naples: E. Anfossi.
—. Gravina (2022).
Harf-Lancner, Laurence. 1999. "Une légende mélusienne dans les *Chroniques* de Froissart: L'histoire du seigneur de Coarraze et de son serviteur Horton." In *Mélusines continentales et insulaires: Actes du colloque international tenu les 27 et 28 mars 1997 à l'Université de Paris XII et au Collège des Irlandais*. Jeanne-Marie Boivin and Proinsias MacCana, ed. Paris: Champion, 205–21.
Heullant-Donat, Isabelle. 2005. "En amont de l'Observance: Les lettres de Sancia, reine de Naples, aux Chapitres généraux et leur transmission dans l'historiographie du XIVe siècle." In *Identités franciscaines à l'âge des réformes*. Frédéric Meyer and Ludovic Viallet, ed. Clermont-Ferrand: Presses Universitaires Blaise Pascal, 73–99.
Hooper, Laurence E. 2016. "Exile and Petrarch's Reinvention of Authorship." *Renaissance Quarterly* 69:1217–56.

CHAPTER 2 ⁊ THE HISTORIANS

Kelly, Samantha. 2004. "Royal Patronage and Royal Propaganda in Angevin Naples: Santa Maria Donna Regina in Contexts." In Elliott–Warr, 27–43.
—. 2013. "The Neapolitan Giovanni Villani: Florence, Naples, and Medieval Historiographical Categorization." In *Renaissance Studies in Honor of Joseph Connors*. Machtelt Israëls et al., ed. Florence: Villa I Tatti, 2:31–38.
Kiesewetter, Andreas. 2005. "Francesco Petrarca e Roberto d'Angiò." ASPN 123:147–74.
Kirkham, Victoria. 2013a. "Chronology of Boccaccio's Life and Works." In Kirkham (2013), xiii–xix.
Kohl, Benjamin G. 2015. "Chronicon Estense." In *Encyclopedia of the Medieval Chronicle*. Graeme Dunphy, ed. Brill Online. At http://referenceworks.brillonline.com/entries/encyclopedia-of-the-medieval-chronicle/chroniconestense-EMCSIM_00582.
Lake, Justin. 2015. "Current Approaches to Medieval Historiography." *History Compass* 13.3:89–109.
Lansing, Richard H. 2000. With Teodolinda Barolini et al., ed. *The Dante Encyclopedia*. New York: Garland.
Looney, Dennis. 2009. "The Beginnings of Humanistic Oratory: Petrarch's Coronation Oration *(Collatio laureationis).*" In Kirkham (2009), 131–40.
Maddox, Donald. 1998. With Sara Sturm-Maddox. *Froissart Across the Genres*. Gainesville: University Press of Florida.
Mazzotta, Giuseppe. 2018. "Boccaccio's Critique of Petrarch." In Candido (2018), 270–85.
Menache, Sophia. 2009. "Written and Oral Testimonies in Medieval Chronicles: Matthew Paris and Giovanni Villani." TMC 6:1–30.
Mercuri, Roberto. 1997. "Avignone e Napoli in Dante, Petrarca e Boccaccio." In A&N, 117–28.
Monteleone, Duca di. 1895. *Diurnali detti del Duca di Monteleone nella primitiva lezione da un testo a penna posseduto dalla Società Napoletana di Storia Patria*. Nunzio Federico Faraglia, ed. Naples: Società Napoletana di Storia Patria.
—. 1958. *I Diurnali del Duca di Monteleone*. Michele Manfredi, ed. Bologna: Zanichelli.
—. 1960. *I Diurnali del Duca di Monteleone*. Giosuè Carducci and Michele Manfredi, ed. Bologna: Zanichelli.
Montuori, Francesco. 2012.2. "La scrittura della storia a Napoli negli anni del Boccaccio angioino." In BA, 171–97.
Moretti, Felice. 1989. *Cultura e società in Puglia in età sveva e angioina: Atti del convegno di studi, Bitonto, 11–12–13 dic. 1987*. Bitonto: Centro ricerche di storia e arte bitontina.
Morosini, Roberta. 2012. "La 'bona sonoritas' di Calliopo: Boccaccio a Napoli, la polifonia di Partenope e i silenzi dell'Acciaiuoli." In BA, 69–87.
Mutini, Claudio. 1972. "Buccio di Ranallo." DBI 14. At www.treccani.it/enciclopedia/buccio-di-ranallo_(Dizionario_Biografico).
Palmer, John Joseph Norman. 1981. *Froissart, Historian*. Woodbridge: Boydell.
Petoletti, Marco. 2018. "Boccaccio, the Classics and the Latin Middle Ages." In Candido (2018), 226–43.
Porta, Giuseppe. 1989. "Giovanni Villani storico e scrittore." In *I racconti di Clio: Tecniche narrative della storiografia*. Pisa: Nistri-Lischi, 147–56.

—. 1999."La construzione della storia in Giovanni Villani." In *Il senso della storia nella cultura medievale italiana (1100–1350)*. Pistoia: Centro Italiano di Studi di Storia e d'Arte, 125–38.

Potestà, Gian Luca. 1990. *Angelo Clareno: Dai poveri eremiti ai fraticelli*. Rome: ISIME.

Sabatini, Francesco. 1992."Lingue e letterature volgari in competizione." In *Italia linguistica delle origini*. V. Coletti et al., ed. 2 vols. Lecce: Argo, 2:507–68.

Sancricca, Arnaldo. 2015. *I "Fratres" di Angelo Clareno: Da Poveri eremiti di papa Celestino a Frati minori della provincia di s. Girolamo "de Urbe" attraverso la genesi del Terz'ordine regolare di s. Francesco in Italia*. Macerata: Edizioni Simple.

Skorge, Kristel Mari. 2006. *Ideals and Values in Jean Froissart's* Chroniques. Bergen: University Press.

Smarr, Janet Levarie. 1987."Life of the Author." In Boccaccio (1987), viii–xxii.

—. 2013."Introduction: A Man of Many Turns." In Kirkham (2013), 1–20.

Solomon, Jon. 2013."Gods, Greeks and Poetry *(Genealogia deorum gentilium)*." In Kirkham (2013), 235–44.

Spinelli, Matteo. 1874. *I Notamenti di Matteo Spinelli*. Camillo Minieri Riccio, ed. Naples: Rinaldi e Sellitro.

Summit, Jennifer. 2000."Topography as Historiography: Petrarch, Chaucer, and the Making of Medieval Rome." *Journal of Medieval and Early Modern Studies* 30:211–46.

Taylor, Matthew. 1986. *Matteo Palmieri (1406–1475): Florentine Humanist and Politician*. Florence: European University Institute.

Tocco, Francesco Paolo. 2001. *Niccolò Acciaiuoli: Vita e politica in Italia alla metà del XIV secolo*. Rome: ISIME.

Tuchman, Barbara W. 1978. *A Distant Mirror: The Calamitous Fourteenth Century*. New York: Random House.

Villani, Giovanni. 1990–91. *Cronica Nuova*. Giuseppe Porta, ed. 3 vols. Parma: Guanda.

—. 2016. *The Final Book of Giovanni Villani's New Chronicle*. Matthew Sneider and Rala Diakite, ed. and trans. Kalamazoo: Medieval Institute.

Villani, Matteo and Filippo Villani. 1995. *Cronica*. Giuseppe Porta, ed. 2 vols. Parma: Guanda.

Walsingham, Thomas. 2005. *The Chronica Maiora of Thomas Walsingham, 1376–1422*. David Preest and James G. Clark, ed. Woodbridge: Boydell.

Wilkins, Ernest Hatch. 1961. *Life of Petrarch*. Chicago: University of Chicago Press.

Winterthur, Johanns von. 1866. *Die Chronik Johann's von Winterthur*. Bernard Freuler, ed. Winterthur: Ziegler.

Wood, Charles T. 1998. "Froissart, Personal Testimony, and the Peasants' Revolt of 1381." In Maddox (1998), 40–49.

Zak, Gur. 2015."Boccaccio and Petrarch." In Armstrong (2015), 139–54.

3. SOURCES

INTRODUCTION

This chapter examines the sources for trecento historians of the Mezzogiorno. These sources ranged from classical remains through medieval world chronicles, local monastic and urban annals and formal histories. We will also discuss religious sources, including Scripture, sermons and saints' lives. In addition, many of these historians, whether lay or religious, urban or court writers, had access to large amounts of archival material ranging from private and public letters and other correspondence to local, legal, notarial, diplomatic and royal records.

Trecento historians also demonstrate knowledge of contemporary law, science, medicine and cosmology, and these influences were brought to bear on both larger narrative schemes and on particular details of plot and character. As with borrowings from literature to be discussed in Chapter 5, these elements were often integrated seamlessly into accounts to lend authenticity to particular episodes and to establish larger truth claims.

Finally, much of the narration in these southern histories includes the strong presence of orality and of first-hand testimony. Thus, the roles of common knowledge, gossip, rumor, widespread opinion, folk and popular memory will be balanced against testimony either gathered by these authors or witnessed by them first-hand. The use and value of such forms of evidence were not solely the product of individual historian's circumstances or talents but a carefully delineated aspect of the rhetorical traditions in which they were trained.[1] Here again the consensus account that northern historiography reflected urban and lay outlooks and that southern reflected religious and monarchical outlooks falls short. We will discuss the important role of southern urban centers and their writers — often notaries[2] — in establishing verifiable documentary history as well as in bridging the gap between oral traditions, urban narrative and learned histories. There have already been extensive studies on many of the sources under discussion here. We will therefore group these authors thematically to highlight common approaches.

We have depended on the best critical editions available and used their apparatus to provide us with clear references to sources. We have quoted from standard English translations as available and translated and cited from the original language when necessary. We have depended on interpretative studies in numerous ways, always verifying their interpretations against our own examination of the best critical editions available.

THE CLASSICAL TRADITION: TEXTS

Renaissance humanism has long been interpreted as revamping historical writing by tapping into the rich works of antiquity. Several elements of the classical tradition are often cited to distinguish this new humanist historiography: Latinity, classical structural and narrative strategies, broad thematic unities, classical character constructions and rhetorical devices, such as fictive speeches and other dialogue.[3] A closer look at southern historiography during the trecento, however, reveals that the classical tradition was never abandoned in the Mezzogiorno.

The record of antiquity remained alive in several ways, including architectural and archeological (particularly epigraphical) remains, as well as the literary traditions of Virgil, Statius and other classical authors. The survival of Greek language and literature — whatever their continuity with the ancient Greek culture of the South — kept alive traditions of historiography and literary and religious writing. Throughout the Middle Ages classical historians remained established sources, if often in vernacular translations or compendia. These authors included Lucan, Valerius Maximus, Sallust, Tacitus, Suetonius, Caesar, Justinus and Josephus.[4]

Livy survived in about ten manuscripts throughout the Middle Ages, and an Italian vernacular translation existed that was quoted by several of our authors, including the Anomino romano.[5] But only with Petrarch's groundbreaking philological research into Livy's works in the 1320s did a reliable text begin to form and to become part of the common source material.[6] Such sources provided general narrative structures, style, rhetorical devices, such as the use of oratory, and elements of character and motivation.

Other, more literary, sources were also available to Italians of the trecento.[7] Among the classics, Cicero, Virgil, Ovid, Horace, Seneca, both Plinys, Apuleius, Varro, Frontinus, Macrobius, Statius, Vitruvius and fragments of the plays of Plautus and Terence offered excellent examples of style and language, narrative strategies, incident and character that went beyond the events and personalities narrated in ancient histories.[8] These were often included in florilegia. Later authors included Eusebius, Lactantius, Augustine, Lucius Anneus Florus, Orosius and Procopius (in translation).[9] Though Petrarch attempted unsuccessfully to learn Greek, Boccaccio had enough knowledge to be able to use existing manuscripts of Homer and to excerpt Theodontius.[10] At the same time, Angelo Clareno was completing his own Latin translations of the Greek Fathers; and at least one of his translations, of John Climacus' *Scala paradisi*, was rendered into Tuscan by Gentile da Foligno.[11] A small core of sources were especially treasured in the South of Italy. These included Florus, Statius and most prominently Virgil for his associations with Naples and Campania.[12]

The types of references to the classics varied considerably and provide us with a unique ability to compare trecento classicism with what generally has been considered the unique contribution of the Renaissance. Such classical use could range from isolated citations, sometimes derived from florilegia, to lengthy citations derived either from the original texts or again from florilegia, to more deeply assimilated practices of adopting true classical style and the self-conscious methods of the classical historians. While many of the sources discussed here used the classics in isolated citations or in "disjunctive" ways that mirror Erwin Panofsky's analysis of medieval approaches to the ancient world,[13] others like the Anonimo romano, Boccaccio, the *Cronaca di Partenope* and Petrarch used both classical references and classical figures to underscore the moral issues facing their times or to bolster arguments with classical authorities in ways that went far beyond the isolated citations of northern chroniclers and that shared the early humanist impulses of northern Italian historiography.[14] Dario Internullo[15] has assembled clear evidence of these types of classical appropriation for trecento Rome, while various authors in the recent collection *Le cronache volgari in Italia*[16] have also noted this variety of use for writers throughout the peninsula, including the trecento Regno. We will attempt to offer examples of all types of classical influence below.

Johanns von Winterthur could cite both Isidore of Seville and Aristotle in a discussion of the famine of 1343/44.[17] But he did so along with citations from Scripture as simply other authorities in a typically scholastic form of argumentation. On the other hand, Thomas Walsingham was the author of four works of classical scholarship, including commentaries on Ovid's *Metamorphoses* and Dictys Cretensis' history of the Trojan war.[18] He constantly cited Virgil, Horace, Ovid, Juvenal and Lucan to illustrate moral virtues and shortcomings or to compare contemporary deeds against a yardstick of ancient achievements, incorporating similes taken from classical sources throughout his work.[19] Similarly, Angelo Clareno was able to call directly upon his own translations of the Greek Fathers to support his major themes, as in his use of Gregory of Nazianzenus' *Orations*.[20]

Among the classicist[21] circles of the trecento, we include the Anomino romano. He filled his narrative with references to classical Latin authors, exemplars and incidents.[22] Like many of his Roman contemporaries, he could both imitate classical style and incorporate texts seamlessly into his work, often from memory.[23] He begins Rienzo's biography recounting Cola's knowledge of Livy, Seneca, Cicero, Julius Caesar and Valerius Maximus, his interest in Rome's classical remains and his facility in reading its ancient inscriptions.[24] In his story of one of Cola's prophetic dreams,[25] the Anonimo digresses to discuss classical ideas on dreams, paraphrasing Gregory the Great,[26] Martinus Polanus[27] and Valerius Maximus,[28] concluding with a lengthy summary of Aristotle's theory.[29] The Anonimo romano summoned up from memory Livy 21–22 to compare Rienzo's victory at Porta San Lorenzo to Hannibal's at Lake Trasimene and Cannae.[30] He directly quoted Valerius Maximus on the tyrant Dionysius of Sicily[31] in his account of the food shortage in Rome of 1353.[32] He digressed to an episode from Livy 5.41 to comment on Rienzo's attempt to flee the Capitoline on the day of his murder.[33] His descriptions of torn and mutilated human bodies may have owed much to Lucan and to Sallust for the vividness of his characterizations.[34]

The *Cronaca di Partenope* makes its classical roots and interests apparent in its very title, recalling the ancient name of Naples and summoning up mythology, social memory and textual traditions that link the present history of the city intimately with its classical past. The first sixteen chapters of the work address the city's Greek foundations and its Greek and Roman history, ending with a paraphrase of Florus' praise of Campania and then continuing on for the next sixteen chapters with a recounting of Naples' Virgilian traditions and legends. After narrating the city's conversion to Christianity, it returns in Chapters 38 and 39 to a discussion of the Cumaean Sibyl. Chapters 40–49 then discuss the city's late ancient history under Constantine and the Byzantines. Chapter 50 begins the city's medieval history from the report of a Saracen siege of 787. The remaining 25 chapters bring the city's history up to the succession of Giovanna I.

Samantha Kelly has carefully examined the *Cronaca's* sources,[35] noting the first two parts' reliance on classical florilegia, a "Commentary V" on Virgil and on Horace, Ovid, Seneca, Lactantius and Livy. While titled a "chronicle," the work focuses not on the annual details of reigns, floods or battles but on an overarching narrative linked by the themes of an ancient city's development from pagan to Christian capital. Classical sources are used not as mere citations to bolster authority or to provide historical comparison but as the essential elements of much of the early narrative and the deep foundation of later developments. Yet there are important differences. Chiara De Caprio, for example, has drawn a distinction between the *Cronaca*'s open, vernacular narrative based on compendia, popular myth and cultural memory and the more formal Latin historiography of the next century that viewed history not as changing process but as formal, finished product. Such a distinction applied also to the use of classical sources and the independent authority given to them in sharp contrast with the "contextual" use of the classics in such trecento works.[36]

※

The author of the *Vita Nicolai Acciaioli,* Matteo Palmieri, had a minimal facility with Greek sources and knew most in Latin translations. But he was thoroughly familiar with his Latin sources, including Cicero, Sallust, Livy, Quintilian, Pliny, Aulus Gellius, as well as Virgil, Ovid, Horace, Juvenal, Plautus and Terence. While drawing on the Villani's *Cronaca nuova,* Acciaiuoli's letters, other contemporary documents and firsthand accounts, Palmieri structured his *Vita* directly on Plutarch's *Lives.*[37] Passages in Acciaiuoli's biography speak not of the trecento but of the classical world, using ancient geographical names and other vocabulary to describe his parentage and youth.[38] While Palmieri belonged to the early Florentine humanist circle and wrote of a fellow Florentine for a Florentine audience, his *Vita* remains an essential document of southern historiography.

※

Petrarch and Boccaccio fully modeled their works on classical genres and employed a wide range of classical sources and devices. Even more importantly, they wrote in a style that was consciously based on classical models: especially Cicero and Virgil. As noted above,[39] Petrarch's historical works under consideration here include his Letters, especially his *Familiares*[40] and *Seniles,*[41] his *Itinerary*[42] and *Eclogue* 2 of his *Bucolicum carmen.*[43] He had set the standard for a revived classical historiography in all these works with his ongoing *De viris illustribus.* He began the work in 1338 and expanded and revised it until his death in 1374. In it Petrarch went far beyond the biographical collections of his contemporaries like Giovanni Colonna's *De viris illustribus*[44] both in the length and detail of his biographies and in his Latin style, which remained the "most consistent classicizing found in his corpus,"[45] asserting that "what else, then, is all history if not the praise of Rome?"[46] He also fully embraced the ancient view that historiography's central goal was moral example and that Latin style was inextricably linked to that high moral purpose.[47] Of all the historians discussed here, Petrarch was also the most clear concerning his "cut-and-paste" methodology, bringing together evidence from a wide variety of classical authors, collating differing sources to create a cohesive and complete narrative and expanding source accounts to more clearly explain an event or make a moral point.[48]

His 638 extant letters, including the *Epistolae rerum familiarium,* the *Epistolae rerum senilium* and the *Epistolae sine nomine,* are important primary source documents about contemporary people and events, letters sent to friends and other contemporaries and to his "familiars" among the ancients: Cicero, Seneca, Horace, Virgil, Homer and others. Together the *Familiares* and *Seniles* form what Ascoli has called a "megamacro-text" and a self-consciously formulated "project of recovering and reproducing the classical past."[49] We will examine the historiographical implications of Petrarch's correspondence and their classical foundations at greater length in our discussion of the black legend of the Angevins in Chapter 8.[50]

Boccaccio was inspired to write his *De mulieribus claris* by Petrarch's *De viris illustribus*. The form of his text derives both from Petrarch and from the classical models of biography established by Plutarch and passed on to the Latin world through Jerome's *De viris illustribus*, the only classical source Boccaccio mentions by name. However, Virginia Brown's examination of the text[51] reveals that he also used Livy, Ovid, Pliny the Elder, Statius, Suetonius, Valerius Maximus and Virgil as well as late ancient and early Christian writers such as Justinus, Lactantius, Orosius and a compendium assembled under the name of Theodontius. He used the same method for his *De casibus virorum illustrium*, which explicitly used classical texts, drawn from Greek and Roman sources, for the majority of his examples. In short, Boccaccio relied on much the same classical sources as other trecento authors, mining the available Latin texts for both their historical and narrative details and for their language and themes. Except for his last six "modern" women, all his examples in *De mulieribus claris* are drawn from classical authors. As Brown indicates, however, Boccaccio did not hesitate to amplify his sources, perhaps from his own creative resources or from other classical and literary sources.[52]

Boccaccio used his specific classical sources in much the same way as his contemporaries: specific citations to bolster moral arguments, silent borrowings from their works, sometimes at great length — as in his borrowing from Virgil to recount the story of Camilla, queen of the Volscians,[53] or from Livy to recount that of the Roman matron Veturia[54] — to fill in details of events, personalities and character, as background or as motivation for plot. Following Petrarch's lead, however, Boccaccio also based his style on classical models and modes. Boccaccio used the classical epideictic form in parallel fashion to conclude both his collections of lives: of praise in the *Vita* of Giovanna I in *De mulieribus claris* and of condemnation in the life of her handmaiden Filippa of Catania in *De casibus virorum illustrium*. He also framed some of his most pointed references to individuals and events in Naples in the classical form of *Eclogues* 3–6, again taking his lead from Petrarch and his "Argus."[55]

CHAPTER 3 ↭ SOURCES

Other classical devices also survived, including the construction of dialogue and speeches and the narration of characters' emotional conditions. In his *Historia septem tribulationum,* Angelo Clareno often deployed both set speeches, including those of Christ to Francis and of Francis to his followers[56] or of Brother Elias to Pope Gregory IX.[57] Dialogues between many of his characters have little or no historical basis but move forward the narrative and themes of his grand history and reflect classical practice. The Anonimo romano's recounting of Rienzo's oratory was probably from first-hand experience, but his construction of characters' inner lives relied heavily on classical sources. His description of Rienzo's inner thoughts[58] and of his decisions during the riots that destroyed the Senate Place on the Capitoline and ended with his death[59] drew on Livy V.41.[60]

THE CLASSICAL TRADITION: ANCIENT REMAINS

Like Rome, Naples and neighboring Campania were also rich in the physical remains of the classical past: temples, amphitheaters, bath complexes, ancient walls, gates and roads all survived often almost intact as far afield as Benevento, Pozzuoli and Baia or as near as the Temple of the Dioscuri in Naples. Massive architectural remains, statuary, inscriptions and other *spolia* of all types offered daily reminders of the long surviving classical past that could freshly evoke formal history, legend and folk memory.[61] Physical remains joined the oral traditions of the city's ciceroni and more learned guides who reported Naples' Virgilian associations. All became source material for a textual community centered around the living traditions of antiquity that performed quite differently from the chronicle of Thomas Walsingham in far-off St. Albans, for example. We have already mentioned the Anonimo romano on Cola's reading of inscriptions. In this the Anonimo shared Giovanni Cavallini's appreciation of antiquities as contested actors in the struggle against of the barons' cultural hegemony.[62] Here we will focus on two other authors: the *Cronaca di Partenope* on Naples' Virgilian tradition and Petrarch on Naples' classical remains around Baia and the Phlegraean Fields.

The *Cronaca's* third chapter narrates Naples' foundation, recounting the flight of many settlers at Cumae after an outbreak of plague to the siren Parthenope's tomb on Monte Eschia.[63] This marks the ancient umbilical from which Naples' life flowed, fixing its history and special identity firmly upon its ancient monuments. The later founding of Neapolis is attested by the survival of an ancient Greek inscription, translated by King Robert's physician,[64] an act of cultural discovery tying the city's greatness under Robert the Wise to antiquity with the same cultural re-appropriation that Petrarch claimed in his friendship with the king.[65] It also echoes Cola di Rienzo's first act of Roman revival narrated by the Anonimo romano.[66] The *Cronaca* reviews many sites in Campania and the Phlegraean Fields that attest to the city's ancient heritage and history, from the castle of Somma[67] to the city's grid plan, its ancient fortresses and *seggi*[68] to the city and Campania's many Virgilian sites.[69] Chapter 8 will analyze how Petrarch's letters and his *Itinerary* similarly deploy Naples' and Campania's classical remains to bolster his narrative of Angevin greatness under Robert the Wise and the king's support for Petrarch's coronation as poet laureate and reviver of antiquity.[70]

EARLIER MEDIEVAL HISTORIOGRAPHY

These chronicles draw strongly on the work of predecessors, either in continuing or compiling a text or in collating various accounts to fill in missing gaps of years and events or to create a new, cohesive narrative. Thomas Walsingham compiled accounts from various textual sources, especially for the years 1377–81,[71] but he relied almost exclusively on first-hand accounts and archival materials for later portions of his work.[72] We do not know what sources or informants he used for his accounts of the Mezzogiorno, however. Jean Froissart also based large parts of his *Chroniques* on earlier works, such as the *Vrayes Chroniques* of Jean Le Bel or the Chandos Herald's *Life of the Black Prince*. For the years 1379–85, he relied on his own sources for events, including those around the reign of Giovanna I. Aside from his own eyewitness, we know only one of the sources used by the author/compiler of the *Diurnale (Diario) di Duca di Monteleone* for the last events of Giovanna I's reign.[73]

※

Giovanni Villani is clear at the outset that his work was based on "compiling the deeds and acts of the Florentines from more ancient and diverse books, both chronicles and [other] authors."[74] For the earlier sections of his work[75] up to about 1275, Giovanni relied on a version of the *Chronica de origine civitatis*, Martin of Troppau's *Chronicon Pontificum et Imperatorum*, a now lost *Gesta Florentiorum*, Brunetto Latini's *Livres dou Tresor*, the pseudo-Latini *Chronicle* and Ricold of Monte Croce's *Liber Peregrinationis*. For later periods, Villani may have used an anonymous *Chronichetta* or have drawn on a common source now lost. He relied on his own recollections of contemporary events after about 1309. Scholars continue to investigate his literary reliance on Dante.[76] For the Regno and the Angevin period, Villani may have used a version of the Tuscan *Leggenda di Messer Gianni di Procida* for the Sicilian Vespers. Thereafter he probably drew on first-hand accounts from associates in Naples and the South.[77]

※

The Anonimo romano based much of his work on eyewitness and oral testimony.[78] He rarely relied on other medieval sources, and no direct influence can be detected from Villani or other urban chronicles. Seibt had speculated that the *Liber Pontificalis*, Martin of Troppau and the Mirabilian tradition might be remote sources, but clear evidence is lacking.[79] There are, however, traces of other sources that reverberate though the Anonimo's text, including Giovanni Colonna's *Mare historiarum*.[80] The author also seems to have been familiar with Rolandino da Padova's thematic approach to the tyrants of the Romagna but so wove his sources into the fabric of his work that no direct citations or borrowings are apparent.[81]

Agnolo di Tura del Grasso took entire tracts from Villani when discussing Florentine topics for his portion of the *Cronaca Senese,* and one would assume that he did the same for other locations, but these sources have not been identified.[82] Likewise, the *Chronicon siculum incerti authoris* relied heavily on the *Cronaca di Partenope* for events from the duecento through the first part of the trecento,[83] but its other written sources have not been established.[84] The *Diurnale (Diario) di Duca di Monteleone* used a wide variety of sources for Naples and the South, including Guglielmo Marramaldo's *Breve chronicon de rebus neapolitanis,* Tommaso Loffredo's *Annales* and the *Diarium regum Neapolis et Siciliae.*

Whatever its ultimate authorship, the *Cronaca di Partenope*[85] takes its late ancient materials from Procopius and the Commentary V, its early Christian sections from the *Gesta episcoporum neapolitanum,* its Virgilian traditions from a wide variety of sources including Gervaise of Tilbury and Alexander of Neckham, its later medieval events from the *Chronicon di Santa Maria del Principio,* the *Vita Athanasii,* the lives of Sant'Aspreno, Sta. Patricia, Sant'Agrippino and others. The Norman sections includes borrowings from the *Romualdi salernitani chronicon,* while sections for the end of the Hohenstaufen and Angevin periods rely almost verbatim on the "Southernized Villani."[86] Likewise, Matteo Palmieri's *Vita* supplemented Acciaiuoli's own correspondence with extensive use of the Villani's *Cronache,* Filippo Villani's *Vita del Gran Siniscalco* and fragments from other contemporary sources.[87]

ARABIC, JEWISH, GREEK SOURCES

Southern historiography under the Normans and Hohenstaufen often relied heavily on sources from the non-Christian communities of the Regno, and the accounts of Abû 'Abdallâh al-Idrîsî and Benjamin of Tudela offer important first-hand accounts of the South.[88] But the Angevin reversal of Norman and Hohenstaufen *convivenza* and the dynasty's emphasis on a new Christian kingdom based on both chivalrous might and sacred lineage provided little opportunity for such religious interaction. The papal condemnations of Frederick II and his heirs as heretics and apostates and Charles II's destruction of the Muslim colony of Lucera[89] provide a cogent example of this new emphasis on Christian hegemony. This absence is particularly noticeable in the sources under discussion here. The Anonimo romano's accounts of the crusade against Gibraltar[90] and to Smyrna,[91] for example, appear to rely solely on Christian sources and participants' reports.

LITERARY SOURCES

Froissart is known as the preeminent historian of chivalry, and for good reason.[92] At the English court of Queen Philippa, he composed *chansons, ballades, virelais* and *rondeaux* and the pre-Arthurian romance *Méliador*. His fictive chivalrous world elided seamlessly into his historical work. Green[93] and Clarke[94] have drawn attention to Giovanni Villani's use of the Italian Alexander romance tradition and of French chivalric romances. Buccio di Ranallo wrote his rhymed *Cronaca aquilana rimata*[95] in Alexandrine verse in imitation of French work popular at the Angevin court. Scholars have noted the influence of Dante's *Inferno* in at least one of his other works, the verse *Leggenda di Santa Caterina d'Alessandria*. Buccio may also reflect the influence of French and Provençal *chansons de geste* and romances then being popularized by Provençal minstrels and troubadours in the Angevin Abruzzi.[96] Seibt has analyzed the Anonimo romano's use of contemporary poetic language,[97] linking it to the Roman Mirabilian tradition and perhaps to the *Storie de Troja e de Roma*, the *Fatti di Cesare* and the *Lyber ystoriarum Romanorum*.[98] In Chapter 5, we will offer a detailed example of this type of source by examining the close connection between chivalrous romance and Angevin narratives of legitimacy, religious devotion and military prowess.

RELIGIOUS SOURCES

Scripture,[99] hagiography,[100] sermons and other religious texts were frequently woven into the texture of medieval chronicles as discrete citations aimed at bolstering an argument, underscoring the meaning of an event or highlighting virtues and vices. Such biblical citation was a seamless process for medieval writers trained in the skills of grammar and rhetoric, where memorization and mnemonic devices were part of their education from early childhood and memorized psalms were used to teach basic literacy skills. It is therefore no surprise to see many medieval chronicles, especially those of well-educated clerics, replete with biblical citation or allusion used to bolster arguments, to enliven passages and to convey emotional and moral impact.[101]

CHAPTER 3 ❧ SOURCES

The Anonimo romano,[102] Buccio di Ranallo and the *Chronicon Estense*[103] used the Bible sparingly or via epitomes as occasional citations of authority. The Anonimo romano refers to collections of canon law and commentaries[104] and cites at length Gregory the Great's *Dialogue* IV.49 in his discussion of Rienzo's dreams.[105] He also includes and parses Cola's use of Maccabees in his repartee with the ambassadors of Naples, stressing Rome's faithfulness to its allies,[106] and he uses the description of Nebuchadnezzar in Daniel 4[107] to emphasis Rienzo's physical deterioration on his return to Rome in 1354.

Johanns von Winterthur's Latinity derived much of its narrative style from the Bible,[108] and he employed Scripture in the same way that he used other authorities, often stringing together a variety of biblical citations to construct a moral argument.[109] He also drew on sermon literature, contemporary moral philosophy, canon law and contemporary local chronicles of Nuremberg and other localities and Franciscan accounts of their missions to Asia.[110] An admirer of the Franciscan Spirituals, he included in his discussion of Franciscan affairs, borrowings from a version of the *Vaticinia de summis pontificibus,*[111] the letters of Queen Sancia of Majorca to the Franciscan Order[112] and a description of her death and burial in Naples.[113] Fulvio Delle Donne[114] has noted Domenico da Gravina's use of Scripture not to bolster arguments but for dramatic effect, as, for example, his Gospel citations of Christ's trial[115] or the sufferings of the martyrs to dramatize the trial of Judge Martuccio.[116] While both Boccaccio's *De mulieribus claris* and *De casibus virorum illustrium* focused on classical models, in his lives of Adam and Eve primarily and for Nimrod, Saul, Rehoboam, Athaliah, Zedekiah and Herod, he did employ biblical citation to a greater or lesser extent.[117]

Hagiography could also be excerpted at length and incorporated into a narrative. Angelo Clareno used early versions of the Franciscan Rule, extensive passages from Bonaventure, John and Thomas of Celano and Brother Leo for his life of Francis of Assisi and for the early history of the order and the *Oraculum Cyrilii* and Joachim of Fiore for his "predictive passages." His oral and first-hand accounts of the Spiritual Franciscans wove sacred lives into his historical fabric to give both meaning and direction to the tribulations of the faithful.[118] Petrarch may have used Iacopo da Voragine' *Legenda Aurea* for Roman material.[119] We have already noted the *Cronaca di Partenope's* reliance on extensive passages from the lives of saints Athanasius, Aspreno and others for its early medieval narrative.[120]

ARCHIVAL SOURCES

A common misconception about medieval historiography is that chroniclers wrote primarily from the narrow focus of their monastery's scriptorium or notary's office, recording events indifferently in their order of occurrence with no view of the larger world or of how these elements fit together into the meaningful and intentional narratives that produce history. On closer examination, however, southern historians deployed a wide range of primary source documents.[121] Roberto Delle Donne, Fulvio Delle Donne, Chiara de Caprio, Francesco Montuori and Francesco Senatore have built upon the work of Francesco Sabatini and Bartolommeo Capasso to lay out how the archives of city and royal governments informed southern historiography of the trecento and quattrocento. Several historians discussed here had direct access to state archives as public officials or through their receipt of official announcements, news reports and narrative accounts. As Senatore has noted,[122] late medieval and early modern chancelleries were not sealed offices but permeable spaces within which notaries and other officials constantly crossed the boundary between public and private duties. He reminds us that notarial archives were often the private possession of their creators, and that such public offices and their records often had no permanent seat. Notaries throughout Italy — North and South — therefore had ready access to such "public" sources and could translate, quote, summarize, or incorporate them wholesale into their chronicles both to record events and to lend veracity to their accounts.

French, English and German historiography also built on a long tradition and professional habitus of deep archival research. At one end of the continuum, Johanns von Winterthur makes repeated reference to papal, episcopal and imperial letters without attribution or quotation. Thomas Walsingham used his privileged position at St. Alban's Abbey, close to London and the court and at the center of a network of travelers and courtiers, to gather an impressive number of archival materials not already in the abbey's library.[123] These focus on English events, primarily around London. It remains unclear, however, what documents Thomas used for his account of Giovanna I. Jean Froissart sometimes incorporated archival sources, like the text of the Treaty of Tournai, into his narrative wholesale.

The *Chronicon Mutinense* relied on Modena's records of its podestàs for 1188–1347.[124] Thereafter Giovanni da Bazzano increasingly used papal and Roman letters[125] and other diplomatic correspondence. These could be variably interpreted. For example, Bazzano's narration of Andrew of Hungary's murder and his favorable treatment of Giovanna I differ dramatically from the interpretation of the same dispatches by the *Chronicon Estense*.[126]

The Anonimo romano was a physician, trained also in Latin, and may have worked for the commune at times. He therefore could have had access to its archival materials. We know that on at least one occasion — Rienzo's speech at the Lateran — the Anonimo recorded the use of a written document, a *carta*.[127] Internullo suggests that he may have borrowed from official documents for other episodes.[128] His account of such remote events as the battle of Crécy may also have depended on documentary circulars.

Domenico da Gravina's relationship to his archival sources is complex and often obscured by his own desire for dramatic impact. As a notary he held a *publica fides* charged with the recording, copying and archiving of official documentation.[129] He was also involved in many of the incidents he records — often as the recipient, often as the public reader of official correspondence. Yet in many cases he chose not to incorporate the document into the text but to transform his materials either into dialogue or speeches.[130] Delle Donne has speculated that this may well have been the result of his attempt to both distance himself from the horror of the events he records and to pass on a historical record that sears such memories into his readers' and his own descendants' minds. Gravina's approach to archives made his work less a chronicle than an artful, personal history that fused private and public memory into a cogent narrative.[131]

COSMOLOGY, SCIENCE, MEDICINE

Medieval chronicles are well known for their annual reports of celestial events ranging from eclipses and comets to "blood skies," hail and thunderstorms, unseasonable snow, heat, floods, earthquakes, plagues and famines. They often reported stories of prodigies, monsters and other "unnatural" creatures[132] among their yearly lists of coronations, battles and parliaments. While casually dismissed as superstitions and credulous retellings of folk tales and rumor, such records also reflect a medieval understanding of current scientific thought and demonstrate a deep interest in how the natural world affected human culture. This science included both the accumulated learning embedded in ancient texts and medieval thought on the interaction between the heavenly and eternal and the secular and quotidian spheres. These spheres interacted through the physical inruptions of extraordinary events — prodigies and portents — and through their use as metaphors for wider social, political and spiritual realities.

The Villani's *Cronaca Nuova* shares much with the long tradition of medieval chroniclers. While emphasizing the role of God and the cosmic process of *fortuna* in rewarding virtue and punishing vice, like many of his contemporaries, Giovanni Villani admitted the place of astrology in helping to determine this divine will.[133] Comets, eclipses, planetary conjunctions and earthquakes could all predict plagues, famine, revolution, death and decline, but only to those well versed in the cutting-edge science of the time. Villani therefore regularly consulted with Paolo Dagomari, a noted Florentine astrologer, on planetary conjunctions and their impact on the cycles of human history and individual lives.[134] Judith Collard has argued that Matthew Paris gathered scientific data from both written texts and visual observation. Such recording formed an integral part of his worldview and writing.[135]

※

Another important category of scientific evidence, especially for southern Italian writers, was contemporary medical knowledge,[136] often from Salerno's medical school and from the many practitioners of medicine and surgery in trecento Italian society, including specialists in women's health.[137] Domenico da Gravina uses contemporary knowledge of urology to explain one of the more important episodes in the dynastic struggle between the Angevin houses of Taranto and Durazzo: the use of false urine samples to destroy the reputation of Agnes de Perigord, the matriarch of the house of Durazzo.[138] We have already discussed the Anonimo romano's use of Aristotle's theory of dreams,[139] but it is worth emphasizing here the acceptance of such theory as part of the scientific base of knowledge concerning human psychology and physiology.[140] The episode of Martino di Porto,[141] a baron and brigand arrested and executed by Rienzo despite his claims of illness, reveals the medical knowledge that advanced the Anonimo's narrative, analyzed character and explained historical action. The Anonimo also drew on the *Canone della Medicina* used at the University of Bologna[142] and on Aristotle's *Meteorologica*.[143] Dario Internullo analyzes how the Anonimo used his knowledge of Galen, Avicenna and Aristotle to explain both personal and political changes. Internullo emphasizes the Anonimo's knowledge of diagnostic techniques and vocabulary as essential to his historical style.[144] Victor Formentin[145] offers an insightful reading of the Anonimo's account of the death of Annibale da Ceccano,[146] linking the *Cronaca*'s detailed description of the cardinal's gluttonous last meal with contemporary medical theory of the physiological impact of certain foods on the body and tracking the rhythm of the Anonimo's prose against the pace of Annibale's illness.

While the *Cronaca di Partenope* used contemporary scientific knowledge, it also had negative things to say about physicians. The author recounts a story about Virgil's founding of the medicinal Baths of Baia for the Neapolitans' health and benefit. But the professional physicians of Salerno were apparently jealous to preserve their monopoly on health care and prevent popular dissemination. They therefore sailed up the coast one night to destroy the series of images and inscriptions detailing each of the body parts healed at each station.[147] In another incident during the reign of the Norman king Roger, an English physician attempted unsuccessfully to steal Virgil's bones from his tomb in Naples. As compensation, however, the Neapolitans gave him the books of necromancy resting under the poet's head.[148] Petrarch also used natural elements like thunderstorms and thunderbolts, earthquakes and tsunamis as "metaphorical doubling" for King Robert's death and the ensuing political and moral disasters that befell Naples under Giovanna I. We will analyze these in detail in Chapter 8.

FOLKLORE, POPULAR MEMORY AND ORALITY

The relationship between orality and textuality has been a topic of intense study among medievalists since the pioneering work of Walter Ong.[149] Mary Carruthers has analyzed the dynamic between individual and group memory and the creation of texts and textual communities.[150] Building on these, Alizah Holstein has emphasized the key role of memory in the Anonimo romano and other mid-trecento Roman writers in both defining and then forgetting Rome's imperial past and as a point of contention between the barons and people of Rome.[151] Chiara De Caprio, Fulvio Delle Donne, Francesco Senatore and other scholars at the Università degli Studi di Napoli Federico II have embarked on a long-term, detailed study of the process and mechanisms by which the orality of official proclamation and news, diplomatic dispatch, urban rumor, *infamia*[152] and *damnatio memoriae*[153] becomes transformed into textuality.[154] Eileen Gardiner[155] has discussed the process through which the very personal and highly subjective experience of near-death or visionary events is transmitted from the oral testimony of the visionary into that of a reliable and replicable textual community and tradition. This often involved a process of conforming the experience to its community's viewpoints, translating often confused and unique first-person narrative to standardized genre and extending language's ability to express experience. Such experience differs little in its first-hand relation from that of a witness to war, urban violence, punishment and torture, the experience of plague, earthquake or other extreme natural events under discussion here. With Gardiner's caveat in mind, we must distinguish between such oral evidence, translated into textual form by historians, and the first-hand, eyewitness and oral testimony gathered by such writers as Froissart, the Villani and the Anonimo romano: the differences between *audita*, "what people said," or "what someone told me directly," and *visa*, "what I saw myself."[156]

Such distinctions and the evaluation of their worth as evidence were part of the classical rhetorical tradition that informed historical writing.[157] Senatore has cautioned,[158] however, that the basis of much that is interpreted as "orality" may, in fact, have been the product of diplomatic dispatches and administrative announcements meant specifically for public distribution. Our historians could then take such documents, transform them into direct discourse and apply rhetorical *amplificatio* to give them the aura of direct oral transmission. He notes that we need to interrogate our notions of unmediated record and apply more rigid analyses of language and form to such constructs.

Johanns von Winterthur offers a catalog of orality, summing up many of his usages in one passage concerning the popular reaction to clerical abuse over the dispensation of penance and absolution in Germany in the autumn of 1347.[159] The abuses produced *scandalum fidei, scrupulum, perplexitates, detractiones, murmuraciones, diffidenciam, desperacione, clamorem, commocionem* as well as *timorem et suspicionem*. Nearly half of these involve some form of orality. To these, Johanns added common *(vulgaris)* rumor[160] and widespread celebrity *(celebris fama)*.[161]

Johanns also explicitly relied on oral testimony for some of the episodes he relates, including a story about King Rudolf that was so celebrated and famous that he took care to commit it quickly to writing,[162] stories of the Franciscans he heard as a young boy,[163] the "prediction that I heard, stunned, of the death of King Albert I that a certain Swiss knight related to many people"[164] or a "recent and popular" story of the war between Teutonic Knights and the peoples of the Baltic.[165] Johanns would have obtained his information about Naples and other remote areas from similar oral testimony narrated directly to him, as in the case of a pilgrim to Compostela — a trustworthy compatriot — who related to him events of 1340 in Alfonso XI of Castile's war against the Muslims. The man, "a compatriot of mine and a trustworthy citizen, explained this to me in the most truthful testimony."[166]

※

Many of Thomas Walsingham's "outside sources" included written newsletters, dispatches from the court or the battlefield or the eyewitness testimony of visitors to St. Albans.[167] But other oral evidence certainly played a part. These include rumors *(ut fertur, auditis)*,[168] *scandalum*[169] and *infamia*,[170] popular gossip *(de me dicunt)*[171] and *contumelia*,[172] popular opinion *(multis opinantibus,*[173] *alii vero dicebant*[174]*)*, reports of portents *(populo manifeste)*[175] and tales of wandering spirits *(bene recoluerunt)*[176] as well as the record of more official oral sources, such as proclamations *(proclamatum fuit)*.[177] We do not know whether such oral reports formed part of Walsingham's account of the end of Giovanna's reign, whether he was "reasonably well informed"[178] through visitors to St. Albans (and who they might have been) or whether he depended almost entirely on written reports.

※

Likewise, Jean Froissart was careful to explain his goals and to lay out his sources and his methods in the prologue to his *Chroniques*:

> In order that the honourable deeds and ventures accomplished by arms, which took place during the wars between France and England, might be aptly documented and commended to lasting memory, so that courageous men might follow such

examples to inspire them to good, it is my wish to undertake to record this glorious history.... I have always requested and enquired to the best of my ability for true accounts of the wars and exploits that have occurred.[179]

Froissart chose his sources well: both the mighty and those in lower ranks — heralds and masters of arms — whose profession it was to gather news and information and to convey it in a consistent and trustworthy manner, including its transmission into writing.[180]

How did Froissart construct his courtly and highly inaccurate account of the reign of Giovanna I and events in the kingdom of Naples found in Book II?[181] According to Alberto Varvaro, Froissart possessed little information about southern Italy; and what he had was "incomplete, imprecise and distorted."[182] His few references to the Regno seem to depend upon Jean le Bel and on the false reputation of Robert the Wise as a keen prognosticator of astrological signs and interpreter of Merlin's prophesies.[183] Magic is at the heart of Neapolitan affairs, as demonstrated in Charles of Durazzo's capture of Giovanna I and Otto of Brunswick in Castel Nuovo,[184] at the center of an evil, enchanted land.[185] Froissart might well have based his account on the Virgilian tradition also then current in northern France. His portrait of Giovanna[186] may also have been based on slanderous rumors circulating at the Visconti court of Milan to counter the possibility of renewed Angevin power in the South.[187] In this case, then, Froissart's reliance on oral reports worked to further cloud the historical record of the Mezzogiorno for northern readers.

Giovanni da Bazzano's *Chronicon Mutinense* also appears to have relied on oral testimony for some of its contemporary reportage. Examples include its reference to news *(literae et nova)*[188] arriving at Modena and the announcement *(prenunciatus et proclamatus fuit)*[189] of the 1350 Jubilee. The chronicler notes the *scandalum, damnum et vituperium* caused by the forces of Ferrara in 1317.[190] Giovanni also reports rumor *(ut dicitur)*[191] and *infamia*.[192] We do not know his sources for events in Naples, but he may have depended on first-hand reports from Hungarians accompanying King Lewis through the Romagna, from couriers repeating the official Hungarian line concerning Prince Andrew's murder or from soldiers returning home with their own accounts of events there. Buccio di Ranallo felt little need to trace the origins of Aquila, a recent foundation, citing written sources only for references to the remote past. He relied instead almost solely on oral testimony and his own witness. He even cited records of city council meetings as oral relations,[193] "striving to give an narrative structure" to documents.[194]

The transparency of the Giovanni Villani's use of orality in the *Nuova Cronica* has been questioned by Sophia Menache, who highlights the rhetorical uses of such claims and posits the author's manipulative intent to amplify readers' emotions and attitudes toward the subject matter.[195] While such usage relied on standard rhetorical modes inherited from both ancient sources and medieval handbooks, Villani did use a set group of verbs and nouns as markers for oral evidence.[196] Thus forms of *dicere* could summon up local traditions about pagan and Christian antiquity,[197] fable and folk tale,[198] well-known facts and popular political memory,[199] popular opinion and reputation,[200] rumor[201] or *infamia*.[202] More rarely are such terms used to report the cry of the people to arms or violence[203] and more rarely still to describe public discussions.[204] Villani uses the plural forms, *dicemmo* throughout almost solely to refer back to other sections of his own narrative[205] or *dicono* to cite proverbs, classics and other textual authorities[206] and rarely for reportage.[207] He appears to have relied on current hearsay and rumor (usually *si dice*)[208] or the report of past rumor and hearsay *(si dicea)*[209] for many events concerning the Angevins and the Regno.

In contrast to this language of rumor and insinuation, Villani's variants of *gridare* almost always had a public connotation and context. They record processions and calls for peacemaking or reconciliation,[210] calls to arms, battle cries and the clamor of armies, panic and defeat,[211] urban uprisings and factional conflict[212] or human torment from torture, armed conflict or natural disaster.[213] Villani also deployed such words in their universal sense to speak of nature and the universe: the ominous sounds of birds before the battle of Crécy[214] or the call of blood for revenge crying out through the world.[215]

Villani used variants of *parlare* to describe the process of narrative and his own authorial voice,[216] textual authority or language itself.[217] Less frequent are its uses to describe urban rumor, public conversation or *infamia*.[218] One such example is the gossip around Giovanna I's affair with Louis of Taranto.[219] The most ominous usages in Villani's chronicle appear around the word *romore*. This is not "rumor" in the modern sense or the modern Italian sense of *voci*,[220] nor a conscious speech act, but the sudden occurrence of audible events, more a force than an act, whether of human or natural agency. It could also describe the rumblings of the people on the verge of violent revolt,[221] the rustling and stirring of an army camp, the sound of an approaching enemy[222] or even, rarely, the upsetting or raging of reason itself.[223] The procession returning the body of the murdered Prince Andrew to Naples was met by a *romore di popolo e a baratta a terra*,[224] while the overthrow of Cola di Rienzo on December 15, 1354 began with a cry to arms that Villani described as a *romore* spreading through the city's streets.[225]

In one sense, Villani's constant use of set terms to describe popular report, rumor or the sounds of uprisings locates language within a set social class and moral sphere, dramatically predictive and suspenseful at the same time. Language describing the din and pain of battle or the cries of Disciplinati scourging themselves attempts to dramatize narrative and to impart a sensory, first-hand immediacy and experience to the reader. In another sense, as Menache has noted, by borrowing the rhetorical valences of his well-used terms — of forms of *gridare,* for example, for torture and natural disaster to personal violence and suffering — he could bring to bear an entire world of allusion to, and connotation of, innocent victimhood to such incidents as the assassination of Andrew of Hungary.[226]

Agnolo di Tura uses the same oral language as Villani to describe the same phenomena. The downfall of the Duke of Athens in Florence on 26 July 1343, for example, was accompanied by the same *suspetto e romore.*[227] The uprising was signaled by the same faceless cries heard throughout the city.[228] The news traveled quickly to Siena.[229] Angelo Clareno also made use of second-hand oral testimony, as, for example, accounts in Brother John's account of Hugh de Digne's prophesies.[230] Clareno's fifth tribulation records dialogues between Peter Olivi and his followers and superiors[231] that ultimately relied on first-hand testimony of witnesses.

While Kelly restricts the *Cronaca di Parthenope*'s sources to written texts,[232] De Caprio also contextualizes them within new research of urban orality.[233] She examines the *Cronaca*'s earlier chapters, noting that they reflect popular legend and widespread oral report, while the latter parts of the text are derived from other written sources, especially what Kelly[234] and other scholars of the *Cronaca* now call the "Southernized" Villani. The author uses many of the common terms for oral transmission already seen in Villani: *Dicto è adunche in quillo tempo;*[235] for popular saying and proverb: *Et secundo la sentencia de quillo vulgale et usato proverbio che dice…;*[236] *Alo quale luoco de Nido se dice che…;*[237] common belief: *da lo qualle cavallo se crede che…;*[238] local place names: *in quillo luoco dove ogi se chyama la Petra de lo Pesse;*[239] and local lore: *el lo grosso populo tene che…, gli antichi nostri tennero.*[240]

The Anonimo romano may be the most self-conscious of his role as a historian, and of his methodology, sources and aims. He begins his work with a citation from Isidore of Seville about the origins of history in memory, visual presentation and stone carving to preserve important events *"in segno de perpetua memoria."* Books and literacy were only later developments from visual memory in stone. Cadmus had invented letters due to the weakness of memory *(per la devolezza della memoria).*[241] In contrast to what famous ancient historians had witnessed first-hand, the

Anonimo also pinpoints the alterity of historical events and their remoteness from both the present and the historian. True to the rhetorical tradition, he carefully distinguishes first-hand experience and oral testimony:

> While I take delight in this work, I am remote from and do not experience war and the events that race through the countryside. One feels sad and miserable because of such great tribulations, and not only the one who suffers them, but also the one who hears about them.

He offers equal truth claims for both forms of evidence in his history: *"ché le infrascritte cose fuoro vere. E io le viddi e sentille."*[242]

The Anonimo's Romanesco, though distinct from Villani's Tuscan, mirrors the Florentine's lexicon for describing orality. Porta has already provided so rich a glossary[243] of this usage that we need only give one example of each. Again, variants of *dire* are associated with a variety of voices. The Anonimo often uses the terms to indicate the texts of classic authors,[244] as text labels on the paintings commissioned by Cola di Rienzo[245] or throughout simply to record dialogue.[246] More complex formulations like *si dice* could indicate folk memory,[247] commonly held beliefs or opinions,[248] the voice of the people[249] or unconfirmed or false rumor.[250] Again, as in Villani, variants of *gridare* usually held a public connotation of extreme emotion, physical pain or vocalization of conflict. Thus, *gridava* could express the unconscious moaning of the dreamer,[251] the suffering of humans in duress from famine,[252] the trauma of battle,[253] rising popular anger[254] or, most frequently, the sound of the people in uprising and revolt.[255]

The Anonimo also uses *parlare* almost universally to describe human speech, conversation or narrative. He does, however, use its negative, *sparlare,* to reflect the spread of negative gossip.[256] This is opposed to his use of *romore,* which — as in Villani — almost never means "rumor" as a conscious speech act[257] but as the sudden occurrence of an audible event, more like a natural force than a human act. It can mean the sounds of armies,[258] armed conflict[259] and battle.[260] It could also convey the sounds of humans and animals suffering duress, disaster or torment.[261] But most frequently the Anonimo uses the term *romore* to connote urban discontent, uprising and revolt, not in the sense of voiced opinion or call to battle but as an anonymous, unidentifiable rumbling from below.[262] *Voce* also takes on this meaning. Most often used simply to describe the human voice,[263] it could also mean the "voice of the people" and the popular will.[264] The Anonimo does, however, use it as a more distinct voicing of popular discontent and revolt,[265] more clearly identifiable than *romore* or *sparlare.* The richness of the Anonimo's language again highlights the important role that orality played in his narrative, recalling classical usage and sources, certainly highlighting dramatic effect and increasing rhetorical impact, but also strengthening the author's claims to the truth of his sources and his narrative.

※

The *Chronicon siculum* lacks a prologue or any other indication of authorial intent and offers few oral referents. It employs the standard forms of *dicere* to convey popular place names;[266] forms of *parlare* generally denote a *parlamentum*.[267] It uses explicit variants of *scandalum*[268] or *opinio*[269] rarely. It does, however, heighten dramatic effect and verisimilitude by using forms of *vocifere*[270] or *clamare*[271] to introduce exclamatory phrases quoting the voice of the people, either acclaiming support or protesting officials and their acts. While we do not know many of the sources for the *Diurnale (Diario) di Duca di Monteleone*, we can be certain that he did rely on oral sources from time to time. The author, for example, declares that he had heard from an old man in Naples that as a young man he had heard boys singing in the street a song about the assassination of Gianni Caracciolo.[272] The *Diurnale*'s author here lays out the stages of orality from the street, to the witness, to the writer/compiler.

※

Given Domenico da Gravina's literary aspirations to turn historical account into drama, it is difficult to disentangle his sources from his narrative. We know that he was an eyewitness to, even a participant in, many of the events he recounts in Apulia, but his account of events in Naples around the murder of Andrew of Hungary, the subsequent decimation of Giovanna's court[273] and her later reign reads uniformly in the third person, including sections of dialogue. Yet there are traces of oral transmission. He assumes that news of Andrew's murder was carried to Buda by members of the prince's Hungarian entourage.[274] He claims not to know the name of the archbishop of Naples who recommended Charles of Durazzo's execution.[275] He uses standard terms for oral transmission, such as *fama*,[276] *publica fama*,[277] *fertur enim communiter*[278] and *fama volante infertur*.[279]

※

Roberta Morosini has recently focused on Boccaccio's use of orality in his Neapolitan works. While his language was formed in the elite circles of the Angevin court, his ear sought the street and the plebeian, constructing an auditory realism that uncovered an underground *"altra Napoli."*[280] In such works as his letters,[281] his *Filocolo, Amorosa Visione, Filostrato, Fiammetta, Teseida* and *Caccia di Diana*, he created a series of symbolic spaces designed to capture the sense of festivity, dance, music, song and play in the city's streets, the *voci* of its people.

EYEWITNESS ACCOUNTS

Finally, we discuss the complex issue of our historians' first-hand experience of the personalities and events they narrate and their record of eyewitness testimony by others. Here we bear in mind our distinction between *audita*, "what people said" (rumor and report), or "what someone told me directly" (first-hand report) and *visa*, "what I saw myself" (eyewitness).[282] We also focus on where and how trecento historians deployed their rhetorical training to evaluate such evidence.[283] These distinctions were ancient, supporting the truth claims of narrative but also deriving from both Roman law and the practice and theory of judicial rhetoric where truth claims *(fides)* were valued on a sliding scale from first-hand and eyewitness narrative and testimony under oath to common report and written document.[284] These historians took care to note both their own witness and their informants' eyewitness accounts. As Senatore cautions,[285] such rhetorical tropes often shaped the prologues that offer these eyewitness confirmations. We must therefore attempt to distinguish between actual eyewitness and its formulaic expressions.

These distinctions among what an author himself saw, the testimony of other eyewitnesses and common knowledge reported to him[286] were well-known in the classical and medieval rhetorical traditions.[287] While citing his main written sources, Jean Froissart claimed precedence for his own eyewitness and for the first-hand testimony of those whom he traveled far and wide to interview for his *Chroniques*. He takes pains that his accounts follow such first-hand testimony: "This is what took place, just as I was informed of it."[288] Yet his trip to northern Italy was the extent of his first-hand knowledge of Italian affairs and, as we have noted above, it was probably in Milan that Froissart picked up a good deal of false rumor and incomplete southern history that he later filled out with chivalrous language and motivations. Like Froissart, Thomas Walsingham relied on his own eyewitness for several of the most important events of English history, including the Peasants' Revolt of 1381.[289] Unlike Froissart, Walsingham spent his entire life in an English monastic circuit.[290] Nor do we know whether any of his sources for Italy, including for Giovanna's reign, depended on the eyewitness accounts of others.

Angelo Clareno was an avid collector of the eyewitness and first-hand oral accounts of St. Francis' first disciples, as in his narration in Tribulation 4 of his interviews with Brother John, a companion of Brother Gilles.[291] The later parts of Clareno's *Historia septem tribulationum* rely largely on his first-hand accounts of events, ranging from the Spirituals' mission to Armenia[292] to their persecution in the March of Ancona.[293] Much of what Clareno narrates in Tribulation 5 concerns the Spirituals' presence in the Regno and the diplomatic exchanges between the papacy and Charles II over their fate. Clareno himself was part of the group who

CHAPTER 3 ⚜ SOURCES

dealt with Angevin court officials as they attempted to steer a safe passage between the demands of the papal inquisition and the crown's prerogatives within the Regno. This experience and Clareno's residence both at Subiaco under the patronage of its powerful abbot and in Basilicata for two decades under royal protection[294] provide us with an important firsthand source for the religious life of the kingdom and the Angevin court.

※

Giovanni Villani participated in many of the events he narrates. He worked in the administration of Charles of Calabria and in that of Walter of Brienne, Duke of Athens, and so would have been well informed of Neapolitan personalities and events through the 1340s. In addition, his and his family's banking activities in Naples would have given them important first-hand information, supplemented by the accounts and written reports of their banks' correspondents in Naples and the South. Fellow Florentine Niccolò Acciaiuoli would have been among his other sources for events through the 1340s. Villani's firsthand account of the Black Death in Florence,[295] from which he died, is among the most famous of all historical sources. These same first-hand sources provided solid evidence for his brother Matteo's and his nephew Filippo's continuations into the 1360s. Among these Matteo's are narrations of the triumphal entry of Giovanna I and Louis of Taranto into Naples in late August 1348[296] and their subsequent coronation on May 23, 1352.[297] Both accounts provide vivid details of locations, personalities, dress, music and the "feeling" of the crowds. Matteo makes it clear that "merchants of Florence, Siena and Lucca" were in Naples as witnesses; and these may well have been his informants.

※

Agnolo di Tura lent his *Cronaca Senese* a sense of immediacy both through his record of the sounds of the uprising against the Duke of Athens,[298] for example, but also through the first-hand accounts of witnesses. His juxtaposition of the arrival of a Sienese embassy in Florence during the uprising with the vivid narration of the duke's officials being torn apart by the angry Florentines[299] makes it clear that it was the ambassadors who carried the grisly news back to Siena, protected by both their diplomatic status and their armed guard.[300]

Agnolo is best known, however, for his lengthy first-hand account of the Black Death in Siena:

> The mortality began in Siena in May [1348]. It was a cruel and horrible thing; and I do not know where to begin to tell of the cruelty and the pitiless ways. It seemed to almost everyone that one became stupefied by seeing the pain. And it is impossible for the human tongue to recount the awful thing. Indeed, one who did not see such horror can be called blessed.[301]

The plague claimed five of his own children, as Agnolo recounts with unrestrained grief:

> And I, Agnolo di Tura, called the Fat, buried my five children with my own hands.... And it was all so horrible that I, the writer, cannot think of it and so will not continue.[302]

Gravina was both eyewitness to, and Hungarian partisan in, the civil war in the South, particularly in his native Apulia, during the Hungarian invasion of 1347/48 and the subsequent reconquest of the region by forces loyal to Giovanna I. His account of the devastation in his own region and his forced abandonment of his youngest children offers a heartbreaking first-person witness to the horrors of invasion and civil war:

> Boliarina, my tiny little girl, and my Filippo — not yet two months old — they are children, still neither aware nor knowing pleasure. Why should they be harmed by the death of Duke Andrew? Why should people like me be made exiles in my own country? Why should this little girl and infant be treated like prisoners caught up by Andrew's Hungarian relations, and I and their mother deprived of their loving sight?[303]

As a notary, however, he was also a public official, and he acted both as the public reader of official acts and decrees and as an often reluctant political actor in the events he describes. Fulvio Delle Donne has noted Domenico's frequent retreats into literary convention when describing such incidents, and he ascribes this both to the writer's desire to escape from their psychological trauma and to his literary aspirations.[304] Gravina is explicit on the second-hand sources of his evidence: "as I have heard said, but not seen.... For I've heard it said by many *[ut audivi, non vidi ...Audivi namque dici a pluribus]*."

The *Anonimo romano* stressed his truth claims even more for events taking place in and around Rome:

> I saw these events and heard them. In particular I gathered information about certain events which occurred in my own country from trustworthy people who are unanimous in what they told me. Therefore I shall place certain signs at appropriate places in my text, which will reassure the reader and free me from suspicion in what I say.[305]

CHAPTER 3 ⚜ SOURCES

He sometimes states outright his own memory of events, even as a youngster during the overthrow of Senator Jacopo Savelli in the summer of 1325.[306] He is also careful to assess eyewitness accounts told to him, as in the testimony of a foot-soldier concerning the massacre of Christian forces at Smyrna during the crusade on 17 January 1345.[307] He judges the evidence first on its general likelihood, on truth claims to eyewitness and finally on the witness' oath. He thus included such explicit eyewitnesses as the escaped Bolognese who recounts the sultan of Babylon's fear of Rienzo[308] and his unnamed source for the detailed account of the battle of Crécy on 26 August 1346.[309]

We can be almost certain that his accounts of two of Rienzo's paintings, of his political speeches and of the many public rituals and celebrations during the life of the *buono stato* were reported first-hand. The Anonimo romano's many eyewitness accounts of events in Rome included Cola's festivals, processions and his knighting. During the great festival of Italian unity, the author was apparently among the spectators in the crowds lining the streets, since he describes the processions using the vocabulary of a witness: "first knights from many nations passed by... countless musicians followed... after them came the Tribune's wife." This account bears the unmistakable mark of an eyewitness who delighted in certain clearly bizarre scenes that made a lasting impression: "Among the many entertainers at the feast was one dressed in an ox skin: he had horns on his head; he looked like an ox; he played and leapt."[310]

We know, however, from the natural limitations of first-hand narrative that the Anonimo could not have been on the scene for some of the events he describes. For some, as we have noted, he may have borrowed from official documents. But others seem to be the work of his literary imagination. These include Rienzo's escape from the burning Senate Palace on October 8, 1354, which the Anonimo describes both from outside, on the Campidoglio as the Romans madly attack the palace, and from inside, describing Cola's actions and inner thoughts as he decided to escape incognito from the burning and collapsing building.[311]

※

One of the most vivid passages in trecento historiography is Petrarch's eyewitness account of the devastating earthquake and tsunami on the Bay of Naples on November 25, 1343.[312] This letter both draws on classical sources, such as Pliny the Younger's description of the eruption of Vesuvius,[313] and on Petrarch's oral and visual first-hand experience. Petrarch concludes his account with a final testimony that perfectly encapsulates the truth claims of various forms of evidence: "I did not read about this, nor hear about it, but saw it with my own eyes." We will return to this letter in great depth in Chapter 8.[314]

※

Boccaccio also related his own eyewitness. His narrative of the fall of Filippa of Catania and Roberto and Sancia de'Cabanni in his *De casibus virorum illustrium*[315] demonstrates the various levels of his knowledge of Neapolitan events and personalities. Boccaccio begins his account of the family with stories told to him as a youth, concluding, "I have heard that this was Filippa's start." He then "comes to the things that I myself saw,"[316] recounting his own experience of the de'Cabanni at the Angevin court in the 1330s.[317] Since he did not return to Naples until 1355, his account of their grisly torture and execution in March 1346 was clearly second-hand. Their torture was performed publicly but, according to Boccaccio who described the "ritual,""what was extracted from them is not known."[318] We will discuss Boccaccio's account in detail in Chapter 7.[319] Unlike Petrarch's account of events on the Bay of Naples, which clearly distinguishes forms of evidence and makes explicit his own eyewitness, Boccaccio's historical narrative resembles his fictions: a conflation of eyewitness and oral accounts, drawn seamlessly together with great rhetorical skill and dramatic dynamism, eliding deep and more recent background with current affairs and oral report with eyewitness and other unknown sources.

CONCLUSIONS

In this chapter, we have reviewed the wide variety of sources and the uses to which these trecento writers put them. The materials include everything from the varying incorporation of classical texts, styles and language, to earlier medieval texts, religious, scientific and archival materials, to a sophisticated and consistent use of oral and eyewitness sources. The overall impression from this material helps strengthen the argument that writing of and about the Mezzogiorno was overwhelmingly lay, heavily influenced by the classics and keenly aware of its style, point of view and truth claims. These writers were highly skilled in the historian's craft. In addition, their source materials were deliberately deployed in order to appeal to new lay audiences that shared the tightly knit civic, lay and urban culture that we have described above. Such historiography can therefore be seen as reflecting the general shift in trecento Italian society that Witt restricted to the North but that under closer examination appears to have permeated the entire peninsula to a degree that made southern writers among the most sophisticated historians of the century.

NOTES

1. Kempshall, 284–95 et passim.
2. Zabbia (1997), 6–13, 58–96, examines several notary-chroniclers and synthesizes previous research to conclude that such notaries held high professional and social status and formed a cohesive social class that could turn to historiography to focus on the history of their *universitates*. He admits (120), however, that his sampling is small. Delle Donne (2001a), 129–31, notes that notaries made up about one-quarter of southern historians and cautions against drawing too strong

CHAPTER 3 ⚜ SOURCES

conclusions concerning similarities of genre, style and motivation among them. See also Petrucci (1958); Arnaldi (1966). Internullo (2016), 89–90, 199–202, examines their role in trecento Rome; as does Palmer (2019), 4–7 et passim.

3. Most recently and forcefully by Witt (2012) in which he explicitly dismisses the historiography of the South. See p. 13 and "The Return to Antiquity," 438–71.

4. Grendler (1990), 255–63.

5. Seibt, 87–90; Holstein (2006), 142–43; Internullo, 243–44 et passim.

6. Kirkham (2009), 6; Zak (2015), 141–43; Celenza (2017), 44–53.

7. The basic introductions are Reynolds–Wilson (1968) and subsequent editions; the ongoing *Catalogus Translationum et Commentariorum,* Kristeller (1960), online at http://catalogustranslationum.org/index.php; and Villa (1992). For recent reference work, with bibliographies, see Grafton (2013).

8. Grendler (1989), 240–55.

9. Moreschini (1992), 1:563–604.

10. Solomon (2013).

11. Musto (1983).

12. Ziolkowski–Putnam (2008); Delle Donne (2015.1).

13. Panofsky (1972), 42–113.

14. Holstein (2006), 146–49, argues that trecento Roman historians used classical sources largely as stylistic models.

15. Internullo (2016), 56–63, 90–113, 221–461.

16. Montuori (2017), 64–81; Gualdo (2017), 197–208; Zabbia (2017), 271–76; D'Achille (2017), 347–64.

17. Winterthur, 216–19.

18. Walsingham (2003), xxiv–xxvi.

19. Walsingham (2003), cix–cx.

20. Second Apologetical Oration, Book 3, Tribulation 2, Clareno (1999), 130–31; Clareno (2005), 72; Oration 33, Book 4, Tribulation 3, Clareno (1999), 158–59; Clareno (2005), 97–98.

21. Internullo (2016), 7, 355–57, argues strongly against the designation "proto-humanist" for trecento Rome. Palmer (2021), 18, discusses "a classicism typical of the thirteenth- and fourteenth-century *popolo.*"

22. Internullo (2016), 314–15.

23. Internullo (2016), 355–66.

24. XVIII.7–22; AR, 143; Wright, 31; Palmer (2021), 183.

25. XVIII.824–992; AR, 172–5; Wright, 57–62; Palmer (2021), 208–9.

26. Dialogue 4.49.

27. "Valens," in *Chronicon,* MGH SS 22:454.

28. 1.7.7.

29. *De divinatione per somnum,* 462b–464b.

30. XVIII.1790–1888; AR, 202–6; Wright, 88–90; Palmer (2021), 236–39. See Holstein (2006), 97–99, 112–21.

31. I.1. Ext. 3.

32. XXVI.52–54; AR, 221–22; Wright, 107–8; Palmer (2021), 257–58.

33. XXVII.195b–243b; AR, 259–67; Wright, 147–54; Palmer (2021), 298–99.

34. Seibt, 90–93.

35. Kelly (2011), 55–78, 285–329.

36. De Caprio (2012), 30–40.

69

37. Palmieri (1934), iv–v.
38. Palmieri (1934), 5–6.
39. Chapter 8, pp. 235–50.
40. Petrarch (2004.1); Petrarch (2005.2).
41. Petrarch (2004.2); Petrarch (2005.1).
42. Petrarch (2002).
43. Petrarch (1974), 16–29.
44. Holstein (2006), 133–38; Modonutti (2013); Internullo (2016), 138–40, 233–38, 298–304.
45. Witt (2009), 105.
46. Ibid.
47. Zak (2015), 141–42.
48. Witt (2009), 105.
49. Ascoli (2015a), 121–23.
50. Chapter 8, pp. 229–32.
51. Boccaccio (2003), xvii–xviii, 481–503.
52. Boccaccio (2003), xviii; Boccaccio (2018), esp. xvi–xix.
53. *Aeneid* XI.539–841, Boccaccio (2003), 154–58.
54. II.39.1–40.12, Boccaccio (2003), 222–30.
55. See Chapter 8, pp. 235, 246–47, 250–51.
56. Prologue, 2, 11–16; Clareno (1999), 96–97; Clareno (2005), 44.
57. Book 3, Tribulation 2, Clareno (1999), 132–33; Clareno (2005), 74–75.
58. XVIII.1786–90; AR, 202; Wright, 87; Palmer (2021), 235.
59. XXVII.195b–423b; AR, 259–67; Wright 147–54; Palmer (2021), 291–99.
60. Internullo (2016), 306 n. 47, speculates that it might also have derived from contemporary sources, such as the compilation entitled *L'Aquila*.
61. Hughes–Buongiovanni; Palmentieri (2015); Delle Donne (2015.1).
62. Holstein (2006), 157–67.
63. *Cronaca* 3–6, Kelly (2011), 168–71.
64. *Cronaca* 7, Kelly (2011), 171–72. Also recorded in the original Greek by Ferraiolo in his manuscript copy of the *Cronaca di Partenope*. See Chapter 9, p. 277.
65. Pp. 235–36.
66. Page 46.
67. *Cronaca* 10, Kelly (2011), 174–75.
68. *Cronaca* 13–15, Kelly (2011), 178–82.
69. *Cronaca* 16–32, Kelly (2011), 182–200.
70. Pp. 235–36.
71. Walsingham (1864), xv–xix; Walsingham (2003), 1:xv–xviii.
72. Walsingham (2011), 2:xcii–xcvii.
73. Monteleone (1895), ix.
74. *Nuova cronica* I.1.
75. Green (1972), 155–64.
76. Green (1972), 16-18, 165–66; Diakité (2003); Clarke (2007), 114–16; Anselmi (2017); Cracco (2017); Porta (2017).
77. Below, pp. 207–9, for example.
78. Preface, I.81–90; AR, 5–6; Holstein (2006), 97–98; Campanelli (2013).
79. Seibt, 73–77.
80. Seibt, 228–29; Modonutti (2013).

81. See also Holstein (2006), 147–48.
82. *Cronaca Senese,* xxi–xxiii.
83. Kelly (2011), 89–92.
84. De Blasiis refers frequently to Villani and other parallel works in his notes but does not attribute these as sources.
85. For questions about authorship, De Caprio (2012), 21–26; De Caprio (2015). For specific source citations, Kelly (2011), 292–329.
86. Kelly (2011), 13, 127–30, 318–25 et passim.
87. Palmieri (1934), ix–xi.
88. Musto (2013), 102–7.
89. Taylor (2003).
90. XI, AR, 68–90.
91. XIII, AR, 101–17.
92. "Froissart: Poet, Writer of Romance, Historian?" in Ainsworth (2013).
93. Green (1972), 35–36.
94. Clarke (2007), 118.
95. Buccio di Ranallo (1907), xxxvii–xlvii.
96. Buccio di Ranallo (1907), xxxviii–xlv.
97. Seibt, 46–54.
98. Seibt, 78–79, 205–15; Holstein (2006), 66–77, 148–50; Internullo (2016), 366–82.
99. Lobrichon (1992).
100. For the impact of hagiography as a literary source, Leonardi (1993), 452–62; Grendler (1990), 278–89.
101. Gehl (1993), 82–95, 114–16; Carruthers (1990), 80–99.
102. With the exceptions of Psalms (9:9, 90:13) and his use of the story of Joseph and his brothers from Gen. 42:15–17. See below Chapter 7, pp. 219–20.
103. Only four times.
104. V.96–98, V.115–20, AR, 23–24.
105. XVIII.866–85, AR, 172–73; Wright, 58–59; Palmer (2021), 208–9.
106. XVIII.1090–1178, AR, 179–82; Wright, 66–68; Palmer (2021), 216–17. See Musto (2003), 166–69.
107. XXVII.304–8, AR, 246–47; Wright, 135; Palmer (2021), 280.
108. Winterthur, xxiv.
109. Winterthur, 225, 277.
110. Winterthur, xxiii–xxviii.
111. Winterthur, 226–29.
112. Winterthur, 93–94; Heullant-Donat (2005). Johanns provides independent testimony to the authenticity of these letters.
113. Winterthur, 266.
114. Delle Donne (2001a), 142–46, citing Gravina (1903), 95–96.
115. Mt. 27:22–23; Mark 15:13–14; Luke 23:18–23.
116. Chapter 7, pp. 211–13.
117. For Adam and Eve, see Gen. 2:7–3:23 for *De mulieribus claris;* Gen. 1–11 for *De casibus virorum illustrium.*
118. Clareno (2005), vii–x.
119. Seibt, 216.
120. Above, p. 51.
121. For a general discussion, Ortalli (1989).

122. Senatore (2017), 287–94.
123. Walsingham (2003), cxiii–cxvi.
124. Chapter 2, pp. 23–24.
125. As for example the famous letters sent by Cola di Rienzo immediately after his rise. *Chronicon Mutinense,* 134–39.
126. *Chronicon Mutinense,* 141–46.
127. See Chapter 6, p. 170.
128. Internullo (2016), 313–14.
129. Zabbia (1997), 63–65, 74–75, notes that the Regno's notaries lost this official standing under Frederick II's legislation, but they continued to hold the title and all the functions of the *"publicus notarius,"* including recognition as pubic officials of high social and cultural stature.
130. Delle Donne (2001a), 142–43.
131. Delle Donne (2001a), 146.
132. Bildhauer–Mills (2003).
133. Green (1972), 17–22, 29–35; Clarke (2007), 117–22.
134. Green (1972), 32.
135. Collard (2014).
136. Siraisi (2001); Grendler (2002), 314–23; Siraisi (2007).
137. For example, the license granted to Maria Incarnata by Giovanna I, May 7, 1343, to practice women's medicine throughout the Regno, translated by Monica H. Green, in Jansen (2009), 324–25; reprinted in Musto (2013), 259–61.
138. Chapter 5, p. 221.
139. Above, p. 46.
140. Seibt, 256–61. On medical knowledge in Rome, especially for the Anonimo romano, see Internullo (2016), 180–88; Palmer (2021), 9–13, 25–27.
141. XVIII.567–611; AR 162–64; Wright, 48–50; Palmer (2021), 200–202.
142. VII.125–29; AR, 32.
143. VIII.12–20; AR, 33–34.
144. Internullo (2016), 186–87.
145. Formentin (2012.1), 38–42.
146. XXIII.150–89, AR, 216–17.
147. *Cronaca* 28 (29B), Kelly (2011), 194. The disrepair of these images was already mentioned by Conrad of Querfurt in his description of Naples from c.1196. See Musto (2013), 122.
148. *Cronaca* 32 (33B), Kelly (2011), 199–200.
149. Doane (1991); Vitullo (2000), esp. Chapter 5, "Orality, Literacy, and the Prose Epic;" Ong (2002); Reichl (2016); Reichl (2016a); Foley–Ramey (2016).
150. Carruthers (1990), 156–220.
151. Holstein (2006), 112–210.
152. On *fama* and *infamia,* Migliorino (1985); Stern (2000); Fenster–Smail (2003); Wickham (2003); Phillips (2007); Lori Sanfilippo (2011); Steinberg (2011); Casteen (2015).
153. Kinney (1998); Doležalová (2010).
154. De Caprio (2012), 32–40, 62–65, 69–138.
155. Gardiner (1993), xxv–xxvii. See also her comments on the relationship of the dream/vision to its narrator in Gardiner (1999).
156. See Carruthers (1990); Ong (2002); Althoff (2002); Ricœur (2004); Cubitt

(2007); Brenner (2013); Clanchy (2013). Summarized by Internullo (2016), 302–4.
157. Kempshall, 284–95; De Roberto (2015).
158. Senatore (2017), 292–93.
159. Winterthur, 277
160. Concerning Clement VI, Winterthur, 213; or Frederick II, at 280.
161. 1337, for a well-known weather prognosticator in Germany, Winterthur, 115.
162. 1276, Winterthur, 27.
163. 1313, Winterthur, 66.
164. 1313, Winterthur, 68.
165. 1348, Winterthur, 279.
166. Winterthur, 122.
167. Walsingham (2011), xcii–xcvii.
168. 1376, Walsingham (2003), 10; 1395, Walsingham (2011), 12; 1397, Walsingham (2011), 72–74.
169. 1381, Walsingham (2003), 476; Appendix 3, 1376, Walsingham (2003), 976.
170. 1379, Walsingham (2003), 314.
171. 1377, Walsingham (2003), 94.
172. 1380, Walsingham (2003), 396.
173. 1381, Walsingham (2003), 500.
174. 1380, Walsingham (2003), 362.
175. 1395, Walsingham (2011), 30.
176. 1397, Walsingham (2011), 54–56.
177. 1396, Walsingham (2011), 40.
178. 1382, Walsingham (2003), 582 and n. 643.
179. I, fol. 1r–v, Froissart (2013).
180. "Against Oblivion: Writing, Memory and Ideology," in Ainsworth (2013); Kempshall, 284–85.
181. Besançon BM, MS 865, fol. 9r–10v, Froissart (1901) chap. 346, 1:217–20; Froissart (2013).
182. Varvaro, 137.
183. Varvaro, 132.
184. Varvaro, 134, 137.
185. Varvaro, 138: "Napoli è ancora una strana e pericolosa periferia del mondo civile."
186. Varvaro, 134–35.
187. As suggested by Marchandisse (2008), 115 n. 96.
188. *Chronicon Mutinense*, 74.
189. *Chronicon Mutinense*, 123–24.
190. *Chronicon Mutinense*, 78.
191. 1291–93, *Chronicon Mutinense*, 51; 1345, 129.
192. 1352, *Chronicon Mutinense*, 151.
193. Zabbia (1997), 52–57.
194. The phrase is Senatore's (2017), 291.
195. Menache (2009).
196. For a comprehensive reference to historical vernacular usage, see the *Tesoro della Lingua Italiana delle Origini*, ed. Pietro G. Beltrami et al., online at: http://tlio.ovi.cnr.it/TLIO. My thanks to Prof. Chiara De Caprio for this reference.
197. For example, II.10 (Villani 1991, 1:76); IV.1 (1:113); V.12 (1:181).
198. X.110 (2:776).

199. V.13 (1:182),VII.85 (1:391), IX.36 (2:57), X.61 (2:265).
200. V.28 (1:212), X.132 (2:333).
201. IX.5 (2:18), X.218 (2:402).
202. VI.1 (1:228), X.219 (2:405), XI.150 (2:708).
203. VII.78 (1:378),VIII.14 (1:434).
204. XI.200 (2:763–64).
205. I.6 (1:11), IV.1 (1:114)
206. I.25 (1:30), II.13 (1:60),VII.81 (1:385–86).
207. III.8 (1:119).
208. VIII.41 (1:477), IX.112 (2:203).
209. XI.223 (2:791), XIII.51 (3:417).
210. VII.57 (1:350), IX.121 (2:210).
211. VIII.27 (1:454),VIII.92 (1:551), IX.56 (2:92).
212. VIII.61 (1:510),VIII.114 (1:578), XI.118 (2:670).
213. IX.70 (2:131), IX.92 (2:183), XIII.51 (3:418).
214. XIII.67 (3:453).
215. XIII.109 (3:534).
216. VII.36 (1:325),VIII.76 (1:530).
217. IX.55 (2:89), and especially X.136, in his famous description of Dante's linguistic mastery (2:335–38). For the text, Chapter 4, pp. 88–89.
218. VIII.13 (1:430).
219. XIII.115 (3:552).
220. Not a common usage for Villani, and most frequently simply associated with the human voice in speech (VIII.8, 1:419), song (IX.80, 2:162), but sometimes as public fame (IX.1, 2:10) or news (XIII.18, 3:344).
221. I.28 (1:45),VI.37 (1:265), IX.12 (2:29), X.96 (2:301).
222. VIII.6 (1:415),VIII.27 (1:454), XI.89 (2:632).
223. IX.96 (2:187).
224. XIII.52 (3:420).
225. XIII.105 (3:524).
226. XIII.51 (3:416–19).
227. A. 1343, RIS 15.6:539, l. 45; 540, l. 15: La gente del duca, sentendo e' romore....
228. A. 1343, RIS 15.6:540, ll. 1–2: gridando: "all'arme, all'arme!" incontinente tutte le buttighe si seraro e tutta la città [fu posta] a romore e ad arme...; 540, l. 36: gridando: "viva il popolo e muoia il duca e' suoi!..."
229. A. 1343, *Cronaca Senese,* 540, ll. 44–45: Sanesi avuto la novella come i Fiorentini aveano levato e' romore contra 'l duca loro signore....
230. Book 5, Tribulation 4, Clareno (1999), 184–85; Clareno (2005), 121–22.
231. Book 6, Clareno (1999), 193–255; Clareno (2005), 129–40.
232. Kelly (2011), 55.
233. De Caprio (2012), 32–38.
234. Kelly (2011), 13
235. *Cronaca* 5, Kelly (2011), 170.
236. *Cronaca* 12, Kelly (2011), 177.
237. *Cronaca* 14, Kelly (2011), 181.
238. *Cronaca* 19 (20B), Kelly (2011), 186.
239. *Cronaca* 24 (25B), Kelly (2011), 190.
240. *Cronaca* 29 (30B), Kelly (2011), 197–98.

241. Prologue, I.15–16, I.25–26; AR, 3; Wright, 21; Palmer (2021), 24, 59–61.
242. Prologue I.76–84; AR, 5; Wright, 22; Palmer (2021), 61.
243. AR, 725–822. Formentin (2012.1), 28–38, warns that Porta's lexicon derives from a reconstructed and hypothetical manuscript tradition whose earliest exemplar dates from the cinquecento. Formentin (2013) recommends close reading of trecento archival materials in Romanesco. See also Palmer (2021), 15–16.
244. Prologue, I.1; AR, 3.
245. XVIII.79–80, AR, 145.
246. XII.148, AR, 95.
247. XIII.139–40c, AR, 110.
248. XI.104–5, AR, 72.
249. XI.541, AR, 87: as in *Diceva la iente*.
250. XXIII.165–68, AR, 217.
251. XVIII.826–27, AR, 171.
252. IX.54–55, AR, 47.
253. XI.223–24, AR, 76.
254. V.93–94, AR, 23.
255. XII.204–5, AR, 97.
256. XVIII.1909–10, AR, 206.
257. There are rare exceptions: XVIII, l. 1938, AR, 207.
258. XVIII.1607–8, AR, 196.
259. X.184, AR, 67.
260. XI.220–22, AR, 76.
261. X.104–6, AR, 64.
262. XXIII.48–49, AR, 213.
263. XI.220–21, AR, 76.
264. XXVII.3–4, AR, 237.
265. XXVI.7–9, AR, 220.
266. E.g., 58.2; 61.1; 81.1; 94.1.
267. E.g., 41.1, 42.1, 97.2.
268. 3.2.
269. 40.1√
270. E.g., 3.2, 8.2, 27.2, 52.1, 69.2.
271. E.g, 12.2, 30.1–2, 36.1, 51.1, 57.1–2, 67.2, 69.1.
272. *Diurnali*, xii.
273. AA. 1345–48, Gravina (1903), 14, l. 20–42, l. 38.
274. A. 1345, Gravina (1903), 18, ll. 6–8.
275. A. 1348, Gravina (1903), 36, ll. 18–19.
276. A. 1348, Gravina (1903), 43, l. 8.
277. AA. 1344–45, Gravina (1903), 13, l. 20, on rumors of Giovanna's infidelity reaching Andrew.
278. A. 1348, Gravina (1903), 36 l. 37–37, l. 1.
279. A. 1348, Gravina (1903), 40, l. 32: it was reported that the news of Charles of Durazzo's execution and the arrest of the Angevin royals at Durazzo flew....
280. Morosini, 72.
281. In the sonority of the Neapolitan Letter to Francesco de Bardi. See above, p. 91.
282. The distinctions among the *compilator*, the *assertor* and the *auctor*. See Ainsworth (2003.1), 252; and n. 158 above.

283. For example, Braida (2009).
284. Kempshall, 185–90.
285. Senatore (2017), 290–91.
286. Malaspina (1999), I. Prologus, 89, ll. 16–20: Placuit ergo sine verbose digressionis anfractibus...nec ambages inserere aut incredibilia immiscere, sed vera vel verisimilia, que aut vidi aut videre potui vel audivi communibus divulgata sermonibus stilo prosayco sub ordine contexta narrare.
287. Kempshall, 183–87 et passim.
288. Froissart (2013), II, fol. 6v. Ainsworth (1990); Ainsworth (2003.1), 264–75; Ainsworth (2013).
289. Walsingham (2003), cxii–cxiii.
290. Walsingham (2003), xviii–xxvii.
291. Book 5, Tribulation 4 Clareno (1999), 180–83; Clareno (2005), 117–20.
292. Book 6, Tribulation 5, Clareno (1999), 224–27; Clareno (2005), 152–57.
293. Clareno (2005), 161–78.
294. Musto (1985); Musto (1997).
295. XIII.84 (Villani 1991), 3:485–88.
296. I.21–22 (Villani 1995), 1:41–43; trans. Musto (2013), 283–84.
297. III.8 (Villani 1995), 1:335–36; trans. Musto (2013), 285–86.
298. Below, pp. 202–7, esp. 204.
299. A. 1343, *Cronaca Senese,* 541, ll. 24–45.
300. A. 1343, *Cronaca Senese,* 542, ll. 10–21.
301. A. 1348, *Cronaca Senese,* 555, ll. 7–10; English trans. Bowsky (1971), 13–14.
302. A. 1348, *Cronaca Senese,* 555, ll. 19–23; English trans. Bowsky.
303. A. 1345, Gravina (1903), 19, l. 43–20, l. 4.
304. Delle Donne (2001a), 138.
305. Prologue, I.84–86, 90, AR, 5; Wright, 22; Palmer (2021), 61.
306. II.10–12, 55, AR, 10: Bene me recordo como per suonno. Io stava in Santa Maria dello Piubico e viddi.... Certo da queste cose io non comenzo; ca, benché così fosse, io era in tanta tenerezza de etate, che conoscimento non avea elettivo. See also Holstein (2006), 97–100, 121.
307. XIII.163c–165c, AR, 110–11: Alcuno me dice per aitra via, e ène verisimile. Disse ca·llo vidde perzonalmente, e ciò fermao per sacramento. Disse questo...
308. XVIII.632–40; AR, 165; Wright 1.12, 50–51; Palmer (2021), 202.
309. XIV, AR, 118–35. Campanelli (2013).
310. XVIII.1228–1380, AR 184–89; Wright 1.25, 69–74; Palmer (2021), 219–24.
311. XXVII.195b–423b, AR, 259–67; Wright 147–54; Palmer (2021), 291–99.
312. *Familiares* V.5, Petrarch (2004.1), 1:652–63; Petrarch (2005.2), 1:243–48.
313. Pliny, *Epistulae* VI.16, VI.20.
314. Pp. 241–43.
315. IX.26, Boccaccio (1983.1), 856–65. For an English translation, Boccaccio (2018), 222–40. See Chapter 7, pp. 208–11.
316. Boccaccio (2018), 222–23.
317. Boccaccio (2018), 222–23.
318. IX.26; Boccaccio (2018), 228.
319. Pp. 208–11.

WORKS CITED

Ainsworth, Peter F. 2013. "Jean Froissart: Chronicler, Poet and Writer." In Froissart (2013).
Althoff, Gerd, et al. 2002. *Medieval Concepts of the Past: Ritual, Memory, Historiography.* Washington, DC: German Historical Institute.
Anselmi, Gian Mario. 2017. "Cronaca e narrazione: Dante e l'interpretazione della storia fra impero romano, Europa cristiana e Mediterraneo islamico." In Francesconi–Miglio, 11–27.
Arnaldi, Girolamo. 1966. "Il notaio e cronista e le cronache cittadine in Italia." In *La storia del diritto nel quadro delle scienze storiche.* Florence: Olschki, 293–309.
Ascoli, Albert Russell. 2015a. "Epistolary Petrarch." In Ascoli-Falkeid, 120–37.
Bildhauer, Bettina. 2003. With Robert Mills, ed. *The Monstrous Middle Ages.* Toronto: University of Toronto Press.
Bowsky, William M. 1971. *The Black Death: A Turning Point in History?* New York: Holt, Rinehart & Winston.
Braida, Francesca. 2009. "Le travail de mémoire: *La Cronica de Dino Compagni.* La fiabilité du voir: Le rôle de témoin oculaire et la véridicité du souvenir." TMC 6:125–40.
Brenner, Elma, et al. 2013. *Memory and Commemoration in Medieval Culture.* Farnham: Ashgate.
Campanelli, Maurizio. 2013. "The Preface of the Anonimo Romano's *Cronica:* Writing History and Proving Truthfulness in Fourteenth-Century Rome." *The Mediaeval Journal* 3.1:83–106.
Carruthers, Mary J. 1990. *The Book of Memory: A Study of Memory in Medieval Culture.* Cambridge: Cambridge University Press.
Clanchy, Michael. 2013. *From Memory to Written Record: England 1066–1307.* Chichester: Wiley-Blackwell.
Collard, Judith. 2014. "Art and Science in the Manuscripts of Matthew Paris." TMC 9:79–116.
Cracco, Giorgio. 2017. "Dante e le cronache dell'Italia settentrionale." In Francesconi–Miglio, 139–63.
Cubitt, Geoffrey. 2007. *History and Memory.* Manchester: Manchester University Press.
D'Achille, Paolo. 2017. "Cronache, scritture esposte, testi semicolti." In Francesconi–Miglio, 347–72.
De Roberto, Elisa. 2015. "Dinamiche enunciative nel discorso storico medievale: Il caso delle strategie evidenziali." In *Sul filo del testo: In equilibrio tra enunciato e enunciazione.* Massimo Palermo and Silvia Pieroni, ed. Ospedaletto Pisa: Pacini, 65–88.
Diakité, Rala Isobel. 2003. "Writing Political Realities in Fourteenth-Century Italy: Giovanni Villani's *Nouva Cronica* and Dante's *Commedia.*" Ph.D. diss., Brown University.
Doane, Alger Nicolaus. 1991. With Carol Braun Pasternack, ed. *Vox Intexta: Orality and Textuality in the Middle Ages.* Madison: University of Wisconsin Press.

Doležalová, Lucie, ed. 2010. *The Making of Memory in the Middle Ages*. Leiden: Brill.
Fenster, Thelma S. 2003. With Daniel Lord Smail. Fama: *The Politics of Talk & Reputation in Medieval Europe*. Ithaca, NY: Cornell University Press.
Foley, John Miles. 2016. With Peter Ramey. "Concepts and Approaches: Oral Theory and Medieval Literature." In Reichl (2016), 71–102.
Formentin, Victor. 2013. "A proposito di romanesco antico: La metafonia nel registro di Giovanni Cenci?" *Lingua e Stile* 48:299–315.
Froissart, Jean. 1901–03. *The Chronicle of Froissart*. John Bourchier Berners and W.P. Ker, ed. 1901; *The Chronicle of Froissart*. 6 vols. London: David Nutt. Repr. New York: AMS, 1967.
Gardiner, Eileen. 1999. "Review of Peter Brown, ed. *Reading Dreams: The Interpretation of Dreams from Chaucer to Shakespeare* (New York: Oxford University Press, 1999)." *The Medieval Review* 00.03.06.
Grafton, Anthony, et al. 2013. *The Classical Tradition*. Cambridge, MA: Harvard University Press.
Grendler, Paul F. 1990. *Schooling in Western Europe*. New York: Renaissance Society of America.
Jansen, Katherine L., et al., ed. 2009. *Medieval Italy: Texts in Translation*. Philadelphia: University of Pennsylvania Press.
Kinney, Dale. 1998. "*Spolia, Damnatio* and *Renovatio Memoriae*." *Memoirs of the American Academy in Rome* 42:117–48.
Kristeller, Paul Oskar, et al., ed. 1971. *Catalogus translationum et commentariorum: Mediaeval and Renaissance Latin Translations and Commentaries: Annotated Lists and Guides*. Washington, DC: Catholic University of America Press.
Leonardi, Claudio. 1993. "Agiografi." In Cavallo (1992–93), 2:421–62.
Lobrichon, Guy. 1992. "Gli usi della Bibbia." In Cavallo (1992–93), 1:523–62.
Lori Sanfilippo, Isa. 2011. With Antonio Rigon. Fama *e publica vox nel Medioevo: Atti del convegno di studio svoltosi in occasione della XXI edizione del Premio internazionale Ascoli Piceno, Ascoli Piceno, Palazzo dei Capitani, 3–5 dicembre 2009*. Rome: ISIME.
Malaspina, Saba, 1999. *Die Chronik des Saba Malaspina*. Hannover: Hahn.
Marchandisse, Alain. 2008. "Milan, les Visconti, l'union de Valentine et de Louis d'Orléans, vus par Froissart et par les auteurs contemporains." In *Autour du XVe siècle: Journées d'étude en l'honneur d'Alberto Vàrvaro*. Paola Moreno and Giovanni Palumbo, ed. Geneva: Droz, 93–116.
Menache, Sophia. 2009. "Written and Oral Testimonies in Medieval Chronicles: Matthew Paris and Giovanni Villani." TMC 6:1–30.
Migliorino, Francesco. 1985. Fama *e infamia: Problemi della società medievale nel pensiero giuridico nei secoli XII e XIII*. Catania: Giannotta.
Modonutti, Rino. 2013. *Fra Giovanni Colonna e la storia antica da Adriano ai Severi*. Padua: Coop. Libraria Editrice Università di Padova.
Moreschini, Claudio. 1992. "I Padri." In Cavallo (1992–93), 1:563–604.
Ong, Walter J. 2002. *Orality and Literacy: The Technologizing of the Word*. London: Routledge.

Ortalli, Gherardo. 1989. "Cronache e documentazione." In *Civiltà comunale: Libro, scrittura, documento. Atti della Società ligure di storia patria* n.s. 29 (103.2): 507–39.
Palmentieri, Angela. 2015. "*Marmora Romana* in Medieval Naples: Architectural *Spolia* from the Fourth to the Fifteenth Centuries, A.D." In Hughes–Buongiovanni, 121–51.
Palmer, James A. 2019. *The Virtues of Economy: Governance, Power and Piety in Late Medieval Rome*. Ithaca, NY: Cornell University Press.
Panofsky, Erwin. 1972. *Renaissance and Renascences in Western Art*. New York: Harper & Row.
Petrucci, Armando. 1958. *Notarii: Documenti per la storia del notariato italiano*. Milan: A. Giuffrè.
Phillips, Susan E. 2013. *Transforming Talk: The Problem with Gossip in Late Medieval England*. University Park: Pennsylvania State University Press.
Porta, Giuseppe. 2017. "La cronaca a Firenze: Passione politica e travaglio compositivo." In Francesconi–Miglio, 157–63.
Reichl, Karl, ed. 2016. *Medieval Oral Literature*. Berlin: De Gruyter.
— . 2016a. "Plotting the Map of Medieval Oral Literature." In Reichl (2016), 3–70.
Reynolds, Leighton Durham. 1968. With Nigel Guy Wilson. *Scribes and Scholars: A Guide to the Transmission of Greek and Latin Literature*. Oxford: Oxford University Press.
Ricœur, Paul. 2004. *Memory, History, Forgetting*. Chicago: University of Chicago Press.
Siraisi, Nancy G. 2001. *Medicine and the Italian Universities, 1250–1600*. Leiden: Brill.
— . 2007. *Medieval & Early Renaissance Medicine: An Introduction to Knowledge and Practice*. Chicago: University of Chicago Press.
Solomon, Jon. 2013. "Gods, Greeks and Poetry *(Genealogia deorum gentilium)*." In Kirkham (2013), 235–44.
Steinberg, Justin. 2011. "Dante and the Laws of Infamy." PMLA 126:1118–26.
Stern, Laura Ikins. 2000. "Public Fame in the Fifteenth Century." *American Journal of Legal History* 44:198–222.
Taylor, Julie. 2003. *Muslims in Medieval Italy: The Colony at Lucera*. Lanham, MD: Lexington Books.
Villa, Claudia. (1992). "I classici." In Cavallo (1992–93), 1:479–522.
Villani, Matteo, and Filippo Villani. 1995. *Cronica*. Giuseppe Porta, ed. 2 vols. Parma: Guanda.
Vitullo, Juliann M. 2000. *The Chivalric Epic in Medieval Italy*. Gainesville: University Press of Florida.
Wickham, Chris. 2003. "*Fama* and the Law in Twelfth-Century Tuscany." In Fenster–Smail (2003), 15–26.
Zak, Gur. 2015. "Petrarch and the Ancients." In Ascoli-Falkeid, 141–53.
Ziolkowski, Jan M. 2008. With Michael C.J. Putnam, ed. *The Virgilian Tradition: The First Fifteen Hundred Years*. New Haven: Yale University Press.

4. NARRATIVE COMMUNITIES AND STRATEGIES

INTRODUCTION: NARRATIVE COMMUNITIES

In this chapter, we will discuss narrative communities, their education and impact and how they influence narrative forms and strategies: scholastic and ecclesiastic, notarial and civic, aristocratic or chivalric, and early humanist. We will then examine language choices, whether Latin or the various vernaculars, and the implication of such choices on the types of narrative, audience, form of historiography and the role of the historian. We will next analyze narrative structures and divide them into three types: paratactic (chronological), thematic and symbolic (figurative). We will conclude with a taxonomy of narrative forms: epideictic, forensic and deliberative.

Trecento narrative communities may be defined as the structures of communication and discourse that underlay authors, their writing and the audiences that both received and helped form them. Despite claims of many late medieval historians — and their acceptance at face value by modern scholars — that they were simple people who merely recorded what they saw before them without much art or learning,[1] the past generation of scholarship on medieval rhetoric and grammar has revealed that these claims were themselves highly rhetorical and self-conscious tropes. The form and content of these histories were consciously constructed cultural artifacts largely determined by specific purposes, audiences and themes. These began with the most elemental but still self-consciously crafted purpose: to provide an official record of events and a continuous archiving of the deep physical, cultural and political structures that surrounded institutions. For other audiences and purposes, histories were modeled to celebrate the virtuous lives and chivalrous deeds of famous people. For either aristocratic or civic audiences, complex narratives and chronologies were developed to provide historical underpinnings, moral instruction and exempla.[2] Their writers drew on a wide variety of sources to suit both narrative and thematic needs and to underscore truth claims.

Each of these purposes could be incorporated into one or more forms and styles, and each conformed to carefully articulated norms that reached back to Cicero and Quintilian, who stressed the importance of brevity, lucidity and credibility, all focusing on the plausibility *(fides)* of a narrative. Narrative structures could therefore be both flexible and open to a variety of what today we would consider separate genres, including history, poetry and fable. Evidence could derive from a range of sources, including the verbal and the visual. Most medieval historiography, therefore, accepted the proposition that narrative lay somewhere between the verifiably true and the fable, between fact and construction. Cicero himself had written that truth needed the arts of rhetoric to make it plausible and convincing,[3] and that in the case of many situations — judicial argument, for example — verisimilitude and probability were more important than unadorned truth. Thus the fluid continuum between fact and fiction, between logical argument, rumor and insinuation, remained an important aid in tailoring narratives to particular situations and audiences, from the most sophisticated and learned to the least educated, all serving a common purpose of persuasion and instruction.[4]

Such rhetorical distinctions were not accepted naively, and late medieval historiography reflected a lively debate concerning the proper boundaries between the factual and the fictive and about the proper place of rhetorical form in creating narratives that were persuasive, plausible and truthful.[5] From at least the time of Gregory the Great, biblical exegesis had also informed all reading of texts with the four levels of interpretation — literal, moral (tropological), anagogic and allegorical — that would influence the ways in which medieval historians constructed their narratives and expected them to be received and interpreted by their audiences.[6]

Such narrative communities, focused on common texts, methods of composition and narrative and forms of reception, were thus central to late medieval historiography. They both constrained and liberated historians within a continuum of imitation and invention.

LANGUAGE CHOICE

Language choice and skill were also essential in establishing the truth claims and authority of any particular narrative and placed it firmly within the context of a tradition and a textual community.[7] We employ the word "choice" deliberately. All the Latin narratives considered here were composed by authors who themselves had vernacular literacy and various degrees of fluency. Writers like Petrarch, Boccaccio and Matteo Palmieri were masters of both Latin and the emerging Tuscan vernacular, while Boccaccio was also fluent in Neapolitan. The authors of several vernacular works also appear to have been fluent in Latin, including the Anonimo romano and the author of the *Cronaca di Partenope*.[8] Vernacular authors often had enough Latin to read many of the letters and official government and diplomatic documents that they drew from or incorporated into their narratives. Language use was often therefore not a matter of necessity, or of lack of education, skill or fluency, but a deliberate choice influenced by several factors: profession and narrative community, sources, audience, authorial intent and prestige.[9]

LATIN HISTORIES

Latin, the language of the Bible, of the church and of government, held the highest place in intellectual argument and in its claims to universality and truth. It provided the basis for all secular legal and administrative culture as well. It was the language of record: royal and civil law and charter, legislation and administrative act, official correspondence, summons, subpoena and indictment, diplomacy, treaty and archive. It determined the monastic and ecclesiastical discourse of the anonymous author of the *Chronicon Suessanum,* Thomas Walsingham and Johanns von Winterthur. It informed the deeply eschatological *recordatio* and *speculatio* of Angelo Clareno's *Historia septem tribulationum.* Latin elevated the lay urban histories of the *Chronicon Mutinense,* of the *Chronicon Estense* and the *Chronicon siculum.* It merged classical form and content in the works of Petrarch, Boccaccio and Palmieri.

Rhetoric[10] and various ancient forms of *ars dictaminis,*[11] *ars predicandi*[12] and *ars arengandi*[13] held a central place in this Latinity in church, court and urban lay administration. But until the late duecento, northern Italy remained what Ronald Witt has described as a "documentary culture"[14] that consumed and produced little of the "book culture" of northern Europe and emphasized instead the palace and law court, the contract and the private dealings of individuals certified by notarial instruments. The cathedral schools and then the *studia* and universities of Italy were devoted to law and science and were slow in producing much literary or historical work. While classical works were available, they exercised little influence on new texts and remained textual monuments with their own authority and life.[15] By the late eleventh century, this documentary culture was also becoming increasingly laicized and had begun moving slowly from the episcopal chancellery to that of the new lay communes that formed the narrative communities of the trecento.[16]

Scholars have acknowledged this highly rhetorical character of trecento culture[17] but have also emphasized the importance of *grammatica,* culminating in the study of classical literature, for the urban elites.[18] Once codified in late duecento textbooks,[19] by the trecento this Latinity was taught both outside the university on lower levels and within the university as the only remaining "arts" curriculum. Grammar studies prepared for professional life and served the greater goal of moral instruction for civic engagement in the commune, an "ethical preparation of the student to enter a textual community."[20]

As with the humanists of the quattrocento, Italians of the trecento held that language was intimately tied to ethics and morality: that the form of one's Latinity also reflected one's closeness to sacred history, the word of God, and to the high example of the ancients.[21] A small elite, perhaps ten percent of students, would have had at least several years of education in the long list of classical Latin authors known in the trecento.[22] If not "learned," this elite was well educated in their Donatus, Aesop[23] and *Disticha Catonis,* their Prosper of Aquitaine and Prudentius, their Boethius and *Physiologus* — in whatever order and duration — before going on to the great classical poets and other *auctores*. Upon completion of their curricula, they understood the sophisticated use of Latin vocabulary, syntax, style and diction, prose, poetry and prosody,[24] myth and fable, symbol and emblem, maxim, proverb, epigram, commonplace and *dicta,* classical rhetoric and its modes, figures of speech and tropes,[25] translation and paraphrase, narrative strategies and styles, including direct address, oratory and dialogue. On higher levels they learned the intricacies of biblical narrative and interpretation, iconography, visual representation and ekphrasis.[26]

At almost all levels of reading Latin, up through the *auctores,* students absorbed the elements of intertextuality, of incorporating glosses and other materials from the classics, whether Christian or pagan, into their writing and their intellectual and moral frames.[27] They learned that texts, reading and writing were multi-leveled and multi-valanced. One must first read *literaliter,* for the surface meaning, but this necessitated also reading *sensualiter,* for internal sense and understanding. Students quickly learned that texts provided insights into interior character, emotional and moral life and social relations.[28] Latin opened the door to a Christian citizenship and the responsibility of the writer to search for truth and knowledge.[29] The Latin literate entered a textual community informed not solely or even primarily by their immediate experiences but informed, filtered and acculturated by a highly sophisticated textual tradition and the self-aware use of language and all its structures and devices.[30] They learned to write not as naive recorders of facts and dates but as highly polished creators of narratives for whom the sophisticated principles of composition were "hard-wired."[31]

In their hands, historiography was a form of rhetoric, in which linguistic construction and its persuasive verisimilitude played a major role.[32] Classical and medieval rhetoric recognized three forms of style *(elocutio):* the plain *(subtilis, planus, rusticus, simplex)* for instruction; the grand *(grande)* for emotional impact; and the mixed *(medium)* for pleasing and reconciling.[33] These historians' prefaces and prologues provide the best indications of their language choices, styles and other devices.

ECCLESIASTICS

Styles varied widely among ecclesiastics. On the most basic level, the author of the *Chronicon Suessanum* compiled his annal-like compendium, adding events by the year, month and day, using the most simple style, without adornment, and without any of the usual formal elements that might demonstrate a conscious rhetorical style. The *Chronicon,* in its present edition,[34] lacks any prologue or preface, no testimony to truth claims or invention and no stylistic embellishments. The same may be said of Angelo Crassullo's *Annales de rebus tarentinis.*

Angelo Clareno's Latinity[35] was heavily influenced by his Franciscan sources. In the Prologue to his *Historia septem tribulationum,* Clareno names these writers, including John and Thomas of Celano, Bonaventure and Frater Leo's biographies of Francis, the Franciscan Rules and Testament. By this and by his constant reiteration of the humility and poverty reflected in these writings, one might assume that Clareno wrote in an unadorned, deliberately anti-rhetorical style that reflected early Christian rejection of the classical tradition.[36] Yet it is clear throughout the *Historia* and his other writings that his linguistic style was heavily influenced by his own translations from the Greek Fathers, such as Gregory of Nazianzus and John Climacus, and by writings in the Joachite tradition.[37] In addition, Clareno makes his knowledge of rhetorical modes clear in his appreciation of Francis of Assisi's "open, brief and clear sermons," which reflect both Francis' "pure and holy simplicity" and Clareno's own knowledge of the unadorned rhetorical style.[38] Clareno also knew his classical sources, and he filled his *Historia* with invented speeches and exchanges of dialogue in order to both dramatize and ornament his narrative.

Northern churchmen offer a similar spectrum of style. In his prologue, Johanns von Winterthur notes that his *Chronica* would follow the rules of *historia* and that his language would use plain style in order to confer the greatest utility for his readers. In true classical form, he declares that he lacks the expertise and eloquence of writing with loquacious and pompous words, deploying instead a "rude and uncultivated" speech.[39] Thomas Walsingham also employed a simple style of short sentences or periods and generally unadorned language. Yet his text also contains a great number of classical references, allusions and vocabulary as well as carefully deployed rhetorical devices, such as metonymy and paranomasia, thus making his style more mixed or medium.[40]

LAY WRITERS

Knowledge of Latin among the laity also held the key to attaining the highest ranks in government, diplomacy, law, medicine and other elite professions.[41] This urban elite formed the core audience for the new Latin writings of poets and historians. As their Latin studies had prepared them to do, educated lay professionals composed self-reflective works replete with major rhetorical tropes, classical references and meta-commentary, informed both by their years of education and memorization of sacred and secular texts and by a keen understanding of their multi-layered literary, civic and moral utility.[42] In whatever form, however, this advanced Latinity would have been the exclusive preserve of males, who — except for rare cases of privileged females well into the early modern period — alone went on to learn *grammatica* in urban schools[43] or the *ars dictaminis* at university.[44]

Though his work follows an almost strictly chronological order, bordering on the annal in its earlier sections, the unknown author of the *Chronicon Estense* claims that he is employing the grand style in order to move his readers with moral instruction and to provide exempla of praise and blame for the civic good. He imitates the example of ancient historiography to elucidate the effects of concord and discord in the contemporary world in the mode of Sallust's moral and political narratives.[45] His style, however, is simple and unadorned, his syntax straightforward with little trace of classical influence. The disjunction between claims of grand style and its actual simplicity is instructive and offers a useful caveat in evaluating all these works. In the context of eyewitness report, Francesco Senatore[46] has noted that prefaces to many histories can often be mere tropes: borrowings from classical models that may not match the reality of the works that follow. In the same way, some of our historians, like the author of the *Chronicon Estense*, may also have overly relied on classical precedent to make their truth and stylistic claims. Another possibility is related to this: we have already cited Panofsky's theory of "disjunction" between medieval claims and means.[47]

The *Chronicon siculum* lacks a prologue or any other indication of authorial intent, but it too presents a simple, unadorned Latin style meant to facilitate its annalistic record of events. The *Chronicon Mutinense* by Giovanni da Bazzano also retains its annalistic form, with amplifications at various points, including events during his lifetime. Bazzano's Latin style is therefore generally also plain. As Marino Zabbia has noted,[48] however, he is capable of moving beyond the annalistic style, most especially in events that concern us here: the murder of Andrew of Hungary and the consequent invasion of the Regno by Lewis of Hungary and events around Cola di Rienzo's *buono stato*. Here Giovanni employs a wide range of rhetorical and dramatic devices more appropriate to the medium style, ranging from invented dialogue[49] to the incorporation of documentary evidence meant to bring verisimilitude to his descriptions.

We have already noted the place of notaries as intermediaries between orality, urban memory and official history.[50] Whether Domenico da Gravina in Apulia or Giovanni da Bazzano in Modena, these notaries used a distinct form and style of Latinity that influenced their narrative structures and made their language and world-view accessible to the urban lay elite. They also learned the basic techniques of transforming orality (through constant memorization and spoken repetition) into written textuality,[51] a skill equally essential to such professions as diplomacy[52] and to official record keeping and historiography. Domenico da Gravina's *Chronicon* lacks any prefatory material and offers indications that the original manuscript has significant lacunae, including a missing last gathering.[53] We cannot therefore be certain about his aims and methods of narration.[54] Few specific sources of any kind — biblical, classical or medieval — have been identified.[55] We might characterize his narrative style as notarial austere or simplex. Nevertheless, the work does contain elements of the mixed style. Small details and minor, digressive scenes are used as synecdoche for the larger evils of the realm. As in the work of Sallust, first-hand accounts and documentary evidence are supplemented by constructed dialogue and speeches, and events are embellished with dramatic details of action, character, emotion and psychological states most likely borrowed from romance literature and *chansons de gestes*.[56]

Petrarch, Boccaccio and Matteo de Palmieri exemplify a newly emerging humanist Latinity. Their Latin began to consciously break with medieval tradition and to return to what they considered the pure classical style.[57] Petrarch made clear his debt to the rhetorical styles of the ancients[58] from the time of his early education under Convenevole da Prato, to his earliest poetry and throughout his *Rerum familiarum libri* to his classical heroes: Cicero, Seneca, Varro, Quintilian, Livy, Horace and Virgil. Petrarch's editorial work on Livy's *Ab urbe condita* and his rejection of Dante's typological approach to epic in the *Africa* set the standard for all later humanist philology.[59] His first major Latin work, the *De viris illustribus*, embraced the moral purposes of biography going back to Lucan. In such speeches as the *Collatio laureationis*, Petrarch built upon medieval traditions of the *ars arengandi* by returning directly to Cicero's rhetorical models, including the *Pro Archia*.[60] In others, however, he relied strongly on medieval *ars predicandi*'s rhetorical forms, biblical quotation and moral counsel, sometimes set side-by-side with parallel classical themes.[61]

Petrarch's *Rerum memorandum libri*[62] returned to Aulus Gellius' and Valerius Maximus' collections of *sententiae*, commonplaces and *topica* and to Cicero's rhetorical work, *De inventione*, to discuss such topics as *otium, vita solitaria, memoria*, the four cardinal virtues and others that stressed the rhetorical underpinnings of historical writing.[63] Such stylistic self-awareness is particularly strong in the writings that concern us here: the *Familiares*, in which Petrarch himself distinguished between his "strong" Ciceronian eloquence and his "weak" or Ovidian one with its emphasis on emotional content and appeal,[64] between the classical rhetoric of his favorite authors and the long tradition of Christian anti-rhetorical writing embodied in the biblical *sermo humilis* and Augustine's distrust of rhetorical convention.[65]

Boccaccio's classical erudition in both Greek[66] and Latin[67] developed between his embrace of the vernacular and Petrarch's insistence on classical models and styles. Boccaccio's Latin *Epistolae* had already revealed his thorough familiarity with the *ars dictaminis,* rhetorical styles, language and vocabulary, deliberately showcasing his knowledge of the Latin classics and incipient command of the Greek.[68] Jason Houston notes that the *Epistolae* foreshadowed the grand style of Boccaccio's mature literary works characterized by seamless shifts of tone, hyperbole, florid and formal expression, erudite classical allusion and extravagant vocabulary.[69] But Boccaccio could also employ a variety of styles, including the low or *rusticus* for his *Buccolica carmen*[70] and the *De mulieribus claris.* In the latter and in his *De casibus virorum illustrium,* he also deploys a variety of rhetorical devices aimed at increasing the utility of his epideictic narrative, including amplification and shortening, fictive speeches and episodes, digression and various exempla, depending on the length or brevity of his sources and his didactic intent.[71]

Matteo Palmieri wrote in both Italian and Latin. His Latin *Vita* of Niccolò Acciaiuoli was based on the model of Plutarch's *Parallel Lives* and took on the epideictic or laudatory form. His style was therefore generally the *sermo simplex,* his language straightforward and generally unadorned, in keeping with his goal of recounting Acciaiuoli's *"virtutum et rerum gestarum gloriam"*[72] and providing the best disposition of evidence for moral instruction.

VERNACULAR HISTORIES

Various vernaculars spoke both of authorial background and to audience, to levels of education and to the purpose of text creation. They also spoke of cultural and political allegiances, whether to the Old French embraced by the Neapolitan court or to the Provençal used by Buccio di Ranallo and other troubadour-inspired poets. They might reflect the formal French of the English and French courts for Froissart, the Italian dialects of the urban commercial classes for the Villani or Agnolo di Tura in Tuscany or for the newly emerging professional classes reflected in the Anonimo romano's Rome or the *Cronaca di Partenope*'s Naples. Giovanni Villani's much-quoted survey of schools and literacy in Florence around the year 1343,[73] though probably exaggerating some numbers, provides a clear indication of the extent of lay literacy — both male and female — in that commercial center. While we have little similar evidence for other cities — North or South — the common commercial culture emerging in the Italian communes from the late twelfth century, the interchangeability of urban offices, institutions and personnel (including podestàs and notaries),[74] the constant interaction among these cities in trade, diplomacy and cultural exchange and their accumulated archival records indicate that such a literate vernacular culture and education were widespread.[75] This vernacular production was not merely an inferior version of cultured church and scholarly discourse but an explicit manifesto of an emerging lay and secular society that saw itself as independent of both church and empire, of both traditional hierarchies and powers. It recorded and celebrated urban lay culture's history and accomplishments.[76]

While not the elevated and self-conscious discourse or the *latinantes* who had completed the grammarians' curricula, vernacular literacy drew heavily on the spread of lay Latinity.[77] It also assumed a command of both elements of the *abbaco*.[78] This was a commercial education sufficient to maintain a business, its records and correspondence, a family and a civic life. *Abbaco* schooling, combined with the necessary grammar and literacy skills, also enabled both males and females to spend leisure time reading translations of classical texts, literary romances, histories, saints' lives and other popular sacred texts.[79] While *latinantes* could aspire to elite leadership and professional roles within a pan-European context and textual community, by the later trecento in Italy the varied local vernaculars had supplanted Latin literacy for most civic and literary purposes. Vernacular historians participated in a vibrant and self-conscious textual community nourished both by translations of classical texts and by the creation of new, highly sophisticated works. According to the scholarly consensus, only the new humanist movement slowed the progress of the vernaculars with classically inspired Latinity during the quattrocento.[80]

※

Among Italian vernaculars,[81] Tuscan earned its reputation as the emerging standard only because Dante, Petrarch and Boccaccio used it to compose their most famous literary works. But such a regional designation is premature for the trecento. While Petrarch wrote his sonnets and other poems, his *Triumphi* and his *Rerum vulgarium fragmenta* in the Tuscan vernacular of Dante,[82] all his historical works discussed here were composed in Latin; and Petrarch's later disdain for the vernacular — including that of Boccaccio — would influence all later humanists.[83] Boccaccio's Tuscan, on the other hand, was infused with influences from Latin classics, the *stil nuovo* and French romance and Provençal courtly literature.[84] Despite Boccaccio's artistry, his "historical" works under consideration here were also composed in Latin.

Through most of the trecento, the Tuscan vernacular was only one of several independently developing idioms. In the hands of Giovanni Villani, it was aimed at a newly literate audience that sought out texts for both moral and civic instruction and for entertainment. Villani knew Brunetto Latini's and Dante's work well and attempted to translate his own reading knowledge of Latin into a language that would suit his audience.[85] Villani's brief biography of Dante[86] explicitly addresses language use, poetics, structure, his knowledge of narrative forms, rhetorical modes, stylistics and devices and Dante's impact on contemporary Tuscan usage. Villani's style may also have been influenced by his reading of the chivalric romances then being translated into Tuscan.[87]

Agnolo di Tura wrote in a simple, unadorned Tuscan but was also well aware of the uses and rhetorical qualities of the vernacular. His report on the death of Dante is taken almost word-for-word from Villani's and briefly sums up the poet's life and work. Agnolo also copied Villani's sections on Dante's language use, poetics, structures and rhetorical devices.[88]

The anonymous author or authors of the *Diurnale (Diario) del Duca di Monteleone* borrowed heavily from other sources. The work's most accurate sections, from 1371 to 1443, reflect a highly Tuscanized southern vernacular, but the base manuscript for the modern edition dates from the sixteenth century. This text has been edited so heavily that one cannot accurately draw conclusions as to the vernacular usage of the existing text.[89]

Buccio di Ranallo used the vernacular poetic form almost exclusively. His verse *Leggenda di Santa Caterina d'Alessandria*, commissioned by a local confraternity some time around 1330, shows some knowledge of Dante, especially the *Inferno*.[90] Beginning in 1338, he composed a series of twenty-one political sonnets.[91] De Bartholomaeis[92] attributed much of Buccio's heightened narrative mode to his straightforward, intense and unfiltered patriotic feelings. He saw him as a unique figure isolated from the incipient Tuscan mainstream and made the Rankean claim that Buccio's "was an exposition of truth pure and simple, devoid of any opportunistic element."[93] Yet Buccio's knowledge of the classical rhetorical forms and his inclusion of witticisms, bon-mots, proverbs, admonitions and pithy phrasing points less toward "rustic simplicity" and more toward his conscious use of Ciceronian *sententiae*, biblical and classical maxims, *facetia* and other classical rhetorical forms known throughout the Middle Ages.[94]

The verse epic or *cronicum carmen* form also allowed him to use *amplificatio* to highlight the significance and emotional gravity of events and to draw character even more sharply.[95] Buccio thus adopted the poetic form of Alexandrine verse to compose his *Cronaca aquilana rimata*. Buccio's is the earliest extant example of the vernacular verse history in Italy, well before its appearance in Mantua, Venice, Urbino, Perugia, Arezzo, Lucca, Volterra or Pisa. While these later works demonstrate the impact of Dante's *Commedia* and of Petrarch's and Boccaccio's historical work, Buccio's remains independent of the Tuscan model. To determine the influences on his Aquileian vernacular, one must look to the French *chansons de geste* and the Provençal courtly poetry, most likely under the impact of the new Angevin dynasty, their administrative and creative classes and their tastes and forms.[96]

The Anonimo romano claimed that he first conceived of and had already composed his *historia* in a "medium style"[97] Latin, the language of his professional training and the language in which his classical and late medieval models wrote. He also claims to have redacted this Romanesco version.[98] There is some evidence to confirm this, including a number of glosses written in Latin that were incorporated into the final text by the copyist, but this thesis has been challenged.[99] Whatever the status of an original Latin version, the Anonimo's use of Romanesco language and vocabulary *(elocutio)* was a deliberate choice focused both on reception — aimed directly at his urban, professional and commercial audience — and on the cultural diffusion of ancient learning and models applied to contemporary events.[100]

Trecento Romanesco was not the Tuscan-inflected language spoken in Rome since the Risorgimento but part of the central and southern Italian family of dialects, closer to the written Neapolitan of the *Cronaca di Partenope* than to Villani's language. The Anonimo romano also wrote in the context of an already-forming Romanesco literary tradition. The thirteenth century had produced both the *Storie de Troja et de Roma*[101] and the *Miracole de Roma*[102] in Romanesco.[103] Whether with the Matter of Troy or the Mirabilian Latin traditions, such works shared the cultural project of bringing vernacular translation to a lay, literate audience, highlighting the Roman commune's historical links to its ancient cultural and political traditions in much the same way as the *Cronaca di Partenope* was to do for Naples. The Anonimo romano's declaration of intent to create a vernacular translation of his work therefore fit into the same cultural project of Roman revival and communal identity that would mark Cola di Rienzo's *buono stato*.[104] Neither project was therefore unique but shared the same impulses as those of the northern Italian communes and their historiography.

Gustav Seibt has analyzed the Anonimo romano's literary forms[105] and has highlighted the author's use of highly emblematic language that appeals to the reader's senses. It is also a dramatically visual and gestial language, both mimetic and illustrative. The Anonimo's sentences use short, concise periods that are both paratactic and concatenate, aided by poetic use of trochaics and dactyls. The Anonimo was well versed in contemporary poetic narrative and a master of rhetorical devices that build dramatic effect and join narrative periods with a fast-paced series of adverbial clauses.[106] The net effect of such pacing, quick cutting and visual device resembles what we might call "cinematic" and what Seibt compares to contemporary Sienese painting. Typologies and *figurae,* concatenations and repetitions and the author's ironic tone show a clear understanding of the place of rhetoric in constructing a convincing narrative.

The Angevins' political, commercial and cultural connections to Provence, Liguria and Tuscany brought people and ideas that used their vernaculars in Naples. Neapolitan, therefore, began to assimilate these influences from the mid-duecento.[107] Francophone administrators and Provençal literary works exerted cultural and formal influences on the language and its textual presentation.[108] Boccaccio was quite conscious of his use of Neapolitan vernacular, citing Queen Giovanna I's use of Neapolitan as a sign of her close ties to the people of Naples. He left us one of the earliest samplings of Neapolitan in his letter from the fictional Jannetto Parisse to Francesco de' Bardi, demonstrating his proficiency in the local language, its richness and the particularly crunchy character of its local surnames.[109] As Samantha Kelly notes, up until the trecento, Campania had little vernacular literary tradition,[110] and most official and notarial documents continued to be composed in Latin. She speculates that the *Cronaca* itself is a "civic Neapolitan"[111] response to the strong vernacular tradition embodied in Villani's chronicle.[112] The *Cronaca di Partenope* is therefore one of the first works in any genre composed in a Tuscanized Neapolitan[113] and gives it formal recognition as a literary language. Neapolitan usage confirms a key aim of the *Cronaca*: to emphasize the special place of Naples as a distinct political and cultural capital with both ancient origins and long traditions of continuity that informed both its civic and communal history and the language used to express it.[114] Though different in many stylistic and syntactic aspects, the *prosa media* used by Neapolitan vernacular chroniclers[115] paralleled that of the Anonimo romano in purpose and intended audience. In this regard, as we have already noted in other contexts, both works cast doubt on the uniqueness of northern Italian communal historiography.[116]

Jean Froissart used the Middle French vernacular for both his poetry and his historical work. But he insisted that poetry, with its propensity toward invention and entertainment, could not have the same claims to truth as a prose style.[117] His purpose, instead, was to commit to perpetual memory noble deeds and to instruct his readers in chivalrous virtues:

> To that end I will not omit, forget, alter, or abridge anything at all in this history for want of language, but will rather enrich and elaborate where I am able, and thoroughly relate every event, point by point.[118]

In order to highlight both character and events he therefore embellished his prose with many rhetorical devices: dramatic, almost cinematic descriptions and set pieces for battles,[119] fictional dialogue and speeches, the use of *dicta*, exempla, of digressions to Arthurian and classical myth.

Yet Froissart was also a critic of many of the moral faults of his times. As Peter Ainsworth notes,[120]

> by a curious paradox, the more the chronicler's prose approximates to poetry, by dint (in particular) of its deployment of metonymical figures that are beginning to transform themselves into metaphors… the more his critique of the society of his times seems to deepen and sharpen.

NARRATIVE STRUCTURES

In this section, we will discuss narrative structures, that is the form in which our historians wrote, as opposed to the three main narrative modes, which we will discuss in the next section. The mode of a narrative — whether one of praise, the argument of a case or of constructing a narrative useful to public life — can often suggest the structure of a narrative but is not determinative of it. Citing Carlo Ginzburg, Chiara De Caprio has noted[121] that for Neapolitan civic chroniclers and their audiences, truth claims relied both on the plausibility of their narratives and on their structure.

The work of Roland Barthes, Hayden White, Paul Ricoeur and Gabrielle Spiegel, among others, has recently re-opened to historians the essentially rhetorical nature of historical narrative.[122] As Barthes put it, "does this form of narration really differ, in some specific trait, in some indubitably distinctive feature, from imaginary narration, as we find it in the epic, the novel, and the drama?"[123] Ricoeur distinguished three types of narrative — the historical, the fictional and the mythic — that all ultimately refer back to the real world of human experience but also to the three rhetorical categories — *historia, argumentum, fabula* — made standard by Cicero, Quintilian and the *Rhetorica ad Herennium*.[124] While the immediate referents of history and literature might differ, the human experience of time unites them and creates deep resemblances in their discursive forms. Both ultimately speak symbolically or allegorically of the same human realities. As White states,

> historical stories and fictional stories resemble one another because whatever the differences between their immediate contents (real events and imaginary events, respectively), their ultimate content is the same: the structures of human time.[125]

Matthew Kempshall[126] and Nancy Partner[127] have reminded us that this linguistic turn is less a revolutionary divergence in historiographical theory than a complex return to medieval and early modern epistemological understandings of the language-based, constructive nature of history writing based on ancient rules of rhetoric. The narrative structures below often coincide with these classical forms but more suit our purposes in distinguishing among the historical works discussed here. The "paratactic," or brief chronicle entry, recounts events linearly, often, like the annal, demarcated by dating elements. The "thematic" shows the hand of the author more clearly as broadly arranged and narrated history focuses on key ideas rather than linear narration. Finally, the "symbolic" narration of historical characters and events offers a series of exempla as the manifestation of divine *invisibilia* — or more broadly for a contemporary audience, of forces over and beyond human agency. Here the linearity of the paratactic seems to disappear, and the narrative is so constructed that themes appear to emerge not through the guiding hand of the author but through some revelation of a higher reality. As we will see below, none of these categories are air-tight, and many of the histories discussed here will demonstrate elements of each.

PARATACTIC

The first — the paratactic or chronological — structure emphasizes one technique by which readers are led to make their own connections between discrete events placed "one after another without coordinating or subordinating connectives."[128] From the time of Aulus Gellius, critics have noted that this structure appears simply to record events without any further reflection or ordering on the part of the writer.[129] As Partner explains it,

> Parataxis seems to have been the stylistic expression of a generalized inability, or humble reluctance, to order experience.... Medieval histories...often leave us feeling that the best parts have been left on the cutting room floor.[130]

Here events are recorded without any apparent authorial intervention and might include births and deaths, battles and coronations, parliaments and councils, plagues, celestial events and portents, famines and floods.

Among Italian writers of Latin histories, the *Chronicon Estense* can serve as a prime example of the paratactic type. The *Chronicon* moves from a purely annalistic structure in its entries from 328 CE to 1190,[131] then jumps ahead to 1207, where it becomes a chronicle, entering various incidents in order of year, month, day or saint's feast, including wars and battles, civil uprisings, truces and treaties, miracles, fires and major building projects and destructions, floods, blood moons, eclipses and natural disasters, food shortages, famines, deaths and plagues, marriages and coronations, papal elections, church councils and religious movements. All are posted linearly as they occur. This structure continues, becoming more detailed after the 1250s and as the work moves through the trecento, devoting lengthy amplifications including invented dialogue and excursus to individuals and events touching on the history of Ferrara and the Romagna. The Hohenstaufen, the Malatesta, Ezzolino da Romano, the Este, Pepoli, della Scala, Gonzaga and Visconti all come in and out of focus as randomly as natural disasters. For the Mezzogiorno, particular attention is devoted to the Angevin conquest, events in the reign of Giovanna I and day-to-day developments in Rome during Cola di Rienzo's *buono stato*.

Given its civic nature, however, the *Chronicon* focuses overwhelmingly on political and secular personalities and events, providing only short annalistic entries for all other items. But this reflects less a thematic unity of writing and structure than a matter of selectivity among a diverse universe of data. No single family, individual or narrative thread is privileged over any other, no form of civil virtue or vice: all are recorded as sources of information and as they rise or fall on the chronicler's horizon. No connections are drawn between events or persons. Deeper causalities and motivations remain unexamined.

The *Chronicon Mutinense* employs a similar structure, dictated by a similar ongoing event horizon. An annalist series of entries by podestà ranges from 1188, gradually amplifying the entries, to 1311.[132] The entries then begin to feature occasional year, month and day markers. Only in 1352[133] is the podestà dating abandoned for dating elements, including indictions. Throughout, the chronicle focuses almost strictly on Mantuan political events and persons, incorporating the same natural and human data into its podestà entries. Bazzano amplifies his account with occasional documents, including official state letters of Cola di Rienzo, and fictionalized dialogue to bolster truth claims and dramatic impact.

The *Chronicon Suessanum* uses an annalistic form, providing year, month and date, from the first entry for 1103 (the diocese of Sessa Aurunca's founding) to 1251,[134] when it begins to amplify the narration with an account of Conrad's descent to the Regno. Entries are similarly full thereafter, supplemented with occasional evidence, such as Queen Sancia's tomb inscription, and fictionalized dialogue. To its conclusion at the end of 1348, the *Chronicon*'s focus remains the political and military events of the Regno that affect the diocese. Angelo Crassullo's *Annales de rebus tarentinis* are just that, with little amplification or any other structural embellishment. Major divisions are by year with subordinate entries by month or date, often introduced by variations of the phrase, *"Fit mentio."* Their horizon and narrative scope are limited to events that touch on Apulia.

The *Chronicon siculum* uses essentially the same structure. After a brief series of paragraphs beginning in CE 340 around the legend of Pope Silvester I and Emperor Constantine, the work moves directly to a political-chorographic survey of the provinces of the Regno and then launches into the history of the Normans, Hohenstaufen and early Angevins.[135] It then begins its annalist entries in 1343 with the reign of Giovanna I, offering extensive, daily detail around the murder of Andrew of Hungary and the punishment of his accused assassins.[136] It

CHAPTER 4 NARRATIVE COMMUNITIES & STRATEGIES

then records events, rarely out of chronological order, to 1396 arranged by year, month and often by day. It provides great detail on the end of Giovanna I's reign, the Neapolitan role in the Great Schism and the reigns of Charles III, Regent Queen Margaret and Ladislaus. It focuses almost purely on political, military and diplomatic events both among the elite and the citizens of Naples. Records of natural events like earthquakes, storms and floods are rare and often linked (if only by entry order) to their political consequences.[137]

Among the Italian vernacular histories, the most prominent example is Agnolo di Tura's *Cronaca Senese*. Agnolo uses a chronological structure but departs from an annalistic account in his attempt to create a synchronic narrative of events within an annual frame, quick cutting, for example, in his opening year of 1300 between Rome and Pistoia, Florence and Siena[138] in an almost cinematic parataxis.[139] Again, while the emphasis is firmly on civic history — the factional struggle between the Guelphs and Ghibellines, Blacks and Whites — each year claims its share of comets, prodigies and plagues, storms, floods and earthquakes, food shortages, fires and building collapses, construction work, artistic projects and university events, battles, uprisings and executions, religious dissent, prophesies and charitable donations. All are recorded in strictly chronological order of occurrence. All are given equal narrative weight if not equal length. Events in France, the Low Countries, the British Isles, the papacy and empire, Naples and the Mediterranean are also duly recorded as time and place emerge into, and fall back out of, focus. Synopses of truce documents, orders of battle and battle deaths and composed speeches amplify and add verisimilitude to the annalist structure.

The *Diurnale (Diario) di Duca di Monteleone* survives in a highly edited text that is based on a sixteenth-century manuscript. We therefore have little reliable indication of the original structure of the work independent of its current editions. As such, and as one would expect from a diary, the work uses a chronological structure, ordered by year, indiction and increasingly as it proceeds by month and day. Within this frame, the author ranges freely among persons and incidents, amplifying the account with lengthy episodes and with rich — if frequently inaccurate — details of people and events, often borrowing freely from other historians. Unlike many annalistic histories, it focuses almost exclusively on one topic: the political fate of the later Angevins.

The northern historians discussed here embraced the paratactic structure of most traditional medieval chronicles. Johanns von Winterthur adopted the annal structure but complemented it with a chronological ordering, dating his entries with papal and episcopal reigns much in the tradition of the *Liber pontificorum* composed since the early Middle Ages. Johanns also states that he has ordered his account of the acts and deeds of his times not according to strict chronological order but to his own sense. He also called out new and various events by the paragraph as designated in his marginalia.[140] Johanns amplified his narrative with detailed accounts of political and religious personalities and events, as well as with occasional digressions to deepen the emotional impact of his history. Such digressions include the progress of Charles of Anjou's conquest of the Regno,[141] the career of the Franciscan preacher Berthold von Regensburg[142] and the lengthy account of the reign of Rudolph of Hapsburg.[143] We have already discussed Johanns' detailed coverage of the reign of Giovanna I.[144] Such excursus take up nearly two-thirds of Johanns' chronicle. Events and individual lives are also sometimes narrated out of chronological sequence if they bear upon other matters covered around the same time or place. While the underlying structure remains that of a linear account, certain thematic concerns that fit Johanns' purpose in writing about papal and imperial history push the boundaries of his parataxis.

Thomas Walsingham wrote his history as a continuation of St. Albans Abbey's chronicles and therefore also adopted a similar chronological structure, but with similar thematic excursus. His accounts of English history provide a complete narrative centered around the chief political personalities and events of his times, including his detailed account of the Peasants' Revolt of 1381. He also acknowledged the historian's duty to rise above the simple chronicle and to emphasize the thematic unities over the ordering of multiple events and diversity of places by employing synecdoche and compelling exempla.[145] Within the major annual headings, Thomas provides thematic rubrics,[146] each devoted to a sub-topic around a person or event within that year. Entire documents are also incorporated into this framework, making the chronicle less an annal than a historical compendium arranged by year and topic, an unfolding of history as viewed by Thomas' monastic and royalist perspective. Thomas would therefore complete his narration of an event or his profile of a person, even if this took course over several places, months or years, before returning to his strict chronology.[147] Such a structuring followed the advice of the *Rhetorica ad Herennium* or Quintilian. Both stressed utility and reader reception over linear order.[148]

THEMATIC

The second, thematic, structure was used by the majority of our writers. Here the historian approaches the subject matter in terms of moral and political examples and lessons, laying out the narrative in broad strokes under thematically unified rubrics or numbered chapters that introduce discrete episodes.

CHAPTER 4 ❧ NARRATIVE COMMUNITIES & STRATEGIES

Quintilian had noted that chronological order was most natural to historiography but that a writer could follow whatever order seemed expedient or advantageous to further an argument or analysis.[149] A thematic ordering was often employed in medieval historiography or combined with a broad chronology in order to include what was necessary, to insure brevity and clarity and to meet audience expectation of plausibility and utility. Narratives might be re-arranged to emphasize the deeds of individuals or the unfolding of events. Events themselves could be narrated using the norms of history, argument or fable.[150] Each of these cases might best be expressed in one of the three "narrative modes" described in the section below.[151]

As Domenico da Gravina notes,[152] his account of events is less a complete chronological record than an attempt to understand the progress of the Regno's political and moral corruption as it spreads from the head and the center of Giovanna I's court throughout the kingdom. Gravina opens his narrative like a play,[153] with his main characters already on the stage as the curtain rises. It moves quickly from the childhood of Princesses Maria and Giovanna to Giovanna's betrothal to Andrew of Hungary, portrayed as Robert of Anjou's rightful heir. Youthful lovers betrothed, a jealous aunt "inspired by a devilish spirit," the exit of one after another of Giovanna's positive influences leads to the unleashing of the new queen's vices. Corruption spreads from the head to the rest of the body. Betrayal, murder, vengeance, invasion, civil war and devastation follow in a fast-paced narrative that moves from the capital to the provinces and then to Gravina's own city and home. Like the works of Sallust and Lucan, it presents a history of disaster filled with moral judgment,[154] focused on the evil effects on the realm caused by the rule of a woman. As self-interest replaces the common good, moral corruption and civil strife spread like a disease from the royal court to the nobility, to the rest of the Regno and its people, down to the youngest children.[155]

After his account of the death of Sancia of Majorca in 1345, Gravina eliminates almost all the paratactic chronographic markers that usually separate events and descriptions of individuals.[156] He seems to assume that his readers will know the dates of the events he frames here and provides neither chapter heads nor rubrics.[157] Gravina's narrative is held together and moved forward simply by his dramatic momentum through what Zabbia calls "concentric movements."[158] Temporal conjunctions like *tunc, sequenti die, et dum, post haec, deinde,* along with causal conjunctives — *igitur, itaque* — transition one paragraph to the next. Related, parallel and simultaneous events are introduced by coordinating or subordinating conjunctions, such as *interea* or *autem* or by verb forms like *contigit*. Day-by-day developments in the action are clearly marked: *sequenti die, post vero dies tres, lucescente igitur die, elapso itaque biduo.*

Petrarch chose two forms — the letter and the eclogue — to narrate his account of Angevin Naples' decline under Giovanna. In both classical and Renaissance modes, the letter was among the most rhetorical of forms, closely related to oratory. C. Julius Victor had expanded Cicero's work on rhetoric to include a section *"de epistolis,"* in which he distinguished official letters from *familiares*.[159] Each had its own formal qualities, and these would later be developed into the medieval *ars dictaminis*. In Italy, this remained firmly Ciceronian, and Petrarch marks the revival of a more pure understanding and use of the letter structure to narrate and to persuade, and he developed this connection between letter writing and historiography.[160] While presenting his interpretation of Neapolitan affairs after King Robert's death as a series of discrete letters to friends and patrons,[161] Petrarch combined these to form a thematic arc of decline and fall focused on the inheritance and reign of Giovanna I.

He supplemented this narrative with his *Eclogues*.[162] Poetry was recognized as a possible form of historiography from the time of the *Rhetorica ad Herennium* and of Quintilian, but one whose verisimilitude and utility were long debated.[163] That Petrarch chose the bucolic or eclogue form underscored the tragic mode in which he sought to frame Neapolitan affairs from the death of Robert through Giovanna's reign. Poetry also allowed him to the create a historical account that amplified certain themes and yet still maintained plausibility and verisimilitude.

Boccaccio's narratives of Naples also used two forms — the epideictic biography and the eclogue — to different effect but with the same grand thematic structure. The first, in his *De mulieribus claris* and his *De casibus virorum illustrium*, examined Giovanna I's life and reign not chronologically but thematically according to a set classical structure as refined in the Middle Ages and intended to examine character and deeds.[164] We will discuss these two works in further detail under our section on narrative modes. The second, eclogue, form followed Petrarch's lead in using a poetic structure to trace the same tragic arc of Angevin decline. We will examine these in greater detail in Chapter 8.[165]

Similarly, Matteo Palmieri's humanist *Vita Nicolai Acciaioli* announces its unified, thematic approach at the outset: "I have therefore determined to interweave and to collect together in one volume the facts of his life and character that I have read scattered separately in various places."[166] Palmieri does so in a continuous biography, arranged chronologically with no further thematic groupings common to the epideictic mode. His account concentrates on Acciaiuoli's career in the Regno and moves forward with the usual temporal and causal adverbs and conjunctions. He omits chapters and dating elements but constructs his narrative in brief paragraphs that move the action seamlessly from scene to scene and from episode to episode. The *Vita* eschews synchronicity. *Interea, interim* or other markers introduce a few paragraphs, but Palmieri prefers to unfold his tale in a single temporal order with few embellishments other than occasional dialogue.

CHAPTER 4 ⚜ NARRATIVE COMMUNITIES & STRATEGIES

Among the Italian vernacular writers, Giovanni Villani is the most difficult to fit into one of these structural categories, and his work points to an intermediary form of historiography as he attempts to move beyond the bounds of genre. Villani frequently incorporated paratactic dating elements by year, month and day, but they do not delineate his entries. Instead, he separated his books and chapters by thematic rubrics that introduce discrete episodes.[167] These episodes are generally carried forward to their dramatic conclusion as far as contemporaneity allows *(nel detto anno, in questi tempi e anno)*, and then sometimes picked up again where the fabric of the narrative requires. Cross references to previous episodes *(e come adietro dicemmo, tornando a raccontare…)* attempt to bind disparate events into a unified narrative. On the whole, however, his history does follow events as they emerge, and largely in chronological order. As Green characterizes it,

> where patterns show in the form of interpretation they do so unintentionally — unthinkingly accepted assumptions materialize in the shaped outlines of events. It neither captures a single historical moment nor expresses one crystallized state of its author's consciousness but, like one of Uccello's panoramic perspectives, follows the confusion of action from successive, uncoordinated points of vision. Its clarity derives not from any kind of ordering through structure.[168]

Nevertheless, as Green goes on to note, Villani's work is unified by the theme of divine justice. "The idea of justice…a law compelling the restoration of moral equilibrium, pervades the historical narrative and gives each of its segments, that is amenable to being moulded by it, unity and meaning."[169] Villani's extended recitation of every variety of historical and natural event, character portrait, excursus on urban life and culture, all underscore his central theme of natural and civic balance disturbed and restored.

The *Cronaca di Partenope* follows Villani's model closely, and many of its manuscripts incorporate about eighteen chapters directly from the *Cronaca nuova*.[170] Chapter divisions are rubricated, numbered and/or titled in various manuscripts, but all the extant manuscripts are late, and we do not know if their structure follows the author's original intent.[171] Part 3 of the *Cronaca*'s heavy indebtedness to Villani, however, probably points to the adoption of the structure that we see today. Again, the *Cronaca di Partenope*'s unifying theme is the rise of Naples from its ancient roots to its current communal richness and fame.[172] Its narrative therefore presents a highly dynamic story of historical progress, embellished with classical descriptions of topography and local legend, sacred record and secular memory unified in its teleological impulse. Few chapters are interwoven with either temporal or causal conjunctions, and structural unity is achieved more by declared intent and narrative flow than by internal markers.

The Anonimo romano's *Cronaca* is a broad history of virtue and vice, of triumph and defeat, the chief portion of which focuses on events and personalities in Rome in the mid-trecento. The Anonimo reveals no apparent influence of Villani's history but adheres to the classical models of Livy, Sallust and Lucan. The Anonimo makes it clear that he intends to conform to a thematic unity and not a purely chronological record. Episodes are re-arranged to fit themes and expand exempla, and the grand sweep of events and the ordered appearance of individual characters are exchanged for a series of chapters used as literary markers to illustrate these themes or to follow the course of an individual's deeds and character.[173] Like Villani, the Anonimo romano attempts to expand the boundaries of the traditional chronicle. Here literary construct and rhetorical disposition rise above chronology, a re-ordering commended by Quintilian and discussed throughout the Middle Ages.[174] The Anonimo notes his rearrangement and division (*dispositio* and *divisio*) in his Prologue: "I am dividing this work into chapters, so that whoever wishes to find beautiful things in it will be able to do so easily."[175] Under these, he often introduces year and other dating elements with the phrase *"in questo tiempo, currevano anni Domini"* or simply *"currevano anni Domini."* The survival of several empty rubrics without accompanying chapters[176] indicates that the Anonimo's thematic structure was unified and preconceived, awaiting only his pen to construct it or that of his copyist to redact his completed project.

Jean Froissart's wrote

> in order that the honourable deeds and ventures accomplished by arms, which took place during the wars between France and England, might be aptly documented and commended to lasting memory, so that courageous men might follow such examples to inspire them to good.[177]

For the sake of his narrative, he therefore structured his book in a series of parts and chapters divided by rubrics.[178] Yet these rubrics stand less as thematic than as place markers. Across this structure, Froissart's episodes flow along with the course of events, loosely joined by temporal conjunctions *(quant, adoncques, adont, aprés, ainsi, lors)* more in the style of literary romance and memoir than of historical narrative linked causally or synchronically. Persons, events, geography, memories and myths all flow with the narrative momentum of a poet rather than a chronicler or a historian. Froissart's work is therefore neither a traditional paratactic chronicle nor a thematically organized history except in the larger sense that he lays out: his loose structure is devoted to providing a series of exempla of his major theme of chivalric deed and character.

CHAPTER 4 ⁂ NARRATIVE COMMUNITIES & STRATEGIES

SYMBOLIC OR FIGURATIVE

The third, symbolic or figurative, structure was a form of tropological exegesis represented here primarily by Angelo Clareno's *Historia septem tribulationum*. Like the Franciscan *Chronicle* of Salimbene da Adam,[179] it offers both a broad thematic approach to personalities and events and also a history of the divine *invisibilia* working their way through the visible events and personalities of history[180] in a symbolic series of *figurae*, exempla and incidents. To modern, empiricist eyes this form most closely resembles the fictions of medieval *fabula*: truth revealed through what appears to be pure invention. But for medievals like Clareno, such narrative was a valid form of *inventio* going back to ancient classical and Christian sources. It depicted eternal, divine truths hung upon the framework of known historical persons and events. These deploy symbol, metaphor, image and vision to depict the events seen by the "mind's eye." While Clareno's work differed from much mendicant historiography in its lack of urban focus,[181] it was not a unique or isolated example of such a symbolic structure. Much of medieval historiography from Eusebius and Augustine through Bede, Otto of Freising and John of Salisbury consciously looked back to both biblical and patristic models to unravel the inscrutable unfolding of the divine plan in human history.[182]

Clareno's *Historia* uses the Apocalypse of John as its basic model: a series of visions and tableaux that gradually provide revelation of the divine and eternal behind the guise of earthly events and appearances. Clareno's narrative employs the same "field of dreams" structure: a freefloating background from which individual persons and events emerge from a higher reality to manifest the eternal *invisibilia* of salvation history "to explain in contingent language the strictly human foreground of history."[183] Francis of Assisi becomes the central symbol, the *figura* of the eternal Christ made manifest in Clareno's own times. Francis' followers become types of the Apostles in a series that binds together sacred history with present tribulations. Such narrative is apocalyptic history in the strict sense: a series of revelations that come to those who understand them. As we will see in Chapter 6,[184] Clareno's written *narratio* resembles the visual narratives of the Neapolitan Apocalypse paintings of Cavallini and Giotto: symbols emerging from a preexisting free-floating field of truths, an assortment of exempla derived from eternal archetypes of good and evil.

Among the most salient aspects of Clareno's *Historia* is this hermetic focus on the inruption of the eternal sacred into the secular realm of time and its narrowing of focus on the Spiritual Franciscans. The secular history of the rest of the world, even of the Franciscan Order, seems to disappear in Clareno's writing, with the very few exceptions of those laymen who actively aid or hinder the apocalyptic mission of the Spirituals. Just as the history of these elect is something special, so too its method of transmission. As with other dissident groups, such as the Waldensians discussed by Stock,[185] the Spirituals form a true textual community united by a largely oral tradition of faithful brothers until Clareno's final redaction to writing in anticipation of the last days.

Equally characteristic of Clareno's account is what Hayden White called

> the poignant moment at which a people or group is forced, by the death of its members, to transfer an experience, existentially determinative of its own image of the nature of its existence as a historical entity, from the domain of memory to that of history.[186]

Clareno's account is filled with this sense of poignancy, of loss and of the isolation of the particular historical moment in the midst of the progress of sacred history. His role models and inspirations, companions and brethren emerge and file past in a procession of sacred memory that must be reduced to written history. It is a reflection upon the passage, within a textual community, from the vibrancy of a movement of reform to one of ideals remembered, betrayals experienced and hopes set up against increasing despair and isolation.

Again, these structures are not air-tight. Johanns von Winterthur made it clear that his *historia* of *rerum gestarum in preteritis temporibus* would not follow the strict *dispositio* of events, but that he would rearrange his *ordo rerum* to provide a more comprehensible narrative for writing papal and imperial history and so increase the usefulness of his narrative and themes.[187] Froissart constructed his theme of chivalrous character and deeds in a narrative space between the paratactic and thematic form. Villani's chronicle traces the emergence of Florence as a brilliant cultural and political capital with its origins in ancient foundation, as does the *Cronaca di Partenope* for Naples. Buccio di Ranallo's poetic narrative seeks to highlight the impact of good and evil character on civil society and to provide example and admonishment to fellow citizens through a linear narration of events. Thomas Walsingham and Agnolo di Tura re-arranged their traditional paratactic structures for similar thematic purposes.

In the end, we cannot draw any clear demarcation between a clerical, annalist and chronicle tradition and a newly emerging, lay thematic history. Quite the opposite case might be made: the most sophisticated southern historians of the trecento, including the Anonimo romano and Domenico da Gravina, were laymen; and the most traditional appear to be the northern, civic chroniclers of Tuscany and the Romagna who used the paratactic and annalistic forms.

CHAPTER 4 ⚜ NARRATIVE COMMUNITIES & STRATEGIES

NARRATIVE FORMS OR MODES

In addition to narrative structures, other factors come into play, most especially plot and tone, both of which were shaped by the cultural, intellectual or political purposes of the writer and the text or by the ideological underpinnings of the master narratives that resolve themselves into various plot types. Several taxonomies of narrative have been proposed. Examples include the tripartite divisions into epic, tragedy and farce;[188] into four "master tropes" of metaphor, synecdoche, metonymy and irony;[189] into epideictic (praise and blame), forensic (judicial) and deliberative (civic) narrative, or into history, poetry and fable forms. All ultimately derive from ancient rhetoric.[190] Medieval historians studied them all and were sophisticated enough to understand them as having entertainment, civic and moral importance.

Here we will employ the most accepted forms of medieval narrative, deriving ultimately from Cicero's three categories of oratory: the epideictic (demonstrative, of praise or blame), the legal (forensic or argumentative), and the deliberative (political or civil).[191] Our brief examination of grammatical and rhetorical traditions has argued that these trecento historians were not transparent recorders of fact and event but that they constructed their narratives with a deep understanding of their craft and according to the classical grammatical models embedded in their "Donatus" and the rhetorical tradition of Cicero, *Ad Herennium,* Quintilian and Boethius.

Epideictic

We will begin with the epideictic form, which these historians used almost exclusively for biography. The best place to begin is with Boccaccio's use of all the classic elements of epideictic rhetoric in his laudatory *Vita* of Giovanna I from the *De mulieribus claris.*[192] This will enable us to clearly distinguish both the narrative form and its constituent elements before examining other examples. Boccaccio was well aware of the rhetorical modes in which he wrote, and he discussed the major differences between *historia* and *fabula* in both early works like the *Allegoria mitologica* and later ones like the *Genealogia deorum gentilium.*[193] In the latter, he noted that *historia* is more closely aligned with the literal truth of persons and events, whereas *fabula* is prone to various forms of *inventio.* At the same time, however, he did see the value of a thematically unified narrative that might need to rearrange the *dispositio* in order to better emphasize virtues and vices and provide moral example and utility.[194]

The ten-part epideictic form that Boccaccio used for biography was developed by Hermogenes and Apthonius and transmitted to medieval writers by Priscian in his *De pre-exercitamentis rhetoricis.*[195] It included: 1. marvelous events at a subject's birth; 2. their nature; 3. their training and education; 4. the nature of their soul (a. justice, b. self-control, c. wisdom, d. courage); 5. the nature of their body (a. beauty, b. stature, c. agility, d. might); 6. pursuits and deeds; 7. external attributes (a. family and friends, b. possessions, c. household, d. fortune); 8. longevity; 9. manner of their end; 10. subsequent events. While not every biography needed to follow all ten steps to lay out what Cicero called the *personae attributa*, depending on the individual described and the audience intended, they did form the basic framework for both royal biography and hagiography.

For example, Matthew of Vendôme's *Ars Versificatoria* (Paris, c.1175) used eleven elements for his ideal description, divided between external attributes, such as beauty *(superficialis)* and internal attributes *(intrinseca)*, either of which might be devoted to praise or vituperation.[196] These included 1. a subject's name; 2. nature (a. body, b. spirit, c. others, including 1. nation, 2. *patria*, 3. age, 4. family, 5. sex); 3. social relations; 4. fortune; 5. deportment; 6. zeal; 7. disposition; 8. counsel; 9. calamity *(casus)*; 10. deeds; and 11. speech. Matthew and other French poetry masters helped influence the new classicism of trecento Italy.[197] Whatever the specific elements, and whatever their order, the epideictic form followed Cicero's and Quintilian's advice that such narration should address a subject's *vita, gesta* and *mores*. The writer can amplify certain aspects, such as virtues and unique achievements, but the essential requirement is to demonstrate how the person's external attributes (birth, family, fortune, etc.) formed and reflected their character, their internal and external virtues and their life and deeds.[198] These rules were applied, for example, in the *Encomium Emmae Reginae* written 1041/42 by an anonymous monk of Saint-Bertin in Saint-Omer in Flanders.

Like the *Encomium*, Boccaccio's biography offers an example of a laudatory or panegyric biography of a queen beset by scandal, constructing a narrative of legitimacy and continuity, drawing on both contemporary events and classical forms. Boccaccio wrote on a difficult subject for a skeptical audience.[199] He therefore skewed the standard ten-part form of epideictic biography, omitting his subject's vices, also drawing on the judicial form of rhetoric, where accusation and defense are central.[200] Like Emma's *Encomium*, Boccaccio's *Vita* focuses on moral character, enumerating the four virtues that constitute inner character *(mores)* and enumerating the external deeds *(res gestae)* that reflect these virtues. Table 4.1 compares the lists from Priscian and Matthew with Boccaccio's *Vita* of Giovanna in Virginia Brown's edition[201] and helps clarify the epideictic form.

As one can see, the epideictic mode need not follow a rigid order, nor include every element. Boccaccio wrote his *Vita* while Giovanna was at her prime, and therefore Priscian's final three items (8–10: the length of her life, her death and her subsequent fame) were elided in Boccaccio's

CHAPTER 4 ⚜ NARRATIVE COMMUNITIES & STRATEGIES

Table 4.1 Epideictic Form in Boccaccio's Vita of Giovanna I

Boccaccio's Vita	Brown, Famous Women (466–72)	Priscian (Murphy, 41)	Matthew of Vendôme (Murphy, 165)
Giovanna's name	466.1		1
Family	466.2–468.4	7.a	2.c.4
Youth & nurture	468.5	2	2.c.3
Nation	468.6	7.c	2.c.1
Riches of realm	468.7	7.b	2.c.2
Spirit & character	470.8	4	2.b.6
External deeds	470.9	6	10
Inner character	470.10	4.b	2.b
Misfortunes	470.11	4.d	9
Appearance	472.12	5.a	2.a
Speech	472.12		11
Deportment	472.12	5b	5
Disposition	472.12	4.b	7
Social relations	472.12		3
Wisdom	472.13	4.c	8
Fame	472.14	8–10	1

last paragraph under her continued fame. Boccaccio also borrowed several elements from the literature of falsely accused queens to make not-so-oblique references to Giovanna's unjust fall, her resilience and her eventual triumph.[202]

Boccaccio used the epideictic form to opposite affect in his *De casibus virorum illustrium*[203] for his life of Giovanna's chief counselor, Filippa of Catania. Here all the elements are reversed: Boccaccio's exordium is one of apology and excuse for including her life.[204] Filippa's birth and youth are lowly and impoverished. She attracts the attention of the Angevin court as a wet-nurse. Her husband, Raymond de'Cabanni — an Ethiopian slave portrayed in one manuscript as physically unattractive[205] — was taken on as a cook, rose through royal service until he, as royal seneschal, and Filippa reached the height of power and influence. Boccaccio uses his narrative to demonstrate how Filippa's and Raymond's inner characters matched their births and external circumstances: intelligent and able but ultimately opportunistic and unscrupulous in their deeds, bringing scandal to the court and realm. While the earlier version of *De casibus* held Giovanna herself guilty, in Boccaccio's final redaction, as we will see below in Chapter 7,[206] Filippa ultimately was held responsible for Prince Andrew's murder and Giovanna's dishonor, bringing calamity to the Angevin dynasty and the realm. Boccaccio carries his biography of Filippa to her grisly execution and death, her subsequent *infamia* and, as Priscian advises, to European-wide events after her end. Here the epideictic form provides moral example of vice rather than virtue, of vituperation rather than praise.

Matteo Palmieri states[207] that his biography of Acciaiuoli will treat "virtues and deeds" in order to commit them to memory and long-lasting glory *(diuturnam gloriam)*. The glory of Acciaiuoli's "life and character" conforms to the epideictic structure. Palmieri treats Acciaiuoli's parentage and birth, his country, city and relations, elements of his fortune, his prudence and other virtues.[208] Matteo then turns to the calamities that beset both Acciaiuoli and the Regno: King Robert's death, Andrew of Hungary's assassination and Lewis of Hungary's invasion.[209] Interwoven into these events is Palmieri's chief interest, a lengthy examination of Acciaiuoli's memorable deeds in response to this crisis: arranging Louis of Taranto's marriage to Queen Giovanna I, attempting to defend Naples, fleeing to Tuscany with Louis and eventually overcoming obstacles to return Louis and Giovanna to their thrones, reconquering the Regno and pressing Angevin claims to Sicily.[210] After discussing these deeds, Palmieri returns to Niccolò's personal traits, including his stature, personal appearance, speech, virtues, manner of dress, deportment and disposition, his piety and pious works.[211] He then proceeds in proper course to Acciaiuoli's longevity, the circumstances and manner of this death and his legacy.[212] Palmieri used all elements of the epideictic form but re-arranged them to suit the rhythm and flow of his dramatic narrative and to amplify episodes with dialogue and further description of events and personalities.

The epideictic form could address cities as well as individuals. As the *Cronaca di Partenope*'s brief prologue states:

> The present chronicle brings together everything about the city of Naples, which has acquired the greatest fame among all other cities of the world for the multitude of its knights and for their delightful and magnificent riches, things that are all narrated in diverse volumes.[213]

In this it followed the lead of both Villani's *Cronaca* and of Naples' Virgilian traditions to develop an epideictic combination of *laus urbis* — or a description of walls, gates, monuments, ruins and other physical features and remains — and *laus civitatis* — or a description of a city's urban life and institutions[214] — outlining the great marvels of the city and singularly praising its sacred and secular foundations and its resulting institutions, leading to its present greatness. Rome's conquest of the city is related alongside the triumphs of Christian saints and martyrs, Virgilian legend and the stormy history of the Hohenstaufen, all given equal weight, if not space, with the Normans and Angevins.

CHAPTER 4 ⚜ NARRATIVE COMMUNITIES & STRATEGIES

JUDICIAL OR FORENSIC

The second major narrative form is the judicial or forensic, derived for the most part from ancient courtroom rhetoric, by which the orator attempts to convince a judge of the speaker's case in defense or in condemnation of an individual or an action. This was the major focus of Cicero's *De Inventione,* for example.[215] In the Middle Ages this became the narrative mode of histories that dealt with a theme of particular controversy or historical notoriety, to either justify or to condemn an individual or a regime, not by praising or blaming an individual life as in the epideictic mode but by mustering plausible, verifiable and trustworthy evidence that would win the reader's faith through carefully arranged argument. The judicial form could be combined with the epideictic when defending a controversial ruler, as the anonymous monk of Saint-Bertin did for the Norman queen of Anglo-Saxon England in his *Encomium Emmae Reginae* (c.1042).[216]

Several southern historians also employed the judicial mode to frame their narratives of the Angevins. The *Diurnale (Diario)* of the Duca di Monteleone moves in its separate parts from a strong advocacy of the Angevins in the entries covering the 1260s through the 1360s, to a second voice, perhaps of a notary and official, in the sections written from 1371 to the ascension of the Aragonese in 1442. In both, evidence is marshaled to support different dynastic claims.[217]

The judicial mode could also be used to devastating effect in condemning an individual ruler. Domenico da Gravina's *Chronicon de rebus in Apulia gestis* is a dramatically focused, often highly embellished indictment of what Gravina portrays as the damage to the Regno caused by the succession of Giovanna I. Within this structure, Gravina deploys a series of synecdoche to create a history of moral decadence and political critique.[218] His dramatic scenes of dynastic infighting, including the murder of a prince, the false accusations of infidelity against a dowager princess and the perils faced by Gravina's own infants are less exempla than stand-ins for the brutality, treachery and devastation that have spread across the kingdom. True to the judicial mode of his writing, these episodes appear less as documentary evidence than as witnesses to the truth of his account, thus allowing him to both embellish with direct apostrophe and to borrow from literary genres to amplify the accusatory thrust of his narrative.

Petrarch's choice of the persuasive, oratorical letter and tragic eclogue forms fit the judicial mode of his interpretation of Neapolitan affairs well, in true classical fashion matching his content to his form as he made his case for the decline and fall of the Angevins under Giovanna I. Boccaccio's *Eclogues* followed Petrarch's example.[219] One could also include the overall structure of Boccaccio's *De casibus virorum illustrium* in this category, since Boccaccio composed it as a procession of witnesses appearing before the writer in a series of visions. The individual chapters either recount individual lives of virtue followed by vice and fall or — like the arguments among Tiberius, Caligula and Messalina in Book VI — are themselves lively, and consciously rhetorical, courtroom debates among those condemned before the court of history and the attacks of *fortuna*.

The judicial form also lent itself well to the apocalyptic thought of Angelo Clareno, whose *Historia septem tribulationum* is essentially a court brief on the terrible mistreatment and injustices committed against the Spiritual wing of the Franciscan Order. Clareno's symbolic structure, like Boccaccio's in *De casibus*, lends itself well to this forensic mode as victim after victim, witness after witness comes forward with narrative and direct dialogue to testify to the faithfulness of the Spirituals and to their persecutors' evil intent. Clareno awaits God's final verdict on the course of the Franciscan Order and the Church as the Last Judgment looms. Clareno's apocalyptic image of Christ's final judgment is one of the most vivid and alarming examples of the forensic style in medieval historiography.[220]

Deliberative

The third major form of historical writing is the deliberative, derived from the ancient rhetorical skill of speaking for or against a matter of civic importance: of *civilia negotia* and *civiles questiones*. Cicero's *De Inventione* had again enshrined this form into civil discourse as the best means of serving public utility.[221] By the high Middle Ages, this *utilitas* involved the four major virtues. Historical deeds and character offered exempla of these virtues. Since one of the keys to deliberative discourse was moral and political counsel, this form was particularly appropriate to communal histories, which often depended on foundation myths, narratives of political legitimization and critique in their attempts to justify the rise and prominence of their civil governments and societies. For this reason, the majority of the Italian urban histories discussed here fall into this category, each with elements of the other forms, but all informed by a deep affinity to communal life and thought.

Yet this could also be the mode used by northern ecclesiastical and monarchical narrators. Thomas Walsingham's *Chronicle*, for example, constructs a carefully balanced series of episodes centered around major persons and events to make some order of the confusion of the historical process and to inform both his monastic and his lay audience on matters necessary for proper governance. Johanns von Winterthur sets out to accomplish the same faithful and useful recording for his readers, concentrating on the history of the popes and emperors. Johanns is clear that he seeks to pursue no one point of view and invites his readers to excuse any inaccuracies or inadequacies of his account.[222] In similar manner, Froissart writes a deliberative, even-handed history of the feats of both the English

CHAPTER 4 ▰ NARRATIVE COMMUNITIES & STRATEGIES

and the French so "that all those, men and women, who read it, see it, or hear it read, may take enjoyment and pleasure in it, and that I may prove worthy of their esteem."[223]

The deliberative mode is the norm among both Italian clerical and communal historians. The *Chronicon Suessanum* focuses on the political and military events of the Regno that effect the diocese of Sessa Aurunca. Buccio di Ranallo sought to highlight the impact of good and bad character on civil society and to provide example and admonishment to fellow citizens through a linear narration of events in the Abruzzi. Angelo Crassullo's annals show an even hand in chronicling the events that affected Taranto during the reign of the later Angevins, while the *Chronicon siculum* focuses on the fate of Naples as its people either witness or participate in the shifting political winds of the late trecento.

In northern Italy, urban chronicles reflect similar interest in providing their readers with a complete record of events to inform and enable them to make proper civic choices as the events of the trecento swirled around them. The *Chronicon Estense* focuses overwhelmingly on political and secular personalities and events, both reproving the lives and crimes of evil men and commending the virtues and laudable deeds of the good in order to instruct citizens on what they should elect or avoid and to follow Sallust's advice that they should choose concord and avoid discord.[224] So too Giovanni da Bazzano's *Chronicon Mutinense* examines political events of interest and utility to his fellow citizens. Agnolo di Tura's *Chronicon Senese* keeps the emphasis firmly on civic history and the factional struggle between the Guelphs and Ghibellines, Blacks and Whites.

Giovanni Villani makes it clear in his prologue that he has written his history of Florence

> to give occasion to our successors not to be negligent in preserving records of the notable things which shall happen in the times after us, and to give example to those who shall come after, of changes, and things come to pass, and their reasons and causes; to the end that they may exercise themselves in practicing virtues, and shunning vices, and enduring adversities with a strong soul, to the good and stability of our republic.[225]

The Anonimo romano similarly set out to

> make a special book and narrative. This is a huge and noble task, and I am undertaking it for several reasons. First, the reader may find things written here which will recur in similar fashion in the future.... Second, the reader will find many noble and excellent examples here, which will help him to avoid dangers and emulate

virtue. Third, I am impressed by the magnificence of these events. My fourth reason is one which influenced Livy.... That is to say, my mind has been stirred to write about this material...and it will not rest until I record in writing the beautiful deeds and events which I have seen during my life. My fifth reason is also one which Livy mentions.... while I am enjoying this work I am remote, and I do not experience the wars and the hardships which overrun the country.[226]

The Anonimo sought to write a history that would contain wondrous and terrible events in order to provide his readers with examples of virtues and vices. His claims are directly in the deliberative rhetorical tradition of history writing aimed at civic life[227] or, as the Anonimo himself makes clear, "for the common utility and enjoyment." This form of deliberative rhetoric informed the Anonimo's work in matters beyond language choice, such as tone and emotional appeal, deployment of exempla and the use of history as political critique. In so doing, the Anonimo also provides us with a very modern sense of historiography: to turn memory and emotion into the distanced and objectified material of history, to create a reflective distance between the writer and reader and the events of the past, all set out in true deliberative form for the reader's moral and civic consideration.

CONCLUSIONS

In this chapter, we have examined the narrative forms deployed by trecento historians. This analysis has ranged from narrative communities to authorship, language choice and use, and audience. It has also attempted to lay out the diverse habitus of various ecclesiastical, aristocratic and civic narrative communities. After drawing some conclusions about the similarities of intent and reception among both Latin and vernacular works, it then discussed narrative structures and modes. Chief among our conclusions is to contest the long-standing dichotomies seen in medieval Italian historiography and to find instead the strong commonalities between lay and clerical works and between northern and southern authors and audiences. The uses that these works addressed were also common to the peninsula: civic pride and memory, social utility and individual virtue and vice. Narrative forms and modes addressed these in a variety of ways but consistently with the same audience and utility in mind. While key differences remain among the wide variety of these works, such differences have little to do with geographical determinants and more with the cultural milieu and skill of individual authors. Such considerations again tend to erase the time-worn distinctions between northern and southern historiography.

CHAPTER 4 🙞 NARRATIVE COMMUNITIES & STRATEGIES

NOTES

1. As, for example, the claims of Giovanni Sercambi of Lucca (1348–1424) taken at face value by Green (1972), 3–4.
2. Internullo (2016), 425–61, examines trecento Romans' construction of such "incredible genealogies."
3. *De Inventione* II.53.161; *Orator* LXXI.237. See Ainsworth (2003.2), 387–89.
4. Ainsworth (2003.2), 389–94; Kempshall, 350–427.
5. Kempshall, 364–76.
6. Kempshall, 378–405.
7. For example, Stein (2005), 74–76; Otter (2005), 115–16. On the place of historiography in both classical grammar and rhetoric, Ray (1985), 68–76. On the impact of language choice and social group on narrative, Brandt, esp. 93–95. Stock (1990), 138, remarks that by the fourteenth century medieval readers and writers had few illusions about the factual truthfulness of their texts.
8. Kelly (2011), 75–78.
9. See Barbato (2017), 112–14.
10. Medieval and early-modern rhetoric has been one of the most intensely studied fields of research over the past generation. See Murphy (1974); Murphy (1978); Breisach; Copeland (1991); Morse (1991); Witt (2001); Gersh-Roest (2003); Black (2007); Copeland-Sluiter (2009) for selected texts; Stodola (2010), 42–81; Kempshall.
11. Murphy (1974), 194–268; Witt (2012), 414–18; Internullo (2016), 383–425.
12. Murphy (1974), 269–355; Longère (1983).
13. Witt (2012), 252–59, 418–24.
14. Witt (2012), 59–70.
15. Witt (2012), 93–100.
16. Witt (2012), 291–313; Murphy (1974), 97–114.
17. For the links between medieval rhetorical theory and the modern linguistic turn, Partner (1985), 22–44; Kempshall, 1–3, 31–33, 336–51, 548–51.
18. Murphy (1974), 135–93; Grendler (1989), 162–66; Gehl (1993), 5–19; Grendler (2002), 199–204; Black (2007), 34–63, 82–123, 331–65; Witt (2012); Kempshall, 121–33; Internullo (2016), 46–48, 76–99.
19. Gehl (1993), 43–81; Witt (2012), 259–90, 351–71, 383–97, 411–14.
20. Gehl (1993), 4. See also Grendler (1989), 3–6, 11–22.
21. Gehl (1993), 102–6 et passim; Murphy (1974), 22–88, 130–32.
22. Chapter 3, pp. 44–49.
23. On the history of the animal fable as a genre, Oldoni (1992); Mann (1993).
24. Murphy (1974), 135–93. Grendler (1989), 111–17 notes that the trecento curriculum remained conservative.
25. Murphy (1974), 19–21, 182–93, 365–74; Partner (1985), 11–12; Kempshall, 1–33, 121–264; Internullo (2016), 406–11.
26. Gehl (1993), 143–51; Black (2007), 275–330; Internullo (2016), 383–406. See also Chapter 6, pp. 165–78.
27. Gehl (1993), 74–84, 107–34. Kempshall, 69–70, 75, traces the practice to Orosius.
28. Gehl (1993), 82–106, 120–34, 145–47, 178–79; Murphy (1974), 80–84, 138–39; Partner (1985), 17, 48–49. Grendler (1989), 319 makes the point that such skills were largely the result of rote learning aided by memorization techniques and modes.
29. Gehl (1993), 102–6, 178–201.
30. Witt (2012), 371–82; Kempshall, 25–27.

31. Kempshall, 6.
32. Ward (1985). For a skeptical view of the rhetorical skill of most medieval historiography before the trecento, Partner (1985), 12–13, who advises that it is not enough to demonstrate a knowledge of grammatical and rhetorical forms. We must be able to establish that these medieval historians saw the connections between their learning and their writing. For the affirmative argument, see Kempshall, passim; Internullo (2016), 383–425.
33. Kempshall, 295–99, 315–30.
34. *Chronicon Suessanum.*
35. Clareno (2005), x–xvii.
36. Murphy (1974), 43–61; Kempshall, 91–120.
37. Chapter 3, pp. 44–45.
38. Kempshall, 295–99.
39. [C]um rerum gestarum in preteritis temporibus et retroactis certa congnicio et fidelis conscripcio posteris per continuas successiones sibi succedentibus non paucam, immo multam conferat utilitatem, idcirco… decrevi non immerito, rudi tamen et incocto sermone, cum faleratis et pompaticis verbis loquendi periciam et eloquenciam non habeam (Winterthur, 1).
40. Walsingham (2003), 1:xlii–xlv.
41. Gehl (1993), 202–32; Witt (2012), 351–410.
42. Gehl (1993), 107–34; Murphy (1974), 41–42; Holstein (2006), 133–67; Witt (2012), 383–97, 438–71; Kempshall, 229–64.
43. This topic has been intensely studied over the past fifty years. For example, Ong (1959); Klapisch-Zuber (1984); Green (2007); Black (2008).
44. Grendler (1989), 23–29.
45. *Chronicon Estense*, 1–2:3: Horum que ab initio mundi facta sunt usque nunc, notitiam minime haberemus, nisi proborum virorum diligentia Ystoria descripsisset, in quibus vita et scelera malorum hominum arguuntur, virtutes vero bonorum et opera laudabilia commendantur. Istoriogroforum itaque vestigia pro nostro modullo imitantes, quedam que nostris temporibus facta sunt in partibus Marchie vel Longbardie seu extra fines Ytalie, in prexenti opusculo decrevimus sub compendio declarare; ut posteri hec legentes, preteritorum memoria instruantur, quid circa presentia vel futura eligere debeant vel vitare. Set cum sit omnibus manifestum, quod "concordia parve res crescunt, discordia vero maxime dilabuntur" [Sallust, *Jugurthine War* X], patet igitur, quod concordia est totis viribus eligenda, discordia omnibus est evitanda (Kempshall, 37–47, 298–99).
46. Senatore (2017), 290–91.
47. Chapter 3, p. 45.
48. Zabbia (2001).
49. A good example is the theatrical presentation of characters, dialogue and action during Andrew's murder: A. 1347, *Chronicon Mutinense*, 143, ll. 5–25.
50. Pp. 53–55, 66–69.
51. Gehl (1993), 88–94. See Holstein (2006), 116–21, for Roman authors.
52. Witt (2012), 359–62.
53. Gravina (1903), xvi–xix, 3; Gravina (2022), II. L'opera.
54. Zabbia (1997), 19, 30, notes Gravina's lack of a preface but adds that the historian does comment on the aims of his writing, attempting to use textuality to distance himself from the events he has witnessed. Gravina (1903), 20, ll. 12–15; Gravina (2022), IX.10: Divertens igitur cor meum ad sequendam materiam incepti dictamminis, sicut audivi, seriosus quam potero, quae sequuta sunt ponam in

scriptis. Et licet longum sit omnia ponere seriatim, tamen ad intellectum omnium declarandum ipsius causae misterium sequar sub brevitate sermonum de materia modicum quasi nichil obmittens.

55. Both Gravina (1903) and Gravina (2022) draw numerous parallels but no direct citations to other contemporary sources like Villani, the *Chronicon Suessanum*, *Chronicon Estense* and Palmieri. Scattered citations from the Gospels or Psalms are used for dramatic emphasis or moral commentary, e.g.: Ps. 144:14, 146:3: Gravina (1903), 20, ll. 8–9; Gravina (2022), IX.9; John 12:25: Gravina (1903), 84, ll. 9–10; Gravina (2022), XXXI.87; Ps. 68:24: Gravina (1903), 91, l. 1; Gravina (2022), XXXV.6; Mt. 27:25: Gravina (1903), 95, ll. 39–42; Gravina (2022), XXXIX.38; Rom. 14:14, Phil. 2:24: Gravina (1903), 123, ll. 7–11; Gravina (2022), XLIX.11.

56. Delle Donne (2001a), 138–46.

57. For a good introduction to Petrarch's Latinity, Kirkham (2009a), 5–16.

58. Zak (2015), 143–53.

59. Marchesi (2009); Grendler (1989), 217–22.

60. Looney (2009); Celenza (2017), 53–57.

61. Kirkham (2009b).

62. Cherchi (2009).

63. Cherchi (2009), 160–61.

64. Zak (2015), 146–53.

65. Kempshall, 52–81, 91–120. See Partner (1985), 48–54; Ray (1985) for skepticism both within and toward the classical rhetorical tradition.

66. Solomon (2013).

67. Smarr (2013), 11–17; Kirkham (2013), 53–76; Lummus (2013), 155–69.

68. Houston (2013).

69. Houston (2013), 72.

70. Lummus (2013), 156–57. On Boccaccio's diversity of voice and style, Daniels (2015).

71. Boccaccio (2003), xix–xx; Guido Guarino, "Introduction," Boccaccio (2011), xvi–xvii, xxiii, xxix–xxx; Boccaccio (2018), xix–xxii, 152–56 et passim.

72. Palmieri (1934), 3, l. 1.

73. XII.94, Villani (1991), 3:198: "Trovamo che' fanciulli e fanciulle che stavano a leggere del continuo da 8,000 in 10,000. I garzoni che stavano ad aprendere l'abbaco e algorisimo in sei scuole da 1,000 in 1,200. E quelli che stavano ad aprendere gramatica e loica in quatro grandi scuole da 550 in 600." Grendler (1989), 71–74, argues that Villani's figures could not have been accurate.

74. Zabbia (2017), 274–76, stresses the great mobility of trecento notaries between northern, central and southern Italy.

75. Grendler (1989), 71, notes that this lack of comparative data may be due either to lack of evidence or study. For "merchant textuality," Robins (2004); Branca (2015).

76. For Roman examples, see Holstein (2006), 61–167.

77. Witt (2012), 444–57.

78. Grendler (1989), 306–29.

79. Gehl (1993), 20–27; Grendler (1989), 278–305.

80. Black (2007), 98–123, 225–73. This view has been modified by Rizzi (2017).

81. For an introduction, Dardano (2012).

82. "Part II, Petrarch's Works: Italian," in Ascoli–Falkeid (2015), 39–86, especially Barański (2015); and in Kirkham (2009), including Kirkham (2009a), 1–5; Barolini (2009); Finotti (2009); Steinberg (2009).

83. Ascoli–Falkeid (2015), 37–38.
84. For Boccaccio's use of the Tuscan vernacular, Bruni (2003); Manni (2003); Smarr (2013); Martinez (2013); Wallace (2013); Weaver (2013); Sherberg (2013).
85. Clarke (2007), 116–17.
86. X.136, Villani (1991), 2:336–37. "Questi fue grande letterato quasi in ogni scienza, tutto fosse laico; fue sommo poeta e filosafo, e rettorico perfetto tanto in dittare, versificare, come in aringa parlare, nobilissimo dicitore, in rima sommo, col più pulito e bello stile che mai fosse in nostra lingua infino al suo tempo e più innanzi.... E fece la Commedia ove in pulita rima, e con grandi e sottili questioni morali, naturali, strolaghe, filosofiche, e teologhe, con belle e nuove figure, comparazioni, e poetrie; compuose e trattò in cento capitoli, overo canti, dell'essere e istato dello ninferno, purgatorio, e paradiso così altamente come dire se ne possa sì come per lo detto trattato si può vedere e intendere, chi è di sottile intelletto." See also Imbriani (1891), 25–34.
87. Clarke (2007), 123.
88. *Cronaca Senese*, 387.
89. *Diurnali*, ix–xv.
90. Buccio (1907), xxix–xlvii; Mutini (1972).
91. See also Green's characterization of Giovanni Sercambi "naiveté" discussed above, Preface, pp. 3–4.
92. Pp. xxxiii–xxxvii.
93. "La sua è esposizione pura e semplice della verità, spoglia da qualsiasi elemento avventizio," Buccio (1907), xlv.
94. Discussed by Liutprand of Cremona, for example, Kempshall, 193–94. For their use in trecento Rome, Internullo (2016), 260–63.
95. On medieval verse historiography modeled on the works of Virgil, Lucan or Statius, and the rhetorical mode of amplification for dramatic effect, see Kempshall, 129–30, 361–65.
96. Buccio (1907), xxxvii–xlv.
97. On the middle style in Latin historiography, Kempshall, 199, 294–95.
98. Dunqua per commune utilitate e diletto fo questa opera vulgare, benché io l'aia ià fatta per lettera con uno latino moito. Ma l'opera non ène tanto ordinata né tanto copiosa como questa. Anche questa opera destinguo per capitoli, perché volenno trovare cobelle, senza affanno se pozza trovare. Prologue, I.94–101, AR, 6. Seibt, 29–30. For a translation, see Wright, 23; Palmer (2021), 61. I take the form *"moito"* not as *"molto"* but as defining *"latino,"* meaning "moiety," "mixed," or "medium," which seems to be the only syntactical solution to this construction and makes contextual sense here: a style adopted for both "utility and enjoyment."
99. Internullo (2016), 310–11, and Palmer (2021), 3, posit a Latin original. Formentin (2012.1), 36–44, called for a new edition to examine these issues more fully. See also Coluccia (2017), 118–22. D'Achille (2017), 349–50, suggests that the Anonimo's Latin fragments were not survivals of an original, but insertions from inscriptions or other sources. For manuscript tradition, see now Vaccaro (2021).
100. Internullo (2016), 92–95, 189–90, 314–15, 320–29, 376–82 et passim; D'Achille (2017), 349–50.
101. Monaci (1920).
102. For the text, Monaci (1915).
103. For studies of Romanesco as it emerged in the duecento, Macciocca (1982); Formentin (2008); Formentin (2012.1); Formentin (2012.2); Loporcaro (2012); Formentin (2013); Gualdo (2017), 193–9. Formentin (2008) cautions that one

must examine the archival record for the larger context of trecento Romanesco but that even the notarial protocols are not transparent evidence but highly coded transmitters of orality into formal, judicial textuality.

104. Holstein (2006), 13–111. Gualdo (2017), 198, notes that this project ended with the return of the papacy in the late trecento.
105. Seibt, 37–99, esp. 45–53.
106. On the stylistics of Roman authors, including the use of the *cursus*, see Internullo (2016), 383–406.
107. De Caprio (2012), 19–21.
108. De Caprio (2012), 34–36.
109. De Caprio (2012), 40–48; and Eileen Gardiner's introduction and translation in Musto (2013), 224–27.
110. Kelly (2011), 52–53. De Caprio (2012), 8, notes that there is still no reliable corpus of edited Neapolitan vernacular texts from the trecento and quattrocento.
111. Sabatini (1996a), 485–86, coined the term *"napoletano civile."*
112. Kelly (2011), 52–53. See Kelly (2012) for the *Cronaca*'s impact on this vernacular tradition.
113. Kelly (2011), 3.
114. De Caprio (2012), 29–31.
115. De Caprio (2012), 42–43 n. 74; De Caprio (2014), 439–41, 447–48.
116. Kelly (2011), 8.
117. Ainsworth (2003.1), 268–71. On the use of poetry for historiography, see Kempshall, 356–69.
118. Prologue of MS Besançon 864, fol. 1r–2r, Froissart (2013).
119. Ainsworth (2003.1), 268–69.
120. Ainsworth (2013).
121. De Caprio (2012), 10.
122. For example, Barthes (1981), 1–20; Said (1983); White (1987b); Spiegel (1997); White (2010a). On the fictive nature of archival collections, how even archival recording of the simplest factual events are culturally constructed and received: Davis (1987), esp. 1–41; White (1987b); Strohm (1992), esp. the section, "Fictional Truth," 28–31. On resistance by established medievalists, Stock (1990), esp. 70–74. For a restatement of the positivist position, Logan (2005).
123. Barthes (1981), 7.
124. Murphy (1974), 13; Ainsworth (2003.2); Kempshall, 316–17, 337–38, 433–44.
125. White (1987c), 179–80.
126. Kempshall, 548–51 et passim.
127. Partner (1985), 22–54.
128. "Parataxis," at www.merriam-webster.com/dictionary/parataxis.
129. Kempshall, 441–46.
130. Partner (1985), esp. 17–19.
131. *Chronicon Estense*, 1–6.
132. *Chronicon Mutinense*, 1–61.
133. *Chronicon Mutinense*, 151.
134. *Chronicon Suessanum*, 51–53.
135. *Chronicon siculum*, 1–7.
136. *Chronicon siculum*, 7–11.
137. *Chronicon siculum*, 64.2

138. *Cronaca Senese*, 255–59.
139. Partner (1985), 17–18.
140. "Acta et gesta meorum temporum et paulo ante habita non semper secundum debitum ordinem, sed secundum quod michi occurrerunt, sumatim interdum et curtatim, quandoque singularis et diffusius annotare.... Novitatem et varietatem insuper historiarum scribendarum ab inicio usque ad finem in margine libri huius per paragrafum designabo." Winterthur, 1, ll. 1–22.
141. Winterthur, 13–15.
142. Winterthur, 18–20.
143. Winterthur, 21–33.
144. Chapter 3, p. 58.
145. "[1381] Exigit historiae confusum ordinem confusio rerum in locis plurimis perpetratarum, et vix, pro varietate locorum et diversitate facinorum, uno tempore commisorum, servari potest ordo scribendi. Ecce enim! dum magna et nimis magna facinora scribo...." Walsingham (1864), 2:1.
146. Sometimes added in a later hand. See, for example, Walsingham (2003), 1:962.
147. See Walsingham (2003), 1:lxxxvii.
148. Kempshall, 299–302.
149. *Institutio Oratoria*, II.13. Kempshall, 300–302.
150. Quintilian, *Institutio Oratoria*, XII.2. Kempshall, 301–5, 315–49, esp. 315–23.
151. Pp. xxv–xxviii.
152. Gravina (1903), 20, ll. 11–15; Gravina (2022), IX.10.
153. Folio 1 contains many lacunae. Gravina (1903), 3 n. 1; Gravina (2022), II. Il titolo.
154. Kempshall, 37–47, 130–33, 298–99.
155. For example, Sallust, Cataline; Lucan, Pharsalia.
156. On the medieval debate between chronology and narrative and how each enabled *historia* or *fabula*, Ainsworth (2003.2); Kempshall, 81–91.
157. See Zabbia (1997), 17–18.
158. Zabbia (1997), 22.
159. Murphy (1974), 194–268, esp. 195–97.
160. Murphy (1974), 111–12; Kempshall, 479–85.
161. *Familiares* V.1–6.
162. Chapter 8, p. 247.
163. Kempshall, 356–69, 432–41.
164. Kempshall, 138–71.
165. Pp. 250–51.
166. "Statui igitur de eius vita et moribus, quod in variis sparsum legeram locis, carptim colligere et uni volumini inserere." Palmieri (1934), 4.
167. These are original to Villani's structure, but book and chapter numbers were added by later editors, including Porta. See, for example, BAV, MS Pal. Lat. 939, fols. 1r–273v, later 14th–early 15th c. But BAV, MS Chigi L.VIII.296, a copiously illustrated manuscript from the mid- to later 14th c. (the "Cronaca figurata"), lacks these rubrics. On Villani's use, see Ragone, 135; Barbaro, 100.
168. Green (1972), 19.
169. Green (1972), 39.
170. Kelly (2011), 7, 125–32.
171. Kelly (2011), 103–25, 136–37, 153, 160–61.
172. Kelly (2011), *Cronaca*, 165.
173. Seibt, 37–49.

CHAPTER 4 ❧ NARRATIVE COMMUNITIES & STRATEGIES

174. Kempshall, 299–304.
175. Prologue, 99–101: "Anche questa opera destinguo per capitoli, perché volenno trovare cobelle, senza affanno se pozza trovare." AR, 6; Wright, 23, Palmer (2021), 61.
176. These are IV, XVII, XIX–XXII, XXIV–XXV, XXVIII. Seibt, 26–30, reviews the possibilities of loss, editing or incomplete original Italian or Latin text. Porta argues that the Anonimo's original contained these lacunae. See also Internullo (2016), 311–12.
177. Above, pp. 58–59.
178. There are many manuscripts of Froissart's *Chroniques*. Froissart (2013) will use 114 and currently offers complete codicological descriptions of 17 manuscripts, almost all from c.1400–c.1420 and therefore close chronologically to Froissart's original text. All contain rubricated chapter headings, and most a table of contents.
179. Lewin (2007). On mendicant historiography in general, Barone (2017).
180. Partner (1985), 19–21; Kempshall, 324–48, esp. 327–36.
181. Barone (2017), 305–8.
182. Kempshall, 52–120; Partner (1985), 19–22; Ray (1985), 68–76.
183. Ray (1985), 71.
184. Pp. 174–75.
185. Stock (1990), 24–29.
186. White (1987d), 78, on Vidal-Naquet's reflections on the Holocaust, with implications for Clareno's sense of the historical centrality of the "seven tribulations."
187. "…acta et gesta meorum temporum et paulo ante habita non semper secundum debitum ordinem, sed secundum quod michi occurrerunt, summatim interdum et curtatim, quandoque singularius et diffusius annotare." Winterthur, 1. On the *ordo rerum* and its connections with narrative *dispositio* and *utilitas*, see Kempshall, 53–54, 299–304.
188. White (2010b), 283–92.
189. Partner (1985), 44–54.
190. Kempshall, 34–120, 536–51.
191. Murphy (1974), 9–10; Kempshall, 133–264.
192. Murphy (1974), 41–42, 164–70; Kempshall, 138–71.
193. Grossvogel (2013); Kempshall, 337–39 et passim; Cherchi (2018); Mazzotta (2018).
194. Kempshall, 53–54, 299–305.
195. Murphy (1974), 41–42.
196. Murphy (1974), 164–68.
197. Witt (2012), 438–41.
198. Kempshall, 138–71.
199. Kempshall, 208–18.
200. Kempshall, 215–29.
201. Boccaccio (2003), 467–73.
202. Chapter 5, pp. 140–42.
203. IX.26, Boccaccio (1983.1), 856–65; Boccaccio (2018), 222–28.
204. IX.25, Boccaccio (1983.1), 852–55; Boccaccio (2018), 222–23.
205. Boccace, *Des cleres et nobles femmes*, dated 1488–1496. Paris, Bibliothèque nationale de France, MS Français 599, fol. 93v. Online at http://gallica.bnf.fr/ark:/12148/btv1b10515437z/f190.item.r=Français%20599.
206. Pp. 208–11. See Casteen (2018), 234 and nn., for a summary of the scholarship.
207. Palmieri (1934), 3.X–4.X.
208. Palmieri (1934), 5.3–7.27.

209. Palmieri (1934), 7.28–10.17.
210. Palmieri (1934), 10.18–26.28.
211. Palmieri (1934), 27.16–29.26.
212. Palmieri (1934), 29.29–31.15.
213. Kelly (2011), 165.
214. These can be referred to as *encomium urbis, laudes urbium, encomium civis, laus civis* or *laudes civitatum*. Hyde (1966). For a useful distinction and a good summary of the *laus* tradition, see Benson (2009), 153–54.
215. Murphy (1974), 9–10, 14–15; Kempshall, 171–229.
216. Kempshall, 207–15.
217. Chapter 2, pp. 21–22.
218. Kempshall, 171–229, 254–64.
219. Chapter 8, pp. 250–51.
220. Book 8, Tribulation 7, 309–10; Clareno (2005), 219–20.
221. Kempshall, 229–64.
222. Winterthur, 1.
223. Besançon MS 864, fol. 1v, Froissart (2013).
224. *Chronicon Estense*, 1.
225. I.1, Villani (1906), 1–2; Porta (1991), 3–4.
226. Prologue. 38–81, AR, 4–5; Wright, 21–22; Palmer (2021), 60–61.
227. Holstein (2006), 147–48; Kempshall, 229–64.

WORKS CITED

Barański, Zygmunt G. 2015. "The *Triumphi*." In Ascoli–Falkeid, 74–84.

Barolini, Teodolinda. 2009. "The Self in the Labyrinth of Time *(Rerum vulgarium fragmenta)*." In Kirkham (2009), 33–62.

Barone, Giulia. 2017. "Ordini mendicanti e cronache volgari." In Francesconi–Miglio, 301–11.

Barthes, Roland. 1981. "The Discourse of History." Stephen Bann, trans. and intro. In *Comparative Criticism: A Yearbook*. E.S. Schaffer, ed. Cambridge: Cambridge University Press, 3–20.

Benson, C. David. 2009. "The Dead and the Living: Some Medieval Descriptions of the Ruins and Relics of Rome Known to the English." In *Urban Space in the Middle Ages and the Early Modern Age*. Albrecht Classen, ed. Berlin: De Gruyter, 147–82.

Black, Robert. 2007. *Humanism and Education in Medieval and Renaissance Italy: Tradition and Innovation in Latin Schools from the Twelfth to the Fifteenth Century.* Cambridge: Cambridge University Press.

—. 2008. "Literacy in Florence, 1427." In *Florence and Beyond: Culture, Society and Politics in Renaissance Italy. Essays in Honour of John M. Najemy.* Daniel E. Bornstein and David Spencer Peterson, ed. Toronto: Centre for Reformation and Renaissance Studies, 195–212.

Branca, Vittore, ed. 2015. *Merchant Writers: Florentine Memoirs from the Middle Ages and Renaissance.* Murtha Baca, trans. Cesare de Michelis, ed. Toronto: University of Toronto Press.

Bruni, Francesco. 2003. *Boccaccio: L'invenzione della letteratura mezzana.* Bologna: Il Mulino.

Cherchi, Paolo. 2009. "The Unforgettable Books of Things to Be

Remembered *(Rerum memorandum libri)*." In Kirkham (2009), 151–62.
—. 2018. "The Inventors of Things in Boccaccio's *De genealogia deorum gentilium.*" In Candido (2018), 244–69.
Copeland, Rita. 1991. *Rhetoric, Hermeneutics, and Translation in the Middle Ages: Academic Traditions and Vernacular Texts.* Cambridge: Cambridge University Press.
—. 2009. With I. Sluiter. *Medieval Grammar and Rhetoric: Language Arts and Literary Theory, AD 300–1475.* Oxford: Oxford University Press.
D'Achille, Paolo. 2017. "Cronache, scritture esposte, testi semicolti." In Francesconi-Miglio, 347–72.
Daniels, Rhiannon. 2015. "Boccaccio's Narrators and Audiences." In Armstrong (2015), 36–51.
Dardano, Maurizio. 2012. *Sintassi dell'italiano antico: La prosa del Duecento e del Trecento.* Rome: Carocci.
Davis, Natalie Zemon. 1987. *Fiction in the Archives: Pardon Tales and Their Tellers in Sixteenth-Century France.* Cambridge: Polity.
Finotti, Fabio. 2009. "The Poem of Memory *(Triumphi).*" In Kirkham (2009), 63–83.
Formentin, Vittorio. 2008. "Frustoli di romanesco antico in lodi arbitrali dei secoli XIV e XV." *Lingua e Stile* 43:21–99.
—. 2013. "A proposito di romanesco antico: La metafonia nel registro di Giovanni Cenci?" *Lingua e Stile* 48:299–315.
Gersh, Stephen. 2003. With Bert Roest. *Medieval and Renaissance Humanism: Rhetoric, Representation and Reform.* Leiden: Brill.
Green, Dennis H. 2007. *Women Readers in the Middle Ages.* Cambridge: Cambridge University Press.
Grossvogel, Steven M. 2013. "A Fable of the World's Creation and Phaeton's Fall *(Allegoria mitologica).*" In Kirkham (2013), 63–68.
Houston, Jason. 2013. "A Portrait of a Young Humanist *(Epistolae* 1–4)." In Kirkham (2013), 69–74.
Hyde, John Kenneth 1966. "Medieval Descriptions of Cities." *Bulletin of the John Rylands Library* 48:308–40.
Imbriani, Vittorio. 1891. *Studi danteschi.* Florence: Sansoni.
Kelly, Samantha. 2012. "Medieval Influence in Early Modern Neapolitan Historiography: The Fortunes of the *Cronaca di Partenope,* 1350–1680." *California Italian Studies* 3.1. At www.escholarship.org/uc/item/2sg144x3.
Kirkham, Victoria. 2009a. "A Life's Work." In Kirkham (2009), 1–30.
—. 2009b. "Petrarch the Courtier: Five Public Speeches." In Kirkham (2009), 141–50.
Klapisch-Zuber, Christine. 1984. "Le chiavi fiorentine di barbablù: L'apprendimento della lettura a Firenze nel XV secolo." *Quaderni storici* n.s. 57:765–92.
Lewin, Alison Williams. 2007. "Salimbene de Adam and the Franciscan Chronicle." In Dale (2007), 87–112.
Logan, F. Donald. 2005. *The Medieval Historian and the Quest for Certitude.* Toronto: Pontifical Institute of Mediaeval Studies.
Longère, Jean. 1983. *La prédication médiévale.* Paris: Etudes augustiniennes.

Looney, Dennis. 2009. "The Beginnings of Humanistic Oratory: Petrarch's Coronation Oration *(Collatio laureationis)*." In Kirkham (2009), 131–40.

Loporcaro, Michele. 2012. With Vincenzo Faraoni and Piero A. Di Pretoro. *Vicende storiche della lingua di Roma*. Alessandria: Edizioni dell'Orso.

Macciocca, Gabriella. 1982. "Fonetica e morfologia di *Le miracole de Roma*." *L'Italia Dialettale* 45:38–123.

Mann, Jill. 1993. "La favolistica." In Cavallo (1992–93), 2:171–95.

Manni, Paola. 2003. *Il Trecento toscano: La lingua di Dante, Petrarca e Boccaccio*. Bologna: Il Mulino.

Marchesi, Simone. 2009. "Petrarch's Philological Epic *(Africa)*." In Kirkham (2009), 113–30.

Martinez, Ronald L. 2013. "Also Known as 'Prencipe Galeotto' *(Decameron)*." In Kirkham (2013), 23–39.

Monaci, Ernesto. 1915. *Le miracole de Roma: Versione dei* Mirabilia Romae *in volgare romanesco del dugento*. Rome: Reale Società Romana di Storia Patria.

—. 1920. Storie de Troja et de Roma: *Altrimenti dette* Liber ystoriarum Romanorum: *Testo romanesco del secolo XIII, preceduto da un testo latino da cui deriva*. Roma: Società alla Biblioteca Vallicelliana.

Morse, Ruth. 1991. *Truth and Convention in the Middle Ages: Rhetoric, Representation, and Reality*. Cambridge: Cambridge University Press.

Murphy, James Jerome. 1978. *Medieval Eloquence: Studies in the Theory and Practice of Medieval Rhetoric*. Berkeley: University of California Press.

Mutini, Claudio. 1972. "Buccio di Ranallo." DBI 14. At www.treccani.it/enciclopedia/buccio-di-ranallo_(Dizionario-Biografico).

Oldoni, Massino. 1992. "La tradizione orale e folclorica." In Cavallo (1992–93), 1:633–55.

Ong, Walter J. 1959. "Latin Language Study as a Renaissance Puberty Rite." *Studies in Philology* 56.2:103–24.

Ray, Roger. 1985. "Rhetorical Skepticism and Verisimilar Narrative in John of Salisbury's *Historia Pontificalis*." In Breisach, 61–102.

Robins, William. 2004. "Vernacular Textualities in Fourteenth-Century Florence." In *The Vulgar Tongue: Medieval and Postmedieval Vernacularity*. Fiona Somerset and Nicholas Watson, ed. University Park: Pennsylvania State University Press, 112–13.

Sabatini, Francesco. 1996a. "Volgare 'civile' e volgare cancelleresco nella Napoli angioina." In *Italia linguistica delle origini: Saggi editi dal 1956 al 1996*. In idem and Vittorio Coletti, ed. Lecce: Argo, 467–506.

Said, Edward. 1983. *The World, the Text, and the Critic*. Cambridge, MA: Harvard University Press.

Sherberg, Michael. 2013. "The Girl Outside the Window *(Teseida delle nozze d'Emilia)*." In Kirkham (2013), 95–106.

Smarr, Janet Levarie. 2013. "Introduction: A Man of Many Turns." In Kirkham (2013), 1–20.

Solomon, Jon. 2013. "Gods, Greeks, and Poetry *(Genealogia deorum gentilium)*." In Kirkham (2013), 235–44.

Stein, Robert M. 2005. "Literary Criticism and the Evidence for History." In Partner (2005), 67–87.

CHAPTER 4 ⚜ NARRATIVE COMMUNITIES & STRATEGIES

Steinberg, Justin. 2009. "Petrarch's Damned Poetry and the Poetics of Exclusion *(Rime disperse)*." In Kirkham (2009), 85–100.

Stodola, Denise. 2010. "The Middle Ages." In *The Present State of Scholarship in the History of Rhetoric: A Twenty-First Century Guide*. Lynée Lewis Gaillet and Winifred Bryan Horner, ed. Columbia: University of Missouri Press, 42–81.

Vaccaro, Giulio. 2021. "Text and Transmission in Early Italian Chronicles." *Opera del Vocabolario Italiano*. Florence: CNR.

Wallace, David. 2013. "Love-Struck in Naples *(Filostrato)*." In Kirkham (2013), 77–85.

Ward, John O. 1985. "Some Principles of Rhetorical Historiography in the Twelfth Century." In Breisach, 103–65.

Weaver, Elissa. 2013. "A Lovers' Tale and Auspicious Beginning *(Filocolo)*." In Kirkham (2013), 87–93.

White, Hayden. 1987b. "The Question of Narrative in Contemporary Historical Theory." In White (1987), 26–57.

—. 1987c. "The Metaphysics of Narrativity: Time and Symbol in Ricoeur's Philosophy of History." In White (1987), 169–84.

—. 1987d. "The Politics of Historical Interpretation: Discipline and De-Sublimation." In White (1987), 58–82.

—. 2010a. "The Structure of Historical Narrative." In White (2010), 112–25.

—. 2010b. "Storytelling: Historical and Ideological." In White (2010), 273–92.

Witt, Ronald G. 2001. *Italian Humanism and Medieval Rhetoric*. Aldershot: Ashgate/Variorum.

Zak, Gur. 2015. "Petrarch and the Ancients." In Ascoli-Falkeid, 141–53.

5. THE IMPACT OF ROMANCE[1]

To write history is so difficult that most historians are forced to make concessions to the technique of legend.

— Erich Auerbach[2]

INTRODUCTION

The impact of literary form, language, trope, even character and plot on medieval historical narrative has long been recognized by modern scholars, who have also drawn our attention to the fact that medieval writers and readers were well aware of both direct borrowings and of the permeability of literary boundaries between history and literature.[3] In Chapter 4, we laid out the grammatical and rhetorical forms and genres that underlay and informed medieval historiography. In the Middle Ages, history — like poetry (or fiction) — was always considered part of rhetoric in the classic seven liberal arts.[4] Among these forms were the paratactic use of the "gap,"[5] closely akin to modern film theory and praxis, to help construct convincingly probable narrative and bolster historical truth claims.

Heeding Philippe Buc's admonition that we ought to focus on medieval chronicles and other sources less as transparent and naively written field notes and more like sophisticated literary constructions,[6] it is worthwhile examining the literary context of our sources to weigh whether their accounts may have owed something to the fictional works around them. Paul Strohm, on the other hand, advises against the assumption that "'historical' readings…consist of good literary detective work, leading to the identification of discrete events or occasions to which a work refers."[7] Instead, he stresses the "larger interpretive structures" within which such works are produced. "The historicity of these schemes lies in their origins, and…their transmission and the varied uses to which they are subject."[8] As Strohm notes:

> The paradox of the lie that might as well be true must interest anyone who seeks to understand texts in history or the historical influence of texts. For strictly speaking, most texts — and not just a few celebrated forgeries or esoteric examples — must be regarded as untrue. Were we to shun texts that rely on devices of narrative rearrangement, interested selection of detail, and spurious self-authorization, we would have to discard most of the

written record.... [Fictive texts] offer crucial testimony on other, though no less historical, matters: on contemporary perception, ideology, belief, and — above all — on the imaginative structures within which fourteenth-century participants acted and assumed that their actions would be understood.[9]

Thus literature, fable, myth, ritual and liturgical texts and practice very often did provide a wealth of supporting detail to lend weight and fulness to accounts for which documents alone could not serve to convey a truthful account.[10]

This constructed discourse and its fictionality were manifest on several levels. First, the truth claims of historical narrative were appreciated more on a rhetorical than on a modern evidentiary basis. On another level, medieval narratives themselves incorporated many literary forms and rhetorical devices wholesale. Unlike modern historians, who have almost unlimited access to archives, memoirs, diaries, oral histories, interviews, photos, film, radio and sound recordings in order to plumb and document the inner workings of their subjects' minds — seeking motivations, explanations, denials, excuses and apologia — medieval historians had few if any of these tools at hand.

In Chapter 3, we examined the types of evidence available to medieval authors to construct their narratives of events. But to describe individual motivation and character — *mores* rather than *res gestae* — they could at best rely on some rare personal knowledge, such as the Astrologer's acquaintance with Louis the Pious. But by and large the inner workings of their subjects' minds and the motivations for their actions were blank walls and blind windows. Medievals had therefore to rely upon a small repertoire of rhetorical devices, largely inherited from ancient sources, to attempt to convey their own sense of character, internal thought and motivation.[11] Perhaps the most familiar of these to modern readers is the inclusion of fictionalized speeches: Thucydides' account of Pericles' speech to the Athenians, for example.

But beyond these devices, medieval historians had little of what we today might call accurate data with which to reconstruct the lives of individuals. Medievals therefore turned to what was available to them: from the standardized tropes of royal biography — ranging from that of Charlemagne or Louis the Pious to St. Louis, for example — to the conventions of hagiography: the spiritual contests and inner conflicts of the men and women who suffered martyrdom or great physical and emotional turmoil in order to serve God. By the twelfth century, however, historians began to turn to an increasingly large and vibrant form of writing: the *chansons de geste* and literary romances being created especially in France.[12] Several cycles were available, including those of Charlemagne and Roland, William of Orange and the Arthurian cycle and its variants in Britain, France and the German lands. These offered contemporary, rich and complex portraits of human personality, of moral and spiritual change and growth, of motivation and emotion, of conflict, injustice, treachery, betrayal, depravity, loyalty, honor and moral courage. Many trecento historians therefore turned to such literary works for borrowings — plot structures, motifs, characters, tropes — to fill in the "gaps" where eyewitness or other evidence was lacking or as "metaphorical doublings"[13] of the facts presented in their narratives.

Allegorical, anagogic, topological and tropological forms of reading appropriated from biblical exegesis were also known to all clerical and educated lay writers and continued to be freely available for the construction of secular narratives. As we will discuss below in Chapter 6, historians could also use visual sources in ways that employed multivalent image, symbol, emblem and narrative that went beyond written text to produce powerful associative truth claims. Again, it was not so much the evidentiary basis of the truth that medieval authors often conveyed but the rhetorical truth, perhaps more accurately the human truth of a situation, action or motivation. While medieval readers and writers had no real concept of fiction in the modern sense of a distinct and sale-able product, as opposed to our non-fiction, they certainly understood the classic distinction between *historia* and *fabula* and even more important the fictionality of constructed narratives.[14] Both had different forms of truth value — just as today we recognize the varied claims to truth of our literary fictions and our non-fiction — but in the Middle Ages, the border between the forms and their claims to truth were far more permeable than we allow today.[15]

Focusing on *Manekine, Belle Hélène de Constantinople,* the *Roman du Contesse d'Anjou* and *Melusine,* this chapter will illustrate this permeability with some trecento examples of narratives of accused queens. Where the conventions of hagiography and royal biography failed to provide the necessary motivating factors for historical events, writers like the Villani, Gravina, Petrarch, Boccaccio or Froissart could draw upon a variety of current romance literature[16] in much the same way that they used the available Latin classics. This porosity allowed trecento historians to employ a vocabulary and grammar of available plot elements, characters, motifs and devices to provide the details of interior thought and motivation, to supply missing details of events and to draw out character beyond the available epideictic conventions. In so doing, these writers were able to deploy dramatizations of female inheritance and male privilege, internal dynastic conflict, female perversion or nobility that were readily recognizable to their audiences. Finally, we will return to Boccaccio's biography of Giovanna I from his *De mulieribus claris* to demonstrate how

CHAPTER 5 ❧ THE IMPACT OF ROMANCE

these strands can come together across the boundary of fictive and factual writing to plot the narrative points of medieval romance onto the actual events of a historical reign.

ACCUSED QUEENS

One of the chief themes in medieval historiography is that of the accused queen. False accusation and humiliation of powerful women were not simply the stuff of chroniclers in fourteenth-century Europe. The literature of the thirteenth to the fifteenth centuries abounded in what literary scholar Nancy Black has termed "medieval narratives of accused queens."[17] We will focus here on one example: that of the rumors around, slanders against and trials of Queen Giovanna I of Naples. Although we may not be able to solve the problem of whether the chroniclers consciously framed their narratives of Giovanna's fall and rise within the literary conventions of their day, we can at least lay out the elements of some of the more important examples from particular genres and note their similarities. We therefore seek less the "discrete elements" than Strohm's "larger interpretive structures" that set the tone for accounts of Queen Giovanna's personality and the events of her reign. First, however, we must briefly summarize those events.

THE REIGN OF GIOVANNA I OF NAPLES

Giovanna of Anjou was born in 1326,[18] the elder daughter of Charles, prince of Calabria, the heir of King Robert of Anjou (r.1309–43). On Charles' death in 1328, Giovanna succeeded her father as heir to King Robert of Naples. Raised by her grandmother, Queen Sancia of Majorca, and educated in both Sancia's strict Franciscan piety and in the customs of the court, Giovanna spent her younger years in the usual courtly pastimes as well as in performing continuous acts of charity and piety in the churches in and around Naples. Her beauty, grace and works of mercy earned her the love and respect of the people of Naples from an early age. Meanwhile King Robert of Anjou held lengthy negotiations with his brothers' families in the houses of Taranto and Durazzo to guarantee his granddaughter's inheritance. He also made sure that the rival claims of the Angevin house of Hungary, descended from his elder brother Charles Martel, were also settled. This process involved the betrothal of Giovanna first to Robert's grand-nephew Lewis, king of Hungary, and then when Lewis was engaged to Margaret of Luxembourg, to Lewis' younger brother Andrew. Just before his death on January 20, 1343, Robert summoned the members of his extended family and had them repeat their oaths of loyalty to Giovanna and to the terms of his will.[19]

Despite these careful arrangements and agreements, Giovanna's Angevin relations continued to maneuver to gain the throne. Her rivals included her two great-aunts. Catherine II de Courtenay (de Valois, 1303–46) was the daughter of Charles de Valois and Catherine I de Courtenay and hence the granddaughter of Baldwin II, last Latin emperor of Constantinople. Through him, she had inherited the title of empress of Constantinople. In 1313 she had married King Robert's brother, Prince Philip of Taranto.[20] On Philip's death in 1331, Catherine had already tried to annul Giovanna's future inheritance in favor of her sons, Robert, Louis or Philip II. Opposing Catherine was Giovanna's other great-aunt, Agnes Talleyrand de Perigord (1305–45), widow of King Robert's youngest brother, John of Gravina, and thus the head of the house of Durazzo.

Giovanna and Andrew were married in Naples on August 27, 1342, while Robert still lived. But with Andrew's brutal murder in the royal palace of Aversa on September 18, 1345, Giovanna's rivals — both in Naples and in Hungary — attempted to place the blame for the murder on her and her closest advisors, many of whom had been loyal officials of King Robert of Anjou. Giovanna's sudden widowhood soon led to an open conflict for her hand among her royal cousins in the houses of Taranto and Durazzo, and both houses put forward claims. We know that the attentions of Giovanna's cousins were taken seriously enough to merit warnings from Pope Clement VI in Avignon concerning the incestuous nature of any such unions. King Lewis and Queen Mother Elizabeth of Hungary meanwhile pressed their opposition to Giovanna's remarriage to any of the royal Neapolitan cousins. Using the standard Latin word *"copulari"* to sexualize Giovanna's proposed marriage alliance, they set out the basis for toppling the queen for moral reasons and called attention to the possibly incestuous, rather than dynastic, elements of a marriage between cousins. They underscored this with their claim that a union between Giovanna and one of her Neapolitan relatives would scandalize all of Christendom. Meanwhile Lewis of Hungary prepared to invade the kingdom of Naples both to avenge his brother Andrew's murder and to seize the throne for himself.

Pope Clement VI, the feudal suzerain of Naples, attempted to hold off Lewis' plans and sided with two of Giovanna's cousins in Naples — Charles of Durazzo and Robert of Taranto — to capture many of Giovanna's closest friends and advisors, including Roberto, Filippa and Sancia de'Cabanni, in 1346. These and several other court officials were humiliated, tortured, tried and then brutally executed before the crowds of Naples.[21] Stripped of any real power and isolated from her closest surviving friends and advisors — and leaving historians deprived from any accurate record of her personal life — Giovanna continued to press for her full rights to rule. Her cousins, meanwhile, continued to press for her hand in marriage.

In alliance with Louis of Taranto, Giovanna determined to resist Lewis of Hungary's invasion in 1347/48, but by January 1348, Taranto's

CHAPTER 5 ✳ THE IMPACT OF ROMANCE

forces had been outmaneuvered by the Hungarians, and Giovanna's vassals-in-chief had abandoned her and sided with the invaders. After delivering a moving speech to her court and people, Giovanna departed Naples by ship and crossed the Mediterranean to her Angevin county of Provence. There she traveled to the papal court in Avignon both to exonerate herself of her husband's murder and to raise funds to return and retake the kingdom. Giovanna's stay in Provence and Avignon lasted only about six months and is marked by some confusion in the historical records concerning the queen's actions and whereabouts. The residence was long enough for her to be delayed by wandering, imprisonment at the hands of the barons of Provence, her trial for Andrew's murder and her impoverishment. The record of Giovanna's trial is also somewhat confused, but after the presentation of legal arguments from both Neapolitan and Hungarian ambassadors — most likely with testimony from Giovanna herself (the king of Hungary did not appear) — the pope and his court found no strong evidence of guilt and decided to acquit the queen and restore her freedom. With Clement VI's eventual blessing, Giovanna then married her cousin Louis of Taranto, whose own wanderings had taken him to Siena and Florence to gain supporters. The couple gathered up enough money to rebuild an army and a fleet. Giovanna succeeded in doing this by divesting herself of one of her prime possessions — the city of Avignon — which she sold to the pope for a bargain price of 80,000 florins.

The queen left Avignon on July 24, 1348, the day after the pope took possession, and on July 28, she embarked from Marseilles with thirteen galleys fully armed and supplied for the reconquest of her kingdom. Giovanna's letters from July to October 1348[22] carefully list all expenses for the restoration of the realm derived from the proceeds of the transfer of Avignon to the pope. A letter of September 1349[23] details Giovanna's and Louis' approval of the expenses from these revenues made by their financier and chief political supporter, Niccolò Acciaiuoli.

On their return to the Regno, the couple faced a kingdom still occupied by Hungarian forces and traumatized by months of sack, rape and murder, followed by the devastation and depopulation of the Black Death of 1347/48. Lewis of Hungary's flight from the Regno caused by threats from Venice to his rear and from the arrival of the plague had demonstrated his inability to govern the city and its kingdom, and Giovanna's return had proven that she was a queen whom Neapolitans could love and obey. The reconquest was not easy. Giovanna was coming back to a ruined country and to a capital that had been radically changed both physically and spiritually: its ruling class and governance, trade, communal life, wealth and sense of pride as a capital city had all been mutilated and destroyed on the executioner's scaffold, on the spear points of invaders and in the vilification of diplomatic correspondence and contemporary reporting.[24]

While Lewis had returned to Hungary with the majority of his surviving forces, he had left behind him viceroys (voivode) — the mercenary captains Conrad of Landau and Fra Morreale — with full powers to rule and enough troops to maintain strongholds in Naples and the Regno. Giovanna and Louis would have to take Naples back district by district, fortress by fortress, and then go on to reclaim the remnants of a kingdom overrun by Hungarians and their mercenaries, by civil war and banditry and further hindered by the collapse of state power and authority. Giovanna and Louis arrived back at Naples on August 31, 1348. The royal couple's strategy was clear: while Louis would go on to Basilicata and Apulia to bring the Regno back into obedience and order, Giovanna herself would remain to conquer Naples. Matteo Villani[25] and Domenico da Gravina[26] recount her courageous leadership in retaking the city.

With Louis of Taranto's return to Naples in February 1349, the real struggle for power began. As Louis sought full parity as king in fact, Giovanna maneuvered to keep him consort. Louis' and Giovanna's courts soon began splitting into parties. Amid this court intrigue, on May 23, 1352, Pentecost Day, she and Louis were officially crowned as king and queen of Naples by a papal legate, again amid great public pomp and formal celebration.[27] But as part of Taranto's propaganda aimed at undermining Giovanna's authority, Niccolò Acciaiuoli began to release false rumors about Giovanna's sexual adventures. The cycle of *infamia* and retribution had begun again. The extent of Giovanna's independence and agency during these years is still a matter that requires further research and debate.[28] Louis died on June 5, 1362, and Giovanna then married Jaime IV, titular king of Majorca, on September 26, 1363. Jaime quickly proved to be an unreliable and personally unstable consort.

By the time of Jaime's death at Soria near Roussillon in 1375, Giovanna was also confronted by the political catastrophe of the Great Schism. She had allied with the Avignon line of popes and found herself defenseless against the Roman line. Declaring Giovanna deposed, the Roman pope Urban VI sanctioned an invasion of the kingdom led by the son of her former rival, Charles of Durazzo. Despite the attempts of Giovanna's fourth husband, Otto of Brunswick, to save her and the Regno, Charles III of Durazzo entered Naples in July 1381. With the approach of an army led by Giovanna's adopted heir, Louis of Anjou, Charles had Giovanna removed to a distant fortress in Basilicata and there ordered her strangled to death in the Spring of 1382.

GIOVANNA I: THE FALSELY ACCUSED QUEEN

Most historians agree on the basic events of Giovanna's reign, yet ever since her accession to the throne — and into the twentieth century — her reputation has been beset by a tradition of *infamia*. This involved the rumors, slanders and then outright accusations that the queen was the epitome of vice and depravity who took a series of lovers, both male and female, and that she had viciously and in cold blood arranged the murder of her first husband, Andrew of Hungary. The accusations — whatever their basis in fact — quickly became timeless myth. As Chantal Thomas notes of the eighteenth-century pamphlet literature's portrayal of French queen Marie-Antoinette,

> the diabolical vocation of Marie-Antoinette was to overstep all the limits, to always outdo herself in frivolousness, indecency, denaturation, scorn for her husband and squandering of the realm, sexual audacity, and murderous lunacy. As a pamphlet heroine, Marie Antoinette was a woman whose capacity for evil exceeded, by a long shot, all bounds of plausibility.[29]

As we will examine in Chapter 8, Giovanna has lived on primarily through the fictions created in the mid-fourteenth century.[30] It therefore seems appropriate to use the queen's story as an important example to investigate how these fictions merged both historical narrative and literary trope to produce this legend.

ROMANCE MODELS

Could the trecento historians studied here have used romance literary motifs to "fill in the gaps" for the queen's psychology, for her handling of challenges and threats, for her implementation of justice, for her travels during a period of confused events and unreliable witnesses?[31] Roger Ray discusses the impact of the rhetorical tradition of *Ad Herennium* on medieval historiography and its recommendation that plausibility and probability colored well-made narrative invention and swayed audiences far more than unadorned "truth." We have already discussed the deep rhetorical training of historians and surveyed their multiple sources and evidentiary claims.[32] These included everything from biblical narrative to classical and medieval histories to myth, fable and literary fiction. Everyday knowledge of human character and types could supplement known persons and events through a series of rhetorical figures and tropes to create a *narratio probabilis* that filled in such gaps with an author's skillful *inventio*.[33]

Such melding of literary romance and real politics, for example, lay behind the letters sent by Queen Mother Elizabeth of Hungary to Giovanna shortly after Andrew of Hungary's murder.[34] History, literature and legend, Queen Mother Elizabeth warned, abound with examples of men who claimed their thrones through marriage to an heiress: the king of Aragon, formerly of Sicily; King Manfred, the Hohenstaufen heir of Sicily; and Brenne (Brennius) of Britain. Elizabeth's short list is full of threats to the pope and the queen. The first two examples were papal enemies who seized kingdoms nominally under papal lordship. The third, Brenne, was the historic leader of the Gauls, the Brennus who sacked Rome in 390 BCE and who later became a figure in the Arthurian cycle so popular among the Angevins. His transformation into myth demonstrates the impact of literary sources on fourteenth-century mentalities and events.

Book III of Geoffrey of Monmouth's *History of the Kings of Britain* (1138/39), for example, recounts the harm to the British realm caused by Brennius' quarrel with his brother Belinus after he had been cheated out of his inheritance to the throne. Brennius, expelled from Britain for the danger his quarrel caused, traveled to Gaul and there married the (unnamed) daughter of Segin — who had no male heirs — to become king of the Burgundians. He then invaded Britain, and bloody civil war was averted only by the intervention of Queen Tonwenna, his and Belinus' mother. Brennius and the united Gauls then went on to capture and sack a duplicitous Rome. Elizabeth's literary threats would be hard to misinterpret either in Avignon at the court of Clement VI, steeped in chivalrous romance culture,[35] or at Naples at a court that knew and continued to commission new and sumptuous manuscript versions of these Arthurian romances.[36]

A second example of such obvious borrowing comes from the chronicle of the notary Domenico da Gravina. He relates[37] a scandalous story about Agnes de Perigord. Agnes had become gravely ill. At the urging of her son, Charles of Durazzo, she visited the noted physician Giovanni da Penne. Following standard medieval medical practice, perfected at the University of Salerno just south of Naples, Giovanni asked Agnes to return the next day with a sample of her urine. But unknown to the patient or her physician, her urine sample was switched with that of Giovanna's lady-in-waiting Sancia de'Cabanni, who was then pregnant. Shocked by his findings, the next day the physician revealed the news discreetly to Charles of Durazzo. On hearing the false news of his widowed mother's pregnancy, Charles ordered her expelled from his household. Placed into the power of her enemies in the house of Taranto, Agnes was soon poisoned at the command of Catherine de Courtenay, whose sons Robert and Louis of Taranto were actively courting Queen Giovanna.

Émile Léonard reminded us that such histories, for all their claim to reconstructing and representing the past, are in the end not scientific reports but literary inventions and are influenced by the imaginative literature of their day. He cites[38] the precedent of Chrétien de Troyes' *Cligès* as a possible literary antecedent for Gravina's episode. In the story of Thessala, the magician of the empress of Greece uses a false urine sample to convince others of the princess' death. According to the analyses of Gravina's work by Marino Zabbia[39] and Fulvio Delle Donne,[40] Gravina seems to have been heavily influenced by both the *chansons de geste* for

CHAPTER 5 ⚜ THE IMPACT OF ROMANCE

battle and other action scenes and by the romances for more complex plot and character devices.

Given the great popularity of chivalric romances and their motifs at the Angevin court of Naples and throughout Italy,[41] could the writings of trecento historians have been modeled on such fictions? The sources for Giovanna's reign are sometimes contradictory and often evoke the genre of contemporary literary tales of accused queens already cited. These narratives represented a hybrid of inverted (or perverted) chivalric romance, folk traditions with deep resonances in archetype and fairy tale and a political fiction that only narrowly steered clear of open identification with real figures and events. All focused on the public consequences of powerful women slandered, accused, punished for, or exonerated of, their supposed sexual transgressions within a tightly woven family context of trust and authority, which they had presumably violated or by which they had been victimized.

The specific context of these tales involves several basic elements: the first of sexual abuse — usually incestuous; the second of false charges leveled against the heroines in revenge for rebuffs of sexual advances or out of jealously, often from within their own family; third, their fall from power and grace, their expulsion or flight into exile — usually by ship — and their humiliation and sufferings;[42] and finally their miraculous restoration by some form of religious authority: generally the Virgin Mary through the agency of a powerful male cleric, often the pope himself. The stories also involve the queen's forgiveness of her accusers either while she is still in exile or upon her return and restoration. Many then repeat the cycle of accusation, exile and restoration, making the female ruler an almost perpetual sacrificial offering to the rhythms of decay and renewal within the family or the larger body politic. If the king's body could die and be reborn, it seems that the queen's body must be repeatedly scarred, dismembered and then returned to face yet another round of trial and exoneration at the hands of her male accusers and judges.[43] Deep anxieties over female agency, inheritance and rule underlie all these fictive elements.

THE EMPRESS OF ROME, CONSTANCE, LA MANEKINE

Nancy Black has grouped these characters and plots into two major types: the "Empress of Rome" and "Constance." While they have different textual and reception traditions, one religious and one secular, by the fourteenth and fifteenth centuries the two, like their audiences, had begun to blend. Exemplars of the Empress of Rome genre appear as early as an inclusion in Gautier de Coinci's *Miracles de Notre Dame* of 1218–36, in Vincent of Beauvais' *Speculum historiale* of c. 1244 and in Matthew Paris in the mid-thirteenth century.[44] The genre takes its name from the tale of an empress whose husband has gone off on pilgrimage, leaving her in charge but under the personal protection of his brother, who soon makes sexual advances to her. Rebuffed and imprisoned, but released on the emperor's return, the brother accuses the queen of gross sexual impropriety. The emperor believes his brother and condemns the empress to death. Escaping various threats to her life and virtue, she is restored to her proper place only to be accused a second time and again exonerated. Constantly besieged by the lustful men around her, the empress' only protection is her faith in the Virgin and her eventual grace. Black has offered evidence of medieval chroniclers' inventing such "false accusations" in order to move forward plot or enhance details of character.[45]

The second major type, the tale of mutilation, is widely known as the handless queen[46] and appears in Philippe de Remi's *La Manekine* (c.1278–c.1300),[47] a story with roots in fairy and folk tales,[48] retold in Charles Perrault's *Histoires ou contes du temps passé* (1697), in Grimm's *Household Tales* (1812) as "The Girl without Hands" and more tamely in Andrew Lang's *Grey Fairy Book* (1900).[49] Also appearing in French in the fourteenth-century *chanson de geste*, *La Belle Hélène de Constantinople*,[50] this genre reaches its full expression in the story of Constance. The tale involves a conflict over inheritance to the throne of Hungary. A king without male heir, whose daughter is prohibited from inheriting, is made to promise by his wife on her deathbed that he must not seek a wife so that their daughter may inherit the kingdom. But if he must marry, then it must be a woman who resembles his wife. At the urging of his council, he forms an incestuous infatuation for his own daughter, Joy. Rather than submit, Joy mutilates herself by cutting off her hand so she no longer resembles her mother. The tale has versions in German, English, Spanish and Italian, the last as the *Historia della Regina Oliva* or *Penta Monomozza* of the fourteenth and fifteenth centuries.[51] As "Constance," this is the same character later picked up by Trevet's *Chronicles*, by John Gower in the *Confessio Amantis*, by Chaucer in the "Man of Law's Tale," by Christine de Pizan and by Thomas Hoccleve.[52] As in the Empress cycle, the powerful woman is subject to false accusations and then exile by sea. In some versions a rebuffed lover — often a male relative with incestuous desires — cuts her companion's throat and places the blame for the murder on Constance.

THE CONTESSE D'ANJOU

A powerful example of the falsely accused queen or Empress of Rome story — with heavy influences from the *Manekine* type — appears in the *Roman de la Contesse d'Anjou*[53] written in 1316 by Jean Maillart (d.1323), a secretary to the French royal court. The *roman* was composed under the impact of the fate of Queen Giovanna's female Capetian cousins in the Tour de Nesle affair. In 1314, King Philip IV arrested his three daughters-in-law, Margaret, daughter of Duke Robert II of

CHAPTER 5 ※ THE IMPACT OF ROMANCE

Burgundy, and Blanche and Jeanne, daughters of Otto IV, count of Burgundy, under suspicion of carrying on or of concealing illicit sexual affairs. Blanche and Margaret were publicly tried before the Parliament of Paris, found guilty of adultery and sentenced to life imprisonment. Their purported lovers were castrated and then — depending on the source — either drawn and quartered or broken on the wheel and hung as traitors. Jeanne of Burgundy was eventually cleared of all charges and saved the fate of her sisters-in-law by the power of her husband, the future Philip V. The shock of the alleged betrayals reportedly contributed to King Philip IV's death in November of 1314 and became a rallying cry for French legists who argued for the implementation of the ancient Salic Law that purportedly prohibited women from inheriting the French crown.[54]

While sometimes known as the *roman* of the count of Anjou, medieval manuscripts named it variously the *Roman de la Contesse d'Anjou* and — in a manuscript now lost but once belonging to the Duc de Berry — *La patience de la Comtesse d'Anjou*, both placing proper emphasis on the young heroine. The *roman* opens with a game of chess between an unnamed and recently widowed count of Anjou and his (also unnamed) beautiful daughter. During the game, he develops an incestuous obsession, threatening to take her by force if she will not consent to be his wife. Fleeing with her governess, the young countess is soon reduced to poverty. After several picaresque episodes of escape from her vengeful father, during which the two women suffer great physical afflictions, fall of status and social marginalization — compared by Maillart to a religious martyrdom but explained more fully by the secular turning of Fortune's wheel — they are given refuge by a generous woman and take up silk weaving in Orléans. Again fleeing the advances of sexual predators, they are sheltered by a chatelain of Lorris, a holding of the count of Bourges. At a feast held at the castle, the mysterious young woman attracts the attention and love of that count, who soon marries her with no knowledge of her background or recent past.

Meanwhile, realizing his horrendous sin and condemned by his own vassals, the Angevin count dies of grief, leaving the young woman as his only heir. The count and now countess of Bourges live in great happiness, and while her husband is away on a military campaign, she gives birth to a beautiful son. However, the greatest danger again comes from within the ruling family: the count's aunt, the countess of Chartres, takes a hateful dislike to her nephew's new wife, questioning her unknown lineage, the dynastic impact of the marriage and the newborn son's right to inherit the county. She then forges letters defaming her new niece. The *roman* then briefly moves from politically structured narrative to fairytale motif as the four commoners charged with executing the countess and her son take pity and aid their escape. Yet, even in this episode, the folkloristic element is undercut by the author's strategy of having the four vigorously debate the tension between their duty to obey their lord — and the punishments awaiting them for not doing so — and the injustice of executing an innocent newborn and their countess, who herself has been so just and kind to the common people. The role of the people and their open debates and discussions over obedience, duty and justice underscore the political nature of the narrative and its critique of both real social injustice and of the conventions of romance.

Wandering from town to town, penniless and abandoned, the countess encounters threats to her virtue and unexpected generosity. Meanwhile, the count sets off to seek his wife and child, abandoning all help and all signs of his station, reducing himself to poverty and immersing himself in the life and world of the marginalized. Enduring both physical hardship and personal insult, he finally finds his wife and child, and the reunited family regains its power and inheritance. The couple live happily ever after, and justice and order are restored under royal, and male, rule.

Maillart's *roman* strips out almost all mythic, magical and folkloristic elements to concentrate on human emotions and motivations and their political and social impact. Rather than the passive folklore type of the suffering innocent, the young countess struggles against the adversity of Fortune with her virtue, delivers moving public speeches to her people and lowers her status to support herself and her child. While all but stock characters remain nameless, political units, titles, social institutions, the royal court and its political working are all specifically invoked, highlighting the social nature of the tale and the "networks of real political associations"[55] evoked by it. Maillart draws the reader's attention to his intentions by framing his *roman* first with a lengthy introduction to the story's truth claims and its sources in the affairs of the French court[56] and then at the epilogue by explicitly hiding his own name in the final verses and instructing the reader on how to decipher and uncover his identity by paying special attention to his verses: an invitation to do the same with the characters hidden beneath the lines and to read on multiple levels. His storytelling thus weaves seamlessly together fiction and political narrative and allows multiple interpretations ranging from the simple moral tale to the political critique, from the pure work of fiction to a narrative heavily influenced by legal, political and dynastic history and reporting, thus smoothing over and encoding the line between fiction and history.

While Peggy McCracken has argued that the Tour de Nesle affair effectively ended literary treatment of adulterous queens,[57] historical narrative showed no such distaste, and these tales continued to circulate widely. Black notes that

> in fact, it would seem that slander, for royal women, was something of an occupational hazard and that the more powerful the noblewoman, the more likely she was to face accusations of adultery or treason.[58]

She sees these fictional accounts of the idealized noble, passive, victimized woman by a male author as an attempt to place powerful and independent woman squarely within the male politics of power as a pawn of dynastic interests.[59] These stories also provided moral lessons, often to royalty themselves, as "political commentary and the construction of social ideals."[60] Whatever her alleged crime or its expiation, Black notes, the queen was seen as an essential intercessor, her chastity essential for royal hegemony.[61] Like the queen in the game of chess that opens the *Roman de la Contesse d'Anjou*,[62] she was viewed in the male world of royally sanctioned fiction and political thought as the major bolster to the king, whose power remained central to these stories of queens and their virtues and vices.

These tales had a broad reach among artists and intellectuals and found their way into emerging popular theater. In Paris, elaborately staged plays[63] based on the Empress of Rome (play 27, performed in 1369) and Handless Queen (play 29, performed in 1371) were presented by the guild of goldsmiths in the forty-play cycle produced between 1339 and 1382. Two plays (nos. 4 and 12) were performed between 1339 and 1364 and took up the themes of falsely accused heroines. Their intent was entertainment for their guild members but set within the social and political contexts of their urban bourgeoisie audiences. In such dramas, these urban classes were often sympathetic protagonists who actively helped the queen survive and achieve restoration and who highlighted social and economic inequalities and injustices.

Melusine

While studies of influence have almost solely concentrated on authorship — which texts did a writer use to create his or her own work — recent scholarship has also focused on the role of reception and audience in helping to define textual communities: what Strohm termed "larger interpretive structures," Royle's uncanny resonances, or intertextuality as absence.[64] We therefore include here the romance of *Melusine*. Though later than Queen Giovanna's reign — and with little evidence of a manuscript tradition in the Regno — *Melusine* is instructive less for any direct correlation of influence of fiction or of fictionalized historical events on trecento historiography than for evidence of the overall cultural ambience of the Francophone elites of the fourteenth century, their expectations of fiction and *fabula* and the deep ethical and psychological issues that such works addressed for them.

Eleven years after Queen Giovanna's death in 1382, her cousin Jean, Duc de Berry, commissioned a tale from Jean D'Arras. Sometimes associated with Arthurian legend, this romance of Queen Melusine of Lusignan[65] survives in both Jean D'Arras' version from 1393 and in Coudrette's from c.1403. Both draw from earlier materials that reached their near final form in the early fourteenth century and that were thus current with

Giovanna I's contemporaries.[66] Its central issues — dynastic foundation and legitimacy, the role of the queen, violence and power rivalry within a ruling family and the objectification of the woman ruler's agency and body — bracket the period under discussion here and remain central to the concerns of its historians.

Of *Melusine*'s two versions, Jean D'Arras' was designed to bolster Jean, Duc de Berry's dynastic claims to the Lusignan inheritance. Coudrette's was composed for Guillaume L'Archevêque, the lord of Pathenay and an ally of the English in the struggle over Aquitaine (and Lusignan) during the Hundred Years' War. Both versions explore the origins of the Lusignan dynasty that lie buried deep within foundation myth and the fairie elements of the Arthurian cycle. The narrative is rich in genre convention borrowed from romance and *chanson de geste* and in the details of campaign and battle derived from contemporary chronicle and crusading history.

Nor does that myth shy away from some of the more unsavory elements of the family's history. It is also underscored by several deep anxieties focused on male inheritance through the female line and the effects of violence by extended family members to either bolster or damage dynastic survival. Unlike the romances discussed above, *Melusine* names all its characters, supporting claims to historic and dynastic credibility.

Raymondin, the new count of Poitiers, meets and courts the mysterious Melusine, who agrees to his proposal of marriage on two conditions: first, that he follow her advice in everything and second, that Raymondin never seek her out on any Saturday. He agrees, the couple are wed amid the great splendor that Melusine magically provides; and the castle of Lusignan and the surrounding monuments of the Pathenay area — castles, towers, mills, churches, abbeys — soon rise under her direction. The couple become powerful and wealthy, eventually having ten sons of great prowess and intelligence but almost all marked by certain physical signs (one eye, boar's tooth, lion's paw, etc.) that reveal their descent from fairy folk.

But Raymondin's brother, now count of Forez, reports false rumors and convinces him that Melusine is betraying him sexually during her retreats. Enraged, Raymondin spies upon his wife in her bath only to discover that below her waist Melusine has an enormous serpent tail, revealing her fairy origins. Raymondin soon repents his suspicions, and Melusine forgives him. The story then follows their sons; no daughters are mentioned. All goes well until Raymondin again accuses her of defiling their marriage through her serpentine, deceptive nature. Melusine now resumes her dragon form, makes a tender farewell speech to their court and, amid great lamentation, changes shape and flies off. Although both Raymondin and Geoffrey, his eventual heir, make pilgrimages to Rome to the pope and beg forgiveness, Melusine is never to be seen by Raymondin or his sons again.

CHAPTER 5 ⚜ THE IMPACT OF ROMANCE

Throughout the romance, the image of Queen Melusine both takes on, and in turn supports, the traditional roles of the female ruler: bolstering the position of her husband, bearing and educating his heirs, endowing religious houses, patronizing and overseeing new building both secular and sacred. Like most female rulers of the time, Melusine's life is one caught in tension between exerting her own power and independence, ceding real power to, or withholding it from, her husband and facing the slanders brought against her by her close relatives and rivals. Ultimately, like the Empress of Rome, Constance, La Manekine and the Comtesse d'Anjou, she must flee her own kingdom, abandoning family, children and her carefully constructed realm.

At the same time, Melusine's fairy nature — reflected in her mysterious origins and birth — are manifested in her otherworldly form when she chooses to reveal herself to her mortal husband and family as a fantastic creature possessing the attributes of a woman, a flying dragon and a serpent. In this regard, the recurrent association of the female with the elemental, the earthly and the serpentine retains a thread of ambiguous magical and misogynistic projection that both hearkens back to the positive archetypal female earth goddess and to negative biblical images of the serpent.[67] Whatever the ultimate meaning of her transformative nature, for late medieval audiences, the association of the powerful woman with the imagery of the earthly and seductive serpent was a central aspect of these romances. The strength of such imagery in the Melusine legend underscores the uninterrupted literary tradition and popular mythology of the seductive and destructive female ruler.

Yet this is not the only female anxiety that the tale of Melusine exposes. Throughout the narrative, in what many take as the side adventures of her and Raymondin's sons, the issue of female inheritance and ruling status is addressed over and over again. In the stories of Urian and Guy, Antoine and Renaud most specifically, but also indirectly in those of Eudes, Raymond and Thierry, each tale of high adventure and warfare, when closely read, is a case study in the variations of male inheritance through marriage with a female heir.[68] To make the parallels of the various tales more obvious, Jean D'Arras prefaces both the stories of Urian and Guy and of Antoine and Renaud with Melusine's lengthy and practical advice on gaining and maintaining rule. As Black has also noted,[69] these *chastoiements* provide both advice in the mirror-of-princes tradition and serve as markers to set off each son's adventure as an exemplum for a male assuming rule through marriage to a female heir.

The tale is as explicit concerning these marriage arrangements and the husband's rights to rule on behalf of the legitimate, female heir as it is about military preparations and engagements. Such arrangements would have been of extreme interest and utility to Jean, Duc de Berry, who had received Lusignan as count of Poitou by grant of his brother King Charles V, but whose legitimate claim to it derived less from its seizure from the English than from his inheritance through his mother, Bonne of Bohemia, daughter of King John of Luxembourg (Bohemia) and thus a descendant of the Lusignans. One also cannot dismiss the possibility that, like the *Roman de la Comtesse d'Anjou*, *Melusine* reflected recent political realities, including the events of Giovanna I's reign.

MELIADUS

We have definitive evidence of the direct impact of romances at the court of Naples in the romance of *Meliadus de Leonnois* or *Guiron le Courtois* (part of the cycle also known as *Palamedes*).[70] While we will examine this work more thoroughly in our discussion of visual imagery in Chapter 6, here we will briefly offer it as another example of the crossover between romance motifs and Angevin political themes. *Meliadus de Leonnois* was composed between 1235 and 1240, when it was mentioned in a letter of Frederick II. It derives from the Arthurian prose romances and appears in the *Prose Tristan*. Its Italian tradition includes *Il dui Tristan*, the *Tavolo Ritondo* and the French *Compilation* or *Roman du Roi Artus* (1270–74) by Rustichello da Pisa,[71] prisonmate of Marco Polo, to whom Marco dictated his *Travels*. As *Guiron le Courtois* or *Meliadus*, it was the most popular Arthurian romance in trecento and quattrocento Italy.[72] Roger Lathuillère's edition of the Old French text[73] accounted for thirty manuscripts, of which nineteen date from the trecento or earlier. There exist several illuminated manuscripts of the romance completed in Naples either in the form of *Guiron le Courtois* or *Meliadus*, ranging from the late thirteenth to the mid-fourteenth century.[74]

One manuscript with direct bearing on our study, now British Library, MS Add. 12228,[75] is also Neapolitan and dates from after May 1352 and the official celebration of the coronation of Giovanna I and Louis of Taranto. It was commissioned by the royal seneschal Niccolò Acciaiuoli, who also commissioned several other chivalric romances and histories, including a *Prose Tristan*, a *Roman de Troie* and a *Histoire ancienne jusqu'à César*. Alessandra Perriccioli Saggese has suggested that the illuminator of at least the first two-thirds of BL MS Add 12228 was Cristoforo Orimina and workshop.[76] In Chapter 6, we will therefore investigate how and where Louis of Taranto, as the patron of this manuscript, inserted himself into the visual program of the *Meliadus* story and how these insertions reflect on the male Angevin's attitudes toward and treatment of his ruling queen.[77]

BOCCACCIO'S DE MULIERIBUS CLARIS

All these strands come together in Giovanni Boccaccio's *Vita* of Giovanna I of c.1375 within his *De mulieribus claris*.[78] We have already discussed its epideictic mode in Chapter 4.[79] Boccaccio wrote this collection as a counterpart to his model Petrarch's work on famous

CHAPTER 5 — THE IMPACT OF ROMANCE

men *(De viris illustribus)*. The 106 biographies of both good and evil women mirror Petrarch's combination of mythological, semi-historical and classical figures and, like Petrarch's assemblage of famous men, Boccaccio's brings the collection up to his own time with a handful of medieval women, including the legendary Pope Joan, Empress Constance and the Sienese widow Camiola, concluding with Giovanna I. He used classical, biblical, patristic, medieval chronicle, royal biographical and other sources to match his subject matter and purposes. But, as the work's most recent Anglophone editor, Virginia Brown, asked, "are these additional details the product of his own imagination or did he have recourse to another source as yet unidentified?"[80] In the rest of this chapter, we will propose an answer to Brown's question.

Boccaccio began the series in 1361 and worked toward its completed first draft in 1362. He had first planned to dedicate the work to Louis of Taranto, but Louis died on June 5, 1362. Nevertheless, at the urging of his and Petrarch's old friend Francesco Nelli, who had taken a post at the Neapolitan court, Boccaccio traveled south once again, dedicating his biographies to Andrea Acciaiuoli, countess of Altavilla, Niccolò's sister. Once there, however, Boccaccio was ignored by Andrea and humiliated by Niccolò: badly housed, forced to take his meals with the court servants and left behind during the court's official movements. In addition, many of Boccaccio's associates and informants in Naples were veterans of King Robert's reign and had decidedly taken Giovanna's side in her conflict with Louis, and it was Niccolò Acciaiuoli himself who was held responsible for the second wave of slander against Giovanna during her conflict with Louis. Boccaccio had also hoped that Acciaiuoli would help him obtain the poet laureate's crown, but he was disappointed when it was awarded to his rival Zanobi da Strada in 1355 at the Florentine's urging.[81] Boccaccio therefore recounted his distaste for Niccolò in several works, including his letter to Francesco Nelli.[82] His *Eclogue* 8, "Midas," is a bitter indictment of what he portrayed as Acciaiuoli's corrupt influence on Naples and its court.[83] One can see this within the overall context of Bocaccio's well-known disdain of patronage.[84] His positive treatment of Giovanna can therefore be understood as both a personal rebuff to Acciaiuoli and Louis of Taranto and a sincere encomium for the queen.[85]

Admittedly, along with his changing views of the queen herself, Boccaccio's vision of women is complex and contested. Rodney Lokaj[86] has assembled enough material from Boccaccio's other works, including his letters and the *Corbaccio*, to highlight his misogyny and to cast serious doubt on the sincerity of this final admiring portrait of the queen. Alcuin Blamires sees his *Corbaccio* as "a mordant experiment in unalloyed contempt" for women.[87] Constance Jordan[88] likewise offers a critique of the misogyny Boccaccio shared with his age. Deanna Shemek has noted that the *De mulieribus claris* "stands as one of the most ideologically controversial works in Boccaccio's corpus, precisely for its peculiar relation to Renaissance feminism."[89] Jordan has called the *De mulieribus claris* "devious" and "pervasively critical" of women. Boccaccio's diatribe, "Against Women," in book 1 of his *De casibus virorum illustrium*, encapsulates late medieval misogyny as a literary form.[90]

Yet, as one might expect from the author of the *Decameron*, Boccaccio's Neapolitan women are graceful, dynamic, courtly, courageous and virtuous even as the poet veils only slightly their real-life intrigues and love affairs at court. In his *Amorosa Visione* 42, he calls the young Giovanna *"gaia e leggiadretta,"* the image of grace and lightness, while he records the remarkable beauty of Agnes de Perigord. His *Fiammetta* is reportedly based on a fictionalized Maria d'Aquino, King Robert's daughter, with whom Boccaccio supposedly fell in love after first meeting her at S. Lorenzo Maggiore in Naples.[91] Niccolò Acciaiuoli's affair with Catherine de Courtenay is recounted in his *Eclogue* 8. Sancia de'Cabanni, Giovanna's intimate friend and lady in waiting, is also described in favorable terms, as "noble and gentle" *(Caccia di Diana* I.19).[92]

Boccaccio's literary strategy for Giovanna's biography is similarly complex. He introduces us to a queen, "more renowned than other women of our time for her nobility, power and goodness." After discussing her parentage, Boccaccio does not hesitate to place her firmly within the dynastic context of her Angevin forbearers without the least hint of discontinuity: "Thus, in our days and in those of our fathers no family in the whole world has been more famous than this for its nobility." He then moves on to Giovanna's youth and proceeds to describe the queen's possessions in Naples, Provence and Forcalquier, their natural riches, their peoples and cities. With some knowledge of the growing chorus of condemnation that surrounded the queen, he continues: "If we examine this kingdom closely, our amazement will be as great as its fame, for it is a mighty kingdom and not usually ruled by women." Boccaccio then reverses his reader's anticipation once again: "And what is even more surprising, Giovanna's spirit is equal to ruling it, so that she has preserved the noble character of her ancestors." "Ruling" or "governance" [*imperium*], "spirit" [*animus*], "character" [*indoles*] and "ancestor" [*avus*] would soon all become contested terms in the black legend of the Angevins that we will discuss in Chapter 8.

Again, Boccaccio wrote in the epideictic mode with a standard set of virtues, character traits, deeds and positive effects on their realms. While these also mirror the virtues of Giovanna's grandfather Robert the Wise,[93] it appears that Boccaccio was familiar with another source that Virginia Brown had speculated might yet be discovered. This was the genre of the falsely accused queen. Boccaccio was the author of the Patient Griselda tale (*Decameron* X.10) from which it made its way into Petrarch's *Seniles*[94] and into Chaucer as the "Clerk's Tale." We know

CHAPTER 5 ⚜ THE IMPACT OF ROMANCE

that Boccaccio was familiar with the chivalric romances composed in or copied for the Angevin royal court,[95] as his mockery of Niccolò Acciaiuoli's patronage of these texts makes clear.[96] On careful reading, Boccaccio's characterization of Giovanna[97] could have equally described the countess in the *Roman du Comtesse d'Anjou*, Constance or Griselda herself:

> Moreover, she is so prudent that she can be deceived more easily by treachery than through shrewdness. She is so steadfast and constant that she will not be easily swayed in her just purposes without reason. This has already been shown clearly enough not long ago by the blows of Fortune[98] which have often struck and buffeted her from every direction. For she has endured the internal struggles of petty fellow-princes and foreign wars which at the time were waged within her kingdom. Through the fault of others, she has had to endure flight, exile, the grim ways of her husbands,[99] the envy of noblemen, undeserved ill-repute, the threats of popes, and other things, all of which she has borne bravely. Finally, her indomitable soul has conquered everything; this would have been a great deed for a strong, powerful king, and not only for a women.[100]

Boccaccio's account of Giovanna's reign ultimately moves beyond both rhetorical mode and the accused-queen genre to rely on facts and events, thus eliding the boundaries between literary fiction and recorded history. Boccaccio offers examples of Giovanna's virtues that both match the medieval ideal of *buon governo* spelled out in Lorenzetti's Sienese fresco cycle and by contemporary political thinkers such as Bartolo da Sassoferrato or Remigio de' Girolamo and recounts real events of her reign: she has cleared the realm of brigands, capturing and executing their leaders. "None of the previous kings had wanted or been able to do this." People and goods may now travel the realm without harm; the barons have been brought under control. The fact that Boccaccio had dedicated the work to the Acciaiuoli, first and foremost allies of Louis of Taranto, makes his omission of Louis' role in all this the more apparent. That Boccaccio could concentrate on Giovanna's accomplishments as ruler without fear of contradiction from those who were in the best position to know better makes his praise even more convincing.

Giovanna's personal virtues show her to be "the legitimate heir" of Robert the Wise. She is astute, generous, loyal and rewarding of service, patient, steadfast and "cannot be deflected from her righteous path." He concludes by extolling Giovanna's "charming appearance," grace and eloquence, her majesty and inflexibility when the occasion demands. He adds that "equally she can be affable, compassionate, gentle and kind, so that one could describe her as her people's ally rather than their queen." Then in a clear comparison to her grandfather Robert, he asks:

"What greater qualities would one seek in a most wise king? And if someone wanted to express completely the integrity of her character, his speech would be very long. For these reasons, I not only think that she is noble and of splendid fame, but an eminent glory of Italy such as has never before been seen by any nation."

CONCLUSIONS

Boccaccio framed his life of Giovanna I around the conventions available to him, including classical epideictic writing, medieval biography and hagiography and one tradition sought but unnamed by Brown. This was the literary romance, most especially that of the falsely accused queen. This chapter has provided examples of this genre in *Manekine, Belle Hélène de Constantinople* and the *Roman du Contesse d'Anjou*. We have also indicated parallels to the events in the life of Giovanna I, proposing that such literary sources helped "fill in the gaps" where accurate data was lacking and where dramatic effect helped establish truth claims for medieval readers. Trecento literary conventions made such tropes easily recognizable to a literate audience. Over and above that, the emerging shifts in late medieval culture that produced both the narratives of accused queens and Boccaccio's biography of Giovanna I were grounded in a common appreciation of the issues around female inheritance and rule reflected in the romance of *Melusine*. Strohm's "larger interpretive structures" and Otter's "metaphorical doublings" thus provide us with rich tools with which to understand the supple literary methods and models used by trecento historians in their construction of personalities and motivations.

NOTES

1. This chapter incorporates research previously published in "The Visualization of Power in the Reign of Giovanna I of Naples," *Visual History* 2 (2016): 105–24; I presented this ongoing research in "Chivalric Romances and Narratives in the Reign of Queen Giovanna I," Seminario Internazionale di Studi nel quadro degli Incontri: Scrivere la storia tra medioevo ed età moderna. Naples, Università degli Studi di Napoli "Federico II" (10 Dec. 2014); "BL MS Add. 12228 and an Early View of Naples," University of Bristol, Centre for Medieval Studies Seminar (28 May 2020); "Manuscript Cultures in Naples, 1350–1500," University of Bristol, Centre for Medieval Studies Seminar (11 Oct. 2018); and "An Early Image of Naples from the Campus Neapolitanus in Painting and Drawing and a Possible Attribution to Pisanello," Gateways to Medieval Naples. The Edith O'Donnell Institute of Art History and Franklin University Switzerland Museo e Real Bosco di Capodimonte / La Capraia (9 June 2021).
2. Auerbach (1953), 17.
3. Ainsworth (2003.2); Rubenstein (2005), 31–32; Otter (2005); Holloway (2011). One of the five major focuses of the International Conference on the Medieval Chronicle and The Medieval Chronicle series is "The Chronicle: History or Literature?" http://medievalchronicle.org/themedieval-chronicle.
4 Otter (2005), 109–10; Breisach.
5 On the narrative "gap" in the verbal and visual, Lewis (2010), 90–92. See also

CHAPTER 5 ⚜ THE IMPACT OF ROMANCE

Ray (1985), 77–92; Partner (1985), 13–22; Summerfield (2010).
6. Buc.
7. Strohm (1992), 117.
8. Ibid.
9. Strohm (1992), 3–4. Strohm (1992), 9, called for "discarding outworn categorizations — like 'literary' versus 'nonliterary' or 'fictional' versus 'historical' — that might foreclose conversation among texts or between texts and events."
10. Strohm (1992), 134–36, points out that the influence of various genres may be indirect in the "same imaginative sources that once fostered the fabliau."
11. Murphy (1974), 41–42, 80–84, and his paraphrase of Matthew of Vendôme at 164–68. For others Kempshall, 405–27.
12. Ainsworth (2003.1), 249–51; Ainsworth (2003.2), 394–411; Kempshall, 432–41.
13. Otter (2005), 116–17; Strohm (1992), 34–51.
14. On the distinction between *historia* and *fabula*, "False Fables and Historical Truth," in Strohm (1992), 3–31; Bietenholz (1994); Weimann (1996); Taviani-Carozzi (2002); Ainsworth (2003.2).
15. Otter (2005), 110–15. Menache (2006) examines this issue for Avignon and the South.
16. Gardner (1930); Delcorno Branca (1968); Delcorno Branca (1974); Delcorno Branca (1998); Graf–Casoli (2000); Delcorno Branca (2004); Berthelot–Lecco (2006); de Matteis (2010); Ferrante (2011); Delcorno Branca (2014); Cavallaro (2016).
17. Blamires (1992); Jones (1993); Bak (1997); Blamires (1997); McCracken (1998); Black (2003).
18. The fundamental work is Léonard. For later work Gaglione (2009); Musto (2013), 256–302; Casteen (2015).
19. For the will and its context, Musto (2013), 234–59.
20. Kiesewetter (2001), 74–82 et passim.
21. Chapter 7, pp. 207–11.
22. Léonard, nos. 44, 47–49.
23. Léonard, no. 52.
24. On Rienzo's return to a devastated Rome, Musto (2003), 320–28.
25. I.20–23, Villani (1995), 37.
26. Gravina (1903), 44–47; Gravina (2022), XXI.1–43.
27. III.8, Villani (1995), 335–36; trans. Musto (2013), 285–86.
28. Casteen claims that Giovanna, pushed aside from real power, constructed a series of false personae to insinuate herself back into control.
29. Thomas (1999), 10.
30. Musto (2017), 17–25.
31. Otter (2005).
32. Chapter 4, pp. 107–8.
33. Ray (1985), 82–85; Ward (1985), 103–8.
34. For the background to the Hungarian political, diplomatic and military strategies, Hóman (1938); Léonard, "Pieces justifactives"; and the correspondence of Clement VI in Cerasoli (1896–97). On papal policy, Mollat (1963), 173–85; Léonard, 1:466–538; Rollo-Koster (2015), 75–77.
35. Wood (1989), 59–61; Vingtain (1998), 255–84; Musto (2003), 61–66; Rollo-Koster (2015); Falkeid (2017), 17–18.
36. On the fictive nature of Geoffrey's work and its reception by medieval readers, Hanning, 142–46; Kempshall, 365–66; Partner (1985), 48; Tolhurst (2012).
37. Gravina (1903), 13, l. 26–14, l. 19; Gravina (2022), VI.5–10.

38. Léonard, 1:49
39. Zabbia (1998).
40. Delle Donne (2001a).
41. Perriccioli Saggese (1979); Sabatini (1992); Dunbabin (2011), 269–74; Perriccioli Saggese (2012); Allaire (2014).
42. Otter (2005), 122, calls attention to Matthew Paris' use of such borrowings from folk tale and romance in his *Lives of the Two Offas*.
43. On the king's body as political symbol, Bertelli (2001); on the queen's body, Parsons (2004).
44. Black (2003), 20–36.
45. Black (2003), 68–72.
46. Black (2003), 37–65.
47. For an English edition of *La Manequine,* Beaumanoir (2010). For analysis, Shepherd (1990). For a more recent discussion, Rouillard (2012).
48. Aarne-Thompson type 510B, unnatural love.
49. Illustrated by Gustave Doré in 1862 and filmed in 1970 as *Peau d'Âne (Donkey Skin)* by Jacques Demy. See also Bottigheimer (2008).
50. Edited by Roussel (1995); Roussel (1998). See Black (2000); Black (2003), 167–85.
51. Black (2003), 66–88; Maillart (1998), 16.
52. Black (2003), 109–66.
53. In the French prose edition by Mora-Lebrun in Maillart (1998).
54. McCracken (1998), 171–78; Brown (2000); Black (2003), 68–83; Adams (2012). For general portrayals of the queen in France, Pratt (1997); Raynaud (1999).
55. Black (2000), 48.
56. Lines 1–63, Maillart (1998), 35–36. See Mora-Lebrun's analysis on 235–36; Black (2000), 43.
57. McCracken (1998), 171–72.
58. Black (2003), 67–68.
59. Black (2003), 34–36; Earenfight (2010); Earenfight (2013); Bianchini (2012); Woodacre (2013). For further bibliography, Casteen (2015), 274–86.
60. Black (2003), 10, 167–68.
61. A point detailed in Strohm (1992), 95–119, in which he also offers historical incidents involving Queens Philippa and Anne of England and Chaucer's Alceste.
62. Yalom (2004), 68–75; De Cessolis (2008), 17–23, 108–10. Written before 1300, *The Book of Chess* became an Italian and pan-European bestseller, both for its attempt to regularize the game and for its moralization of the pieces and their roles in society and private life. Yalom recognizes De Cessolis' impact and emphasizes the role of the queen as constantly sexualized and strictly controlled.
63. Edited in Paris (1876–93). See Runnalls (1999); Black (2003), 89–108.
64. N. 7 above; Daniels (2009) for Boccaccio; and Royle (2003). My thanks to Liz McAvoy for the latter reference.
65. For the Old French text, Jean D'Arras (1932). For a modern French edition, Jean D'Arras (2003). For an English version, Jean D'Arras (2012). For critical interpretations, the essays in Maddox (1996); Haines-Courroux (2013).
66. Jean D'Arras (2012), 2–4.
67. On women and the monstrous, Wittkower (1942); Nichols (1996); Cohen (1999), McAvoy-Walters (2002); Bildhauer-Mills (2003); Oswald (2010); Miller (2010); Mittman-Dendle (2012).
68. The variations include: marriage to a king's daughter, Hermine and refusal to remain only a consort to a ruling queen (Urian in Cyprus, Jean D'Arras

CHAPTER 5 ⚜ THE IMPACT OF ROMANCE

[2012], 97–99); marriage to woman as sole heir, Florie, who assumes she is ruler but is put aside (Guyon in Armenia, ibid., 110–12); attempt to capture a ruling woman and to rule by force (king of Alsace against heiress Crestienne of Luxembourg, ibid., 113–15); male assumes the crown from the sole female heiress, Aiglentine (Renaud in Bohemia, ibid., 131–46): "governance of a women is of little value.... you must marry a man fully capable of taking care of you and your land" (ibid., 142–43); female heirs disqualified (Geoffrey in Northumberland, ibid., 186–87).
69. Black (2000), 43–44.
70. On *Meliadus* and the courtly romances in Naples, Lathuillère (1966); Perriccioli Saggese (1979); Wahlen (2006); Wahlen (2010); Cigni (2006); Morato (2010). New editions are available: Bubenicek (2014); and Leonardi and Trachsler (2020). I have not yet been able to access Nevile (2013).
71. Rustichello da Pisa (1994).
72. Cigni (2006), 85–87.
73. Lathuillère (1966), 35–106; Cigni (2004); Cigni (2014).
74. Cataloged and illustrated by Perriccioli Saggese (1979): her nos. 12 (Venice, BNM, MS IX 227); 14 (Paris, BNF, MS fr. 1463); 19 (Vatican, BVA, MS Reg. Lat. 1501); 24 (Venice, BNM, MS fr. XV (228). See also Cigni (2006), 91–105, 114–17.
75. The manuscript of *Meliadus* (London, BL, MS Add. 12228) is online at www.bl.uk/manuscripts/Viewer.aspx?ref=add_ms_12228.
76. This Neapolitan origin was challenged in favor of a Genoese workshop by Cigni (2006), 92 n. 31, relying on Perriccioli Saggese (1985), 62–64. However, Perriccioli Saggese focused her comments there only on the second half of the manuscript and its illustration style. She reiterated the Neapolitan argument in Perriccioli Saggese (2010), 122. See also D'Urso (2021); and Chapter 6 below.
77. Cigni (2014), 24, notes the similar use of the Arthurian cycle by Edward I.
78. Kolsky (2003); Boccaccio (2003), 466–73; Daniels (2009), 6–11, 137–71; Musto (2013), 291–98.
79. Pp. 103–6.
80. Boccaccio (2003), xviii.
81. For a summary, Morosini, 72–73.
82. His letter 13 to Francesco Nelli in Boccaccio (1992a); analyzed in Boccaccio (1987), xviii–xix, 226–27; Boli (2013), 299–300. See also Morosini.
83. Boccaccio (1987), 74–85, and notes on 224–28; Lummus (2013), 158.
84. Daniels (2009), 19–20, citing Leonardo Bruni.
85. Daniels (2009), 6–7; and Daniels (2018), 57–59, argues that Boccaccio sought Acciaiuoli's favor by dedicating the work to his sister Andrea. Casteen (2018), 226 et passim, sees the dedication as motivated by a desire for patronage and by his evolving appreciation of the queen.
86. Lokaj (2000).
87. Blamires (1992), 166. For the contexts, Stillinger–Psaki (2006) and the more nuanced interpretation by Panizza (2013), which balances this rhetorical invective against the *De mulieribus claris*. For recent work, Cagnolati (2014); Migiel (2015); Armstrong (2015), 240–41. On Boccaccio's changing voice, Daniels (2015).
88. Jordan (1987).
89. Shemek (2013), 195.
90. I.18, Boccaccio (1983.1), 90–101; Boccaccio (2018), 38–42. Ficara (2018) examines Petrarch's and Boccaccio's attitudes from a philological viewpoint: "idea, in one of its primitive acceptations, means precisely form and poem" (286).

91. Gaglione (2009), 261–62; Di Franza (2012); Rullo (2012); Wallace (2013), 78; Weaver (2013), 88–89, 378 n. 3.
92. On Sancia and the other de'Cabanni, Musto (2013), readings 65, 74, 76.
93. Kelly (2003), 16–17, for the organization of her study around these virtues.
94. XVII.3 (1372–73). Petrarch (2004.2), 4:2364–95; Petrarch (2005.1), 2:655–68.
95. As in Wallace, Weaver and Sherberg in Kirkham (2013). See also Gardner (1930), 228–38; Delcorno Branca (1985); Delcorno Branca (1990), Delcorno Branca (1991); Barbato (2012); Zinelli (2012); Kleinhenz (2014).
96. Chapter 6, p. 182.
97. From Boccaccio (2011), 249–50.
98. *Fortuna* becomes the central character in *De casibus*. See Marchesi (2013).
99. "Et coniugum austeros mores," Boccaccio (2003), 471, par. 11.
100. See also Boccaccio (2003), 470–72.

WORKS CITED

Adams, Tracy. 2012. "Between History and Fiction: Revisiting the Affaire de la Tour de Nesle." *Viator* 43.2:165–92.

Ainsworth, Peter. 2003.2. "Legendary History: *Historia* and *Fabula*." In Deliyannis (2003), 387–416.

Allaire, Gloria F. 2014. With Regina Psaki, ed. *The Arthur of the Italians: The Arthurian Legend in Medieval Italian Literature and Culture*. Cardiff: University of Wales Press.

Auerbach, Erich. 1953. *Mimesis: The Representation of Reality in Western Literature*. William Trask, trans. Princeton: Princeton University Press.

Bak, János M. 1997. "Queens as Scapegoats in Medieval Hungary." In Duggan (1997), 223–33.

Barbato, Marcello. 2012. With Giovanni Palumbo. "Fonti francesi di Boccaccio napoletano?" In BA, 127–48.

Beaumanoir, Philippe de Remi. 1988. *La Manekine: Text, Translation, Commentary*. Irene Gnarra, ed. and trans. New York: Garland.

—. 1999. *Le roman de la manekine*. Barbara Nelson Sargent-Baur et al., ed. Amsterdam: Rodopi.

—. 2010. *Manekine, John and Blonde, and "Foolish generosity."* Barbara Nelson Sargent-Baur, ed. University Park: Pennsylvania State University Press.

Berthelot, Anne. 2006. With Margherita Lecco. *Materiali arturiani nelle letterature di Provenza, Spagna, Italia*. Alessandria: Edizioni dell'Orso.

Bianchini, Janna. 2012. *The Queen's Hand: Power and Authority in the Reign of Berenguela de Castile*. Philadelphia: University of Pennsylvania Press.

Bietenholz, Peter G. 1994. *Historia and Fabula: Myths and Legends in Historical Thought from Antiquity to the Modern Age*. Leiden: Brill.

Bildhauer, Bettina. 2003. With Robert Mills, ed. *The Monstrous Middle Ages*. Toronto: University of Toronto Press.

Black, Nancy B. 2000. "*La Belle Hélène de Constantinople* and Crusade Propaganda at the Court of Philip the Good." *15th-Century Studies* 26:42–51.

Blamires, Alcuin, ed. 1992. *Woman Defamed and Woman Defended: An Anthology of Medieval Texts*. Oxford: Clarendon.

—. 1997. *The Case for Women in Medieval Culture*. Oxford: Clarendon.

Boccaccio, Giovanni. 1992a. *Epistole e lettere*. Ginetta Auzzas, ed. In Boccaccio (1992).

Boli, Todd. 2013. "Personality and Conflict *(Epistole, Lettere)*." In Kirkham (2013), 295–306.
Bottigheimer, Ruth. 2008. "Before *Contes du temps passé* (1697): Charles Perrault's *Griselidis, Souhaits* and *Peau*." *The Romantic Review* 99.3:175–89.
Brown, Elizabeth A.R. 2000. "The King's Conundrum." In *Medieval Futures: Attitudes to the Future in the Middle Ages*. J.A. Burrow and Ian P. Wei, ed. Woodbridge: Boydell, 115–65.
Bubenicek, Venceslas. 2014. *Guiron le courtois: Roman arthurien en prose du xiiie siècle*. Berlin: De Gruyter.
Cagnolati, Antonella, De S.M. González. 2014. *Boccaccio e le donne*. Rome: Aracne.
Cavallaro, Dani. 2016. *The Chivalric Romance and the Essence of Fiction*. Jefferson, NC: McFarland.
Cerasoli, Francesco. 1896–97. "Clemente VI e Giovanna I di Napoli: Documenti inediti dell'Archivio Vaticano (1343–1352)." ASPN 21:3–41; 227–64, 427–75, 667–707; 22:3–46.
Cigni, Fabrizio. 2004. "Per la storia del *Guiron le Courtois* in Italia." *Critica del Testo* 7.1:295–316.
—. 2006. "Mappa redazionale del *Guiron le Courtois* diffuso in Italia." In *Modi e forme della fruizione della materia arturiana nell'Italia dei sec. XIII–XV: Milano, 4–5 febbraio 2005*. Milan: Istituto lombardo di scienze e lettere, 85–117.
—. 2014. "French Redactions in Italy: Rustichello da Pisa." In Allaire-Psaki (2014), 21–40.
Cohen, Jeffrey Jerome. 1999. *Of Giants: Sex, Monsters, and the Middle Ages*. Minneapolis: University of Minnesota Press.
Daniels, Rhiannon. 2009. *Boccaccio and the Book: Production and Reading in Italy 1340–1520*. London: Legenda.
—. 2015. "Boccaccio's Narrators and Audiences." In Armstrong (2015), 36–51.
—. 2018. "Reading Boccaccio's Paratexts: Dedications as Thresholds between Worlds." In Holmes–Stewart, 48–79.
d'Arras, Jean. 1932. *Melusine: Roman du XIVe siècle*. Louis Stouff, ed. Dijon: Université de Dijon.
—. 2003. *Melusine: Ou, La noble histoire de Lusignan. Roman de XIVe siècle*. Jean-Jacques Vincensini, ed. Paris: Librarie Générale Française.
—. 2012. *Melusine, Or the Noble History of Lusignan*. Donald Maddox and Sara Sturm-Maddox, ed. and trans. University Park: Pennsylvania State University Press.
De Cessolis, Jacobus. 2008. *The Book of Chess*. H.L. Williams, trans. New York: Italica Press.
Delcorno Branca, Daniela. 1968. *I romanzi italiani di Tristano e la Tavola Ritonda*. Florence: Olschki.
—. 1974. *Il romanzo cavalleresco medievale*. Florence: Sansoni.
—. 1985. *Tradizione arturiana in Boccaccio*. Florence: Olschki.
—. 1990. "*De Arturo Britorum rege*: Boccaccio fra storiografia e romanzo." *Studi sul Boccaccio* 19:151–90.
—. 1991. *Boccaccio e le storie di re Artù*. Bologna: Il Mulino.
—. 1998. *Tristano e Lancillotto in Italia: Studi di letteratura arturiana*. Ravenna: Longo.
—. 2004. *La tradizione della* Mort Artu *in Italia*. Rome: Viella.

—. 2014. "The Italian Contribution: *La Tavola Ritonda.*" In Allaire–Psaki (2014), 69–90.
De Matteis, Mario. 2010. With Antonio Trinchese and Giuliana Pianura, ed. Lo re Artu k'avemo perduto: *Storia e mito di Artu e del Graal in Italia.* Oberhausen: Athena.
Di Franza, Concetta. 2012. "'Dal fuoco dipinto a quello che veramente arde': Una poetica in forma di *quaestio* nel capitolo VIII dell' *Elegia di Madonna Fiammetta.*" In BA, 89–101.
Duggan, Anne J. 1997. *Queens and Queenship in Medieval Europe.* Bury St. Edmunds: Boydell.
D'Urso et al., ed. 2021. *Manoscritti miniati della Biblioteca Nazionale di Napoli* 1. *Italia, secoli XIII–XIV.* Rome: Istituto Poligrafico e Zecca dello Stato.
Earenfight, Theresa. 2010. *The King's Other Body: María of Castile and the Crown of Aragon.* Philadelphia: University of Pennsylvania Press.
—. 2013. *Queenship in Medieval Europe.* Basingstoke: Palgrave Macmillan.
Falkeid, Unn. 2017. *The Avignon Papacy Contested: An Intellectual History from Dante to Catherine of Siena.* Cambridge, MA: Harvard University Press.
Ferrante, Joan M. 2011. *The Conflict of Love and Honor: The Medieval Tristan Legend in France, Germany and Italy.* Berlin: De Gruyter.
Ficara, Giorgio. 2018. "The Perfect Woman in Boccaccio and Petrarch." In Candido (2018), 286–312.
Gaglione, Mario. 2009. *Donne e potere a Napoli: Le sovrane angioine. Consorte, vicarie e regnanti (1266–1442).* Catanzaro: Rubbettino, 175–292.
Gardner, Edmund G. 1930. *The Arthurian Legend in Italian Literature.* London: Dent.
Graf, Arturo. 2000. With Andrea Casoli. *Artú e le leggende bretoni in Italia.* Turin: N. Aragno.
Haines, John. 2013. With Pierre Courroux. "Mélusine et les L'archevêque: Légende et historiographie dans le Poitou de la fin du XIVe siècle." *Cahiers de Recherches Médiévales et Humanistes* 26:309–25.
Holloway, Julia Bolton. 2011. "Romancing the Chronicle." TMC 7:1–14.
Hóman, Bálint. 1938. *Gli Angioini di Napoli in Ungheria, 1290–1403.* Rome: Reale Accademia d'Italia.
Jones, Steven Swann. 1993. "The Innocent Persecuted Heroine Genre: An Analysis of Its Structure and Themes." *Western Folklore* 52:13–41.
Jordan, Constance. 1987. "Boccaccio's In-Famous Women: Gender and Civic Virtue in the *De mulieribus claris.*" In *Ambiguous Realities: Women in the Middle Ages and Renaissance.* C. Levin and J. Watson, ed. Detroit: Wayne State University Press, 25–47.
Kiesewetter, Andreas. 2001. "I principi di Taranto e la Grecia, 1294–1383." *Archivio storico pugliese* 54:53–100.
Kleinhenz, Christopher. 2014. "The Arthurian Tradition in the Three Crowns." In Allaire–Psaki (2014), 158–78.
Kolsky, Stephen. 2003. *The Genealogy of Women: Studies in Boccaccio's 'De mulieribus claris'.* New York: Peter Lang.
Lathuillère, Roger. 1966. *Guiron le Courtois: Etude de la tradition manuscrite et analyse critique.* Geneva: Droz.
Lewis, Suzanne. 2010. "Narrative." In Rudolph (2006), 86–105.

Lokaj, Rodney. 2000. "La Cleopatra neapoletana: Giovanna d'Angiò nelle 'Familiares' di Petrarca." *Giornale storico della letteratura italiana* 177:481–521.

Maddox, Donald. 1996. With Sara Sturm-Maddox. *Melusine of Lusignan: Founding Fiction in Late Medieval France.* Athens: University of Georgia Press.

Leonardi, Lino, and Richard Trachsler, ed. *Il ciclo di Guiron le Courtois.* 7 vols. proj. Florence: SISMEL–Edizioni del Galluzzo, 2020–.

Maillart, Jean. 1998. *Le roman du comte d'Anjou.* Francine Mora-Lebrun, ed. Paris: Gallimard.

Marchesi, Simone. 2013. "Boccaccio on Fortune *(De casibus virorum illustrium)*." In Kirkham (2013), 245–54.

McAvoy, Liz Herbert. 2002. With Teresa Walters, ed. *Consuming Narratives: Gender and Monstrous Appetite in the Middle Ages and the Renaissance.* Cardiff: University of Wales Press.

McCracken, Peggy. 1998. *The Romance of Adultery: Queenship and Sexual Transgression in Old French Literature.* Philadelphia: University of Pennsylvania Press.

Menache, Sophia. 2006. "Chronicles and Historiography: The Interrelationship of Fact and Fiction." *Journal of Medieval History* 32.4:333–45.

Migiel, Marilyn. 2015. "Boccaccio and Women." In Armstrong (2015), 171–84.

Miller, Sarah Alison. 2010. *Medieval Monstrosity and the Female Body.* New York: Routledge.

Mittman, Asa Simon. 2012. With Peter Dendle, ed. *The Ashgate Research Companion to Monsters and the Monstrous.* Farnham, Surrey: Ashgate.

Mollat, Guillaume. 1963. *The Popes at Avignon, 1305–1378.* London: Nelson.

Morato, Nicola. 2010. *Il ciclo di Guiron le Courtois: Strutture e testi nella tradizione manoscritta.* Florence: SISMEL-Edizioni del Galluzzo.

Nevile, Anne Elizabeth. 2013. "'A Tapestry Woven by Poets': Narrative in Text and Illustration in the *Meliadus de Leonnois,* British Library MS. Add. 12228." Ph.D. diss., University of Melbourne.

Nichols, Stephen G. 1996. "Melusine Between Myth and History, Profile of a Female Demon." In Maddox (1996), 137–64.

Oswald, Dana. 2010. *Monsters, Gender and Sexuality in Medieval English Literature.* Woodbridge, Suffolk: D.S. Brewer.

Panizza, Letizia. 2013. "Rhetoric and Invective in Love's Labyrinth *(Il Corbaccio).*" In Kirkham (2013), 183–93.

Paris, Gaston. 1876–93. With Ulysse Robert, ed. *Miracles de Notre Dame par personages.* 8 vols. Paris: Société des Anciens Textes Français.

Parsons, John Carmi. 2004. "Violence, The Queen's Body, and the Medieval Body Politic." In *"A Great Effusion of Blood"?: Interpreting Medieval Violence.* Mark D. Meyerson et al., ed. Toronto: University of Toronto Press, 241–67.

Perriccioli Saggese, Alessandra. 1979. *I romanzi cavallereschi miniati a Napoli.* Naples: Società Editrice Napoletana.

—. 1985. "Alcune precisazioni sul 'Roman du roy Meliadus', Ms. Add. 12228 del British Museum." In Sesti (1985), 51–64.

—. 2001. "L'enluminure à Naples au temps des Anjou (1266–1350)." In *L'Europe des Anjou.* Guy Massin Le Goff et al., ed. Paris: Somogy, 123–33.

—. 2005. "Gli *Statuti dell'Ordine dello Spirito Santo o del Nodo*: Immagine e ideologia del potere regio a Napoli alla metà del Trecento." In *Medioevo:*

Immagini e ideologie. Arturo Carlo Quintavalle, ed. Parma: Centro Studi Medievali, 519–24.

—. 2006. "Le illustrazioni di storia nei codici miniati a Napoli tra Duecento e Trecento: Riflessioni sullo stato degli studi." In *Medioevo: Il tempo degli antichi.* Arturo Carlo Quintavalle, ed. Parma: Centro Studi Medievali, 547–56.

—. 2010. "Cristophoro Orimina: An Illuminator at the Angevin Court of Naples." In *Anjou Bible,* 113–25.

—. 2011. "Dall'*Histoire ancienne* al *Roman du roy Meliadus:* L'illustrazione della battaglia nella miniatura napoletana di età angioina." In *La battaglia nel Rinascimento meridionale.* Giancarlo Abbamonte, ed. Rome: Viella, 17–27.

—. 2012. "Romanzi cavallereschi miniati a Napoli al tempo di Boccaccio." In BA, 347–56.

Pratt, Karen. 1997. "The Image of the Queen in Old French Literature." In Duggan (1997), 236–62.

Ray, Roger. 1985. "Rhetorical Skepticism and Verisimilar Narrative in John of Salisbury's *Historia Pontificalis.*" In Breisach, 61–102.

Raynaud, Christiane. 1999. "La reine dans les *Grandes Chroniques de France.*" TMC 1:226–39.

Rollo-Koster, Joëlle. 2015. *Avignon and Its Papacy, 1309–1417: Popes, Institutions, and Society.* Lanham, MD: Rowman & Littlefield.

Rouillard, Linda Marie. 2012. Review of "Jean Wauquelin, *La Manequine,* Maria Colombo Timelli, ed. (Paris: Éditions Classiques Garnier, 2010)." *Speculum* 87.1:288–89.

Roussel, M. Claude. 1995. *La Belle Hélène de Constantinople: Chanson de geste du XIVe siècle.* Geneva: Droz.

—. 1998. *Conter de geste au XIVe siècle: Inspiration folklorique et écriture épique dans La belle Hélène de Constantinople.* Geneva: Droz.

Royle, Nicholas. 2003. *The Uncanny.* Manchester: Manchester University Press.

Rubenstein, Jay. 2005. "Biography and Autobiography in the Middle Ages." In Partner (2005), 22–41.

Rullo, Alessandra. 2012. "L'incontro di Boccaccio e Fiammetta in San Lorenzo Maggiore a Napoli: Un ipotesi di ricostruzione del coro dei frati nel XIV secolo." In BA, 303–16.

Runnalls, Graham A. 1999. "Drama and Community in Late Medieval Paris." In *Drama and Community: People and Plays in Medieval Europe.* Alan Hindley, ed. Turnhout: Brepols, 18–33.

Rustichello da Pisa. 1994. *Il romanzo arturiano di Rustichello da Pisa.* Fabrizio Cigni and Valeria Bertolucci Pizzorusso, ed. Pisa: Pacini.

Sabatini, Francesco. 1992. "Lingue e letterature volgari in competizione." In Carratelli (1992), 401–31.

—. 1996. With Vittorio Coletti. *Italia linguistica delle origini: Saggi editi dal 1956 al 1996.* Lecce: Argo.

Shemek, Deanna. 2013. "Doing and Undoing: Boccaccio's Feminism *(De mulieribus claris).*" In Kirkham (2013), 195–204.

Shepherd, M. 1990. *Tradition and Re-Creation in Thirteenth Century Romance: "La Manekine" and "Jean et Blonde" by Philippe de Rémi.* Amsterdam: Rodopi.

Stillinger, Thomas C. 2006. With Regina Psaki, ed. *Boccaccio and Feminist Criticism.* Chapel Hill, NC: Annali d'Italianistica.

Summerfield, Thea. 2010. "Filling the Gap: Brutus in the *Historia Brittonum*, Anglo-Saxon Chronicle MS F, and Geoffrey of Monmouth." TMC 7:85–102.
Taviani-Carozzi, Huguette. 2002. "Mythe et histoire dans les chroniques d'Italie du Sud (IXe–XIIe siècles)." TMC 2:238–49.
Thomas, Chantal. 1999. *The Wicked Queen: The Origins of the Myth of Marie Antoinette*. Julie Rose, trans. New York: Zone Books.
Tolhurst, Fiona. 2012. *Geoffrey of Monmouth and the Feminist Origins of the Arthurian Legend*. New York: Palgrave Macmillan.
Vingtain, Dominique. 1998. With Claude Sauvageot, ed. *Avignon: Le Palais des Papes*. Saint-Léger-Vauban: Zodiaque.
Wahlen, Barbara. 2006. "Nostalgies romaines: Le parcours de la chevalerie dans le *Roman du roi Meliadus*, première partie de *Guiron le Courtois*." In Bertholot (2006), 165–81.
—. 2010. *L'écriture à rebours: Le* Roman de Meliadus *du XIIIe au XVIIIe siècle*. Geneva: Droz.
Wallace, David. 2013. "Love-Struck in Naples *(Filostrato)*." In Kirkham (2013), 77–85.
Ward, John O. 1985. "Some Principles of Rhetorical Historiography in the Twelfth Century." In Breisach, 103–65.
Wauquelin, Jean. 1913. *Belle Hélène de Constantinople: L'ystoire de Helayne*. J. van den Gheyn, ed. Brussels: Vroman.
—. 2002. La Belle Hélène de Constantinople: *Mise en prose d'une chanson de geste*. Marie-Claude de Crecy, ed. Geneva: Droz.
—. 2010. *La Manequine*. Maria Colombo Timelli, ed. Paris: Garnier.
Weaver, Elissa. 2013. "A Lovers' Tale and Auspicious Beginning *(Filocolo)*." In Kirkham (2013), 87–93.
Weimann, Robert. 1996. *Authority and Representation in Early Modern Discourse*. David Hillman, ed. Baltimore: Johns Hopkins University Press, 105–32.
Wittkower, Rudolf. 1942. "Marvels of the East: A Study in the History of Monsters." *Journal of the Warburg and Courtauld Institutes* 5:159–97.
Wood, Diana. 1989. *Clement VI: The Pontificate and Ideas of an Avignon Pope*. Cambridge: Cambridge University Press.
Woodacre, Elena. 2013. *Queenship in the Mediterranean: Negotiating the Role of the Queen in the Medieval and Early Modern Eras*. New York: Palgrave Macmillan.
Yalom, Marilyn. 2004. *Birth of the Chess Queen: A History*. New York: Harper Collins.
Zabbia, Marino. 1998. "Il contributo dei notai alla codificazione della memoria storica nelle città italiane (secoli XII–XIV)." *Nuova Rivista Storica* 82.1:1–16.
Zinelli, Fabio. 2012. "'Je qui li livre escrive de letre en vulgal': Scrivere il francese a Napoli in età angioina." In BA, 149–73.

6. VISUAL EVIDENCE

INTRODUCTION

This chapter examines how late medieval historiography also drew on visual sources: the common language and grammar of images developed during the trecento throughout the Italian peninsula. Just as these trecento historians used literary conventions to "fill in the gaps" of biography, character and motivation, so too could they rely on a newly developing set of visual symbols, gestures, and scenarios to quickly remind their readers of important themes and tropes. While visual evidence cannot be as clearly linked to sources in the way that textual influence can be traced using standard philological methods, medieval textual communities formed not only around orality and script but also around the visual, and the continuities among all three forms of text helped define such communities.[1]

Reversing Gregory the Great's *dictum* that images are the texts of the illiterate and therefore subordinate to the written word,[2] Herbert Kessler has remarked, "by the High Middle Ages, pictures were, in fact, no longer simply 'books of the illiterate,' but, rather, multivalent devices used by various groups in diverse ways and deeply implicated in oral as well as written culture."[3] Madeline Harrison Caviness has extended this dynamic to issues of visual authorship and reception and called these "viewing communities."[4] Italian elites used various forms of visuality ranging from the public display of political, religious and social values in sculpture, mosaic, fresco, liturgical props to newly emerging panel painting with appeal to both literate and illiterate viewers. These forms addressed various contexts and deployed a recognizable visual grammar and vocabulary to present the public language of virtues and vices, praise, blame, aspiration and power that were understandable to all members of the medieval urban community: nobles and *popolani*, learned, literate or unlettered.[5]

Yet political elites also commissioned more privileged visual forms aimed solely at the literate — whether Latin or vernacular — mostly in the form of manuscript decoration and illumination in both learned literature and more popular genres. Both shared the visual language of public discourse but also contained themes and motifs specifically crafted to promote cultural and political agendas among the powerful. The Angevins of Naples in particular followed the lead of their Capetian cousins and commissioned a wide range of deluxe

CHAPTER 6 ❧ VISUAL EVIDENCE

and lavishly illuminated manuscripts, underscoring ancient lineage, devotion and legitimacy.[6]

The first part of this chapter addresses trecento painting cycles aimed at urban audiences. One is extant: Ambrogio Lorenzetti's *The Effects Good and Bad Government* in the Palazzo Pubblico in Siena (1338–39). One is now lost and known only from scattered references and remnants: Giotto's *De viris illustribus* cycle in Castel Nuovo, Naples (c.1328–33). The last is known only from a detailed verbal description by the Anonimo romano: the three paintings commissioned by Cola di Rienzo in Rome (1346/47). We will then examine common elements and themes for their possible impact on the narrative structures, characterizations and framing techniques of trecento historians. Several of these writers made reference to visual sources: Francesco da Barberino, Petrarch, Boccaccio, Malizia Barattone and the Anonimo romano.

The second half of this chapter analyzes the closer and more circumspect impact of manuscript illumination within one context: Angevin dynastic conflicts around the inheritance and rule of Queen Giovanna I of Naples. Angevin manuscripts, such as the *Anjou Bible* (Maurits Sabbe 1), the *Statutes of the Order of the Holy Spirit* or *Knot* (BNF Fr. 4274) and *Meliadus de Leonnois* (BL Add 12228), demonstrate the ease with which Angevin rulers crossed the boundary between fiction and fact by inserting themselves into the fabric of chivalric romance and sacred history to bolster dynastic claims at home and abroad.

TRECENTO VISUAL LANGUAGE AND ITS THEMES

By the mid-fourteenth century, Italian religious art had begun using a clear symbolic language; and the forms of public, secular art were in the process of becoming more regularized. The lay viewing public was becoming more skilled in, and accustomed to, viewing and reading visual programs with an accessible visual grammar and language that Hans Belting called a "public rhetoric of wall painting."[7] But such a dynamic was hardly universal or consistent. Early attempts at visualizing the governing principles of the new communes, such as at the Sala dei Notari in the Palazzo dei Priori in Perugia, showed mixed results and a lack of ready-made visual vocabulary.[8] It therefore became necessary for public officials like the Florentine notary and doctor of laws Francesco da Barberino (1264–1348) to compose his *Documenti d'amore* (1309–13) [Fig. 6.1] and to attempt to spell out for contemporary artists visual programs relating to secular — and lay — time and space.[9]

Barberino was well traveled in Italy, Avignon and northern France. He was a student of Brunetto Latini, knew Cardinal Pietro Colonna and served as a diplomat at the courts of Pope Clement V, King Philip IV and Louis X of France. He seems to have been part of the pro-Angevin circle of intellectuals around Charles of Calabria during the

Fig. 6.1. Francesco da Barberino, "Iustitia," from Documenti d'amore. Source: MS Vat. Barb. 4076, fol. 87v. Autograph, c.1310. Vatican, Biblioteca Apostolica Vaticana. By permission of Biblioteca Apostolica Vaticana, with all rights reserved.

prince's protectorate in Florence.[10] He was probably acquainted with Dante, Cavalcanti and Cimabue; and he advised the sculptor Tino da Camaino. Barberino certainly knew Giotto. Whether he was a source for some of the iconography of the vices and virtues in Giotto's Arena Chapel in Padua of c.1305 remains unclear, but his images were certainly familiar to artists and intellectuals.[11] He does appear to have collaborated on manuscripts of Dante's *Commedia* and of Villani's *Cronaca*.[12]

He composed his *Documenti* in both Italian and Latin with Latin glosses and included twenty-seven miniatures that present a visual program for painters of public art to instruct them in a standardized symbolic language of civic vices and virtues. Yet Barberino himself admitted the difficulty in rendering these figures. French artists, he claimed, did not have the visual vocabulary to create a unified series of secular allegories and symbols that would relate to the new lay audiences of the Italian communes. Instead, he had to turn to Italian artists who were just then systemizing this language, and in many cases, he had to compose them himself. To make his meanings clear he also attached text labels to his allegorical images, a practice becoming standard in trecento public art.[13]

Such language had several sources, including a standardized set of artists' model books,[14] French Gothic sculpture, theater and legal courts and a rich vocabulary of ancient sculpture just then becoming accessible to trecento artists.[15] Painting, even monumental painting cycles on church walls, was no longer viewed exclusively as illustrative of sacred texts but also as a reflection of external, everyday and lay reality.[16] As imagery began to take on a reality independent of the memory of a sacred text — their *recordatio* — viewers began to understand painting and its imagery on a new level, as an independent medium that could convey not only secular *historia* (persons and events) but also *allegoria* (the deeper meaning of what the artists had portrayed).[17] Moshe Barasch[18] has demonstrated how Giotto could draw upon classical, Byzantine and medieval art, liturgy, legal procedure and theater to create an original language of gesture that revealed both a standardized code and new insights into human emotion and character. Eva Frojmovič has drawn our attention to Petrus Abano's appreciation of his contemporary Giotto's art of expression as a form of rhetoric allowing deeper insights into human character.[19] By the mid-fourteenth century, Italian public art was forging a message and a medium of the highest symbolic complexity meant for an educated public becoming acculturated to both the visual and the verbal signifiers that it contained.

Lorenzetti in Siena

We can still view one of the trecento's most dazzling pieces of public art, secular or religious: Ambrogio Lorenzetti's *Good and Bad Government*.[20] Because it survives nearly intact and has been thoroughly analyzed over the last two generations, we will begin our view with a brief summation of the cycle's public meaning. Lorenzetti's frescoes were not mere decoration meant only for the eyes of the city councilors but were placed where any citizen having business in the town hall could see them. These secular paintings were anchored in everyday reality as surely as biblical history and allegory had been attached to well-known sacred landscapes and kairotic events. They spoke a secular, quotidian truth as surely and adroitly as Giotto's Old and New Testament cycles in Padua conveyed the truths of Scripture. The Sienese needed no clergyman or monk to explain the meaning of these paintings. Ratté has emphasized that because such depictions of Siena and its countryside evoked city- and landscapes well known to their viewers, they acted as mnemonic devices that, like quotations from classical *auctores,* served the moral and civic purpose of reinforcing common identity and purpose.[21]

Such scenes underscored these paintings' truth claims through details known to its viewers. Most could absorb the meaning and importance of the *allegoria* of Good Government and its attendant virtues and comprehend its effects portrayed in the *historia* of the

Fig. 6.2. Ambrogio Lorenzetti. "Iusticia." From the Allegory of Good Government. *Source: Siena, Palazzo Pubblico, 1338–39. Public domain, via Wikimedia Commons.*

real city, well governed under peace and justice. [Fig. 6.2] They could also understand their opposites — the *allegoria* of Tyranny and the city and country in anarchy and desolation, reality beset by Cruelty, War, Treason and Division. These citizens formed Caviness' "viewing community," bringing their own experience and levels of interpretation to bear on the art. For literate viewers, even those labels placed beside the allegorical figures, the word *concordia* next to Concord holding the "chord" of unity, for example, would have been less a necessary sign than an added visual and textual gloss to both delight and reward the attentive citizen and to confirm their own experience and memory.[22] This "structured language of pictorial imagery"[23] helped create history: bringing together private experiences and memories into a common, and comprehensible, public narrative, deploying a standardized vocabulary and set of

CHAPTER 6 ❧ VISUAL EVIDENCE

rhetorical tools and leaving behind a *recordatio* that was constantly verifiable and reproducible in individual memory, in contemplation and in repetition, whether in oral, written or visual form.[24]

Lorenzetti's visual language was translated almost literally into the chroniclers' descriptions of both lawlessness and of justice: the Anonimo romano, the Villani, Cola di Rienzo and Boccaccio use explicitly the very same elements to describe the state of good or bad government. Whether such verbal descriptions influenced the visual, whether the influence came from the opposite direction or whether they all shared a common set of ideas and mental images that informed both verbal and visual, it is clear that the trecento had created a common language to describe virtue, vice, civil peace and war, treachery, betrayal and loyalty, anguish, joy and a host of other human emotions, attitudes, character traits, events and ideas. The visual could effectively fill in such gaps in ways fully acceptable to trecento viewers.[25]

GIOTTO IN NAPLES

Lorenzetti did not create his forceful images in Siena without precedent. Earlier in the century, Giotto di Bondone had completed several secular fresco cycles that spoke directly to public vices and virtues and that helped set their representation in visual and verbal terms.[26] Two were in Padua: one in the Arena (Scrovegni) Chapel, the second in the Palazzo della Ragione.[27] The third was in Naples in the Sala Grande of Castel Nuovo. In Padua's Arena Chapel, on the ground-level tier below his great Life of the Virgin, Giotto painted a series of grisaille panels representing the virtues [Fig. 6.3], each matched with its opposite vice across the hall.[28] Giotto's second Paduan cycle from c.1306–9, now surviving only in fragments, offered four representations of civic virtue, "focusing on the concept of communal rule through justice."[29] Frojmovič places the theoretical origins of the cycle in the context of such political theorists as Brunetto Latini and Remigio de' Girolami whose work would later resonate with Boccaccio, Domenico da Gravina, the Anonimo romano and Cola di Rienzo.

The third was Giotto's *De viris illustribus* in Naples. According to surviving archival records, Giotto made two extended stays in Naples.[30] The first was in 1328/29, perhaps at the invitation of Charles of Calabria (d.1328), the son of Robert the Wise. Since 1325 Charles had been King Robert's chief agent as Protector of Florence and most likely met Giotto there. We know that in 1330 Giotto was named a *familiaris* of Robert's court, which probably meant an extended residence in Castel Nuovo both to oversee projects and to act as a court advisor. The archives also place him in

Fig. 6.3. Giotto. Allegory of Iustitia. *Source: Padua, Arena Chapel, c.1305. Public domain, via Wikimedia Commons.*

CHAPTER 6 ✺ VISUAL EVIDENCE

Naples in 1333.[31] On his first visit, Giotto worked on the frescoes at Sta. Chiara but was soon transferred to work as *protomaestro* for the Capella Palatina within Castel Nuovo.[32] This was a monumental undertaking, with a wall surface half again as large as the St. Francis cycle in Assisi and the Scrovegni Chapel in Padua combined. The work was divided among several important artists, including Maso di Banco.[33] The theme chosen was the interrelationship of Old and New Testaments, a popular theme since the building of Rome's early Christian basilicas.

Some time in 1331/32, however, Robert had Giotto move on to another project, the *De viris illustribus* for the castle's Sala Grande.[34] With the exception of a few fragments excavated below the present Sala dei Baroni,[35] Giotto's *De viris illustribus* in Naples was almost entirely destroyed between 1453 and 1457, during Alfonso I's complete reconstruction of the Sala Grande. The surviving Angevin archives make no reference to Giotto's work, and our earliest knowledge of the fresco cycle comes almost entirely from literary sources.[36] Boccaccio's *Amorosa Visione* of 1341/42 extolls their beauty in the *"gran sala"* of the castle. While at the Neapolitan court, the Florentine Malizia Barattone (Giovanni Fiorentino) described and commented on each of the figures in a sonnet cycle c.1360.[37] In his *I commentarii* begun in 1447, Lorenzo Ghiberti's made brief mentions of Giotto's *"de' uomini famosi"* in Castel Nuovo.

From this evidence, scholars have concluded that across the grand expanse of wall Giotto painted a series of classical and biblical heroes. This motif first appeared in France c.1312 as the "Neuf Preux," or Nine Worthies, in a romance by Jacques de Longuyon entitled *Les voeux du paon*. The "Nine Worthies" included three sets of heroes. Three were classical: Hector of Troy, Alexander the Great and Julius Caesar; three came from the Hebrew Bible: Joshua, David and Judas Maccabaeus; and three drew from Christian history: King Arthur, Charlemagne and Godfrey of Bouillon, crusader king of Jerusalem. The theme appeared in a fresco cycle in Arras in 1336; and in 1337, King Pedro III of Aragon received a cycle painted on cloth from Avignon, most likely as a gift from Pope Benedict XII.[38] As in the Cloisters Hero Tapestries in New York from c.1405 [Fig. 6.4],[39] the portraits of the heroes were often embellished with visual marginalia: soldiers, clergymen, artists, court attendants and the women associated with the heroes, each group intended to enhance the stature of the particular hero and offer deeper context.

King Robert's close ties with both the French and Avignon courts would have given him easy access to examples of the cycles, and by 1335 his library certainly possessed a version of *De viris illustribus* by the fourth-century Roman Aurelius Victor.[40] But under Robert's direction, Giotto's commission quickly veered from Longuyon's original. In Castel Nuovo, the "Nine" portrayed were Alexander the Great, Hector, Achilles, Paris, Aeneas, Hercules, Julius Caesar,

Fig. 6.4. Nine Heroes Tapestry (detail), 1400–1410. Source: The Cloisters Museum, New York. Munsey Fund, 1932; Gift of John D. Rockefeller Jr., 1947. Accession No. 32.130.3a; 47.101.4. Public Domain Mark.

Samson and Solomon. This shifted the emphasis toward the classical and specifically Virgilian traditions so strong in Naples[41] and noted as a special interest of Robert's by Petrarch.[42] The only remaining biblical figure, Samson, symbol of strength, was a special favorite of King Robert and a subject of one of his diplomatic addresses.[43] Solomon, the king known for his wisdom, was singled out for praise and comparison to Robert himself by the Angevin court and its supporters.[44] Most important, however, was the Neapolitan cycle's unique promotion of the heroes' female counterparts — almost all queens in their own right — attested to by Malizia Barattone: the Queen of Sheba, Penthesilea, Dido, Polyxena, Helen, Delilah, Cleopatra and Roxana claimed space equal to the male heroes whom they faced across the Sala Grande.[45] Leone de Castris posits the possible influence of Francesco da Barberino in establishing this visual program.[46]

Serena Romano has speculated[47] that the cycle may also have included a portrait of Robert the Wise, and she cites as parallels the portrait of Robert himself surrounded by the virtues in the *Anjou Bible* (fol. 3v)[48] and the precedent set in Castel Nuovo by the grand fresco portrait of Emperor Frederick II and his chief justiciar Pier delle Vigne in a complex image of secular justice. That portrait may have still existed in the Angevin period and could well have set a precedent for Robert's own appearance in the Giotto cycle.

Robert also spoke at Castel Nuovo, addressing royal guests, the court and the prominent citizens of Naples. It seems likely that the king used the frescoes as a backdrop for several of his speeches.[49] Some were traditional religious sermons on spiritual themes, including Joachite spirituality, so popular at the Angevin court.[50] Others were more secular: to commemorate treaties, to celebrate academic occasions, to address papal and other ambassadors, to discuss domestic and dynastic themes. Robert spoke frequently at the Franciscan church of Sta. Chiara and, as occasion mandated, throughout Naples at its various churches and public spaces. Sermonizing in front of related images had a long medieval tradition, made even more explicit by the Franciscan preachers in their newly frescoed hall churches, and scholars have analyzed several instances of such practice.[51]

The combination of political oratory set against vivid visual imagery with the same themes, delivered by a skilled speaker to a focused textual community, could convey powerful political, religious and social messages.[52] Joost-Gaugier has presented a probable enough argument that Giotto's work on the cycle, and its location in the grand audience hall, may have been a highly coordinated effort by Robert to set the stage for his announcement on November 6, 1330 that his granddaughter Giovanna would inherit the throne and later, on September 18, 1333, for her betrothal to Prince Andrew of Hungary.[53] Bearing in mind that the women portrayed by Giotto in the Sala Grande were almost all queens in their own right, Robert's words before them would have underscored without equivocation Giovanna's sole right to rule. The impact of these messages would not quickly dissipate, and like official court announcements, diplomatic and other news, it would soon be absorbed into both urban news networks and into the written accounts of notaries and chroniclers close to the court or in contact with the streams of news circulated in the city.

While Cathleen A. Fleck draws on Martin Warnke's clear-cut distinction between royal courts and city-states to analyze Giotto's paintings in Naples,[54] it is more important to see this work within the larger context of a common trecento visual language that both relied upon and augmented verbal language across contexts of power, geography and audience. Such a contextualization eschews an outmoded dichotomy between the robust urban communes of the North and the thwarted civic aspirations of the South.[55] Robert the Wise therefore could use Giotto's frescoes of illustrious men and women as the backdrop for his own speeches to the assembled royal court and chief citizens of the realm in order to deliver a similar multimedia message concerning political virtues and agendas, framing such issues as the Angevin Guelph ascendency in Italy, the marriage of granddaughter and heir Giovanna to Prince Andrew of Hungary or the need for Naples' barons to unite their *seggi* in peace and harmony within the context of well known and understood visual exempla of civic virtues and historical figures.

Still, given their limited exposure, how would Giotto's frescoes have influenced trecento historiography? Leone de Castris summarizes previous research to demonstrate their probable influence on Boccaccio in more than his *Amorosa Visione,* providing a key influence for his *De mulieribus claris* and *De casibus virorum illustrium*.[56] Again, given the very public nature of the Sala Grande for both the Angevin court and the citizens of Naples, the examples of public virtue expressed by these royal men and women would easily have made their way into the currency of political discourse within the city, both in oral and eventual written form in chronicles and histories. They would have provided a deep context for historians to construct their views of contemporary Neapolitan issues and personalities.

The obvious historiographical question remains, however: why cannot we trace any influence of Giotto's frescos within the writings or correspondence of Francesco Petrarch, who made the *De viris illustribus* a central theme of humanist historiography? In his *Itinerary to the Holy Land,* Petrarch describes a visit to Naples some time in the 1350s.[57] He claims to have visited many sites in the city, including the Castel Nuovo and its Cappella Palatina, where he says "my countryman [Giotto] has left great monuments of his skill and genius." Yet Petrarch, then still working on his own *De viris illustribus,* makes no mention of Giotto's cycle in the castle's Sala Grande. Leone de Castris has summarized considerable research and debate on this omission, tentatively concluding that Petrarch ignored this cycle and, instead, concentrated on the Cappella Palatina and its sacred art because of the religious pilgrimage theme of his *Itinerary*.[58] Yet the Naples sections of the *Itinerary* concentrate not on Christian but on decidedly non-Christian sites, focusing almost solely on Naples' Virgilian and other classical remains, as well as on the city's secular palaces and *seggi*. Petrarch recounted his visits with King Robert and their conversations about the city's Virgilian past in

CHAPTER 6 ⚜ VISUAL EVIDENCE

preparation for his coronation on Rome's Capitoline in April 1341. Given the classical basis for Petrarch's attachment to Robert and to Naples' past,[59] it seems highly improbable that religious interest could explain his omission of one of the most classical of contemporary fresco cycles in the very Castel Nuovo where Robert had hosted the poet.

Another explanation may be more plausible, therefore. While Petrarch began his *De viris illustribus* in 1338, shortly after Giotto has completed the Naples cycle, the poet had few if any contacts with the Neapolitan court until his campaign to be crowned poet laureate between 1339 and 1341. Thereafter his friendship with King Robert blossomed, as did his almost boundless admiration for the monarch. In Chapter 8, we will detail Petrarch's bitter disappointment at Robert's death, his sudden about-face concerning Naples, the Angevins and Robert's successor Queen Giovanna I and his complex motives for this turnaround. Given Petrarch's outspoken disdain for the queen and her succession, and his campaign to vilify her, her court and her city, it may be as likely that Petrarch ignored these frescoes precisely because of their female heroes' positive connections to Queen Giovanna's succession.[60] Petrarch was also among the first to lay the blame for Prince Andrew's murder on the queen and to interpret it as one of the first signs of what he represented as the Regno's rapid decline.[61] Giotto's allegorical depiction of Queen Giovanna's right to rule and her close ties to Andrew of Hungary ran counter to Petrarch's narrative. Nor can we attribute the omission to a generalized misogyny. Chapter 8 examines his admiration for Countess Maria of Pozzuoli, whom he contrasts to Giovanna.[62] In his 1358 congratulatory letter to Empress Anna on the birth of a girl,[63] Petrarch explicitly lays aside male privilege and offers a brief treatise on "famous women" ranging from Minerva and Sappho, through the Amazon queen Orithya to Penthesilea, Cleopatra, Zenobia to Camilla and Countess Matilda of Tuscany.[64] In his carefully edited image of Naples, this always self-conscious craftsman of personal and cultural narrative excluded one woman in particular: Giovanna I. He therefore had ample reason to ignore one of the very first and most important examples of the *De viris illustribus* tradition that was to become central to his later reputation.[65]

RIENZO'S POLITICAL FRESCOES IN ROME

Like Francesco da Barberino, Cola di Rienzo was a well-educated notary. He was a renowned student and interpreter of Rome's ancient remains, an ambassador to the papal court in Avignon in 1343–44, a friend of Petrarch and eventually a *familiaris* of the papal court and household. At Avignon he had the opportunity either to meet, or to see and study the paintings of, Simone Martini, Rico d'Arezzo, Pietro da Viterbo and Matteo Giovanetti. He was the pope's official representative on Rome's civic council from 1344 to 1347 and secretly received substantial funding from the papal treasury to push forward the pope's agenda of reform.[66]

We know Cola di Rienzo's political paintings in Rome[67] solely through textual descriptions in the chronicle of the Anonimo romano, who created a *recordatio* that spans the verbal and the visual. The Anonimo also provides us with both the social and political contexts of these paintings and with his and the audience's reaction, making these images a unique monument to the trecento's urban language of visual symbol. We know neither the artists nor the exact datings of these paintings; nor do we know their media or longevity. Like contemporary *pitture infamanti*, they may have been quite current and ad hoc, quickly completed and just as quickly removed from public view after they had served their purposes. Nor can we completely trust the descriptions provided by the Anonimo romano at the dawn of Renaissance art analysis. We do know that these paintings were commissioned and completed sometime between 1344 and 1347 in preparation for Rienzo's nonviolent overthrow of Rome's baronial government and that their exhibitions were attended by large numbers of Romans.

As Amy Schwartz has already made clear,[68] the Anonimo romano's descriptions, despite their sometimes confused interpretations, are so highly detailed that one can recreate not only the art but trace its origins back to other well-known trecento works.[69] In addition, as the Anonimo romano narrates, they were linked to Cola's own series of speeches intended to explain this public art's meaning to his audience of Rome's lay middle class and barons. They were also accompanied by a series of rhymed text labels — *tituli* or *didascalia*, probably in Romanesco — to help identify their allegorical figures and the actions unfolding around them.[70] They thus formed the core of an extended textual community constructed around the political, religious and social ideals of Cola's new *buono stato*. Underscored by Cola's highly skilled rhetoric and set within carefully chosen and well revered sites associated with Rome's sacred and secular history, they became a highly laicized version of Gregory the Great's "bibles for the laity" or of Franciscan preaching against a backdrop of sacred fresco cycles. Cola's visual texts — like Barberino's treatise and Giotto's and Lorenzetti's cycles — spoke to urban vices and virtues. They also set the context for contemporary narratives of Rienzo's *buono stato* and for the politics of Rome in the mid-trecento. Though usually overlooked in modern discussions of trecento art, they formed one of that century's most important portrayals of civic culture and so lent themselves easily to framing both political agendas and narratives.[71]

Rienzo commissioned three grand paintings or cycles to outline his ideas on Rome's current political and social decline, its ancient past and its apocalyptic future as the New Jerusalem. While the Anonimo romano makes it clear that Rienzo commissioned them,[72] it is not clear who painted them. Given Rome's geographical and cultural position mid-way between Tuscany and Naples, its continued ties to papal Avignon (which employed and secretly funded Rienzo) and his personal acquaintance with some of the era's most important culture workers, it is reasonable to assume that Rienzo would have contracted one or more of the finest artists of the trecento then making the circuit of communes and courts, following commissions and patronage up and down the peninsula. Bearing in mind Francesco da Barberino's testimony to the innovative visual language that such cycles contained,[73] it is also probable that only a few of Italy's workshops could have completed the highly detailed paintings that Cola commissioned.

But could we expect the Anonimo, at this stage of late medieval ekphrasis,[74] to describe or analyze visual styles and techniques in enough detail to even begin to conjecture who Cola's artists might have been? The answer seems to be a tentative "yes." If the *grammatica* curriculum in Florence's schools is indicative of the rest of the peninsula[75] — and Dario Internullo has recently suggested it was for trecento Rome[76] — the inclusion of Prudentius' *Dittochaeon* and its highly condensed verse ekphrasis of a now-lost mosaic cycle of biblical narratives[77] would almost guarantee that the developing Latinist would be familiar with the techniques of visualization and of transforming visual experience into written narration and analysis and of recording an audience's emotional reaction. From Prudentius and Boethius' use of allegorical figures like Philosophia, such *latinantes* would have mastered narratives of fabulistic and iconic rhetoric and understood the meaning and use of personification, emblems, animal symbolism, allegorical figures and other visual tools already part of the trecento's visual rhetoric. Gehl notes that both Petrarch and Boccaccio certainly felt such influence.[78]

Rienzo commissioned the first of his paintings — on Rome's present corruption and decline — for the wall of the Senate Palace atop the Capitoline [Fig. 6.5].[79] This would have been visible to many inhabitants of Rome's *abitato*, even if individual details might be unreadable at a distance. Here in medieval Rome's most public space, Rienzo set his secular *Navicella*,[80] borrowing heavily from Giotto's *Navicella* mosaic of c.1300 [Fig. 6.6], just inside the main entry arch of Old St. Peter's atrium. While Giotto visualized Christ's miracle on the Sea of Galilee and his salvation of the Church, Rienzo's substituted Rome itself for the Church and its political turbulence for the storm at sea. He used Italy's current visual language for his portrayal and, like Giotto in Padua and Naples and Lorenzetti in Siena, secularized its allegorical valences.

Common to much trecento civic art, Cola's visual quotations from St. Peter's served as rhetorical synecdoche, evoking both Rome current situation and calling on its recent past through selective architectural and pictorial quotation.[81] Rome had recently been personified, for example, as the pleading matron

Fig. 6.5. Cola di Rienzo and the Capitoline Painting *by Lodovico Pogliaghi.* L'Illustrazione Italiana *22.17 (April 28, 1895). Source: Author's Collection.*

in the illuminated text known as the *Carmina regia* or *Panegyric to Robert of Anjou from the Citizens of Prato*.[82] Of the surviving exempla, the one probably closest to the Neapolitan original, perhaps completed by Neapolitan artists in Prato about 1335, is now in the British Library (Royal 6E.IX).[83] Tomei offers evidence of close ties to other Angevin manuscripts discussed below.[84] The manuscript offers a *"zibaldone"*[85] of allegorical representations of the virtues, images of the Capetian and Angevin dynasties, of Florence and Prato, and on fol. 10v, the famed profile portrait of Robert of Anjou enthroned against a backdrop of golden fleur-de-lis. The *Carmina* also presents the well-known image of Rome [fol. 11v, Fig. 6.7] as a widow dressed in black, urging Robert to rescue justice, bring the papacy back to Italy and restore Rome to its proper grandeur. The figure had been used as early as Bernard of Clairvaux's letter to the Roman people in 1145 and had become canonical with Dante's use in *Purgatorio* VI.112–14.[86] Her gesture of desperate mourning and imploring also borrowed heavily from the visual language that Giotto and his followers had already established in the Arena Chapel and in the *Navicella* at St. Peter's. Long

Fig. 6.6. Giotto, Navicella *mosaic, Old St. Peter's, c. 1420. Source: Copy by Parri Spinelli (1387–1453). New York, Metropolitan Museum of Art. Accession No. 19.76.2. Hewitt Fund, 1917. The file of this image was donated to Wikimedia Commons as part of a project by the Metropolitan Museum of Art.*

attributed to Convenevolo da Prato (c.1270–1338), Petrarch's Latin teacher, the text is now believed by some to be Petrarch's.[87] The illuminations have been attributed to Pacino di Bonaguida, a follower of Giotto, active in Florence c.1300–c.1350.[88]

In Cola's fresco — accompanied by his own metrical text labels *(didascalia)* probably composed in Romanesco[89] — the Widow Rome tells the story of the sinking, storm-tossed ship and the spiritually desperate condition of the city. The painting thus evoked Giotto's *Navicella* and combined *historia, allegoria* and *infamia* in a style and a rhetorical language that would be immediately readable by his viewers. Giotto had already provided what the Anonimo romano described as the "tremendous sea with horrible waves, storming violently,"[90] as he had the storm-tossed ship. But Rome here is not the eternal Church but the earthly city, sailless and rudderless, about to founder. Instead of the apostles of sacred history, Rome herself sails the choppy waves of secular history amid the shipwreck of earlier empires: the successive *tempora* of secular history.

While the image of the shipwrecked Rome goes back at least to Gregory I, Cola's inspiration was more direct. In 1335

Fig. 6.7. Rome as an aged widow. From the Carmina regia *or* Panegyric to Robert of Anjou from the Citizens of Prato, *c.1335. Source: London, British Library, MS Royal 6.E.IX, fol. 11v. Public Domain Mark. www.bl.uk/catalogues/illuminatedmanuscripts/ ILLUMIN.ASP?Size=mid&IllID=50479.*

— contemporary with the *Carmina regia* — Petrarch had written a lengthy letter in verse, his *Epistola metrica* (I.2) to Pope Benedict XII, urging him to return the papacy to Rome, personified as the same distressed and disheveled matron. In 1342, with the arrival of Stefano Colonna's Roman embassy at Avignon, Petrarch wrote another *Epistola metrica* (II.5) to the newly elected Clement VI warning of the impending shipwreck of the Roman church, which he portrayed again as a distressed matron. The verbal and visual thus continued to cross-reference one another, enriching both and the appreciation and understanding of their audiences. The Roman author Giovanni Cavallini dei Cerroni would later include the image of the "ship of state" in his *Polistoria* of 1345–47, but it is uncertain whether this derives from Petrarch and Cola's usage, whether Cola borrowed from Cavallini, or whether such verbal and visual imagery was part of Roman's common discourse.[91]

Cola's painting substituted the twin towers to the left of Giotto's *Navicella* with two islands — Italy, as the label read — and, like the *Carmina regia*,[92] the four civic virtues. On the right, on another island, a kneeling woman replaces the image of the pope in Giotto's *Navicella*. She represents the suffering Christian faith, whose safety and well-being, her verse label reveals, depend on the health and safety of Rome itself. Devils might beset the universal Church on the cosmic level in Giotto's painting, but here in the real Rome, more earthly beasts replace the tempests and threaten to wreck the city and its church. These beasts carried the traditional meanings of medieval symbolism common both to humble bestiaries and to Dante's opening canto, but they are also uncomfortably close to the lions, bears and wolves on the heraldic devices of the baronial families known to all of Rome's citizens. The barons are not alone in sharing a place in this *infamia*.[93] Less powerful, if still dangerous, creatures also have their labels, and every social status, every profession responsible for Rome's present corruption is put up for public condemnation.

As we have already noted, the Anonimo romano had very little precedent for his account of these paintings, yet the fact that he was able to construct a comprehensive and comprehensible narrative of both their action and meaning indicates that he was relying on a factor over and above Cola's in-person exposition or the text labels embedded in the paintings. That factor was the readily understandable visual language then current in the mid-trecento that made the ekphrastic translation from visual to written text an apparently seamless endeavor for an educated layperson.

For the second painting — that of Rome's great past — Rienzo chose the site of the city's cathedral and the intersection of papal and Roman imperial power: the church of St. John Lateran where in legend

Emperor Constantine had donated his imperial powers in the West to Pope Sylvester I. As his text Rienzo chose the *lex de imperio Vespasiani,* an ancient bronze tablet dating from 69 CE, now in the Capitoline Museum, that records the earlier transfer of that imperial power from the Roman Senate and people to the emperor. Here Cola combined two of the most potent symbols of Roman power and authority over the secular and sacred.[94] For the Lateran meant not only the seat of their bishop but also the act whereby Constantine had transferred to the pope both spiritual authority and political power over the western empire.

There is evidence to suggest that the Anonimo was not present at this event, however. Unlike his painting at the Senators' Palace, open and visible to all, here Rienzo chose the apse, "behind the choir," the private space of church and lay elites, of former imperial palace and papal church. There Cola "gathered many of the powerful together, including the Colonna, among the most expert and magnificent of Rome" as well as "many learned men: judges and canon lawyers and many other people of authority." He delivered an oration to this invited elite on the very foundational authority of their power. While the Anonimo was a learned physician and may have even worked for the commune, he was not among this elite and may have derived his description from copies made of Rienzo's speech. He notes that Cola read from a *carta*.

The Anonimo's account of the Lateran address included no visual ekphrasis other than vague details about the elements of the assembled presentation.[95] In the middle of the piece hung the surviving bronze tablet of the *lex de imperio Vespasiani,*[96] which was known to Roman intellectuals like Giovanni Cavallini dei Cerroni[97] but which Rienzo himself had first transcribed. Yet the Anonimo only relates that:

> Around this tablet he had *figurae* painted, showing how the Roman Senate conceded authority to the Emperor Vespasian.... When [Cola] had finished and descended [from the pulpit], he was praised warmly by all the people.

Here the difference between ekphrasis and the Anonimo's purely verbal description is obvious: we have no sense of what the installation looked like, what the *figurae* could have been.

He probably set the tablet up on one of the choir walls. Around this object of political veneration he then imposed a painted *recordatio,* a visual meditation on the inscription that explained its meaning to an audience variously learned in classical history, and he placed it within the *historia* being portrayed. This would be recognizable to the elites present as a large-scale version of the text, gloss and image of one of the manuscripts they studied at university or used in their professional lives. Cola's painting fit into a trecento practice of using visual quotations of familiar landmarks, architecture or other "mimetic details" as synecdoche to involve

CHAPTER 6 ⚜ VISUAL EVIDENCE

the viewer's own experience and memory into the scene being depicted and to break down spatial and temporal boundaries.[98]

The message could not have been lost: here the present meets the past — and in a sense the present has a chance to undo, or edit, the actions of the past. For what the Senate could give in the name of the Roman people, it could now take back. So Cola read his transcription of the tablet — again, the Anonimo is clear that he used a *carta* — and delivered his secular sermon as he bade the assembled senators, officials and professionals to contemplate the historical scene, the center of which was the very reality that the painted *historia* portrayed, the very tablet by which such authority had been granted. In this way, Cola re-contextualized the tablet as Rome's secular sacrament of political authority whose power heretofore only the popes and clergy in their Lateran Palace had grasped. In so doing, Rienzo also challenged the sole privilege of Rome's clerical and lay elites to interpret such classical remains.[99]

Cola's lecture has been recognized by scholars as the first example of the Renaissance's understanding of ancient inscriptions and historical sources in their proper civic and historical context. Cola may also have had sections of the inscription no longer available to modern scholars, but his own legal knowledge as a notary and that of several of his closest advisers made even these unnecessary. The theory of a *lex regia* that had granted authority to the emperors was actively debated among Cola's contemporaries. But Rienzo's own interpretation of the event and his reliance on an actual inscription to document his interpretation underscored his attempt to reverse the Church's co-optation of this legislative concession and to return it to its historical, civil context and use. His coupling the tablet, the visual *recordatio* of the event narrated in the tablet and his oral presentation of both in front of the very audience historically charged with making this grant drew on long medieval tradition of religious sermonizing. But it also helped create a new secular textual community that could now form around common written sources, common images and common interpretations to produce ethical meaning, social identity and political memory and action.[100]

❦

Rienzo's third and final installation moved away from present political disaster and ancient Roman history to the apocalyptic future. The Anonimo states that Rienzo commissioned this painting for the Colonna church of Sant'Angelo in Pescheria,[101] within the Portico of Octavia in the busy commercial port of Rome. Cola's images — the Anonimo writes *"queste figure"* — contained neither lofty *historia* drawn from the annals of ancient Rome nor the *allegoria* used in his secular *Navicella*. Here instead the apocalyptic images were direct, the church portrayed was Sant'Angelo itself, built in 1290/91, and dedicated to the Archangel Michael, with its well-known and lofty campanile.

Fig. 6.8. *Apocalyptic Christ,* Maiestas. *Anagni Cathedral Crypt, Chapel of St. Magnus, c.1250. Source: Photograph by author.*

The painting's symbolism was complex and not completely standard.[102] But the image of final conflagration and the destruction of Babylon in a blaze of heavenly fire does appear in at least two fresco cycles illustrating the text of Apocalypse 18 and 19 and within a day's journey of Rome: at Anagni to the south (c. 1250, Fig. 6.8) and at Castel Sant'Elia to the north.

Such scenes were also painted by three trecento artists who traveled between Florence, Rome and Naples during this period: Cavallini, Maso di Banco and Giotto.[103] Our first example [Fig. 6.9] is attributed to the workshop of Pietro Cavallini.[104] This *Last Judgment* of c.1320 in the choir of Sta. Maria Donna Regina in Naples has been analyzed by Janis Elliott.[105] It includes the standard elements of the Last Judgment made canonical by Giotto in Padua. But here in Sant'Angelo in Rome, Cola employed imagery that was unusual for the Italian trecento and included such features as the "two witnesses" (Peter and Paul) and the woman of Apocalypse 12 (the Anonimo's "old woman," two-thirds burnt). Elliott has analyzed Cavallini's use of this "Madonna of the Apocalypse" in Donna Regina [Fig. 6.10] and has also noted its rarity

CHAPTER 6 ⚜ VISUAL EVIDENCE

Fig. 6.9. Pietro Cavallini, Last Judgement. *Naples, Sta. Maria Donna Regina, 1317–23. Source: Photograph by author.*

Fig. 6.10. Madonna of the Apocalypse. Cavallini workshop. Sta. Maria Donna Regina, Naples. 1317–23. Source: Image courtesy of the Complesso Monumentale Donnaregina.

Fig. 6.11. Passion cycle, Sta. Maria Donna Regina, Naples. Cavallini workshop. 1317–23. Source: Photograph by author.

in Italian art of the period. She attributes its presence directly to the Franciscan Joachite influences of Queen Sancia of Naples.[106] Next to the Madonna, the Archangel Michael (the "angel dressed in white") slays the dragon with his sword (Apoc.12:7–9). Prominent among the elect below is St. Francis. Elliott traces this program to the Angevins' devotion to the mendicants,[107] especially the Franciscans, the Anonimo's brown "sparrows."

In addition to the content of these paintings, there are also striking structural parallels to Cola's visual narrative. In his Passion cycle in Donna Regina, Cavallini had deployed a traditional framing structure to separate scenes [Fig. 6.11],[108] a standard visual device similar to the "thematic" structure of most conventional trecento histories, which divided their narratives into discrete chapters with clear topical distinctions.[109] By contrast [Fig. 6.12], Cavallini painted his *Apocalypse* over the doorway to Donna Regina's Loffredo Chapel with its figures and scenes arranged in a dreamlike free form, without ground lines or borders.[110] Such a "symbolic" narrative structure resembles the *Historia septem tribulationum* by the Franciscan Joachite Angelo Clareno.[111] Written c.1325, this employed just such a "field of dreams" from which individuals and events emerge from a higher reality to manifest the eternal *invisibilia* within human history.[112] In this regard, the

CHAPTER 6 ⚜ VISUAL EVIDENCE

Fig. 6.12. Pietro Cavallini, Apocalypse. Naples, Sta. Maria Donna Regina, Loffredo Chapel, 1317–23. Source: Photograph by author.

narrative structure of Cavallini's Loffredo *Apocalypse* also resembles the Anonimo's descriptions of such free-flowing *figurae* in Cola's painting.

The second painter brought to mind is Maso di Banco [Fig. 6.13]. Comparable in naturalistic intent and close in style to Giotto's — but far different in its spirit of ghostly evocation — is Maso's fresco in the Bardi di Vernio Chapel of Sta. Croce in Florence.[113] Working between the 1330s and 1350, documented as an assistant to Giotto in Naples, and contemporary to Cola's career in Rome, Maso painted scenes of Pope Sylvester binding and sealing the dragon that explicitly invoke Apocalypse 19.

Almost all the elements of Cola's apocalyptic vision can be found together in our third example: the *Stuttgart Apocalypse* [Fig. 6.14a-b].[114] Similar in their free-form composition and style to Cavallini's Loffredo *Apocalypse*, these two panel paintings, each about 35 × 86 cm., depict the episodes of the Apocalypse in a series of discrete *figurae* again floating in a "field of dreams" that departs from the set arrangements of medieval Apocalypses and Last Judgments in significant and original ways.[115] Pierluigi Leone de Castris, Alessandro Tomei and Victor Schmidt have synthesized previous research to conclude that these were Neapolitan — model panels presented c.1330 to King Robert and Queen Sancia for Giotto's now destroyed fresco cycle in Santa Chiara[116] — and that

175

Fig. 6.13. Maso di Banco, St. Silvester and the Dragon. *Bardi di Vernio Chapel of Sta. Croce, Florence. c.1340. Source: Photograph by author.*

Giotto's program followed faithfully the royal couple's Joachite spirituality, again influenced by Angelo Clareno.[117]

The frescoes would have been well known, and members of Giotto's school would have been fluent in the Joachite apocalyptic imagery employed by Cola's artist for the Sant'Angelo fresco. In addition, the familiarity of this imagery to those working or traveling between Avignon, Rome and Naples in the first half of the trecento would have made their visual language comprehensible enough for the Anonimo romano and others to have understood their overall program and major episodes. Leone de Castris has again synthesized recent research to demonstrate the influence of these programs on deluxe manuscript production in Naples.[118] Fleck has closely examined both the Stuttgart panels and the Cavallini *Apocalypse* in relation to these manuscripts and has concluded their visual programs are particular to Neapolitan manuscripts.[119]

As Lewis has noted for English Apocalypse narratives, such cycles acted as allegorical repositories for "problematic contemporary experiences...in which visual representation becomes an agent rather than a reflector of social change."[120] The Anonimo romano reported that some Romans were convinced by Cola's visual arguments, some thought them meaningless and mockable, and some thought that art and symbols alone could not change society. But Cola had finally achieved what he wanted: everyone in Rome who "poured into" the exhibit at Sant'Angelo came out talking not art but politics and religion. In bringing the Romans to openly discuss and to debate what most had given up for dead — the basis of a just

CHAPTER 6 ⚜ VISUAL EVIDENCE

Fig. 6.14. The Stuttgart Apocalypse.
(a) Neapolitan Master (now attributed to Giotto and studio), Apocalypse of John (Chapters 1–13), c.1332/34. Staatsgalerie Stuttgart, Inv. Nr. 3082. Tempera, 34.9 × 86.3 cm.
(b) Neapolitan Master (now attributed to Giotto and studio), Apocalypse of John (Chapters 14–22), c.1330/40. Staatsgalerie Stuttgart, Inv. Nr. 3100. Tempera, 34.9 × 86.3 cm. Source: Photo © Staatsgalerie Stuttgart. Used by permission of Staatsgalerie Stuttgart.

society, the *buono stato* — he had achieved what he had come back to the shattered city to do: to make possible once again what three decades of depression and civil war had destroyed, the common ground of civil society, from which he knew all other change must follow.

Whatever their iconographic antecedents, visual sources or creators, Cola's three paintings confirm both the impact of the visual on lay society and the active role that an urban population took in viewing, interpreting and then incorporating the visual into a textual community. In cities small enough so that every family shared connections with almost every other one, in which rumor, report, formal and informal conversation, public debate, *infamia,* preaching and official announcements became magnified by proximity and thick social networks, text and its interpretation — whether written, oral or visual — took on a broad definition that effected the ephemeral, day-to-day communication of the street and the marketplace and the more permanent record of the chronicle and history.

ANGEVIN MANUSCRIPTS AND THE VISUALIZATION OF POWER

This common language of civic virtues and vices, gesture, *historia* and *recordatio* also informed the production of deluxe manuscripts intended for a small audience of royals and other elites. In the rest of this chapter, we will therefore discuss such manuscript production for Angevin Naples. We hope to demonstrate the ease with which Angevin rulers used this codified language of civic virtues and vices, of gesture, of well-known historical characters, events and moral situations to insert themselves into the fabric of chivalric romance and sacred history.

While Jens Wollesen noted that earlier trecento manuscript production did not share this common language,[121] the Angevins themselves had a clear-cut precedent in the works commissioned by their cousins, the Capetian kings of France. The *Grandes Chroniques de France,* for example, offer several examples of lavishly produced and illuminated manuscripts documenting the history of the French monarchy in both verbal and visual form.[122] One such example, BL, Royal MS 16.G.VI,[123] one of nine illuminated exempla of the *Chroniques* dating from before 1350, was produced between 1332 and 1350 for John, duke of Normandy, before his succession as King John II (the Good). It covers the history of the French monarchy from its mythical origins in Troy, through Clovis to the death of Louis IX in 1270. Its 453 folios in double-column French Gothic script contain 418 one- or two-column miniatures. These illustrate every aspect of French royal history. In doing so, they codified a visual language of battles, sieges and sacks; royal births, coronations, marriages and funerals; betrayals, murders, assassinations, torture and mutilations; sacred visions and miracles, martyrdoms and liturgies; parliaments, coronations and councils; celestial events, portents and wonders. All levels of society are represented: royals, aristocrats, city-folk and rural workers, soldiers, popes, bishops and monks, men, women and children. Such lavish manuscripts were produced for and viewed by a very small royal elite. Yet the precedent they set for visualizing history in both broad stroke and the minute details of action and gesture was profound and easily accessible to the Neapolitan Angevin branch of the family as it set off to establish its own dynastic claims, venerable origins and hard-fought right to rule. Such influence is also evident in Paris BNF, MS Fr. 9561, a *Bible moralisée,* that follows long French tradition but is clearly the product of Angevin Naples.[124]

We must not draw too close a comparison to these French royal manuscripts, however. The *Grandes Chroniques* spoke a visual language of the north and of the Gothic. By the time of BL, Royal MS 16.G.VI, their abstract and stylized backgrounds, highly standardized forms and language of gesture, derived from long French traditions of sculpture and illustration,[125] were already being supplanted in Italy with the new language of Giotto and his followers. With the unfolding of the trecento, this Italian visual language was also being firmly established in manuscript production, and court artists and illuminators were learning its style and techniques. It remains important to remember, however, that such French royal manuscripts offered a rich source of visualization for events and personalities that could easily be translated into a new original language of Neapolitan Angevin manuscripts. One intermediate example is again the work of Francesco da Barberino, where his figure of *Iustitia* [fol. 87v, Fig. 6.1] presents a classically inspired Giottesque figure set against a traditionally French geometrical tapestry background.

Scholars have debated the provenance of a number of these Neapolitan manuscripts.[126] Our analysis, however, is concerned less with the precise origins of manuscripts discussed than their textual communities and the uses to which these manuscripts and their texts and images were put. We will thus speak of manuscript production not strictly in Angevin Naples but of Angevin Naples, what Tomei describes as a koinè of influence.[127] Here we will focus on three such texts: the *Anjou Bible* (Leuven, Maurits Sabbe 1), the *Statutes of the Order of the Holy Spirit* or *of the Knot* (Paris, BNF, MS Fr. 4274) and *Meliadus de Leonnois* (London, BL, MS Add. 12228). These examples provide a clear-cut demonstration of the visualization of power, placing real historical personalities and events within literary settings in order to bolster claims to legitimacy and rule through an interlacing of sacred and secular associations.

THE ANJOU BIBLE

The *Anjou Bible* of 1340[128] is one of the most lavish and well-known illustrated manuscripts of the later Middle Ages. It was commissioned in the late 1330s by King Robert and largely completed by 1340 by two of the court's artists, the scribe Iannucius de Matrice and the illuminator Cristoforo Orimina. It was probably intended as a wedding present for Robert's granddaughter and heir Giovanna I and his grandnephew Andrew of Hungary, but it was completed under the patronage of royal counselor and later chancellor Niccolò d'Alife at Queen Giovanna's request after Andrew's assassination in 1345. D'Alife then bequeathed the bible to the Celestine house of the Ascension before his death in 1367. From there it entered the collection of Jean, Duc de Berry. In this context, Duke Jean's acquisition of the *Anjou Bible* fits well within the duke's interests in family lineage.[129] The bible was already in the possession of the duke by the time of the February 9, 1402 library inventory, and its inventory description at that time speaks less of the manuscript's design and illuminations than of its heraldic and genealogical information on these Angevin royal cousins.

There are miniature portraits of the Angevin royal family throughout, including the frontispiece portrait of Robert enthroned among the virtues overcoming the vices, the figures clearly showing parallels to Barberino, Giotto and Lorenzetti (fol. 3v), the famed Angevin pictorial genealogy (4r) [Cover], Robert commissioning the Bible (217r) and a delightful scene of Robert and Queen Sancia of Majorca playing chess (257r). Of greatest interest here, however, is the insertion into the codex of King Robert's attempts to bolster the position of his granddaughter's future inheritance.[130] Just as Robert could use Giotto's *De viris illustribus* frescoes in Castel Nuovo to support Giovanna I's succession, he firmly identifies her as his heir apparent in several illustrations. On the pictorial genealogy, in the second range, King Charles II turns toward his heir Robert, while Robert himself passes the rule to Giovanna, who kneels with her sister Maria, embraced by their deceased father, Charles of Calabria. The gesture is underscored by Charles II's queen, Marie of Hungary, explicitly pointing to the act of succession pictured. In the third range, along with her younger sister Maria, Giovanna is again pictured receiving the grace and clear indication of succession from Queen Sancia and King Robert.[131] On folio 231v Giovanna is portrayed seated on a royal throne, the heraldic arms of the Neapolitan Angevins behind her. On folio 309r [Fig. 6.15], she sits, crowned, with Robert, in the left of three panels in front the Neapolitan Angevin arms. Giovanna and Robert examine a text, while Prince Andrew kneels in the right-hand panel as Robert hands him the text that Robert and Giovanna have prepared together. On folio 309r, Giovanna is shown seated, crowned and reading, in clear imitation of her grandfather's well-known wisdom, a theme picked up later by Boccaccio in his biography of the queen in *De mulieribus claris*.

The *Bible* — like Giotto's *De viris illustribus* in Castel Nuovo — counters the already growing opposition to Giovanna's inheritance among her royal rivals in the houses of Durazzo, Taranto and Hungary and demonstrates the love and respect between Giovanna and her future consort Andrew of Hungary.[132] In the tender miniatures of young Giovanna and Andrew conversing (249r), Giovanna wears the royal crown, while Andrew's head is bare, as they appear again on folio 289v. On folio 278r, Andrew caresses the princess' chin in a gesture of intimacy but also holds her arm in the ancient Roman gesture of *restitutio*. Barasch has analyzed how Giotto reinterpreted this to indicate loyalty and support. Indeed, Giovanna wears the royal crown, and Andrew's

CHAPTER 6 ⚜ VISUAL EVIDENCE

head is bare. Even though the bible appears to have been commissioned as a present for Andrew, nowhere does he appear crowned or set within any context of rule.[133] Throughout the manuscript, in or around key images of rule, the arms of the Neapolitan Angevins are consistently repeated and associated with Giovanna.

THE STATUTES OF THE ORDER OF THE HOLY SPIRIT

Quite different are the intentions and symbolism in Louis of Taranto's *Statutes of the Order of the Holy Spirit* or *of the Knot* of 1352.[134] These were composed in Old French by Florentine banker and royal seneschal Niccolò Acciaiuoli, who had also commissioned several other chivalric romances and histories, including a *Prose Tristan*, a *Roman de Troie* and a *Histoire ancienne jusqu'à César*. The *Statutes* are written in an Italian Gothic hand and fill only 10 folios of the 55-folio codex.

Fig. 6.15. Robert of Anjou and Giovanna I. Source: Anjou Bible, *c.1340. Leuven, Maurits Sabbe 1, fol. 309r. Public domain, via Wikimedia Commons.*

Again illuminated by Cristoforo Orimina, these folios constitute "one of the most sumptuous among those illuminated in Naples during the Angevin age, and it is the only illuminated example known of the statutes of an order of chivalry."[135] The *Statutes* attempt to visualize as fact the fictive world of the chivalric romances so popular in Naples, as Louis attempts to project himself as another King Arthur and to plant this chivalric world firmly on Neapolitan soil.[136] Like many of the chivalric orders created during the late fourteenth century, Louis here attempts to use the order to strengthen the bonds between a presumptive monarch and his powerful vassals-in-chief.[137] He projects himself as another Arthur and leader of his own chivalric order.

The *Statutes* project the royal presence onto various fictive scenarios: at feast, Mass, induction of new members, battle against enemies. On behalf of Holy Church, the order's knights embark upon ships decorated with the royal arms of Queen Giovanna and those of the house of Taranto to crusade in the Holy Land, joined by the arms of England, Leon and Castile, France, the papacy and others. Louis required the careful rendition of the hospital rooms where the wounded convalesce, along with the chapel where the tombs and hanging swords of (projected) deceased brothers line the walls. Boccaccio gives vivid testimony to the risible elements of these cross-overs between fact and fiction, explicitly comparing the fictive *"fatti"* of the knights of the Holy Spirit to those of the knights of the Round Table. But Boccaccio's testimony is even more explicit: he notes that Niccolò Acciaiuoli composed the *Statutes* in French in the same style used by those who had written the Arthurian romances[138] and attributes Acciaiuoli's leading role in their composition to Louis of Taranto's own ignorance. Another hand might also have been behind Acciaiuoli's composition: in his letter to the seneschal of February 20, 1352 on the "education of a prince,"[139] Petrarch had urged Acciaiuoli to instruct Louis in precisely this form of martial valor, to earn his crown, to be "tenacious with his own fame" and to "behave as he wishes to appear."[140]

Women are invisible, with one exception. This is the sumptuous carpet page that opens the *Statutes*, the famous double portrait (fol. 2v), [Fig. 6.16] of Louis of Taranto and Queen Giovanna I kneeling at the foot of the mandorla revealing the crucified Christ upheld by God the Father. Behind Louis kneels an attendant bearing a standard upon which rises Louis' helmet, crowned and adorned with high wings, bearing the Angevin royal arms. Giovanna presence in the otherwise all-male confraternity of arms is important: it both legitimizes the new order and acknowledges that in 1352 the queen still ruled Naples. On folio 3r, however, Louis sits alone, enthroned, the Holy Spirit descending upon him. Behind him hangs a tapestry bearing the Angevin arms and Jerusalem Cross below the elaborate knot of the order. He also wears the royal red with golden bands, mirroring Giovanna's red robe

CHAPTER 6 ❧ VISUAL EVIDENCE

Fig. 6.16. Double portrait of Giovanna I and Louis of Taranto. Statutes of the Order of the Holy Spirit *or* of the Knot. *c.1352. Source: Paris, Bibliothèque nationale de France, MS Fr. 4274, fol. 2v. ark:/12148/ btv1b8551130g. Public Domain. Source: gallica.bnf.fr/BnF.*

bordered with white ermine on folio 2v. Louis thus sought to use the visual program of the *Statutes* to highlight his chivalric prowess, to tie the knots that bind a male king directly to his vassals-in-chief and to underscore the sacred underpinnings of his Angevin bloodline, its *beata stirps*.[141] All were essential foundations of royal power.

Louis modeled his own image of kingship not on his dependent relationship to his wife or the Angevin dynasty but to literary sources: a conflation of Arthurian romance and crusading *gestes* with the omnipresence of Jerusalem clearly indicated. In this he sought to create his own base of power and loyalty, independent of his wife's claims to the throne. He had already secured the alliance of Niccolò Acciaiuoli and the financial and diplomatic power that this Florentine embodied. But above all, as Petrarch had advised, he needed to appear and to become the chief male of the realm.

MELIADUS DE LEONNOIS

A third example, *Meliadus de Leonnois*,[142] provides evidence of the direct impact of Arthurian romance at the court of Naples. Alessandra Perriccioli Saggese has identified several illuminated manuscripts of this work completed in Naples either in the form of *Guiron le Courtois* or of *Meliadus,* ranging from the late duecento to the mid-trecento. One manuscript with direct bearing on our study, now BL, MS Add. 12228,[143] is Neapolitan and dates from after May 1352 and the marriage of Giovanna I and Louis of Taranto. It was also commissioned by Acciaiuoli and written in Old French, in the same Italian Gothic hand as the *Statutes*. Perriccioli Saggese has suggested that the illuminator of at least the first two-thirds of Add. 12228 was again Cristoforo Orimina and workshop.

The BL manuscript of *Meliadus de Leonnois* discussed here falls into the *Palamedes* version of the cycle and takes up 352 double-columned folios of Old French. It ends incomplete at fol. 352v,1.[144] The work falls into two major parts. The first involves the many adventures of the knights of Arthur's Round Table and their forbearers among the *Tavola Vecchia*. Meliadus, the father of Tristan, emerges as the chief champion and best knight of his time. This first half reveals an externalized rhetoric of masculinity that promotes kingship as a matter of personal glory and mastery of arms and again reflects feudal anxiety over the power of vassals-in-chief.

In Chapter 5, we analyzed how literary romances like the *Contesse d'Anjou* and the tradition of *La Manekine* and *Melusine*[145] are thick with political and social context. They make explicit reference to the virtues and responsibilities of the ruler and of social peace and justice, giving equal platform to the skills, trials and accomplishments

CHAPTER 6 VISUAL EVIDENCE

of their female protagonists.[146] *Meliadus,* by contrast, embodies a male culture based on the idealization of knighthood, personal honor, revenge and violent confrontation through repeated cycles of encounter with new characters, challenges and jousts. Female characters remain nameless and passive. "Damsels" are captured, rescued, slain, used to convey news or arrange entrapment. They are servants, wives, mistresses, temptresses and queens but never active agents. The murder of one damsel (fol. 56v) becomes the occasion of a hearty reconciliation among male heroes, and she is promptly forgotten amid dialogues of praise for the chivalric careers of knights errant.

The second half of *Meliadus,* beginning with the bas-de-page image of the elaborate royal procession on folio 212v [Fig. 6.17], uses a more traditional romance structure. Meliadus meets the (unnamed) queen of Scotland during a festival and falls in love with her. Their secret love is discovered, and Arthur's sister Morgana falsely accuses the queen of physical relations with the hero. In disgrace, the queen is taken from Arthur's court by her husband, but then Meliadus attacks the Scots' entourage, wounds the king and takes the queen to Leonnois (Lohenois or Lothian). Arthur and the king of Scotland ally to avenge this dishonor and invade Leonnois. The subtext of secret love, betrayal and *infamia,* foreign invasion and male heroism all underscored Louis' role in courting, wedding and defending Giovanna against the invasion of Lewis of Hungary in 1347/48.

Fig. 6.17. Royal procession. Meliadus de Leonnois, *c.1352. Source: London, British Library, MS Add. 12228, fol. 212v. Detail. Public Domain Mark. www.bl.uk/manuscripts/Viewer. aspx?ref=add_ms_12228_f212v.*

185

The manuscript's visual program reveals a consistent and emphatic projection of Louis of Taranto's claims to rule into the fabric of the romance. On folio 4r, there is a bas-de-page illustration taking up the full two columns of the text with an elaborate portrait of Louis of Taranto [Fig. 6.18] that replicates almost exactly that on fol. 3r of the *Statutes of the Order of the Holy Spirit*. In this image, he is again enthroned and bearing the full regalia of crown, scepter and orb. Behind him a tapestry bears the arms of the Angevin rulers of Naples: the golden fleur-de-lis set in a blue field, impaled with the Jerusalem Cross. These arms — most often with the fleur-de-lis field capped by a red bar — was borne by every Neapolitan ruler from Charles II to Queen Giovanna I and used by her over the portals of her church of Sta. Maria Incoronata, for example. To bring home the comparison, above Louis is the elaborately drawn symbol of his new chivalrous Order of the Knot. To his right stands a crowd of beleaguered women, children and elders. To his left Asian peoples, flanked by camels and lions, offer open coffers holding what appears to be tribute monies,

Fig. 6.18. Louis of Taranto. Meliadus de Leonnois, *c.1352. Source: London, British Library, MS Add. 12228, fol. 4r. Public Domain Mark. www.bl.uk/ manuscripts/Viewer. aspx?ref=add_ms_12228_f004r.*

again perhaps directly influenced by Petrarch's letter to Acciaiuoli on the education of a prince. Petrarch explicitly states that the wealth of Asia is brought to a true king's feet.[147] Queen Giovanna I is nowhere visible, but the scene represented here obviously alludes both to Louis' relationship with the queen (who with papal backing refused to make Louis king, but only consort)[148] and to the heroic male qualities praised in the *chansons de geste:* the successful conquest of the pagan Muslims and the aiding of supplicants. The bas-de-page is set against the introduction to the tale of Meliadus. As it begins, Arthur is the only king whom the Roman emperor has not been able to subjugate and who has gained his special hatred.

Louis of Taranto thus inserted himself into two key Angevin themes: first their mastery not only of the Regno but also of the Holy Land and its peoples. The second theme is the Neapolitan Angevin role on behalf of the papacy and the Italian Guelphs as champions against the Roman emperors, in this case of the German attempts to reconquer the Mezzogiorno and assert inherited Hohenstaufen claims over both Rome and Naples. Robert of Anjou had resisted Emperor Lewis of Bavaria with diplomacy and military force, and his heir Queen Giovanna would inherit this same pro-papal stance against imperial and Italian Ghibelline power. By extension, Louis assumes the role of Arthur: the king who has led his country and its nobility against the threat of imperial aggression and whose rule is bolstered by divine agency.

Louis' identification with Meliadus is clear: his arms, which appear frequently through the rest of the manuscript,[149] bear the Angevin royal arms [Fig. 6.19] that also appear on folio 2v of the *Statutes* [Fig. 6.16]. The consistency of the heraldic and other iconography in the bas-de-page runs across changes of illuminator, visual style, costume and detail from mid-trecento to mid-quattrocento and points to a clearly determined visual program for the manuscript. Perriccioli Saggese has argued that Orimina and his workshop completed the illuminations up to folio 259 and that Orimina reserved for himself the bas-de-page illustrating the procession of the queen of Scotland (fol. 212r) [Fig. 6.17],[150] probably using as his model actual historical events in the triumphant processions of Queen Giovanna's and Louis of Taranto's return to Naples in 1348 or their wedding in Naples on Pentecost Sunday (May 23) 1352.[151] The permeable boundary between fiction and historiography comes to the fore: these same rich details of ornament and dress are also described by Matteo Villani in his *Cronaca*.[152] The placement of the procession illumination at the center of the codex and its assignment to Orimina's own hand points to the importance of the historical event and of the fictive episode both to the royal couple and to Louis' strategy for the *Meliadus* manuscript.

Louis sought to inject his career into this fictional account for two chief reasons: the first, reflecting the first part of the tale, is to

Fig. 6.19. *Meliadus bearing Angevin royal arms.* Meliadus de Leonnois, c.1352. Source: London, British Library, MS Add. 12228, fol. 68v. Public Domain Mark. www.bl.uk/manuscripts/Viewer.aspx?ref=add_ms_12228_fo68v.

mythologize his gradual rise to prominence among the high nobility of the Angevin court, to prove his worthiness to rule through martial valor. The second focuses on yet another tale of a falsely accused queen as the queen of Scotland becomes a fictionalized stand-in for Queen Giovanna. Her relationship with Meliadus and the false accusations in the fictional version become metaphorical doublings of the slanders surrounding Louis and Giovanna's relationship from the time of Prince Andrew's murder in 1345, through Lewis of Hungary's invasion of 1347/48 to Giovanna's and Louis' coronation in 1352. As in *Meliadus*, Louis claimed to have saved both the queen's life and her reputation. Through Louis' military defeats, his wanderings in search of aid and his final reunion with his beloved, he shares the suffering and travails of the fictive count of Anjou in the *Roman de la Comtesse d'Anjou*.[153] BL, MS Add 12228 thus becomes a manifesto of the new royal couple's union and of Louis' fitness to rule.[154]

CONCLUSIONS

In this chapter, we have drawn on the new visuality turn in medieval studies and its broader definitions of textual and visual communities to focus on how the visual was used in the late Middle Ages to project both cultural values and political power. We have examined the common

CHAPTER 6 ❦ VISUAL EVIDENCE

visual language emerging in trecento civic culture throughout the Italian peninsula and offered the examples of Lorenzetti's *Buon Governo* cycle in Siena, Giotto's *De viris illustribus* in Naples and Cola di Rienzo's political paintings in Rome to demonstrate this unity of language, expression and reception. We have also argued for the permeable boundary between such visual expression and verbal narratives in this common civic culture.

The same visual language could also be used to express the more courtly ideals of Italian feudal elites because they shared its textual referents with the urban commercial and professional classes who read the same romances and *chansons de geste*. For such elites, this found expression especially through manuscript illumination in both sacred and secular texts. Bringing together the visual evidence of the *Anjou Bible*, the *Statutes of the Order of the Holy Spirit* and *Meliadus* we have indicated how the permeable border between fiction and history, and between the verbal and the visual, was crossed by the Angevins to insert themselves into the fabric of sacred history and chivalric romance in order to visualize political legitimacy and power. Within the broader context of this study, we have also shown how trecento historiography drew on this variety of visual sources that shared the language of vices and virtues, political loyalty and legitimacy then being developed for Italian civic culture and commonly understood by audiences North and South.

NOTES

1. The need for such an investigation for trecento verbal and visual sources had already been signaled by Zorzi (1994), 420.
2. In two letters of c.600 CE to Serenus, bishop of Marseilles.
3. Kessler (2006), 160.
4. Caviness (2006), 68. We retain the broader term "textual community" as more inclusive of both author and reader and of oral, verbal and visual.
5. Kessler (2006), 161. Lewis (2006), 93, stated for northern medieval art, "Images can only evoke a story the viewer already knows; the narrative lies in the perception of the pictorial rhetoric of bodies, gestures, and gazes enacting the drama of the moment within a strategically constructed framed space."
6. On the medieval ideas of royal legitimacy, see the essays in Alfonso (2004).
7. Belting (1985).
8. Wollesen (1990), 187–88.
9. Francesco's autograph manuscript, from the first half of the trecento, survives in BAV, Barb. Lat. 4076, and 4077, online at http:// digi.vatlib.it/view/ MSS_Barb.lat.4076 (4077). See Pasquini (1997); Barberino (2006); Barberino (2008). Barberino's images have been analyzed in Nardi (1993); Frojmovič (2007); MacLaren (2007); Ciccuto (2011); Schmid (2014); Schmid (2015); Blume (2015); Lavin (2020), 92–100.
10. Leone de Castris (2006), 30.
11. Wollesen (1990), 199; Blume (2015); Lavin (2020), 100–101.
12. Barbato (2017), 98; Holloway (2020).
13. Wollesen (1990), 198–201; Frojmovič (2007); Boucheron (2018), 48–59.

14. Schneller (1963).
15. For example, Tronzo (2004).
16. Schmid (2014), 20.
17. Schmid (2015), 11–12.
18. Barasch (1987).
19. Frojmovič (2007), 204.
20. See Musto (2003), 104–39, 357–61; Bertone (2006); Riklin (2017); Boucheron (2018). Norman (2018) emphasized the close relationship between Lorenzetti's art and Angevin patronage and political agendas throughout the peninsula.
21. Ratté (2006), 100–161.
22. Kessler (2006), 158; Schmid (2015), 10–11; Boucheron (2018), 80–88.
23. Ratté (2006), 109.
24. Carruthers (1990), 156–220.
25. Lewis (2006), 91. Partner (1985), 13, 17–22, qualifies comparisons to modern film theory. Boucheron (2018), 5–11 et passim, demonstrates the continued legacy of these common referents through the sermons of Bernardino da Siena.
26. For representation in rhetorical tradition, Partner (1985); Kempshall, 245–52.
27. Frojmovič (1996).
28. Tronzo (2004) notes both the history of interpretation of these paintings and the classical sculptural models for the language of the vices and virtues portrayed.
29. Frojmovič (1996), 24.
30. Aceto (1992); Bruzelius (2004), 103–5; Leone de Castris (2006); Fleck (2010.3); Romano (2017), 182–84.
31. On dating, Leone de Castris (2006), 16–23; for the documents, 234–40.
32. Leone de Castris (2006), 168–216.
33. Leone de Castris (1995), 45–49; Leone de Castris (2006), 172–85; De Marchim (2013).
34. Bologna, 219–23; Joost-Gaugier (1980); Joost-Gaugier (1982); Joost-Gaugier (1984); Donato (1985); Leone de Castris (1986), 318–20; Ciccuto (1988); Leone de Castris (2006), 217–33; Fleck (2010.3), 45–48; Tomei–Paone (2010).
35. Leone de Castris (2006), 187 figs. 167–168, 226 n. 2.
36. Leone de Castris (2006), 13–14. Romano (2017), 183–84, accepts Leone de Castris' reconstruction.
37. *Sonetti composti per..., il quale essendo nella sala del Re Ruberto a Napoli vide dipinti questi famosi uomini;* in Leone de Castris (2006), 228–29 n. 13. We do not know whether the figures prefacing Petrarch's *Triumfi* in Florence, Biblioteca Medicea Laurenziana, MS Strozzi 174 bear resemblance to Giotto's originals. See Leone de Castris (2006), 223, fig. 182; Pignatti (2001); Di Simone (2012–13); Lavin (2020), 71–72.
38. Romano (2017), 227 n. 64.
39. Barnet–Wu (2005), 116–17.
40. Leone de Castris (2006), 221–22.
41. Hughes–Buongiovanni.
42. Petrarch (2002), 9.8–10.1.
43. To the Genoese, 27 July 1328. Musto (2013), 196–99.
44. Kelly (2003), 242–86.
45. A ninth woman is missing. Joost-Gaugier (1980), 312. Leone de Castris (2006), 217, 222, cites the full Italian title: *Uomini illustri dell'antichità e dei loro amori*.
46. Leone de Castris (2006), 231 n. 25; Lavin (2020), 69–105, for the historiography.

CHAPTER 6 ⚜ VISUAL EVIDENCE

47. Romano (2017), 183–84.
48. The winged vices mirror "Timor" in Lorenzetti's *Mal Governo*.
49. Few of the sermons analyzed and cataloged in Pryds (2000) provide locations. Among those that do at Castel Nuovo, see Pryds for Schneyer sermon numbers 73, 108, 110, 255. From context, we may also add 76 and 131.
50. Musto (1985); Musto (1997).
51. Owst (1933), 139–41; Wollesen (1990), 184–87; Caviness (2006), 71–74; Boucheron (2018), 5–11, on Bernardino's references to the Siena frescoes.
52. Caviness (2006), 72, emphasizes this interactivity of the visual with sermon texts.
53. Joost-Gaugier (1980), 317; Leone de Castris (2006), 221–24.
54. Fleck (2010.3), 39–40.
55. See Feniello (2015). For this theme in Rome, see Internullo (2016), 5–9. For Angevin connections to Sienese pubic painting, Norman (2018).
56. Leone de Castris (2006), 218–20, 227–28 nn. 9–11.
57. Petrarch (2002), 10.0–10.4.
58. Leone de Castris (2006), 217–26 and 227 n. 8.
59. On Petrarch's letters with Robert leading up to the coronation, *Familiares* IV.1-9. For his bitterness on Robert's death and Giovanna I's succession, V.1–6.
60. Musto (2013), lvi–lxi, 261–69. Citing *Familiares* XXIII.17, Casteen (2018), 226, reconstructs Petrarch's changing views on Queen Giovanna in the 1350s, just when he was completing his *Itinerary*, but even here his praise is pro forma and includes Giovanna only as a shadow of King Robert's splendor.
61. Chapter 8, pp. 244–46.
62. Chapter 8, pp. 240–41.
63. Milan, 23 May. *Familiares* XXI.8, Petrarch (2005.2), 3:175–79.
64. Had Boccaccio seen a copy of this letter while planning the first draft of his *De mulieribus claris* in 1361? Of the twenty-three women named in the letter, Boccaccio included biographies of all but Countess Matilda of Tuscany. Brown, Boccaccio (2003), xviii, suggests that Boccaccio would have had access to Petrarch's library while composing the work.
65. Witt (2009), 103–11, focuses on the textual sources for Petrarch's work.
66. "Della monete non dubitete, ca la Cammora de Roma hao moite riennite inestimabile.... Allo presente comenzaremo con quattro milia fiorini, li quali hao mannati missore lo papa, e ciò sao lo vocario sio." AR XVIII, ll. 256–90, Porta, 151–53. Giotto's expenses for the Castel Nuovo paintings, 15 Jan. 1330, were app. 515 florins: Leone de Castris (2006), (234, d.); April 1, 1331, app. 520 florins, (236, g.).
67. Musto (2003), 104–34.
68. Schwarz (1994).
69. Seibt, 48–49, discusses ekphrasis in the Anonimo romano's narrative technique.
70. AR 18. See Internullo (2016), 318–19, 327–29, 380–81; D'Achille (2017), 352–53, 364–66.
71. Examined by Holstein (2006), 151–67.
72. "Per una similitudine la quale fece pegnere." XVIII.66–67, AR 145; Wright, 33; Palmer (2021), 185.
73. Above, pp. 153–55.
74. Baxandall (1971), 51–78; Rosand (1987); Heffernan (1993); Johnston (2015).
75. See reservations in Witt (2012), 488–90; Gehl (1993), 14–15, 234–40.
76. Internullo (2016), 199–213 et passim.

77. Gehl (1993), 143–51, 165.
78. Gehl (1993), 152, 180–92.
79. The ease with which Lodovico Pogliaghi was able to produce this engraving from the Anonimo's ekphrasis is discussed in a presentation this author gave at the third Early Modern Rome Conference in October 2017. See above p. xxxii.
80. For Cola's "Navicella" painting, Anonimo romano XVIII, ll. 64–249, AR, 147–51. For its antecedents and imagery, Sonnay (1982); Musto (2003), 104–12; Tomei (2016), 211 nn. 28–30; Internullo (2016), 327–29.
81. Ratté (2006), 1–15, 46–47.
82. The others are Vienna, Österreichisches Nationalbibliothek, Series Nova 2639; and Florence, BN, Banco Rari 38. Tomei (2016), 201.
83. Online, with complete catalog information at www.bl.uk/manuscripts/FullDisplay.aspx?ref=Royal_MS_6_E_IX.
84. Tomei (2016), 209.
85. Tomei (2016), 204.
86. Holstein (2006), 19–20, 70–71; Falkeid (2018), 98–102, 133–34 et passim.
87. Petrarch (1996), 28 n. 14, notes the pervasive use of Rome as widow in his works.
88. I thank Julia Holloway for this identification. See Labriola (2004); Sciacca (2012). Pasut (2014) makes no reference to the *Carmina*.
89. See Internullo (2016), 327–28.
90. Wright, 33; Palmer (2021), 185–86.
91. Laureys (1997); Collins (2002), 31; Internullo (2016), 338–39; Falkeid (2018), 98–102.
92. Tomei (2016), 205.
93. On *infamia*, see above p. 72 n. 152. On *pitture infamanti*, Masi (1931); Ortalli (1979); Antoine (1988); Lori Sanfilippo–Rigon (2011); Ortalli (2015); Behrmann (2016).
94. On Cola's lecture on the *lex de imperio Vespasiani*, Beneš (1999); Collins (2002), 41–47 et passim; Musto (2003), 112–17; Holstein (2006), 72–74, 126–27, 162–67.
95. Musto (2003), 114. Modigliani (2012), 101, attributed this to Rienzo' imperialist ambitions but in Modigliani (2014), 244, re-contextualized his work into an Italian communal federalism.
96. Internullo (2016), 338.
97. Internullo (2016), 338.
98. Ratté (2006), 46–47, 111–14; Boucheron (2018), 49–59.
99. Holstein (2006), 160–65.
100. Ratté (2006), 83–90.
101. XVIII, ll. 213–49, AR, 150–51. See Musto (2003), 126–29 and 360 n. 17.
102. This is not the most common iconography for the period. It is missing, for example, in Giotto's *Last Judgment* in the Arena Chapel in Padua and Cavallini's in Sta. Cecilia in Rome. There are late medieval examples, including the Angers Tapestry of 1377–82 and the Estense *Apocalypse,* a block book of c.1450.
103. Collins (2002), 105–8, drawing on Musto (1985), Schwartz (1994), and Elliott (2004) discussed Neapolitan connections. See also Schwartz (2007).
104. Elliott–Warr (2004), 6–8.
105. Elliott (2004).
106. Elliott (2004), 181–82.
107. Elliott (2004), 185.
108. Hoch (2004) 132–33.
109. Chapter 4, pp. 96–100.

110. Elliott (2004), 182. Schmid (2015), 5, also calls attention to this free-floating composition in Barberino's fragmentary visualization of Constantia in heaven.
111. Chapter 4, pp. 96–100.
112. As Ray (1985), 71, puts it, such a structure "explain[s] in contingent language the strictly human foreground of history." Leone de Castris and Fleck synthesized research to demonstrate the unique influence of these programs on deluxe manuscript production in Naples.
113. Luchinat–Lusanna (1998); Ratté (2006), 114–17; Long (2009).
114. Stuttgart, Staatsgalerie, inv. 3082, 3100, previously in the possession of Erbach von Fürstenau. For bibliography and historiography, Leone de Castris (2006), 160–61 nn. 40–1.
115. Schmid (2015), 6, notes the eschatological associations in Barberino's visualizations of Constantia and other virtues.
116. Leone de Castris (2006), 128–29.
117. Leone de Castris (2006), 125–56, concurs with Musto (1997).
118. Leone de Castris (2006), 143–48, for Cristoforo Orimina's Apocalypse in the *Hamilton Bible* (Berlin, Staatliche Museen, MS 78 E 3).
119. Fleck (2010.1), 54–67.
120. Lewis (2006), 94.
121. Wollesen (1990), 188.
122. Morrison (2002), 104–5; Morrison (2010.a), 19–20, compares the visual cycles in the *Roman de Troie* and their influence on the *Grandes Chroniques*. No sharp distinctions were made between fiction and history. Their boundary was permeable.
123. At www.bl.uk/manuscripts/FullDisplay.aspx?index=0&ref=Royal_MS_16_G_VI. with full description. See Hedeman (1991); Raynaud (1999); Hedeman (2006), 432–36; Martellucci (2012); Field–Gaposchkin (2014).
124. See Besseyre and Christe, *Bible moralisé* (2011); Tomei (2016), 209.
125. Stones (1976) notes that French visual motifs moved from sacred and secular texts to become building blocks of the stock of visual narrative in either realm.
126. Musto (2016), 92 n. 3. Tristano (1993), 14, 18, notes that it is nearly impossible to identify the provenance of southern Gothic manuscripts based solely on hands.
127. Tomei (2016), 209.
128. The *Malines Bible*. Leuven, Maurits Sabbe Library, MS 1, previously online at: www.anjoubible.be/thebibleonline. Access now limited. See Musto (2016), 93–94.
129. Chapter 5, pp. 135–38.
130. Other MSS document the social and political use of the visual at the Neapolitan court. The analysis of Giovanna I's *Book of Hours* (Vienna, Österreichische Nationalbibliothek, Ms. Cod. 1921) in Duran (2010), 87–91, calls attention to the prominent place of the Empress Helen as a model for Giovanna's right to rule. The *Hours* were also produced in Orimina's workshop.
131. Fleck (2010.2), 46–47.
132. Casteen (2015), 12 n. 27, argues against this interpretation.
133. Fleck (2010.2), 48, suggests that the figure on fol. 308v, enthroned and crowned with orb and scepter, may be Andrew. But the figure's dress and gender are ambiguous: the bobbed red hair could equally be Giovanna's.
134. Paris, BNF, MS 4274. At: http://gallica.bnf.fr/ark:/12148/btv1b8551130g/f1.item.r=4274. For analyses, Musto (2016), 94–96; Di Cerbo (2016).

135. Perriccioli Saggese (2010), 121.
136. In 13th-century French MSS, scenes of biblical and literary action became freely associated in the minds of illustrators and readers, so that biblical imagery could be seen through the narrative lens of French romance: Mann (2002), 55.
137. Di Cerbo (2016), 12–14, proposes this affinity for the Orsini of Nola and notes their marriage alliance to the Acciaiuoli.
138. Formisano–Lee (1993), 139–42, 160–61; Musto (2016), 94–95.
139. *Familiares* XII.2, Petrarch (2004.1), 3:1628–55; Petrarch (2005.2), 2:132–40.
140. Petrarch (2004.1), 3:1642; Petrarch (2005.2), 2:136.
141. Musto (2013), lvii and n. 137.
142. Musto (2016), 97–100.
143. BL, MS Add. 12228 at www.bl.uk/manuscripts/Viewer.aspx?ref=add_ms_12228.
144. Federico Torregiani's Venetian translation, *Gli Egregi Fatti del Gran Re Meliadus*, takes 1,224 pages in the Aldine edition of 1559/60. See also *Guiron le Courtois* (1966, 2014, 2020–).
145. Pp. 129–38.
146. Chapter 5, pp. 134–35.
147 *Familiares* XII.2, Petrarch (2004.1), 3:1653; Petrarch (2005.2), 2:139.
148. Matteo Villani, *Cronica* I.20, for this conflict.
149. Fully recognizable from folio 68v onward.
150. Perriccioli Saggese (2010), 122.
151. Perriccioli Saggese (2010), 122. See Chapter 5, p. 128.
152. III.8. For an English translation, Musto (2013), 285–86.
153. Chapter 5, pp. 133–34.
154. Musto (2016), 100–102, examines the probable insertion of Naples as the stand-in for Leonnois in the visual program of the last third of the codex.

WORKS CITED

Aceto, Francesco. 1992. "Pittori e documenti della Napoli angioina: Aggiunte ed espunzioni." *Prospettiva* 67:53–65.

Alfonso, Isabel, et al., ed. 2004. *Building Legitimacy: Political Discourses and Forms of Legitimacy in Medieval Societies.* Leiden: Brill.

Antoine, Jean-Philippe. 1988."*Ad perpetuam memoriam:* Les nouvelles fonctions de l'image peinte en Italie, 1250–1400." *Mélanges de L'ecole française de Rome. Moyen Âge, Temps Modernes* 100.2:541–615.

Barasch, Moshe. 1987. *Giotto and the Language of Gesture.* Cambridge: Cambridge University Press.

Barberino, Francesco da. 2006. I documenti d'amore *di Francesco da Barberino secondo i mss. originali.* 4 vols. Francesco Egidi, ed. Rome: Società Filologica Romana, 1905–27. Repr. Milan: Archè.

—. 2008. *I documenti d'amore. Documenta amoris.* 2 vols. Marco Albertazzi, ed. Lavis: La finestra.

Barnet, Peter. 2005. With Nancy Wu. *The Cloisters: Medieval Art and Architecture.* New York: Metropolitan Museum of Art.

Baxandall, Michael. 1971. *Giotto and the Orators: Humanist Observers of Painting in Italy and the Discovery of Pictorial Composition, 1350–1450.* Oxford: Clarendon.

Behrmann, Carolin, ed. 2016. *Images of Shame: Infamy, Defamation and the Ethics of* Oeconomia. Boston: De Gruyter.

Besseyre, Marianne, and Yves Christe. 2011. *Bible moralisée of Naples*. Barcelona: Moliero.

Belting, Hans. 1985. "The New Role of Narrative in Public Painting of the Trecento: *Historia* and Allegory." *Studies in the History of Art*. Washington, DC: National Gallery of Art, 151–68.

Beneš, Carrie E. 1999. "Cola di Rienzo and the *Lex Regia*." *Viator* 30:231–51.

Bertone, Giorgio. 2006. "Il 'Buon Governo' come paesaggio testuale: Note di un lettore dell'affresco di Ambrogio Lorenzetti." In *Per un Giardino della Terra*. Antonella Pietrogrande, ed. Padua: Università di Padova, 223–28.

Blume, Dieter. 2015. "Francesco da Barberino: The Experience of Exile and the Allegory of Love." In *Images and Words in Exile*. Elisa Brilli et al., ed. Florence: SISMEL-Edizioni del Galluzzo, 171–92.

Boucheron, Patrick. 2018. *The Power of Images: Siena, 1338*. Andrew Brown, trans. Cambridge: Polity.

Carruthers, Mary J. 1990. *The Book of Memory: A Study of Memory in Medieval Culture*. Cambridge: Cambridge University Press.

Caviness, Madeline Harrison. 2006. "Reception of Images by Medieval Viewers." In Rudolph (2006), 65–85.

Ciccuto, Marcello. 1988. "*Trionfi* e *Uomini illustri* fra Roberto e Renato d'Angiò." *Studi sul Boccaccio* 17:343–402.

———. 2011. "Francesco da Barberino: Un pioniere del Bildercodex tra forme del gotico cortese e icone della civiltà comunale." *Letterature & Arte* 9:83–95.

Collins, Amanda. 2002. *Greater than Emperor: Cola di Rienzo (ca. 1313–54) and the World of Fourteenth-Century Rome*. Ann Arbor: University of Michigan Press.

D'Achille, Paolo. 2017. "Cronache, scritture esposte, testi semicolti." In Francesconi–Miglio, 347–72.

De Marchi, Andrea. 2013. *Maso di Banco in Giotto's Workshop in Naples and an Unpublished Saint Dominic*. Florence: Centro Di.

Derbes, Anne. 2004. With Mark Sandona. *The Cambridge Companion to Giotto*. Cambridge: Cambridge University Press.

Di Cerbo, Cristiana. 2016. "La Campagnia del Nodo, o di Santo Spirito, e la commitenza di Niccolò Orsini nella chiesa di Santa Maria Jacobi a Nola (1354–1359)." *Intrecci d'arte* 1:44–60.

Di Simone, Paolo. 2012–13. "Giotto, Petrarca e il tema degli *uomini illustri* tra Napoli, Milano e Padova: Prolegomeni a un'indagine." *Rivista d'arte* 5.2:39–76; 5.3:35–55.

Donato, Maria Monica. 1985. "Gli eroi romani tra storia ed 'exemplum': I primi cicli umanistici di *Uomini Famosi*." In *Memoria nell'antico nell'arte italiana*. Salvatore Settis, ed. Turin: Einaudi, 2:97–152.

Duran, Michelle M. 2010. "The Politics of Art: Imaging Sovereignty in the Anjou Bible." In *Anjou Bible*, 73–93.

Elliott, Janis. 2004. "The 'Last Judgement': The Cult of Sacral Kingship and Dynastic Hopes for the Afterlife." In Elliott–Warr, 175–93.

Field, Sean L. 2014. With M. Cecilia Gaposchkin. "Questioning the Capetians, 1180–1328." *History Compass* 12.7:567–85.

Formisano, Luciano. 1993. With Charmaine Lee. "Il 'Francese di Napoli' in opere di autori italiani dell'età angioina." In Trovato–Gonelli (1993), 133–62.

Frojmovič, Eva. 1996. "Giotto's Allegories of Justice and the Commune in the Palazzo della Ragione in Padua: A Reconstruction." *Journal of the Warburg and Courtauld Institutes* 59:24–47.
—. 2007. "Giotto's Circumspection." *The Art Bulletin* 89.2:195–210.
Guiron le courtois. 1966. *Guiron le Courtois: Étude de la tradition manuscrite et analyse critique*. Roger Lathuillère, ed. Geneva: Droz.
—.2014. *Guiron le courtois: Roman arthurien en prose du xiiie siècle*. Venceslas Bubenicek, ed. Berlin: De Gruyter.
—.2020–. *Il ciclo di Guiron le Courtois*. 7 vols. proj. Lino, Leonardi and Richard Trachsler, ed. Florence: SISMEL–Edizioni del Galluzzo.
Hedeman, Anne D. 1991. *The Royal Image: Illustrations of the Grandes Chroniques de France, 1274–1422*. Berkeley: University of California Press.
—. 2006. "Gothic Manuscript Illustration." In Rudolph (2006), 421–42.
Heffernan, James A.W. 1993. *Museum of Words: The Poetics of Ekphrasis from Homer to Ashbery*. Chicago: University of Chicago Press.
Holloway, Julia. 2020. "Il *buon governo: Il Tesoretto, il Tesoro* e *la Rettorica* di Brunetto Latino come *paideia* a Guido Cavalcanti, Dante Alighieri e Francesco da Barberino." *Letteratura italiana antica* 21:79–94.
Johnston, Andrew James, et al., ed. 2015. *The Art of Vision: Ekphrasis in Medieval Literature and Culture*. Columbus: Ohio State University Press.
Joost-Gaugier, Christiane L. 1980. "Giotto's Hero Cycle in Naples: A Prototype of *donne illustre* and a Possible Literary Connection." *Zeitschrift für Kunstgeschichte* 43:311–18.
—. 1982."The Early Beginning of the Notion of *'Uomini Famosi'* and the *'De Viris Illustribus'* in Greco-Roman Tradition." *Artibus et Historiae* 5:97–115.
—. 1984. "The History of a Visual Theme as Culture and the Experience of an Urban Center: *Uomini famosi*." *Antichità Viva* 22.1:5–14.
Kessler, Herbert L. 2006. "Gregory the Great and Image Theory in Northern Europe During the Twelfth and Thirteenth Centuries." In Rudolph (2006), 151–72.
Labriola, Ada. 2004. "Pacino di Buonaguida." In *Dizionario Biografico dei Miniatori Italiani: Secoli IX–XVI*. Milvia Bollati and Miklós Boskovits, ed. Milan: Sylvestre Bonnard, 841–43.
Lavin, Irving. 2020. *The Art of Commemoration in the Renaissance: The Slade Lectures*. Marilyn Aronberg Lavin, ed. New York: Italica Press.
Leone de Castris, Pierluigi. 1986. *Arte di corte nella Napoli angioina*. Florence: Cantini.
—. 1995. "A margine di 'I pittori alla corte angioina': Maso di Banco e Roberto d'Oderisio." In *Napoli, l'Europa: Ricerche di storia dell'arte in onore di Ferdinando Bologna*. Francesco Abbate and Fiorella Sricchia Santoro, ed. Catanzaro: Meridiana, 45–49.
—. 2006. *Giotto a Napoli*. Naples: Electa.
Lewis, Suzanne. 2006. "Narrative." In Rudolph (2006), 86–105.
Long, Jane Collins. 2009. "Franciscan Chapel Decoration: The St. Silvester Cycle of Maso Di Banco at Santa Croce in Florence." *Studies in Iconography* 30:72–95.
Lori Sanfilippo, Isa. 2011. With Antonio Rigon. *Fama e publica vox nel*

Medioevo. Rome: ISIME.
Luchinat, Cristina Acidini. 1998. With Enrica Neri Lusanna, ed. *Maso Di Banco: La cappella di San Silvestro*. Milan: Electa.
MacLaren, Shelley. 2007. "Shaping the Self in the Image of Virtue: Francesco da Barberino's *I Documenti d'amore*." In *Image and Imagination of the Religious Self in Late Medieval and Early Modern Europe*. Reindert Falkenburg et al., ed. Turnhout: Brepols, 71–104.
Mann, C. Griffith. 2002. "The Morgan Picture Bible and the Art of Narrative: Picturing the Bible in the Thirteenth Century." In *The Book of Kings: Art, War, and the Morgan Library's Medieval Picture Bible*. William Noel and Daniel H. Weiss, ed. Baltimore: The Walters Art Museum, 39–59.
Martellucci, Myriam. 2012. "Images et pouvoir monarchique au sein d'un manuscrit des *Grandes chroniques de France*." In *La puissance royale: Image et pouvoir de l'Antiquité au Moyen Âge*. Emmanuelle Santinelli-Foltz and Christian-Georges Schwentzel, ed. Rennes: Presses universitaires, 129–39.
Masi, Gino. 1931. *La pittura infamante nella legislazione e nella vita del comune fiorentino (secc. XIII–XVI)*. Rome: Società editrice dell' "Foro italiano."
Modigliani, Anna. 2012. "Cibo e potere a Roma: I banchetti imperiali di Cola di Rienzo e di Paolo II." *Archivi e Cultura* n.s 45:99–111.
—. 2014. "Lo ogliardino de Roma: Il progetto italiano di Cola di Rienzo." In *Roma nel Rinascimento*, 241–53.
Morrison, Elizabeth. 2002. "Illuminations of the *Roman de Troie* and French Royal Dynastic Ambition (1260–1340)." Ph.D. diss., Cornell University.
—. 2010. With Anne Dawson Hedeman and Elisabeth Antoine, ed. *Imagining the Past in France: History in Manuscript Painting, 1250–1500*. Los Angeles: J. Paul Getty Museum.
—. 2010a. "From Sacred to Secular: The Origins of History Illumination in France." In Morrison (2010), 9–26.
Nardi, Valeria. 1993. "Le illustrazioni dei *Documenti d'Amore* di Francesco da Barberino." *Ricerche di storia dell'arte* 49:75–91.
Norman, Diana. 2018. *Siena and the Angevins, 1300–1350: Art, Diplomacy and Dynastic Ambition*. Turnhout: Brepols.
Ortalli, Gherardo. 1979. *Pingatur in Palatio: La pittura infamante nei secoli XIII–XVI*. Rome: Jouvence.
—. 2015. *La pittura infamante: Secoli XIII–XVI*. Rome: Viella.
Owst, Gerald R. 1933. *Literature and Pulpit in Medieval England*. Cambridge: Cambridge University Press.
Pasquini, Emilio. 1997. "Francesco da Barberino." DBI 49. At www.treccani.it/enciclopedia/francesco-da-barberino_(Dizionario-Biografico).
Pasut, Francesca. 2014. "Pacino di Buonaguida." DBI 80. At www.treccani.it/enciclopedia/pacino-di-buonaguida_(Dizionario-Biografico).
Pignatti, Franco. 2001. "Giovanni Fiorentino." DBI 56. At www.treccani.it/enciclopedia/giovanni-fiorentino_(Dizionario-Biografico).
Ratté, Felicity. 2006. *Picturing the City in Medieval Italian Painting*. Jefferson, NC: McFarland.
Ray, Roger. 1985. "Rhetorical Skepticism and Verisimilar Narrative in John of Salisbury's *Historia Pontificalis*." In Breisach, 61–102.

Raynaud, Christiane. 1999. "La reine dans les *Grandes Chroniques de France*." TMC 1:226–39.
Riklin, Alois. 2017. *Etica repubblicana nel Palazzo Pubblico di Siena, 1315–1535: Simone Martini, Ambrogio Lorenzetti, Taddeo di Bartolo, Domenico Beccafumi.* Venice: Marsilio.
Rosand, David. 1987. "Ekphrasis and the Renaissance of Painting: Observations on Alberti's Third Book." In *Florilegium Columbianum*. Karl-Ludwig Selig and Robert Somerville, ed. New York: Italica Press, 147–65.
Schmid, Petra. 2014. "*I Documenti d'Amore* von Francesco da Barberino Trecenteske: Bildfindungen zwischen politischen und ästhetischen Tugenddiskursen." *ALL-OVER: Magazin für Kunst und Ästhetik* 7:15–24.
—. 2015. "*I Documenti d'Amore* von Francesco da Barberino: Zur politischen Funktion interpiktorialer Bildstrategien im frühen Trecento." *kunsttexte.de. Sektion Politische Ikonographie* 4:1–18.
Schneller, Robert W. 1963. *A Survey of Medieval Model Books*. Haarlem: E.F. Bohn.
Schwartz, Amy. 1994. "Images and Illusions of Power in Trecento Art: Cola di Rienzo and the Ancient Roman Republic." Ph.D. diss., State University of New York at Binghamton.
—. 2007. "Eternal Rome and Cola di Rienzo's Show of Power." In *Acts and Texts: Performance and Ritual in the Middle Ages and the Renaissance.* Laurie and Wim Husken, ed. Amsterdam: Rodopi, 63–76.
Sciacca, Christine, ed. 2012. *Florence at the Dawn of the Renaissance Painting and Illumination, 1300–1350*. Los Angeles: J. Paul Getty Museum. At www.getty.edu/art/exhibitions/florence/introduction.html.
Sonnay, Philippe. 1982. "La politique artistique de Cola di Rienzo (1313–1354)." *La Revue de l'art* 55:35–43.
Stones, Alison. 1976. "Secular Manuscript Illumination in France." In *Medieval Manuscripts and Textual Criticism*. Christopher Kleinhenz, ed. Chapel Hill: University of North Carolina Press, 83–102.
Tomei, Alessandro. 2010. With Stefania Paone. "Paintings and Miniatures in Naples: Cavallini, Giotto and the Portraits of King Robert." In *Anjou Bible*, 53–71.
—. 2016. "I *Regia Carmina* dedicati a Roberto d'Angiò nella British Library di Londra: Un manoscritto tra Italia e Provenza." *Arte Medievale* ser. 4.6:201–12.
Tristano, Caterina. 1993. "Scrivere il volgare in Italia meridionale (secc. XII– XIV)." In Trovato-Gonelli (1993), 7–26.
Tronzo, William. 2004. "Giotto's Figures." In Derbes–Sandona (2004), 63–75.
Wollesen, Jens T. 1990. "'*Ut poesis pictura*?' Problems of Images and Texts in the Early Trecento." In *Petrarch's Triumphs: Allegory and Spectacle*. Konrad Eisenbichler and Amilcare A. Iannucci, ed. Toronto: Dovehouse, 183–210.

7. CASE STUDIES
INTRODUCTION
This chapter presents case studies for the narrative elements we have discussed in previous chapters. These include the fall of the Duke of Athens, the punishments of Queen Giovanna I's inner circle, the trial of Judge Martuccio in Apulia and the murder of Cola di Rienzo. It will devote special attention to what I have termed "rituals of punishment," including descriptions of ritual cannibalism. It will then examine what I have termed "prison dialogues," including the private discussions among the captured barons of Rome awaiting their execution in 1347, the exchanges among the brothers of Fra Morreale awaiting their own execution in 1354 and the heated arguments among the condemned courtiers of Queen Giovanna I. These case studies are intended both to illustrate and to test the arguments that we have made throughout this book concerning authorship, genre, truth claims and audience reception.

CEREMONY AND RITUAL
The past generation has produced groundbreaking research on the role of ritual in all forms of medieval life, both private and public.[1] Ceremony and ritual served private and public social functions — bringing together communities and commemorating individual or political events — as well as symbolic and representational ones. They bolstered personal and official memory, projected power, authority and social structures and underscored social and cultural cohesion. They were defined by a highly explicit and coded set of gestures, actions, signs and symbols.

Despite these apparently standardized meanings and functions, Philippe Buc[2] has warned against too facile a reliance on medieval accounts of ritual and performance as if they were transparent field notes or naive recordings of events. Ritual descriptions, he argues, were highly charged constructs presenting less actual occurrence than ideal representations reflecting political, cultural and religious agendas and views. As such, authorial intent and textuality are far more apparent in these descriptions than is the ground of Rankean reality. Lawrence Bryant has noted that not all such forms of action were firmly set to single meanings or easily interpreted systems of belief, that meanings were constantly contested, that the agency of participants changed the meanings of rituals and that no single polarity ever gave final definition to public or private acts.[3] Ritual and ceremony could also be consciously invented to reflect new social or political realities.[4] Thus what Lévi-Strauss has termed a "bricolage" of meanings must be considered when attempting to interpret any historical record of such rituals and ceremonies. As we have seen above,[5] this was nothing unusual for medieval historians who worked along the well established and frequently crossed borderline between *historia* and *fabula*: accounts of such ceremony and ritual might be based strictly on eyewitness experience or testimony, but they could as well be based on ancient sources, on literary borrowings, on rhetorical embellishments, amplifications or condensations to provide both a historical record and an emotional effect designed to encourage personal virtue and civic responsibility.

Brigitte Bedos-Rezak has reminded us that such rituals took place within tightly knit urban contexts that were themselves textual communities. These communities bridged the gap between private and public experience largely through the role of the written text as an interpreter and authenticator of public acts.[6] Within this context, Charles Burroughs[7] and Kiril Petkov[8] have emphasized the special role of the notary in overseeing many of the secular public rituals of trecento Italian cities.[9] Notaries, for example, presided over the frequent ceremonies of arbitration and reconciliation[10] and over the betrothals that unified trecento urban society. They also officially witnessed and recorded such public ceremonies as elections and charitable donations and knew the highly symbolic visual and gestural language that both law and custom required for these public acts. This role made several of the authors discussed here keenly aware both of the ritual nature of many of the episodes they describe and fully capable of combining their rhetorical toolkits and knowledge of the classics with a language of formal ritual in either describing or inventing many of the narratives and details presented below.[11] Both in the written space of their texts and in the public spaces of these rituals, the city itself then became a theatrical stage for all types of trecento rituals.

RITUALS OF PUNISHMENT

Since the late 1990s, historians have applied theories of medieval "rituals of violence" and Artaud's "theater of cruelty" in a variety of anthropological, literary, performative, art-historical and liturgical frames.[12] Many scholars have used similar texts to construct a taxonomy of the very public, almost theatrical rehearsal of key elements of physical torture and execution that appear to flow like anthropological field notes from some object culture under study. One needs to take care to distinguish two terms, however. "Rituals of violence" could include the freeform loss of social controls associated with interregna, carnival and other festivities that symbolically or physically attacked and subverted the body politic.[13] The "theater of cruelty," on the other hand, more strictly describes both theatrical and public violence against the private body. The descriptions of public rituals found in several trecento texts appear to follow a set form of third-person description — even of first-person narration — placing the narrator among the self-conscious public community of celebration and witness. Alternately, accounts of certain rituals of violence — which I term "rituals of punishment" — combine both rituals of violence and the theater of cruelty. They seem to isolate the narrators as the lonely voice outside the crowd, deliberately alienating and separating themselves from the events being narrated, both out of an unspoken sense of horror at the event and from an attempt to create a truth claim from distance and separation.

These authors also often made it clear that they were not on the scenes that they describe, most especially in the instances of ritual dismemberment and cannibalism described below. That is, they are not agents, passive participants or even spectators but detached reviewers who can therefore dispassionately relate what this theater of cruelty has performed. This recalls the Anonimo romano's preface to his *Cronaca*, that among his reasons for writing was "also one which Livy mentions...while I am enjoying [reading or composing] this work I am remote, and I do not experience the wars and the hardships which overrun the country."[14] The Anonimo's comment offers a profound insight into the classical mode, for the medieval theater of pain largely served the same function as the ancient tragic theater in both its pull toward empathy for, and its ultimate separation from, its tragic figures.[15] As such, the narrators become like scribes *(scriptores)* recording a medieval passion play, and the events and sufferings they portray take on the quality of formalized, but theatrical, pain.

Such accounts of trial and punishment may be genuine documentary evidence of fourteenth-century Italy.[16] But there are elements of these accounts that speak to us rather as tropes and genre pieces. Here we will examine narratives of the Florentine mob's execution and ritual cannibalism of the retainers of the deposed Duke of Athens; the execution of Giovanna's inner circle in Naples; the trial, torture and execution of Judge Martuccio in Apulia; and the account of the brutal assassination and ritual hanging of Cola di Rienzo in Rome. The repetition of these set acts of public cruelty, of a sadistic and very participatory vengeance against public officials, may indeed speak to the reality of fourteenth-century judicial procedure and symbolic retribution.[17] But they may also reveal the indebtedness of one medieval historian to another or to rhetorical forms, to literary, biblical and hagiographical traditions and to visual conventions. They may not be transparent artifacts but deliberate constructions meant to indicate their authors' less obvious intent.[18]

Paul Strohm[19] has called attention to the carnivalesque language and actions of the rebels described by Thomas Walsingham and other chroniclers of the Peasants' Revolt in England in 1381.[20] Though Walsingham's description certainly reflects the realities of the uprising and incidents witnessed at St. Albans itself,[21] Strohm notes that the textual descriptions cast the actions of the rebels in light of the deliberate inversions that were characteristic of carnival throughout the European Middle Ages. In addition, these descriptions also caricatured the rebels — of several classes, professions and localities, but mostly London burghers — as peasants and rustics, who actions revealed their animalistic, "grotesque" and barbaric nature. This "ludic or theatrical analogy"[22] manifested itself both in the language of carnival inversion used by Walsingham to condemn the rebels in terms of a "grotesque realism,"[23] and inversely in the rebel's own consciousness of their transgressive actions, attitudes and cultural models. These informed and lent their political and military deeds a ritualistic quality that was understood clearly by both the actors and their chroniclers.

On another level, Enders demonstrated that the "medieval theater of cruelty," while perhaps based on the reality experienced by medieval audiences, owed much to the rhetorical conventions of stage plays depicting the passion of Christ and the martyrs.[24] Graphic violence and punishments that included explicit sexual mutilations of women were common on stage as they were in visual portrayals of martyrdoms and of the punishments in hell.[25] Dante's visions of hell were only the most perfect of a taxonomy of ghastly torture and punishments in medieval spiritual writings and images that have been documented by Gardiner and visualized by Pilgun and Gamberini.[26] Their brutality may have owed much to the daily life around them — art imitating life — but this very inversion points to the tendency of writers to imitate literary sources in constructing their record of reality.[27]

THE DUKE OF ATHENS

Our first case study examines the descriptions of the fall of Walter VI of Brienne (1311–56), known as the Duke of Athens, and his followers in Florence in July 1343.[28] The grandson of Hughes de Brienne, regent of the kingdom of Jerusalem, he had inherited wide swaths of territory in France and the Mediterranean. Walter married Beatrice, daughter of Prince Philip of Taranto and niece of King Robert of Naples. He gained some reputation but little success in pursuing Angevin and his own family claims to Latin Greece either as Angevin vicar-general or as the legendary Duke of Athens. As such he appears as a character in Boccaccio's *Decameron* (II.7) as Theseus, duke of Athens (conflated with the classical hero), and as the same in the "Knight's Tale" of Chaucer's *Canterbury Tales* and so eventually made his way into Shakespeare's *Midsummer Night's Dream* as the vengeful father and duke. The duke's rise and fall was one of the most arresting historical episodes for trecento Italian audiences. We are fortunate to have four overlapping accounts of his fall: from Villani, Agnolo di Tura, the Anonimo romano and Boccaccio. Giovanni Villani provides the base narrative.[29]

When King Robert's son and heir Charles, duke of Calabria, was proclaimed signor of Florence (1326–36) in order to protect Guelph interests in Tuscany, Walter was named his vicar. In 1342 he was again invited to Florence to take control of the city and to alleviate its severe economic depression caused by the recent collapse of its international banks. Walter ruled efficiently but strictly, imposing high taxes and forced loans, allowing his lieutenants too free a hand. He soon lost the loyalty of all classes in the city, while his experience in the Angevin East added to his growing reputation as an oriental despot. On July 26, 1343, a conspiracy of the magnates joined those of the *popolani grassi* and *populi minuti*. The whole city soon took up arms against the duke. Walter and his troops took refuge in the Palazzo Vecchio (della Signoria). As the rebellion spread, the Florentines besieged both the Palazzo Vecchio and the Palazzo del Podestà (Bargello). They elected their own committee of fourteen, and the duke's hated officials were hunted down throughout the city. Tensions — and Villani's detail — grew as an unnamed notary for the Altoviti, infamous for his cruelty and crimes, was seized by the people and torn into little pieces, as was Judge Simone da Norcia, a treasury official known for his cruel tortures and executions of citizens. A Neapolitan notary, appointed captain of the duke's foot sergeants and known for his thefts and felonies, was also torn into little pieces. Sir Arrigo Feo, superintendent of the hated gabelle tax, attempted to flee dressed as a friar. But he was recognized and killed. The older boys of the city then dragged his naked body through the streets until they reached the Piazza dei Priori, where they hung it upside down, gutted and split open like a slaughtered pig.[30]

But the most gruesome events were still to come. After a protracted siege by Florentine forces, followed by lengthy negotiations aided by the Sienese, Walter agreed to surrender his most hated lieutenant, Guglielmo d'Assisi, and Guglielmo's eighteen-year-old son. Both stood accused by the Florentines of extortion and acts of violence and outrage against citizens. Handed over to the fury of the assembled people, the son was dismembered and cut into little pieces before his father's eyes. Guglielmo next suffered the same fate. According to Villani, the Florentines then committed acts of ritual cannibalism on their victims: "One carried a piece on his lance, another on his sword all through the city, and they behaved so cruelly and with so much bestial fury and hatred that they ate their flesh raw or cooked."[31] Walter quickly resigned his post, barely escaped alive from the city, and on August 5 fled via Bologna to Venice and there took ship back to the Regno.

Agnolo di Tura's description[32] follows Villani's in its most important aspects. He does provide several new embellishments, however. Once Arrigo Feo's body had been hung and gutted like a pig, Agnolo reports, the citizens then proceeded to cut off and skewer small slices of the body, which they then carried around like pieces of porchetta.[33] Similarly, once Guglielmo d'Assisi's son was surrendered, Agnolo reported that he was torn apart alive, "as he begged for mercy."[34] When Guglielmo suffered the same fate, "the pieces of his body were also skewered and traded around from one person to the next like meat in a butcher shop, eaten raw and cooked."[35]

The Anonimo romano also summarized the incident in his *Cronaca* and called out for special attention the act of ritual cannibalism reported by Villani and repeated by Agnolo di Tura.[36] The Anonimo, however, embellishes his account with dialogue and further details that borrow freely from both classical references to tyrants like Dionysius of Syracuse and from medieval fabliaux. He provides new details of the character and avarice of Arrigo da Feo and of discussions among the conspirators. We learn that Judge Simone da Norcia was killed and his body cut into four pieces and distributed to the four "Anziani" of the people. We read that Guglielmo d'Assisi and his son, now an angelic-looking creature of twelve years old, had reached extremes of cruelty in mistreating the Florentines. When Guglielmo's son was expelled from the Palazzo dei Priori, like a swine to the slaughterhouse, he was set upon by the citizens, but not before he was able to exchange a mournful dialogue with his father. A priest was the first to strike: severing the boy's arm from his body and cursing out his retributive justice. A thousand wounds followed. Guglielmo was dismembered, and the slices of their bodies were carried around the city, sold by weight, roasted and eaten.[37]

Boccaccio also included the duke's downfall in his *De casibus virorum illustrium*.[38] He appears to have based his account on Villani's but compressed the narrative to emphasize Walter's moral failings and cowardly response to the uprising in order to stress his theme of republican liberty versus tyranny. He does, however, add telling details, including the death and dismemberment of Guglielmo d'Assisi and his son and the slaughter of Arrigo da Feo, "hung upside down like a pig, gutted, and finally cut into pieces."[39]

CHAPTER 7 ☙ CASE STUDIES

These accounts coincide so closely that only minor details differ: all offer unambiguous evidence of urban rituals of punishment meted out in horrible detail specific enough that later historians[40] could build theories around late medieval retributive "rituals of violence" using these sources. Yet are these the transparent anthropological "field notes" that modern historians make them out to be? Or are they rather the inventions that Buc has cautioned us to deconstruct? They could be the factual accounts that many have taken them to be; but our examination of the truth claims of trecento historians and of their presentation of evidence argues against a literal interpretation on several counts, a critical stance that has been most strongly stated by William Arens.[41]

The first count is the obvious textual borrowing from Villani by Agnolo di Tura, Boccaccio and perhaps the Anonimo romano. Neither Agnolo nor the Anonimo romano were at the scene when these events took place. Nor, when we examine Villani's and Boccaccio's accounts, do they claim to have witnessed these events themselves, though both were in the city at the time. This is important, because as we have seen, medieval historians from Villani, to the Anonimo romano, to Agnolo di Tura, from Froissart to Domenico da Gravina and Boccaccio were explicit and careful about noting either their own first-hand witness to the events they describe or about the reliability and testimony of others who claimed to witness them. None missed the opportunity to make such claims to truth, and none were casual in omitting them.

Further, Villani himself was among those implicated in the misrule of the Duke of Athens, and he greeted the new government that replaced him with outspoken contempt.[42] He might therefore be inclined to exaggerate the brutality of the uprising. By the same token, Agnolo di Tura took a decidedly partisan viewpoint to the events of 1343, extolling the role of the Sienese in restoring order and achieving a political settlement and not hesitating to exaggerate the barbarity of the Florentines.[43] The Anonimo romano's obvious rhetorical embellishments, including invented dialogues and additional details of the murders, follow his usual style and method for events in Rome and the Regno, as does Boccaccio's candid use of apostrophe to stress moral character, virtue and vice.

While all the sources seem to agree on the public execution of the duke's chief lieutenants, they differ on the details of the supposed ritual cannibalism upon their remains. Boccaccio, who was in Florence, speaks only of dismemberment but not of any ritual consumption. This would be a difficult detail to omit, even from the point of view of classical decorum. Classical sources, in fact, whether Christian or pagan, spoke frequently of cannibalism in various forms.[44] It appears in the Hebrew Bible in stories or admonitions against devouring one's children,[45] in classical literature in Josephus' account of the siege of Jerusalem, which Boccaccio himself used for the story of the Jewish woman Marie's devouring her own child

205

during Titus' siege of Jerusalem into his *De casibus virorum illustrium*. It was transmitted via Eusebius and Hegesippus and in Ovid's tale of Lycaon in the *Metamorphoses*. Classical philosophers assumed a historical cannibalism that was superseded by either animal sacrifice or vegetarianism.[46] Roman writers known to the trecento, including Cicero[47] and Sallust,[48] also focused on cannibalism as a sign of social disruption and subversion.[49]

Jerome recorded hearing in his youth during a visit to Gaul that the Attacotti of Scotland were cannibals,[50] as Strabo in his *Geography* said of the Sarmatians and Scythians.[51] The most frequent accusations of cannibalism leveled in the Roman world were against Christians due to a misunderstanding of the Eucharistic feast and recorded by several early Christian apologists.[52] The apologists also relied on classical sources for stories of exotic and barbarian peoples who indulged in human flesh. These tales would have been known to most medieval Italian authors through such works as the Alexander legend in the Pseudo-Callisthenes and other versions. So too in the apocalyptic prophesies of the Pseudo-Methodius, the cannibalistic peoples, the "children of Japhet," long held at bay by Alexander's gates, would be released on the civilized world. Geographical lore and apocalyptic legend merged with anti-Semitic polemic in the late Middle Ages to see both internal subversion and external threat, such as the Tartars in Matthew Paris' *Chronica Majora* or the story of the Christian Tarfurs in Guibert of Nogent's account of the first crusade. Cannibalism was also projected on the Saracens by several Latin sources.[53]

Dante used the story of the imprisoned Count Ugolino della Gherardesca, forced to devour his own children, not as an example of cannibalism but of treason to family and society.[54] Medieval vision literature offers numerous images of humans being torn into bits, roasted and consumed by demons in frenzied retribution for sins. But aside from Ugolino gnawing at Archbishop Ruggiero's head, no humans devour human flesh in Dante or any other hell visions.[55] Thomas of Celano's *Second Life* of Francis of Assisi speaks of starving parents eating their dead child.[56] Significantly, however, medieval penitentials, canon law and civil law carried no injunctions against or penances for cannibalism.[57]

We are therefore left with the distinct impression that such stories were precisely that: invented narratives. A generation ago, Arens made the case that while "survival" cannibalism has existed in all periods with reliable evidentiary bases, "ritual" cannibalism raises this one insurmountable obstacle: from the earliest records in Herodotus to the most recent in Papua New Guinea, we possess not a single record by a first-hand eyewitness. Ritual cannibalism has always been practiced by the next people, the "other" across the water, up the river or across the border, but never by "us"; while the cultural contexts and symbolic valences of such reports had gone largely unexamined until recent critical turns.[58]

CHAPTER 7 ⚜ CASE STUDIES

Such narratives and story elements therefore could have come to trecento historians from any number of directions. Though it is difficult to know the sources for all of Villani's episodes, we know that Agnolo di Tura relied both on Villani's written text and on reports from Sienese ambassadors. The Anonimo romano borrowed often from his classical sources and is explicit is making direct comparisons during his account of 1343 to the tyranny of Dionysius of Sicily, perhaps from Dante or florilegia of classical authors.[59] All could be true accounts based on the most recent news from Florence and later embellished with details from written sources, popular legend or passion plays. Or, again, they could be constructed whole to rhetorically emphasize the enormity of the crimes committed against the body politic under the Duke of Athens and to elicit the proper emotional and then moral response.

If the textual offers no answers, the visual might. Yet in no instance of Italian trecento art are there depicted instances of ritualistic cannibalism. In Lorenzetti's *Good and Bad Government, Mal Governo,* a satanic tyrant, presides over scenes of arson, murder, assault, rape and pillage.[60] Yet there are no scenes resembling the descriptions in the Villani, Gravina or the Anonimo romano. In the same period and place, hell images, which present to the viewer every conceivable torture and punishment, also appear to lack scenes of ritualistic cannibalism, of playing sport with the remains of defeated enemies or of the sinners condemned to even the lowest levels of hell. While Satan and his devils are often portrayed consuming the damned, and hell itself is portrayed as a gaping mouth devouring men, women and children, rich and poor, no sinner feasts on human flesh. Still, such omnipresent hell imagery might have influenced details in written accounts.

Lack of evidence cannot constitute proof, especially given the disappearance of so many fresco cycles due to age, war and other damage; but the examples that we have cited generally include every form of human violence. So if we can also find no direct visual sources for ritual cannibalism, can we conclude that these descriptions reflect unmediated reality on the ground? As Arens has noted, when the evidence is lacking, we must seek other explanations for such narratives within cultural contexts, systems of symbol and narrative conventions.[61]

GIOVANNA I'S COURTIERS

By the time Giovanna's first husband, Prince Andrew of Hungary, had been brutally murdered at the Angevins' country retreat at Aversa on September 18, 1345, tensions among the Hungarian Angevins, Giovanna's Neapolitan cousins and the Angevin court bureaucracy had reached their peak. Whatever source one believes, the circle of suspects in the murder quickly grew wider and wider and rose through higher and higher levels of King Robert's and Queen Giovanna's trusted advisors and officials.

As Nikolas the Hungarian told Villani[62] in Florence, the conspirators also included Filippa de'Cabanni's son Roberto, the count of Eboli and seneschal of the realm. The *Cronaca di Partenope*[63] corroborates this. According to the *Chronicon Mutinense*,[64] de'Cabanni himself had seized Andrew by the testicles to thrust him over the parapet that night. The *Mutinense* also named Admiral Corrado de Catanzaro, while the *Chronicon Suessanum* added Carlo Artus to the list.[65] Villani added retainers of the counts of Leonessa and Stella.[66] It seemed everyone close to the royal household had a hand in the crime. But it was the ladies of Giovanna's court who earned the particular venom of the prosecutors and of trecento historians

The de'Cabanni, who under King Robert had risen up from the ranks of slaves and kitchen staff to the highest offices of the Regno, were special targets. The accusation that Roberto de'Cabanni was himself the perpetrator of Andrew's castration and sexual mutilation played on and added to the association of the de'Cabanni with their African origins and the sexual abandon and licentiousness projected onto Africans in the European imagination. Thus in one family were concentrated most of the sexual vices one can imagine: Filippa's raising Giovanna to become a sexual wanton, Sancia de'Cabanni's affair with Giovanna, Sancia's bisexuality and use of her own pregnancy to spread the poison of evil, Roberto de'Cabanni's rumored affair with Giovanna — adding incest to Giovanna's dealings with uncle and niece — and finally Roberto's ultimate sexual crime: the mutilation of Andrew, the innocent Christian prince. Gravina had already implicitly characterized the poison that spread throughout the kingdom as a feminine effusion. He now explicitly condemns the women of Giovanna's court for their stereotypical physicality: pregnant with evil that if not checked leads to the destruction of individuals and then of kingdoms. Whatever the truth of the accusations, Sancia and her mother Filippa were quickly and almost automatically implicated in Andrew's death.

A papal inquest slowly attempted to ascertain the truth of the accusations. But on March 6, 1346, riots broke out in the center of Naples and spread like a tidal wave against the Castel Nuovo and Giovanna's court. Without warning, mobs shouting for the death of Giovanna as *"la gran puttana"* or *"magna meretrix"*[67] burst into the neighboring Largo delle Corregge. The count of Terlizzi himself was quickly captured and brought to the palace of the duke of Durazzo.[68] On March 11, with some regret but with the full assurance from her justiciar Bertrand des Baux and the papal legate Bertrand des Deaulx, Giovanna gave up custody of her inner circle. The prisoners were led outside the water gate of Castel Nuovo and transferred to one of Hugues des Baux's (Ugo del Balzo) galleys waiting in the harbor. In the course of transfer from Castel Nuovo to Castel del'Ovo, however, Hugues had the prisoners seized and, in full view of the population of the city watching from the shore, had

CHAPTER 7 ⚜ CASE STUDIES

Filippa, Sancia and Terlizzi stripped naked and tied to the masts.[69] There they were tortured in order to extract their confessions. Their torture was performed publicly and by a state official and was thus legal. But according to Boccaccio, who recounted the "ritual" in his *De casibus virorum illustrium*, "what he extracted from them is not known."[70]

The prisoners were brought ashore along with their confessions duly recorded by a notary. But then, as they were being transferred to confinement, a band of mercenaries under Fra Morreale rode up to the shore and seized them by order of the Angevin princes. They were brought to the palaces of Durazzo and Taranto in the Largo delle Corregge. There they were publicly tortured again and retained overnight. On the morning of March 12, Giovanna sent Roberto de'Cabanni, as seneschal of the royal court,[71] with a small force to quell the unrest, but he was captured by her royal cousins. Roberto was then publicly tortured, out of hearing range of the assembled people, and he purportedly confessed to being part of the conspiracy to murder Andrew. A notary recorded his testimony.[72] Not surprisingly, Roberto named all those already on the Angevin princes' proscription lists. Those soon condemned to death included the old civil servants of Robert the Wise and now of Giovanna.[73] The execution procession, the cart and the place of execution all have historical evidence and are illustrated by the chronicler Ferraiolo in the next century.[74] But several details are unusual.

Domenico da Gravina offers this description:[75]

> Then the justiciar [Bertrand des Baux] gave orders to his retainers: the carts were prepared and irons were put in the forges and the instruments of torture were placed aboard.[76] The grand justiciar ordered the count of Terlizzi put in one cart, bound by iron chains, and the seneschal of the royal court [Roberto de'Cabanni] in the other. But he ordered that Lord Roberto be stripped of his clothes and his flesh sliced off piece by piece all the way to Piazza Sant'Eligio [about a kilometer, to the present Piazza del Mercato]. Then he ordered him to be burned alive, along with the two counts. The grand justiciar condemned Lady Filippa to a similar punishment.

> Listen to this: the condemned were led to their punishment, and the executioners mercilessly ripped their flesh repeatedly with burning meat hooks. While others lashed their bodies with whips, they were led through each and every street corner of Naples. At each stop, from the smallest to the largest intersection, the executioners cried out: "Each and every one of you traitors should suffer this and worse!" Some people spat right into their faces, others struck them with rocks.

> When they reached the place of execution, where the fire was prepared, even through the burning hooks had left precious little of the flesh on their bodies, Lord Roberto [de'Cabanni] quickly

gave up the ghost. But the count of Terlizzi was still alive. They were therefore pulled off the carts, and there they were hacked to pieces. Then as much of them as could be gathered up was thrown onto the fire. But the Neapolitans watching the execution were moved to frenzy. Pulling the bodies — dead or alive — from the fire, they fell on them with swords and axes and then threw them back into the flames. Many took home their bones: some made dice, some knife handles for the perpetual memory of the event.

But because Lady Sancia was pregnant, the laws mandated that her sentence be deferred until she gave birth. Nevertheless she was kept in jail under tight security.[77]

🙢

Gravina's description of the Neapolitan mob's frenzy matches Villani's and Agnolo di Tura's after the Florentines' execution of the Duke of Athens' henchmen. Gravina is also clear that the execution served the purposes of both public exemplum and vivid historiography that Zorzi emphasizes: some in the crowd made dice, some knife handles "for the perpetual memory of the event."[78] Such memory then served not only to reinforce the effects of justice on the people but on a rhetorical level to use *enargeia* to rouse the reader's emotions and make Gravina's narrative come alive with a vividness and particularity that appealed to the mind's eye.[79] On another level, Gravina's deploying dice as such a mnemonic could also be making a reference to the Crucifixion in Matthew 27:35, where the soldiers "cast lots" for Christ's clothing.[80] Gravina uses Matthew 27 directly in his account of the trial of Judge Martuccio below.[81] The Vulgate is clear that the soldiers, "diviserunt vestimenta eius sortem mittentes." There are many depictions of the scene in trecento painting. The Louvre *Crucifixion* by Giotto of c.1330, for example, shows two soldiers stretching out the garment into a gaming surface as a third prepares to throw the dice.[82] Is Gravina then not recording actual events but using synecdoche to emphasize the unjust lengths to which the crowd eventually went?

Boccaccio[83] bears out these details of burning pincers[84] and dismemberment but adds to them. Both Roberto and then Filippa de'Cabanni were sent to the flames. Barely alive, Filippa was drawn and quartered. Her heart and her innards were then torn from her body, carried through the city and displayed prominently on one of the city's gates. Roberto's heart was also torn from his burning flesh, but then the Neapolitans devoured it in a "lugubrious ritual of sacrifice" that seemed to mock the Eucharist itself. Whatever was left of their bodies was dragged through every sewer and vile pit in Naples until the remains were left to rot.[85]

Boccaccio's narrative takes on the inevitable dynamic of tragic drama that would certainly lend itself to a ritualistic public event. But

CHAPTER 7 ❧ CASE STUDIES

Boccaccio is explicit and careful to distinguish what he narrates of the victims' torture and executions from what he himself claims to have known and experienced first-hand. Boccaccio had begun his account of Filippa's life with an explicit truth claim, clearly distinguishing what he had witnessed from what he has heard:

> I described what I saw with my own eyes, and I know that I was not deceived. In what I have heard, I have related the more truthful, and so I will not come to be refuted, I have sought out those who were more truthful.[86]

He then introduces Filippa with a recollection from his own youth: "while I was still a boy and employed at the court of [King] Robert …Marinus of Bulgaria…[and] Calaber Constantine da Rocca… recounted the antiquity and nobility of the courtiers. Among other things they told how"[87] the de'Cabanni family, African in origin, had risen from a life of slavery to the highest offices in the Regno. Boccaccio concludes, "I have heard that this was Filippa's start." He next "comes to the things that I myself saw."[88] Boccaccio recounts the life of the de'Cabanni at court, their stature and bearing. "What a ridiculous thing to see an African from a slave prison, from the vapor of the kitchen, standing before Robert, the king, performing royal service for the young noblemen, governing the court and making laws for those in power!"[89] These are the elements of the de'Cabanni's lives that he himself witnessed. How he knew of their ultimate fates he does not say.

The gruesome rituals of public torture, mutilation, dismemberment — even the eating of the victims' remains — are narrated in meticulous detail. But again, no one of our sources — from the far-off *Chronicon Mutinense* or Villani to Domenico da Gravina and Boccaccio — claimed to be present at the events they describe. Boccaccio was in Florence at the time, while Gravina never seems to have left his native Apulia. His account's confusion between Raimondo de'Cabanni and his son Roberto reflects his second-hand reportage. We are then once again led to question the open space between the historical facts — the arrest and execution of Giovanna's inner circle — and the details of their executions. This is again the space of medieval historiography, a porous borderland between *historia* and *fabula* that was crossed with the metaphorical, symbolic and other rhetorical tools available to trecento authors to amplify emotional impact, to invoke moral exempla and to construct compelling and convincing history.

JUDGE MARTUCCIO

Gravina was a protagonist in many of the incidents that he describes first-hand during the civil war in Apulia. As his chronicle makes clear, he was a bitter enemy and detractor of Queen Giovanna I and a staunch adherent of the Hungarian faction. In Gravina itself, he played a leading role in public assemblies and debates, translating Latin letters and official communications. His eyewitness accounts of the shifting fortunes of the Neapolitan and Hungarian parties offer a vivid picture of both partisans and innocent civilians caught in the web of violence and revenge. Domenico himself was forced to flee Gravina, abandoning his wife, mother and children to their fates as the Neapolitan forces under Robert of San Severino and the duchess of Durazzo closed in on the town and other Hungarian strongholds. Gravina's fast-paced account of battles and sieges, late-night meetings around the dinner table and fireside, escapes out rear windows, hiding in neighbors' houses and wells reads like the popular French romances that so influenced his style. But Gravina's account is more than adventure. It is also a moral tale of ethical choices and the cowardice and heroism attending them.

Because Domenico witnessed so many of these events, his episode of the execution of Judge Martuccio in Gravina in Apulia in May 1349[90] provides us with a needed contrast and control to the above narratives of torture and execution. Martuccio was one of the judges presiding over the assembly of citizens in Gravina in the spring of 1349 when they voted with heavy hearts and with an eye to self-preservation to shift their loyalty to the Hungarian forces occupying Apulia.[91] Martuccio expressed reservations but declared the majority vote valid. With the changing tide and the triumph of Neapolitan forces, however, all the Hungarian party who had not fled, including Martuccio, were rounded up and their goods confiscated. They were accused of treason, jailed and condemned to the gruesome execution of traitors.[92]

Martuccio defended his decision to allow the commune of Gravina to side with the Hungarians, and he told his judges that all the remaining citizenry assembled before them had shared in that decision. Yet, Domenico explains, greed and rivalry moved the judges to recommend Martuccio's torture and execution. The new city captain, realizing Martuccio's innocence, at first refused to pass judgment, and then, in a scene that recalls Jesus' trial before Pilate (Mt. 27:25), surrendered to the people's demands for Martuccio's death, declaring "May his blood be upon you and upon your children." Martuccio was then placed on a cart, stripped naked, tortured with burning pincers and paraded through the city. Amid the clamor, as the crowd shouted, "Let the traitor die as every traitor deserves!" Martuccio could be heard praying as he was led to the fork. Reprieving his own description of the execution of Giovanna I's courtiers, Gravina reports that by the time Martuccio arrived in the center of the square, all his flesh had been pulled off by the burning pincers, and he was hung on the fork. At that point, a certain Master Lorenzo Chaccharello, one-eyed and disabled, unsheathed his sword and struck him in the legs, hacking them like wood. Martuccio's body hung on the fork for about a month. No one dared cut him down.

CHAPTER 7 ✥ CASE STUDIES

Gravina then breaks off his narrative to reveal his construct of the episode: "I've written this in the order of events, but not everything, since it would take too long to write it all. I've written it partially at least as a memorial for his children and their followers to seek revenge for their father."[93] And a construct this surely was, for, by his own admission, Gravina was not on the scene: "I heard it said by many who saw him suffer like this."[94] Once again, therefore, the most horrible details of this ritual of violence are reported second-hand, and the author is careful to distance himself from the event. No witness is named, and no truth claims are put forward for their reliability. We might expect Gravina's narration of events in distant Naples to rely on reportage and hearsay, amplified by dramatic detail and dialogue. For events in his own hometown, involving associates and neighbors, however, this reliance on second-hand reports only underscores the rhetorical form of such stories. Gravina is explicit in recording his desire to sear the event into the memory of Martuccio's heirs, and he is clear about how he selected incidents and constructed his narrative to do so.[95] Surely the judge was executed for treason, but his Christ-like defense and suffering, as well as the similarity of his death to those of the martyrs, again cloud our ability to discern the unadorned facts "as they really happened" from the historical and literary construct before us.[96]

COLA DI RIENZO

This section's final case study is the execution of Cola di Rienzo, the most famous example of these rituals of punishment.[97] Similarities between the Anonimo romano's account[98] and the examples above will be apparent. In 1347 Rienzo had successfully reestablished the Roman commune as the new *buono stato*, defeating the armed opposition of the barons, restoring order and purpose to the city and making it a renewed center of diplomacy and apocalyptic expectation. After exile and trial in Avignon, Rienzo returned to the city as a papal agent. But Cardinal Albornoz's[99] fears of an independent Rome, baronial opposition and the increased pressures of pan-Italian politics finally led to a conspiracy that rose up in arms on October 8, 1354. Rioters from the Colonna districts of the city converged on the Capitoline and set the Senate Palace ablaze. Rienzo was able to escape in disguise but was recognized, seized and brought to the place of execution on the Capitoline slope, near where his statue now stands. After a silent standoff of almost an hour, out of the crowd one man, Cecco dello Viecchio, approached the tribune and thrust his knife into his gut. Then another — Laurentio de Treio, a notary just like Cola — took a sword and split his skull. Then one man after another approached; some were even brave enough to press their blades into Rienzo's bleeding body.

But Cola had died at once, and the Anonimo romano asserts, "He felt no pain." Someone else then came and tied his feet together with a rope. Cola's body was cast to the ground, and then began the ritual desecration of his corpse. The crowd dragged the body down the slope, piercing him with their swords and knives as he passed along the dirt path, his clothing and then his skin peeling off behind him all the way to the Piazza San Marcello, up the Via Lata, today's Corso, to the heart of the Colonna district. By the time the crowd reached San Marcello, they were making merry: the tribune's body had been stabbed so many times that it "looked like a sieve." His head, already split by the first sword, oozing his brains, had melted along the Corso, and by the time the mob had hoisted up his body, feet first, it no longer had a head. As his body hung there, bleeding, skinless, "his guts dangled from his belly. He was horribly fat. He was white as bloody milk. He was so fat that he looked like a giant buffalo or cow in a slaughterhouse." Cola's remains were then brought to the Mausoleum of Augustus where the Colonna ordered the Jews of the city[100] (Cola's neighbors in the Arenula) to burn the body and to toss the remaining ashes into the Tiber to prevent any cult of remembrance or political opposition.

Again, the Anonimo romano was careful to lay out his motivations and methods[101] and was explicit about events to which he was an eyewitness.[102] We can also be fairly certain of those others to which he was probably an eyewitness.[103] There are other incidents, however, that the Anonimo describes when he could not have been on the scene. These include the battle of the Porta San Lorenzo, in which he tracks the action both inside and outside the city as well as the mental state and thoughts of protagonists on both sides of the conflict.[104] These could be garnered from public documents or from other witnesses or participants, but in almost every case, the Anonimo does not specify who these might have been. The same applies to his account of Cola's death. This shifts dramatically from the viewpoint of the mob surging up to the Senate Palace, to the inner thoughts and conflicts of Cola trapped inside, to the drama of Cola's final moments on the Capitoline slope, to his ritual dismemberment and hanging. While the Anonimo might have witnessed some of these scenes, he could not have witnessed them all, and he makes no claim to have done so. He therefore chose to embellish his account of Cola's actions inside the Senate Palace with references from his classical sources, for example. But his account of the subsequent desecration of Rienzo's body again shows so many similarities to our other examples above that one might either posit Zorzi's standardized form of ritual behavior or some literary borrowings, such as the Anonimo had already done for his account of the death of the Duke of Athens' lieutenants.

How then are we to judge these narratives? If they are not accurate first-hand accounts, to what sources or narrative conventions do we

CHAPTER 7 ※ CASE STUDIES

owe this richness of detail? Gardiner has noted that such punishments are key to western descriptions of hell from at least as early as Virgil.[105] Zorzi has also noted the similarities among such accounts, emphasizing their ritualistic and symbolic valences to underscore the role of justice in supporting the commune and the symmetry between the types of crimes described and their retribution: the removal of tongues for blasphemers, amputation of hands for notaries or accountants who kept false records, castration for sexual crimes, dismemberment for those who divide the commune, fire and finally burning at the stake for crimes considered most poisonous to the body politic, those who would defile its purity. Heretics, witches and homosexuals met the same fate in the flames that were seen both to cleanse society and to foreshadow the fires of hell. The degradation of the offender's body and its comparison to those of animals underscored the deterrent value of such extreme punishment.[106]

Yet Zorzi also emphasizes the highly regulated nature of such expressions of communal justice and punishment, turning the modes of punishment themselves into forms of representation and social construction parallel to the new visual language of virtues, vices, good and bad government, rewards and punishments then being constructed by Giotto and his followers.[107] The extremity of the punishments described in these episodes may well have been used as a form of rhetorical *amplificatio* or *enargeia*[108] and as shocking exempla designed to appeal to the immediacy of the mind's eye. As Zorzi observes,[109] the horrific detail and intense drama of such scenes may well have been a conscious construct, part of a "circularity of images and models," that served the same rhetorical purposes of civic education and admonition. But again, was such admonition written in the flesh or only on parchment and paper?

Enders has noted the classification of torture as just such a rhetorical device as early as Aristotle and the *Rhetorica ad Herennium*[110] and notes Isidore of Seville's linkage of public torture to drama.[111] The rhetorical deployment of suffering as a heuristic device, as a representation of truth, lay behind both the medieval passion play and the public execution, and their representations allowed a wide variety of rhetorical amplification and exaggeration to bring home their messages as both individually exemplary and socially commemorative.

In the end, if anthropological findings, literary theory, visual studies, ancient and medieval rhetorical traditions, classical sources and source criticism itself cannot resolve our conundrum, we are therefore left with the age-old problem of the historian: to what extent can we believe our sources? This deals not so much with the dichotomy between true recording of actual events and the construction of fictional narratives as with the art of the historian as intermediary in imposing meaning on the real world of events, establishing plausibility and verisimilitude and attempting to extract moral and civic lessons from them.

PRISON DIALOGUES

Our next series of case studies involves what appears to be set pieces in two of our sources, Domenico da Gravina and the Anonimo romano. These record secret conversations among groups of the condemned awaiting execution in prison, what I have termed "prison dialogues." These brief conversations are candid, highly emotional yet assumed to be private. Two very similar exchanges come from the Anonimo romano's account of Cola di Rienzo's career: one involves discussions among the Colonna and other captured barons of Rome awaiting their execution in 1347,[112] the other among the brothers of Fra Morreale awaiting their own execution in 1354.[113] Domenico da Gravina offers us a highly charged conversation among Queen Giovanna's inner circle awaiting execution for treason.[114] But if these conversations were secret, and among those who would soon die, how did the authors of these histories know what transpired? The Colonna and their allies were later released and pardoned, so the Anonimo romano could have interviewed them; and all the rest could have had personal or prison attendants who might have overheard these conversations. Yet trecento social norms seems to argue against Roman nobles revealing their doubts and fears to commoners; and neither the Anonimo romano nor Gravina say who their sources were or even that they were reporting accurate and trustworthy second-hand accounts.

These prison dialogues, supposedly candid, give the air of even greater reliability: they are not public, there is no notary or other official witness to the words spoken. They lack even the "one witness" that was considered barely adequate for testimony by Roman and Jewish law[115] and that medieval historians took as the minimally reliable source of evidence. They are thus highly unreliable narratives but are paradoxically offered as even more true accounts: like scenes of the final hours in the Führer Bunker so often conjured up on screen and in fiction recently. All the major players cited in these fourteenth-century prison dialogues were dead when the authors wrote. But because of their intimate point of view, for both medieval and modern readers, they take on the air of true, first-hand accounts. They may thus exhibit one of the most prominent attempts at historical truth in the rhetorical tradition: the plausible and verisimilar constructed to offer a truth claim that relied almost exclusively on rhetorical *inventio*.

They may be, as White[116] and Frisch[117] have observed, narrative constructions reflective more of social solidarity, domination — or estrangement — than factual, epistemic records. The dialogues simply take place in the course of the narratives with no further commentary from the historian. But because of their intimate point of view, they take on the air of the "lived stories" that, White posits, historians often believe are possible to uncover from the past. One therefore again suspects that rhetorical invention, including dramatic dialogue similar to that of romances, is at work here. Other literary sources might be traced as well.

The Bible offers some basic elements of this narrative type, for example in the story of Joseph and his brothers in Genesis 42:15–17 or in Paul's letter to the Colossians 4. Accounts of tribunes placing patricians in prison appear in Livy III.13, of prisoner's gold being seized for the public good in Livy XXX.21 and of dialogues among prisoners in Josephus, *Antiquities* II.53–74. One of the most influential "prison dialogues" was that of Boethius in *The Consolation of Philosophy*,[118] as we have already noted, a work known in whole or excerpt to every student from their *grammatica* and studied intensely by rhetoricians throughout the Middle Ages.[119] Elements of this form also appear in late medieval literature, as in Maillart's *Roman du Comte d'Anjou*.[120] In one episode, four countryfolk who had saved the countess and her child from death are falsely accused of her murder.[121] Interrogated by the count of Anjou, they are thrown into his most secure and dark prison, deprived of all nourishment except bread and water, left frightened, hungry and sleepless. In the subsequent dialogue, they wonder aloud why they have been subjected to such "martyrdom" and debate what course of action to take.

THE ROMAN BARONS

Our first example concerns the rebellious barons of Rome whom Rienzo arrested at a state dinner party and imprisoned on the Capitoline on September 15, 1347, following a failed assassination attempt upon the tribune. On September 17, Cola wrote to the papal notary, Rinaldo Orsini, on the outcome of that dinner party:[122]

> We have conducted courteously to our prison on the Capitoline — not restraining them in the least — several of the barons of the City who were regarded with a certain suspicion by us and the Roman people and who were taken into our custody: Lord Stefano Colonna [il Vecchio], Lord Rinaldo Orsini, Count Bertoldo, Giordano, Cola, and Orso of Lord Jacopo de Filiis Ursi [Orsini] and Giovanni Colonna. After purging any scruples of our growing suspicion from our conscience, in order that they might be reconciled not only with us, but also with God, we employed the following stratagem to cause them to be confessed most devoutly:
>
> On the fifteenth of September, as many as there were, we sent that many friars and chosen religious to the prison. They were ignorant of our pure intention and they believed that we were ready to employ the harshest severity on the barons. Just as we had ordered them, the clerics said to these barons: "The Lord Tribune intends to

sentence you to death." Meanwhile the parliament bell kept tolling loudly and continuously. The barons were terrified and believed that they were in danger of imminent death. Not expecting any outcome but death, they tearfully made their confessions.

As we had prearranged, at the assembly to which the entire Roman people had come at our invitation and request, we not only forgave these barons in their absence in this public parliament, indeed we also had them heaped with praise and offices. And so, with the benevolence of the peaceable people already bestowed on them, we caused them to come before the entire people, who unanimously forgave them of whatever and in whatever way they were obliged to restore or to make amends to them. And by our will and the will of the entire people, we gave to these barons consecrated rings, honors and offices.

Recalling the same event years afterward, the Anonimo romano sets the episode not in the public forum but inside the prison cell:

When the barons heard this news [of their execution] along with the pealing of the bell, they became so frozen with fear that they couldn't speak. Most of them humbled themselves and did penance and took communion. Messer Ranallo delli Orsini and another baron, because they had eaten fresh figs earlier in the morning, could not take communion. Messer Stefano [il Vecchio] della Colonna refused to confess or take communion. He said that he was not prepared and had not yet arranged his affairs....[123]

It was the third hour. All the barons, sad, like condemned men, went down to the audience hall. They stood before the people. The tribune, changed in his purpose, ascended the platform and made a beautiful speech. It was based on the Paternoster: "Forgive us our trespasses." Then he pardoned the barons and he said that they wished to be of service to the people and make peace with the people. One by one they bowed their heads to the people.[124]

The triangulation of witness is important here. The first point is Rienzo's own account, reported clearly via intermediaries, perhaps the unsuspecting mendicants whom he had sent to confess the barons. The second point of the triangulation is the Anonimo romano's narration of the private emotions among the barons, and the third, the public account of their reconciliation with the people of Rome atop the Capitoline. In none of these cases does it seem improbable that the accounts of the barons' actions, first inside their prison, and then once released, are accurate and likely relayed by eyewitnesses. Only the barons' own emotions and certain small details might be subject to some embellishment.

CHAPTER 7 ⚜ CASE STUDIES

Fra Morreale and His Brothers

In the second instance of a prison dialogue, however, the Anonimo romano appears less trustworthy. It involves the arrest and imprisonment of the notorious mercenary leader Fra Morreale and his brothers in 1354. Morreale was instrumental in helping Rienzo regain power in Rome, but he and his brothers only planned to use Cola to seize power for themselves. At this point the Anonimo's account begins to read like film noir. Morreale, being the gangster he was, kept a mistress whom he insulted and mistreated. She therefore went to Rienzo to reveal the mercenaries' plot. And so Fra Morreale entered Rome, presumably to collect on Cola's debt to him. But once inside the gates, he was immediately arrested and brought to the prison on the Capitoline. There he joined both his brothers Bettrone and Arimbaldo, whom Cola had already ordered seized. The Anonimo continues:

> Now Fra Morreale, seeing that he had been caught by the work of his maidservant and realizing how much she could say, was very much afraid that she would be the ruin of him. However, he took heart. Knowing that the Tribune needed money, he decided to see if he could free himself in some way. He informed Messer Cola di Rienzo that if he let him go he would provide him with all the money and soldiers he needed and would give him everything he wanted.
>
> And so Fra Morreale, thinking he would be pardoned, said to his imprisoned brothers, Messer Arimbaldo and Messer Bettrone, "Let one or two of us stay here. Let me go. I'll come back with ten thousand, twenty thousand florins for him...as much money and as many men as he pleases." His brothers answered, "Let's do it, for God's sake!"[125]

Several elements of this narrative are different. The first is the completely private nature of the brothers' deliberations. One might argue that a guard overheard the speakers, but mercenaries as clever and ruthless as Morreale and his lieutenants surely would have been more wary than to reveal their plans in front of a guard. Nor are these likely to have been details revealed by the brothers themselves under torture (not recorded) or in a confession aimed at securing pardon. The second element is the carefully staged nature of the dialogue itself. Both the actions and the dialogue immediately strike the reader as both forceful and dramatic in ways that strongly resemble the fictional. The basis for the dialogue among the brothers and their agreement to let one of their party go appears to be taken almost directly from the story of Joseph's test of his brothers in Genesis 42:9–25. Verses 14–17 are key.

> [14] But Joseph said to them, "It is just as I have said to you; you are spies! [15] Here is how you shall be tested: as Pharaoh lives, you shall not leave this place unless your youngest brother

comes here! [16] Let one of you go and bring your brother, while the rest of you remain in prison, in order that your words may be tested, whether there is truth in you; or else, as Pharaoh lives, surely you are spies." [17] And he put them all together in prison for three days.

The story, one of the most famous of the Bible, would have surely resonated among the Anonimo romano's readers. But, though the structure of the stories is similar, there are significant differences between them. In both cases, the brothers are compelled by their desire for wealth. In both cases, the protagonist — Joseph or Rienzo — uses some form of deception to exact justice (or revenge). In both cases, the imprisoned brothers enter into a desperate dialogue concerning their next moves. And in both cases, one of the brothers is released to accomplish the brothers' goals and unknowingly to further the protagonist's device. Yet in Joseph's case, his brothers are ultimately rewarded and shown mercy; in Rienzo's, they are lead only to their final doom. In Joseph's case, the state's wealth is distributed downward, in Rienzo's, the outlaws' wealth is seized to benefit the state.

The Anonimo is clear about his intentions in creating such a striking contrast: mercy and the Jewish virtue of anonymous charity is contrasted with a terrible and unpopular justice. The wealth that Cola brings the *buono stato* is by implication stained with the brothers' blood and tainted by Rienzo's subsequent need to appear before the people to explain their execution. But the Anomino seeks not only to contrast individual action and motivation here but also to make a stark contrast that fits within the ironic tone of his story and its Sallustian pessimism. Cola's action, though unpalatable and unpopular, is ultimately for the good of the state, and the Anonimo's use of the biblical story both provides a well-known frame for his narrative and deploys a ready point of moral comparison that his readers could not fail to understand. In Joseph's case, the seeds of mercy later yield prosperity, peace and reconciliation; in Rienzo's, the seeds of terrible justice yield nothing but horrible revenge from the people whom the *buono stato* had sought to aid.

Giovanna I's Courtiers (Again)

The third major example of the prison dialogue involves the interactions of Queen Giovanna I's court officials accused and found guilty of the murder of her first husband, Prince Andrew of Hungary. Domenico da Gravina provides the account. The de'Cabanni — Roberto, Filippa and Sancia — along with the count of Terlizzi were brought together to Castel del'Ovo to await their trial. Gravina relates an exchange among them deep within their dungeon. This is an unusual piece of reportage, since Gravina was nowhere on the scene. Nor does he disclose his sources; and

CHAPTER 7 ❧ CASE STUDIES

none of the speakers long survived. As Gravina relates it, while the prisoners were awaiting their torture and inquisition, they began to exchange recriminations over the guilt for Andrew's murder. Finally:

> the malign Sancia [de'Cabanni] — confident in her evildoing — asked "why are you going at one another like this? No excuse will keep us from dying for our guilt. We deserve even worse for our crime. But I at least die happy that while I was on this earth I took my full of sexual pleasure."
>
> And then laughingly taunting the count of Terlizzi, she said, "Come on, old man, think about how you used to screw me in your bedroom. That's right: I'm pregnant and you're the father. But some people know that Duchess Agnes of Durazzo died because of my pregnancy. I switched her urine for mine when I was pregnant. So the duke of Durazzo, when his physician told him that his mother was pregnant — based on the urine sample that the doctor showed him — no longer cared a hoot about his mother's illness but made plans to hasten her death. To make sure the duchess died even more quickly, he put poison in the ointment they prepared for her. And I've done a lot of other things that I deserve to die for. But I'm content. So don't mourn, take comfort and live until the day you die!"[126]

Two key elements here parallel those in the Anonimo romano's story of Fra Morreale brothers: the privacy of the prisoners and the vibrant realism of their dialogue. Once again, it seems highly unlikely that they would have displayed their mutual recriminations in front of witnesses or guards. How Sancia herself knew the private dealings of the house of Durazzo is also never revealed. The otherwise full account of their arrest, torture and execution makes no mention of any informants. Their guilt appears to have been established by the public inquests — however they may have been trumped up — conducted by the Angevin princes. One is therefore again left with the sense of a fictive narrative, constructed by the chronicler to reflect what likely occurred, and probably borrowed from some commonly known literary sources. But which those might have been remain unclear.

CONCLUSIONS

We have provided seven selected case studies under two broad rubrics — rituals of punishment and prison dialogues — to examine core issues of trecento historiography in the dynamic tension between fact and fiction. Truth claims, reliability and verisimilitude of evidence and witnesses and rhetorical embellishments must be measured against modern methodologies, including anthropological findings, form and literary criticism and recent studies in medieval ritual, theater, hagiography and narrative practice. While we propose various approaches to deconstructing our sources, it is clear that trecento historians reported a bedrock of fact and event: historical conflict and change occured, individuals suffered and died as a result of both legal and extra-legal actions. Though we have no way of ultimately verifying details of their private dialogues, their tortures and executions, they certainly met the fates that our historians describe. Equally important, however, is the light that these episodes shed on the trecento art of writing history and the methods, sources, inventions and expectations of audience reception that they embodied. We therefore come away with deeper sense of persons and events and with a more tangible understanding of the forms and methods of historiography that these writers employed.

NOTES

1. Among the more useful works for urban ritual are Hanawalt–Reyerson (1994); Kipling (1998); Bertelli (2001); Petkov (2003); Postlewate–Husken (2007); Brown (2011). Ratté (2006), 119–92, focuses on trecento Italian communes.
2. Buc, 1–12.
3. Bryant (1994), 3–9.
4. See Kempers (1994).
5. Chapter 4.
6. Bedos-Rezak (1994), 34–55; Zabbia (1997), 10, 37–39, 47–49, 96–97.
7. Burroughs (2000).
8. Petkov (2003), 82–92.
9. Recent work on Italian urban rituals includes specific analysis of southern Italian evidence. See Cohn (2013); Zchomelidse (2014).
10. Musto (2003), 157–59, 363 n. 15; Jansen (2013); Palmer (2014); Palmer (2019) Kumhera (2017). On Rienzo's use of ritual, see Schwartz (2007).
11. See Seibt for the Anonimo romano; Zabbia (1999), Delle Donne (2001a), Gravina (2022) for Gravina and Ranallo. On narrative truth and reliability, see the works of White and Frisch (2004). Ginzburg (1992), 96, makes clear the problematic nature of eyewitness account and historical record but criticizes White's "relativism" and invokes the Holocaust to stress that "an unlimited skeptical attitude toward historical narratives is therefore groundless." On misinterpretations of White and his strict adherence to the factual ground of historical accounts, White's "middle voice," see Doran, "Editor's Introduction" in White (2010), xiii–xxxiv, at xxv–xxxii.
12. Among the works that engage "rituals of evidence" are Bynum (1992); Bynum (2002) with Merback's (2002) response; Baraz (2003). Cohen (2000) offers valuable insights into medieval perceptions and descriptions of physical pain and torture. Important studies include Edgerton (1985); Flynn (1994); Enders (1999); Merback (1999); Rollo-Koster (2003); Groebner (2004); Meyerson (2004); Parsons (2004); Owens (2005); Rollo-Koster (2008).
13. Essential are Zorzi (1988); Zorzi (1994); "Rituals of Violence," in Bertelli (2001), 39–61, esp. 39–40, 58–61; Zorzi (2012).
14. See above, Chapter 4, pp. 109–10. Flynn (1994), 153–58 discusses this externalizing function of public ritual and its commemoration yet notes the permeability of this commemorative firewall.
15. Flynn (1994), 163–4; Enders (1999), 183–85.

16. For background, Vallerani (2012).
17. What Merback (2002), 43, summarizes as a "historical economy of violence."
18. They may reflect what Cohen (2000), 34, calls "stylized ritualized gestures" rather than factual descriptions. Buc, 51–87, warns against the seeming transparency of these accounts and emphasizes their consciously constructed, and contested, nature.
19. "'A Revelle!': Chronicle Evidence and the Rebel Voice," in Strohm (1992), 33–56.
20. Walsingham (2003), 1:410–523.
21. Walsingham (2003), 1:442–510.
22. Strohm (1992), 46.
23. Strohm (1992), 47, borrowing from Bakhtin.
24. Enders (1992).
25. Cohen (2000) finds a similar reliance on visual and verbal performance.
26. Gardiner (1989); Gardiner (1993); Owen (2001); Mallegni (2003); Gardiner (2006); Ricci (2018); Pilgun (2019); Gamberini (2021).
27. Ginzburg (1992) addressed narrative debt in medieval Jewish massacre stories.
28. See Sestan (1972). On Chaucer's Italian influences, see now Fulton (2021).
29. *Cronica* XIII.1–4, 8, 16–17; Villani (1991), 3:291–303, 306–18, 325–42.
30. XIII.17. "Fu preso uno notaio del conservadore per li Altoviti stato crudele e reo, fu tutto tagliato a bocconi… e poi da' fanciulli tranato ignudo per tutta la città, e poi in sulla piazza de' priori impeso per li piedi, e sparato e sbarrato come porco." Villani (1991), 3:338.
31. XIII.17: "e chi•nne portava un pezzo in sulla lancia e•cchi in sulla spada per tutta la città; ed ebbevi de' sì crudeli, e con furia bestiale e tanto animosa, che mangiaro delle loro carni cruda e cotta." Villani (1991), 3:339.
32. *Cronaca Senese*, 538–42.
33. "E tagliato a pezi e minuzato e infilato, i pezuoli de la carne portando in mano come carne di porco" *Cronaca Senese*, 541, ll. 33–34.
34. "Gridando misericordia, lo tagliaro e lo smenbrarono a minuti pezi." *Cronaca Senese*, 542, ll. 15–17.
35. "E tale portava infilata e vendevalla all'uno all'altro come carne di becharia e tali furono di tanto animo, che cruda e cotta mangiaro di detta carne." *Cronaca Senese*, 542, ll. 18–21.
36. XII. In tiempo de questo papa, anni Domini MCCCXLII[I], in die de santa Anna, fu cacciato de Fiorenza missore Gottifredo, conte de Brenna, duca de Atena, signore perpetuale de Fiorenza; e folli fatta moita onta e moito despiacere e detuperio e danno; e fuoro muorti uomini e loro carne fu manicata. La quale novitate fu per questa via.
37. XII: Milli vocconi ne fuoro fatti. Po' lo figlio veo lo patre moito onoratamente vestuto con vari. Uno calice d'ariento avea 'naorato in mano colla ostia. Male volentieri veniva; ma quelli de drento lo premevano, quelli de fòra lo tiravano. Così lo tagliano como foglia menutelle. La carne soa e dello figlio fu portata per Fiorenza e fu vennuta a peso e fu arrostita; e fu chi nemanicao.
39. IX.24.38, Boccaccio (1983.1), 850–51.
40. Zorzi (1994), 401–2.
41. In Arens (1979). See also McGowan (1994); Price (2003); Blurton (2007). Coudert (2012), 523–24, reflects critiques of Arens' thesis, especially by Marshall Sahlins. While she seems to conflate Arens' important distinction between "survival" and "ritual anthropophagy" (523), she otherwise agrees with his conclusions.

42. Green (1972), 13.
43. Such *damnatio memoriae* of one commune by the historians of another was not unusual. See, for example, Francesconi (2010).
44. McGowan (1994), 427–31; Price (2003), 1–8, 69–70.
45. E.g., Lev. 26:29, Deut. 28:53, 2 Kings 6:28–29, Jer. 19:9, Lament. 2:20, Ezech. 5:10.
46. McGowan (1994), 423–25. Boccaccio included Josephus' account in his chapters 3, "Some Lamenters," and 9 "Against the Hebrews," of book 2. See Hedeman (2008), 116–27.
47. *In Vatinium* 6.14.
48. Catalinus 22.
49. McGowan (1994), 432–34: "To be a 'cannibal' meant to be lawless, primitive foreign, immoral, secretive and violent."
50. *Adversus Jovinianum* 2.7.
51. VII.3.8.
52. McGowan (1994), 417–22.
53. Blurton (2007), 108–14 et passim.
54. Canto XXXIII. See Freccero (1977); Owen (2001); Pilgun (2019), 239, fig. 284; Gamberini (2021), 163, fig. 6.
55. For example, "The Vision of Tundale," in Gardiner (1989), 149–95, at 155–80.
56. Celano II, 2.23.53, does not name the man confessed or the circumstances.
57. According to the Cornell University Legal Information Institute, there is still no specific law against cannibalism in US law, and the British outlawed it only in 1800. See www.law.cornell.edu/wex/cannibalism.
58. Arens (1979), 5–22, 43–80, 97–98, 172–77. Even Margaret Mead believed second-hand reports about the "tribe" next door.
59. *Inferno* XII.107–8.
60. Analysis, with annotation to secondary work, in Musto (2003), 132–34. For a vision of anthrophagy, Gamberini (2021), 103, fig. 8.
61. Arens (1979), 110–15, 139–61, 181–85. Arens wrote before the literary turns of the 1980s had provided a critical language to apply to such approaches.
62. XIII.51.
63. *Cronaca di Partenope* III.26.
64. 612D–E.
65. SN 3:239.
66. XIII.51.
67. *Chronicon Estense*, 422E.
68. Gravina (1903), 21, ll. 22–26; Gravina (2022), X.10.
69. Boccaccio (1983.1), IX.26, calls the ship "an immense oak barge." See also Gravina (1903), 21, ll. 27–33; Gravina (2022), X.11.
70. IX.26.23. Nec mora, erecto quippe in navi aculeo, in conspectu neapolitane urbis, medio maris in sinu, ritu regionis spectante populo et Phylippa, torsit misellam Sanciam et Robertum. Quid exhauserit incertum est; ex secutis tamen hos in mortem Andree fuisse noxios pro constanti habitum est.... Boccaccio (1983.1), 862–63; Boccaccio (2018), 228.
71. Gravina confuses Raimondo and Roberto; but Boccaccio, who knew them both, relates the correct story: Raimondo, husband of Filippa, had died several years earlier with full royal honors. His son Roberto was first named seneschal of the royal household and then grand seneschal of the realm.

CHAPTER 7 ❦ CASE STUDIES

72. Gravina (1903), 21, l. 33–22, l. 27; Gravina (2022), X.12–16.
73. According to the *Annales Pistorienses,* Villani, Gravina and the later papal commission.
74. New York, Morgan Library, MS 801, fols. 95v–96r.
75. Gravina (1903), 23, ll. 15–37; Gravina (2022), X.27.
76. Such punishment for traitors was pictured on the *Cronaca* of Ferraiolo for the year 1486 in New York, Morgan Library, MS 801, fols. 94r–98r.
77. The sparing of pregnant criminals until delivery was also standard practice in England at the time. Strohm (1992), 129–30.
78. "…aliqui taxillos, aliqui manicas cultellorum fecerunt, ad rei memoriam sempiternam." Gravina (1903), 23, ll. 33–34; Gravina (2022), X.27.
79. Kempshall, 328–34.
80. See also Lev. 16:8; Prov. 16:33, 18:18; Acts 1:24–26.
81. Pp. 211–13.
82. Depictions varied. Andrea di Bartolo, for example, shows the soldiers pulling straws in his *Crucifixion* (c. 1400): Metropolitan Museum of Art (Rogers 12.6).
83. *De casibus* IX.26.24–28, Boccaccio (1983.1), 864–65. Boccaccio (2018), 228 omits the last gruesome details.
84. See a print by Lucas Meyer, dated 1589. See Merback (1999), 214, fig. 86.
85. IX.26.27, Boccaccio (1983.1), 864–65.
86. *De casibus* IX.25.4–5, Boccaccio (1983.1), 854–55; Boccaccio (2018), 223.
87. IX.26.1, Boccaccio (1983.1), 856–57; Boccaccio (2018), 223.
88. IX.26.7–8, Boccaccio (1983.1), 858–59; Boccaccio (2018), 224–25.
89. IX.26.10–11, Boccaccio (1983.1), 858–59; Boccaccio (2018), 224–25.
90. Gravina (1903), 94, l. 14–96, l. 12; Gravina (2022), XXXIX.1–49.
91. Gravina (1903), 59, l. 12–62, l. 24; Gravina (2022), XXVI.1–44.
92. Gravina (1903), 84, l. 21–94, l. 13; Gravina (2022), XXXII.1–XXXVIII.13.
93. "Hoc autem scripsi ita seriatim, non licet in totum, cum totum scribere longum foret; saltim in parte scripsi, ut sit ad memoriam filiorum patris vindictam querere et suorum sequacium, qui fuerunt." Gravina (1903), 96, ll. 9–11; Gravina (2022), XXXIX.48.
94. "Audivi namque dici a pluribus qui viderunt eundem sic pati." Gravina (1903), 96, l. 3; Gravina (2022), XXXIX.45.
95. See also Gravina (1903), 20, ll. 11–15; Gravina (2022), IX.10.
96. See also Delle Donne (2001a), 141–46.
97. Zorzi (1994); Musto (2003), 341–46. Holstein (2006), 179–85, also emphasizes the ritualistic elements of the narrative and considers it (200–205) a turning point from pubic memory to one of "social forgetting."
98. XXVII.195b–376b, AR, 259–65; Wright, 146–54; Palmer (2021), 291–99.
99. Cardinal-legate for the reconquest of the papal states. Musto (2003), 312–17, 342, 346.
100. On Rome's trecento Jewish community, Internullo (2016), 216–20, 350–51.
101. Pp. 90–91, 100.
102. Pp. 66–67.
103. P. 67.
104. XVIII.1599–1888, AR, 196–206; Wright, 80–88; Palmer (2021), 229–36.
105. *Aeneid* VI.
106. Zorzi (1994), 395–406.

107. Zorzi (1994), 406–22. See also Chapter 6.
108. Kempshall, 330–34.
109. Zorzi (1994), 422–25.
110. Enders (1999), 28–30.
111. Enders (1999), 48–49.
112. AR XVIII, ll. 1431–54.
113. AR XXVII, ll. 503–5b.
114. Gravina (1903), 22, l. 26–23 l. 1; Gravina (2022), X.17–21.
115. Ginzburg (1992), 84–85.
116. White (1987); White (2010).
117. Frisch (2004).
118. Phillips (2014).
119. See Kempshall, Gehl, Murphy.
120. Maillart (1998), 147–53.
121. See above, pp. 133–34.
122. 40, Rienzo (1913–29), 2.3:145–47, ll. 11–69.
123. XVIII.1431–40, AR, 190–91; Wright, 76; Palmer (2021), 225–26.
124. XVIII.1445–54, AR, 191; Wright, 76; Palmer (2021), 225–26.
125. XXVII.503–5b, AR, 253; Wright, 141–42; Palmer (2021), 285–86.
126. Gravina (1903), 22, l. 28–23, l. 1; Gravina (2022), X.17–21.

WORKS CITED

Baraz, Daniel. 2003. *Medieval Cruelty: Changing Perceptions, Antiquity to the Early Modern Period*. Ithaca: Cornell University Press.

Bedos-Rezak, Brigitte. 1994. "Civic Liturgies and Urban Records in Northern France, 1100–1400." In Hanawalt–Reyerson (1994), 34–55.

Blurton, Heather. 2007. *Cannibalism in High Medieval English Literature*. Basingstoke: Palgrave Macmillan.

Brown, Warren. 2011. *Violence in Medieval Europe*. Harlow: Longman.

Bryant, Lawrence. 1994. "Configurations of the Community in Late Medieval Spectacles: Paris and London During the Dual Monarchy." In Hanawalt–Reyerson (1994), 3–33.

Burroughs, Charles. 2000. "Spaces of Arbitration and the Organization of Space in Late Medieval Italian Cities." In *Medieval Practices of Space*. Barbara A. Hanawalt and Michal Kobialka, ed. Minneapolis: University of Minnesota Press, 64–100.

Bynum, Caroline Walker. 1992. *Fragmentation and Redemption: Essays on Gender and the Human Body in Medieval Religion*. New York: Zone Books.

—. 2002. "Violent Imagery in Late Medieval Piety." *German Historical Institute. Bulletin* 30:3–36.

Cohen, Esther. 2000. "The Animated Pain of the Body." *American Historical Review* 105:36–68.

Cohn, Samuel Kline, et al., ed. 2013. *Late Medieval and Early Modern Ritual: Studies in Italian Urban Culture*. Turnhout: Brepols.

Coudert, Allison P. 2012. "The Ultimate Crime: Cannibalism in Early Modern Minds and Imagination." In *Crime and Punishment in the Middle Ages and Early Modern Age*. Albrecht Classen and Connie L. Scarborough, ed. Berlin: De Gruyter, 521–54.

Edgerton, Samuel Y. 1985. *Pictures and Punishment: Art and Criminal Prosecution During the Florentine Renaissance*. Ithaca: Cornell University Press.

Enders, Jody. 1992. *Rhetoric and the Origins of Medieval Drama*. Ithaca, NY: Cornell University Press.

Flynn, Maureen. 1994. "The Spectacle of Suffering in Spanish Streets." In Hanawalt–Reyerson (1994), 153–68.

Frisch, Andrea. 2004. *The Invention of the Eyewitness: Witnessing and Testimony in Early Modern France*. Chapel Hill: University of North Carolina Press.

Francesconi, Giampaolo. 2010. "*Infamare per dominare:* La costruzione retorica fiorentina del conflitto politico a Pistoia." In *Lotta politica nell'Italia medievale*. Federico Canaccini and Isa Lori Sanfilippo, ed. Rome: ISIME, 95–106.

Freccero, John. 1977. "Bestial Sign and Bread of Angels (*Inferno* 32 and 33)." *Yale Italian Studies* 1:53–66.

Gamberini, Andrea. 2021. *Inferni medievali: Dipingere il mondo dei morti per orientare la società dei vivi*. Rome: Viella.

Gardiner, Eileen. 1989. *Visions of Heaven and Hell Before Dante*. New York: Italica Press.

—. 2006. "Hell-on-Line." At www.hell-on-line.org.

Ginzburg, Carlo. 1992. "Just One Witness." In *Probing the Limits of Representation: Nazism and the "Final Solution."* Saul Friedländer, ed. Cambridge, MA: Harvard University Press, 82–96.

Groebner, Valentin. 2004. *Defaced: The Visual Culture of Violence in the Late Middle Ages*. Pamela Selwyn, trans. New York: Zone Books.

Hanawalt, Barbara. 1994. With Kathryn Reyerson. *City and Spectacle in Medieval Europe*. Minneapolis: University of Minnesota Press.

Hedeman, Anne D. 2008. *Translating the Past: Laurent de Premierfait and Boccaccio's De casibus*. Los Angeles: Getty Publications.

Jansen, Katherine L. 2013. "'Pro bono pacis': Crime, Conflict, and Dispute Resolution: The Evidence of Notarial Peace Contracts in Late Medieval Florence." *Speculum* 88.2:427–56.

Kempers, Bram. 1994. "Icons, Altarpieces, and Civic Ritual in Siena Cathedral, 1100–1530." In Hanawalt–Reyerson (1994), 89–136.

Kipling, Gordon. 1998. *Enter the King: Theatre, Liturgy, and Ritual in the Medieval Civic Triumph*. Oxford: Clarendon Press.

Kumhera, Glenn. 2017. *The Benefits of Peace: Private Peacemaking in Late Medieval Italy*. Leiden: Brill.

Maillart, Jean. 1998. *Le roman du comte d'Anjou*. Francine Mora-Lebrun, ed. Paris: Gallimard.

Mallegni, Francesco. 2003. With M. Luisa Ceccarelli Lemut. *Il conte Ugolino Della Gherardesca tra antropologia e storia*. Pisa: PLUS.

McGowan, Andrew. 1994. "Eating People: Accusations of Cannibalism Against Christians in the Second Century." *The Journal of Early Christian Studies* 2:413–42.

Merback, Mitchell B. 2002. "Reverberations of Guilt and Violence, Resonances of Place: A Comment on Caroline Walker Bynum's Lecture." *German Historical Institute. Bulletin* 30:37–50.

Meyerson, Mark Douglas, et al., ed. 2004. *A Great Effusion of Blood?: Interpreting Medieval Violence*. Toronto: University of Toronto Press.

Owen, Rachel. 2001. "Dante's Reception by 14th- and 15th-Century Illustrators of the *Commedia*." *Reading Medieval Studies* 27:163–225.

Owens, Margaret E. 2005. *Stages of Dismemberment: The Fragmented Body in Late Medieval and Early Modern Drama*. Newark: University of Delaware Press.

Palmer, James A. 2014. "Piety and Social Distinction in Late Medieval Roman Peacemaking." *Speculum* 89.4:974–1004.

—. 2019. *The Virtues of Economy: Governance, Power and Piety in Late Medieval Rome*. Ithaca, NY: Cornell University Press.

Parsons, John Carmi. 2004. "Violence, the Queen's Body, and the Medieval Body Politic." In Meyerson (2004), 241–67.

Petkov, Kiril. 2003. *The Kiss of Peace: Ritual, Self, and Society in the High and Late Medieval West*. Leiden: Brill.

Phillips, Philip Edward. 2014. "Boethius, the Prisoner, and *The Consolation of Philosophy*." In *Prison Narratives from Boethius to Zana*. Philip Edward Phillips, ed. New York: Palgrave Macmillan.

Pilgun, Andry. 2019. *The Otherworldly World of the Middle Ages: Paradise, Purgatory and Their Characters in Visionary Texts and Miniatures from Western Manuscripts, IX–XV Centuries*. Moscow: Gamma Press.

Postlewate, Laurie. 2007. With Wim Husken. *Acts and Texts: Performance and Ritual in the Middle Ages and the Renaissance*. Amsterdam: Rodopi.

Price, Merrall Llewelyn. 2003. *Consuming Passions: The Uses of Cannibalism in Late Medieval and Early Modern Europe*. New York: Routledge.

Ratté, Felicity. 2006. *Picturing the City in Medieval Italian Painting*. Jefferson, NC: McFarland.

Ricci, Lucia Battaglia. 2018. *Dante per immagini: Dalle miniature trecentesche ai giorni nostri*. Turin: Einaudi.

Rienzo, Cola di. 1913–29. *Die Briefwechel des Cola di Rienzo*. Konrad Burdach and Paul Piur, ed. In *Vom Mittelalter zur Reformation* 2.1–5. Berlin: Weidmann.

Rollo-Koster, Joëlle. 2003. "The Politics of Body Parts: Contested Topographies in Late Medieval Avignon." *Speculum* 78.1:66–98.

—. 2008. *Raiding Saint Peter: Empty Sees, Violence, and the Initiation of the Great Western Schism (1378)*. Leiden: Brill.

Sestan, Ernesto. 1972. "Gualtieri di Brienne." DBI 14. At www.treccani.it/enciclopedia/gualtieri-di-brienne_(Dizionario-Biografico).

Schwartz, Amy. 2007. "Eternal Rome and Cola di Rienzo's Show of Power." In Postlewate (2007), 63–76.

Vallerani, Massimo. 2012. *Medieval Public Justice*. Washington, DC: Catholic University of America Press.

Zchomelidse, Nino Maria. 2014. *Art, Ritual, and Civic Identity in Medieval Southern Italy*. University Park: Pennsylvania State University Press.

Zorzi, Andrea. 1988. *L'amministrazione della giustizia penale nella Repubblica Fiorentina: Aspetti e problemi*. Florence: Olschki.

—. 2012. "Justice." In *The Italian Renaissance State*. Andrea Gamberini and Isabella Lazzarini, ed. Cambridge: Cambridge University Press, 490–514.

8. CONSTRUCTING GRAND NARRATIVES: THE BLACK LEGEND OF THE ANGEVINS

INTRODUCTION

This chapter examines one grand narrative that unites several strains of trecento historiography: what I have termed the "black legend of the Angevins."[1] The following pages will also analyze its closely related themes of the use of nature imagery as metaphor for female rule and women's role in political change. For the historiography of the South, this imagery focuses on pollution and disease.

The Angevins ruled throughout the period covered here.[2] Their reign colored all perceptions of the kingdom of Naples, including the larger cultural discourse during the trecento and quattrocento over the meanings of humanism and cultural rebirth and their application to contemporary life. This discourse among early modern historians, philosophers, artists and political theorists focused on many of the key aspects of culture that were central for late medieval and early modern Italians: the verbal and visual representations of political, civic, moral and religious virtues encoded in both classical rhetorical forms[3] and the emerging visual language[4] of the trecento. It remains key today to our understanding of the historiography of Naples and the South. This chapter argues that the Question of the South had its ultimate origins not only in the politico-economic debates during the Risorgimento over *meridionalismo* but also in far older and more deeply rooted themes and tropes developed in the trecento.

The original black legend — of Spanish atrocity and genocide in the conquest of the Americas — was first formulated in the sixteenth century in the works of the Spanish missionary to the Americas, Fra Bartolomé de Las Casas, OP (1474–1566) and then taken up and elaborated over subsequent centuries by Spain's political and religious enemies.[5] Like the Spanish legend, the black legend of the Angevins is based largely on contemporary reportage and filtered through the selective lenses of politically motivated writers. Like the Spanish black legend, its outline and conclusions were accepted by nearly all subsequent writers and historians in the scholarly consensus regarding their nature and extent. How was the Angevin black legend formed, and how has it survived? A brief narrative follows.

Raised up by Pope Urban IV against the excommunicated Hohenstaufen, Charles I of Anjou conquered Naples and executed the surviving heirs of Frederick II without pity or justice. For many contemporaries, including Dante, his dynasty was thus based on usurpation and blood.[6] But Charles and his son Charles II gradually replaced a heterodox and heterogeneous Hohenstaufen court and culture with the new, orthodox culture of the French. Their new Gothic architecture, the chivalric romance literature that their dynasty favored, their vigorous crusading culture and the religiously sanctioned bloodline *(beata stirps)* of Saint Louis of France remade Naples and the South in the image of the emerging great kingdoms of the North: France and (Angevin) England.[7]

The process of nation and culture building saw continual forward motion and ascent toward modernity, culminating in the reign of Robert of Anjou, called "the Wise" even in his own lifetime. According to this historiography, Robert was the richest, most competent, cultured and just ruler of his age. He brought Naples to the center of European (i.e., French) culture and surrounded himself with Christendom's best artists and writers, intellectuals, jurists, architects and religious leaders. He brought the Regno to the apogee of wealth and influence and made his kingdom a model of late medieval rule. He also personified the high moral and ethical standards so prized in a medieval ruler and made his court a model of probity. So thorough and conscious was his notion of statecraft that some modern historians have seen him as among the first Renaissance (or proto-Renaissance) rulers of Italy.

According to the black legend, this upward trajectory was marred both by the blood stain of the Angevins' original usurpation and by the continued stigma of illegitimacy that dogged the dynasty. Robert himself was so conscious of his brother Charles Martel of Hungary's prior claims to the throne that he deliberately set out to legitimize his rule by fashioning a persona of the wise and rational ruler that essentially made him a modern political figure. But the Angevin ascendancy was tragically cut short by the premature death of Robert's only surviving son, Charles of Calabria, in November 1328 and then by the inability — or refusal — of his second wife, Queen Sancia of Majorca, to bear an heir.[8] The Angevins' steady progress toward a modern, rational state therefore halted abruptly. Sancia has been held largely responsible for this failure based on her allegedly traditionalist, obscurantist Franciscan religiosity, a spiritual inclination that new interpretations claim was not shared by her rational, more modern, husband Robert.[9]

The result was the most important of several abrupt period changes in the history of the Regno. According to this historiography, the reign of Giovanna I (1343–82) marked a sudden and irrevocable decline in

CHAPTER 8 ❧ GRAND NARRATIVES

Angevin fortunes. All the blood-soaked guilt that had founded the dynasty and that its male rulers long held in check now suddenly emerged again. In the narratives of trecento writers, irrationality and perversity at the Neapolitan court were matched by growing lawlessness and immorality among the Regno's people, by a selfish disregard for the common good by its nobility[10] and by the South's slippage back into the immobility of timelessness first broken by the Northmen.

While the male Angevins had projected agency and masculine virtues, the South now assumed Giovanna's feminine character. Her fickleness and unfaithfulness permeated the body politic. Giovanna I brought promiscuity, murder, disloyalty, secretiveness and religious irrationality to court life, while her betrayals, political incompetence and indecisive paralysis brought collapse to the Regno. As the head was corrupted, so corruption flowed like a polluted stream through the body politic, the land and its people. The Angevin dynasty fell back into southern obscurity, feeding upon itself and its own blood, ruined by self-inflicted wounds and the mutilation of the royal person and the body politic.

Even recent cultural histories of the Angevin kingdom of Naples, including its artistic, intellectual and political life, stop at 1343, the year of Robert's death.[11] All else of the medieval Regno, beginning with Giovanna I's reign, is seen as a tragic afterword to an era of brilliance and reason. History would have to wait until the emergence of the Aragonese dynasty and the final eradication of the last Angevins to witness the Renaissance in the Regno. But even with this revival, Naples and the South would forever remain fallen from grace: an ignorant, strange and vengeful land, full of mystery, corruption, lust and violence, a culture maimed and thwarted at home into a-historical immobility, only periodically resuscitated but inevitably altered through foreign force and spirit.

Unlike a similar dynastic history — that of the Plantagenets of England and their heirs among the houses of Lancaster, York and Tudor — the story of the Angevins and of Naples never achieved the high level of noble tragedy that the same tale of conflicting bloodline and inheritance, treachery, usurpation, illegitimacy and murder did among the English royal line. Perhaps this is because the kingdom of Naples never found its Shakespeare and his history plays to ennoble the trajectory of dynastic crisis into the stuff of individual and national rebirth. The England that emerged from these troubles in the literary and political imagination of the late sixteenth century, John of Gaunt's "blessed plot," was a land and nation made wiser and more mature by its travails. By the same period, however, Naples and the South were already marked, like their master Spain, as a land of depravity and corruption: their time of troubles had brought them nothing but a reputation for decline and damnation. Late medieval England has since been framed by the history play, the South of Italy by the

Jacobean theater of cruelty[12] and the Gothic novel of the eighteenth and nineteenth centuries.[13]

Where did the legend begin? As with so much of the history of the mid-fourteenth century in Italy, we should start with Petrarch. This chapter will therefore focus on the poet's evolving views of Robert of Anjou and his heirs, taking some time to carefully lay out the shift in Petrarch's thinking about Naples and its Angevin dynasty. But if Petrarch was the most forceful to formulate the black legend, he was certainly not the first or only contemporary. Dante had already cast a shadow on the Angevins. Giovanni Villani, Domenico da Gravina and Giovanni Boccaccio later joined Petrarch in creating this legend.

In Chapter 7, we discussed the arrest, imprisonment and execution of Giovanna's household familiars and chief administrative officers in the grisly murder of her consort, Prince Andrew of Hungary. Our sources are almost unanimous in laying ultimate blame and *infamia* for the murder on Giovanna herself.[14] We have also followed the consequences of that murder and of Giovanna's marriage to her cousin Prince Louis of Taranto and their subsequent history and its literary embellishments. Here we will follow the construction of the narrative around Giovanna's supposed moral depravity, her incompetence to rule and their consequences for Naples and the Regno.

INFAMY: WOMEN MURDERERS

The motif of women arranging the murder of their husbands follows several well-worn tropes. One nearly contemporary example is the *Westminster Chronicle*'s account of Elizabeth Wauton's murder of her own husband Andrew on June 24, 1387. Embellishing the official indictment in the chronicle account — whether via direct access to the records or via gossip — "the location of the crime shifts from an outdoor ambuscade near a footpath in an open field to the symbolically charged confines of the nuptial bed."[15] This pattern of transference is formulaic and raises suspicions over its authenticity on formal grounds alone. Strohm notes:

> The most apparent thing about the chronicler's perspective is its extreme antifeminism: women are creatures of appetite, rage out of control, seduce men, act out their antagonism and rebellion within the relations and at the sites of greatest trust, gratify themselves unrepentantly (and slumber untroubled) at the very locations they have desecrated.... So powerful is this lurid fantasy that it is realized in a number of accounts, fervent in their narration but uncertain in their particular historicity.[16]

In such accounts, the facts of the case are soon overwhelmed by rumor, gossip, *infamia* and deliberate, often malicious distortion. According to changing sources, the scene of Prince Andrew of Hungary's murder also shifts from exterior hallway to marriage chamber, while Giovanna herself claimed to have slumbered through the apparently clamorous event.[17]

The sources of these changes are often the natural result of the gossip network and the workings of individual or group memory. Yet the strikingly similar descriptions of female behavior leads one to consider other more immediate sources that might have stirred the imaginations of literate readers and writers. As Strohm notes of Elizabeth Wauton:

> like her distant cousins in the fabliaux, she is held up to mockery, her motivations recorded as sex-driven, out of control, beneath reason. For hers is a threat that needed diffusing, a deep disturbance of patriarchy that required redress by a narratively refashioned community of disapproval.[18]

When the threat was to the supreme patriarchal structures of royal bloodline and inheritance, and when the accounts were placed into the hands of hostile royal propagandists, this refashioning became a dangerous weapon that would threaten not only individual women but dynasties and kingdoms.

HUNGARIAN ROYAL PROPAGANDA

After the initial shock, deep grief, and rising anger at hearing that their brother and son had been so viciously slaughtered, the Angevin King Lewis of Hungary and his mother Queen Elizabeth Piast set their court's full propaganda apparatus into motion.[19] Through the Spring of 1346, a flow of letters[20] streamed from the Hungarian court at Visegrad and Buda to the papal court at Avignon, decrying the assassination, constructing the ideal persona of the slain Andrew — a martyred Christian prince, an innocent among wolves — naming the responsible parties, laying out the early stages of the revived Hungarian claim to the crown of Naples and calling on the pope to take immediate and decisive action to bring the criminals to justice.

As Lewis of Hungary prepared his invasion to claim the kingdom of Naples, he and his mother developed four main themes: first, Lewis was the legitimate heir of Charles Martel, whose throne Robert of Anjou had usurped. Hungary asserted that the marriage arrangements for King Robert's granddaughters was the object of long negotiation between Robert and his nephew Carobert concerning the essence of the Angevin inheritance. They claimed that if Andrew and Giovanna died, then inheritance would pass to her younger sister, Princess Maria, and another of the sons of Carobert (namely Lewis). With Andrew dead, Lewis was "the first born of the first born of the ruling house of the kingdom of Naples," and therefore had the strongest claim on the throne. Lewis' assertions, however, flatly contradicted the widely circulated terms of King Robert's last will and testament.[21]

Second, no woman should rightly take on a man's role and a kingdom's crown. Queen Mother Elizabeth quoted from St. Paul (1 Cor. 11:3), "since the man is the woman's head," and set the keystone to the Hungarian propaganda edifice: the male naturally has a prior claim to the crown. She does not say so specifically, but she does not need to, for all knew that male inheritance had been the age-old custom of the royal house of France and all its cadet lines. The shock of the Tour de Nesle affair had very recently prompted France's legists to reassert the supposedly ancient claims of the *lex salica*.[22] History, literature and legend also abounded with examples of men who claimed their thrones through marriage to an heiress.

As we have already seen,[23] Elizabeth offered several examples of males who received their crowns through their wives: the king of Aragon, formerly of Sicily; King Manfred, the Hohenstaufen heir of Sicily; and Brennius of Britain. Elizabeth reminded the pope that her own son Lewis was a defender of the faith in a world surrounded by pagans. He was a crusader who knew how to defend his own. Elizabeth did not have to reiterate that it was through a papal crusade to defend the faith that the Angevins toppled the faithless Hohenstaufen and won Naples. Nor did she need to remind him that Brennius' success ultimately ended in a bloody reign. History could well repeat itself.[24]

Third, Lewis and Elizabeth pressed their opposition to Giovanna's remarriage, either with any of the royal Neapolitan cousins — Robert, Louis or Philip of Taranto — or with any living man. Using the standard Latin word *"copulari"* to sexualize Giovanna's proposed marriage alliance, they set out the basis for toppling the queen for moral reasons and called attention to the possibly incestuous, rather than dynastic, elements of a marriage between cousins. They underscored this with their claim that a union between Giovanna and one of her Neapolitan relatives would scandalize all of Christianity. Pro-Hungarian historians, such as the Villani, would soon pick up this official line and add the details to fill out the narrative: a depraved queen who murders her husband, then enters into new sexual union with her own relative to the scandal of all of Christendom.[25]

Fourth, they asserted that Giovanna was unfit to rule since it was she who plotted Andrew's murder. She is a "husband killer" *(viricida)* and is notorious *(infama)* for the act. The accusation of *infamia* is ominous, for in the Italian context of the fourteenth century, it meant a publicly acknowledged criminal who had lost all right to further judicial review, who could be brought to justice dead or alive.[26] Since the pope had refused to depose her and had delayed the necessary inquests, Lewis himself would have to claim his rights by vendetta *(vindicta)* and force of arms.

The chief elements of the case that Lewis pleaded against Giovanna before the supreme court and judge of Christendom were therefore in place within one year of Andrew's murder. But they still lacked the necessary cohesion in mustering plausible, verifiable and trustworthy evidence that wins over the judge's approval and the public's consent. This could only be accomplished through carefully arranged forensic argument set in the accusatory mode. This required a broader rhetorical framework, one that implicated both the female ruler and her realm in a grand narrative of Neapolitan decline and corruption, making the individual and debatable details of the case less important than the ontological incapacity of a woman to rule. This is what we have termed the black legend of the Angevins, and it was ready at hand.

PETRARCH

Like so much in the history of trecento thought, we can also attribute much of the black legend of the Angevins to Petrarch. We can trace this development in his thinking about Naples and its Angevin rulers in his "Argus," Eclogue 2 of his *Bucolicum carmen*,[27] and in a small group of letters later re-arranged thematically by the poet in books 4 and 5 of his *Letters on Familiar Matters (Familiares)* and his *Letters of Old Age (Seniles)*. We have already noted his "cut-and-paste" methodology, collating evidence and argument from a wide variety of classical sources to create a cohesive and complete narrative.[28] Together the *Familiares* and *Seniles* form what Albert Ascoli has called a "mega-macro-text," a "project of recovering and reproducing the classical past."[29]

Given Petrarch's sharply focused intent to mold his image to match the ancients' and to carefully edit and glean his correspondence to highlight this connection, it is little wonder that Petrarch's letters reflect such a sharp turnabout in his views of Naples and the Regno from his outright admiration of King Robert[30] and his court to his bitter condemnation of Giovanna I and her rule.[31] These letters trace Petrarch's trajectory from a place of privilege and prestige to one of rejection: from King Robert's intimate and learned interlocutor on the city's Virgilian past[32] to the disappointed papal ambassador to Giovanna's court and eyewitness to the early days of her rule, no longer the chief but only one of the court's important guests. The *Familiares* also portray the temporary downfall of the man of classical letters and the erasure of his bonds to his ancient models, a disappointment to him as bitter as the ruin of Cola di Rienzo and the dream of ancient Rome's revival.[33] Both disappointments were expressed through the narration of events and the projection of failure unto third persons — whether Rienzo or Giovanna — but both had their foundations in the same classical impulse that informed all the poet's works.

Petrarch's narrative construct begins with his epideictic letter *Familiares* IV.2 of c.1340 to Dionigio da Borgo San Sepolcro.[34] As Petrarch prepares for his upcoming coronation in Rome as poet laureate on April 8, 1341 — beginning a new enlightened age — he asserts his spiritual and cultural affinity to King Robert the Wise, the archetypal ruler who is the culmination of Christian virtues, closely akin to the monastic virtues that he praises to Dionigio. Robert is the epitome of the male who "takes command of the passions which rebel against the mind and would crush him if he yielded."[35] The king's virtues include self-control, magnanimity, freedom from desire, patience, moderation and love of peace.

In letter IV.3[36] of December 26, 1340, Petrarch addresses Robert directly on what concerned them both: the miseries of the world and their expectation of spiritual rebirth.

> For what greater blessing can one conceive than, once divested of our garment of flesh and thus free from these chains, reaching the day... when we, having overcome death, put on immortality, thereby restoring indissolubly and reforming the rotten garment of our flesh half eaten by worms and altogether rotten?[37]

Petrarch again wrote to Robert in *Familiares* IV.7 from Pisa on April 30, 1341. This time the theme was Robert as the patron of arts and culture. The king has recalled the ancient Muses and brought about a "rebirth... worthy to be numbered among philosophers and poets, one can say with even greater truth, what Suetonius said about Augustus: 'He fostered the talents of his century in every possible way'."[38]

Robert's death on January 20, 1343 would therefore become a disaster of the worst kind. In his letter to Barbato da Sulmona of May 29, 1343 (*Fam.* V.1),[39] Petrarch uses the rhetoric of predictive historiography long familiar through biblical and early Christian writing[40] to set up the self-fulfilling prophesy that repeats the imagery of innocent lambs and wolves already developed by the Hungarian court:

> What I feared [Robert's death] has happened.... [H]ow I fear that those other presentiments of mine may also come true, presentiments which my distressed mind, always a too certain prophet of evils, now suggests to me. I am really alarmed about the youthfulness of the young queen, about the talents and ways of the courtiers. I wish I could be a lying prophet about these things, but I see two lambs entrusted to the care of a multitude of wolves, and I see a kingdom without a king. How can I call someone a king [Andrew] who is ruled by another [Giovanna]? and who is exposed to the greed of so many and (I sadly add) to the cruelty of so many?... what should be seen in the death of that man [Robert] who was by nature another Plato, and in his wisdom and glory second to no other king, and whose death

CHAPTER 8 ⚜ GRAND NARRATIVES

furthermore has opened the way to so many dangers on all sides?[41]

It did not take long for Petrarch to see the results of his own foresight. As Robert's declared heir, Giovanna I had came to the throne amid the rival claims of royal cousins in Naples and Hungary. Pope Clement VI therefore sent Petrarch to Naples as a special envoy to evaluate the governing council and test the atmosphere at court. Petrarch's patron Cardinal Giovanni Colonna had also entrusted him with a private mission to win the release of the Pippini, Colonna clients, local barons and infamous brigands of Basilicata and Apulia whom King Robert had outlawed and Queen Giovanna had imprisoned. Petrarch tracked the progress of his mission for Cardinal Colonna in *Familiares* V.

During this second journey to Naples in the Fall of 1343, Petrarch portrayed a court in disarray, beset by natural disasters, superstitious and incapable of response, dominated by corrupt courtiers, presiding over a city and kingdom where moral depravity seemed the rule of the day. Barely six months had passed since Robert's death, but the signs of decline were everywhere. Yet Petrarch's strongest condemnation of Giovanna and her court was not direct. The Regno remained under the firm control of King Robert's appointed regency council, headed by his widow Queen Sancia of Majorca on behalf of Giovanna I. Instead, the poet focused on the influence at court of Fra Roberto da Mileto OFM, an Italian Spiritual Franciscan, a follower of Angelo Clareno, one of Queen Sancia's most trusted advisors and among the first testators of King Robert's will.[42] In so doing he constructed an image of corruption that would frame the black legend.

Through Petrarch's pen, Roberto became the infamous *"horrendum tripes,"* the horrible and cruel monster of *Familiares* V.3,[43] which Petrarch wrote to his patron Cardinal Giovanni Colonna:

> I came to Naples where I visited the queens [Sancia and Giovanna] and participated in their Council meeting. Alas, what a shame, what a monster! May God remove this kind of plague from Italian skies! I thought that Christ was despised at Memphis, Babylon, and Mecca. I feel pity for you, my noble Parthenope, for you truly resemble any one of them since you reflect no piety, no truth, no faith. I saw a terrible three-footed beast, with its feet naked, with its head bare, arrogant about its poverty, dripping with pleasures....
>
> ...To be sure you know his sacred name; he is called Roberto. In the place of that most serene Robert who was recently king, this other Roberto has arisen who will be an eternal dishonor of our age just as the other was its only glory. I shall now consider it less unbelievable that a serpent can arise from the remains of a buried man since this insensitive asp has sprung up from the royal tomb.

Oh supreme shame! See who has dared invade your royal throne, most excellent king! But this is the trust one can have in Fortune. She not only turns human affairs around but overturns them. It was not sufficient that she should remove the sun from the world, thereby superimposing dark shadows over it, but after having snatched away our unparalleled king she did not simply replace him with someone inferior in virtue, but instead with a horrible and cruel monster.

Is this how you look upon us, Lord of the stars? Is this a suitable successor for such a king? After the Dionysii and Agathocles and Phalaris, was this person (who is more repulsive and underneath more monstrous) a proper legacy of destiny to the Sicilian court, this "most unmerciful oppressor," to use the words of Macrobius? With an extraordinary type of tyranny he wears not a crown, or a habit, or arms, but a filthy mantle, and, as I said, not completely wrapped in it but only half-way, and curved over not so much because of old age but because of his hypocrisy. Relying not as much on eloquence as on silence and on arrogance, he wanders through the courtyards of the queens, and, supported by a staff, he pushes aside the more humble, he tramples upon justice, and he defiles whatever remains of divine or human rights. Like a new Tiphys and another Palinurus he controls the helm of the unrestrained ship of state which, in my opinion, will soon perish in a huge shipwreck....

The matter has now reached the point where I have no hope in human assistance, especially with respect to the surviving Roberto who in his excessive treachery and because of the strangeness of his dress deserves the name and rank of the foremost monster in courtly circles. As a fitting conclusion, pass on to [the pope] this one particular thought of mine: would he believe that the Saracen centers of Susa or Damascus might receive his apostolic exhortations more reverently, as I believe they would, than Christian Naples?...

In truth, while I am trying to relieve my angry stomach with these sputtering words, I fear that I might also be moving you to anger. If this proves of no avail, and if the temerity of such people and your patience can lead to nothing more than our getting upset, of what avail is it to try to relay the insolence of the matter with our words, something which neither Cicero himself nor Demosthenes could accomplish? Even if it were possible, such damage would accrue to the person who undertakes it that he would lose his peace of mind while the perpetrators of the crimes remain unpunished. Therefore it would be wise to bring our words to a conclusion.

Petrarch portrays Fra Roberto as a foul and wretched man who dresses in filthy rags and in his filth personifies the regency council and the vile influence that now surrounds the young queen. Borrowing from stock classical condemnations of the Orient as despotic, corrupt and evil,[44] the poet makes repeated illusion to Giovanna's court as a "Saracen Susa, or a Damascus," Fra Roberto a tyrant like Dionysius of Syracuse or Agatiocle and Phalaride. Giovanna has become Cleopatra and Andrew her Ptolemy. Petrarch's orientalizing would set the frame for both contemporaries and for later Italian thought on the alterity of the Mezzogiorno. To this otherness he adds Roberto's monstrous nature. Often associated in the Middle Ages with the female and its appetites, this metaphor adds to the degradation of Naples as beyond the pale of civilized Christendom.[45]

Petrarch's most devastating image, however, is of Roberto as the reptilian offspring of King Robert, the serpent slithering out of the grave of the first, royal Robert. The image conjures up the horrible corruption of death as it spreads over the kingdom. This is the heart of the black legend and its intellectual foundation. If King Robert had symbolized all that was good and attractive about the Regno — and the kingdom itself was embodied in the king's own body, as medievals believed — then in Robert's death, it became a corpse putrefying and spreading a noxious disease. Petrarch had already used the image of the serpent or the worm that issues from the rotting body in a letter to King Robert himself.[46]

Petrarch's images are deliberate and conscious constructs. As he himself tells Cardinal Colonna, he has used the rhetorical tradition of Cicero and Demosthenes to enrage his reader's emotions. His words also fit aptly into the rhetorical traditions of medieval literature and painting. The slithering snake is the first of the devil's creatures escaping from the grave, for example, in Orcagna's painting of *The Triumph of Death* (c. 1350) in the Campo Santo in Pisa or in the torments of hell so well documented by Eileen Gardiner. On a deeper level, this imagery conjures up the manifestation of Satan himself finally being unmasked by death. Petrarch is brilliant in his use of a single image to show the full spectrum of moral corruption, political disintegration of the body politic and, by transference, the jump to the embodiment of the realm in a new female body. His second metaphor of the "unrestrained ship of state which, in my opinion, will soon perish in a huge shipwreck," is a clear reference to Giotto's *Navicella* in the Vatican and — as Petrarch had designed his narrative in these letters — a foreboding of the deadly tsunami of *Familiares* V. 5.

Though he composed an entire corpus to his unknown "Laura" and thus made the sonnet the ideal form of love poem, Petrarch seems to have left behind little reference to women as his intellectual equals.[47] His corpus of public letters, the 350 in the *Familiares* and the 128 in the *Seniles*, contain only one to a woman, to Empress Anna (*Fam.* XXI. 8, Milan, May 23, 1352). In his letter to Dionigio da Borgo San Sepolcro (*Fam.* IV. 2)[48] of January 4, 1339, he focuses on women within the context of his praise of the monastic virtues of Robert the Wise: "A single law governs all females: they desire silly things and they dread things of small account."[49] To be fair, one cannot make too much of this: Petrarch was no exception to his time and place, and his attitudes were commonplace. Yet their very "normalcy" reveals much of Barthes' "what goes without saying," the deep structures of attitude and mentality that give rise to myths.

Just as fairly, it is not too far a leap to see Petrarch's view of the new, queen's body of Giovanna as the corruption inherent in her very female nature. In this regard, the viper creeping out of the tomb of the dead king is a deeply troubling psychological image: abhorrence of the woman issuing from the body of the male. Giovanna was spawned not naturally by a regular process of succession through her own father, who had predeceased Robert, but unnaturally from her grandfather. In this sense, she has been spawned from his grave. Roberto da Mileto becomes Petrarch's proxy for Giovanna; and the poet describes Fra Roberto with stereotypical female characteristics, such as *perfidia* and hypocrisy. Indeed, Roberto's dress — supposedly so shocking to Petrarch but so familiar to Italians of the fourteenth century as typical of the strict Franciscans — his demeanor and his odor are all reminiscent of late medieval misogynist descriptions of "female" corruption.

Petrarch also expressed these themes through his descriptions of the city's architecture,[50] artistic heritage and natural setting. In *Familiares* V.4 of November 23, 1343,[51] he recounts to Cardinal Giovanni Colonna his excursion with fellow scholars around the Bay of Naples. Petrarch sings the praises of antiquity described by Virgil: Lago Averno and Lucrinus, Caligula's highway across the bay, the Sibyl's cave at Cumae, Monte Falerno and the Neapolitan grotto described by Seneca. These impressions would form the core of his description of Naples in his latter *Itinerary*.[52] Just as his journey required him to then turn completely around the Bay, Petrarch turned the tone of his letter back to his original criticism of Queen Giovanna by next focusing on the remains of the baths at Baia and their "effeminate elegance."[53] Pompey, Caesar, Marius and Scipio Africanus had all turned their backs on its pleasures.

This leads Petrarch immediately to his encounter with Maria, the countess of Pozzuoli, a proud and independent noblewoman of enormous beauty and physical strength, a fierce warrior in her own right, protector of her inheritance, whom Petrarch then compares to the Amazons and to Camilla, queen of the Volscians.[54] But his unspoken comparison and contrast is the main point, for Petrarch used both the classical settings of the Bay of Naples and references to the Amazons to draw out his contrast to that other female ruler across the bay, Queen Giovanna. Maria, Petrarch tells Colonna, is "marked not by signs of kisses and the lascivious signs of the bold teeth of lovers, but wounds and scars" won while waging "an hereditary war with her neighbors." To further the contrast and to reemphasize what Petrarch considered the true Angevin legacy, he adds

CHAPTER 8 *✥* GRAND NARRATIVES

that King Robert had once traveled across the bay to visit Maria and to meet this illustrious woman himself.

Petrarch was not casually narrating his voyage around the bay. Its natural sequence would have led from the Phlegraean Fields to Pozzuoli and then to Baia before returning across the bay to Naples, as he would have known from his own experience and from his classical sources' descriptions: a route he followed in reverse in his *Itinerary*. Instead, he reconstructed his epistolary narrative to conclude with the Pozzuoli episode. *Familiares* V.5 and 6 explain this inversion. The first describes a devastating earthquake and tsunami on the Bay of Naples on November 25, 1343, and what he portrayed as Queen Giovanna's helplessness in the face of adversity. The second, of November 30, 1343, portrays the violence and disorder that beset Naples under Giovanna, barely six months after Robert's death. Petrarch unites these episodes into a watery text of shifting valences and moods for his developing narrative of the rapid decline of the Angevins.

Familiares V.5[55] is worth examining at some length in order to highlight the forms of language that the poet used. After citing classical sources for natural disasters, Petrarch recounts not only a dramatic unfolding of calamity, but a self-conscious construct tracing the steps of narrative from the orality of the city street, to the sounds of panic and uncontrolled nature, to first-person testimony of the feeling and sounds of the quake, to the eyewitness of disaster, to the written record. The impending calamity was first predicted in the streets by a bishop, well versed in astrology, visiting from an island in the bay. Paralleling the Anonimo romano's account of Rienzo's painting cycles, Petrarch then reports the reactions of the crowds: from fear to mockery to indifference. He next moves on to signs and sounds in the skies on the night before, the rising public alarm as Neapolitans left their homes to gather at local churches, and then his own view of Vesuvius, covered in darkening cloud. The narrative then turned to the night of the earthquake: the shaking, the calling out to companions in the pitch dark of their rooms, the terror of the community at San Lorenzo where he was lodged, and then the downpour, winds, lightning and thunder, the roaring of the sea and the shrieking of the populace. The destruction became clear with the new day.

> Good God! When was anything like this ever heard of? The oldest sailors asserted that what had happened was indeed without parallel. The port was filled with frightening and dismal wreckage. The unfortunate victims, who had been scattered by the water and had been trying to grasp the nearby land with their hands, were dashed against the reefs and were broken like so many tender eggs. The entire shore line was covered with torn and still living bodies: someone's brains floated by here, someone else's bowels floated there. In the midst of such sights the yelling of men and wailing of women were so loud that they overcame the sounds of the seas and the heavens.

To all this was added the destruction of buildings, many of whose foundations were overturned by the violent waves against which that day respected no bounds and respected no work of man or nature. They overflowed their natural limits, the familiar shoreline, as well as that huge breakwater which had been constructed by zealous men and which, with its outstretched arms, as Maro [Virgil] says, constitutes the port, and all that portion of the region which borders the sea. And where there had been a path for strolling there was now something dangerous even for sailing.

A thousand or more Neapolitan horsemen had gathered there as if to assist at the funeral of their homeland. Having joined this group, I had begun to feel somewhat less frightened of perishing amidst so many. But suddenly a new clamor could be heard. The very place on which we stood, weakened by the waves that had penetrated beneath, began to give way. We hurried to a higher elevation. No one raised his eyes to the heavens, for the band of men could not bear to look at the angry faces of Jove and of Neptune.

Thousands of mountainous waves flowed between Capri and Naples. The channel appeared not dark or, as is usual in great storms, black, but grayish with the frightening whiteness of sea foam. Meanwhile the younger queen [Giovanna],[56] barefooted and uncombed, and accompanied by a large group of women, departed from the royal palace unconcerned about modesty in the face of great danger, and they all hastened to the church of the Virgin Queen [Sta. Maria Donna Regina], praying for her grace amidst such dangers.

Unless I am mistaken, I imagine that you now fearfully await the outcome of such a calamity. On land we could scarcely find an escape and neither on the deep nor in port could a ship be found to equal those waves....

Only one of so many survived. It was loaded with robbers who had been spared their rightful punishment so that they could be sent on an expedition to Sicily, and who, having been spared the sword of the executioner, were to be exposed to the sword of battle.... The exhausted prisoners hastened from all sides to the keel because of the threatening dangers.... they were powerful persons who, freed from death, feared nothing more than death, which they resisted even more obstinately and boldly.... Suddenly beyond all hope the skies began to clear and the exhausted sea began to slacken its roughness. Thus, so many having perished, only the worst seemed to escape, whether because "Fortune saves many guilty ones," as Lucan says, or because "the gods thought otherwise" as Virgil says; or, as may be the case, those are most free from the dangers of death who consider life worth little.[57]

The poet peppered his eyewitness account with classical allusions — to book 2 of Pliny the Elder's *Natural History* and to Pliny the Younger's description of the Bay of Naples during Vesuvius' destruction of Pompeii, for example. Natural disaster also became a backdrop for the foundering ship of state, an image already well known in art and made famous by Giotto's contemporary mosaic of the *Navicella* in the Vatican [Fig. 6.6]. Here the works of civilization, "constructed by zealous men," were overturned to their foundations by unleashed forces "which that day respected no bounds and respected no work of man or nature." The waters of the sea, recalling those of untamed Chaos before Creation, become a metaphor for the rule of the untamed, "monstrous" woman. Sarah Alison Miller,[58] citing Julia Kristeva, called attention to this deeply imbedded idea of medieval writers of the female body as "abject," "which 'disturbs identity, system, order', that 'does not respect boundaries, positions, rule'," and that is closely associated with bodily fluids. Petrarch juxtaposes his relief at being among noble males with the irrational rushing of the queen and her ladies. Giovanna's image also conjures up that of Petrarch's fallen Rome from the *Carmina Regia* [Fig. 6.7].

Even Petrarch's image of citizens broken "like so many tender eggs" sardonically recalls the most important of Naples' legends: his hero Virgil's magic egg in Castel dell'Ovo, whose wholeness guaranteed the integrity of the city and Regno. Petrarch is clear that his intent is to offer an exemplum on human behavior from the book of nature: the fall of civil society and the inversion of justice, where the innocent are slain and condemned criminals are spared. The doubling here is less classical, but its strength derives from this metaphorical intent: the disruption of the cosmic order, nature broken out of all bounds to the destruction of individuals, communities and kingdoms under Naples' female ruler. In this way, Petrarch turned observation of the natural world into personal and political metaphor that became the underlying driving force of the narrative arc for his experience of Naples under Giovanna I.

In *Familiares* V.6,[59] the poet turns to the case of the Pippini, robber barons and infamous brigands of Basilicata and Apulia whom King Robert had outlawed and Queen Giovanna had imprisoned. Petrarch had traveled to Naples both to reconnoiter the situation at Giovanna's court for the pope and to seek the Pippini's release on behalf of their protectors, the Colonna. Despite Giovanna's commands, they had been released by Prince Consort Andrew. In 1347 they would be instrumental in toppling Cola di Rienzo's *buono stato* on behalf of the Colonna. During the civil war in Apulia following Lewis' invasion, the Pippini and their local clients — including Domenico da Gravina — would side with the Hungarians against Giovanna. In 1355, Janni Pippino, count of Minervino and count palatine of Rome, would end on a gibbet in his native Altamura. He had joined the mercenary free companies ravaging the Mezzogiorno and was finally captured by Giovanna. The Anonimo romano reports that, instead of being beheaded like a noble, Janni was hung like a common thief.[60] But in 1343, Petrarch asserts that these men would now be free "if the poisonous serpent [Roberto da Mileto] had not overcome the minds of the judges." Petrarch then proceeds from this metaphor to that of disease to assert deep structural flaws in the Regno and the breakdown of its social life and norms under Giovanna. He makes explicit the connection between the failure of his mission and the depravity of Naples itself.

> Perhaps last night I might have obtained the courtesy even of rejection had the [Regency] Council not adjourned because of the approaching darkness, and had not the incurable disease of the city compelled everyone to return home early. Though very famous for many reasons, the city possesses one particularly dark, repulsive, and inveterate evil: to travel in it by night, as in a jungle,[61] is dangerous and full of hazards because the streets are beset by armed young nobles whose dissoluteness cannot be controlled by the discipline of their parents, by the authority of their teachers, or by the majesty and command of kings. But is it any wonder that they act brazenly under the cover of darkness without witnesses, when in this Italian city in broad daylight, with royalty and the populace as spectators, infamous gladiatorial games are permitted of a wildness that is greater than we associate with barbarians? Here human blood flows like the blood of cattle and often, amidst the applause of the insane spectators, unfortunate sons are killed under the very eyes of their wretched parents.[62]

When King Robert and his Angevin ancestors had staged elaborate and normally bloody tournaments in the Largo delle Corregge, these were seen as the highpoint of the chivalrous life, celebrated in the courtly romances commissioned by the court.[63] But now Petrarch takes on the righteous persona of his hero St. Augustine and makes his own *Confessions,* turning his offended eyes away from the blood and cries of the arena. Naples itself has become the archetypal urban "jungle," its public spaces unsafe to travel by night, a trope on Naples and the Mezzogiorno that continues to resonate.

The poet made this image of Neapolitan depravity and corruption explicit, describing Prince Andrew's murder on September 18, 1345 in *Familiares* VI.5 to Barbato da Sulmona.[64] Writing from the Fountain of the Sorgue outside Avignon shortly after the event, Petrarch portrayed the atmosphere of the kingdom and its court as the human manifestation of the same storm that had destroyed the bay and its ships two years earlier. Again, Pliny the Elder's description of the signs of impending natural disaster (*Natural History* 2.83) might be a literary source. Petrarch also combines the image of the ship of state with that of poison streaming through the body politic. Neapolitan society now takes on the evil that nature itself had manifested once Giovanna had assumed rule:

CHAPTER 8 ⚜ GRAND NARRATIVES

The awful slime of evil had penetrated so deeply into all the veins of the kingdom as now to be fatal, so far advanced are the boldness and the dissoluteness of the evildoers, and the despair and grief of the pious. Everywhere the signs of the approaching storms were numerous: disturbing clouds shaded serious faces; stubborn winds pressed upon disturbed hearts; glowing eyes flashed; mouths thundered and uttered menaces; it was almost as though ungodly hands were hurling lightning. The seas of the royal court at times were swollen with anger; at times a horrible glow and crashing of waves resounded and foul birds and strange portents seemed widely to encompass your shores. With the death of its king the face of the kingdom has changed and with the soul of a single man the vigor and resolution of everything seems to have vanished. We witnessed all these things and were distressed no less by future than by present evils.[65]

His description of Andrew's murder gave final shape to this frame:

Would that my prediction had been less true! Of course I viewed the rage and gnashing of the wolves as things common to doomed men — contempt, envy, deceit, theft, prison, and exile. But I had never learned to conceive of nor fear such a death for such a man, and indeed could not recall in any tragedies I had read such abominable and insidious savagery....

Oh Naples, so suddenly changed!... Alas, not you, but those harsh and savage — I don't know what to call them — men or beasts or some other kind of rare monster living within your walls....

You, however, dear Robert, greatest of all kings of our day who I believe behold and commiserate with our affairs from some portion of the heavens, with what eyes did you behold this abomination? And how were you able to endure this horrible injustice to your blood?

For indeed your regal presence would have been the salvation of the kingdom, the conciliator of minds, the fountain of justice and the expeller of treachery, and like a salutary shade over your flock you would have been as propitious to shepherds as fatal to serpents....[66]

All the imagery of objectification is here: Naples under Queen Giovanna is a city of bestiality, savagery, monstrosity and abomination where the Christ-like innocent are slaughtered like beasts, where injustice rules and where the "awful slime of evil has penetrated so deeply." On a more profound level, even the Angevin bloodline has now been tainted. Both images have a long history in medieval portrayals of the serpentine female body.[67]

In 1367 the poet encapsulated his version of the black legend in his *Seniles* X.2[68] written from Venice to Guido Sete, archbishop of Genoa. Though it is a general lament on the sorry state of the world, Petrarch reiterates his image of Naples' decline by recounting his first-hand experience of journeys there. He prefaces his reflections with a reference to Horace's *Ars Poetica,* contrasting sharply the "joys of the kingdom" under King Robert and the "disaster" that ensued with his death and the succession of Giovanna I.[69] He deploys references to ancient authors and characters and the classical language of auguries, lightning bolts and Fortune to project a sense of tragedy.

> After another four years [1341], I journeyed to Naples.... Robert was then king of Sicily, or rather of Italy, or better king of kings, whose life was the joy of the kingdom, and whose death its downfall.... Four [two?] years later... I did indeed see the walls and squares, the sea, the port, the surrounding vine-clad hills...but I did not find the Naples I knew. I did notice the seeds of many calamities and clear signs of impending disaster, and I regret being so accurate a prophet. What I felt about it I reported not only orally, but in letters, while Fortune was already thundering, but not yet shooting its lightening bolts; and it was all fulfilled so soon afterward, along with so many other evils, that my own prophesy, however terrible, was surpassed by an infinite series of evils that are much easier to deplore than to enumerate.[70]

Petrarch's bitterness toward Queen Giovanna herself appears to have diminished in a later series of letters[71] that the poet wrote to Niccolò Acciaiuoli and other members of the court, extolling and encouraging their place in the revival of the Regno after 1352, urging their friendship and unity, praising their diplomatic and military deeds, outlining the virtues needed for the education of "king" Louis of Taranto.[72] *Familiares* XXIII.17 to Ugo, count of San Severino and one of Giovanna's supporters, may have been a response to renewed royal overtures or to the poet's renewed bid for the queen's patronage sent through the count. It sympathizes with Giovanna's current plight under Louis' harsh treatment, acknowledges her "generous, noble and beneficent mind" and pledges continued allegiance to King Robert's "blood descendant." But it decries what Petrarch has foreseen as Naples' decline after Robert's death, its "wretchedness" and its rule by "Egyptian monsters" and "court dogs." Despite pro-forma courtesies for the again-embattled queen, Petrarch's imagery of the Regno's growing depravity remained unchanged.

Petrarch's narrative was also constructed explicitly in two other works: his *Itinerary to the Holy Land* and Eclogue 2, "Argus," from the *Bucolicum carmen*. His *Itinerary* was completed in 1358 and continued this classical project but in a very different mode: not of vertical memory and connection to the past but a spatial one, a "textual territory"[73] of horizontal construction, the re-creation of an Italy that existed in the classical past as a distinct social, political and cultural ideal, as a metaphor of travel in time and space.[74] Where Petrarch had attempted several times to bring about a newfound awareness of Italy's political and cultural unity through his alliance with political leaders as diverse as Cola di Rienzo[75] and Emperor Charles IV,[76] here he is concerned with a more intellectual unity, beginning with his own self-identity[77] and extending out to a mental world set apart from the rest of Christendom both by its geography and by its deep roots in social and cultural memory.

Essential to this unity was his prized laurel crown won on Rome's Capitoline at Italy's center and the sponsorship of this crown by King Robert of Naples, "famous for his kingdom, but still more illustrious for his intelligence and his literary culture." Petrarch also recalled his discussions with Robert on Naples' Virgilian remains; and his descriptions of Naples and its environs in his *Itinerary* 9.7–10.3 reinforced both his laureate crown and Naples' deep classical associations, linking Petrarch to Virgil in one direction and to Rome and Italy in the other. These sections are full of classical place names, incidents and references to Virgil, Homer, Suetonius, Seneca and Pliny the Elder. They place the Mezzogiorno not in the history of Christian salvation denoted by Petrarch's supposed pilgrimage to Jerusalem but firmly within the classical tradition.

The *Eclogues* were written over the course of nearly twenty years and completed in 1364. They continue his project and adopt the strict classical form of Virgil's own *Eclogues*, follow the twelve-fold division of the *Aeneid* and employ a similar classical form and language to discuss deeply personal and political issues. Eclogue 2, "Argus," from 1346[78] uses classical names for contemporary people and events in a thinly veiled account of Robert of Anjou's death and what Petrarch saw as the rapid decline of the Regno. Here "Silvius" is Petrarch, "Idaeus" Giovanni Barrili and "Pythias" Barbato da Sulmona. "Argus" himself is King Robert, whose death and the subsequent ruin of the Regno is presaged by the thunderstorm that uproots the "lofty cypress…shaking the hills and fields." The shepherds' subsequent dirge recalls Virgil's fifth eclogue mourning the death of Augustus[79] and returns Petrarch to both the spirit and content of the classics and to his Virgilian interpretation of Naples and its tragic history.

VILLANI

Villani concurred in Petrarch's assessment of Robert the Wise. In Book XIII.10 of his *Cronaca,* he narrates Robert's death and the public mourning in Florence and describes the king in glowing terms:

> This King Robert was the wisest who had reigned among Christians in the past five hundred years, both in natural wisdom and in learning, like the greatest master in theology and highest

philosophy. He was a sweet and lovable lord, and most friendly toward our commune, and endowed with every virtue.[80]

Like Petrarch, Villani saw the great storm of November 1343 as an omen of bad events to come.[81] Throughout his account of Neapolitan affairs Villani never mentions Giovanna as queen, but only as "the wife of King Andrew," the "granddaughter of King Robert" or the "cousin of the prince of Taranto."[82] Villani also takes a very unfavorable view of the queen, seeing her as lost in *"disordinata lussuria."*[83] *Lussuria* (Latin *luxuria*) was the sin associated with the lustful. She had been a woman from at least the fifth century. Her representation appears in the twelfth-century sculpture program at Moissac: a long-limbed, smooth-bellied gamine, her flowing hair gathered in braids. Naked and swirling, vipers clinging to her breasts and licking at her genitals, she spins in dance with the devil himself. *Luxuria* was also long conflated with the unrepentant Mary Magdalene,[84] the archetype of the red-haired wanton. Dante devoted Canto 5 of the *Inferno* to the punishments of this particular sin: Semiramis, Cleopatra, Helen and Paris, Tristan, Dido and most famously Francesca da Rimini were chief examples of *luxuria*. Boccaccio provides ample examples of this sin throughout his *De casibus*.

The Villani had particular reasons to bear a grudge against Giovanna. Partisans of the Bardi banking family, they shared the anger set off by Giovanna's refusal to honor the huge debts incurred by her grandfather Robert to the Florentine banking establishment.[85] Villani's report of Giovanna's marriage to Louis of Taranto[86] informs the reader that her sensuality caused her first husband Andrew's murder and, echoing Hungarian royal propaganda, that her incestuous marriage to her cousin had evil effects for the kingdom. Like Petrarch, Villani focuses on the queen's body as the source of corruption for the entire body politic.

DOMENICO DA GRAVINA

Gravina sets the stage for his condemnation of Naples under Queen Giovanna by first introducing us to the corrupt women around her. He used the imagery of poisonous fluids — with special reference to the female body — to describe the disease that had begun to spread throughout the Regno.[87] Sources for such imagery reach back to biblical, patristic and contemporary literature, as well as to papal and Italian communal theory. In his letter to the Romans of June 24, 1347, for example, Petrarch urged very harsh measures against the barons: "The republic must be relieved of these as a body would be freed of its poisonous excretions. Thus the republic, though diminished in numbers, will be stronger and healthier."[88]

The metaphor of the body, "relieved of its poisonous excretions," justified the persecution of heretics, witches and homosexuals, and it served — as Foucault, Cohen, Zorzi and other students of ceremonies

CHAPTER 8 ⚜ GRAND NARRATIVES

of punishment emphasize — to provide one of the deeply symbolic underpinnings of the communes' extreme treatment of criminals and political traitors. As we have seen in Chapter 7, public punishment, harsh and violent, played out trecento rituals involving purification of the body politic and exemplary warning to future malefactors. In the next century, the sermons of Bernardino da Siena continued to excoriate these — and members of factions — as "poisons" to the body politic.

We have already examined Gravina's episode of Agnes de Perigord's illness:[89] the false urine sample provided by Sancia de'Cabanni, Agnes' son Charles of Durazzo's shock at his widowed mother's supposed pregnancy, her expulsion from his household and murder soon thereafter. As we have seen, Gravina repeats this account almost verbatim in the mouth of Sancia de'Cabanni as Giovanna's courtiers await their execution in prison,[90] and this becomes the leitmotif for his treatment of Giovanna's court in the aftermath of Prince Andrew's murder. Gravina describes the cover-up of the conspiracy and its gradual exposure:

> And because the perpetrators of the crime were not revealed, but instead were hidden, each and every one of them knew where the tiny stream of bitter water came from. And so, once that water was spread throughout the Regno, it killed many, it destroyed many others, and it wasted away many more. And that tiny stream crossed seas and mountains, plains and forests until it reached Hungary and widened into the Danube. And then it crossed into Germany and aroused all of Hungary and Germany upon the kingdom of Naples, and its rising flood reached this Regno and washed away the blood of the innocent duke.[91]

The body of water is not a neutral element here, but a narrow bitter stream that spreads through the body politic like a poison through a vein.[92] Just as Petrarch used the Bay of Naples to emphasize the changing and unreliable nature of Angevin rule under Giovanna I,[93] here Gravina deploys watery imagery of a nature perverted, but insidiously, like Fra Roberto's worm emerging from King Robert's tomb. Just as the bitter rivulet is a female image of pollution,[94] of silent, hidden and spreading corruption, the mighty Danube, like a river god, is its male counterpart that will cleanse the body politic of this poison. The flood that reaches Naples and washes away the blood of the innocent duke may also have been a reference to the Neapolitan tsunami of November 1343.

Like Petrarch and Villani, Gravina also matched this body imagery with an equally forceful picture of decline after the reign of Robert the Wise and Queen Sancia of Majorca:

> These youths, the duke [Andrew] and the queen [Giovanna] were absorbed by the games and pastimes of the young. Meanwhile,

the other royal cousins adorned themselves in splendid cloths, now making public appearances, now joking, riding around on horseback through the splendid city of Naples, never caring about a thing. And in the midst of their gay life, the worst cabal of counselors was constantly seen looting the great treasury of King Robert, which had been left neglected....

Meanwhile in the city of Naples itself Queen Giovanna was seduced by the games of the young, always dancing, constantly riding on horseback, everything was always gay and given up to pleasurable pastimes. She was seduced by her vain youth. Seeing that she could not tear her away from these activities, after the death of her husband King Robert in the year 1343, Queen Sancia quickly turned to God and entered the monastery of Santa Croce in Naples as a nun, renouncing her royal dignity. There shortly afterward she ended her days in Christ.

Sancia had restrained the young queen and her companions. But after her death they became completely unbridled and under Queen Giovanna Castel Nuovo was held in contempt by everyone, as if it were a common tavern. Her councilors became like wolves among the sheep of this kingdom, and the city of Naples devoured the entire realm, and there the entire treasure of the kingdom perished.[95]

Pollution, corruption, faction and egotism, unbridled pleasure-seeking at the expense of the public good, the inversion of justice as the wolves take charge of the sheep, decay, bankruptcy and moral and political ruin spread across the realm in ever widening circles: the royal family itself, the daily life of the capital, and finally the kingdom of Naples as a whole, its lands and its peoples. All derive from the corruption and frivolity of the female and the loss of male agency and control.

BOCCACCIO

Giovanni Boccaccio's relation to the black legend of the Angevins is more ambiguous. Aside from his classically inspired forms, Boccaccio relied almost entirely on contemporary sources, written and oral, and from his own first-hand knowledge of the queen and her court. We have discussed these aspects of his writing and have already seen his high praise of Giovanna in the epideictic *Vita* of the queen, completed in 1362.[96] But earlier Boccaccio had framed some of his most pointed references to individuals and events in Naples in the classical form of Eclogues 3–6 of his *Buccolicum carmen,* perhaps conceived soon after his move from Naples to Florence in 1341 but completed only in 1346/47.[97]

Perhaps taking his lead from Petrarch's "Argus," Boccaccio drew directly from Virgil's *Bucolica* and from Severus' gloss, as well as Catullus, Ovid and Horace and two ancient pastorals by Calpurnius and Nemesianus.[98] Eclogue 3, "Faunus,"[99] recounts events in Naples

CHAPTER 8 ⚜ GRAND NARRATIVES

following the death of Robert the Wise (again, Argus), the murder of Andrew of Hungary (Alexis) and the invasion of the Regno by Lewis of Hungary (Tytirus) told from the perspective of Francesco degli Ordelaffi (Faunus), lord of Forlì (Testilis) as he attempted to both placate the Hungarians passing through his territories and avoid being swept up in the invasion of the Regno. Boccaccio himself (Palemon) and Petrarch (Mopsus) take on the self-conscious role of classical authors, both weaving their Virgilian verses around actual historical events.

Eclogue 4, "Dorus,"[100] takes up the narrative, relating the flight of Louis of Taranto (Dorus) and Nicolo Acciaiuoli (Phytias) from the Regno as Lewis of Hungary (here Polyphemus) approached Naples. Again Argus represents King Robert, Alexis the murdered Prince Andrew and Liquoris Queen Giovanna, a clear allusion to Virgil's Eclogue 10 in which Lycoris has abandoned her lover and escaped to the North with a new man.[101] Other figures include Charles of Durazzo (Paphus) and Princess Maria of Anjou (Nays).

Eclogue 5, "Silva Cadens" ("The Falling Forest"),[102] relates a dialogue between two citizens of Naples — Caliopus and Pamphylus[103] — in the disastrous wake of Louis and Giovanna's flight and the city's conquest by Lewis of Hungary. The speakers recall Petrarch's own "Argus" and his trope of Naples' dramatic decline after King Robert's death. They discuss the lament of Parthenope (Naples)[104] as she watches the glorious garden of the Regno laid waste by war. Finally, Eclogue 6, "Alcestus,"[105] is a dialogue between Amintas and Melibeus, two shepherds who appear often in Virgil's *Eclogues*.[106] They discuss the return to Naples of Giovanna and Louis of Taranto (Alcestus) and the happiness that ensues in the Regno.

Boccaccio thus applied the classical bucolic form, language, meter and direct quotations from Virgil to discuss the most controversial of events, personalities and political issues during the early years of Giovanna's reign. Strongly influenced by Petrarch, he demonstrated a clear-cut preference for Louis of Taranto and Acciaiuoli and a marked concern over the decline of the Regno under Giovanna. As we have seen, in his later years, he would reverse these opinions and turn squarely against both the prince consort and grand seneschal. But his image of the Regno as tragically wasted after the death of King Robert contributed forcefully to the creation of the black legend. While he might ultimately cast Queen Giovanna in a positive light, he did so as he finally turned his back on Naples in bitterness and refused offers to rejoin its court. Just as for Petrarch, for Boccaccio the glory of Naples under Robert the Wise lay far in the past, irretrievably lost.

CONCLUSIONS

In this chapter we have traced how Petrarch, Boccaccio, Giovanni Villani and Domenico da Gravina brought together the various strands of historical narrative, reportage, political propaganda, literary citation, misogynistic tradition and nature imagery to construct the black legend of the Angevins. They did so by deploying many of the narrative modes and rhetorical devices that we have analyzed in previous chapters. Their constructs were also so powerful because they resonated with trecento audiences' understanding of the ready-made vocabulary of personal and civic virtue and vice that derived from classical sources; contemporary social and political thought; and the tropes, plots and characters of romance literature.

Shakespeare's history plays cover the course of England's Plantagenet dynasty: murder, rape, assassination, rebellion and usurpation, incest, lust, dynastic rivalry and illegitimacy, treachery and deceit, egotism, ambition and incompetence are all essential elements of both characters and plots. Yet, when the curtain descends on the actors in *Richard III* and the Tudor dynasty takes its place on the throne and in history, England has become a greater nation, made wiser and stronger by its travails. Shakespeare's genius was to take his sources and to combine them into a seamless grand narrative — a continuous arc of progress to a new age of enlightenment and justice under Henry Tudor and his heirs.

But the Plantagenets' contemporaries, the Angevins of Naples, had no such poet of tragic greatness and redemption. Though Petrarch and Boccaccio took their places of greatness beside Shakespeare even in the Anglophone world, they and their contemporaries created a far different narrative: one sharing the all-too-human elements of Shakespeare's histories but one in which a crown, a capital and a kingdom were forever lost amid the narrative of treachery and depravity that its trecento historians constructed. While Plantagenet England paved the way for the Tudors and their English Renaissance, the Angevins of Naples had to be eradicated like a disease in order for the new Renaissance dynasty of the Aragonese to seize, cleanse and renew the city and kingdom.

This black legend of the Angevins was as much a literary and historical construct as Shakespeare's plays, and it was created by equal genius and deep moral purpose. But the image of Naples and the Regno that trecento writers left to posterity remains with us as firmly as Shakespeare's "sceptered island" does for England. Shakespeare wrote under the reign of the world's most famous female monarch, and his tale of corrupt and fallen men and women only served to strengthen the contrasts to the reign of the glorious Elizabeth. Petrarch, the Villani, Gravina and Boccaccio, however, took the reign of Giovanna I — the first female ruler of Naples, the longest lived of her century — and turned it into a narrative of debasement and incompetence that would forever mark the Mezzogiorno.[107]

CHAPTER 8 ⚜ GRAND NARRATIVES

NOTES

1. Musto (2013), 256–58; Musto (2017), 11–17.
2. See Gaglione (2009); Musto (2013), lvi–lxxiii, 144–302; and Hall–Willette.
3. Chapter 4, pp. 80–121.
4. Chapter 6, pp. 152–98.
5. Hanke (1949), esp. 88–91, 195–96; Keen (1971). For the Spanish black legend in England: Maltby (1971); Greer (2007); Lawrance (2009); Samson (2020).
6. On Dante and the Angevins, Cooper (2008).
7. This was reiterated by Dunbabin (1998), 3–8, 181–224. Dunbabin (2011), 1–9, posited influence in both directions to demonstrate European-wide cultural and political spheres. See also Hall–Willette.
8. Musto (1985).
9. Dunbabin (1998), 8, 203–24; Kelly (2003); Kelly (2004); Pryds; restated by Fleck (2010.1); Fleck (2010.2); Romano (2017), 180–84.
10. The tale of decline after the reign of the good monarch is not unique to Naples. See Brandt, 76–79, for the narrative after the death of Henry I of England.
11. Kelly (2003); Kelly (2004); Pryds; Bruzelius (1991); Bruzelius (2004), which covers the years 1266–1343; and Bruzelius–Tronzo (2011), 110–11. More recent scholarship repeats this trope. See "Chronology," in Barański (2015), xxiii: "1343: Death of Robert of Anjou and End of Angevin Dynasty in Naples."
12. Shakespeare's *The Tempest* is set into motion by the cruelty and deceptions of the Neapolitan royal house. The play premises these events, without elaboration, as natural elements of Neapolitan politics. But the prime example, set in Amalfi, remains *The Duchess of Malfi* of 1612/13, Webster (2009). For Artaud's theater of cruelty in the later Middle Ages: Enders (1999) and Merback (1999).
13. Romanticism recast the fallen South to its own tastes. Decadence and the frailty of human endeavor in the face of nature became a hallmark of the Mezzogiorno in such works as Walpole's *Castle of Otranto* of 1764, Radcliffe's *The Italian* (1797), de Staël's *Corinne, or Italy* (1807) and Dumas' *Jeanne de Naples* (1839–41).
14. Analyzed by Casteen (2015), 29–66.
15. Strohm (1992), 136.
16. Strohm (1992), 136–37.
17. For her official letter, see Musto (2013), 275.
18. Strohm (1992), 136.
19. Lewis was the son of Charles Martel, King Robert of Anjou's elder brother, and potential claimant to Naples' crown. Charles had been persuaded to give up claims to Naples to pursue the Hungarian crown. See Léonard, 466–538.
20. Léonard no. 9, December 1343; Léonard, no. 24 and 25, Visegrad, January 16, 1346; Léonard, no. 26, Visegrad, January 15, 1346; Léonard, no. 27, March 18, 1346; Léonard, no. 39, Buda, March 27, 1347; Léonard, no. 40, Buda, March 27, 1347.
21. Pars. 1–4, and 7 of Robert's last will and testament, from 1343, Musto (2013), 241–45.
22. Chapter 5, pp. 132–33.
23. Chapter 5, pp. 129–30.
24. Hanning, 136–41, notes Geoffrey's obsession with cyclical patterns.
25. XIII.99, Villani (1991), 511.
26. Above, p. 72 n. 152.
27. Petrarch (1974); Carrai (2009).

28. Chapter 3, pp. 47–48.
29. Ascoli (2015a), 121–23.
30. *Familiares* IV.2–8, Petrarch (2004.1), 1:487–531; Petrarch (2005.2), 1:181–96.
31. *Familiares* V.1–6, Petrarch (2004.1), 1:616–69; Petrarch (2005.2), 1:228–50.
32. *Itinerarium,* in Petrarch (2002), 10.0–10.1.
33. *Familiares* XIII.6, Petrarch (2004.1), 3:1840–61; Petrarch (2005.2), 2:193–98; Petrarch (1996), 130–48.
34. *Familiares* IV.2, Petrarch (2004.1), 1:488–97, probably written after King Robert had appointed the friar professor of theology at the University of Naples.
35. Petrarch (2004.1), 1:492; Petrarch (2005.2), 1:182.
36. Petrarch (2004.1), 1:498–505.
37. Petrarch (2004.1), 1:500; Petrarch (2005.2), 1:185–86.
38. *Familiares* IV.7, Petrarch (2004.1), 1:524; Petrarch (2005.2), 1:195.
39. Petrarch (2004.1), 1:616–21.
40. Kempshall, 56–59, 276–83.
41. Petrarch (2004.1), 1:616–18; Petrarch (2005.2), 1:228.
42. Musto (2013), 240, 252.
43. Petrarch (2004.1), 1:626–39; Petrarch (2005.2), 1:234–36; Forcellini (1926).
44. Ganim (2008).
45. Arens, 26–33, 157–58 et passim, stresses female rule in depictions of societies beyond the pale of civilization. In many accounts, women are the agents or instigators of ritual cannibalism. On research on the role of the monstrous and its medieval associations with the female and the Orient in redefining the Other, above, p. 145 n. 67.
46. Above, p. 236.
47. Alfie (2014).
48. Petrarch (2004.1), 1:488–97.
49. "Muliercularum omnium una lex est: inepta cupiunt, ridenda formidant." Petrarch (2004.1), 1:488.2; Petrarch (2005.2), 1:181.
50. Ratté (2006) argues that portraits of urban architecture were designed to reflect civic virtues or vices.
51. Petrarch (2004.1), 1:640–51; Petrarch (2005.2), 1:238–42.
52. Petrarch (2002) 9.7–10.3.
53. "Non immersi sed subducti effeminantibus animos munditiis." Petrarch (2004.1), 1:644.8; Petrarch (2005.2), 1:240.
54. Virgil, *Aeneid* XI.539–841; Boccaccio (2003), 154–59.
55. Petrarch (2004.1), 1:652–63; Petrarch (2005.2), 1:243–48.
56. Petrarch (2004.1), 1:658.15:"Regina… iunior."The "older queen," Sancia of Majorca, still held the senior role as regent.
57. Petrarch (2004.1), 1:658–60; Petrarch (2005.2), 1:243–47.
58. Miller (2010), 139.
59. Petrarch (2004.1), 1:664–69; Petrarch (2005.2), 1:249–50.
60. XVII.2003–30, AR, 209–10. "His head was crowned with a paper miter." On it was written, "Messer Janni Pippino, knight of Altamura, Paladin, the count of Minervino, lord of Bari, liberator of Rome."Wright, 94; Palmer (2021), 242–43.
61. "Inter densissimas silvas." Petrarch (2004.1), 1:664.2. The allusion is to Dante, *Inferno* I.1–60 and its moral peril.
62. Petrarch (2004.1), 1:664–66; Petrarch (2005.2), 1:249.
63. Above, Chapter 6. Such tournaments are pictured in the *Meliadus* of BL Add.

CHAPTER 8 ⚜ GRAND NARRATIVES

12228, for example on fols. 213r–216r.
64. Petrarch (2004.1), 2:852–65; Petrarch (2005.2), 1:318–23.
65. Petrarch (2004.1), 2:854–56; Petrarch (2005.2), 1:318–19.
66. Petrarch (2004.1), 2:858–62; Petrarch (2005.2), 1:320–22.
67. Miller (2010), 132, quotes the *Ancrene Wisse:* "Are you not come from foul slime? Are you not a vessel of filth? Are you not worm's food? *'Philosophus: Sperma es fluidam, vas stercorum, esca vermium'.*" Melusine again comes to mind.
68. Petrarch (2004.2), 2:1210–59; Petrarch (2005.1), 2:359–74.
69. Petrarch (2005.1), 2:368.
70. Petrarch (2004.2), 2:1238.36–1240.37; Petrarch (2005.1), 2:368.
71. *Familiares* XI.13 to Niccolò Acciaiuoli; XII.2 to Niccolò Acciaiuoli; XII.14 to Giovanni Barrili; XII.15 to Niccolò Acciaiuoli; XII.16 to Niccolò Acciaiuoli and Giovanni Barrili; XII.17 to Zanobi da Strada; XXII.6 to Zanobi da Strada; XXIII.17 to Ugo, count of San Severino; XXIII.18 to Niccolò Acciaiuoli; *Seniles* III.3 to Niccolò Acciaiuoli. Petrarch re-edited and rearranged the letters by thematic unity rather than by strict chronology.
72. *Familiares* XII.2, Petrarch (2004.1), 3:1628–55; Petrarch (2005.2), 2:132–40.
73. Cachey (2009), 229. Petrarch's mention that the church and convent of Sta. Chiara "is the work of the elderly queen" (10.2) points to the composition of at least part of the *Itinerary* from after Giovanna I's ascension in 1343 and before Sancia of Majorca's death in 1345.
74. Petrarch (2002), 4, 7.
75. Petrarch (1996); Musto (2003); Modigliani (2014), 16–17.
76. Bayley (1942); Ascoli (2011).
77. Petrarch (2002), 230, 237–38.
78. For an English edition, see Petrarch (1974). See Martinez (2015), 90–92.
79. Carrai (2009), 165–66, 170–71.
80. Villani (1906), 320.
81. XIII.27.
82. XIII.51.
83. Villani (1991), 417, l. 14.
84. Haskins (1994), 151–70.
85. Baddeley (1897), 306–7; Green (1972), 13–14; Clarke (2007), 116; Musto (2013), 200–201, 231–34.
86. XIII.96.
87. For analyses, Cuffel (2007); Vaught (2010), 1–14; Nohrnberg (2010), 43–64.
88. *Variae* 48 *(Hortatoria),* in Petrarch (1996), 17–18.
89. Above, pp. 130–31.
90. Above, p. 221.
91. Gravina (1903), 17, ll. 10–15; Gravina (2022), VII.16.
92 The connection between private actions and the public good was a special concern of the mid-trecento. In England, for example, the Statute of Treason of 1352 extended the definition of treason to household affairs, especially the insubordination of women, children and employees. Strohm (1992), 121–44.
93. Above, pp. 240–43, for example.
94. Elliott (1999).
95. Gravina (1903), 8, l. 16–19, l. 4; Gravina (2022), III.6–10.
96. Above, pp. 103–6.

97. Boccaccio (1987), xi–xiii; Lummus (2013), 155 and n. 4; Casteen (2018), 226–31.
98. Boccaccio (1987), liii–lv; Lummus (2013), 156–59.
99. Boccaccio (1987), 22–29.
100. Boccaccio (1987), 30–41.
101. Boccaccio (1987), 215.
102. Boccaccio (1987), 42–51.
103. Boccaccio (1987), 217–18, suggested that these represent a dialogue between the muse of poetry and Boccaccio, anxious for news of his beloved Naples.
104. Boccaccio (1987), 44–49, ll. 27–119.
105. Boccaccio (1987), 52–63.
106. Boccaccio (1987), 219.
107. Musto (2017), 17–25.

WORKS CITED

Alfie, Fabian. 2014. "Love and Misogamy in the Age of Dante and Petrarch." In *Approaches to Teaching Petrarch's* Canzoniere *and the Petrarchan Tradition.* Christopher Kleinhenz and Andrea Dini, ed. New York: MLA.
Ascoli, Albert Russell. 2011. "Petrarch's Private Politics: *Rerum Familiarium Libri* 19." In *A Local Habitation and a Name: Imagining Histories in the Italian Renaissance.* New York: Fordham University Press, 118–58.
—. 2015a. "Epistolary Petrarch." In Ascoli–Falkeid, 120–37.
Baddeley, Welbore St Clair. 1897. *Robert the Wise and His Heirs, 1278–1352.* London: W. Heinemann.
Barański, Zygmunt G. 2015. With Lino Pertile, ed. *Dante in Context.* Cambridge: Cambridge University Press.
Bayley, Charles Calvert. 1942. "Petrarch, Charles IV, and the *Renovatio Imperii.*" *Speculum* 17:323–41.
Bruzelius, Caroline. 2011. With William Tronzo. *Medieval Naples: An Architectural & Urban History, 400–1400.* New York: Italica Press.
Bynum, Caroline Walker. 1998. "Men's Use of Female Symbols." In *Debating the Middle Ages: Issues and Readings.* Lester K. Little and Barbara H. Rosenwein, ed. Malden: Blackwell, 277–89.
Cachey, Theodore J., Jr. 2009. "The Place of the *Itinerarium.*" In Kirkham (2009), 229–41.
Carrai, Stefano. 2009. "Pastoral as Personal Mythology in History *(Bucolicum carmen).*" In Kirkham (2009), 165–77.
Cooper, Richard. 2008. "The French Dimension in Dante's Politics." In *Dante and Governance.* John Robert Woodhouse, ed. Oxford: Clarendon Press, 59–83.
Cuffel, Alexandra. 2007. *Gendering Disgust in Medieval Religious Polemic.* Notre Dame: University of Notre Dame Press.
Dunbabin, Jean. 1998. *Charles I of Anjou: Power, Kingship and State-Making in Thirteenth-Century Europe.* London: Longman.
—. 2011. *The French in the Kingdom of Sicily, 1266–1305.* Cambridge: Cambridge University Press.
Elliott, Dyan. 1999. *Fallen Bodies: Pollution, Sexuality, and Demonology in the*

Middle Ages. Philadelphia: University of Pennsylvania Press.
Forcellini, Vincenzo. 1926. "'L'horrendum tripes animal' della lettera 3 del libro V delle *Familiari* di Petrarca." In *Studi di storia napoletana in onore di Michelangelo Schipa*. Naples: I.T.E.A., 167–99.
Ganim, John M. 2008. *Medievalism and Orientalism*. Basingstoke: Palgrave Macmillan.
Greer, Margaret Rich, et al., ed. 2007. *Rereading the Black Legend: The Discourses of Religious and Racial Difference in the Renaissance Empires*. Chicago: University of Chicago Press.
Hanke, Lewis. 1949. *The Spanish Struggle for Justice in the Conquest of America*. Philadelphia: University of Pennsylvania Press.
Haskins, Susan. 1994. *Mary Magdalen: Myth and Metaphor*. New York: Harcourt, Brace.
Keen, Benjamin. 1971. "Approaches to Las Casas, 1535–1970." In *Bartolomé de Las Casas in History*. Juan Friede and Benjamin Keen, ed. DeKalb: Northern Illinois University Press, 3–63.
Kelly, Samantha. 2004. "Religious Patronage and Royal Propaganda in Angevin Naples: Santa Maria Donna Regina in Context." In Elliott–Warr, 25–43.
Lawrance, Jeremy. 2009. *Spanish Conquest, Protestant Prejudice: Las Casas and the Black Legend*. Nottingham: Critical, Cultural and Communications Press.
Maltby, William S. 1971. *The Black Legend in England: The Development of Anti-Spanish Sentiment*. Durham: Duke University Press.
Martinez, Ronald L. 2015. "The Latin Hexameter Works: *Epystole, Bucolicum carmen, Africa*." In Ascoli–Falkeid, 87–99.
Miller, Sarah Alison. 2010. *Medieval Monstrosity and the Female Body*. New York: Routledge.
Modigliani, Anna. 2014. "Lo ogliardino de Roma: Il progetto italiano di Cola di Rienzo." In *Roma nel Rinascimento*, 241–53.
Nohrnberg, James C. 2010. "'This Disfigured People': Representations of Sin as Pathological Bodily and Mental Affliction in Dante's *Inferno* XXIX–XXX." In Vaught (2010), 43–64.
Ratté, Felicity. 2006. *Picturing the City in Medieval Italian Painting*. Jefferson, NC: McFarland.
Samson, Alexander. 2020. *Mary and Philip: The Marriage of Tudor England and Habsburg Spain*. Manchester: Manchester University Press.
Vaught, Jennifer C. ed. 2010. *Rhetorics of Bodily Disease and Health in Medieval and Early Modern England*. Aldershot: Ashgate.
Webster, John. 2009. *The Duchess of Malfi*. Arden Shakespeare. London: Thompson Learning.

9. MEDIEVAL TO RENAISSANCE: THE HISTORIOGRAPHICAL QUESTION

RENAISSANCE HISTORIOGRAPHY

This final chapter begins by briefly examining the Anglophone consensus on Renaissance historiography[1] and the influence of Leonardo Bruni on such writers as Flavio Biondo. It then focuses on humanists at the Aragonese court of Naples[2] who wrote *historia,* biography, commentary, urban description and *laudatio.* These include Antonio Beccadelli (Panormita), Bartolomeo Facio, Lorenzo Valla, Giannozzo Manetti and Giovanni Pontano. We will then return to the basso continuo of southern historiography found among civic writers of Naples, including Loise de Rosa, the Notar Giacomo and Ferraiolo. These urban chroniclers provide continuity to the works examined in previous chapters and a contrast against which we may judge Renaissance historiography of the Mezzogiorno. Such contrast is central to this chapter, especially in light of the consensus view asserting stark differences between a local, clerical and annalist tradition of the monasteries and courts of the South and the new spirit of true historiography emerging from the lay, mercantile and then humanist urban centers of the North.[3]

We use the term "Renaissance" where we might more accurately use "quattrocento," "early modern" or "humanist." We do so first because modern historiography has enshrined the term, and secondly, because these historians shared the humanist conviction that they offered a dramatic break from the past. According to the consensus view, Renaissance historiography involved changes in narrative form and structure, linguistic and stylistic developments and methodological advances in the discovery, use and interpretation of sources that marked a decided shift from trecento historiography.[4] According to the consensus view, such quattrocento narratives were innovative because they were also unified by authorial voice and intent. They were based on ancient models, such as Sallust and Livy, but also the newly discovered Greek historians including Thucydides, Xenophon, Polybius and Procopius. Stylistically informed by Cicero and the classical rhetorical tradition, the new humanist histories were structured by topical order and arranged into books around single themes. These included the cycles of *fortuna*, the place of *virtù* as human agency in history and the role of illustrious men, including potential patrons and lords.

These writers focused on political history, human character and motivation to the exclusion of almost every other cultural context and causality. Even institutional and constitutional history was largely ignored in this concentration on the illustrious man. At the same time, historians like Bruni and Biondo saw their own times within the context of a strict periodization, a historical consciousness of progression and change, separation and distance that could be dated and verified via the careful examination of archeological remains, original documents and narratives and via a rigorous philological study of language and its contexts and evolution.[5]

By contract, consensus scholarship has viewed medieval historiography as universal and limited by the writer's personal experience. The secular world was important only as a reflection of the divine. Humans were passive spectators rather than agents, and notions of causality were practically nonexistent. It ignored classical historiography.[6] According to the model established by Cochrane and still widely accepted, the general historiography of the trecento was thus backward.[7] But it was nothing like that of the Mezzogiorno. There

> political development... took place in a manner exactly the opposite the way it did in northern Italy.... Hence, the kind of urban chronicle typical of pre-humanist historiography in the North never emerged in the South.

Exclusively monastic and monarchical, southern chronicles were "disorderly, uncertain, and stuffed with spurious names." What did emerge was "misguided," informed by "plagiarizing," and "reverted" to the old annalist catalogues.

Only the coming of the Northmen brought a new "impulse" and "afforded a new opportunity for further development" to southern historiography, weighed down as it was by the oriental culture of the Greeks and Arabs.[8] "Not only, then, did the Normans fully satisfy the longing of southern Italians for internal peace and protection against foreign foes, they also provided them with new and, in some aspects, more advanced models of historical writing."[9] Later, on the mainland, the Angevin period produced little of broad value, aside from Gravina's account of events in Apulia. While in Sicily, the Christians were "grateful" for the Norman conquest, "these contacts were not always fruitful, largely because the chronicle-writing Christian subjects of the new kingdom turned out to be far less open-minded than their immigrant princes" from the North.[10]

The coming of the Aragonese in the quattrocento revived historiography. As Cochrane again proposed:
> Thus history writing had been dead for over a hundred years by the time Southerners once again began to take an interest in it in the second quarter of the fifteenth century, and few if any of them seem to have been at all aware of the rich historiographical heritage left them by their ancestors of the age of the Normans or the Vespers.[11]

Expanding on Cochrane's research, Bentley[12] applied these categories to the work of quattrocento historians of Naples. He concluded that the chief focus of this school included the rebirth of the Regno under the Aragonese, the revival of urban life, the arts and letters, the role of the individual and the political and ethical issues that motivate individual action. These, he stressed, were not mere imitations or imports of Tuscan developments but grew out of the unique context of Aragonese history and the practical experience of these authors in education, royal administration, diplomacy and war. Whether initially attracted from elsewhere in Italy or home grown, they reflected a lay, political and civic ethic that informed all their broadly historical work. Bentley accepted and expanded on Hans Baron's theory of civic humanism[13] as a key to Neapolitan historiography in the quattrocento. Manetti's stylistics, Pontano's Sallustian approach to focused narrative, Panormita's political realism and Valla's philological researches and analysis together marked Neapolitan historiography of the quattrocento as something new for the South and for humanist writing in general.

According to Bentley, almost all Neapolitan historiography during the quattrocento imitated classical historians like Livy, Caesar, Suetonius and Xenophon. It reflected a coherent political narrative; a new critical attitude toward the sources enabled by the discovery of new texts and careful philological study; a clear-cut deployment of rhetorical skills to advance both utility and truthfulness; and an almost exclusive concentration on political themes that pitted the character, virtues and agency of Naples' rulers against the vicissitudes of *fortuna*.[14] What made Neapolitan historiography unique, Bentley observed, were the most startling examples of changing fortunes experienced by the Aragonese as they won and attempted to maintain their kingdom and its influence on Italy in the face of internal dissent, revolt, rival Italian machination and foreign invasion.[15]

HISTORICAL INTRODUCTION

The transformation of the kingdom of Naples from the most powerful state of the Italian trecento into an appendage first of the Aragonese empire and then of the new Spanish crown has been well recorded

CHAPTER 9 ❧ MEDIEVAL TO RENAISSANCE

and need detain us only to identify the chief events and personalities of the quattrocento around which these historians wrote.[16]

During the Great Schism between the rival Roman and Avignon popes (1378–1417), Queen Giovanna I took the side of Avignon Pope Clement VII against Urban VI, former archbishop of Bari and now the Roman pope. Urban retaliated by excommunicating the queen and crowning Charles of Durazzo (Charles III), the son of Robert the Wise's nephew, as king of Naples. Charles conquered Naples in 1381 and had Giovanna murdered in 1382. By that time, however, Giovanna had adopted Duke Louis I of Anjou as her heir. He, however, died in 1384. Charles III then went off to assert Angevin claims to the crown of Hungary and was assassinated there in 1386. Louis II of Anjou then invaded the Regno, but Charles' young son, Ladislaus of Durazzo, managed to retain the throne by allying with the Roman papacy in 1399. On Ladislaus' death in 1414, his younger sister, Giovanna II (r.1414–35), came to power. Heirless, in 1421 she adopted Alfonso V, king of Aragon and Sicily since 1416, but quickly disowned him and drove him out in 1423, turning instead to her French cousin, Louis III of Anjou (d.1434), and then to his brother, René of Anjou. With Giovanna II's death in 1435, claims to the kingdom were divided between the house of Anjou through dynastic lineage and the adoptive claims of Duke, now King, René and the house of Aragon through Alfonso's adoption in 1421. After years of war, Alfonso took Naples on June 6, 1442, and René abandoned the Regno.

As Alfonso I, the Magnanimous (1442–58),[17] he made Naples a major center of the new verbal and visual culture of the quattrocento.[18] The king built new infrastructure, squares and palazzi and patronized the arts. He established a humanist center at the rebuilt Castel Nuovo and at the revived university. Alfonso patronized the new humanists, refurbished the royal library, which had been moved from Castel Capuano to Castel Nuovo after its renovation, vastly increased its size and importance, sponsored philosophical and literary discussions at the academy there and opened it up to selected students at the *studium*. Alfonso also turned Naples into one of the first capitals of an early modern state, establishing a permanent class of well-educated professionals and a bureaucracy drawn from the urban middle class, which he utilized to check the barons' power.[19]

Alfonso was succeeded by Ferdinand I or Ferrante (1458–94). In 1459, Ferrante was faced with a serious revolt of the barons in league with the aged René and Jean of Anjou that was finally subdued in 1465. In the 1470s and 1480s, Naples was a key player in the Italian balance of power. But the 1490s brought catastrophe to Naples and to Italy as a whole. With Lorenzo de' Medici's death in 1492, the fragile balance of the peninsula wobbled, and an alliance between Lodovico Sforza of Milan and King Charles VIII of France finally tipped it.

Charles hoped to extend French rule over the old Angevin Regno; and Sforza's invitation to intervene gave him the opportunity when Ferrante died in January 1494. Ferrante's son, Alfonso II (1494–95), quickly allied with the papacy. But Charles turned south with a huge army, panicking Alfonso, who in 1495 abdicated in favor of his son Ferdinand II (Ferrante II or Ferrandino, r. 1495–96). With barons in revolt and Naples in anarchy, Charles entered the city, almost without a fight, in February 1495.

Yet by July, Ferdinand II had retaken the city, and by 1496, he had added most of the kingdom. Success seemed to be blessing him when Ferdinand fell ill and died in October. The throne passed to Ferdinand's uncle Frederick (r. 1496–1501); but by then the papacy had allied with the French, and in 1500 the French in turn had signed the Treaty of Granada to divide the Regno with a newly unified Spain under Ferdinand and Isabella. By 1502, however, the French and Spanish were fighting one another, and by 1504 Ferdinand the Catholic's lieutenant in Italy, Gonzalo Fernandez de Córdoba, had won the entire kingdom for Spain, fighting off a new French invasion, this time under Louis XII. The last Aragonese claimant to the throne died in 1550.

These events struck contemporaries in as startling a fashion as the Angevin defeat of the Hohenstaufen has done two centuries earlier, and they gave rise to similar speculations on virtue and fate, on good and bad character, on the life cycle of realms and on good and bad government. How quattrocento historians dealt with these startling turns — and how they did so in the same or new manners from those of the trecento — will be our final consideration.

HUMANIST HISTORIANS OF THE QUATTROCENTO: FLAVIO BIONDO

Though based in Rome and Florence, Flavio Biondo (1392–1463)[20] wrote extensively on the history and chorography of the Regno and played a major part in constructing the new humanist historiography. He was born in Forlì in 1392. After a standard education in grammar, rhetoric and poetics, the young Flavio moved to Padua. There he came under the influence of Petrarch's humanist successors before relocating to Piacenza, then to Pavia.

Flavio had taken up his father's profession as an itinerant chancellery notary.[21] By 1427 he had become secretary to the papal governor of the Romagna and entered the papal curia in Rome in 1432. Like many humanists, Biondo continued to travel widely, a practice that would become part of his research into the history and geography of all the Italian regions. But Biondo's most permanent home was Florence, and there he joined the circle of Leonardo Bruni (c. 1370–1444)[22] and began to write history in the new humanist mode. When he died in Rome in 1463, his reputation was European-wide, and his books continued to be used as basic texts for at least the next century.

CHAPTER 9 ⚜ MEDIEVAL TO RENAISSANCE

After studying Orosius, Tacitus and Jerome, Flavio began his *Historiarum ab inclinatione romani imperii decades*, first composed between 1439 and 1453[23] and planned variously to cover the period from 410 to sometime between 1410 and 1443. Flavio considered this period not a continued last world empire of medieval tradition but something "fallen" and lost. Using Livy's *Decades* as a model, Biondi built on Bruni's concept of separate periods and concluded that the year 1410 — the rounded thousandth anniversary of Alaric's sack of Rome — marked the beginning of an age of renewal after the "middle age."[24] He amplified this idea in his historical works on the city of Rome, carefully collating and critiquing the known narrative sources with the archeological remains of the city, debunking the Roman Mirabilian tradition and borrowing from humanist colleagues like Poggio Bracciolini. The result was two massive works, the *Roma Instaurata*[25] (1443–46) and the *Roma Triumphans*[26] (1452–59). Flavio's work fused Roman imperial and Christian history with the city's new status as humanist capital. It continued Bruni's broad humanist enterprise of "pragmatic history."[27]

Biondo followed this up with his general history of Italy and its regions, the *Italia Illustrata*, begun in 1447 and completed in 1453. In his dedication to Pope Nicholas V,[28] Flavio asserted that history provides "a wealth of models and precedents" and insures the reputations of illustrious men to "eternal memory." While "the art of history writing alone failed utterly and was snuffed out" over the barbarian centuries, the new age encouraged by Pope Nicholas has revived the arts and "a passion to study history."[29]

But the project also derived from Biondo's relationship with King Alfonso.[30] Flavio was writing to Alfonso as early as 1443 to secure patronage and advising him on the importance of history as a guide to rule and reputation.[31] He sent the first eight books of his *Decades* to Alfonso in June 1443. He at first planned to end this work with Alfonso's triumphal entry into Naples the previous year, but his emphasis on neat periodization moved his end date. Alfonso had urged Biondo to create a catalog of illustrious men, to "travel across and illuminate Italy" and to reconcile ancient and modern names and usage.[32] Flavio accepted the commission, wrote to Bartolomeo Facio at the Neapolitan court for advice on revisions[33] and applied his previously successful methodologies with a chorographic comprehensiveness to all the regions of ancient Roman Italy. Flavio finally visited Naples for several months in 1451/52; and in 1453, shortly after the fall of Constantinople to the Turks, he wrote a treatise urging Alfonso to lead a crusade against them.[34]

Flavio's *Italia Illustrata* demonstrates many of the tensions between strict adherence to classical style, language and modern realities, most especially in place names and in numerous modernizations of vocabulary. In this he was neither original nor alone, but he built on a long medieval tradition of attempts to define the nature and extent of Italy.[35] His Regno, however, remains the ancient Roman provinces, and his discussion focuses on a careful study of ancient sources and archeological remains. In this sense, Flavio follows the humanist approach favored by Petrarch: Italy as a place of common memory and identity only insofar as it reflected the greatness of antiquity.[36] Despite this plan, Flavio's work remained selective, determined to some extent by the location of powerful patrons.[37] Sicily barely appears, and he makes no mention of Sardinia.[38]

His descriptions of the South contain great detail on the geography and history of the Abruzzo, of Campania and the Bay of Naples and of Apulia. But when Biondo turns to the Regno as a unit, he immediately equates identity with geography:

> Now over the four-hundred-year period that these seven regions[39] have been fused into a single entity called the Kingdom, what took place there and how precisely the Kingdom was established may be told in a single detailed narrative.[40]

The Regno is "fused into a single entity" and its history told "in a single detailed narrative." The Regno is an "appellation," the product of a single binding narrative. It is not the subject of its own will or history but a construct forced into being by an external power: the Normans. *Italia Illustrata*'s lengthy narrative of the rise of the Normans in southern Italy[41] — to the exclusion of almost all other events and dynasties — is a treatise on the creation of a territorial state through cunning, tenacity and the proper application of force and diplomacy upon an ancient geography robbed of its agency by the debilitating process of time. Biondo makes clear the Normans' roots in the North and their superiority to a southern mix of Italians, Greeks, Muslims and Lombards. His tale of state-building predates, and anticipates in miniature, Machiavelli's narrative of the rise of Cesare Borgia in *The Prince*. It also offers the Mezzogiorno as a historical exemplum of statecraft and of the building of a territorial principality directed not only to the Aragonese of Naples, but to the Medici in Florence, the Sforza in Milan and the papacy in Rome. The Hohenstaufen merit hardly three paragraphs,[42] while his treatment of the Angevins covers the entire 200 years of the dynasty in another three.[43]

The South becomes the object of analysis, both endlessly fascinating, steeped in its geography and history but also remote, separate and bound by sensuous physicality. Biondo anticipates and helps extend the narrative of the black legend and prepares the intellectual ground of *meridionalismo*.[44] The heart of the "loveliest plain in all Italy,"[45] Capua, is living proof of "Campanian lasciviousness…the source of cruelty and arrogance,"[46] a region reflected in its pornographic theater, in its "lewd smuttiness…its lather of debauchery."[47] Biondo's intent is clear: immediately after this portrait of sensual decadence, he brings the reader back to the Norman prince Robert Guiscard, "the first to reduce into the form of a kingdom that large and magnificent portion of Italy known as the Kingdom of Sicily." The Regno is a construct of northern invaders who rescue the South from its decadent sensuousness.

Biondo's treatment of the Bay of Naples, including Baiae, the Campi Flegrei and Vesuvius[48] is based to an extent on his own travels to the court of Alfonso,[49] his own archeological investigations[50] and what he could glean "from the local inhabitants"[51] and "experts in local geography."[52] He also arranged with King Alfonso to call upon his court humanists for further details. But his account largely derives from his own critical and philological examination of ancient sources — Livy, Plutarch, Pliny, Virgil, Horace, Servius, Cicero, Aulus Gellius, Macrobius, Juvenal, Suetonius and others — and from contemporary sources like Pier Candido Decembrio. His discussion of Naples,[53] on the other hand, begins with his ancient sources' narration of the original Greek colony, its conflicts with neighbors and then its alliance with Rome. Aside from a brief mention of Virgil's tomb, which he says he could not find,[54] he omits the medieval Virgilian tradition prized by the *Cronaca di Partenope*.[55]

Naples[56] itself becomes synecdoche for the Mezzogiorno: a passive object as a colony of Greeks, as an intruder in conflict with neighbors, as a Roman ally. After a brief mention of Virgil's tomb, Biondo segues to the city's medieval history in a free association connecting Virgil to Petrarch and then to Petrarch's immortalization of King Robert.

> I can demonstrate...that outside Naples itself, very few men... know who King Robert was...except by reason of having read about him in the Latin or vernacular works of his close friend Francesco Petrarca.[57]

Biondo thus makes clear two key elements of his treatment of the South: first, the role of writers like Petrarch and himself in preserving the perpetual memory of great men like King Robert and Alfonso; and second, that his own narrative of Naples and the Angevin Regno is highly indebted to Petrarch's narrative.[58] To bring home this point of historical precedent and doublings, Biondo then narrates Procopius' account of Belisarius' capture of the city and recalls King Alfonso's own use of Belisarius' stratagem, entering the city through a disused aqueduct.[59] He concludes his account with a quick tour of Naples' chief monuments, ending with an encomium to Castel Nuovo, "a work worthy of the glorious memory of King Alfonso...superior to all other works, monuments, and edifices ancient or modern now extant in Italy."[60]

HUMANISTS AT THE NEAPOLITAN COURT

The life and works of the humanist historians at the Aragonese court of Naples have been well analyzed by Bentley and more recently by Senatore,[61] Delle Donne[62] and others. In contrast to what Bentley has termed a Neapolitan civic humanism, Delle Donne and Cappelli instead echo Burckhardt's concept of the "state as a work of art" and label the work of Naples' humanists as a *"umanesimo monarchico"*[63] that aimed to construct the image of Alfonso and his successors as legitimate heirs to the Regno and their state as this work of art. Contrary to Bentley's thesis, they assert that this royal ideology can neither be compared easily with communal/republican or with aristocratic ideas of governance nor viewed as inferior types of a Florentine norm.

Panormita

Antonio Beccadelli (1394–1471),[64] known as Panormita from the Latin name of his native Palermo, served throughout the reign of Alfonso the Magnanimous and into that of the king's heir Ferrante. His family fled their native Bologna to Sicily, but in 1419 Beccadelli traveled to Florence and in 1420 returned to Bologna to study law at the university. He began his writing career at about that time. He returned to Palermo in 1434 and entered the service of Alfonso the Magnanimous as librarian at the royal palace of Ziza. Alfonso quickly entrusted Panormita with a variety of important administrative and diplomatic posts, including the presidency of the royal Sommaria (exchequer).[65] The humanist remained close to the king throughout Alfonso's conquest of the Regno and served as royal ambassador through much of the 1450s. He soon became the dean of Naples' intellectual life, culminating in 1447 with the establishment of the Neapolitan Academy, which then passed on to the leadership of Giovanni Pontano, whose name has since been attached to it.

His most important historical work was his *De dictis et factis Alphonsi regis* of c.1456.[66] Panormita followed Xenophon's epideictic model in the *Memorabilia,* which collected anecdotes and events in the life of Socrates, but Panormita noted that he based his account solely on what he himself had witnessed or what trustworthy and reliable witnesses related. He praised Alfonso's virtues and deeds: his courage, justice, modesty, prudence, wisdom, mercy, piety and faith. He also highlighted Alfonso's personal qualities of humor, gravity, patience, diligence and liberality, all following the classical form.[67]

Panormita followed this in 1462 with two letters to King Ferrante following the *speculum principis* form, urging the king to practice both the ancient and Christian virtues of justice, moderation, chastity, gratitude, kindness, humanity and liberality.[68] In 1469 he began his *Liber rerum gestarum Ferdinandi regis*[69] in the same epideictic mode, based on

CHAPTER 9 ⚜ MEDIEVAL TO RENAISSANCE

both Xenophon and Suetonius. This work covered Ferrante's youth, his virtues and his military prowess and his deeds. But before he could complete it, Panormita died in Naples on January 15, 1471.

In his works for both kings, Panormita sought to legitimize the Aragonese dynasty against both Angevin claims and threats from rival Italian states. In so doing, he combined traditional medieval causality with the emerging early modern emphasis on contingency. He equated *fortuna* with the will of God to explain the vicissitudes of the Aragonese and such calamitous events as the recurrence of the plague. Like Villani, he was pessimistic of the role of human *virtù* in the face of such divine will.

BARTOLOMEO FACIO

A close associate of Panormita, Facio (c.1405–57) was born at La Spezia near Genoa, into a family of notaries.[70] Bartolomeo received his *grammatica* training at La Spezia and then around 1420 went on to Verona where he became a student of the humanist Guarino Veronese. With Guarino's recommendation, in 1426 he moved to Venice to become the tutor for the children of Doge Francesco Foscari. There in 1427 he met Panormita and began his lifelong friendship and collaboration with the Neapolitan humanist. He spent the remainder of the 1420s and 1430s in Florence, where he learned Greek, then in Lucca, Milan and Genoa, where he served as a notary, chancellor and ambassador. In 1443, Facio joined King Alfonso's military entourage in the March of Ancona as a Genoese ambassador and in September 1443 traveled to Naples as Genoese chancellor and ambassador. There he again met Panormita, who recruited him into Alfonso's service in 1445.

Facio is best known at the Neapolitan court for his notorious literary conflict with Lorenza Valla that produced his *Invective in Laurentium Vallam*,[71] but his philosophical and historical works place him at the forefront of humanist writing in the Regno.[72] In 1445 he composed his *De humane vitae felicitate*, dedicated to Alfonso and based on his readings of Plato, Aristotle, Cicero, Seneca, Lactantius, Augustine and Isidore of Seville. In 1448 he completed his *De excellentia ac praestantia hominis*, dedicated to Pope Nicholas V, and by 1454 he had finished his chief historical work, the *De rebus gestis ab Alfonsi primo neapolitanorum rege*,[73] based on Caesar but supplemented by close readings of documentary and diplomatic evidence. Facio made it clear that his work was not a rhetorical *laudatio* but a work of true historical narrative *(rerum gestarum narratio)*.[74] Following the prime rules of humanist historiography, Facio focused on the deeds and character of his illustrious subject as a contest between *fortuna* and personal *virtù*. He followed this up in 1455–57 with his own *De viris illustribus liber*, again dedicated to Alfonso, and then another epideictic work in praise of King Ferrante. Facio devoted his last years to translations of ancient Greek works, including Arrian's life of Alexander the Great and the writings of Isocrates. He died in Naples toward the end of 1457.

Lorenzo Valla

The most famous of all Neapolitan humanists, and among the most influential of all Renaissance authors, was Lorenzo Valla (1407–57). As such he has been the subject of countless studies over the past century on every aspect of his work:[75] translation, philosophical, moral and philological, exegetical and religious, polemical and historical.[76] Here we will concentrate only on those works that relate to the humanist historiography of the Neapolitan Regno.[77]

Valla was born in Rome in 1407 into a family of lawyers and papal curialists and grew up amid the new humanist culture. He studied under Giovanni Aurispa and Leonardo Bruni, but his outspoken and abrasive manner earned the animosity of curial humanists Antonio Loschi and Poggio Bracciolini, who prevented him from gaining a papal appointment. In 1431, through Panormita's influence, he therefore moved to Pavia to teach rhetoric at the university. During this period, he wrote his *De vero et falso bono*,[78] an Epicurean dialogue on pleasure. But he was forced to flee for his life after publishing a treatise attacking the trecento legist Bartolus of Sassoferrato. Moving to Milan again to teach, he met Bartolomeo Facio, and in 1435 he moved to the Regno in time to accompany Alfonso of Aragon into defeat and imprisonment in Genoa following the Aragonese defeat at Ponza. During this period, he probably served as a tutor to Prince Ferrante and began for him a translation of Xenophon's *Cyropaedia* as a "mirror of princes."

Once established at the Aragonese court, in the 1440s Valla began to produce a series of moral and philosophical treaties, including his *Dialectical Disputations*,[79] in which he stressed the literary and rhetorical arts, his dialogue *On Free Will*[80] and his polemic *The Profession of the Religious*.[81] In all of these, he sought to promote a lay, civic ethics while advancing philological studies. His *Elegantiae linguae latinae* of 1441 used the study of words and their historical development and contexts to correct errors about the past and to reform individual ethics and institutions in the present.[82] His *Collatio Novi Testamenti* of 1442[83] was a comparative study of the Latin Vulgate and the Greek New Testament that would have an enormous influence on Erasmus' and all later exegetical studies.

Valla combined his philological, polemical and historical interests in one of the most important Renaissance texts, his *Declamation on the Donation of Constantine* of 1440.[84] While there has been some debate over the intent of the work,[85] its Neapolitan context and thrust seems to support Bentley's contention that "it seems to me impossible to doubt the political implications of Valla's treatise."[86] These were intended to bolster Alfonso of Aragon's claims to the throne against Pope Eugenius' assertions of papal sovereignty and his backing the claims of René of Anjou. Bentley concedes that Valla's letters indicate that Alfonso pressured the reluctant humanist to compose the work, and Valla acknowledged its controversial nature and the personal danger into which it placed him.[87]

This groundbreaking political application of philological method examined the text of Constantine's supposed grant of the Western Empire to Pope Sylvester I.[88] Valla demonstrated that the work was actually composed around the mid-eight century, thus undermining papal pretensions to secular power. As important, he deployed rhetorical arguments and changing historical contexts to demolish the *Donation*'s claims to verisimilitude.[89] His defense of the Regno against papal claims to secular sovereignty is clear,[90] as is his emphasis on true historiographical method that insists on facts over legend, *historia* over *fabula*, whether this derives from ancient historians or Christian hagiography.[91]

Despite Alfonso's support, Valla's own rash personality and uncompromising search for truth brought him into conflict both with the inquisition in Naples and with fellow Neapolitan humanists Panormita and Facio. Facio and Valla's invectives[92] against one another form one of humanism's more unsavory, if skilled, exchanges. But the bad feelings resulted in Panormita and Facio's harsh criticisms of the methodology, form and factual errors in Valla's life of Alfonso's father, the *Gesta Ferdinandi regis Aragonum,* composed between April 1445 and February 1446.[93] The controversy is instructive since it ranges from stylistics to the new humanist historical method. Beneath the vituperation emerged a new sense of scholarly debate focused on texts and their interpretations.

Valla had sought to compose a collection of heroic *gesta* in the epideictic tradition. But in his prologue, he revealed a far larger project: to question Aristotle's contentions in the *Poetics* and *Rhetoric* that historical narratives are inferior to poetry and to philosophical precept.[94] Instead, Valla argued, history has higher claims to utility, pleasure and truth. Contrary to Aristotle's claim, history is essentially the record of exempla with universal application. Sallust, Livy, Quintilian, Moses and the evangelists all demonstrated the superiority of history writing to philosophy.

Valla then moves on to the methodology of history: the difficulties of comparing varying accounts and interpretations and the proper tools of the historian. History "requires no less accuracy and wisdom than that which is shown by a judge or a doctor."[95] Whether demonstrative or deliberative, forensic or judicial, in its use of rhetoric in the tradition of Cicero, Sallust and Thucydides, Quintilian and Pliny, historical narrative establishes truth, and rhetoric itself is the mother of history. The judicious choice of evidence and witnesses and the rhetorical use of digression, ornamentation, *amplificatio*, invented speeches and *sententiae* to construct narrative is, contrary to Facio's assertions, fully within the proper bounds of verisimilitude. On the other hand, *res gestae* — he pointedly replies to Facio's criticisms of inappropriate language and choice of incidents — is not the same as panegyrics to famous men, and historical truth must retain its honesty. History demonstrates that events are not the result of divine interventions but of the decisions and intelligence of men, portrayed with all their virtues and faults.[96]

Such controversies and pressures led Valla to ask Alfonso to be released from his service. He returned to Rome after the election of his friend Tommaso Parentucelli as Pope Nicholas V. There he devoted the last decade of his life to scholastic, liturgical and biblical studies.

GIANNOZZO MANETTI

Manetti (1396–1459)[97] was born in Florence into a family of prosperous merchant bankers. He was first educated in the *abbaco* to take his place in the family business, and he soon entered the city's administration, serving as one of the Twelve Good Men in 1429. By 1421, he had begun his studies of Latin, Greek and Hebrew. By the 1440s, he was already recognized as among the most important Florentine humanists, and in 1444 he served as the orator of Leonardo Bruni's funeral. During this period, he began composing humanist tracts and philological studies of the Greek and Hebrew scriptures, on the Greek philosophers, historical work[98] and biographies.[99]

Alfonso of Aragon invited Manetti to Naples in 1443 and again in 1445 to attend the wedding of Ferrante and Isabella di Chiaromonte. Manetti served in Rome as papal secretary until Nicholas V's death and finally moved to Naples to join Alfonso's court in 1455. There he served as a highly rewarded court councilor and as president of the Sommaria. He remained in Naples until his death on October 27, 1459.

Though he never wrote any history directly focused on Naples, Manetti did write works in praise of Alfonso and his life in several genres marked by a highly rhetorical style.[100] His *Oration to Pope Calixtus III* of 1455, urging the selection of King Alfonso to lead a new crusade, uses the deliberative mode to paint a picture of Turkish cruelty and the need for Christian unity and service. Alfonso, he argued, was the best leader for such a crusade, since he possessed all the proper Christian and civic virtues and, like the ancient Pompey, had years of experience as both a political and military leader.[101] Such deliberative rhetoric fit well with Manetti's epideictic orations in praise of Alfonso. In his dedication to the *Vita Socratis et Senecae*,[102] he praised Alfonso's patronage of the arts and letters. His *Oration to Alfonso* of 1452 followed the strict classical order laid down by Cicero, Quintilian, Priscian and Matthew of Vendôme[103] to cover Alfonso's birth and family, his physical prowess and intellect, his military skills and deeds, and his virtues, including the mercy he displayed after capturing the city in the same manner as Belisarius.

Giovanni Pontano

Pontano (1426–1503) best exemplifies humanist historiography in Naples.[104] He was born on 7 May 1426 in Cerrato in Umbria, where he received his *grammatica* education. Giovanni went on to study at Perugia, and in September 1447, he took the opportunity of Alfonso's campaign in Tuscany to introduce himself to the Neapolitan king. Alfonso took the young man into his entourage and brought him to Naples in October 1448. There Pontano continued his studies in Greek and astrology. He so favorably impressed the court with his learning and eloquence that Panormita included him in his diplomatic missions to Florence and Venice in 1451. From 1452 to 1457, he was back in Naples as tutor to Alfonso's nephew, Juan de Navarre.

Despite Alfonso's death and Ferrante's accession, Pontano's career remained assured. He accompanied the new king during his campaigns against both Angevin claimants and rebel barons, and by the 1460s, he was serving in the offices of the royal chamberlain, protonotary and royal councilor. After a teaching appointment in Perugia (1466–68), he returned to Naples. Ferrante granted him Neapolitan citizenship in 1471 and named him to the royal Sommaria in 1475. Pontano soon succeeded Panormita as tutor to Duke Alfonso of Calabria, and in 1471 he succeeded Panormita as president of the Neapolitan Academy, which stills bears his name.[105] From 1475 to 1482, he served as secretary to Alfonso's wife, Ippolita Sforza, and from May 1482, to Alfonso himself. In that capacity, Pontano traveled with the duke to the Abruzzi and Lombardy during the War of Ferrara and acted as the chief inspiration and negotiator for the Peace of Bagnolo in 1484 that reestablished the Italian balance of power. In 1486, in the aftermath of the second barons' revolt, Pontano became royal secretary to Ferrante and chief ambassador.

Pontano later career coincides with the collapse of the Italian balance of power, the French invasion, the end of the Aragonese dynasty and the beginning of the Spanish hegemony. Though wealthy enough by the 1490s to own his own urban palazzo and country villa and to build the Capella Pontano in the city center, he continued in active and loyal service to the Aragonese. On Ferrante's death in 1494, he served as royal secretary to Alfonso II and then to King Ferrandino. He devoted all his diplomatic, oratorical and military experience to preventing the French conquest but was on hand to present the keys of Naples to French King Charles VIII with the plea that the French spare the city from sack. He retired from active service in 1495 but maintained his civic loyalty to Naples. His last known letter, dated May 1503,[106] urged the French King Louis XII to come to the starving city's relief as Spanish troops under Gran Capitán Gonsalvo de Córdoba advanced against it.

Cochrane summarized his negative portrayal of southern historiography by declaring that Pontano saved it from "succumbing to its own inherent weaknesses upon the death of the sole patron [Alfonso] who had called it into existence."[107] Yet more focused studies by Bentley, Ginzburg and most recently Roick and Cappelli[108] offer a positive assessment, aligning Pontano and his intellectual circle fully with both the classical influence and civic humanism of the time and with a new pragmatic history that anticipated both Guicciardini's and Machiavelli's emphasis on human motivation, political realism, prudence[109] and fortitude. Most of Pontano's works reflect this civic humanism, methodically treating the public and private virtues of citizens and rulers.[110]

In only one work, *De bello neapolitano* (1465–69),[111] did Pontano turn explicitly to history writing. This focused on Ferrante's struggle to keep the throne after Alfonso's death. Rejecting the epideictic mode, Pontano based his narrative on his own eyewitness and on his access to diplomatic and archival materials. Like most humanist historians, he emphasized political developments and great deeds, personalities and character but balanced these against the conflict of individual will and *virtù* and the power of *fortuna*, expressed through a series of contingencies not the least of which was the agency of other humans.

Pontano did not publish *De bello napoletano* until 1495, accompanied by a theoretical discussion on the art of history writing *(De conscribenda historia)*. Explicitly invoking Sallust and Livy, Pontano calls on the long rhetorical tradition to assert that history is a form of literature, close to poetry. Its goals are to teach, to delight and to stir the emotions. To accomplish this, the historian must structure the work into distinct books based on set themes, deploy rhetorical devices such as *amplificatio*, invent speeches and dialogue, dramatize events like battles and use embellished language, including inventing neologisms to properly convey the reality described.[112] In his dialogue *Actius*, he echoed Quintilian's description of history as a prose song *(carmen solutum)*.[113]

Pontano expanded on his ideas in *De fortuna* (1501) in which *fortuna* was the working of the natural world on human agency. But the *homo fortunatus*, through reason and will, can overcome such contingency. Like Machiavelli, Pontano used his *De principe* (1468)[114] to argue that the ruler can overcome *fortuna* through his own virtues, most especially *prudentia*. All other civic virtues revolve around this key to successful rule.[115] To the end of his career and of the Aragonese dynasty, Pontano reflected the Neapolitan humanists' concern with combining civic virtue with service to the new monarchical state.[116] In this, he reflected the general trend of humanist historiography since Bruni to acknowledge, come to terms with and serve the emerging oligarchies of the cinquecento.

CHAPTER 9 ⚜ MEDIEVAL TO RENAISSANCE

CIVIC HISTORIANS OF THE QUATTROCENTO

After the *Cronaca di Partenope,* the most prominent "citizen chronicles" of Naples[117] were written by a growing number of Neapolitan authors in the quattrocento.[118] Here we will discuss the minor court official Loise de Rosa, the Notary Giacomo and the writer known as Ferraiolo. Like the author(s) of the *Partenope,* they also chose to write in the Neapolitan vernacular and took their place among a circle of well-informed public figures who gave voice to the aspiring middle and professional classes of the city. Unlike the humanist historians discussed above, they reflected not official Aragonese policy or aspiration but the oral and visual life of the street, the documentary record of everyday life and their own perceptions of civic life and power. Without stretching such differences too far, one can say that such work reflected the existential situation of the writer immersed in the thick social context of the city.[119] As opposed to the finely crafted product of humanist work, such a space maintained a constant dialogue with the reader and created text not as finished artifact but as a continuous process of selection, extension and revision. These texts also created a dialogue between the official state documents to which their authors had access via local municipal, *seggio* and church records,[120] the printing press and local gossip, report, memory, tradition and historical and literary writing.[121]

These works differed from contemporary humanist texts in another very important regard: the incorporation of previous histories into their narratives. While Bruni might re-use Villani, or Biondo any number of classical, medieval and humanist accounts, one was never in doubt as to whose ego and authorial pen had organized the narrative and its themes. These civic chroniclers, on the other hand, did so in a way that submerged their authorial presence and questioned the very notion of single authorship in much the same way as today's online writing can often obscure individual authorship and authority.[122] For these urban historians, there existed no notion of an "original text" as an abstract ideal. In addition, they molded their texts in accordance with audience expectation and contexts. While the humanists sought to enhance their own reputations — and their patronage and position — these urban historians sought rather to create a patrimony for their fellow citizens out of shared memory and experience.[123]

LOISE DE ROSA

While Cochrane relegates Loise de Rosa to an index entry, Jerry Bentley opened his authoritative analysis of Neapolitan historiography with an account of Rosa's encomium to the city.[124] Born in Pozzuoli around October 15, 1385,[125] Loise was brought up in Naples. The family fled to Aversa during the sack of Naples by Alfonso I. We know little of his education, though the fact that he wrote exclusively in the Neapolitan vernacular, without trace of Latin, indicates that he may have received a standard *abaco* education. He was apparently back in Naples, serving at the royal court at the age of twenty, when he was arrested and falsely accused of having abused a maid of Queen Giovanna II. He died in 1475.

Loise claimed to have served in the royal bureaucracy for the Angevin, Angevin-Durazzan and Aragonese dynasties, including the courts of Otto of Brunswick, Ladislaus, James II of Bourbon (the husband of Giovanna II), Louis III, René of Anjou and Alfonso and Ferrante of Aragon. He also claimed to have served Margherita, queen of Charles III of Durazzo, Ladislaus' queens Maria of Cyprus and Maria of Taranto, Queen Giovanna II, René of Anjou's regent-queen Isabelle of Lorraine and Ferrante's queen Isabella di Chiaramonte. Loise listed himself as household seneschal of King James II, of Grand Seneschal Gianni (Sergianni) Caracciolo, of Cardinal Latino Orsini, of Hugh de Lusignan the cardinal of Cyprus, of Giovanni Vitelleschi the patriarch of Alexandria, of the princes of Salerno, of the Orsini and Sanseverino, of the dukes of Sora and Vasto, of the counts of Troia and Ariano and of other great lords. De Rosa also recorded his service as viceroy of Bisceglie and the Val di Gaudo and two terms as vice-admiral of the Neapolitan fleet.

Whatever the variety and scope of his duties and experience,[126] like several Neapolitan historians of the trecento and the humanists of the quattrocento, he was a royal administrator who knew and understood the personalities, events, official narratives and archives of the dynasties and their courts. He produced three major works,[127] which he himself dates from between 1467 and 1475, though he seems to have conceived them some time around 1452. These included his *Memorie* or *Ricordi,* his *Elogio di Napoli* and a *Cronaca di Napoli* concluding with his tract *Lodi della donna*. The manuscript belonged to Ippolita Sforza, wife of Ferrante's heir, Duke Alfonso of Calabria, and seems to have been the product of Loise's service to the duke and duchess, duties that both Panormita and Pontano also fulfilled. His *Lodi* were written for Ippolita, while he notes that his *Ricordi* were begun as a result of a request from Don Alfonso.

Loise adopted various rhetorical modes for his works. His *Lodi* for Ippolita is clearly in the epideictic, while his *Elogio* develops the urban *laudatio* with a taxonomy of thirteen characteristics that any great city must possess.[128] His *Ricordi,* however, resemble more the commentary form, eschewing chronological order for a chapter arrangement by themes, including the role of *fortuna* and the tragic fall of great emperors, kings, popes and nobles, thus echoing Boccaccio's own *De casibus*. His *Cronaca* ranges across the history of the Regno from Robert Guiscard to Ferrante and combines a political focus with the workings of extra-human causality, such as miracles, prodigies and astrological influences. His tale of Neapolitan history — of its victories, treasons, wars and treaties, its marriages and births — leads to the life and praises of Duchess Ippolita. The *Cronaca* thus lies somewhere between history and private *ricordanza*. As such, its memories open a space for the legendary and fantastic, living along the well-worn medieval boundary between *historia* and *fabula*.

Unlike that of the court humanists, Loise's work is based closely on orality and enlivened with details drawn from every level of Neapolitan society: from the conversations of the powerful in the Regno and the humanists at Castel Nuovo, to the sermons of popular preachers, deliberations of the *seggi* and the echoing chatter in the *vicoli* of Naples. His Neapolitan vernacular was apparently untouched by the Tuscan-inflected *medio* dialect used at court or by writers like Diomede Carafa, Masuccio Salernitano and others.[129]

Notar Giacomo

We know very little of his life. Cochrane remarks that aspects of his account "would have made Orosius blush."[130] Chiara De Caprio, however, has presented a meticulously detailed picture in various studies.[131] Giacomo lived during the last years of Aragonese rule and into that of the Spanish viceroys. De Caprio ultimately rejects speculations that he may have been Giacomo della Morte, identified as a Neapolitan notary during the period.[132] His wrote his *Cronica di Napoli* in a Neapolitan–Campanian vernacular that avoided many localisms but included numerous insertions from Latin authors. Like the *Cronaca di Partenope*, which provided a major source,[133] Giacomo narrated events from the origins of the Regno but continued his account until 1511. Like many of the trecento urban chronicles we have already discussed,[134] he employed a thematic form to carry his political focus on events of the French invasion of 1494 and the end of Aragonese rule. But he also included events further afield in Europe and reported later events from the streets of Naples. Following in the tradition of Quintilian, he constructed a continuous chronological narrative divided by discrete paragraphs in the original and single manuscript.[135]

The uniqueness of this manuscript and its structure offers several good indications of its development, use and purpose. Giacomo copied from previous sources but eliminated most notices of natural calamities and meteorological events and deleted most borrowings from literary traditions, including fables and Virgilian materials. He included a detailed narration of Lewis of Hungary's invasion and the reconquest of the Regno, which he attributed to Louis of Taranto. He did this as part of a project to construct the first draft of a political narrative that would create a new event horizon for the citizens of Naples, one that accounted not only for the great men and deeds but for the civic role of the everyday incident and of the average citizen.[136] Giacomo concentrated on the years 1476–1511 not by chance but to demonstrate these two key interrelated themes: the history of the Aragonese juxtaposed against its contexts both within the Italian peninsula and Europe and within the newly emerging society of late quattrocento Naples. He used both administrative and public documents to narrate these themes in complex, simultaneously synchronic and diachronic, "barycentric" patterns. Ultimately his intent was to demonstrate how the wide world of Italian and European events intersect along the narrow streets of Naples.[137] Here the grand themes of quattrocento historiography come alive: the synchronic experiences of *fortuna* and its attendant disasters of battle and siege — Dooley's "contemporaneity"[138] and De Caprio's "shared simultaneity"[139] — are met by the citizens of Naples who can summon up their deep diachronic history of civic virtue and honor.

To accomplish this rapid change of focal length and to establish his truth claims, Giacomo relied on every available source: from earlier histories and local memory, to official documentation filtered down to local administrators, to the urban networks of oral transmission[140] that connect the palace to the street. In the other direction, his own eyewitness and his professional role as a notary took oral testimony and transformed it into the official documentation of the court and archive.[141] While the humanist historians at court formed their textual community synchronically among the elite and their colleagues and diachronically with the writers of antiquity with whom they imagined themselves in constant dialogue, the urban chroniclers worked synchronically with the local and the oral and diachronically with older chronicle texts and popular memory. As we have already noted in discussing the *Cronaca di Partenope*,[142] in the case of Naples this diachronicity could also be informed by Naples' Virgilian tradition only partially altered, if at all, by new humanist historical and philological learning.

Ferraiolo

The *Cronaca* of Ferraiolo[143] focuses on the fate of the Aragonese from 1423 through Alfonso's conquest of Naples in 1442 to February 1498 and the coming of the French. We do not know much about Ferraiolo's life.[144] He seems to have come from a family of goldsmiths active in the city through the end of the cinquecento. He notes that his father Francesco witnessed Alfonso I's triumphal entry into the city in 1442, and Ferraiolo family names appear in the registers of the Aragonese chancellery from 1479 to 1500. There is little evidence to bolster the claim that he was the Melchionne named in contemporary legal and financial records.[145] Whatever his education, Ferraiolo appears to have known Latin. He may have served as a minor court official under Alfonso and his successors, a lower level majordomo or seneschal, and claimed to have witnessed "with my own eyes"[146] events around the royal family. But he was not privy to the humanist circle around the king, and his access to deliberations at court was probably second-hand. He also sometimes misinterpreted[147] official documentary material made available through local administration and print.

His *Cronaca* survives in a single manuscript[148] that incorporates several works: the *Fasciculus temporum*, a Latin world chronicle attributed to Werner Rolewinck,[149] a hand copy of the first print edition (1486–90) of the *Cronaca di Partenope*,[150] Ferraiolo's father's description of Alfonso's entry into Naples,[151] an Italian translation of *The Baths of Pozzuoli*[152] and finally Ferraiolo's *Cronaca*.[153] This array of materials enabled Ferraiolo to construct a history of Naples and its environs based on information garnered from official circles but given life by his perspective of the city's streets and marketplaces, its topography and local lore. In this regard Ferraiolo's work reflects the voice of Naples' urban classes and the orality that underlay their community of communications and memory. Poetry and rhymed prose, popular sayings and metaphors from folk tale, all in the popular style of Neapolitan vernacular, make his text one of the most important monuments of vernacular prose of the late quattrocento.[154]

At the same time, Ferraiolo's manuscript provides vivid testimony to the still porous boundaries between oral, manuscript and new print cultures of the cinquecento.[155] Its version of Rolewinck's *Fasciculus temporum* copies both the text and images in Erhard Ratdolt's printed edition (Venice 1481); while his versions of the *Cronaca di Partenope* and the *Baths of Pozzuoli* are based on the first printed Neapolitan edition of 1486–90 by Francesco del Tuppo.[156] But he also revised the *Cronaca*, for example, with a fresh transcription of the original Greek inscription on the pediment of the Temple of the Dioscuri and a note on its columns.[157] Ferraiolo's own Neapolitan text is accompanied by 120 well-known pen-and-wash drawings of varying sizes that provide a vivid picture of events in quattrocento Naples. The fact that between fols. 128r and 145v spaces were left for another 53 drawings that were never completed negates any sense of random assemblage but indicates a clear-cut plan for a collection whose ultimate uses and audience can only be surmised. So too does the manuscript's lavish size (420 × 230 mm.), its consistent mis-en-page and its single professional humanist hand used throughout the manuscript for both Latin and Neapolitan texts. Such usage also demonstrates the new access to various forms of popular and more learned texts made available to a broader public through the printing press.

Ferraiolo's manuscript thus testifies to a sense of fluidity of medium, genre, language, textuality, orality and visuality in this more popular genre of historiography.[158] The skilled (if idiosyncratic) richness of its decoration and illustrations,[159] many showing clear mastery of classical style and motifs,[160] also points to more than a naive private book of *ricordanze*. This evidence may indicate the creation of a presentation copy for a member of the court,[161] or a publication plan,[162] a work of "recuperation"[163] designed to succeed the *Cronaca di Partenope* to bolster civic pride, knowledge of the city's geography, topography and traditions while confirming the place of the Aragonese in a tumultuous phase of its illustrious history.

De Caprio[164] focuses on three episodes to analyze Ferraiolo's construction of narrative and truth claims. His account of Alfonso's triumphal entry into Naples[165] depends on oral transmission: his father's eyewitness memory. His report of the recovery of Otranto from the Turks[166] is based on a popular Neapolitan song. His record of the trial and punishment of the rebellious barons in 1486[167] derives verbatim from the official court documentation printed by Francesco Del Tuppo. This was no naive bricolage, the product of chance or lack of skill: Ferraiolo had opportunity to copy print editions completely[168] and to draw indirectly on official documentation and other written accounts — both Latin and vernacular — but chose instead to turn his history into a reflection of his own life as a citizen of Naples, committing to perpetual memory oral recollections,[169] the traditions of popular song and poetry and the transmission of official documentation and propaganda through the city's streets and piazzas via the new medium of print.

Like the narratives constructed by the woman historians of the nineteenth century,[170] this was a history of the "web" of thick social relationships, a network that addressed events, their transmission and impact on people and cities; that considered the agents of history, their reporters and their audience; and that wove a far richer fabric of reality "as it actually happened" than the linguistically correct, methodologically innovative, but backward-looking Latin histories of court humanists.

CONCLUSIONS

The humanists treated above present clear-cut examples of a newly developing classical scholarship set within their European republic of letters that devoted it energies to discovering, collating and establishing authoritative editions of classical works, fixed in print[171] and subject to repeated revision by a community of skilled philologists. Their historical works tended to emphasize the single authorship of the classical scholar, unified around set themes of vice and virtue, and the exemplary lives of illustrious men. Their work lent itself well to what Pettitt has called the "Gutenberg parenthesis" of fixed editions and standardized format that clearly distinguished a synchronic distance between the author, the text and the audience in much the same way as their historical sense clearly distinguished a newly fixed diachronic distance between their contemporary world and antiquity.

Naples' urban chroniclers offer something different and not inferior to the modern eye. Italian work[172] has brought to bear much recent research on documents and histories as more fluid performative and social texts. Urban historians like De Rosa, Notar Giacomo and Ferraiolo incorporated official texts into their chronicles and recorded their reception, whether the reaction at court to the latest news or diplomatic dispatch or of the people on the streets to decrees and reports. Like the Romans' reaction to Rienzo's painting cycles that the Anonimo romano reported,[173] such reception formed an essential part of the urban chroniclers' textual community, their intellectual and social world.

NOTES

1. Hay (1977), 87–132; Cochrane.
2. Bentley; Cochrane, 134–59.
3. Senatore (2014), 51–53, assesses the strengths and weaknesses of this monastic historiography but stresses their essential historical methodologies.
4. Cochrane, 3–15.
5. On this sense of difference and change, Wilcox (1985), 167–71, 189–200, 215–26.
6. Cochrane, xv.
7. Cochrane, 134–37.
8. Cochrane, 136–38.
9. Cochrane, 140.
10. Cochrane, 139.
11. Cochrane, 144.
12. Bentley, 1–7. For amplification and revision, see Cappelli (2016).
13. Baron (1955); Baron (1988). This thesis has been criticized and modified, for example, by Siegel (1966); Rabil (1988); Hankins (1995).
14. Bentley, 222–41; Cappelli (2016), 43–59, 187–224.
15. Bentley, 241–52.
16. This account is based largely on Bentley, 7–39; Musto (2017), 3–7.
17. Delle Donne (2015).
18. Giannetti (2017), 59–76.
19. Senatore (2012); Delle Donne (2015.2).
20. See Cochrane, 34–40; Fubini (1968); Biondo (2005), vii–xxvii; Pellegrino (2007); Caster (2016); Mazzocco (2016.a).
21. White, viii–ix.
22. Cochrane, 3–9, 17–20; Vasoli (1972); Hankins (1997); Ianziti (2007); Ianziti (2010); Ianziti (2016); Kempshall, 486–89, 495–97.
23. Pellegrino, 285–98.
24. Hay (1958); Pontari (2016).
25. Biondo (1542).
26. Biondo (2016.1).
27. Ianziti (2007), 264.
28. Biondo (2005), 4.5–9.7.
29. Biondo (2005), 3.1–5.3.
30. Pellegrino, 274 n. 7; 281.
31. Bentley, 47, 54, 222.
32. Fubini (1968); White in Biondo (2005), xi.
33. Bentley, 104.
34. Bentley, 164–65.
35. Laureys (1997), 110–11; Airò (2013), 34–35.

36. Ascoli (2011); and above, pp. 162–63, 246–47.
37. Castner (1998); Pellegrino (2007), 281.
38. Biondo never completed his plan to describe all seven regions. He references his hasty conclusion in his later Appendix. Biondo (2016.2), 362–63.1.2.
39. "Abruzzo, Campania, Puglia, Lucania and the territories of the Salentini, the Calabri, and the Brutii." Biondo (2016.2), 178–79.1.
40. "Quae vero a quadrigentis annis postquam septem hae regiones in unicam regni appellationem sunt confusae, in eo acciderint et qua ratione facta sit ipsa regni constitutio videtur unico contextu diligentius enarrandum." Biondo (2016.2), 178–79.1.
41. Biondo (2016.2), 178.1–193.11.
42. Biondo (2016.2), 194.12–199.14.
43. Biondo (2016.2), 199.15–203.17.
44 Naples' physicality is also central to its depiction in the pages of *Illustrazione italiana* during the Risorgimento: Moe, 85–125, 187–223; Musto (2017), 25–26.
45. "Totius Italiae amoenissimum." Biondo (2016.2), 298–99.19.
46. "Quam Capua in magnis parebuit Campane luxuriae documenta, siquidem pro superbiae et crudelitatis origine." Biondo (2016.2), 300–301.21.
47. "Satis superque fuerit obscoenam norare lasciviam." Biondo (2016.2), 300–301.21.
48. Biondo (2016.2), 304.25–341.51.
49. Biondo (2016.2), 288–89.11.
50. For example, Biondo (2016.2), 306–7.25; 310.28–327.39.
51. "Ab his qui inhabitant civibus scire potuimus." Biondo (2016.2), 298–99.18.
52. "Et periti regionis…cives affirmant." Biondo (2016.2), 300–301.19.
53. Biondo (2016.2), 326.40–337.49.
54. Biondo (2016.2), 326–27.39.
55. Above, pp. 51, 56–57, 106–7 et passim.
56. Biondo (2016.2), 326–37 n. 42.
57. Biondo (2016.2), 330–31.42.
58. Above, pp. 235–47 et passim.
59. Biondo (2016.2), 334–35.47.
60. Biondo (2016.2), 334–35.48.
61. Senatore (2012).
62. Delle Donne (2016).
63. Delle Donne (2015.2), viii–xii; Cappelli (2016), 7–9, 125–45.
64. Resta (1970); Ryder (1976); Cochrane, 146–48; Bentley, 84–100.
65. Ryder (1976), 126.
66. Beccadelli (1990).
67. Above, pp. 103–6.
68. Bentley, 204–5, 224–28, 243–46.
69. Beccadelli (1968).
70. Kristeller (1965); Bentley, 100–108, 118–20, 228–32, 290–97 et passim; Viti (1994); Kraye (1996); Delle Donne (2012).
71. Facio (1978); Bentley, 117–18, 229–30.
72. Albanese–Pietragalla (1999).
73. Facio (2004).
74. See Dall'Oco (1995).
75. Izbicki (1993); Kallendorf (2011).
76. Rossi (2007). For a new survey of translation work conducted in early modern Naples, see Rizzi (2017), 57–74.

77. Cochrane, 147–57, 256–58; Bentley, 108–22, 233–38; Kempshall, 496–509, 545–46.
78. Valla (1970.2); Lorch (1985).
79. Valla (2012).
80. Valla (1948).
81. Valla (1985).
82. Cochrane, 148.
83. Valla (1970.1).
84. Valla (1993); Valla (2007).
85. Valla (1993), 3–4; Bentley, 113–15. Bowerstock, Valla (2007), vii–x, agrees that it was written under Alfonso's patronage but asserts it was "more reasonably seen as an extension of his literary and philosophical interests than as a political weapon" and that the work had neither impact nor appeal at the time, an interpretation laid out by Setz (1975). For a political interpretation, see Fois (1969).
86. Bentley, 114.
87. Valla (2007), 2–5.1.
88. Kempshall, 497.
89. Valla (2007), 6–7.4; Janik; Bentley, 237.
90. Valla (2007), 52–53.33
91 For example, his discussion of Valerius Maximus and Livy's treatments of the legend of the Lacus Curtius in Chapter 5, Valla (2007), 126.77–131.79.
92. Facio (1978); Valla (1981).
93. Valla (1973).
94. Bentley, 233–36; Kempshall, 497–505.
95. Proemium, p. 7, quoted in Kempshall, 499.
96. Cochrane, 148–49.
97. Cochrane, 26–27; Bentley, 122–27, 209–12; Foà (2007); Kallendorf (2014).
98. Manetti (2014).
99. Manetti (2003).
100. Wittschier (1968); Bentley, 209–12.
101. Botley (2006).
102. Manetti (1979), 113–18.
103 Above, pp. 104–5.
104. Bentley, 127–37, 176–94, 241–54, 261–65, 297–99 et passim; Pontano (2012), 1:vii–xxvii; Figliuolo (2015).
105. Furstenberg-Levi (2016).
106. Bentley, 134; citing Sabia (1980).
107. Cochrane, 151.
108. Roick (2017); Cappelli (2016).
109. Ginzburg (2009).
110. Bentley, 132–33, 220–22, 249–52; Pontano (1999); Pontano (2006); Pontano (2012), xi–xii.
111. Sabia (1995); Pontano (1996).
112. Bentley, 239–41; Figliuolo (2015).
113. Kempshall, 505–6.
114. Pontano (2003); Cappelli (2016), 91–98; English translation in Nichols–McGregor (2019), 119–38.
115. Kahn (1983); Bentley, 206–8, 246–52.
116. Finzi (2004); Cappelli (2016), 200–224.
117. For these *cronache cittadine,* Senatore (2014); De Caprio (2014); Coluccia, 122–32. For the larger contexts of vernacular writing in Naples, Rizzi (2017), 57–74.

118. The list might also include Silvestro Guarino and Giuliano Passaro. See De Caprio (2014), 43–44.
119. De Caprio (2014), 39–42, reminds us that both Machiavelli and Pontano made clear their immersion in the daily life that informed their ideas and work.
120. De Caprio–Senatore (2016), 138–42.
121. De Caprio (2012), 32–40; Senatore (2014); De Caprio–Senatore (2016).
122. Gardiner notes similarities to today's digital journalism, where a story in the online *New York Times* might lead with breaking news and then supplement it with already reported background from several reporters. See Gardiner–Musto (2015), 135–39. Pettitt (2012) termed the print hiatus between manuscript and digital cultures the "Gutenberg parenthesis."
123. Senatore (2014), 280.
124. Bentley, 3–7.
125. De Nichilo (1991); De Rosa (1998).
126. Croce (1948), at 125, attributes much of De Rosa's record of his achievements to the "illusions of servants." Bentley, 3, also questions his accuracy on this count.
127. All contained in Paris, BnF, Cod. Ital. 913 (ex 10171). For editions, De Rosa (1971), superceded by De Rosa (1998).
128. Bentley, 4–5. Naples earned 12 out of 13, a higher score than any other Italian or Mediterranean city. For a translation, see Nichols–Mc Gregor (2019), 68–76.
129. De Rosa (1998), 13–64.
130. Cochrane, 146.
131. Among these are De Caprio (2004); De Caprio (2012), esp. 15, 48–62, 76–84, 139–57; De Caprio–Montuori (2013); De Caprio (2017), 132. De Caprio (2017), 24 n. 60.
133. Montuori (2017), 40–41.
134. Chapter 4, pp. 96–100.
135. Naples, BN, MS Brancacciano II.F.6.
136. De Caprio (2007), 20–25.
137. De Caprio (2007), 36–38.
138. Dooley (2010), xiii; De Caprio (2014), 48.
139. I thank Prof. De Caprio for bringing this idea to my attention.
140. On the place of aurality and the new aural history, Atkinson (2016).
141. On the role of the notariate as intermediary between official royal power and the life of the streets, De Caprio (2012), 94–104; De Caprio (2017), 25–38.
142. Above, pp. 49–51, 56–57, 106–7 et passim
143. Ferraiolo (1956); Ferraiolo (1987).
144. Ferraiolo (1987), xxiv–xxxv; Pignatti (1996).
145. De Caprio (2012), 76 n.11.
146. Ferraiolo (1987), § 247, p. 118.
147 De Caprio–Senatore (2016), 142, note his uneven understanding of the documents.
148. New York, Morgan Library, MS 801. Many images of the manuscript are now online at: http://ica.themorgan.org/manuscript/page/1/146991. The following comments are based on my physical examination of the Morgan MS; the Morgan description; and the detailed description, much revised, at corsair.morganlibrary.org/msdescr/BBM0801a.pdf. See also Ferraiolo (1987), li–lxi.
149. Fols. 1r–51v; Ferraiolo (1987), liii–liv.
150. Fols. 52r–83r; Ferraiolo (1987), liv–lvi; Barbato–Montuori (2014).

151. Fol. 84r–v. Ferraiolo (1987), § 1–2, pp. 3–4, conflates this entry with the main body of the *Cronaca*.
152. *Trattato de li bagni di Pezola*, fols. 85r–87v; Ferraiolo (1987), lvi.
153. Fols. 88r–150r; Ferraiolo (1987), 3–118.
154. De Caprio (2012), 62–68, 75–76.
155. Senatore (2014), 307–8; Montuori (2017), 41–43.
156. Barbato–Montuori (2014), 53–54; Montuori (2017), 37–39.
157. Ferraiolo (1987), x–xi.
158. Montuori (2012.1), 21–28; Senatore (2014), 297–98; De Caprio–Senatore (2016), 142–43; De Caprio (2017), 30–31.
159. De Caprio (2012), 76 nn. 11–12 for bibliography.
160. For example, fols. 35r, 36r, 36v, 41r, 43r, 104r, 104v, 105r, 107r, 108r, 115v, 116r.
161. Barbato–Montuori (2014), 67, citing Bühler.
162. Barbato–Montuori (2014), 67, argues for its audience as a small textual community of family or neighbors, for which a print edition's rigidity was inadequate.
163. Montuori (2017), 43.
164. De Caprio (2012), 79–80.
165. Ferraiolo (1987), § 1–2, pp. 3–4.
166. Ferraiolo (1987), § 15, pp. 8–12. For a detailed analysis, Coluccia (2017), 129–32.
167. Ferraiolo (1987), § 16–28, pp. 13–19.
168. Barbato–Montuori (2014), 67–68.
169. De Caprio (2012), 93–104; De Caprio (2014), 68–69.
170. Smith (2001).
171. Bearing in mind the caveats of Johns (1998), 10–40 et passim.
172. Zabbia (1999); Delle Donne (2001); Delle Donne (2012); De Caprio (2012), 112–18; Delle Donne (2015).
173. See above, pp. 165–78.

WORKS CITED

Airò, Anna. 2013. "'*Italia, Italie, Italicae Gentes:* Particolarismi, varietà e tensioni all'unitas nella cronistica tardomedievale." In *Unità d'Italia e Istituto storico italiano: Quando la politica era anche tensione culturale*. Elisabetta Caldelli et al., ed. Roma: ISIME, 33–55.

Albanese, Gabriella, and Daniela Pietragalla. 1999. "*In honorem regis edidit:* Lo scrittoio di Bartolomeo Facio alla corte napoletana di Alfonso il Magnanimo." *Rinascimento* 39:293–336.

Ascoli, Albert Russell. 2011. "Petrarch's Private Politics: *Rerum Familiarium Libri* 19." In *A Local Habitation and a Name: Imagining Histories in the Italian Renaissance*. New York: Fordham University Press, 118–58.

Atkinson, Niall. 2016. *The Noisy Renaissance: Sound, Architecture, and Florentine Urban Life*. University Park: The Pennsylvania State University Press.

Barbato, Marcello. 2014. With Francesco Montuori. "Dalla stampa al manoscritto: La iv parte della *Cronaca di Partenope* trascritta dal Ferraiolo (1498)." In *Dal manoscritto al web: Canali e modalità di trasmissione dell'italiano. Tecniche, materialie e usi nella storia della lingua*. E. Garavelli and E. Suomela-Härmä, ed. Florence: Cesati, 51–70.

Baron, Hans. 1955. *The Crisis of the Early Italian Renaissance: Civic Humanism and Republican Liberty in an Age of Classicism and Tyranny*. 2 vols. Princeton: Princeton University Press.

—. 1988. *In Search of Florentine Civic Humanism: Essays on the Transition from Medieval to Modern Thought*. 2 vols. Princeton: Princeton University Press.
Beccadelli, Antonio (Panormita). 1538. *De dictis et factis Alphonsi regis Aragonum et Neapolis, libri quatuor.* Basel: Hervagius.
—. 1968. *Antonii Panhormitae liber rerum gestarum Fernandi regis.* Gianvito Resta, ed. Palermo: Centro di studi filologici e linguistici siciliani.
—. 1990. *De dictis et factis Alfonsi regis.* M. Vilallonga, ed. Barcelona: Barcono.
—. 2021. *Alfonsi regis Triumphus: Il Trionfo di re Alfonso. Introduzione, edizione, traduzione.* Fulvio Delle Donne, ed. Potenza: Basilicata University Press.
Biondo, Flavio. 1542. *Roma ristaurata et Italia illustrata di Biondo.* Lucio Fauno, ed. Venice: Tramezzino.
—. 2005. *Italy Illuminated* 1. Jeffrey A. White, ed. and trans. Cambridge, MA: Harvard University Press.
—. 2016.1. *Rome in Triumph.* Maria Agata Pincelli and Frances Muecke, ed. and trans. Cambridge, MA: Harvard University Press.
—. 2016.2. *Italy Illuminated* 2. Jeffrey A. White, ed. and trans. Cambridge, MA: Harvard University Press.
Botley, Paul. 2006. "Giannozzo Manetti, Alfonso of Aragon and Pompey the Great: A Crusading Document of 1455." *Journal of the Warburg and Courtauld Institutes* 67:129–56.
—. 2008. *Latin Translation in the Renaissance: The Theory and Practice of Leonardo Bruni, Giannozzo Manetti and Desiderius Erasmus.* Cambridge: Cambridge University Press.
Cappelli, Guido. 2016. Maiestas: *Politica e pensiero politico nella Napoli aragonese (1443–1503).* Rome: Carocci.
Castner, Catherine J. 1998. "Direct Observation and Biondo Flavio's Additions to *Italia Illustrata:* The Case of Ocriculum." *Medievalia et Humanistica* n.s. 25:93–108.
—. 2016. "The *Fortuna* of Biondo Flavio's *Italia Illustrata.*" In Mazzocco-Laureys (2016), 177–96.
Croce, Benedetto. 1948. "Sentendo parlare un vecchio napoletano del Quattrocento." In *Storie e leggende napoletane.* Bari: Laterza.
Da Bisticci, Vespasiano. 1963. *Renaissance Princes, Popes, and Prelates.* W. G. Waters and Emily Waters, ed. New York: Harper & Row; repr., *The Vespasiano Memoirs: Lives of Illustrious Men of the XVth Century.* Toronto: University of Toronto Press, 1997.
Dall'Oco, Sondra. 1995. "La 'laudatio regis' nel *De rebus gestis ab Alphonso primo* di Bartolomeo Facio." *Rinascimento* 35:243–51.
De Caprio, Chiara. 2004. "Fra codice e testo: Il caso della *Cronica di Napoli* di Notar Giacomo, con una riflessione sulla categoria di 'codice-archivio'." *Medioevo romanzo* 28:390–419.
—. 2007. "La *Cronica* di Notar Iacobo: Codice, testo e *dehors texte.*" *Filologia e Critica* 32:59–74.
—. 2010. "Giacomo, Notar." In *Encyclopedia of the Medieval Chronicle.* R. G. Dunphy, ed. Boston: Brill, 704.
—. 2012. *Scrivere la storia a Napoli tra Medioevo e prima età moderna: Tre studi.* Rome: Salerno.
—. 2013. With Francesco Montuori. "Copia, riuso e rimaneggiamento

della Quarta Parte della *Cronaca di Partenope* tra Quattro e Cinquecento." In *Actas del XXVI Congreso Internacional de Lingüística y Filología Románica: Valencia 2010*. Emili Casanova and Cesáreo Calvo, ed. Berlin: De Gruyter, 89–102.

—. 2014. "Spazi comunicativi, tradizioni narrative e storiografia in volgare: Il Regno negli anni delle guerre d'Italia." *Filologia Critica* 39:39–72.

—. 2016. With Francesco Senatore. "Orality, Literacy, and Historiography in Neapolitan Vernacular Urban Chronicles of the Fifteenth and Sixteenth Centuries." In *Interactions Between Orality and Writing in Early Modern Italian Culture*. Luca Degl'Innocenti et al., ed. London: Routledge, 129–43.

Delle Donne, Fulvio. 2012. "Facio, Bartolomeo." In *Encyclopedia of the Medieval Chronicle*. Leiden: Brill. At http://dx.doi.org/10.1163/2213-2139_emc_SIM_00985.

—. 2015.2. *Alfonso il Magnanimo e l'invenzione dell'umanesimo monarchico: Ideologia e strategie di legittimazione alla corte aragonese di Napoli*. Rome: ISIME.

—. 2016. "Il re e i suoi cronisti: Reinterpretazioni della storiografia alla corte aragonese di Napoli." *Humanistica* 11 (n.s. 5) 1–2:17–34.

De Nichilo, Mauro. 1991. "De Rosa, Loise." DBI 39:171–4. At www.treccani.it/enciclopedia/loise-de-rosa_(Dizionario-Biografico).

De Rosa, Loise. 1971. *Napoli aragonese nei ricordi di Loise De Rosa: Edizione del ms. parigino 913 con glossario e indici*. Antonio Altamura, ed. Naples: Libreria scientifica.

—. 1998. *Ricordi: Edizione critica del Ms. Ital. 913 della Bibliothèque Nationale de France*. Vittorio Formentin, ed. Rome: Salerno.

Dooley, Brendan M. 2010. *The Dissemination of News and the Emergence of Contemporaneity in Early Modern Europe*. Farnham-Burlington: Ashgate.

Facio, Bartolomeo. 1978. *Invective in Laurentium Vallam: Critical Edition*. Ennio I. Rao, ed. Naples: Società Editrice Napoletana.

—. 2004. *Rerum gestarum Alfonsi regis libri: Testo latino, traduzione italiana, commento e introduzione*. Daniela Pietragalla, ed. Alessandria: Edizioni dell'Orso.

Ferraiolo. 1956. *Una cronaca napoletana figurata del Quattrocento*. Riccardo Filangieri di Candida, ed. Naples: L'Arte tipografica.

—. 1987. *Cronaca*. Rosario Coluccia, ed. Florence: Accademia della Crusca.

Figliuolo, Bruno. 2015. "Pontano Giovanni." DBI 84. At www.treccani.it/enciclopedia/giovanni-pontano_(Dizionario-Biografico).

Finzi, Claudio. 2004. *Re, baroni, popolo: La politica di Giovanni Pontano*. Rimini: Il Cerchio.

Foà, Simona. 2007. "Manetti, Giannozzo." DBI 68. At www.treccani.it/enciclopedia/giannozzo-manetti_(Dizionario-Biografico).

Fois, Mario. 1969. *Il pensiero cristiano di Lorenzo Valla nel quadro storico-culturale del suo ambiente*. Rome: Libreria Editrice dell'Università Gregoriana.

Fubini, Ricardo. 1968. "Biondo Flavio." DBI 10:536–59. At www.treccani.it/enciclopedia/biondo-flavio_(Dizionario-Biografico).

Furstenberg-Levi, Shulamit. 2016. *The Accademia Pontaniana: A Model of a Humanist Network*. Leiden: Brill.

Gentile, Salvatore. 1961. *Postille ad una recente edizione di testi narrativi napoletani del '400*. Naples: Liguori.

Giannetti, Anna. 2017. "Urban Design and Public Spaces." In Hall–Willette, 46–100.

Ginzburg, Carlo. 2009. "Pontano, Machiavelli and Prudence: Some Further Reflections." In *From Florence to the Mediterranean and Beyond: Essays in Honour of Anthony Mohlo.* Diogo Ramada Curto and Niki Koniordos, ed. 2 vols. Florence: Olschki, 1:117–25.

Haan, Annet den. 2016. *Giannozzo Manetti's New Testament: Translation Theory and Practice in Fifteenth-Century Italy.* Leiden: Brill.

Hankins, James. 1995. "The 'Baron Thesis' after Forty Years, and Some Recent Studies of Leonardo Bruni." *Journal of the History of Ideas* 56:309–38.

—. 1997. *Repertorium Brunianum: A Critical Guide to the Writings of Leonardo Bruni.* Rome: ISIME.

Hay, Denys. 1958. "Flavio Biondo and the Middle Ages." *Proceedings of the British Academy* 45:97–125.

—. 2007. "Challenging Chronicles: Leonardo Bruni's *History of the Florentine People.*" In Dale (2007), 249–72.

Ianziti, Gary. 2010. *Writing History in Renaissance Italy: Leonardo Bruni and the Uses of the Past.* Cambridge, MA: Harvard University Press.

—. 2016. "Leonardo Bruni and the Rise of Official Historiography in Renaissance Florence." In *Studies on Florence and the Italian Renaissance in Honour of F.W. Kent.* Peter Howard and Cecilia Hewlett, ed. Turnhout: Brepols, 431–48.

Izbicki, Thomas M. 1993. "Lorenzo Valla: The Scholarship in English through 1992." In *Humanity and Divinity in Renaissance and Reformation: Essays in Honor of Charles Trinkaus.* John W. O'Malley et al., ed. Leiden: Brill, 287–301.

Janik, Linda Gardiner. 1973. "Lorenzo Valla: The Primacy of Rhetoric and the Demoralization of History." *History and Theory* 12:389–404.

Johns, Adrian. 1998. *The Nature of the Book: Print and Knowledge in the Making.* Chicago: University of Chicago Press.

Kahn, Victoria Ann. 1983. *Giovanni Pontano's Rhetoric of Prudence.* University Park: Pennsylvania State University Press.

Kallendorf, Craig. 2011. "Lorenzo Valla." In *Oxford Bibliographies Online.* New York: Oxford University Press. At http://oxfordbibliographiesonline.com/view/document/obo-9780195399301/obo-9780195399301-0129.xml.

—. 2014. "Giannozzo Manetti." In *Oxford Bibliographies Online.* New York: Oxford University Press. At http://dx.doi.org/10.1093/OBO/9780195399301-0091http://dx.doi.org/10.1093/OBO/9780195399301-0091.

Kraye, Jill. 1996. "Facio, Bartolomeo." *Grove Art Online.* New York: Oxford University Press. At www.oxfordartonline.com/subscriber/article/grove/art/T027321.

Kristeller, Paul Oskar. 1965. *The Humanist Bartolomeo Facio and His Unknown Correspondence.* New York: Random House.

Lorch, Maristella de Panizza. 1985. *A Defense of Life: Lorenzo Valla's Theory of Pleasure.* Munich: Fink.

Manetti, Giannozzo. 1979. *Vita Socratis et Senecae.* Alfonso De Petris, ed. Florence: Olschki.

—. 2014. *Storia di Pistoia.* Stefano Ugo Baldassarri and William J. Connell, ed. Alessandria: Edizioni dell'Orso.

Mazzocco, Angelo. 2016. With Marc Laureys, ed. *A New Sense of the Past: The Scholarship of Biondo Flavio (1392–1463).* Leuven: Leuven University Press.

—. 2016.a. "Introduction." In Mazzocco-Laureys (2016), 9–34.
Nichols, Charlotte 2019. With James H. Mc Gregor, ed. *Renaissance Naples: A Documentary History, 1400–1600*. New York: Italica Press.
Notar Giacomo. 1845. *Cronica di Napoli*. Paolo Garzilli, ed. Naples: Stamperia reale.
—. 2006. "La *Cronica di Napoli* di Notar Giacomo: Edizione critica del ms. brancacciano II F 6 della Biblioteca Nazionale di Napoli." Chiara De Caprio, ed. Ph.D. diss., University of Naples.
Pellegrino, Nicoletta. 2007. "From the Roman Empire to Christian Imperialism: The Work of Flavio Biondo." In Dale (2007), 273–98.
Petrucci, Armando. 1985. "La scrittura del testo." In *Letteratura Italiana*. 4. *L'Interpretazione*. Alberto Asor Rosa, ed. Turin: Einaudi, 283–308.
Pettitt, Thomas. 2012. "Bracketing the Gutenberg Parenthesis." *Explorations in Media Ecology* 11.2:95–114.
Pignatti, Franco. 1996. "Ferraiolo." DBI 46. At www.treccani.it/enciclopedia/ferraiolo_(Dizionario-Biografico).
Pontano, Giovanni. 1996. *La "guerra d'Ischia" nel "De bello Neapolitano."* Antonietta Iacono, ed. Naples: Accademia Pontaniana.
—. 1999. *I libri delle virtù sociali*. Francesco Tateo, ed. Rome: Bulzoni.
—. 2003. *De principe*. Guido M. Cappelli, ed. Rome: Salerno.
—. 2006. *Baiae*. Rodney G. Dennis, ed. Cambridge, MA: Harvard University Press.
—. 2012. *Dialogues*. Julia Haig Gaisser, ed. Cambridge, MA: Harvard University Press.
—. 2021. *La guerra nel regno di Napoli di Giovanni Pontano*. Francesco Tateo, ed. and trans. Rome: Roma nel Rinascimento.
Pontari, Paolo. 2016. "'Nedum mille qui effluxerunt annorum gesta sciamus'. L'Italia di Biondo e l'invenzione' del Medioevo." In Mazzocco–Laureys (2016), 151–76.
Rabil, Albert, Jr. 1988. "The Significance of 'Civic Humanism' in the Interpretation of the Italian Renaissance." In idem, *Renaissance Humanism*. 3 vols. Philadelphia: University of Pennsylvania Press, 1:141–74.
Rao, Ennio I. 1981. *The Invectives of Bartolomeo Facio Against Lorenzo Valla: A Contribution to the History of Italian Humanism*. Ann Arbor: University Microfilms.
Resta, Gianvito. 1970. "Beccadelli, Antonio, detto il Panormita." DBI 7. At www.treccani.it/enciclopedia/beccadelli-antonio-detto-il-panormita_(Dizionario Biografico).
Rizzi, Andrea. 2017. *Vernacular Translators in Quattrocento Italy: Scribal Culture, Authority, and Agency*. Turnhout: Brepols.
Roick, Matthias. 2017. *Pontano's Virtues: Aristotelian Moral and Political Thought in the Renaissance*. London: Bloomsbury Academic.
Rossi, Marielisa. 2007. "Bibliografia degli scritti su Lorenzo Valla." In *Lorenzo Valla: Edizioni delle opere (sec. XV–XVI)*. Marielisa Rossi, ed. Rome: Vecchiarelli, 176–206.
Ryder, Alan Frederick Charles. 1976. "Antonio Beccadelli: A Humanist in Government." In *Cultural Aspects of the Italian Renaissance: Essays in Honour of Paul Oskar Kristeller*. Cecil H. Clough, ed. Manchester: Manchester University Press, 123–40.

Sabia, Liliana Monti. 1980. "L'estremo autografo di Giovanni Pontano." *Italia medioevale e umanistica* 23:293–314.

—. 1995. *Pontano e la storia: Dal* De bello Neapolitano *all'*Actius. Rome: Bulzoni.

Senatore, Francesco. 2012. "The Kingdom of Naples." In *The Italian Renaissance State*. Andrea Gamberini and Isabella Lazzarini, ed. New York: Cambridge University Press, 30–49.

—. 2017. "Cronaca e cancellerie." In Francesconi–Miglio, 285–99.

Setz, Wolfram. 1975. *Lorenzo Vallas Schrift gegen die konstantinische Schenkung: De falso credita et ementita Constantini donatione: Zur Interpretation und Wirkungsgeschichte.* Tübingen: Niemeyer.

Siegel, Jerrold E. 1966. "'Civic Humanism' or Ciceronian Rhetoric? The Culture of Petrarch and Bruni." *Past and Present* 34:3–48.

Smith, Bonnie G. 2001. *The Gender of History: Men, Women, and Historical Practice*. Cambridge: Harvard University Press.

Trinkaus, Charles Edward. 1985. *The Astrological Cosmos and Rhetorical Culture of Giovanni Gioviano Pontano*. New York: Renaissance Society of America.

Valla, Lorenzo. 1948. "*De libero arbitrio,* trans. as *The Dialogue on Free Will.*" In *The Renaissance Philosophy of Man*. Charles Trinkaus and Ernst Cassirer, ed. Chicago: University of Chicago Press, 145–82.

—. 1970.1. *Collatio Novi Testamenti*. Alessandro Perosa, ed. Florence: Sansoni.

—. 1970.2. *De vero falsoque bono*. Maristella de Panizza Lorch, ed. Bari: Adriatica.

—. 1973. *Laurentii Valle Gesta Ferdinandi regis Aragonum*. Ottavio Besomi, ed. Padua: Antenore.

—. 1981. *Laurentii Valle Antidotum in Facium*. Mariangela Regoliosi, ed. Padua: Antenore.

—. 1985. *The Profession of the Religious*. Olga Z. Pugliese, trans. Toronto: University of Toronto Press.

—. 1993. *The Treatise of Lorenzo Valla on the Donation of Constantine*. Christopher B. Coleman, ed. and trans. Toronto: University of Toronto Press.

—. 2007. *On the Donation of Constantine*. G.W. Bowerstock, ed. and trans. Cambridge, MA: Harvard University Press.

—. 2012. *Dialectical Disputations*. Brian P. Copenhaver and Lodi Nauta, ed. and trans. 2 vols. Cambridge, MA: Harvard University Press.

Vasoli, Cesare. 1972. "Bruni, Leonardo." DBI 14:618–33. At www.treccani.it/enciclopedia/bruni-leonardo-detto-leonardo-aretino_(Dizionario-Biografico).

Viti, Paolo. 1994. "Facio, Bartolomeo." DBI 44. At www.treccani.it/enciclopedia/bartolomeo-facio_(Dizionario-Biografico).

Wilcox, Donald J. 1985. "The Sense of Time in Western Historical Narratives from Eusebius to Machiavelli." In Breisach, 167–237.

Wittschier, Heinz Willi. 1968. *Gianozzo Manetti, das corpus der Orationes*. Cologne: Bohlau.

10. CONCLUSIONS

This book has invited readers to consider the writers and forms of history-writing of the trecento that helped shape our modern perceptions of the Italian Mezzogiorno. These perceptions include both popular ideas about the South of Italy encountered in almost daily reportage and in more scholarly discourse around culture and its representations. This book has attempted to synthesize both synchronic issues — the differences or similarities between the historiography produced within the Regno and that of the North of Italy and the rest of Europe — and diachronic issues, including contrasts and similarities with humanist historiography of the quattrocento. These comparisons and contrasts have allowed us to distinguish many key characteristics of trecento writing.

Except for the comparative Chapter 9, we have limited the scope of our study strictly to fourteenth-century writers and to those who focused on the historical figures and events of the mainland Mezzogiorno. We have excluded prominent historical writers of the duecento and those who focused on Sicily, the long-severed member of the original Regno. This focus has allowed us to examine in detail a variety of issues from numerous methodological approaches that we hope have provided readers with a more clear understanding of these writers and their works. We have discussed social backgrounds, educations, professions, skills, historical works and their sources, subject matter and scope, language, style, narrative forms and structures, influences, interests, themes, audience and reception. For the most part, these have been covered in Chapters 1 through 4.

Chapters 5 and 6 have discussed the influences of literature and the visual arts on the construction of historical narratives. These chapters have delineated the porous boundaries between the *fabula* and *historia* and between the visual and the verbal. Both chapters underscore the flexibility of trecento historiography in its sources and its means of emplotment, character development and narrative construction.

Chapters 7 and 8 applied these insights to specific case studies in order to test our findings. Chapter 7 developed around several key incidents that involve what I have termed "rituals of punishment" and "prison dialogues" and examined trecento criteria for verisimilitude and the reliability of oral and first-hand witness testimony. Chapter 8 traced the development of what we have termed the "black legend of the Angevins" and deployed a variety of methods from feminist critique and the study of queenship to recent work on reputation and infamy, the metaphorical doublings offered by nature imagery and female embodiment for the fate of a dynasty and a kingdom.

Chapter 9 concluded with contrasts. Beginning with the consensus view of Renaissance historiography, it offered a survey of the humanists at the Aragonese court. These deployed classical models and language to describe and analyze the lives and actions of princes and the role of virtue and vice in the face of *fortuna* and other historical contingency. It then turned to the continuing tradition of urban, civic chroniclers who wrote mostly in the vernacular and constructed their works as more open-ended, ongoing narratives of life in particular communities impacted both by the grand events of the quattrocento and by the perceptions and voices of the streets and neighborhoods of Naples.

Chapters 1 through 8 dealt with the synchronic issue of comparing the writers of the Regno with their northern counterparts. By contrast, Chapter 9 addressed the diachronic issue of trecento historiography both in comparison to earlier medieval traditions and to the humanist writing of the quattrocento. It attempted to demonstrate that the writers of the Mezzogiorno shared much with northern writers and that the issues and outlook of trecento historiography differed from "Renaissance" historiography in several ways. These differences revolved around the humanists' re-embrace of the classical Latin style and language and a new philological understanding of the distant past.

If one defines Renaissance humanism as formed around such stylistics and methods, divorced from larger social, cultural and political contexts, one can see a distinct break from trecento historiography c. 1450. If, however, one defines quattrocento historiography and its attendant humanism as the embrace of the classics as a means of understanding and fostering both civic life and individual virtues, then there appears less to differentiate the two historiographies. As the previous chapters have shown, even that most revered category of humanist historiography, its sense of the past, has been pushed backward into the trecento and earlier medieval writing.[1]

Should we perhaps attempt to resolve one of these issues by following current trends to eliminate the term "Renaissance" from our discussion, focusing instead on "early modern"? As useful, and as focused on continuities and discontinuities as this is, it elides a basic fact of quattrocento historiography itself: that humanist writers — whether or not accurately — saw themselves essentially and intrinsically as breaking with their late medieval pasts and reviving the achievements of antiquity.

CHAPTER 10 ⚜ CONCLUSIONS

This also elides the fact that we now live and think well past the impulse of either "Renaissance" or "modern," and that the debates generated in all fields of the humanities by the post-modern have altered our notions of *historia* and *fabula*, of scientific and rhetorical writing. Whatever our framing terminology, one could still assert that quattrocento historiography on its most official levels, as expressed by the Neapolitan humanists, was in many regards a distinct break from that of the trecento. But this may no longer be the most valid criterion for judging such work. A statement that an author "wrote in the style and spirit of the ancients" and that "these are the deeds of famous men" will be met with indifference by the vast majority of even educated people today. For it is not the humanist writing of the quattrocento and its "fixed" editions in the "Gutenberg parenthesis" but the trecento tradition of medieval historiography that is, ironically, bringing new life to historical studies in the age of the digital.[2]

As Francesco Senatore has noted,[3] with the digital turn these studies have moved away from analyses of individuals and their impact on institutions and toward a "culture of information" and its modes of transmission. Trecento historiography shares this porosity to influence, addition and emendation, these broad-based interests and diverse audiences, these open-ended methodologies and multivalent sources, and this understanding of the text as a multipolar and multimedia process and not the final, fixed product of exchange and prestige that it was for quattrocento humanists. In this sense, trecento historiography presages both the condition of the twenty-first century and the deep continuities of cultural and intellectual life, of human agency and its limitations that continue to shape and inform history.

More broadly, humanist historiography's focus on the political and ethical — inherited by Ranke and the "empiricist" school of the nineteenth century — has been replaced by recent historiography's embrace of the natural world, of events, peoples and historical sources that reflect the patterns and structures of everyday life, of the cycles, representations and rituals of the body and gender, of symbol and performance of the body cultural and civic, of economic, religious and other belief systems, of classes and groups long outside the scope and view of humanist writing. In this, current historiography resembles and returns to the broad web of connectedness among peoples and between peoples and the natural world encompassed by trecento writers.[4]

What precisely these trends mean has not yet been fully settled and will remain a matter of some speculation as long as history writing remains a humanistic endeavor and as long as history itself is seen as useful for our civic lives and characters and as necessary in informing and helping mold our present and future.

⚜

NOTES
1. See Kempshall, 503–4.
2. See the introduction to Gardiner–Musto (2015), 1–13.
3. Senatore (2017), 296–99, also drawing on the work of Isabella Lazzarini.
4. On the old and new historiography and the distinct web-like quality of non-humanist writing, see Smith (2001); Gardiner–Musto (2015), 135–39.

CHRONOLOGY

This chronology provides the dates of significant persons and events in order to set the context for the historians, artists, and political figures discussed in the text. Birth years are provided for individuals. Approximate dates are marked in *italics*. Death dates are indicated by "d.," marriages by "m.," abdications by "ab." Papal dates are those of their election and death.

1250. Frederick II Hohenstaufen (d. Dec. 13)
1255. Angelo Clareno, OFM (d. June 15, 1337)
1264. Francesco da Barberino (d. 1348)
1265. Clement IV, pope (d. Nov. 29, 1268)
    Charles I of Anjou crowned king of Naples (d. Jan. 7, 1285)
1265. Dante Alighièri (d. 13/14 Sept. 1321)
1266. Battle of Benevento (Feb. 26)
1267. Giotto di Bondone (d. Jan. 8, 1337)
1280. Giovanni Villani (d. 1348)
1282. Sicilian Vespers (Mar. 30–April 28)
1285. Giovanni da Bazzano (d. 1363)
1285. Charles II of Anjou, king (d. May 5, 1309)
1286. Sancia of Majorca (d. July 28, 1345)
1294. Buccio di Ranallo (d. 1363)
1295. Boniface VIII, pope (d. Oct. 11, 1303)
1300. Domenico da Gravina (d. 1351)
    Agnolo di Tura.
    Johanns von Winterthur (d. 1348)
1303. Benedict XI, pope (d. July 7, 1304)
1304. Francesco Petrarch (d. July 18/19, 1374)
1305. Elizabeth of Poland, queen of Hungary (d. Dec. 26, 1380)
    Clement V, pope (d. April 20, 1314)
1309. Robert of Anjou, king (d. Jan. 20, 1343)
1310. Nicolò Acciaiuoli (d. Nov. 8, 1365)
1313. Cola di Rienzo (d. Oct. 8, 1354)
1313. Giovanni Boccaccio (d. Dec. 21, 1375)
1316. John XXII, pope (d. Dec. 4, 1334)

1318. Anonimo romano (d. October 1360)
1319. Ambrogio Lorenzetti (d. *1348*)
1325. Filippo Villani (d. *1407*)
1326. Giovanna I of Anjou (b. January)
1328. Charles of Calabria d. (Nov. 9)
1330. Angelo Crassullo
1335. Benedict XII, pope (d. April 25, 1342)
1337. Hundred Years War begins
    Jean Froissart (d. *1404*)
1340. Battle of Rio Salado (Oct. 30)
    Thomas Walsingham (d. *1422*)
1341. Petrarch crowned poet laureate in Rome (April 8)
1342. Clement VI, pope (d. Dec. 6. 1352)
    Giovanna I m. Prince Andrew of Hungary (Aug. 27)
1343. Smyrna Crusades (1351)
    Giovanna I, queen (Jan. 20)
    Cola di Rienzo in Roman embassy to Avignon (Jan. 27)
    Duke of Athens overthrown in Florence (July 26)
1345. Murder of Andrew of Hungary (Sept. 18)
1346. Battle of Crécy (Aug. 26)
1347. Lewis of Hungary invades Regno
    Cola di Rienzo establishes *buono stato* in Rome (May 20)
    Battle of Porta San Lorenzo (Nov. 20)
    Cola di Rienzo ab. (Dec. 13/14)
1348. Giovanna I sells Avignon to Pope Clement VI (July 23)
    Black Death
1349. Civil war in Apulia
1352. Giovanna I m. Louis of Taranto (May 23)
    Innocent VI, pope (d. Sept. 12, 1362)
1354. Rienzo returns to Rome (Aug. 1)
    Rienzo murdered on Capitoline (Oct. 8)
1356. Battle of Poitiers (Sept. 19)
1362. Louis of Taranto d. (June 5)
    Urban V, pope (d. Dec. 19, 1370)
1363. Giovanna I m. Jaime IV of Majorca
    Matteo Villani d.

CHRONOLOGY

1370. Leonardo Bruni (d. Mar. 9, 1444)
1371. Gregory XI, pope (d. Mar. 27, 1378)
1375. Giovanna I m. Otto of Brunswick
1378. Urban VI, pope (d. Oct. 15, 1389)
   Great Schism (ends 1417)
1381. Charles III of Durazzo, king (d. Feb. 24, 1386)
   Peasants' Revolt in England
1382. Giovanna I d.
1385. Loise de Rosa (d.*1475*)
1386. Margaret of Durazzo, queen regent (d. Aug. 6, 1412)
1389. Boniface IX, pope (d. Oct. 1, 1404)
1392. Flavio Biondo (d. June 4, 1463)
1393. Ladislaus of Durazzo, king (d. Aug. 6, 1414)
1394. Antonio Beccadelli (Panormita) (d. Jan. 19, 1471)
1396. Giannozzo Manetti (d. Oct. 27, 1459)
1404. Innocent VII, pope (d. Nov. 6, 1406)
1405. Bartolomeo Facio (d. Nov. 1457)
1406. Matteo Palmieri (d. April 13, 1475)
   Gregory XII, pope (d. July 4, 1415)
1407. Lorenzo Valla (d. Aug. 1, 1457)
1414. Giovanna II, queen (d. Feb. 2, 1435)
1417. Martin V, pope (d. Feb. 20, 1431)
1426. Giovanni Pontano (d. Sept. 1503)
1431. Eugenius IV, pope (d. Feb. 23, 1447)
1435. René of Anjou, king (d. July 10, 1480)
1442. Alfonso I, of Aragon, king (d. June 27, 1458)
1447. Nicholas V, pope (d. Mar. 24, 1455)
1450. Ferraiolo (d. c.1498)
1453. Hundred Years War ends
   Fall of Constantinople (April. 6)
1455. Calixtus III, pope (d. Aug. 6, 1458)
1458. Pius II, pope (d. Aug. 15, 1464)
   Ferrante I, king (d. Jan. 25, 1494)
1459. First Revolt of Barons
1464. Paul II, pope (d. July 26, 1471)
1471. Sixtus IV, pope (d. Aug. 12, 1484)

1474. Bartolomé de las Casas, OP (d. July 18, 1566)
1480. Turks capture Otranto (July 28)
1484. Innocent VIII, pope (d. July 25, 1492)
1485. Second Revolt (Conspiracy) of Barons
1492. Fall of Granada to Ferdinand and Isabella (Jan. 2)
　　　Alexander VI, pope (d. Aug. 18, 1503)
1494. Alfonso II, king (ab. Jan. 23, 1495)
1495. Ferrante II (ab. Sept. 7, 1496)
　　　Charles VIII of France conquers Naples.
1496. Frederick I, king (ab. Aug. 1, 1501)
1501. Louis XII of France conquers Regno.
1504. Ferdinand the Catholic of Spain conquers Regno.
1511. Notar Giacomo d.

BIBLIOGRAPHY

MANUSCRIPT & ARCHIVAL MATERIALS

Archivio della Latinità Italiana del Medioevo, at http://alim.dfll.univr.it.
Berlin. Staatliche Museen, MS 78 E 3
Besançon. Bibliothèque Municipale, MS 865
Florence. Biblioteca Medicea Laurenziana, MS Strozzi 174
Florence. Biblioteca Nazionale Centrale, Banco Rari 38.
Leuven. Maurits Sabbe Library, MS 1
London. British Library, MS Add 12228
—. MS Royal 6.E.IX
—. MS Royal 16.G.VI
Naples. Biblioteca Nazionale Vittorio Emmanuele III, MS Brancacciano II.F.6
New York. Morgan Library, MS 801
Paris. Bibliothèque Nationale de France, MS Français 599
—. MS Français 1463
—. MS Français 4274
Vatican. Biblioteca Apostolica Vaticana, MS Chigi L.VIII.296
—. MS Pal. Lat. 939
—. MS Reg. Lat. 1501
—. MS Vat. Barb. 4076
—. MS Vat. Barb. 4077
Venice, Biblioteca Nazionale Marciana, MS IX 227
—. MS Fr. XV
Vienna, Österreichische Nationalbibliothek, MS Cod. 1921
—. MS Series Nova 2639

PRIMARY SOURCES

Anonimo romano. 1928. *La Vita di Cola di Rienzo*. Alberto M. Ghisalberti, ed. Florence: Olschki.
—. 1975. *The Life of Cola di Rienzo*. John Wright, ed. and trans. Toronto: Pontifical Institute of Mediaeval Studies.
—. 1979. *Cronica*. Giuseppe Porta, ed. Milan: Adelphi.
—. 1999. *Anonimo Romano. Cronica: Vita di Cola di Rienzo*. Ettore Mazzali, ed. Milan: Rizzoli.
—. 2021. *The Chronicle of an Anonymous Roman: Rome, Italy, and Latin Christendom, c.1325–1360*. James A. Palmer, ed. and trans. New York: Italica Press.
Bacco, Enrico. 1991. With C. d'Engenio Caracciolo. *Naples: An Early Guide*. Eileen Gardiner, ed. and trans. Introductions by Caroline Bruzelius and Ronald G. Musto. New York: Italica Press.

Barberino, Francesco da. 2006. *I documenti d'amore di Francesco da Barberino secondo i mss. originali*. 4 vols. Francesco Egidi, ed. Rome: Società Filologica Romana, 1905–27. Repr. Milan: Archè.

—. 2008. *I documenti d'amore. Documenta amoris*. 2 vols. Marco Albertazzi, ed. Lavis: La finestra.

Bazzano, Giovanni da. 1917. *Chronicon Mutinense AA. 1188–1363*. Tommaso Casini, ed. RIS 15:551–634.

Beaumanoir, Philippe de Remi. 1988. *La Manekine: Text, Translation, Commentary*. Irene Gnarra, ed. and trans. New York: Garland.

—. 1999. *Le roman de la Manekine*. Barbara Nelson Sargent-Baur et al., ed. Amsterdam: Rodopi.

—. 2010. *Manekine, John and Blonde, and "Foolish Generosity."* Barbara Nelson Sargent-Baur, ed. University Park: Pennsylvania State University Press.

—. 2010.1. *La Manequine*. Maria Colombo Timelli, ed. Paris: Garnier.

Beccadelli, Antonio (Panormita). 1968. *Antonii Panhormitae liber rerum gestarum Fernandi regis*. Gianvito Resta, ed. Palermo: Centro di studi filologici e linguistici siciliani.

—. 1990. *De dictis et factis Alfonsi regis*. M. Vilallonga, ed. Barcelona: Barcono.

—. 2021. *Alfonsi regis Triumphus: Il Trionfo di re Alfonso. Introduzione, edizione, traduzione*. Fulvio Delle Donne, ed. Potenza: Basilicata University Press.

Biondo, Flavio. 1542. *Roma ristaurata et Italia illustrata di Biondo*. Lucio Fauno, ed. Venice: Tramezzino.

—. 2005. *Italy Illuminated* 1. Jeffrey A. White, ed. and trans. Cambridge, MA: Harvard University Press.

—. 2016.1. *Rome in Triumph*. Maria Agata Pincelli and Frances Muecke, ed. and trans. Cambridge, MA: Harvard University Press.

—. 2016.2. *Italy Illuminated* 2. Jeffrey A. White, ed. and trans. Cambridge, MA: Harvard University Press.

Boccaccio, Giovanni. 1949. Letter 2. "Neapolitan." In *Testi Napoletani dei secoli XIII e XIV.* Antonio Altamura, ed. Naples: Libreria Perrella, 143–47.

—. 1983. *De casibus virorum illustrium*. Pier Giorgio Ricci and Vittorio Zaccaria, ed. Milan: Mondadori.

—. 1983.2. Letter 2. "Neapolitan." "Prospettive sul parlato nella storia linguistica italiana, con una lettura dell'Epistola napoletana del Boccaccio." In *Italia Linguistica: Idee, Storia, Strutture*. Francesco Sabatini, ed. Bologna: Il Mulino, 167–201.

—. 1987. *Eclogues*. Janet Levarie Smarr, trans. New York: Garland.

—. 1992. *Rime, Carmina, Epistole e Lettere, Vite, De Canaria*. In *Tutte le opere* 5.1. Vittore Branca et al., ed. Milan: Mondadori.

—. 1992a. *Epistole e lettere*. Ginetta Auzzas, ed. In Boccaccio (1992).

—. 2003. *Famous Women*. Virginia Brown, ed. and trans. Cambridge, MA: Harvard University Press.

—. 2011. *On Famous Women*. Guido A. Guarino, ed. and trans. New York: Italica Press.

BIBLIOGRAPHY

—. 2018. *The Downfall of the Famous*. Louis Brewer Hall, ed. and trans. Rev. ed. New York: Italica Press.
Buccio di Ranallo. 1907. *Cronaca aquilana rimata di Buccio di Ranallo di Popplito di Aquila*. Vincenzo De Bartholomaeis, ed. Rome: Forzani.
—. 1969. *Poemetti sacri dei secoli XIV e XV.* Erasmo Pèrcopo, ed. Bologna: Commissione per i testi di lingua.
—. 2008. *Cronica*. Carlo De Matteis, ed. Florence: SISMEL-Edizioni del Galluzzo.
Cerasoli, Francesco. 1896–97. "Clemente VI e Giovanna I di Napoli: Documenti inediti dell'Archivio Vaticano (1343–1352)." ASPN 21:3–41; 227–64, 427–75, 667–707; 22:3–46.
Chronicon Estense. 1908. RIS 15.3, fasc. 1–2.
—. 1937. *Chronicon Estense cum additamentis usque ad annum 1478*. G. Bertino, ed. RIS 15.3, fasc. 1–2.
Chronicon Suessanum. In Pelliccia, 1:51–78.
Clareno, Angelo. 1959. *Chronicon seu Historia septem tribulationum ordinis minorum*. Alberto Ghinato, ed. Rome: Pontificia Ateneo Antoniano.
—. 1983. *The Chronicle or History of the Seven Tribulations of the Order of Friars Minor.* Mary Bartholomew McDonald, OSF and George Marcil, OFM, trans. St. Bonaventure: Franciscan Institute.
—. 1998. *Liber chronicorum sive tribulationum ordinis minorum*. Giovanni Boccali, OFM and Felice Accrocca, ed. Marino Bigaroni, OFM, Italian trans. Assisi: Edizioni Porziuncula.
—. 1999. *Historia septem tribulationum Ordinis minorum*. Orietta Rossini and Hanno Helbling, ed. Rome: ISIME.
—. 2005. *A Chronicle or History of the Seven Tribulations of the Order of Brothers Minor.* David Burr and E.R. Daniel, ed. and trans. St. Bonaventure, NY: Franciscan Institute.
Crassullo, Angelo. *Annales de rebus tarentinis*. In Pelliccia, 5:111–25.
Cronaca di Partenope: An Introduction to and Critical Edition of the First Vernacular History of Naples (c.1350). 2011. Samantha Kelly, ed. Leiden: Brill.
Cronaca Senese. Andrea Dei and Agnolo di Tura del Grasso. RIS 15.6:253–94.
Da Bisticci, Vespasiano. 1963, 1997. *Renaissance Princes, Popes, and Prelates.* W.G. Waters and Emily Waters, ed. New York: Harper & Row. Repr., *The Vespasiano Memoirs: Lives of Illustrious Men of the XVth Century.* Toronto: University of Toronto Press.
D'Arras, Jean. 1932. *Melusine: Roman du XIVe siècle.* Louis Stouff, ed. Dijon: Université de Dijon.
—. 2003. *Melusine: Ou, La noble histoire de Lusignan: Roman de XIVe siècle.* Jean-Jacques Vincensini, ed. Paris: Librarie Générale Française.
—. 2012. *Melusine, Or the Noble History of Lusignan*. Donald Maddox and Sara Sturm-Maddox, ed. and trans. University Park: Pennsylvania State University Press.
De Blasiis, Giuseppe, ed. 1887. *Cronicon siculum incerti authoris ab anno 340 ad annum 1396 in forma diary [sic]: Ex inedito Codice ottoboniano vaticano*. Naples: Giannini.

De Cessolis, Jacobus. 2008. *The Book of Chess*. H.L. Williams, trans. New York: Italica Press.
Del Re, Giuseppe. 1868. *Cronisti e scrittori sincroni napoletani*. Naples: Iride.
De Rosa, Loise. 1971. *Napoli aragonese nei ricordi di Loise De Rosa: Edizione del ms. parigino 913 con glossario e indici*. Antonio Altamura, ed. Naples: Libreria scientifica.
—. 1998. *Ricordi: Edizione critica del Ms. Ital. 913 della Bibliothèque Nationale de France*. Vittorio Formentin, ed. Rome: Salerno.
Edizione nazionale dei testi della Storiografia umanistica. 2008. At www.ilritornodeiclassici.it/ensu/index.php?type=opera&op=fetch&id=478&lang=it.
Facio, Bartolomeo. 1978. *Invective in Laurentium Vallam: Critical Edition*. Ennio I. Rao, ed. Naples: Società Editrice Napoletana.
—. 2004. *Rerum gestarum Alfonsi regis libri: Testo latino, traduzione italiana, commento e introduzione*. Daniela Pietragalla, ed. Alessandria: Edizioni dell'Orso.
Ferraiolo. 1956. *Una cronaca napoletana figurata del Quattrocento*. Riccardo Filangieri di Candida, ed. Naples: L'Arte tipografica.
—. 1987. *Cronaca*. Rosario Coluccia, ed. Florence: Accademia della Crusca.
Froissart, Jean. 1901–03. *The Chronicle of Froissart*. John Bourchier Berners and W.P. Ker, ed. 6 vols. London: David Nutt. Repr. New York: AMS, 1967.
—. 1991. *Chroniques*. George T. Diller, ed. Geneva: Droz.
—. 2003–15. *Chroniques de Jean Froissart*. Nathalie Desgrugillers-Billard, ed. Clermont-Ferrand: Éditions Paléo.
—. 2013–. *The Online Froissart*. Peter Ainsworth and Godfried Croenen, ed. v. 1.5 (Sheffield: HRIOnline, 2013), www.hrionline.ac.uk/onlinefroissart/apparatus.jsp?type=intros&intro=f.intros.PFA-Froissart.
Gardiner, Eileen, ed. 1989. *Visions of Heaven and Hell Before Dante*. New York: Italica Press.
—. 1993. *Medieval Visions of Heaven and Hell: A Sourcebook*. New York: Garland.
Gravina, Domenico da. 1781. "Chronicon de rebus in Apulia gestis." In Pelliccia, 3:193–486.
—. 1890. *Chronicon e rebus in Apulia gestis*. Naples: E. Anfossi.
—. 1903. *Dominici de Gravina notarii Chronicon de rebus in Apulia gestis (aa. 1333–1350)*. RIS 12.3. Albano Sorbelli, ed. Città di Castello: S. Lapi.
—. 2022. *Chronicon de rebus in Apulia gestis*. Fulvio Delle Donne et al., ed. Florence: SISMEL-Edizioni del Galluzzo.
Guiron le courtois. 1966. *Guiron le Courtois: Étude de la tradition manuscrite et analyse critique*. Roger Lathuillère, ed. Geneva: Droz.
—. 2014. *Guiron le courtois: Roman arthurien en prose du xiiie siècle*. Venceslas Bubenicek, ed. Berlin: De Gruyter.
—. 2020–. *Il ciclo di Guiron le Courtois*. 7 vols. proj. Lino Leonardi and Richard Trachsler, ed. Florence: SISMEL–Edizioni del Galluzzo.
Jansen, Katherine L., ed. 2009. With Joanna Drell and Frances Andrews, ed. *Medieval Italy: Texts in Translation*. Philadelphia: University of Pennsylvania Press.
Maillart, Jean. 1998. *Le roman du comte d'Anjou*. Francine Mora-Lebrun, ed. Paris: Gallimard.
Malaspina, Saba, 1999. *Die Chronik des Saba Malaspina*. Hannover: Hahn.

Manetti, Giannozzo. 1979. *Vita Socratis et Senecae.* Alfonso De Petris, ed. Florence: Olschki.

—. 2014. *Storia di Pistoia.* Stefano Ugo Baldassarri and William J. Connell, ed. Alessandria: Edizioni dell'Orso.

Monaci, Ernesto. 1915. *Le miracole de Roma: Versione dei* Mirabilia Romae *in volgare romanesco del dugento.* Rome: Reale Società Romana di Storia Patria.

—. 1920. Storie de Troja et de Roma: *Altrimenti dette* Liber ystoriarum Romanorum: *Testo romanesco del secolo XIII, preceduto da un testo latino da cui deriva.* Roma: Società alla Biblioteca Vallicelliana.

Monteleone, Duca di. 1895. *Diurnali detti del Duca di Monteleone.* Nunzio Federico Faraglia, ed. Naples: Società Napoletana di Storia Patria.

—. 1958. *I Diurnali del Duca di Monteleone.* Michele Manfredi, ed. Bologna: Zanichelli.

—. 1960. *I Diurnali del Duca di Monteleone.* Giosuè Carducci and Michele Manfredi, ed. Bologna: Zanichelli.

Muratori, Ludovico Antonio, ed. 1723–51. *Rerum Italicarum Scriptores.* 25 vols. Milan: RIS, 5th ed. Giosuè Carducci and Vittorio Fiorini, ed. Bologna: Zanichelli, 1931–33.

Musto, Ronald G., ed. 2013. *Medieval Naples: A Documentary History, 400–1400.* New York: Italica Press.

Nichols, Charlotte. 2019. With James H. Mc Gregor, ed. *Renaissance Naples: A Documentary History, 1400–1600.* New York: Italica Press.

Notar Giacomo. 1845. *Cronica di Napoli.* Paolo Garzilli, ed. Naples: Stamperia reale.

Palmieri, Matteo. 1934. *Vita Nicolai Acciaioli.* Gino Scaramella, ed. RIS 13.2.

— 2001. *La vita di Niccolò Acciaioli.* Alessandra Mita Ferraro, ed. Bologna: Il Mulino.

Paris, Gaston. 1876–93. With Ulysse Robert, ed. *Miracles de Notre Dame par personages.* 8 vols. Paris: Société des Anciens Textes Français.

Pelliccia, Alessio A. 1780–81. *Raccolta di varie croniche, diarj, ed altri opuscoli cosi italiani, come latini appartenenti alla storia del regno di Napoli.* 5 vols. Naples: Perger.

Petrarch, Francesco. 1974. *Petrarch's Bucolicum Carmen.* Thomas Goddard Bergin, trans. New Haven: Yale University Press.

—. 1996. *The Revolution of Cola di Rienzo.* Mario Emilio Cosenza, ed. Ronald G. Musto, 3rd rev. ed. New York: Italica Press.

—. 2002. *Guide to the Holy Land: Itinerary to the Sepulcher of Our Lord Jesus Christ.* Theodore J. Cachey, Jr., ed. and trans. Notre Dame: University of Notre Dame Press.

—. 2004. *Le familiari: Familiarium rerum libri.* Vittorio Rossi and Umberto Bosco, Latin ed. Ugo Dotti and Felicita Audisio, Italian trans. 5 vols. Turin: N. Aragno.

—. 2004.1. *Le senili: Rerum senilium libri.* Elvira Nota, Latin ed. Ugo Dotti, Italian trans. 3 vols. Turin: N. Aragno.

—. 2005.1. *Letters of Old Age: Rerum senilium libri.* 2 vols. Aldo S. Bernardo et al., trans. New York: Italica Press.

—. 2005.2. *Letters on Familiar Matters: Rerum familiarium libri.* 3 vols. Aldo S. Bernardo, trans. New York: Italica Press.

Pontano, Giovanni. 1509. *Pontani De Sermone et De Bello Neapolitano*. Naples: Mayr.
—. 1996. *La "guerra d'Ischia" nel "De bello Neapolitano."* Antonietta Iacono, ed. Naples: Accademia Pontaniana.
—. 1999. *I libri delle virtù sociali*. Francesco Tateo, ed. Rome: Bulzoni.
—. 2003. *De principe*. Guido M. Cappelli, ed. Rome: Salerno.
—. 2006. *Baiae*. Rodney G. Dennis, ed. Cambridge, MA: Harvard University Press.
—. 2012. *Dialogues*. Julia Haig Gaisser, ed. Cambridge, MA: Harvard University Press.
—. 2021. *La guerra nel regno di Napoli di Giovanni Pontano*. Francesco Tateo, ed. and trans. Rome: Roma nel Rinascimento.
Rienzo, Cola di. 1913–29. *Die Briefwechel des Cola di Rienzo*. Konrad Burdach and Paul Piur, ed. In *Vom Mittelalter zur Reformation* 2.1–5. Berlin: Weidmann.
Rustichello da Pisa. 1994. *Il romanzo arturiano di Rustichello da Pisa*. Fabrizio Cigni and Valeria Bertolucci Pizzorusso, ed. Pisa: Pacini.
Spinelli, Matteo. 1874. *I Notamenti di Matteo Spinelli*. Camillo Minieri Riccio, ed. Naples: Rinaldi e Sellitro.
Valla, Lorenzo. 1948. "*De libero arbitrio*, trans. as The Dialogue on Free Will." In *The Renaissance Philosophy of Man*. Charles Trinkaus and Ernst Cassirer, ed. Chicago: University of Chicago Press, 145–82.
—. 1970.1. *Collatio Novi Testamenti*. Alessandro Perosa, ed. Florence: Sansoni.
—. 1970.2. *De vero falsoque bono*. Maristella de Panizza Lorch, ed. Bari: Adriatica.
—. 1973. *Laurentii Valle Gesta Ferdinandi regis Aragonum*. Ottavio Besomi, ed. Padua: Antenore.
—. 1981. *Laurentii Valle Antidotum in Facium*. Mariangela Regoliosi, ed. Padua: Antenore.
—. 1985. *The Profession of the Religious*. Olga Z. Pugliese, trans. Toronto: University of Toronto Press.
—. 1993. *The Treatise of Lorenzo Valla on the Donation of Constantine*. Christopher B. Coleman, ed. and trans. Toronto: University of Toronto Press.
—. 2007. *On the Donation of Constantine*. G.W. Bowerstock, ed. and trans. Cambridge, MA: Harvard University Press.
—. 2012. *Dialectical Disputations*. Brian P. Copenhaver and Lodi Nauta, ed. and trans., 2 vols. Cambridge, MA: Harvard University Press.
Villani, Giovanni. 1906. *Selections from the First Nine Books of the* Croniche Fiorentine. Rose E. Selfe, trans. Philip H. Wicksteed, ed. London: Constable.
— 1990–91. *Cronica Nuova*. Giuseppe Porta, ed. 3 vols. Parma: Guanda.
—. 2016. *The Final Book of Giovanni Villani's* New Chronicle. Matthew Sneider and Rala Diakite, ed. and trans. Kalamazoo: Medieval Institute.
Villani, Matteo, and Filippo Villani. 1995. *Cronica*. Giuseppe Porta, ed. 2 vols. Parma: Guanda.
Walsingham, Thomas. 1864. *Thomae Walsingham, quondam monachi S. Albani, historia anglicana*. Henry Thomas Riley, ed. London: Longman, Green.

—. 2003–11. *The St Albans Chronicle: The* Chronica Maiora *of Thomas Walsingham.* John Taylor et al., ed. and trans. 2 vols. Oxford: Clarendon.
—. 2005. *The Chronica Maiora of Thomas Walsingham, 1376–1422.* David Preest and James G. Clark, ed. Woodbridge: Boydell.
Wauquelin, Jean. 1913. *Belle Hélène de Constantinople: L'ystoire de Helayne.* J. van den Gheyn, ed. Brussels: Vroman.
—. 1995. *La Belle Hélène de Constantinople: Chanson de geste du XIVe siècle.* M. Claude Roussel, ed. Geneva: Droz.
—. 2002. La Belle Hélène de Constantinople: *Mise en prose d'une chanson de geste.* Marie-Claude de Crecy, ed. Geneva: Droz.
Webster, John. 2009. *The Duchess of Malfi.* London: Thompson.
Winterthur, Johanns von. 1866. *Die Chronik Johann's von Winterthur.* Bernard Freuler, ed. Winterthur: Ziegler.
—. 1982. *Die Chronik Johanns von Winterthur.* Friedrich Baethgen and C. Brun, ed. MGH n.s. 3. Berlin: Weidmann.

SECONDARY WORKS

Abbamonte, Giancarlo. 2015. "Naples, A Poet's City: Attitudes towards Statius and Virgil in the Fifteenth Century." In Hughes-Buongiovanni, 170–88.
Abulafia, David. 1979. "The Reputation of a Norman King in Angevin Naples." *Journal of Medieval History* 5.2:135–47.
—. 1997. *The Western Mediterranean Kingdoms 1200–1500: The Struggle for Dominion.* Harlow: Longman.
Aceto, Francesco. 1992. "Pittori e documenti della Napoli angioina: Aggiunte ed espunzioni." *Prospettiva* 67:53–65.
—. 2012. "Boccaccio e l'arte: La novella di Andreuccio da Perugia (*Decameron* II, 5) e il sepulcro di Filippo Minutolo." In BA, 289–302.
Adams, Tracy. 2012. "Between History and Fiction: Revisiting the Affaire de la Tour de Nesle." *Viator* 43.2:165–92.
Ainsworth, Peter F. 1990. *Jean Froissart and the Fabric of History: Truth, Myth, and Fiction in the* Chroniques. Oxford: Clarendon.
—. 2013. "Jean Froissart: Chronicler, Poet and Writer." In Froissart (2013).
—. 2003.1. "Contemporary and 'Eyewitness' History." In Deliyannis (2003), 249–76.
—. 2003.2. "Legendary History: *Historia* and *Fabula.*" In Deliyannis (2003), 387–416.
Airò, Anna. 2013. "*Italia, Italie, Italicae Gentes:* Particolarismi, varietà e tensioni all'unitas nella cronistica tardomedievale." In *Unità d'Italia e Istituto storico italiano: Quando la politica era anche tensione culturale.* Elisabetta Caldelli et al., ed. Roma: ISIME, 33–55.
Albanese, Gabriella. 1999. With Daniela Pietragalla. "*In honorem regis edidit:* Lo scrittoio di Bartolomeo Facio alla corte napoletana di Alfonso il Magnanimo." *Rinascimento* 39:293–336.
Alfano, Giancarlo, et al., ed. 2012. *Boccaccio angioino: Materiali per la storia culturale di Napoli nel trecento.* Brussels: Peter Lang.

Alfie, Fabian. 2014. "Love and Misogamy in the Age of Dante and Petrarch." In *Approaches to Teaching Petrarch's* Canzoniere *and the Petrarchan Tradition*. Christopher Kleinhenz and Andrea Dini, ed. New York: MLA.
Alfonso, Isabel. 2004. With Julio Escalona and Hugh Kennedy, ed. *Building Legitimacy: Political Discourses and Forms of Legitimacy in Medieval Societies*. Leiden: Brill.
Allaire, Gloria F. 2014. With Regina Psaki, ed. *The Arthur of the Italians: The Arthurian Legend in Medieval Italian Literature and Culture*. Cardiff: University of Wales Press.
Althoff, Gerd, et al. 2002. *Medieval Concepts of the Past: Ritual, Memory, Historiography*. Washington, DC: German Historical Institute.
Ambrasi, Domenico. 1969. "La vita religiosa." SN 3:437–574.
Andreolli, Bruno. 1991. *Repertorio della cronachistica emiliano-romagnola: Secc. IX–XV.* Rome: ISIME.
The Anjou Bible: A Royal Manuscript Revealed, Naples 1340. Lieve Watteeuw and Jan Ven der Stock, ed. Leuven: Peeters, 2010.
Anselmi, Gian Mario. 2017. "Cronaca e narrazione: Dante e l'interpretazione della storia fra impero romano, Europa cristiana e Mediterraneo islamico." In Francesconi–Miglio, 11–27.
Antoine, Jean-Philippe. 1988. "*Ad perpetuam memoriam:* Les nouvelles fonctions de l'image peinte en Italie, 1250–1400." *Mélanges de L'ecole française de Rome. Moyen Âge, Temps Modernes* 100.2:541–615.
Arens, William. 1979. *The Man-Eating Myth: Anthropology and Anthropophagy*. Oxford: Oxford University Press.
Armstrong, Guyda, et al., ed. 2015. *The Cambridge Companion to Boccaccio*. Cambridge: Cambridge University Press.
—. 2015.1. With Rhiannon Daniels and Stephen J. Milner. 2015. "Boccaccio as Cultural Mediator." In Armstrong (2015), 3–19.
Arnaldi, Girolamo. 1966. "Il notaio e cronista e le cronache cittadine in Italia." In *La storia del diritto nel quadro delle scienze storiche*. Florence: Olschki, 293–309.
—. 1970. "Bonifacio da Morano." In DBI 12 (1970):188–90.
—. 1992–93. "Annali, Cronache, Storie." In Cavallo (1992–93), 2:463–513.
Ascoli, Albert Russell. 2011. "Petrarch's Private Politics: Rerum Familiarium Libri 19." In idem, *'A Local Habitation and a Name': Imagining History in the Italian Renaissance*. New York: Fordham University Press, 118–58.
—. 2015. With Unn Falkeid. *The Cambridge Companion to Petrarch*. Cambridge: Cambridge University Press.
—. 2015a. "Epistolary Petrarch." In Ascoli-Falkeid, 120–37.
Asor Rosa, Alberto, ed. 1987. *Storia e geografia* 1. *L'età medievale*. Turin: Einaudi.
Atkinson, Niall. 2016. *The Noisy Renaissance: Sound, Architecture, and Florentine Urban Life*. University Park: The Pennsylvania State University Press.
Auerbach, Erich. 1953. *Mimesis: The Representation of Reality in Western Literature*. William Trask, trans. Princeton: Princeton University Press.
Avignon & Naples: Italy in France, France in Italy in the Fourteenth Century. 1997. Marianne Pade et al., ed. Rome: "L'Erma" di Bretschneider.

Baddeley, Welbore St Clair. 1897. *Robert the Wise and His Heirs, 1278–1352*. London: W. Heinemann.
Bak, János M. 1997. "Queens as Scapegoats in Medieval Hungary." In Duggan (1997), 223–33.
Baker, Nicholas Scott. 2015. With Brian Jeffrey Maxson. *After Civic Humanism: Learning and Politics in Renaissance Italy*. Toronto: Centre for Reformation and Renaissance Studies.
Barański, Zygmunt G. 2015. "The *Triumphi*." In Ascoli–Falkeid, 74–84.
—. 2015.1. With Lino Pertile, ed. *Dante in Context*. Cambridge: Cambridge University Press.
Barasch, Moshe. 1987. *Giotto and the Language of Gesture*. Cambridge: Cambridge University Press.
Baraz, Daniel. 2003. *Medieval Cruelty: Changing Perceptions, Antiquity to the Early Modern Period*. Ithaca: Cornell University Press.
Barbato, Marcello. 2012. With Giovanni Palumbo. "Fonti francesi di Boccaccio napoletano?" In BA, 127–48.
—. 2014. With Francesco Montuori. "Dalla stampa al manoscritto: La iv parte della *Cronaca di Partenope* trascritta dal Ferraiolo (1498)." In *Dal manoscritto al web: Canali e modalità di trasmissione dell'italiano. Tecniche, materialie e usi nella storia della lingua*. E. Garavelli and E. Suomela-Härmä, ed. Florence: Cesati, 51–70.
—. 2017. "Testo e codice: Le cronache volgari fino a Villani." In Francesconi–Miglio, 89–115.
Barbero, Alessandro. 1994. "La propaganda di Roberto d'Angiò, re di Napoli." In Cammarosano, 111–31.
Barnet, Peter. 2005. With Nancy Wu. *The Cloisters: Medieval Art and Architecture*. New York: Metropolitan Museum of Art.
Barolini, Teodolinda. 2009. "The Self in the Labyrinth of Time *(Rerum vulgarium fragmenta)*." In Kirkham (2009), 33–62.
Baron, Hans. 1955. *The Crisis of the Early Italian Renaissance: Civic Humanism and Republican Liberty in an Age of Classicism and Tyranny*. 2 vols. Princeton: Princeton University Press.
—. 1988. *In Search of Florentine Civic Humanism: Essays on the Transition from Medieval to Modern Thought*. 2 vols. Princeton: Princeton University Press.
Barone, Giulia. 2017. "Ordini mendicanti e cronache volgari." In Francesconi–Miglio, 301–11.
Barthes, Roland. 1981. "The Discourse of History." Stephen Bann, trans. & introduction. In *Comparative Criticism: A Yearbook*. E.S. Schaffer, ed. Cambridge: Cambridge University Press, 3–20.
Baxandall, Michael. 1971. *Giotto and the Orators: Humanist Observers of Painting in Italy and the Discovery of Pictorial Composition, 1350–1450*. Oxford: Clarendon.
Bayley, Charles Calvert. 1942. "Petrarch, Charles IV, and the *Renovatio Imperii*." *Speculum* 17:323–41.
Bedos-Rezak, Brigitte. 1994. "Civic Liturgies and Urban Records in Northern France, 1100–1400." In Hanawalt–Reyerson (1994), 34–55.

Behrmann, Carolin, ed. 2016. *Images of Shame: Infamy, Defamation and the Ethics of* Oeconomia. Boston: De Gruyter.
Belting, Hans. 1985."The New Role of Narrative in Public Painting of the Trecento: *Historia* and Allegory." *Studies in the History of Art.* Washington, DC: National Gallery of Art, 151–68.
Beneš, Carrie E. 1999."Cola di Rienzo and the *Lex Regia.*" *Viator* 30:231–51.
Benson, C. David. 2009. "The Dead and the Living: Some Medieval Descriptions of the Ruins and Relics of Rome Known to the English." In *Urban Space in the Middle Ages and the Early Modern Age.* Albrecht Classen, ed. Berlin: De Gruyter, 147–82.
Bentley, Jerry H. 1987. *Politics and Culture in Renaissance Naples.* Princeton: Princeton University Press.
Bertelli, Sergio. 2001. *The King's Body: Sacred Rituals of Power in Medieval and Early Modern Europe.* R. Burr Litchfield, trans. State College: Pennsylvania State University Press.
Berthelot, Anne. 2006. With Margherita Lecco. *Materiali arturiani nelle letterature di Provenza, Spagna, Italia.* Alessandria: Edizioni dell'Orso.
Bertolini, Paolo. 1988. "Dei, Andrea." DBI 36. At www.treccani.it/enciclopedia/andrea-dei_(Dizionario_Biografico).
Bertone, Giorgio. 2006. "Il 'Buon Governo' come paesaggio testuale: Note di un lettore dell'affresco di Ambrogio Lorenzetti." In *Per un Giardino della Terra.* Antonella Pietrogrande, ed. Padua: Università di Padova, 223–28.
Besseyre, Marianne. 2011. With Yves Christe. *Bible moralisée of Naples.* Barcelona: Moliero.
Bianchini, Janna. 2012. *The Queen's Hand: Power and Authority in the Reign of Berenguela de Castile.* Philadelphia: University of Pennsylvania Press.
Biddick, Kathleen. 1994. "Bede's Blush: Postcards from Bali, Bombay, and Palo Alto." In *The Past and Future of Medieval Studies.* John Van Engen, ed. Notre Dame: University of Notre Dame Press, 16–44.
Bietenholz, Peter G. 1994. Historia *and* Fabula: *Myths and Legends in Historical Thought from Antiquity to the Modern Age.* Leiden: Brill.
Bildhauer, Bettina. 2003. With Robert Mills, ed. *The Monstrous Middle Ages.* Toronto: University of Toronto Press.
Black, Jeremy. 2003. *Italy and the Grand Tour.* New Haven: Yale University Press.
Black, Nancy B. 2000. "*La Belle Hélène de Constantinople* and Crusade Propaganda at the Court of Philip the Good." *15th-Century Studies* 26:42–51.
—. 2003. *Medieval Narratives of Accused Queens.* Gainesville: University Press of Florida.
Black, Robert. 2007. *Humanism and Education in Medieval and Renaissance Italy: Tradition and Innovation in Latin Schools from the Twelfth to the Fifteenth Century.* Cambridge: Cambridge University Press.
—. 2008. "Literacy in Florence, 1427." In *Florence and Beyond: Culture, Society and Politics in Renaissance Italy. Essays in Honour of John M. Najemy.* Daniel E. Bornstein and David Spencer Peterson, ed. Toronto: Centre for Reformation and Renaissance Studies, 195–212.
Blamires, Alcuin, ed. 1992. *Woman Defamed and Woman Defended: An Anthology of Medieval Texts.* Oxford: Clarendon.

—. 1997. *The Case for Women in Medieval Culture*. Oxford: Clarendon.
Blume, Dieter. 2015. "Francesco da Barberino: The Experience of Exile and the Allegory of Love." In *Images and Words in Exile*. Elisa Brilli et al., ed. Florence: SISMEL-Edizioni del Galluzzo, 171–92.
Blunt, Anthony. 1974. *Naples as Seen by French Travellers 1630–1780*. Oxford: Clarendon.
—. 1975. *Neapolitan Baroque and Rococo Architecture*. London: Zwemmer.
Blurton, Heather. 2007. *Cannibalism in High Medieval English Literature*. Basingstoke: Palgrave Macmillan.
Boli, Todd. 2013. "Personality and Conflict *(Epistole, Lettere)*." In Kirkham (2013), 295–306.
Bologna, Ferdinando. 1969. *I pittori alla corte angioina di Napoli, 1266–1414, e un riesame dell'arte nell'età fridericiana*. Rome: Ugo Bozzi.
Botley, Paul. 2006. "Giannozzo Manetti, Alfonso of Aragon and Pompey the Great: A Crusading Document of 1455." *Journal of the Warburg and Courtauld Institutes* 67:129–56.
—. 2008. *Latin Translation in the Renaissance: The Theory and Practice of Leonardo Bruni, Giannozzo Manetti and Desiderius Erasmus*. Cambridge: Cambridge University Press.
Bottigheimer, Ruth. 2008. "Before *Contes du temps passé* (1697): Charles Perrault's *Griselidis, Souhaits* and *Peau*." *The Romantic Review* 99.3:175–89.
Boucheron, Patrick. 2018. *The Power of Images: Siena, 1338*. Andrew Brown, trans. Cambridge: Polity.
Bowsky, William M. 1971. *The Black Death: A Turning Point in History?* New York: Holt, Rinehart & Winston.
Bragantini, Renzo. 2018. "Petrarch, Boccaccio, and the Space of Vernacular Literature." In Candido (2018), 313–39.
Braida, Francesca. 2009. "Le travail de mémoire: *La Cronica de Dino Compagni*. La fiabilité du voir: Le rôle de témoin oculaire et la véridicité du souvenir." *TMC* 6:125–40.
Branca, Vittore, ed. 2015. *Merchant Writers: Florentine Memoirs from the Middle Ages and Renaissance*. Murtha Baca, trans. Cesare de Michelis, ed. Toronto: University of Toronto Press.
Brandt, William J. 1966. *The Shape of Medieval History: Studies in Modes of Perception*. New Haven: Yale University Press.
Breisach, Ernst. 1985. *Classical Rhetoric & Medieval Historiography*. Kalamazoo, MI: Medieval Institute Publications.
Brenner, Elma, et al. *Memory and Commemoration in Medieval Culture*. Farnham: Ashgate.
Brentano, Robert. 1974. *Rome before Avignon: A Social History of Thirteenth-Century Rome*. New York: Basic Books.
Brown, Elizabeth A.R. 2000. "The King's Conundrum: Endowing Queens and Loyal Servants, Ensuring Salvation, and Protecting the Patrimony in Fourteenth-Century France." In *Medieval Futures: Attitudes to the Future in the Middle Ages*. J.A. Burrow and Ian P. Wei, ed. Woodbridge: Boydell, 115–65.
Brown, Warren. 2011. *Violence in Medieval Europe*. Harlow: Longman.

Bruni, Francesco. 2003. *Boccaccio: L'invenzione della letteratura mezzana.* Bologna: Il Mulino.

Bruzelius, Caroline. 1991. "Art, Architecture and Urbanism in Naples." In Bacco, lxv–lxxix.

——. 2004. *The Stones of Naples: Church Building in Angevin Italy, 1266–1343.* New Haven: Yale University Press.

——. 2011. With William Tronzo. *Medieval Naples: An Architectural & Urban History, 400–1400.* New York: Italica Press.

Bryant, Lawrence. 1994. "Configurations of the Community in Late Medieval Spectacles: Paris and London During the Dual Monarchy." In Hanawalt–Reyerson (1994), 3–33.

Buc, Philippe. 2001. *The Dangers of Ritual: Between Early Medieval Texts and Social Scientific Theory.* Princeton, NJ: Princeton University Press.

Burckhardt, Jacob. 1958. *The Civilization of the Renaissance in Italy.* S.G.C. Middlemore, trans. New York: Harper & Row.

Burgess, Richard W. 2013. With Michael Kulikowski. "Medieval Historiographical Terminology: The Meaning of the Word *Annales*." TMC 8:165–92.

Burroughs, Charles. 2000. "Spaces of Arbitration and the Organization of Space in Late Medieval Italian Cities." In *Medieval Practices of Space.* Barbara A. Hanawalt and Michal Kobialka, ed. Minneapolis: University of Minnesota Press, 64–100.

Bynum, Caroline Walker. 1992. *Fragmentation and Redemption: Essays on Gender and the Human Body in Medieval Religion.* New York: Zone Books.

——. 1998. "Men's Use of Female Symbols." In *Debating the Middle Ages: Issues and Readings.* Lester K. Little and Barbara H. Rosenwein, ed. Malden: Blackwell, 277–89.

——. 2002. "Violent Imagery in Late Medieval Piety." *German Historical Institute. Bulletin* 30:3–36.

Cachey, Theodore J., Jr. 2009. "The Place of the *Itinerarium*." In Kirkham (2009), 229–41.

Cagnolati, Antonella, De S.M. González. 2014. *Boccaccio e le donne.* Rome: Aracne.

Cammarosano, Paolo, ed. 1994. *Le forme della propaganda politica nel Due e nel Trecento.* Rome: École Française de Rome.

Campanelli, Maurizio. 2013. "The Preface of the Anonimo Romano's *Cronica*: Writing History and Proving Truthfulness in Fourteenth-Century Rome." *The Mediaeval Journal* 3.1:83–106.

——. 2014. "The Anonimo Romano at His Desk: Recounting the Battle of Crécy in Fourteenth-Century Italy." TMC 9:33–78.

Candido, Igor. 2018. *Petrarch and Boccaccio: The Unity of Knowledge in the Pre-Modern World.* Berlin: De Gruyter.

Capano, A.M. Compagna Perrone. 1981. With Alberto Varvaro. "Capitoli per la storia linguistica dell'Italia meridionale e della Sicilia." *Medioevo romanzo* 8:91–132.

Capasso, Bartolomeo. 1902. *Le fonti della storia del provincie napolitane dal 568 al 1500.* Naples: Riccardo Marghieri.

Cappelli, Guido. 2016. Maiestas: *Politica e pensiero politico nella Napoli aragonese (1443–1503)*. Rome: Carocci.
Caravale, Mario. 1991. "Domenico da Gravina." DBI 40. At www.treccani.it/enciclopedia/domenico-da-gravina_(Dizionario-Biografico).
Carpetto, George M. 1984. *The Humanism of Matteo Palmieri*. Rome: Bulzoni.
Carrai, Stefano. 2009. "Pastoral as Personal Mythology in History *(Bucolicum carmen)*." In Kirkham (2009), 165–77.
Carratelli, Giovanni Pugliese. 1992. *Storia e civiltà della Campania 2. Il medioevo*. Naples: Electa.
Carruthers, Mary J. 1990. *The Book of Memory: A Study of Memory in Medieval Culture*. Cambridge: Cambridge University Press.
Casteen, Elizabeth. 2015. *From She-Wolf to Martyr: The Reign and Disputed Reputation of Johanna I of Naples*. Ithaca, NY: Cornell University Press.
—. 2018. "On She-Wolves and Famous Women: Boccaccio, Politics and the Neapolitan Court." In Holmes–Stewart, 219–45.
Castner, Catherine J. 1998. "Direct Observation and Biondo Flavio's Additions to *Italia Illustrata:* The Case of Ocriculum." *Medievalia et Humanistica* n.s. 25:93–108.
—. 2016. "The *Fortuna* of Biondo Flavio's *Italia Illustrata.*" In Mazzocco-Laureys (2016), 177–96.
Cataudella, Michele. 2006. *Petrarca e Napoli: Atti del convegno, Napoli, 8–11 dicembre 2004*. Pisa: Istituti editoriali e poligrafici internazionali.
Cavallaro, Dani. 2016. *The Chivalric Romance and the Essence of Fiction*. Jefferson, NC: McFarland.
Cavallo, Guglielmo. 1992–93. With Claudio Leonardi and Enrico Menestò, ed. *Lo spazio letterario del medioevo: Il medioevo latino 1. La produzione del testo*. Rome: Salerno.
Caviness, Madeline Harrison. 2006. "Reception of Images by Medieval Viewers." In Rudolph (2006), 65–85.
Celenza, Christopher. 2017. *Petrarch: Everywhere a Wanderer*. London: Reaktion Books.
Cherchi, Paolo. 2009. "The Unforgettable Books of Things to Be Remembered *(Rerum memorandum libri)*." In Kirkham (2009), 151–62.
—. 2018. "The Inventors of Things in Boccaccio's *De genealogia deorum gentilium*." In Candido (2018), 244–69.
Ciccuto, Marcello. 1988. "*Trionfi* e *Uomini illustri* fra Roberto e Renato d'Angiò." *Studi sul Boccaccio* 17:343–402.
—. 2011. "Francesco da Barberino: Un pioniere del Bildercodex tra forme del gotico cortese e icone della civiltà comunale." *Letterature &Arte* 9:83–95.
Cigni, Fabrizio. 2004. "Per la storia del *Guiron le Courtois* in Italia." *Critica del Testo* 7.1:295–316.
—. 2006. "Mappa redazionale del *Guiron le Courtois* diffuso in Italia." In *Modi e forme della fruizione della materia arturiana nell'Italia dei sec. XIII–XV: Milano, 4–5 febbraio 2005*. Milan: Istituto lombardo di scienze e lettere, 85–117.
—. 2014. "French Redactions in Italy: Rustichello da Pisa." In Allaire-Psaki (2014), 21–40.

Cilento, Nicola. 1969. "La cultura e gli inizi dello studio." SN 2.2:521–640.
Clanchy, Michael. 2013. *From Memory to Written Record: England 1066–1307*. Chichester: Wiley-Blackwell.
Clark, James G. 2004. *A Monastic Renaissance at St Albans: Thomas Walsingham and His Circle, c.1350–1440*. Oxford: Clarendon.
Clarke, Paula. 2007. "The Villani Chronicles." In Dale (2007), 113–43.
Cochrane, Eric. 1980. *Historians and Historiography in the Italian Renaissance*. Chicago: University of Chicago Press.
Cohen, Esther. 2000. "The Animated Pain of the Body." *American Historical Review* 105:36–68.
Cohen, Jeffrey Jerome. 1999. *Of Giants: Sex, Monsters, and the Middle Ages*. Minneapolis: University of Minnesota Press.
Cohn, Samuel Kline, et al., ed. 2013. *Late Medieval and Early Modern Ritual: Studies in Italian Urban Culture*. Turnhout: Brepols.
Collard, Judith. 2014. "Art and Science in the Manuscripts of Matthew Paris." TMC 9:79–116.
Collins, Amanda. 2002. *Greater than Emperor: Cola di Rienzo (ca. 1313–54) and the World of Fourteenth-Century Rome*. Ann Arbor: University of Michigan Press.
Coluccia, Rosario. 1994. "Il volgare nel Mezzogiorno." In *Storia della lingua italiana*. L. Serianni and P. Trifone, ed. 3. *Le altre lingue*. Turin: Einaudi, 373–405.
—. 2017. "Testi storici e fatti linguistici." In Francesconi–Miglio, 117–36.
Cooper, Richard. 2008. "The French Dimension in Dante's Politics." In *Dante and Governance*. John Robert Woodhouse, ed. Oxford: Clarendon, 59–83.
Copeland, Rita. 1991. *Rhetoric, Hermeneutics, and Translation in the Middle Ages: Academic Traditions and Vernacular Texts*. Cambridge: Cambridge University Press.
—. 2009. With I. Sluiter. *Medieval Grammar and Rhetoric: Language Arts and Literary Theory, AD 300–1475*. Oxford: Oxford University Press.
Coudert, Allison P. 2012. "The Ultimate Crime: Cannibalism in Early Modern Minds and Imagination." In *Crime and Punishment in the Middle Ages and Early Modern Age*. Albrecht Classen and Connie L. Scarborough, ed. Berlin: De Gruyter, 521–54.
Cracco, Giorgio. 2017. "Dante e le cronache dell'Italia settentrionale." In Francesconi–Miglio, 139–63.
Croce, Benedetto. 1948. "Sentendo parlare un vecchio napoletano del Quattrocento." In *Storie e leggende napoletane*. Bari: Laterza.
Cubitt, Geoffrey. 2007. *History and Memory*. Manchester: Manchester University Press.
Cuffel, Alexandra. 2007. *Gendering Disgust in Medieval Religious Polemic*. Notre Dame: University of Notre Dame Press.
D'Achille, Paolo, et al. 2012. *Lasciatece parlà: Il romanesco nell'Italia di oggi*. Rome: Carocci.
—. 2017. "Cronache, scritture esposte, testi semicolti." In Francesconi–Miglio, 347–72.

Dale, Sharon, et al., ed. 2007. *Chronicling History: Chroniclers and Historians in Medieval and Renaissance Italy.* University Park: Pennsylvania State University Press.

Dall'Oco, Sondra. 1995. "La 'laudatio regis' nel *De rebus gestis ab Alphonso primo* di Bartolomeo Facio." *Rinascimento* 35:243–51.

Daniels, Rhiannon. 2009. *Boccaccio and the Book: Production and Reading in Italy 1340–1520.* London: Legenda.

—. 2015. "Boccaccio's Narrators and Audiences." In Armstrong (2015), 36–51.

—. 2018. "Reading Boccaccio's Paratexts: Dedications as Thresholds between Worlds." In Holmes–Stewart, 48–79.

Dardano, Maurizio. 2012. *Sintassi dell'italiano antico: La prosa del Duecento e del Trecento.* Rome: Carocci.

Davis, Natalie Zemon. 1987. *Fiction in the Archives: Pardon Tales and Their Tellers in Sixteenth-Century France.* Cambridge: Polity.

De Blasi, Nicola. 2012. *Storia linguistica di Napoli.* Rome: Carocci.

De Caprio, Chiara. 2004. "Fra codice e testo: Il caso della *Cronica di Napoli* di Notar Giacomo, con una riflessione sulla categoria di 'codice-archivio'." *Medioevo romanzo* 28:390–419.

—. 2006. "La *Cronica di Napoli* di Notar Giacomo: Edizione critica del ms. brancacciano II F 6 della Biblioteca Nazionale di Napoli." Ph.D. diss., University of Naples.

—. 2007. "La *Cronica* di Notar Iacobo: Codice, testo e *dehors texte.*" *Filologia e Critica* 32:59–74.

—. 2010. "Giacomo, Notar." In *Encyclopedia of the Medieval Chronicle.* R.G. Dunphy, ed. Boston: Brill, 704.

—. 2012. *Scrivere la storia a Napoli tra Medioevo e prima età moderna: Tre studi.* Rome: Salerno.

—. 2013. With Francesco Montuori. "Copia, riuso e rimaneggiamento della Quarta Parte della *Cronaca di Partenope* tra Quattro e Cinquecento." In *Actas del XXVI Congreso Internacional de Lingüística y Filología Románica: Valencia 2010.* Emili Casanova and Cesáreo Calvo, ed. Berlin: De Gruyter, 89–102.

—. 2014. "Spazi comunicativi, tradizioni narrative e storiografia in volgare: Il Regno negli anni delle guerre d'Italia." *Filologia e Critica* 39:39–72.

—. 2015. "La storiografia angioina in volgare: Lessico metaletterario, modalità compositive e configurazioni stilistiche nella *Cronaca di Partenope.*" In *Boccaccio e Napoli: Nuovi materiali per la storia culturale di Napoli nel Trecento.* Giancarlo Alfano et al., ed. Florence: Cesati, 427–48.

—. 2016. With Francesco Senatore. "Orality, Literacy, and Historiography in Neapolitan Vernacular Urban Chronicles of the Fifteenth and Sixteenth Centuries." In *Interactions Between Orality and Writing in Early Modern Italian Culture.* Luca Degl'Innocenti et al., ed. London: Routledge, 129–43.

—. 2017. "La scrittura cronachistica nel Regno: Scriventi, tesi e stili narrativi." In Francesconi–Miglio, 227–68.

Delcorno Branca, Daniela. 1968. *I romanzi italiani di Tristano e la Tavola Rotonda.* Florence: Olschki.

—. 1974. *Il romanzo cavalleresco medievale.* Florence: Sansoni.

—. 1985. *Tradizione arturiana in Boccaccio*. Florence: Olschki.
—. 1990. "*De Arturo Britorum rege:* Boccaccio fra storiografia e romanzo." *Studi sul Boccaccio* 19:151–90.
—. 1991. *Boccaccio e le storie di re Artù*. Bologna: Il Mulino.
—. 1998. *Tristano e Lancillotto in Italia: Studi di letteratura arturiana*. Ravenna: Longo.
—. 2004. *La tradizione della Mort Artu in Italia*. Rome: Viella.
—. 2014. "The Italian Contribution: *La Tavola Ritonda*." In Allaire–Psaki (2014), 69–90.
Delle Donne, Fulvio. 2001. *Politica e letteratura nel Mezzogiorno medievale: La cronachistica dei secoli XII–XV.* Salerno: Carlone.
—. 2001a. "Austerità espositiva e reelaborazione creatrice nel *Chronicon* di Domenico da Gravina." In Delle Donne (2001), 128–46.
—. 2012. "Facio, Bartolomeo." In *Encyclopedia of the Medieval Chronicle*. Leiden: Brill. At http://dx.doi.org/10.1163/2213-2139_emc_SIM_00985.
—. 2015.1. "*Virgiliana Neapolis Urbs:* Receptions of Classical Naples in the Swabian and Early Angevin Ages." In Hughes–Buongiovanni, 152–69.
—. 2015.2. *Alfonso il Magnanimo e l'invenzione dell'umanesimo monarchico: Ideologia e strategie di legittimazione alla corte aragonese di Napoli*. Rome: ISIME.
—. 2016. "Il re e i suoi cronisti: Reinterpretazioni della storiografia alla corte aragonese di Napoli." *Humanistica* 11 (n.s. 5) 1–2:17–34.
—. 2021. With Guido M. Cappelli. *Nel regno delle lettere: Umanesimo e politica nel Mezzogiorno aragonese*. Rome: Carocci.
Del Treppo, Mario. 2006. *Storiografia nel Mezzogiorno*. Naples: Guida.
Deliyannis, Deborah Mauskopf, ed. 2003. *Historiography in the Middle Ages*. Leiden: Brill.
De Marchi, Andrea. 2013. *Maso di Banco in Giotto's Workshop in Naples and an Unpublished Saint Dominic*. Florence: Centro Di.
De Matteis, Mario. 2010. With Antonio Trinchese and Giuliana Pianura, ed. *Lo re Artu k'avemo perduto: Storia e mito di Artu e del Graal in Italia*. Oberhausen: Athena.
Dembowski, Peter F. 1983. *Jean Froissart and His Meliador: Context, Craft, and Sense*. Lexington, KY: French Forum.
De Nichilo, Mauro. 1984. "Angelo Filippo Crassullo." DBI 30. At www.treccani.it/enciclopedia/angelo-filippo-crassullo_(Dizionario_Biografico).
—. 1991. "De Rosa, Loise." DBI 39:171–4. At www.treccani.it/enciclopedia/loise-de-rosa_(Dizionario-Biografico).
Derbes, Anne. 2004. With Mark Sandona. *The Cambridge Companion to Giotto*. Cambridge: Cambridge University Press.
De Roberto, Elisa. 2015. "Dinamiche enunciative nel discorso storico medievale: Il caso delle strategie evidenziali." In *Sul filo del testo: In equilibrio tra enunciato e enunciazione*. Massimo Palermo and Silvia Pieroni, ed. Ospedaletto Pisa: Pacini, 65–88.
Diakité, Rala Isobel. 2003. "Writing Political Realities in Fourteenth-Century Italy: Giovanni Villani's *Nouva Cronica* and Dante's *Commedia*." Ph.D. diss., Brown University.
Di Cerbo, Cristiana. 2016. "La Campagnia del Nodo, o di Santo Spirito, e la

commitenza di Niccolò Orsini nella chiesa di Santa Maria Jacobi a Nola (1354–1359)." *Intrecci d'arte* 1:44–60.
Di Franza, Concetta. 2012. "'Dal fuoco dipinto a quello che veramente arde': Una poetica in forma di *quaestio* nel capitolo VIII dell' *Elegia di Madonna Fiammetta*." In BA, 89–101.
Di Simone, Paolo. 2012–13. "Giotto, Petrarca e il tema degli *uomini illustri* tra Napoli, Milano e Padova: Prolegomeni a un'indagine." *Rivista d'arte* 5.2:39–76; 5.3:35–55.
Doane, Alger Nicolaus. 1991. With Carol Braun Pasternack, ed. *Vox Intexta: Orality and Textuality in the Middle Ages.* Madison: University of Wisconsin Press.
Doležalová, Lucie, ed. 2010. *The Making of Memory in the Middle Ages.* Leiden: Brill.
Donato, Maria Monica. 1985. "Gli eroi romani tra storia ed 'exemplum': I primi cicli umanistici di *Uomini Famosi*." In *Memoria nell'antico nell'arte italiana*. Salvatore Settis, ed. Turin: Einaudi, 2:97–152.
Dooley, Brendan M. 2010. *The Dissemination of News and the Emergence of Contemporaneity in Early Modern Europe.* Farnham–Burlington: Ashgate.
Duggan, Anne J. 1997. *Queens and Queenship in Medieval Europe.* Bury St. Edmunds: Boydell.
Dumville, David. 2002. "What Is a Chronicle?" TMC 2:1–27.
Dunbabin, Jean. 1998. *Charles I of Anjou: Power, Kingship and State-Making in Thirteenth-Century Europe.* London: Longman.
—. 2011. *The French in the Kingdom of Sicily, 1266–1305.* Cambridge: Cambridge University Press.
Duran, Michelle M. 2010. "The Politics of Art: Imaging Sovereignty in the Anjou Bible." In *Anjou Bible*, 73–93.
D'Urso et al., ed. 2021. *Manoscritti miniati della Biblioteca Nazionale di Napoli* 1. *Italia, secoli XIII–XIV.* Rome: Istituto Poligrafico e Zecca dello Stato.
Earenfight, Theresa. 2010. *The King's Other Body: María of Castile and the Crown of Aragon.* Philadelphia: University of Pennsylvania Press.
—. 2013. *Queenship in Medieval Europe.* Basingstoke: Palgrave Macmillan.
Edgerton, Samuel Y. 1985. *Pictures and Punishment: Art and Criminal Prosecution During the Florentine Renaissance.* Ithaca, NY: Cornell University Press.
Elliott, Dyan. 1999. *Fallen Bodies: Pollution, Sexuality, and Demonology in the Middle Ages.* Philadelphia: University of Pennsylvania Press.
Elliott, Janis. 2004. With Cordelia Warr, ed. *The Church of Santa Maria Donna Regina: Art, Iconography, and Patronage in Fourteenth-Century Naples.* Burlington, VT: Ashgate.
—. 2004a. "The 'Last Judgement': The Cult of Sacral Kingship and Dynastic Hopes for the Afterlife." In Elliott–Warr, 175–93.
Emerson, Catherine, ed. 2001. With Edward A. O'Brien and Laurent Semichon. *Auctoritas: Authorship and Authority.* Glasgow: University of Glasgow French and German Publications.
Encyclopedia of the Medieval Chronicle. Graeme Dunphy et al., ed. Brill Online, 2015. At http://referenceworks brillonline. com/entries/encyclopedia-of-the-medieval-chronicle.

Enders, Jody. 1992. *Rhetoric and the Origins of Medieval Drama*. Ithaca, NY: Cornell University Press.
—. 1999. *The Medieval Theater of Cruelty: Rhetoric, Memory, Violence*. Ithaca, NY: Cornell University Press.
Epstein, Stephan R. 1992. *An Island for Itself: Economic Development and Social Change in Late Medieval Sicily*. Cambridge: Cambridge University Press.
Faini, Enrico. 2008. "Alle origini della memoria comunale: Prime ricerche." *Quellen und Forschungen aus italienischen Archiven und Bibliotheken* 88:61–81.
Falconieri, Tommaso di Carpegna. "Note sulla cronachistica in volgare a Roma." In Francesconi–Miglio, 215–26.
Falkeid, Unn. 2017. *The Avignon Papacy Contested: An Intellectual History from Dante to Catherine of Siena*. Cambridge, MA: Harvard University Press.
Felici, Lucio. 1972. "Le vicende del dialetto romanesco." *Capitolium* 47.4:26–33.
Feniello, Amedeo. 2015. *Napoli 1343: Le origini medievali di un sistema criminale*. Milan: Mondadori.
Fenster, Thelma S. 2003. With Daniel Lord Smail. *Fama: The Politics of Talk & Reputation in Medieval Europe*. Ithaca, NY: Cornell University Press.
Feo, Michele. 1994. "L'epistola come mezzo di propaganda politica in Francesco Petrarca." In Cammarosano, 203–26.
Ferguson, Wallace K. 1948. *The Renaissance in Historical Thought: Five Centuries of Interpretation*. Boston: Houghton Mifflin.
Ferrante, Joan M. 2011. *The Conflict of Love and Honor: The Medieval Tristan Legend in France, Germany and Italy*. Berlin: De Gruyter.
Ferraro, Alessandra Mita. 2005. *Matteo Palmieri: Una biografia intellettuale*. Genoa: Name.
Ficara, Giorgio. 2018. "The Perfect Woman in Boccaccio and Petrarch." In Candido (2018), 286–312.
Field, Sean L. 2014. With M. Cecilia Gaposchkin. "Questioning the Capetians, 1180–1328." *History Compass* 12.7:567–85.
Figliuolo, Bruno. 2015. "Pontano Giovanni." DBI 84. At www.treccani.it/enciclopedia/giovanni-pontano_(Dizionario-Biografico).
Finotti, Fabio. 2009. "The Poem of Memory *(Triumphi)*." In Kirkham (2009), 63–83.
Finzi, Claudio. 2004. *Re, baroni, popolo: La politica di Giovanni Pontano*. Rimini: Il Cerchio.
Fleck, Cathleen A. 2010.1. *The Clement Bible at the Medieval Courts of Naples and Avignon: A Story of Papal Power, Royal Prestige, and Patronage*. Farnham: Ashgate.
—. 2010.2. "Patronage, Art, and the *Anjou Bible* in Angevin Naples (1266–1352)." In *Anjou Bible*, 37–51.
—. 2010.3. "The Rise of the Court Artist: Cavallini and Giotto in Fourteenth-Century Naples." In Warr–Elliott, 38–61.
Fleischman, Suzanne. 1983. "On the Representation of History and Fiction in the Middle Ages." *History and Theory* 22:278–310.
Flynn, Maureen. 1994. "The Spectacle of Suffering in Spanish Streets." In Hanawalt–Reyerson (1994), 153–68.

Foà, Simona. 2007. "Manetti, Giannozzo." DBI 68. At www.treccani.it/enciclopedia/giannozzo-manetti_(Dizionario-Biografico).
Fois, Mario. 1969. *Il pensiero cristiano di Lorenzo Valla nel quadro storico-culturale del suo ambiente*. Rome: Libreria Editrice dell'Università Gregoriana.
Foley, John Miles. 2016. With Peter Ramey. "Concepts and Approaches: Oral Theory and Medieval Literature." In Reichl (2016), 71–102.
Fontana, Emanuele. 2014. "Paolino da Venezia, vescovo di Pozzuoli." DBI 81. At www.treccani.it/enciclopedia/paolino-da-venezia-vescovo-di-pozzuoli_(Dizionario-Biografico).
Foote, Sarah. 2005. "Finding the Meaning of Form: Narrative in Annals and Chronicles." In Partner (2005), 88–108.
Forcellini, Vincenzo. 1926. "'L'horrendum tripes animal' della lettera 3 del libro V delle *Familiari* di Petrarca." In *Studi di storia napoletana in onore di Michelangelo Schipa*. Naples: I.T.E.A., 167–99.
Formentin, Vittorio. 2008.1. "Frustoli di romanesco antico in lodi arbitrali dei secoli XIV e XV." *Lingua e Stile* 43:21–99.
—. 2008.2. "Schede lessicali e grammaticali per la *Cronica* d'Anonimo romano." *La Lingua Italiana* 4:25–43.
—. 2010. "Sfortuna di Buccio di Ranallo." *Lingua e Stile* 45.2:185–221.
—. 2012. "Approssimazioni al testo e alla lingua della *Cronica* d'Anonimo romano." In idem, *Leggere gli apparati: Testi e testimoni dei classici italiani*. Milan: Unicopli, 27–71.
—. 2013. "A proposito di romanesco antico: La metafonia nel registro di Giovanni Cenci?" *Lingua e Stile* 48:299–315.
Formisano, Luciano. 1993. With Charmaine Lee. "Il 'Francese di Napoli' in opere di autori italiani dell'età angioina." In Trovato–Gonelli (1993), 133–62.
Francesconi, Giampaolo. 2010. "*Infamare per dominare:* La costruzione retorica fiorentina del conflitto politico a Pistoia." In *Lotta politica nell'Italia medievale*. Federico Canaccini and Isa Lori Sanfilippo, ed. Rome: ISIME, 95–106.
—. 2017. With Massimo Miglio, ed. *Le cronache volgari in Italia: Atti della VI Settimana di studi medievali (Roma, 13–15 maggio 2015)*. Rome: ISIME.
—. 2017.a. "Una toscana senza autori: Siena e dintorni." In Francesconi–Miglio, 165–86.
Freccero, John. 1977. "Bestial Sign and Bread of Angels (*Inferno* 32 and 33)." *Yale Italian Studies* 1:53–66.
Frisch, Andrea. 2004. *The Invention of the Eyewitness: Witnessing and Testimony in Early Modern France*. Chapel Hill: University of North Carolina Press.
Frojmovič, Eva. 1996. "Giotto's Allegories of Justice and the Commune in the Palazzo della Ragione in Padua: A Reconstruction." *Journal of the Warburg and Courtauld Institutes* 59:24–47.
—. 2007. "Giotto's Circumspection." *The Art Bulletin* 89.2:195–210.
Fubini, Ricardo. 1968. "Biondo Flavio." DBI 10:536–59. At www.treccani.it/enciclopedia/biondo-flavio_(Dizionario-Biografico).
Fulton, Helen, ed. 2021. *Chaucer and Italian Culture*. Cardiff: University of Wales Press.
Furstenberg-Levi, Shulamit. 2016. *The Accademia Pontaniana: A Model of a Humanist Network*. Leiden: Brill.

Gaglione, Mario. 2009. Converà ti que aptengas la flor: *Profili di sovrani angioini, da Carlo I a Renato (1266–1442)*. Milan: Lampi di stampa.

—. 2009.1. *Donne e potere a Napoli: Le sovrane angioine. Consorte, vicarie e regnanti (1266–1442)*. Catanzaro: Rubbertino.

Gamberini, Andrea. 2012. With Isabella Lazzarini, ed. *The Italian Renaissance State*. Cambridge: Cambridge University Press.

—. 2021. *Inferni medievali: Dipingere il mondo dei morti per orientare la società dei vivi*. Rome: Viella.

Ganim, John M. 2008. *Medievalism and Orientalism*. Basingstoke: Palgrave Macmillan.

Gardiner, Eileen. 1999. "Review of Peter Brown, ed. *Reading Dreams: The Interpretation of Dreams from Chaucer to Shakespeare* (New York: Oxford University Press, 1999)." *The Medieval Review* 00.03.06.

—. 2006. "Hell-on-Line." At www.hell-on-line. org.

—. 2015. With Ronald G. Musto. *The Digital Humanities: A Primer for Students and Scholars*. New York: Cambridge University Press.

Gardner, Edmund G. 1930. *The Arthurian Legend in Italian Literature*. London: Dent.

Gardner, Julian. 1976. "Saint Louis of Toulouse, Robert of Anjou, and Simone Martini." *Zeitschrift für Kunstgeschichte* 39:12–33.

—. 2004. "Santa Maria Donna Regina in Its European Context." In Elliott–Warr, 195–201.

Gehl, Paul F. 1993. *A Moral Art: Grammar, Society, and Culture in Trecento Florence*. Ithaca, NY: Cornell University Press.

Gentile, Salvatore. 1961. *Postille ad una recente edizione di testi narrativi napoletani del '400*. Naples: Liguori.

Gersh, Stephen. 2003. With Bert Roest. *Medieval and Renaissance Humanism: Rhetoric, Representation and Reform*. Leiden: Brill.

Giannetti, Anna. 2017. "Urban Design and Public Spaces." In Hall–Willette, 46–100.

Ginzburg, Carlo. 1992. "Just One Witness." In *Probing the Limits of Representation: Nazism and the "Final Solution."* Saul Friedländer, ed. Cambridge, MA: Harvard University Press, 82–96.

—. 2009. "Pontano, Machiavelli and Prudence: Some Further Reflections." In *From Florence to the Mediterranean and Beyond: Essays in Honour of Anthony Mohlo*. Diogo Ramada Curto and Niki Koniordos, ed. 2 vols. Florence: Olschki, 1:117–25.

Girgensohn, Dieter. 2007. "Maramaldo (Maramauro), Landolfo." DBI 69. At www.treccani.it/enciclopedia landolfo-maramaldo_ (Dizionario-Biografico).

Gittes, Tobias F. 2008. *Boccaccio's Naked Muse: Eros, Culture, and the Mythopoetic Imagination*. Toronto: University of Toronto Press.

—. 2015. "Boccaccio and Humanism." In Armstrong (2015), 155–70.

Godi, Carlo. 1970. "La *Collatio laureationis* del Petrarca." *Italia medioevale e umanistica* 13:1–27.

Graf, Arturo. 2000. With Andrea Casoli. *Artú e le leggende bretoni in Italia*. Turin: N. Aragno.

Grafton, Anthony, et al. 2013. *The Classical Tradition.* Cambridge, MA: Harvard University Press.
Green, Dennis H. 2007. *Women Readers in the Middle Ages.* Cambridge: Cambridge University Press.
Green, Louis. 1972. *Chronicle into History: An Essay on the Interpretation of History in Florentine Fourteenth-Century Chronicles.* Cambridge: Cambridge University Press.
Greenblatt, Stephen. 1980. *Renaissance Self-Fashioning: From More to Shakespeare.* Chicago: University of Chicago Press.
Greer, Margaret Rich, et al., ed. 2007. *Rereading the Black Legend: The Discourses of Religious and Racial Difference in the Renaissance Empires.* Chicago: University of Chicago Press.
Grendler, Paul F. 1989. *Schooling in Renaissance Italy: Literacy and Learning, 1300–1600.* Baltimore: Johns Hopkins University Press.
—. 1990. *Schooling in Western Europe.* New York: Renaissance Society of America.
—. 2002. *The Universities of the Italian Renaissance.* Baltimore: Johns Hopkins University Press.
Groebner, Valentin. 2004. *Defaced: The Visual Culture of Violence in the Late Middle Ages.* Pamela Selwyn, trans. New York: Zone Books.
Grossvogel, Steven M. 2013. "A Fable of the World's Creation and Phaeton's Fall *(Allegoria mitologica)*." In Kirkham (2013), 63–68.
Gualdo, Riccardo. 2017. "Le cronache dell'Italia mediana." In Francesconi–Miglio, 187–213.
Guenée, Bernard. 1973. "Histoire, Annales, Chroniques: Essai sur les genres historiques au moyen âge." *Annales: Economies, Sociétés, Civilisations* 4:997–1016.
Haan, Annet den. 2016. *Giannozzo Manetti's New Testament: Translation Theory and Practice in Fifteenth-Century Italy.* Leiden: Brill.
Haines, John. 2013. With Pierre Courroux. "*Mélusine* et les L'archevêque: Légende et historiographie dans le Poitou de la fin du XIVe siècle." *Cahiers de Recherches Médiévales et Humanistes* 26:309–25.
Hall, Marcia B. 2017. With Thomas Willette, ed. *Artistic Centers of the Italian Renaissance: Naples.* New York: Cambridge University Press.
Hanawalt, Barbara. 1994. With Kathryn Reyerson. *City and Spectacle in Medieval Europe.* Minneapolis: University of Minnesota Press.
Hanke, Lewis. 1949. *The Spanish Struggle for Justice in the Conquest of America.* Philadelphia: University of Pennsylvania Press.
Hankins, James. 1995. "The 'Baron Thesis' after Forty Years, and Some Recent Studies of Leonardo Bruni." *Journal of the History of Ideas* 56:309–38.
—. 1997. *Repertorium Brunianum: A Critical Guide to the Writings of Leonardo Bruni.* Rome: ISIME.
Hanning, Robert W. 1966. *The Vision of History in Early Britain: From Gildas to Geoffrey of Monmouth.* New York: Columbia University Press.
Harf-Lancner, Laurence. 1999. "Une légende mélusienne dans les *Chroniques* de Froissart: L'histoire du seigneur de Coarraze et de son serviteur Horton." In *Mélusines continentales et insulaires: Actes du colloque international tenu les 27 et 28 mars 1997 à l'Université de Paris XII et au Collège des Irlandais.* Jeanne-Marie Boivin and Proinsias MacCana, ed. Paris: Champion, 205–21.

Haskins, Susan. 1994. *Mary Magdalen: Myth and Metaphor.* New York: Harcourt, Brace.
Hay, Denys. 1958. "Flavio Biondo and the Middle Ages." *Proceedings of the British Academy* 45:97–125.
—. 1977. *Annalists and Historians: Western Historiography from the Eighth to the Eighteenth Centuries.* London: Methuen.
—. 2007. "Challenging Chronicles: Leonardo Bruni's History of the Florentine People." In Dale (2007), 249–72.
Hedeman, Anne D. 1991. *The Royal Image: Illustrations of the Grandes Chroniques de France, 1274–1422.* Berkeley: University of California Press.
—. 2006. "Gothic Manuscript Illustration." In Rudolph (2006), 421–42.
—. 2008. *Translating the Past: Laurent de Premierfait and Boccaccio's De casibus.* Los Angeles: Getty Publications.
Heffernan, James A.W. 1993. *Museum of Words: The Poetics of Ekphrasis from Homer to Ashbery.* Chicago: University of Chicago Press.
Hendrix, Harald. 2015. "City Branding and the Antique: Naples in Early Modern City Guides." In Hughes-Buongiovanni, 217–41.
Hersey, George L. 1969. *Alfonso II and the Artistic Renewal of Naples, 1485–1495.* New Haven: Yale University Press.
—. 1973. *The Aragonese Arch at Naples, 1443–1475.* New Haven: Yale University Press.
Heullant-Donat, Isabelle. 2005. "En amont de l'Observance: Les lettres de Sancia, reine de Naples, aux Chapitres généraux et leur transmission dans l'historiographie du XIVe siècle." In *Identités franciscaines à l'âge des réformes.* Frédéric Meyer and Ludovic Viallet, ed. Clermont-Ferrand: Presses Universitaires Blaise Pascal, 73–99.
Hoch, Adrian. 2004. "The Passion Cycle" in Elliott–Warr, 129–53.
Holloway, Julia. 2011. "Romancing the Chronicle." TMC 7:1–14.
—. 2020. "Il buon governo: *Il Tesoretto, il Tesoro* e *la Rettorica* di Brunetto Latino come *paideia* a Guido Cavalcanti, Dante Alighieri e Francesco da Barberino." *Letteratura italiana antica* 21:79–94.
Holmes, Olivia, and Dana E. Stewart, ed. 2018. *Reconsidering Boccaccio: Medieval Contexts and Global Intertexts.* Toronto: University of Toronto Press.
Holstein, Alizah. 2006. "Rome During Avignon: Myth, Memory, and Civic Identity in Fourteenth-Century Roman Politics." Ph.D. diss., Cornell University.
Holtz, Louis. 1992–93. "Autore, Copista, Anonimo." In Cavallo (1992–93), 1:325–52.
Hóman, Bálint. 1938. *Gli Angioini di Napoli in Ungheria, 1290–1403.* Rome: Reale Accademia d'Italia.
Hooper, Laurence E. 2016. "Exile and Petrarch's Reinvention of Authorship." *Renaissance Quarterly* 69:1217–56.
Houston, Jason. 2013. "A Portrait of a Young Humanist (*Epistolae* 1–4)." In Kirkham (2013), 69–74.
Hughes, Jessica. 2015. With Claudio Buongiovanni, ed. *Remembering Parthenope: The Reception of Classical Naples from Antiquity to the Present.* Oxford: Oxford University Press.

BIBLIOGRAPHY

Hyde, John Kenneth 1966. "Medieval Descriptions of Cities." *Bulletin of the John Rylands Library* 48:308–40.

Ianziti, Gary. 2010. *Writing History in Renaissance Italy: Leonardo Bruni and the Uses of the Past.* Cambridge, MA: Harvard University Press.

—. 2016. "Leonardo Bruni and the Rise of Official Historiography in Renaissance Florence." In *Studies on Florence and the Italian Renaissance in Honour of F.W. Kent.* Peter Howard and Cecilia Hewlett, ed. Turnhout: Brepols, 431–48.

Imbriani, Vittorio. 1891. *Studi danteschi.* Florence: Sansoni.

Internullo, Dario. 2016. *Ai margini dei giganti: La vita intellettuale dei romani nel Trecento (1305–1367 ca.).* Rome: Viella.

Izbicki, Thomas M. 1993. "Lorenzo Valla: The Scholarship in English through 1992." In *Humanity and Divinity in Renaissance and Reformation: Essays in Honor of Charles Trinkaus.* John W. O'Malley et al., ed. Leiden: Brill, 287–301.

Janik, Linda Gardiner. 1973. "Lorenzo Valla: The Primacy of Rhetoric and the Demoralization of History." *History and Theory* 12:389–404.

Jansen, Katherine L. 2013. "'Pro bono pacis': Crime, Conflict, and Dispute Resolution: The Evidence of Notarial Peace Contracts in Late Medieval Florence." *Speculum* 88.2:427–56.

Johns, Adrian. 1998. *The Nature of the Book: Print and Knowledge in the Making.* Chicago: University of Chicago Press.

Johnston, Andrew James. 2015. With Ethan Knapp and Margitta Rouse, ed. *The Art of Vision: Ekphrasis in Medieval Literature and Culture.* Columbus: Ohio State University Press.

Jones, Steven Swann. 1993. "The Innocent Persecuted Heroine Genre: An Analysis of Its Structure and Themes." *Western Folklore* 52:13–41.

Joost-Gaugier, Christiane L. 1980. "Giotto's Hero Cycle in Naples: A Prototype of *donne illustre* and a Possible Literary Connection." *Zeitschrift für Kunstgeschichte* 43:311–18.

—. 1982. "The Early Beginning of the Notion of *'Uomini Famosi'* and the *'De Viris Illustribus'* in Greco-Roman Tradition." *Artibus et Historiae* 5:97–115.

—. 1984. "The History of a Visual Theme as Culture and the Experience of an Urban Center: *Uomini famosi.*" *Antichità Viva* 22.1:5–14.

Jordan, Constance. 1987. "Boccaccio's In-Famous Women: Gender and Civic Virtue in the *De mulieribus claris.*" In *Ambiguous Realities: Women in the Middle Ages and Renaissance.* C. Levin and J. Watson, ed. Detroit: Wayne State University Press, 25–47.

Kahn, Victoria Ann. 1983. *Giovanni Pontano's Rhetoric of Prudence.* University Park: Pennsylvania State University Press.

Kallendorf, Craig. 2011. "Lorenzo Valla." In *Oxford Bibliographies Online.* New York: Oxford University Press. At http://oxfordbibliographiesonline.com/view/document/obo-9780195399301/obo-9780195399301-0129.xml.

—.2014. "Giannozzo Manetti." In *Oxford Bibliographies Online.* New York: Oxford University Press. At http://dx.doi.org/10.1093/OBO/9780195399301-0091http://dx.doi.org/10.1093/OBO/9780195399301-0091.

Keen, Benjamin. 1971. "Approaches to Las Casas, 1535–1970." In *Bartolomé de Las Casas in History.* Juan Friede and Benjamin Keen, ed. DeKalb: Northern Illinois University Press, 3–63.
Kelly, Samantha. 2003. *The New Solomon: Robert of Naples (1309–1343) and Fourteenth-Century Kingship.* Leiden: Brill.
—. 2004. "Religious Patronage and Royal Propaganda in Angevin Naples: Santa Maria Donna Regina in Context." In Elliott–Warr, 27–43.
—. 2012. "Medieval Influence in Early Modern Neapolitan Historiography: The Fortunes of the *Cronaca di Partenope*, 1350–1680." *California Italian Studies* 3.1. At www.escholarship.org/uc/item/2sg144x3.
—. 2013. "The Neapolitan Giovanni Villani: Florence, Naples, and Medieval Historiographical Categorization." In *Renaissance Studies in Honor of Joseph Connors.* Machtelt Israëls et al., ed. Florence: Villa I Tatti, 2:31–38.
Kempers, Bram. 1994. "Icons, Altarpieces, and Civic Ritual in Siena Cathedral, 1100–1530." In Hanawalt–Reyerson (1994), 89–136.
Kempshall, Matthew. 2011. *Rhetoric and the Writing of History, 400–1500.* Manchester: Manchester University Press.
Kessler, Herbert L. 2006. "Gregory the Great and Image Theory in Northern Europe During the Twelfth and Thirteenth Centuries." In Rudolph (2006), 151–72.
Kiesewetter, Andreas. 1998. "La cancelleria angioina." In EA, 360–415.
—. 2001. "I principi di Taranto e la Grecia, 1294–1383." *Archivio storico pugliese* 54:53–100.
—. 2005. "Francesco Petrarca e Roberto d'Angiò." ASPN 123:147–74.
Kinney, Dale. 1998. "*Spolia, Damnatio* and *Renovatio Memoriae.*" *Memoirs of the American Academy in Rome* 42:117–48.
Kipling, Gordon. 1998. *Enter the King: Theatre, Liturgy, and Ritual in the Medieval Civic Triumph.* Oxford: Clarendon.
Kirkham, Victoria. 2009. With Armando Maggi, ed. *Petrarch: A Critical Guide to the Complete Works.* Chicago: University of Chicago Press.
—. 2009a. "A Life's Work." In Kirkham (2009), 1–30.
—. 2009b. "Petrarch the Courtier: Five Public Speeches." In Kirkham (2009), 141–50.
—. 2013. With Michael Sherberg and Janet Levarie Smarr, ed. *Boccaccio: A Critical Guide to the Complete Works.* Chicago: University of Chicago Press.
—. 2013a. "Chronology of Boccaccio's Life and Works." In Kirkham (2013), xiii–xix.
Klapisch-Zuber, Christine. 1984. "Le chiavi fiorentine di *barbablù*: L'apprendimento della lettura a Firenze nel XV secolo." *Quaderni storici* n.s. 57:765–92.
Kleinhenz, Christopher. 2014. "The Arthurian Tradition in the Three Crowns." In Allaire–Psaki (2014), 158–78.
Knape, Joachim. 2002. "Historiography as Rhetoric." TMC 2:117–29.
Kohl, Benjamin G. 2015. "Chronicon Estense." In *Encyclopedia of the Medieval Chronicle.* Graeme Dunphy, ed. Brill Online. At http://referenceworks.brillonline.com/entries/encyclopedia-of-the-medieval-chronicle/chroniconestense-EMCSIM_00582.

Kolsky, Stephen. 2003. *The Genealogy of Women: Studies in Boccaccio's 'De mulieribus claris'*. New York: Peter Lang.
Kraye, Jill. 1996. "Facio, Bartolomeo." *Grove Art Online*. New York: Oxford University Press. At www.oxfordartonline.com/subscriber/article/grove/art/T027321.
Kristeller, Paul Oskar. 1965. *The Humanist Bartolomeo Facio and His Unknown Correspondence*. New York: Random House.
—. 1971. With F. Edward Cranz and Virginia Brown. *Catalogus translationum et commentariorum: Mediaeval and Renaissance Latin Translations and Commentaries: Annotated Lists and Guides*. Washington, DC: Catholic University of America Press.
Kumhera, Glenn. 2017. *The Benefits of Peace: Private Peacemaking in Late Medieval Italy*. Leiden: Brill.
Labriola, Ada. 2004. "Pacino di Buonaguida." In *Dizionario Biografico dei Miniatori Italiani: Secoli IX–XVI*. Milvia Bollati and Miklós Boskovits, ed. Milan: Sylvestre Bonnard, 841–43.
Lake, Justin. 2015. "Current Approaches to Medieval Historiography." *History Compass* 13.3:89–109.
Lansing, Richard H. 2000. With Teodolinda Barolini et al., ed. *The Dante Encyclopedia*. New York: Garland.
Laureys, Marc. 1997. "Between *Mirabilia* and *Roma Instaurata:* Giovanni Cavallini's *Polistoria*." In AN, 100–115.
Lavin, Irving. 2020. *The Art of Commemoration in the Renaissance: The Slade Lectures*. Marilyn Aronberg Lavin, ed. New York: Italica Press.
Lawrance, Jeremy. 2009. *Spanish Conquest, Protestant Prejudice: Las Casas and the Black Legend*. Nottingham: Critical, Cultural and Communications Press.
Léonard, Emile G. 1932–37. *Histoire de Jeanne I, reine de Naples, comtesse de Provence (1343–1382): Mémoires et documents historiques*. 3 vols. Paris–Monaco: Imprimerie de Monaco, 1932–37. 1. *La jeunesse de la reine Jeanne*.
Leonardi, Claudio. 1993. "Agiografi." In Cavallo (1992–93), 2:421–62.
Leone de Castris, Pierluigi. 1986. *Arte di corte nella Napoli angioina*. Florence: Cantini.
—. 1995. "A margine di 'I pittori alla corte angioina': Maso di Banco e Roberto d'Oderisio." In *Napoli, l'Europa: Ricerche di storia dell'arte in onore di Ferdinando Bologna*. Francesco Abbate and Fiorella Sricchia Santoro, ed. Catanzaro: Meridiana, 45–49.
—. 2006. *Giotto a Napoli*. Naples: Electa.
L'état Angevin: pouvoir, culture et société entre XIIIe et XIVe siècle: Actes du colloque international organisé par l'American Academy in Rome (Rome–Naples, 7–11 novembre 1995). Rome: École française de Rome & ISIME, 1998.
Lewin, Alison Williams. 2007. "Salimbene de Adam and the Franciscan Chronicle." In Dale (2007), 87–112.
Lewis, Suzanne. 2010. "Narrative." In Rudolph (2006), 86–105.
Lobrichon, Guy. 1992. "Gli usi della Bibbia." In Cavallo (1992–93), 1:523–62.
Logan, F. Donald. 2005. *The Medieval Historian and the Quest for Certitude*. Toronto: Pontifical Institute of Mediaeval Studies.

Lokaj, Rodney. 2000. "La Cleopatra neapoletana: Giovanna d'Angiò nelle 'Familiares' di Petrarca." *Giornale storico della letteratura italiana* 177:481–521.
Long, Jane Collins. 2009. "Franciscan Chapel Decoration: The St. Silvester Cycle of Maso Di Banco at Santa Croce in Florence." *Studies in Iconography* 30:72–95.
Longère, Jean. 1983. *La prédication médiévale*. Paris: Etudes Augustiniennes.
Looney, Dennis. 2009. "The Beginnings of Humanistic Oratory: Petrarch's Coronation Oration *(Collatio laureationis)*." In Kirkham (2009), 131–40.
Loporcaro, Michele, et al. 2012. *Vicende storiche della lingua di Roma*. Alessandria: Edizioni dell'Orso.
Lorch, Maristella de Panizza. 1985. *A Defense of Life: Lorenzo Valla's Theory of Pleasure*. Munich: Fink.
Lori Sanfilippo, Isa. 2011. With Antonio Rigon. Fama *e* publica vox *nel Medioevo: Atti del convegno di studio svoltosi in occasione della XXI edizione del Premio internazionale Ascoli Piceno, Ascoli Piceno, Palazzo dei Capitani, 3–5 dicembre 2009*. Rome: ISIME.
Loud, Graham. 2007. "History Writing in the Twelfth-Century Kingdom of Sicily." In Dale (2007), 29–54.
Luchinat, Cristina Acidini. 1998. With Enrica Neri Lusanna, ed. *Maso Di Banco: La cappella di San Silvestro*. Milan: Electa.
Lumley, Robert. 1997. With Jonathan Morris, ed. *The New History of the Italian South: The Mezzogiorno Revisited*. Exeter: University of Exeter Press.
Lummus, David. 2013. "The Changing Landscape of the Self *(Buccolicum carmen)*." In Kirkham (2013), 155–69.
Macciocca, Gabriella. 1982. "Fonetica e morfologia di *Le miracole de Roma*." *L'Italia Dialettale* 45:38–123.
MacLaren, Shelley. 2007. "Shaping the Self in the Image of Virtue: Francesco da Barberino's *I Documenti d'amore*." In *Image and Imagination of the Religious Self in Late Medieval and Early Modern Europe*. Reindert Falkenburg et al., ed. Turnhout: Brepols, 71–104.
Maddox, Donald. 1996. With Sara Sturm-Maddox. *Melusine of Lusignan: Founding Fiction in Late Medieval France*. Athens: University of Georgia Press.
—. 1998. With Sara Sturm-Maddox. *Froissart Across the Genres*. Gainesville: University Press of Florida.
Mallegni, Francesco. 2003. With M. Luisa Ceccarelli Lemut. *Il conte Ugolino Della Gherardesca tra antropologia e storia*. Pisa: PLUS.
Maltby, William S. 1971. *The Black Legend in England: The Development of Anti-Spanish Sentiment*. Durham, NC: Duke University Press.
Mann, C. Griffith. 2002. "The Morgan Picture Bible and the Art of Narrative: Picturing the Bible in the Thirteenth Century." In *The Book of Kings: Art, War, and the Morgan Library's Medieval Picture Bible*. William Noel and Daniel H. Weiss, ed. Baltimore: The Walters Art Museum, 39–59.
Mann, Jill. 1993. "La favolistica." In Cavallo (1992–93), 2:171–95.
Manni, Paola. 2003. *Il Trecento toscano: La lingua di Dante, Petrarca e Boccaccio*. Bologna: Il Mulino.
Marchandisse, Alain. 2008. "Milan, les Visconti, l'union de Valentine et de Louis d'Orléans, vus par Froissart et par les auteurs contemporains." In

Autour du XVe siècle: Journées d'étude en l'honneur d'Alberto Vàrvaro. Paola Moreno and Giovanni Palumbo, ed. Geneva: Droz, 93–116.
Marchesi, Simone. 2009. "Petrarch's Philological Epic *(Africa).*" In Kirkham (2009), 113–30.
—. 2013. "Boccaccio on Fortune *(De casibus virorum illustrium).*" In Kirkham (2013), 245–54.
Marco, Costantino. 2008. *Meridione e meridionalismo: Dal mito storiografico alla politica della formazione civile*. Lungro di Cosenza: Ibis.
Marino, John A. 2013. "Constructing the Past of Early Modern Naples: Sources and Historiography." In *A Companion to Early Modern Naples*. Tommaso Astarita, ed. Leiden: Brill, 11–34.
Martellucci, Myriam. 2012. "Images et pouvoir monarchique au sein d'un manuscrit des *Grandes chroniques de France*." In *La puissance royale: Image et pouvoir de l'Antiquité au Moyen Âge*. Emmanuelle Santinelli-Foltz and Christian-Georges Schwentzel, ed. Rennes: Presses universitaires, 129–39.
Martinez, Ronald L. 2013. "Also Known as 'Prencipe Galeotto' *(Decameron).*" In Kirkham (2013), 23–39.
—. 2015. "The Latin Hexameter Works: *Epystole, Bucolicum carmen, Africa*." In Ascoli–Falkeid, 87–99.
Marzano, Annalisa. 2015. "Reshaping the Past, Shaping the Present: Andrea de Jorio and Naples' Classical Heritage." In Hughes–Buongiovanni, 266–83.
Masi, Gino. 1931. *La pittura infamante nella legislazione e nella vita del comune fiorentino (secc. XIII–XVI)*. Rome: Società editrice dell "Foro italiano."
Mazzamuto, Pietro. 1983. "Il cronotopo dell'isola nel *Decameron* e la vicenda siciliana di Lisabetta." In *Boccaccio e dintorni: Miscellanea di studi in onore di Vittore Branca*. Florence: Olschki, 161–68.
Mazzocco, Angelo. 2016. With Marc Laureys, ed. *A New Sense of the Past: The Scholarship of Biondo Flavio (1392–1463)*. Leuven: Leuven University Press.
—. 2016.1. "Introduction." In Mazzocco–Laureys (2016), 9–34.
Mazzotta, Giuseppe. 2018. "Boccaccio's Critique of Petrarch." In Candido (2018), 270–85.
McAvoy, Liz Herbert. 2002. With Teresa Walters, ed. *Consuming Narratives: Gender and Monstrous Appetite in the Middle Ages and the Renaissance*. Cardiff: University of Wales Press.
McCracken, Peggy. 1998. *The Romance of Adultery: Queenship and Sexual Transgression in Old French Literature*. Philadelphia: University of Pennsylvania Press.
McGowan, Andrew. 1994. "Eating People: Accusations of Cannibalism Against Christians in the Second Century." *The Journal of Early Christian Studies* 2:413–42.
Menache, Sophia. 2006. "Chronicles and Historiography: The Interrelationship of Fact and Fiction." *Journal of Medieval History* 32.4:333–45.
—. 2009. "Written and Oral Testimonies in Medieval Chronicles: Matthew Paris and Giovanni Villani." TMC 6:1–30.
Merback, Mitchell B. 1999. *The Thief, the Cross, and the Wheel: Pain and the Spectacle of Punishment in Medieval and Renaissance Europe*. Chicago: University of Chicago Press.

—. 2002. "Reverberations of Guilt and Violence, Resonances of Place: A Comment on Caroline Walker Bynum's Lecture." *German Historical Institute. Bulletin* 30:37–50.
Mercuri, Roberto. 1997. "Avignone e Napoli in Dante, Petrarca e Boccaccio." In A&N, 117–28.
Meyerson, Mark Douglas, et al., ed. 2004. *A Great Effusion of Blood?: Interpreting Medieval Violence.* Toronto: University of Toronto Press.
Migiel, Marilyn. 2015. "Boccaccio and Women." In Armstrong (2015), 171–84.
Migliorino, Francesco. 1985. *Fama e infamia: Problemi della società medievale nel pensiero giuridico nei secoli XII e XIII.* Catania: Giannotta.
Miller, Sarah Alison. 2010. *Medieval Monstrosity and the Female Body.* New York: Routledge.
Mittman, Asa Simon. 2012. With Peter Dendle, ed. *The Ashgate Research Companion to Monsters and the Monstrous.* Farnham, Surrey: Ashgate.
Modigliani, Anna. 2012. "Cibo e potere a Roma: I banchetti imperiali di Cola di Rienzo e di Paolo II." *Archivi e Cultura* n.s 45:99–111.
—. 2014. "Lo ogliardino de Roma: Il progetto italiano di Cola di Rienzo." In *Roma nel Rinascimento,* 241–53.
Modonutti, Rino. 2013. *Fra Giovanni Colonna e la storia antica da Adriano ai Severi.* Padua: Coop. Libraria Editrice Università di Padova.
Moe, Nelson. 2002. *The View from Vesuvius: Italian Culture and the Southern Question.* Berkeley: University of California Press.
Mollat, Guillaume. 1963. *The Popes at Avignon, 1305–1378.* London: Nelson.
Montuori, Francesco. 2012.1. "Immagini di Napoli fra trecento e quattrocento." In *Il viaggio a Napoli tra letteratura e arti.* Pasquale Sabbatino, ed. Naples: Edizioni Scientifiche Italiane, 13–37.
—. 2012.2. "La scrittura della storia a Napoli negli anni del Boccaccio angioino." In BA, 171–97.
—. 2017. "Come 'si costruisce' una cronaca." In Francesconi–Miglio, 31–87.
Morato, Nicola. 2010. *Il ciclo di* Guiron le Courtois: *Strutture e testi nella tradizione manoscritta.* Florence: Edizioni del Galluzzo.
Moreschini, Claudio. 1992. "I Padri." In Cavallo (1992–93), 1:563–604.
Moretti, Felice. 1989. *Cultura e società in Puglia in età sveva e angioina: Atti del convegno di studi, Bitonto, 11–12–13 dic. 1987.* Bitonto: Centro ricerche di storia e arte bitontina.
Morosini, Roberta. 2012. "La 'bona sonoritas' di Calliopo: Boccaccio a Napoli, la polifonia di Partenope e i silenzi dell'Acciaiuoli." In BA, 69–87.
Morrison, Elizabeth. 2002. "Illuminations of the *Roman de Troie* and French Royal Dynastic Ambition (1260–1340)." Ph.D. diss., Cornell University.
—. 2010. With Anne Dawson Hedeman and Elisabeth Antoine, ed. *Imagining the Past in France: History in Manuscript Painting, 1250–1500.* Los Angeles: J. Paul Getty Museum.
—. 2010a. "From Sacred to Secular: The Origins of History Illumination in France." In Morrison (2010), 9–26.
Morse, Ruth. 1991. *Truth and Convention in the Middle Ages: Rhetoric, Representation, and Reality.* Cambridge: Cambridge University Press.

Mortensen, Lars Boje. 2015. "Comparing and Connecting: The Rise of Fast Historiography in Latin and Vernacular (12th–13th cent.)." *Medieval Worlds* 1:25–39.
Murphy, James Jerome. 1974. *Rhetoric in the Middle Ages: A History of Rhetorical Theory from Saint Augustine to the Renaissance.* Berkeley: University of California Press.
—. 1978. *Medieval Eloquence: Studies in the Theory and Practice of Medieval Rhetoric.* Berkeley: University of California Press.
Musca, Giosuè. 1985."Cronisti meridionali nell'età angioina." In *Civiltà del Mezzogiorno: La cultura angioina.* Milan: Silvana, 31–74.
Musella, Luigi. 2005. *Meridionalismo: Percorsi e realtà di un'idea, 1885–1944.* Naples: Guida.
Musto, Ronald G. 1983. "Angelo Clareno, O.F.M.: Fourteenth-Century Translator of the Greek Fathers. A Checklist of Manuscripts and Printings of His 'Scala paradisi'." *Archivum Franciscanum Historicum* 76:589–645.
—. 1985."Queen Sancia of Naples (1286–1345) and the Spiritual Franciscans." In *Women of the Medieval World: Essays in Honor of John H. Mundy.* Julius Kirshner and Suzanne F. Wemple, ed. New York: Blackwell, 179–214.
—. 1991."An Introduction to Neapolitan History." In Bacco, xix–lxii.
—. 1997. "Franciscan Joachimism at the Court of Naples, 1305–1345: A New Appraisal." *Archivum Franciscanum Historicum* 90.3–4:1–86.
—. 2003. *Apocalypse in Rome: Cola di Rienzo and the Politics of the New Age.* Berkeley: University of California Press.
—. 2016. "The Visualization of Power in the Reign of Giovanna I of Naples." *Visual History* 2:105–24.
—. 2017."Naples in Myth and History." In Hall–Willette, 1–33.
Mutini, Claudio. 1972. "Buccio di Ranallo." DBI 14. At www.treccani.it/enciclopedia/buccio-di-ranallo_(Dizionario_Biografico).
Nardi, Valeria. 1993."Le illustrazioni dei *Documenti d'Amore* di Francesco da Barberino." *Ricerche di storia dell'arte* 49:75–91.
Nevile, Anne Elizabeth. 2013. "'A Tapestry Woven by Poets': Narrative in Text and Illustration in the *Meliadus de Leonnois,* British Library MS. Add. 12228." Ph.D. diss., University of Melbourne.
Nichols, Stephen G. 1996. "Melusine Between Myth and History, Profile of a Female Demon." In Maddox (1996), 137–64.
Nitti, Francesco Saverio. 2004. With Domenico De Masi. *Napoli e la questione meridionale, 1903–2005.* Naples: Guida.
Nohrnberg, James C. 2010. "'This Disfigured People': Representations of Sin as Pathological Bodily and Mental Affliction in Dante's *Inferno* XXIX–XXX." In Vaught (2010), 43–64.
Norman, Diana. 2018. *Siena and the Angevins, 1300–1350: Art, Diplomacy and Dynastic Ambition.* Turnhout: Brepols.
Oldoni, Massino. 1992."La tradizione orale e folclorica." In Cavallo (1992–93), 1:633–55.
Ong, Walter J. 1959."Latin Language Study as a Renaissance Puberty Rite." *Studies in Philology* 56.2:103–24.

—. 2002. *Orality and Literacy: The Technologizing of the Word.* London: Routledge.
Ortalli, Gherardo. 1979. *Pingatur in Palatio: La pittura infamante nei secoli XIII–XVI.* Rome: Jouvence.
—. 1989. "Cronache e documentazione." In *Civiltà comunale: Libro, scrittura, documento. Atti della Società ligure di storia patria* n.s. 29 (103.2): 507–39.
—. 2015. *La pittura infamante: Secoli XIII–XVI.* Rome: Viella.
Oswald, Dana. 2010. *Monsters, Gender and Sexuality in Medieval English Literature.* Woodbridge, Suffolk: D.S. Brewer.
Otter, Monica. 2005. "Functions of Fiction in Historical Writing." In Partner (2005), 109–30.
Owen, Rachel. 2001. "Dante's Reception by 14th- and 15th-Century Illustrators of the *Commedia.*" *Reading Medieval Studies* 27:163–225.
Owens, Margaret E. 2005. *Stages of Dismemberment: The Fragmented Body in Late Medieval and Early Modern Drama.* Newark: University of Delaware Press.
Owst, Gerald R. 1933. *Literature and Pulpit in Medieval England.* Cambridge: Cambridge University Press.
Palmentieri, Angela. 2015. "*Marmora Romana* in Medieval Naples: Architectural *Spolia* from the Fourth to the Fifteenth Centuries, A.D." In Hughes–Buongiovanni, 121–51.
Palmer, James A. 2014. "Piety and Social Distinction in Late Medieval Roman Peacemaking." *Speculum* 89.4:974–1004.
—. 2019. *The Virtues of Economy: Governance, Power and Piety in Late Medieval Rome.* Ithaca, NY: Cornell University Press.
Palmer, John Joseph Norman. 1981. *Froissart, Historian.* Woodbridge: Boydell.
Panizza, Letizia. 2013. "Rhetoric and Invective in Love's Labyrinth *(Il Corbaccio).*" In Kirkham (2013), 183–93.
Panofsky, Erwin. 1972. *Renaissance and Renascences in Western Art.* New York: Harper & Row.
Parsons, John Carmi. 2004. "Violence, the Queen's Body, and the Medieval Body Politic." In Meyerson (2004), 241–67.
Partner, Nancy F. 1985. "The New Cornificius: Medieval History and the Artifice of Words." In Breisach, 5–59.
—. 1986. "Making Up Lost Time: Writing on the Writing of History." *Speculum* 61:90–117.
—. 2005. *Writing Medieval History.* London: Hodder Arnold.
Pasquini, Emilio. 1997. "Francesco da Barberino." DBI 49. At www.treccani.it/enciclopedia/francesco-da-barberino_(Dizionario-Biografico).
Pasut, Francesca. 2014. "Pacino di Buonaguida." DBI 80. At www.treccani.it/enciclopedia/pacino-di-buonaguida_(Dizionario-Biografico).
Pellegrino, Nicoletta. 2007. "From the Roman Empire to Christian Imperialism: The Work of Flavio Biondo." In Dale (2007), 273–98.
Peri, Illuminato. 1981. *La Sicilia dopo il Vespro: Uomini, città e campagne, 1282–1376.* Bari: Laterza.
Perriccioli Saggese, Alessandra. 1979. *I romanzi cavallereschi miniati a Napoli.* Naples: Società Editrice Napoletana.

—. 1985. "Alcune precisazioni sul 'Roman du roy Meliadus', Ms. Add. 12228 del British Museum." In Sesti (1985), 51–64.

—. 2001. "L'enluminure à Naples au temps des Anjou (1266–1350)." In *L'Europe des Anjou*. Guy Massin Le Goff et al., ed. Paris: Somogy, 123–33.

—. 2005. "Gli *Statuti dell'Ordine dello Spirito Santo o del Nodo*: Immagine e ideologia del potere regio a Napoli alla metà del Trecento." In Quintavalle, (2005), 519–24.

—. 2005.1. "Le illustrazioni di storia nei codici miniati a Napoli tra Duecento e Trecento: Riflessioni sullo stato degli studi." In Quintavalle (2005), 547–56.

—. 2010. "Cristophoro Orimina: An Illuminator at the Angevin Court of Naples." In *Anjou Bible*, 113–25.

—. 2011. "Dall'*Histoire ancienne* al *Roman du roy Meliadus:* L'illustrazione della battaglia nella miniatura napoletana di età angioina." In *La battaglia nel Rinascimento meridionale*. Giancarlo Abbamonte, ed. Rome: Viella, 17–27.

—. 2012. "Romanzi cavallereschi miniati a Napoli al tempo di Boccaccio." In BA, 347–56.

Petkov, Kiril. 2003. *The Kiss of Peace: Ritual, Self, and Society in the High and Late Medieval West*. Leiden: Brill.

Petoletti, Marco. 2018. "Boccaccio, the Classics and the Latin Middle Ages." In Candido (2018), 226–43.

Petrucci, Armando. 1958. Notarii: *Documenti per la storia del notariato italiano*. Milan: A. Giuffrè.

—. 1985. "La scrittura del testo." In *Letteratura Italiana. 4. L'Interpretazione*. Alberto Asor Rosa, ed. Turin: Einaudi, 283–308.

—. 1992–93. "Dalla minuta al manoscritto d'autore." In Cavallo (1992–93), 1:353–72.

Petrucci, Livio. 1993. "Il volgare a Napoli in età angioina." In Trovato–Gonelli (1993), 27–72.

Pettitt, Thomas. 2012. "Bracketing the Gutenberg Parenthesis." *Explorations in Media Ecology* 11.2:95–114.

Phillips, Philip Edward. 2014. "Boethius, the Prisoner, and the Consolation of Philosophy." In idem, ed. *Prison Narratives from Boethius to Zana*. New York: Palgrave Macmillan.

Phillips, Susan E. 2013. *Transforming Talk: The Problem with Gossip in Late Medieval England*. University Park: Pennsylvania State University Press.

Pignatti, Franco. 1996. "Ferraiolo." DBI 46. At www.treccani.it/enciclopedia/ferraiolo_(Dizionario-Biografico).

—. 2001. "Giovanni Fiorentino." DBI 56. At www.treccani.it/enciclopedia/giovanni-fiorentino_(Dizionario-Biografico).

Pontari, Paolo. 2016. "'Nedum mille qui effluxerunt annorum gesta sciamus'. *L'Italia* di Biondo e l'"invenzione' del Medioevo." In Mazzocco–Laureys (2016), 151–76.

Porta, Giuseppe. 1989. "Giovanni Villani storico e scrittore." In *I racconti di Clio: Tecniche narrative della storiografia*. Pisa: Nistri-Lischi, 147–56.

—. 1999. "La construzione della storia in Giovanni Villani." In *Il senso della storia nella cultura medievale italiana (1100–1350)*. Pistoia: Centro Italiano di Studi di Storia e d'Arte, 125–38.

—. 2017. "La cronaca a Firenze: Passione politica e travaglio compositivo." In Francesconi–Miglio, 157–63.
Postlewate, Laurie. 2007. With Wim Husken. *Acts and Texts: Performance and Ritual in the Middle Ages and the Renaissance*. Amsterdam: Rodopi.
Potestà, Gian Luca. 1990. *Angelo Clareno: Dai poveri eremiti ai fraticelli*. Rome: ISIME.
Pratt, Karen. 1997. "The Image of the Queen in Old French Literature." In Duggan (1997), 236–62.
Price, Merrall Llewelyn. 2003. *Consuming Passions: The Uses of Cannibalism in Late Medieval and Early Modern Europe*. New York: Routledge.
Pryds, Darleen. 2000. *The King Embodies the Word: Robert d'Anjou and the Politics of Preaching*. Leiden: Brill.
Quinones, Ricardo J. 2016. *North/South: The Great European Divide*. Toronto: University of Toronto Press.
Quintavalle, Arturo Carlo, ed. 2005. *Medioevo: Immagini e ideologie*. Parma: Centro Studi Medievali.
Rabil, Albert, Jr. 1988. "The Significance of 'Civic Humanism' in the Interpretation of the Italian Renaissance." In idem, *Renaissance Humanism*. 3 vols. Philadelphia: University of Pennsylvania Press, 1:141–74.
Ragone, Franca. 1998. *Giovanni Villani e i suoi continuatori: La scrittura delle cronache a Firenze nel Trecento*. Rome: ISIME.
Rao, Ennio I. 1981. *The Invectives of Bartolomeo Facio Against Lorenzo Valla: A Contribution to the History of Italian Humanism*. Ann Arbor: University Microfilms.
Ratté, Felicity. 2006. *Picturing the City in Medieval Italian Painting*. Jefferson, NC: McFarland.
Ray, Roger. 1985. "Rhetorical Skepticism and Verisimilar Narrative in John of Salisbury's *Historia Pontificalis*." In Breisach, 61–102.
Raynaud, Christiane. 1999. "La reine dans les *Grandes Chroniques de France*." TMC 1:226–39.
Rehberg, Andreas. 2004. With Anna Modigliani. *Cola di Rienzo e il Comune di Roma*. 2 vols. Rome: Inedita.
Reichl, Karl, ed. 2016. *Medieval Oral Literature*. Berlin: De Gruyter.
—. 2016a. "Plotting the Map of Medieval Oral Literature." In Reichl (2016), 3–70.
Resta, Gianvito. 1970. "Beccadelli, Antonio, detto il Panormita." DBI 7. At www.treccani.it/enciclopedia/beccadelli-antonio-detto-il-panormita_(Dizionario Biografico).
Reynolds, Leighton Durham. 1968. With Nigel Guy Wilson. *Scribes and Scholars: A Guide to the Transmission of Greek and Latin Literature*. Oxford: Oxford University Press.
Ricci, Lucia Battaglia. 2018. *Dante per immagini: Dalle miniature trecentesche ai giorni nostri*. Turin: Einaudi.
Ricœur, Paul. 2004. *Memory, History, Forgetting*. Chicago: University of Chicago Press.
Riklin, Alois. 2017. *Etica repubblicana nel Palazzo Pubblico di Siena, 1315–1535: Simone Martini, Ambrogio Lorenzetti, Taddeo di Bartolo, Domenico Beccafumi*. Venice: Marsilio.

Rizzi, Andrea. 2017. *Vernacular Translators in Quattrocento Italy: Scribal Culture, Authority, and Agency.* Turnhout: Brepols.
Robins, William. 2004. "Vernacular Textualities in Fourteenth-Century Florence." In *The Vulgar Tongue: Medieval and Postmedieval Vernacularity.* Fiona Somerset and Nicholas Watson, ed. University Park: Pennsylvania State University Press, 112–13.
Roick, Matthias. 2017. *Pontano's Virtues: Aristotelian Moral and Political Thought in the Renaissance.* London: Bloomsbury Academic.
Rollo-Koster, Joëlle. 2003. "The Politics of Body Parts: Contested Topographies in Late Medieval Avignon." *Speculum* 78.1:66–98.
—. 2008. *Raiding Saint Peter: Empty Sees, Violence, and the Initiation of the Great Western Schism (1378).* Leiden: Brill.
—. 2015. *Avignon and Its Papacy, 1309–1417: Popes, Institutions, and Society.* Lanham, MD: Rowman & Littlefield.
Romano, Serena. 2017. "Patrons and Paintings from the Angevins to the Spanish Hapsburgs." In Hall–Willette, 171–232.
Rosand, David. 1987. "Ekphrasis and the Renaissance of Painting: Observations on Alberti's Third Book." In *Florilegium Columbianum.* Karl-Ludwig Selig and Robert Somerville, ed. New York: Italica Press, 147–65.
Rossi, Marielisa. 2007. "Bibliografia degli scritti su Lorenzo Valla." In *Lorenzo Valla: Edizioni delle opere (sec. XV–XVI).* Marielisa Rossi, ed. Rome: Vecchiarelli, 176–206.
Rouillard, Linda Marie. 2012. Review of "Jean Wauquelin, *La Manequine,* Maria Colombo Timelli, ed. (Paris: Éditions Classiques Garnier, 2010)." *Speculum* 87.1:288–89.
Roussel, M. Claude. 1998. *Conter de geste au XIVe siècle: Inspiration folklorique et écriture épique dans* La belle Hélène de Constantinople. Geneva: Droz.
Royle, Nicholas. 2003. *The Uncanny.* Manchester: Manchester University Press.
Rubenstein, Jay. 2005. "Biography and Autobiography in the Middle Ages." In Partner (2005), 22–41.
Rudolph, Conrad. 2006. *A Companion to Medieval Art: Romanesque and Gothic in Northern Europe.* Malden, MA: Blackwell.
Rullo, Alessandra. 2012. "L'incontro di Boccaccio e Fiammetta in San Lorenzo Maggiore a Napoli: Un ipotesi di ricostruzione del coro dei frati nel XIV secolo." In BA, 303–16.
Runnalls, Graham A. 1999. "Drama and Community in Late Medieval Paris." In *Drama and Community: People and Plays in Medieval Europe.* Alan Hindley, ed. Turnhout: Brepols, 18–33.
Ryder, Alan Frederick Charles. 1976. "Antonio Beccadelli: A Humanist in Government." In *Cultural Aspects of the Italian Renaissance: Essays in Honour of Paul Oskar Kristeller.* Cecil H. Clough, ed. Manchester: Manchester University Press, 123–40.
Sabatini, Francesco. 1975. *Napoli angioina: Cultura e società.* Naples: Edizioni scientifiche italiane.
—. 1992. "Lingue e letterature volgari in competizione." In *Italia linguistica delle origini.* V. Coletti et al., ed., 2 vols. Lecce: Argo, 2:507–68.

—. 1996. With Vittorio Coletti. *Italia linguistica delle origini: Saggi editi dal 1956 al 1996*. Lecce: Argo.

—. 1996a. "Volgare 'civile' e volgare cancelleresco nella Napoli angioina." In idem, (1996), 467–506.

Sabia, Liliana Monti. 1980. "L'estremo autografo di Giovanni Pontano." *Italia medioevale e umanistica* 23:293–314.

—. 1995. *Pontano e la storia: Dal De bello Neapolitano all'*Actius. Rome: Bulzoni.

Said, Edward. 1983. *The World, the Text, and the Critic*. Cambridge, MA: Harvard University Press.

Samson, Alexander. 2020. *Mary and Philip: The Marriage of Tudor England and Habsburg Spain*. Manchester: Manchester University Press.

Sancricca, Arnaldo. 2015. *I "Fratres" di Angelo Clareno: Da Poveri eremiti di papa Celestino a Frati minori della provincia di s. Girolamo "de Urbe" attraverso la genesi del Terz'ordine regolare di s. Francesco in Italia*. Macerata: Edizioni Simple.

Santini, Emilio. 1940. "La Sicilia nel *Decameron*." *Archivio storico per la Sicilia* 6:239–52.

Santore, John. 2001. *Modern Naples: A Documentary History, 1799–1999*. New York: Italica Press.

Schmid, Petra. 2014. "*I Documenti d'Amore* von Francesco da Barberino Trecenteske: Bildfindungen zwischen politischen und ästhetischen Tugenddiskursen." *ALL-OVER: Magazin für Kunst und Ästhetik* 7:15–24.

—. 2015. "*I Documenti d'Amore* von Francesco da Barberino: Zur politischen Funktion interpiktorialer Bildstrategien im frühen Trecento." *kunsttexte.de. Sektion Politische Ikonographie* 4:1–18.

Schneller, Robert W. 1963. *A Survey of Medieval Model Books*. Haarlem: E.F. Bohn.

Schwartz, Amy. 1994. "Images and Illusions of Power in Trecento Art: Cola di Rienzo and the Ancient Roman Republic." Ph.D. diss., State University of New York at Binghamton.

—. 2007. "Eternal Rome and Cola di Rienzo's Show of Power." In Postlewate (2007), 63–76.

Sciacca, Christine, ed. 2012. *Florence at the Dawn of the Renaissance Painting and Illumination, 1300–1350*. Los Angeles: J. Paul Getty Museum. At www.getty.edu/art/exhibitions/florence/introduction.html.

Seibt, Gustav. 2000. *Anonimo romano: Scrivere la storia alle soglie del Rinascimento*. Rome: Viella.

Senatore, Francesco. 2012. "The Kingdom of Naples." In Gamberini and Lazzarini (2012), 30–49.

—. 2014. "Fonti documentarie e costruzione della notizia nelle cronache cittadine dell'Italia meridionale (secoli XV–XVI)." *Bullettino* ISIME 116:279–333.

—. 2017. "Cronaca e cancellerie." In Francesconi–Miglio, 285–99.

Sestan, Ernesto. 1972. "Gualtieri di Brienne." DBI 14. At www.treccani.it/enciclopedia/gualtieri-di-brienne_(Dizionario-Biografico).

Setz, Wolfram. 1975. *Lorenzo Vallas Schrift gegen die konstantinische Schenkung: De falso credita et ementita Constantini donatione: Zur Interpretation und Wirkungsgeschichte*. Tübingen: Niemeyer.

Shemek, Deanna. 2013. "Doing and Undoing: Boccaccio's Feminism *(De mulieribus claris)*." In Kirkham (2013), 195–204.
Shepherd, M. 1990. *Tradition and Re-Creation in Thirteenth-Century Romance: "La Manekine" and "Jean et Blonde" by Philippe de Rémi.* Amsterdam: Rodopi.
Sherberg, Michael. 2013. "The Girl Outside the Window *(Teseida delle nozze d'Emilia)*." In Kirkham (2013), 95–106.
Siegel, Jerrold E. 1966. "'Civic Humanism' or Ciceronian Rhetoric? The Culture of Petrarch and Bruni." *Past and Present* 34:3–48.
Siraisi, Nancy G. 2001. *Medicine and the Italian Universities, 1250–1600.* Leiden: Brill.
—. 2007. *Medieval & Early Renaissance Medicine: An Introduction to Knowledge and Practice.* Chicago: University of Chicago Press.
Skorge, Kristel Mari. 2006. *Ideals and Values in Jean Froissart's Chroniques.* Bergen: University Press.
Smarr, Janet Levarie. 1987. "Life of the Author." In Boccaccio (1987), viii–xxii.
—. 2013. "Introduction: A Man of Many Turns." In Kirkham (2013), 1–20.
Smith, Bonnie G. 2001. *The Gender of History: Men, Women, and Historical Practice.* Cambridge: Harvard University Press.
Solomon, Jon. 2013. "Gods, Greeks and Poetry *(Genealogia deorum gentilium)*." In Kirkham (2013), 235–44.
Sonnay, Philippe. 1982. "La politique artistique de Cola di Rienzo (1313–1354)." *La Revue de l'art* 55:35–43.
Spiegel, Gabrielle M. 1997. *The Past as Text: The Theory and Practice of Medieval Historiography.* Baltimore: Johns Hopkins University Press.
—. 2005. *Practicing History: New Directions in Historical Writing after the Linguistic Turn.* New York: Routledge.
Stein, Robert M. 2005. "Literary Criticism and the Evidence for History." In Partner (2005), 67–87.
Steinberg, Justin. 2009. "Petrarch's Damned Poetry and the Poetics of Exclusion *(Rime disperse)*." In Kirkham (2009), 85–100.
—. 2011. "Dante and the Laws of Infamy." *PMLA* 126:1118–26.
Stern, Laura Ikins. 2000. "Public Fame in the Fifteenth Century." *American Journal of Legal History* 44:198–222.
Stillinger, Thomas C. 2006. With Regina Psaki, ed. *Boccaccio and Feminist Criticism.* Chapel Hill, NC: Annali d'Italianistica.
Stock, Brian. 1990. *Listening for the Text: On the Uses of the Past.* Philadelphia: University of Pennsylvania Press.
Stodola, Denise. 2010. "The Middle Ages." In *The Present State of Scholarship in the History of Rhetoric: A Twenty-First Century Guide.* Lynée Lewis Gaillet and Winifred Bryan Horner, ed. Columbia: University of Missouri Press, 42–81.
Stones, Alison. 1976. "Secular Manuscript Illumination in France." In *Medieval Manuscripts and Textual Criticism.* Christopher Kleinhenz, ed. Chapel Hill: University of North Carolina Press, 83–102.
Strohm, Paul. 1992. *Hochon's Arrow: The Social Imagination of Fourteenth-Century Texts.* Princeton: Princeton University Press.

Summerfield, Thea. 2010. "Filling the Gap: Brutus in the *Historia Brittonum, Anglo-Saxon Chronicle* MS F, and Geoffrey of Monmouth." TMC 7:85–102.

Summit, Jennifer. 2000. "Topography as Historiography: Petrarch, Chaucer, and the Making of Medieval Rome." *Journal of Medieval and Early Modern Studies* 30:211–46.

Taylor, Julie. 2003. *Muslims in Medieval Italy: The Colony at Lucera.* Lanham: Lexington Books.

Taviani-Carozzi, Huguette. 2002. "Mythe et histoire dans les chroniques d'Italie du Sud (IXe–XIIe siècles)." TMC 2:238–49.

Taylor, Matthew. 1986. *Matteo Palmieri (1406–1475): Florentine Humanist and Politician.* Florence: European University Institute.

Thomas, Chantal. 1999. *The Wicked Queen: The Origins of the Myth of Marie Antoinette.* Julie Rose, trans. New York: Zone Books.

Tocco, Francesco Paolo. 2001. *Niccolò Acciaiuoli: Vita e politica in Italia alla metà del XIV secolo.* Rome: ISIME.

Tolhurst, Fiona. 2012. *Geoffrey of Monmouth and the Feminist Origins of the Arthurian Legend.* New York: Palgrave Macmillan.

Tomei, Alessandro. 2010. With Stefania Paone. "Paintings and Miniatures in Naples: Cavallini, Giotto and the Portraits of King Robert." In *Anjou Bible,* 53–71.

—. 2016. "I *Regia Carmina* dedicati a Roberto d'Angiò nella British Library di Londra: Un manoscritto tra Italia e Provenza." *Arte Medievale* ser. 4.6:201–12.

Trinkaus, Charles Edward. 1985. *The Astrological Cosmos and Rhetorical Culture of Giovanni Gioviano Pontano.* New York: Renaissance Society of America.

Tristano, Caterina. 1993. "Scrivere il volgare in Italia meridionale (secc. XII–XIV)." In Trovato-Gonelli (1993), 7–26.

Troncarelli, Fabio. 1992–93. "L'attribuzione, il plagio, il falso." In Cavallo (1992–93), 1:373–90.

Tronzo, William. 2004. "Giotto's Figures." In Derbes–Sandona (2004), 63–75.

Trovato, Paolo. 1993. With Lida Maria Gonelli, ed. *Lingue e culture dell'Italia meridionale, 1200–1600.* Rome: Bonacci.

Tuchman, Barbara W. 1978. *A Distant Mirror: The Calamitous Fourteenth Century.* New York: Random House.

Vaccaro, Giulio. 2021. "Text and Transmission in Early Italian Chronicles." *Opera del Vocabolario Italiano.* Florence: CNR.

Vallerani, Massimo. 2012. *Medieval Public Justice.* Washington, DC: Catholic University of America Press.

Varvaro, Alberto. 1997. "L'Italia meridionale nelle cronache di Jean Froissard." In A&N, 131–39.

Vasoli, Cesare. 1972. "Bruni, Leonardo." DBI 14:618–33 At www.treccani.it/enciclopedia/bruni-leonardo-detto-leonardo-aretino_(Dizionario-Biografico).

Vaught, Jennifer C. ed. 2010. *Rhetorics of Bodily Disease and Health in Medieval and Early Modern England.* Aldershot: Ashgate.

Villa, Claudia. (1992). "I classici." In Cavallo (1992–93), 1:479–522.
Vingtain, Dominique. 1998. With Claude Sauvageot, ed. *Avignon: Le Palais des Papes*. Saint-Léger-Vauban: Zodiaque.
Viti, Paolo. 1994. "Facio, Bartolomeo." DBI 44. At www.treccani.it/enciclopedia/bartolomeo-facio_(Dizionario-Biografico).
Vitolo, Giovanni. 2004. With Aurelio Musi. *Il Mezzogiorno prima della questione meridionale*. Florence: Le Monnier.
Vitullo, Juliann M. 2000. *The Chivalric Epic in Medieval Italy*. Gainesville: University Press of Florida.
Wahlen, Barbara. 2006. "Nostalgies romaines: Le parcours de la chevalerie dans le *Roman du roi Meliadus*, première partie de *Guiron le Courtois*." In Bertholot (2006), 165–81.
—. 2010. *L'écriture à rebours: Le* Roman de Meliadus *du XIIIe au XVIIIe siècle*. Geneva: Droz.
Wallace, David. 2013. "Love-Struck in Naples *(Filostrato)*." In Kirkham (2013), 77–85.
Ward, John O. 1985. "Some Principles of Rhetorical Historiography in the Twelfth Century." In Breisach, 103–65.
Warr, Cordelia. 2010. With Janis Elliott. *Art and Architecture in Naples, 1266–1713*. Malden, MA: Wiley-Blackwell.
Weaver, Elissa. 2013. "A Lovers' Tale and Auspicious Beginning *(Filocolo)*." In Kirkham (2013), 87–93.
Weimann, Robert. 1996. *Authority and Representation in Early Modern Discourse*. David Hillman, ed. Baltimore: Johns Hopkins University Press, 105–32.
White, Hayden. 1987. *The Content of the Form: Narrative Discourse and Historical Representation*. Baltimore: Johns Hopkins University Press.
—. 1987a. "The Value of Narrativity in the Representation of Reality." In White (1987), 1–25.
—. 1987b. "The Question of Narrative in Contemporary Historical Theory." In White (1987), 26–57.
—. 1987c. "The Metaphysics of Narrativity: Time and Symbol in Ricoeur's Philosophy of History." In White (1987), 169–84.
—. 1987d. "The Politics of Historical Interpretation: Discipline and De-Sublimation." In White (1987), 58–82.
—. 2010. *The Fiction of Narrative: Essays on History, Literature, and Theory, 1957–2007*. Robert Doran, ed. Baltimore: Johns Hopkins University Press.
—. 2010a. "The Structure of Historical Narrative." In White (2010), 112–25.
—. 2010b. "Storytelling: Historical and Ideological." In White (2010), 273–92.
Wickham, Chris. 2003. "*Fama* and the Law in Twelfth-Century Tuscany." In Fenster–Smail (2003), 15–26.
—. 2015. *Sleepwalking into a New World: The Emergence of the Italian City Communes in the Twelfth Century*. Princeton: Princeton University Press.
Wilcox, Donald J. 1985. "The Sense of Time in Western Historical Narratives from Eusebius to Machiavelli." In Breisach, 167–237.
Wilkins, Ernest Hatch. 1961. *Life of Petrarch*. Chicago: University of Chicago Press.

Witt, Ronald G. 2001. *Italian Humanism and Medieval Rhetoric.* Aldershot: Ashgate/Variorum.

—. 2009. "The Rebirth of the Romans as Models of Character *(De viris illustribus).*" In Kirkham (2009), 103–11.

—. 2012. *The Two Latin Cultures and the Foundation of Renaissance Humanism in Medieval Italy.* Cambridge: Cambridge University Press.

Wittkower, Rudolf. 1942. "Marvels of the East: A Study in the History of Monsters." *Journal of the Warburg and Courtauld Institutes* 5:159–97.

Wittschier, Heinz Willi. 1968. *Gianozzo Manetti, das corpus der Orationes.* Cologne: Bohlau.

Wollesen, Jens T. 1990. "'*Ut poesis pictura?*' Problems of Images and Texts in the Early Trecento." In *Petrarch's Triumphs: Allegory and Spectacle.* Konrad Eisenbichler and Amilcare A. Iannucci, ed. Toronto: Dovehouse, 183–210.

Wood, Charles T. 1998. "Froissart, Personal Testimony, and the Peasants' Revolt of 1381." In Maddox (1998), 40–49.

Wood, Diana. 1989. *Clement VI: The Pontificate and Ideas of an Avignon Pope.* Cambridge: Cambridge University Press.

Woodacre, Elena. 2013. *Queenship in the Mediterranean: Negotiating the Role of the Queen in the Medieval and Early Modern Eras.* New York: Palgrave Macmillan.

Yalom, Marilyn. 2004. *Birth of the Chess Queen: A History.* New York: Harper Collins.

Zabbia, Marino. 1997. *Notai-cronisti nel Mezzogiorno svevo-angioino: Il "Chronicon" di Domenico da Gravina.* Salerno: Laveglia.

—. 1998. "Il contributo dei notai alla codificazione della memoria storica nelle città italiane (secoli XII–XIV)." *Nuova Rivista Storica* 82.1:1–16.

—. 1999. *I notai e la cronachistica cittadina italiana nel Trecento.* Rome: ISIME.

—. 2001. "Giovanni da Bazzano." DBI 55. At www.treccani.it/ enciclopedia/giovanni- da bazzano_ (Dizionario_Biografico).

—. 2017. "Cronaca e mondo notarile." In Francesconi–Miglio, 271–84.

Zak, Gur. 2015. "Boccaccio and Petrarch." In Armstrong (2015), 139–54.

—. 2015.1. "Petrarch and the Ancients." In Ascoli-Falkeid, 141–53.

Zchomelidse, Nino Maria. 2014. *Art, Ritual, and Civic Identity in Medieval Southern Italy.* University Park: Pennsylvania State University Press.

Zinelli, Fabio. 2012. "'Je qui li livre escrive de letre en vulgal': Scrivere il francese a Napoli in età angioina." In BA, 149–73.

Ziolkowski, Jan M. 2008. With Michael C.J. Putnam, ed. *The Virgilian Tradition: The First Fifteen Hundred Years.* New Haven: Yale University Press.

Zorzi, Andrea. 1988. *L'amministrazione della giustizia penale nella Repubblica Fiorentina: Aspetti e problemi.* Florence: Olschki.

—. 1994. "Rituali di violenza, ceremoniali penali, rappresentazioni della Giustizia nelle città italiane centro-settentrionali (secoli xiii–xv)." In Cammarosano, 395–425.

—. 2012. "Justice." In Gamberini and Lazzarini (2012), 490–514.

INDEX

A

Acciaiuoli: Andrea 139; Donato 32; Niccolò 29, 106, 127; Boccaccio 29, 31, 139–41, 182, 250–51; Giovanna I 128; manuscript commissions 138, 141, 181–88; Palmieri 31–32, 47, 51, 87, 98, 106; Petrarch 187, 246; reconquest of Regno 127; Villani 26, 65

Alfonso I, king 159, 261–73; Duca di Monteleone 21; Palmieri 32

Anagni *Apocalypse* 171, **172**

Andrew of Hungary: *Anjou Bible* 179–81; Bazzano 54, 85; Boccaccio 31, 105–6, 251; *Chronicon Estense* 24; *Chronicon Mutinense* 24, 59, 85; *Chronicon Suessanum* 16–17; *Cronaca di Partenope* 17; *Cronaca Senese* 27; *Cronicon siculum* 94–95; Gravina 18, 63, 97; marriage 125, 161–63, 180; murder 126, 129, 163, 207–8, 232–35; Palmieri 106; Villani 60–61; Winterthur 33. *See also* Giovanna I.

Angevins: *beata stirps* 184, 230; black legend 8, 229–52, 290; Durazzo 18, 34, 56, 59, 63, 75, 125–26, 128, 130, 180, 208–9, 212, 221, 249, 251, 261, 274; Holy Land 182, 187; Hungary 8, 125, 180, 233–35, 248; manuscripts 178–88; *Pictorial Genealogy* **iv**, 180; Taranto 21, 22, 125–26, 130, 180, 234–35. *See also* Giovanna I; Louis of Taranto; Robert the Wise.

Anjou Bible 7, 161, 179–80, **181**

Anonimo romano: Cola di Rienzo 213–16; *Cronaca* 19–20; crusade accounts 52; Duke of Athens 203–7; ekphrasis 153, 157, 164–78; eyewitness 66–67; Fra Morreale 216, 219–21; invented speech 49; language choice and style 46, 81, 90–91; Latin classics 19–20, 44–46; life and work 15, 19–20; memory 57; narrative form and structure 100, 102, 109–10; Roman barons 217–18; sources 49–56, 61–63

audience: Anonimo romano 110; aristocratic 178–79, 189; Boccaccio 104; civic 68, 85–93, 218, 252, 273, 277–78; Froissart 34; Gravina 97; Latin 82; Palmieri 47; reception 7, 80–81, 199; ritual 202–3, 222; romance 124, 129, 131, 135, 137, 142; visual 153–54, 161, 164–65, 169, 171; Walsingham 108

authorship 1, 8, 17, 22, 27, 37, 60, 110, 135, 152, 199, 258, 273, 278

B

Barberino, Francesco da 153–55, 161, 163–65, 179; "Iustitia" **154**

Barratone, Malizia (Giovanni Fiorentino) 153, 159, 161

Bazzano, Giovanni da 5, 14; archival sources 54; Latinity and style 85; life and work 23–24. *See also Chronicon Mutinense*.

Beccadelli, Antonio (Panormita) 8, 266–67

Belle Helene de Constantinople 124, 132, 142

Biondo, Flavio 8, 258, 262–66

black legend: Angevin 140, 229–52; Spanish 229–30

Boccaccio, Giovanni: Acciaiuoli 29, 31, 140–41, 182, 250–51; "Against Women" 140; *Allegoria mitologica* 103; "altra Napoli" 63; ambassador 30; *Amorosa Visione* 30, 63, 140, 159, 162; Andrew of Hungary 31, 105–6, 251; Angevin court 30; Black Death 30; black legend of Angevins 250–51; *Buccolicum carmen* 87; *Caccia di Diana* 30, 63, 140; *Corbaccio* 139; *Cronaca di Partenope* 31; Dante 30; de' Cabanni 31, 140, 208–11; *Decameron* 2, 29, 30, 31, 140, 202; *De casibus virorum illustrium* 31, 48, 53, 68, 71, 87, 98, 105, 107–8, 140, 162, 209; *De mulieribus claris* 7, 30, 48, 53, 71, 87, 98, 103, 124,

138–42, 162, 191; *De vita et moribus Francisci Petracchi de Florentia* 30; *Eclogues* 48, 107, 139–40, 250–51; epideictic mode 87, 140; *Epistolae* 87; eyewitness 68; *fabula* 31; *Fiammetta* 30, 63, 140; *Filocolo* 30, 63; *Filostrato* 63; *Genealogia deorum gentilium* 30, 103; Giovanna I 7–8, 30–31, 38, 48, 103–6, 138–42, 250–51; Greek 30, 44, 48, 87; historiography 5, 23; language choice 81, 88; Latinity and style 30, 45, 47–48, 82, 86–87; lectures on Dante 30; *lieta brigata* 30; life and works 29–31; Louis of Taranto 31, 141; "Midas" 31; misogyny 30, 139–40, 146; Naples 29–31, 139; narrative form and structure 98, 103–8; Neapolitan 31, 91; *Ninfe fiorentine* 31; Ordelaffi 31; "Patient Griselda" 140–41; Petrarch 27, 30, 250–51; Robert the Wise 29, 31; romance literature 31; sources 53, 63; *Teseida* 63; Tuscan 3; vernacular 30, 88

Buccio di Ranallo (Boezio di Rainaldo di Poppleto): bible 53; *chansons de geste* 52; *Cronaca aquilana rimata* 20, 52, 89; Dante 52; language choice 89; *Leggenda di Santa Caterina d'Alessandria* 20, 52, 89; life and works 20–21; narrative form 109; sources 52, 59

C

cannibalism 7, 199–207, 254

Cavallini: Giovanni 49, 169, 170; Pietro 101, 172–76, 193 n. 102; "Last Judgement," Naples **173**; "Madonna of the Apocalypse," Naples **173**; Passion cycle, Naples **174**; "Apocalypse," Loffredo Chapel, Naples **175**

character: Anonimo romano 56, 204; Boccaccio 48, 98–100, 104, 140–42, 205; Buccio di Ranallo 89, 102, 109; civic chroniclers 15, 43, 83, 122–23; Froissart 34, 91, 100; Gravina 19, 86; humanists 8, 14, 44, 259–62, 267, 272; Palmieri 106; rhetorical tradition 104, 108; romances 6–7, 129, 131–32;

visual arts 155, 157; Winterthur 102

Charles of Calabria, prince 25, 65, 153–54, 157, 180, 203, 230

Chronicon Estense 5; authorship and contents 24–25; Cola di Rienzo 94; Giovanna I 94; Latinity and style 82, 85; narrative form and structure 93–94, 109; sources 53–54

Chronicon Mutinense 23; Cola di Rienzo 24; Duke of Athens 208; invented dialogue 85; Latinity and style 82, 85; Lewis of Hungary 24; narrative form and structure 94, 109; sources 54, 59. See also Bazzano, Giovanni da.

Chronicon Suessanum 5, 16; cleric 14; Duke of Athens 208; Latinity and style 82, 84; narrative form and structure 94, 109

Cicero: Anonimo romano 20, 48; Boccaccio 47; civic chroniclers 44, 81; *De inventione* 86, 107–8; humanists 259, 265, 267, 269–70, 290; Palmieri 47; Petrarch 27, 47–48, 86, 238–39; *Pro Archia* 86; rhetorical tradition 92, 98, 103–4

Clareno, Angelo, OFM 5; clerical culture 14; eyewitness 64–65; Greek 16, 45, 94; *Historia septem tribulationum* 16, 64, 174–76; invented speeches 49, 82; Latinity and style 82, 84; life and works 15; narrative form and structure 101–2, 108; sources 53, 61

Clement VI, pope 28, 126–27, 130, 237

Cola di Rienzo 7, 8, 10, 90, 189, 219, 235; Anonimo romano 19, 62, 67; archeology 49; Avignon 163–64; *buono stato* 24, 28–29, 67, 85, 90, 94, 164, 177, 213, 220, 243; *Chronicon Estense* 24; *Chronicon Mutinense* 72, 85; Fra Morreale 219–20; frescos 7, 157, 163–78, **166**; letters 19; murder 213–16; Roman barons 217–18; Spiritual Franciscans 16; Villani 25, 60

Colonna: Agapito 27; Giacomo, cardinal 15, 27; Giovanni, cardinal 28, 237–38; Giovanni, *De viris illustribus* 47, *Mare*

historianum 51–52; Pietro, cardinal 153
Constance 7, 22, 131–32, 137, 141
Contesse d'Anjou, la (Roman du Comtesse d'Anjou) 7, 124, 132–35, 138, 141–42, 184, 217
Convenevole da Prato 86, 167, **168**
Crassullo, Angelo 5, 14; *Annales de rebus tarentinis* 21; Latinity and style 84; life and work 21; narrative form and structure 94, 109
critical interpretations: Ainsworth 92; Artaud 200; Ascoli 29, 235; Auerbach 122; Barasch 155; Barthes 92; Bedos-Rezak 200; Belting 153; Bentley 260; Billanovich 19; Black 125, 132, 134–37; Blamires 139; Brown 48, 104, 139, 140, 142; Bryant 199; Buc 122, 199; Burroughs 200; Capasso 22, 54; Carruthers 57; Casteen 38; Caviness 152, 156; Clarke 52; Cochrane 259–60; Collard 56; De Bartholomaeis 89; De Caprio 17, 46, 54, 57, 61, 92; Delle Donne, F. 53, 54, 55, 57, 66, 130; Delle Donne, R. 54; Del Treppo 1; Elliott 172–74; Fleck 161–62; Formentin 56; Frojmovič 155; Gardiner 57, 202, 235; Gehl 165; Ginzburg 92, 222 n. 11, 223 n. 27, 272; Green 52, 99; Holloway 192; Holstein 57; Houston 87; Internullo 45, 54, 56, 165; Joost-Gaugier 161; Jordan 139–40; Kelly 21, 46, 61, 91; Kempshall 92; Kessler 152; Kohl 24; Lathuillère 138; Leone de Castris 161–62, 175–76; Leonard 130; Levi-Straruss 200; Lokaj 139; McCracken 134; Menache 60, 61; Moe 3, 10 n. 25; Montuori 17, 54; Morosini 63; Ong 57; Otter 142; Panofsky 45, 85; Partner 92, 112 n. 32, 190 n. 26; Perriccioli Saggese 138, 145 n. 74, 145 n. 76, 184, 187; Petkov 200; Porta 62, 75 n. 243, 117 n. 176; Ranke 89, 199; Ratté 155; Ray 129; Ricoeur 92; Romano 161; Royle 135; Sabatini 17, 54, 115 n. 111; Schmidt 175–76; Schwartz 164; Seibt 20, 51–52, 90; Senatore 54, 57, 64, 85, 291; Shemek 139; Spiegel 92; Strohm 122, 125, 142, 202, 232–33; Thomas 129; Tomei 166, 175; Tuchman 34; Varvaro 59; White 11 n. 34, 92, 102, 115 n. 122, 216–17, 222 n. 11; Witt xxix–xxx, 2, 68, 69, 82; Zabbia 85, 97, 130; Zorzi 210
Cronaca di Partenope 5, 17–18; archeological remains 49; authorship 51; classics 45, 46; *Cronicon siculum* 51; Duke of Athens 208; language choice 81, 90; narrative form and structure 99–100, 102, 106; Neapolitan 91; sources 46, 51, 53, 56–57, 61; Villani 26, 99
Cronaca Senese 5; authorship and contents 27; Dei 27; eyewitness 65; sources 51; Villani 27
Cronicon siculum incerti authoris 5; *Cronaca di Partenope* 21; Latinity and style 82, 85; narrative form and structure 94–95, 109; sources 51, 63

D

Dante Alighieri: Boccaccio 30; Brunetto Latini 36 n. 48; Buccio di Ranallo 20, 52; *Commedia* 23, 89, 154, 166, 169, 202; historiography 5, 23; Petrarch 27, 86; religious life 16; Tuscan 3, 88; Villani 26
de'Cabanni 208–11, 220–21; Filippa (of Catania, La Catanese) 31, 68, 126; Raymond 105; Roberto 31, 68, 126; Sancia 31, 68, 126
deeds *(res gestae)*: Anonimo romano 100, 110; Boccaccio 98, 104–8, 140; chivalric 80; *Chronicon Estense* 109; deliberative form 108; epideictic form 104–8; Froissart 58, 91, 100, 102; Gravina 96; humanists 266–67, 271–72, 275, 291; Palmieri 106; Villani 50; Winterthur 96
Duca di Monteleone, *Diurnale (Diario)* 5, 21–22, 51; language choice 89; narrative form and structure 95, 107; sources 63

Duke of Athens (Walter VI of Brienne): 7, 19, 199, 201–7, 210, 214; Agnolo di Tura 61, 65, 204; Anonimo romano 204; Boccaccio 204–5; *Cronaca Senese* 65; Villani 25, 65, 203–5

E

education: 182, 187, 215, 246, 260, 274, 276; *abbaco* 88, 113, 270; *Disticha Catonis* 83; Donatus 83, 103; *grammatica* xxv, 7, 31, 52, 80, 82, 85, 88, 111, 124, 152–53, 165, 217, 262, 271; instruction 80–83, 85, 87–88; legal 82; literacy xxv, xxvi, 14, 22–23, 52, 61, 81, 83, 87–90, 142, 152, 156; Priscian 103–6; Prudentius 83, 165; textbooks xxv, 82

ekphrasis 7, 83, 165, 170, 192 n. 79. *See also* Anonimo romano; visuality.

Elizabeth of Hungary, queen 126, 129–30, 233–35

Empress of Rome 7, 131–32, 135, 137

F

fable *(fabula)*: Boccaccio 31, 103, 211; Clareno 101; De Rosa 275; humanists 269; rhetorical tradition 60, 81, 83, 92, 97, 103; romances 123–24, 129, 135, 200; Villani 37. *See also* literature.

Facio, Bartolomeo 8, 258, 263, 267–68

falsely accused queens 7, 105, 124–25, 140, 142

Ferraiolo 276–78

fiction 7, 81, 122, 124, 129, 131, 134–35, 141, 153, 182, 187, 189, 193, 216, 221

first-hand testimony: 43, 51, 206, 216; Agnolo di Tura 27, 64–65; Anonimo romano 49, 57, 61–62, 67; Bazzano 59; Boccaccio 5, 23, 31, 205, 211, 250; Clareno 14–16, 53, 61, 64; *Cronaca di Partenope* 17; Gravina 18, 86, 205, 211–12; Froissart 33–34, 64; Petrarch 5, 23, 29, 67, 246; Roman law 641; Villani 50, 61, 64; Walsingham 34, 64. *See also* orality.

Florence: Agnolo di Tura 65, 95; Angevins 127, 154, 157, 166; banking 25; Barberino 153–54; Black Death 65; Boccaccio 29–30, 205, 211, 250; *Cronaca Senese* 65; Duke of Athens 7, 19, 61, 202–7; education 87, 165; Mezzogiorno 2; painting 167, 172, 175–76; Palmieri 31–32; Petrarch 27, 28; Villani 25–26, 65, 87, 102, 109, 208, 247

Fortune *(fortuna)* 55, 108, 133, 134, 146, 238, 242, 246, 272, 284

Franciscan Order 16, 33, 49; Rule 53, 84; Sancia of Majorca 53; Spirituals xxiv, 15, 53, 101, 108

Froissart, Jean 5; *Chroniques* 33; eyewitness 64; language choice 91–92; life and works 33–34; *Meliador* 34, 52; narrative form and structure 100, 102, 108–9; Petrarch 33; sources 50, 52, 54, 58–59; Virgilian tradition 59

G

Giotto di Bandone: Barberino 154–55; *De viris illustribus*, Naples 7, 29, 157–63, 180; "Iustitia," Padua **158**; Navicella, Rome 165–69, **167**, 239; Padua 154–56, 159, 165, 172, 193 n. 102; *Crucifixion*, Paris 210; *Stuttgart Apocalypse* 101, 175–76, **177**; Villani 26

Giovanna I, queen: accession 17; Anjou Bible 179–80, **181**; Bazzano 54; Boccaccio 30, 98, 103–6, 124, 138–42, 250–51; *Chronicon Estense* 24; courtiers 7, 8, 126, 207–11, 220–21; *Chronicon Suessanum* 16; *Cronaca di Partenope* 46; *Cronicon siculum* 21, 94–95; Duca di Monteleone 50; economic influence 22; Froissart 34, 50, 59; Giotto 161–62; Gravina 18, 97, 107, 248–50; Hungarians 233–38; *infamia* 8, 232–35; intellectual circle 29; life and reign 125–29, 138, 261; literary sources 131; *Meliadus* 184–89; Neapolitan 91; northern Italian historians 23; Palmieri 32, 106; Petrarch 57, 97–98, 163, 235–47; *Statutes of Order of the Holy Spirit (Knot)* 181–84, **181, 183**; Villani 25, 60, 65, 247–48; Walsingham 34, 54; Winterthur 96. *See also* Andrew

of Hungary; de'Cabanni; Louis of Taranto; Robert the Wise.
Gravina, Domenico da *(Chronicon de rebus in Apulia gestis)* 5, 8, 14, 216, 232; Agnes of Perigord 130, 249; black legend of Angevins 248–50; de'Cabanni 208–10, 220–21, 248–49; eyewitness 66; Giovanna I 128, 209–10, 248–50; Judge Martuccio 211–13; Latinity and style 85–86; life and work 18–19; narrative form and structure 97, 102, 107; sources 7, 55–56, 63, 66, 86

H
historia and *fabula* 37, 103, 124, 200, 275. See also fable *(fabula)*.
Hohenstaufen 2, 3, 11, 51, 187, 230, 234, 262, 264

J
Jean, Duc de Berry 133, 135–37, 179–80
Joachim of Fiore 16, 53, 84, 161, 174, 176
language choice 80–92; Agnolo di Tura 87; Anonimo romano 87; *Cronaca di Partenope* 87; dialects 3, 87, 90; Neapolitan 6, 17, 31, 81, 90–91; Old French 87, 138, 145, 181, 184; Provençal 52, 87–89, 91; Romanesco 6, 62, 75, 90, 115, 164, 167; Tuscan 3, 6, 25, 27, 32, 45, 50, 81, 114, 260, 275; Tuscanized southern 89; vernacular use 26, 37, 44, 46, 73, 95, 99, 110, 115, 152, 265, 273–78, 282, 290; Villani 87
Latini, Brunetto 5, 26, 36, 50, 88, 153
Latinity and style 44; Ciceronian 86; civic 15; ecclesiastic 84; gender 85; historiography 82–87; lay 84–87; literacy *(latinantes)* 88, 165; notarial 85–86; quattrocento 88; *sermo humilis* 87. See also education; individual authors and works; rhetoric.
legend: cannibalism 206–7; *Cronaca di Partenope* 49, 61, 99, 106; *Cronicon siculum* 94; romance 122, 129, 135 137, 234–35; Rome 169–70; Valla 269; Villani 25
legitimacy 3, 52, 104, 136, 153, 179, 189–90

Lewis of Hungary, king: Anomino romano 19; Boccaccio 31, 250–51; *Chronicon Estense* 24; *Chronicon Mutinense* 59, 85; *Chronicon Suessanum* 16–17; Gravina 18–19; invasion of Regno 22, 24, 31, 125–27, 185, 233–35, 251; Palmieri 32, 106. See also Angevins: Hungary.
literature: Acciaiuoli 138, 181–82; Angevins 6–7, 19, 131, 153, 178, 181–85, 230; Arthurian 52, 91, 124, 130, 135–36, 145; Boccaccio 29, 141; *chansons de geste* 19, 86, 89, 124, 184, 187, 189; civic chroniclers 15; Froissart 33–34, 52, 100; poetry 4, 30, 31, 81, 83, 85, 87, 89, 92, 103, 104, 115, 236; romance 29, 88, 122–45, 159, 194, 212, 217, 244, 252; *stil novo* 88. See also orality.
Livy: Anonimo romano 20, 49, 100, 110, 201, 217; Boccaccio 48; Cola di Rienzo 46–49; *Cronaca di Partenope* 46; humanists 258, 260, 263, 265, 269, 272; manuscripts 44; Palmieri 47; Petrarch 28, 44, 86; vernacular translation 44
Lorenzetti, Ambrogio 7, 141, 153, 155–57, 207; "Iustitia" **156**
Louis of Taranto 16–17, 126–30, 232, 246, 275; Boccaccio 139, 251; Buccio di Ranallo 20; coronation 138; *Cronicon siculum* 21; death 128; *Meliadus* 138, 184–89, **186, 188**; Palmieri 32, 106; *Statutes of Order of the Holy Spirit (Knot)* 181–84, **183**; Villani 60, 65. See also Giovanna I.
Lucan 20, 44–46, 86, 97, 100, 114 n. 95, 116, 242

M
Manekine, La 7, 124, 131–32, 137, 142, 184
Manetti, Giannozzo 8, 258, 270–71
manuscripts; Berlin: SM, MS 78 E 3 193; Florence: BML, MS Strozzi 174 191; BN, MS Banco Rari 38, 192; Leuven: Maurits Sabbe, MS 1 7, 153, 179–80, **181**; London: BL, MS Add 12228 7, 138, 145, 153,

179, 184–88, *185*, *186*, *188*, 194; BL, MS Royal 6.E.IX 166, *168*; BL, MS Royal 16.G.VI 178; Naples: BN, MS Brancacciano II.F6 282; New York, Morgan Library, MS 801 276–80, 283; Paris: BnF, MS fr. 599 118; BnF, MS fr. 1463 145; BnF, MS fr. 4274 7, 153, 179, 181–84, *183*, 194; BnF, MS fr. 9561 178; Vatican: BAV, MS Barb. Lat. 4076 and 4077 153–55, *154*, 190; BAV, MS Chigi L.VIII.296 117; BAV, MS Pal. Lat. 939 117; BAV, MS Reg. Lat. 1501 145; Venice: BNM, MS IX 227 145 n. 74; BNM, MS fr. XV 145 n. 74; Vienna: ONB, MS Cod. 1921 194; ONB, MS Series Nova 2639 192; Villani, *Cronaca figurata* 117

Maria of Pozzuoli, countess 163, 240–41

Martuccio, Judge 7, 53, 199, 201, 210–13

Maso di Banco 159, 172, 175; "St. Silvester and Dragon" *176*

Meliadus de Leonnois 7, 138, 153, 179, 184–89, *185*, *186*, *188*

Melusine 7, 33, 124, 135–38, 142, 184, 255

memory *(memoria)* 43, 57, 233; Anonimo romano 46, 61–62, 67, 110; Boccaccio 31; *Chronicon Estense* 112 n. 45; civic 273, 275–78; Clareno 16, 102; *Cronaca di Partenope* 21, 46, 49, 99; Froissart 58, 91, 100; Gravina 19, 55, 213; humanists 263–65; notaries 85–86; Palmieri 106; Petrarch 86, 246–47; ritual 199, 210, 225–26 n. 97; Villani 25, 60; visual 155–57, 170–71

Mezzogiorno: Angevin 1; Aragonese 4; Biondo 264; Byzantine 2, 3, 155; definitions 1–4, 14; Froissart 34; German imperial 187; modern historiography xxviii–xxix, 3, 4, 8, 10, 27, 252, 258–59, 272, 289–90; Norman 2, 3, 259, 265; Petrarch 27, 239, 244, 247

Morreale, Fra 8, 128, 199, 209, 216, 219–21

N

Naples: Anonimo romano 19; Aragonese 260–79; archeological remains 49; archives 3; Bazzano 23–24; black legend 229–52; Byzantine 46; Capella Palatina 29; capital 3; Castel Nuovo 29, 153, 157, 180, 191–92, 208, 250, 261, 265, 275; *Chronicon Estense* 24; civic historians 20, 273–78; Constantine 46; *Cronaca di Partenope* 17, 46; *Cronicon siculum* 21; Duca di Monteleone 21–22; Florence 25; Gravina 18; Hungarian invasion 127–28; manuscripts 152–53, 178–89; northern European historiography 22, 32–34, 59; revolt against Giovanna I 208–11; romance literature 129–42; Regno 1–4, 14; *seggi* 17, 21, 22, 61; Sta. Chiara 160, 161; Sta. Maria Donna Regina 172–75; Temple of the Dioscuri 49; tsunami of 1343 67, 239–43; university 29, 57, 142; Villani 25, 65; Virgil 45, 46, 49. See also Angevins; Boccaccio; Giovanna I; Petrarch; Robert of Anjou.

narrative: communities construction 278, 290; deliberative (civic) 108–10; epideictic (praise or blame) 48, 103–6, *105*; fictional 123–25, 137; forms 6, 15, 80, 89, 103–10, 289; "gap" 6–7, 43, 50, 122, 124, 129, 142–43, 157, 200, 207; grand 229–52; judicial (or forensic) 107–8; prison 216–22; paratactic 93–96; punishment 199–215; structures 7, 44, 80–82, 92–102, 103, 110, 153; symbolic or figurative 101–2; thematic 96–100; visual 152–78, 190

natural phenomena and disasters 60, 61, 244; Black Death 20, 24–27, 33, 65–66, 127; blood moons and skies 55, 93; comets 55, 95; earthquakes 20, 55–57, 67, 95, 239–41; eclipses 55, 93; famine 20, 45, 55, 62, 93; floods 93, 95; hail 55; monstrosities 25, 55, 246; plague 49, 55, 57, 93, 95, 237, 267; pollution 250; portents 55, 58, 93, 178, 245; prodigies 26, 55, 95, 274; storms 95, 242, 245

INDEX

Nine Heroes *(Neuf Preux)* 159–61, **160**
Notar Giacomo 8, 258, 275–76, 279
notaries: archives 18, 53–55; authors 15, 21, 22, 24, 130, 153, 163, 262; class 27, 43, 54, 68–69 n. 2, 80, 82, 86, 91, 113 n. 74, 115, 267, 275; culture 6; Latinity 21, 85–86, 171; public office 18, 55, 66, 72 n. 129, 87, 107, 271, 276; orality 85, 161; ritual 200, 203, 209, 213–17

O

orality 1, 6, 115, 152, 241, 275; *admonitio* 89, 205; *audita* and *visa* 57, 64; battle cries 60; bon mots 89; *clamor* 60, 212, 242; commonplace and knowledge 43, 83, 86; *contumelia* 58; conversation xxv, 60, 62, 143, 216; *damnatio memoriae* 224; dialogue and oratory 44, 49, 55, 62–63, 83–84, 86, 94, 98, 103, 106, 108, 112, 161, 204, 213, 217, 219–21, 251, 256, 268, 272–73, 276; *dicta* 83, 91; *fama* 58, 63, 72; folk memory and tales 2, 31, 43, 55, 58, 60, 131–35, 137, 144, 206, 277; gossip xxv, 43, 58, 62, 273; hearsay 60, 213; infamy *(infamia)* 8, 59–60, 106, 128, 167, 169, 177, 185, 192, 232–34, 290; insinuation 60, 81; myth 46, 83, 91, 100, 108, 123, 129–30, 136, 240; news xxv, 27, 34, 54, 59, 61, 63, 65, 74, 130, 161, 185, 207, 218, 256, 279, 282; opinion 43, 58, 60, 62; proclamation 57, 58; proverb 60, 61, 83, 89; report 5, 24, 46, 61, 64, 68, 85, 89, 140, 177, 248, 273, 278; reputation 28, 56, 59–60, 88, 128, 163, 188, 202–3, 231, 262, 263, 290; *romore* 60–62, 74; rumor 5, 43, 55, 57–60, 62, 64, 75, 81, 125, 128, 136, 177, 233; scandal 58, 59; song 30, 63, 74, 272, 278; speech act 60; tradition 15, 102; *voci* 60, 62, 63
Orimina, Cristoforo 138, 179, 182, 184, 193, **181, 183, 185, 186, 188**

P

Palmieri, Matteo 5, 51; *Della vita civile* 32; Greek 47; language choice 81, 87; Latinity and style 47, 82, 86; narrative form and structure 98, 106; *Vita* of Niccolò Acciaiuoli 31–32, 87
Panegyric to Robert of Anjou (Carmina regia) 165–69; Rome as widow **168**
Petrarch, Francesco: Acciaiuoli 182, 184, 187; Andrew of Hungary 244–46; "Argus" 31, 48, 246; black legend of Angevins 27, 235–47; Biondo 265; Boccaccio 30–31, 37 n. 82, 48, 191–92; *Bucolicum carmen* 47; Cicero 27, 238–39; classical remains 49–50; Cola di Rienzo 28–29, 235; Colonna 27, 28, 29, 243–44; coronation 28, 86, 162, 191 n. 59; Dante 86; *De viris illustribus* 28, 30, 47–48, 86, 139, 162–63; *Eclogues* 29, 97–98, 107, 247, 251; *Epistola metrica* 169; *Epistolae sine nomine* 47; eyewitness 67; *Familiares* 7, 29, 47, 48, 86, 235–46; Giovanna I 8, 28, 162–63, 235–47; Greek 28, 44; historiography 23; *Itinerary* 29, 47, 162–63, 246; Latinity and style 30, 45, 47, 81, 82, 86–88, 98; life and works 27–29; Livy 28, 44, 86; Maria of Pozzuoli 240–41; misogyny 146 n. 90, 239–40; Naples 28–29, 67–68, 232, 235–47; narrative 47, 97–98, 107–8; *Panegyric* 167–69; Robert of Anjou 29, 49, 56–57, 235–40; Roberto da Mileto 237–40; Rome 28–29, 248–49; *Seniles* 29, 47, 48, 140, 235, 239, 245, 255; sources 53, 56–57, 86, 124; *Triumphi* 88, 191 n. 17; Tuscan 3, 88; Villani 26; Virgil 28, 160, 162–63; visuality 153, 165
Pontano, Giovanni 8, 271–73
prison dialogues 7, 199, 216–21, 289
punishment: judicial 94, 242; ritual 7–8, 31, 199–215, 289; report 57. See also ritual; torture; violence.

Q

Quintilian 47, 81, 86, 92, 96, 97, 98, 100, 103–4, 269–70, 272, 275

R

rhetoric: *amplificatio* 57, 89, 270; archetype 131, 248; *ars arengandi* 86; *ars dictaminis* 82, 85, 87, 98; *ars predicandi* 86; *brevitas* 81, 87, 97; credibility 81;

341

dispositio 100, 102, 103, 117; *divisio* 100; education 31, 64, 262, 268; *elocutio* 83, 90; emblem 83, 124; epigram 83; exempla 80, 85, 87, 91, 93, 96, 100, 101, 108, 110, 162, 166, 178, 211, 215, 269; *fides* (plausibility) 81, 92, 97, 98, 129, 215; *inventio* 101, 103; judicial argument 81; *laudatio* 267; lucidity 81; maxim 83; medieval debate on 81; metaphor xxvi, 55, 277; *narratio probabilis* 129; notarial 14; *personae attributa* 104; persuasion 81; plausibility 81, 92, 97, 98, 129, 215; predictive 236; probability 81, 129; *Rhetorica ad Herennium* 92, 96, 98, 103, 129; *res gestae* 87, 102, 104, 112, 266; style 83–84; synecdoche 86, 96, 103, 107, 165, 170, 210, 265; *topica* 86; tropes 7, 29, 64, 80, 83, 85, 103, 122–24, 129, 142, 201, 229, 232, 244, 251, 252–53; truth claims 8, 43, 66, 81, 84, 94, 199, 205, 213; utility *(utilitas)* 84, 85, 87, 96–98, 103, 108, 109–10, 114, 117, 137, 260, 269; verisimilitude 8, 32, 63, 81, 83, 85, 95, 98, 215, 221, 270 289; visual 153, 155, 157; *vita, gesta* and *mores* 104. *See also* allegory; education; orality.

ritual 1, 68, 123, 221–24, 254; ceremony 7, 199–200, 248; coronations 93; dance 30, 63, 248; dismemberment 7, 214; festivity 63, 207; music 63, 65; performance 199, 291; processions 60, 67, 187. *See also* cannibalism; punishment; violence.

Robert the Wise (of Anjou), king: *Anjou Bible* 178–80, **181**; Anomino romano 19; archeology 49, 50; *Chronicon Estense* 24; court officials 126, 209; economic influence 22; Florence 157; intellectual circle 29; Joachimism 175–76; Palmieri 106; *Panegyric* 166; patronage 236; prognosticator 59; romance literature 19; Sicily 2; Villani 25; Virgil 28, 160–62; virtues and wisdom 140–41, 230, 239; will and testament 10, 125. *See also* Andrew of Hungary; Boccaccio; Giovanna I; Petrarch.

Roberto da Mileto, OFM 237–40

Rome: archeology 49; archives 20; barons 8; Brennius 130; *Chronicon Estense* 24; classical studies 45–46; District 1, 3, 14; English 34; Jubilees 20, 25; Lateran 169–71; medical knowledge 72; medieval empire 19, 187; memory 57; *Mirabilia* 51–52; notaries 69; "proto–humanists" 69; S. Angelo in Pescheria 171–78; St. Peter's 165–69; Villani 25; Widow 167–69, **168**. *See also* Anonimo romano; Cola di Rienzo; Petrarch.

Rosa, Loise de 8, 273–75

S

Sallust: Anonimo romano 20, 46, 100; cannibalism 206; *Chronicon Estense* 85, 106, 112 n. 45; Gravina 86, 97; humanists 258, 269, 272; Palmieri 47

Sancia of Majorca, queen: Clareno 16; Franciscans 125; Gravina 97; regent 237, 249–50; Robert of Anjou 180, 230; *Stuttgart Apocalypse* 175–77; Winterthur 33, 53

Sicily: Angevin claims 196, 242; Aragonese 2, 234, 261, 266; *Cronicon siculum* 21; historiography 5, 259; kingdom of 2, 21, 129, 246, 265; separateness 1, 9, 14, 264, 289; Vespers 2, 5, 14, 36, 50

sources: archeological 49–50; archival 3, 6, 14, 15, 23, 43, 50–55, 68, 75, 115, 157, 272; *auctores* 83, 155; biblical 45, 52, 53, 81, 83, 86, 89, 101, 124, 129, 137, 155, 159–60, 165, 194, 201, 220, 236, 248, 270; classical 44–49, 129; diplomatic 43, 54, 57, 64; epigraphic 49; evidence 81, 152; eyewitness 15, 23, 32, 50, 57–58, 63–68, 85, 107, 124, 129, 172, 200, 206, 212–16, 221–22, 235, 241, 243–44, 266, 269, 272; florilegia 44, 45, 46; Greek 16, 17, 19, 29, 32, 44; hagiography 7, 52, 53, 71, 88, 104, 123, 124, 142, 222, 269; legal 43; letters 23; literary 43, 44, 52, 53, 131–37; medical 19, 27, 43, 56–57, 72, 130; medieval 50–51; oral (including folklore and memory) 43, 49, 50,

53, 55, 57–68, 277; *recordatio* 155, 157, 164, 170–71, 178; scientific 6, 26, 43, 55–57, 82, 217; scholastic 45; second-hand report 34; *sententiae* 86, 89, 270; sermons 6, 52, 84, 161, 190, 191, 249, 275; translation 32, 37, 44, 83, 88, 90, 169, 194, 268, 277, 281. *See also* legend; literature; orality; textuality; visuality.

Statutes of the Order of the Holy Spirit (Knot) 7, 153, 179, 181–82, **183**, 184, 186–89

Stuttgart Apocalypse 175–76, **177**, 178

T

textuality 86, 113, 115, 199, 277; allegorical 81, 124, 154, 156, 163–67, 171, 176, 207; anagogic 81, 124; literal 81, 103, 205; moral (tropological) 81; textual community 16, 49, 57, 81, 88, 102, 161, 164, 177, 189, 276, 279, 283; textual interpretation 83, 85; topological 124; tropological 81, 101, 124; typologies 90. *See also* authorship; orality; rhetoric; visuality.

torture 57, 60, 61, 68, 178, 200, 201, 207, 209, 211–12, 215, 219, 221–22. *See also* punishment.

Tura del Grasso, Agnolo di 27, 65; eyewitness 66; language choice 89; narrative form and structure 95, 102, 109; sources 51, 61. *See also Cronaca Senese.*

V

Valerius Maximus 20, 44, 46, 48, 86

Valla, Lorenzo 8, 258, 268–70

Villani: Giovanni 8, 25, 47, 232; Anonimo romano 20; Barberino 154; black legend of Angevins 234, 247–48; *Cronaca di Partenope* 17; Dante 23, 50, 89; Duke of Athens 203–5; eyewitness 65; Filippo 25, 26, 51, 65; *fortuna* 26, 267; Giovanna I 128, 247–8; Matteo 25–26, 187; narrative form and structure 99, 102, 109; orality 60; Palmieri 47; sources 50, 52, 55–56, 60–61, 89, 100, 124; "Southernized" 51, 61; survey of Florence schools 87, 113 n. 73; Tuscan vernacular 62–63, 88–90

violence 57, 61, 136, 201–3, 205, 207, 212–13, 223, 231, 241. *See also* punishment; ritual.

Virgil: Biondo 265, Boccaccio 47–48, 250–51, *Cronaca di Partenope* 44, 46, 56; Palmieri 47–48; Petrarch 28, 47, 86, 240, 242–43, 247; Walsingham 45

virtues and vices: Barberino 154, 161–62, 164; Boccaccio 103–4, 106, 108, 140–45, 205; cardinal 86, 108; chivalric 91, 132, 134–35, 231; civic 7, 20, 94, 100, 109–10, 178, 200, 252, 254 n. 50, 272, 274, 276; Giotto 157, **158**, 161–62; humanists 260, 262, 266, 270–72; Lorenzetti 154–57, **156**; *Panegyric* 166, 169; Petrarch 236, 238, 239, 246; religious 26, 52, 55, 220, 229, 236, 238; Villani 248–49; visual imagery 152, 166, 189, 215; Winterthur 45

visuality 1, 4, 7, 11, 61, 67, 81, 138, 143, 152–97, 200, 223, 229, 261, 273, 289; *Anjou Bible* 179–80, **181**; *figurae* 90, 101, 160, 162–66, 170–71, 175, 179; images xxvi, 56, 72, 137, 202, 206–7, 215, 239, 245, 277, 283; *Meliadus de Leonnois* 184, **185**, **186**, 187, **188**; Rienzo's Roman frescoes 163–78, **166**; *Statutes of the Order of the Holy Spirit* 181–82, **183**, 184; symbols 83, 101, 124, 144, 154, 160, 164, 170, 176, 186, 199, 207, 291; trecento visual language 153–55; visions 101, 108, 178, 202. *See also* Anagni *Apocalypse*; Barberino; Cavallini; Giotto; Lorenzetti.

W

Walsingham, Thomas 5, 49; eyewitness 64; Latinity and style 45, 82, 84; life and works 34, 50; narrative form and structure 96, 102, 108, 202; sources 50, 54, 58

Winterthur, Johanns von 5; Latinity and style 82, 84; life and works 33; narrative form and structure 95–96, 102, 108; sources 45, 53, 54, 58

*Production of This Book Was Completed
on 21 December 2021 at Italica Press,
Clifton, Bristol, United Kingdom.
It Was Set in Adobe Bembo,
Adobe Bembo Expert &
Monotype Botanical*

www.ingramcontent.com/pod-product-compliance
Lightning Source LLC
Chambersburg PA
CBHW030101170426
43198CB00009B/445